introduction TO
MANAGERIAL ACCOUNTING

7TH EDITION

PETER C. BREWER
Lecturer, Wake Forest University

RAY H. GARRISON
Professor Emeritus, Brigham Young University

ERIC W. NOREEN
Professor Emeritus, University of Washington

McGraw Hill Education

INTRODUCTION TO MANAGERIAL ACCOUNTING

Published by McGraw-Hill Education, 2 Penn Plaza, New York, NY 10121. Copyright © 2016 by McGraw-Hill Education. All rights reserved. Printed in the United States of America. No part of this publication may be reproduced or distributed in any form or by any means, or stored in a database or retrieval system, without the prior written consent of McGraw-Hill Education, including, but not limited to, in any network or other electronic storage or transmission, or broadcast for distance learning.

Some ancillaries, including electronic and print components, may not be available to customers outside the United States.

This book is printed on acid-free paper.

1 2 3 4 5 6 7 8 9 0 DOW/DOW 1 0 9 8 7 6 5

ISBN 978-1-25925312-6
MHID 1-259-25312-0

All credits appearing on page or at the end of the book are considered to be an extension of the copyright page.

The Internet addresses listed in the text were accurate at the time of publication. The inclusion of a website does not indicate an endorsement by the authors or McGraw-Hill Education, and McGraw-Hill Education does not guarantee the accuracy of the information presented at these sites.

www.mhhe.com

DEDICATION

To our families and to our colleagues who use this book.
—Peter C. Brewer, Ray H. Garrison, and Eric W. Noreen

About the Authors

Peter C. Brewer is a Lecturer in the Department of Accountancy at Wake Forest University. Prior to joining the faculty at Wake Forest, he was an accounting professor at Miami University for 19 years. He holds a BS degree in accounting from Penn State University, an MS degree in accounting from the University of Virginia, and a PhD from the University of Tennessee. He has published 40 articles in a variety of journals including *Management Accounting Research*; the *Journal of Information Systems; Cost Management; Strategic Finance*; the *Journal of Accountancy; Issues in Accounting Education*; and the *Journal of Business Logistics*.

Professor Brewer has served as a member of the editorial boards of the *Journal of Accounting Education* and *Issues in Accounting Education*. His article "Putting Strategy into the Balanced Scorecard" won the 2003 International Federation of Accountants' Articles of Merit competition, and his articles "Using Six Sigma to Improve the Finance Function" and "Lean Accounting: What's It All About?" were awarded the Institute of Management Accountants' Lybrand Gold and Silver Medals in 2005 and 2006. He has received Miami University's Richard T. Farmer School of Business Teaching Excellence Award.

Prior to joining the faculty at Miami University, Professor Brewer was employed as an auditor for Touche Ross in the firm's Philadelphia office. He also worked as an internal audit manager for the Board of Pensions of the Presbyterian Church (U.S.A.).

Ray H. Garrison is emeritus professor of accounting at Brigham Young University, Provo, Utah. He received his BS and MS degrees from Brigham Young University and his DBA degree from Indiana University.

As a certified public accountant, Professor Garrison has been involved in management consulting work with both national and regional accounting firms. He has published articles in *The Accounting Review, Management Accounting,* and other professional journals. Innovation in the classroom has earned Professor Garrison the Karl G. Maeser Distinguished Teaching Award from Brigham Young University.

Eric W. Noreen has taught at INSEAD in France and the Hong Kong Institute of Science and Technology and is emeritus professor of accounting at the University of Washington. Currently, he is the Accounting Circle Professor of Accounting, Fox School of Business, Temple University.

He received his BA degree from the University of Washington and MBA and PhD degrees from Stanford University. A Certified Management Accountant, he was awarded a Certificate of Distinguished Performance by the Institute of Certified Management Accountants.

Professor Noreen has served as associate editor of *The Accounting Review* and the *Journal of Accounting and Economics*. He has numerous articles in academic journals including: the *Journal of Accounting Research; The Accounting Review;* the *Journal of Accounting and Economics; Accounting Horizons; Accounting, Organizations and Society; Contemporary Accounting Research;* the *Journal of Management Accounting Research;* and the *Review of Accounting Studies*.

Professor Noreen has won a number of awards from students for his teaching.

Pointing Students in the Right Direction

"Why do I need to learn Managerial Accounting?"

Brewer's *Introduction to Managerial Accounting* has earned a reputation as the most accessible and readable book on the market. Its manageable chapters and clear presentation point students toward understanding just as the needle of a compass provides direction to travelers.

However, the book's authors also understand that everyone's destinations are different. Some students will become accountants, while others are destined for careers in management, marketing, or finance. Not only does the Brewer text teach students managerial accounting concepts in a clear and concise way, but it also asks students to consider how the concepts they're learning will apply to the real world situations they will eventually confront in their careers. This combination of conceptual understanding and the ability to apply that knowledge directs students toward success, whatever their final destination happens to be.

Here's how your colleagues have described Brewer's *Introduction to Managerial Accounting:*

"The **best introductory managerial accounting book** on the market. Plain and simple."
—Paige Paulsen, Salt Lake Community College

"This is an **excellent, high quality text** that uses **state-of-the-art technologies** to enhance the learning experience for students."
—Olen L. Greer, Missouri State University

"It is the **best textbook for introductory managerial accounting to date.** It is concise, well-written and well-organized. With an abundance in real-world flavors, students will see the material as interesting and relevant."
—Minwoo Lee, Western Kentucky University

"This is a **well organized and written textbook.** It is easy to read and provides **excellent illustrations.** The coverage is clear and presented very well."
—Gloria Stuart, Georgia Southern University

Brewer's *Introduction to Managerial Accounting* is an **excellent managerial accounting text** that is written with the student in mind. The practical examples, review problems, helpful hints and incorporation of the Excel application all serve to motivate the student to learn the topic.
—Blair Arthur William, Slippery Rock University

"The **best resource to making your job in the classroom easier.** If students read the text and utilize the supplements, they are going to learn Managerial Accounting easier and faster than with any other text."
—Tom Hrubec, Franklin University

". . . **excellent depth and breadth of topic coverage** that will prepare the students for their advanced business and accounting classes. The textbook will also lay the foundation to ensure the students have the ability to successfully apply managerial accounting concepts in their full-time professional jobs!"
—Michael Hammond, Missouri State University

"I would describe this text as very well written and organized. Topics covered have been updated nicely to reflect most current business trends. I would say this book is **very student and professor friendly!**"
—Matthew Muller, Adirondack Community College

Introduction to Managerial Accounting, 7th edition,
by **BREWER/GARRISON/NOREEN** empowers
your students by offering:

CONCISE COVERAGE

Your students want a text that is concise and that presents material in a clear and readable manner. *Introduction to Managerial Accounting* keeps the material accessible while avoiding advanced topics related to cost accounting. Students' biggest concern is whether they can solve the end-of-chapter problems after reading the chapter. Market research indicates that Brewer/Garrison/Noreen helps students apply what they've learned better than any other managerial accounting text on the market. Additionally, the key supplements are written by the authors ensuring that students and instructors will work with clear, well-written supplements that employ consistent terminology.

DECISION-MAKING FOCUS

All students who pass through your class need to know how accounting information is used to make business decisions, especially if they plan to be future managers. That's why Brewer, Garrison, and Noreen make decision making a pivotal component of *Introduction to Managerial Accounting*. In every chapter you'll find the following key features that are designed to teach your students how to use accounting information: Each chapter opens with a **Decision Feature** vignette that uses real-world examples to show how accounting information is used to make everyday business decisions; **Decision Point boxes** within the chapters help students to develop analytical, critical thinking, and problem-solving skills; and end-of-chapter **Building Your Skills** cases challenge students' decision-making skills.

A CONTEMPORARY APPROACH TO LEARNING

Today's students rely on technology more than ever as a learning tool, and *Introduction to Managerial Accounting* offers the finest technology package of any text on the market. From study aids like narrated, animated Guided Examples to online grading and course management, our technology assets have one thing in common: they make your class time more productive, more stimulating, and more rewarding for you and your students. McGraw-Hill *Connect® Accounting* is an online assignment and assessment solution that connects students with the tools and resources they'll need to achieve success, including *Connect Accounting* provides an online, media-rich, searchable version of the text in addition to access to *Connect*, giving students a convenient way to access everything they need to succeed in their course. The *Connect* library provides your students with a variety of multimedia aids to help them learn managerial accounting. includes quizzes, audio and visual lecture presentations, and course-related videos. Students also can download an iPad® app for LearnSmart®, an adaptive tool that helps students learn faster, study more efficiently, and retain more knowledge.

*"The book's **number one feature is the real world examples** it incorporates in each chapter."*

—Meghna Singhvi, Florida International University

Introduction to Managerial Accounting is full of pedagogy designed to make studying productive and hassle-free. On the following pages, you'll see the kind of engaging, helpful pedagogical features that have made Brewer one of the best-selling Managerial Accounting texts on the market.

APPLYING EXCEL

This exciting end-of-chapter feature **links the power of Excel with managerial accounting concepts** by illustrating how Excel functionality can be used to better understand accounting data. Applying Excel goes beyond plugging numbers into a template by providing students with an opportunity to build their own Excel worksheets and formulas. Students are then asked "what if" questions in which they analyze not only **how** related pieces of accounting data affect each other but **why** they do. Applying Excel immediately precedes the Exercises in eleven of the thirteen chapters in the book and is also **integrated with McGraw-Hill *Connect Accounting,*** allowing students to practice their skills online with algorithmically generated datasets and to watch animated, narrated tutorials on how to use formulas in Excel.

> *"An excellent pedagogical feature that helps **further reinforce students' knowledge** of key concepts in the text book, while **strengthening students' Excel skills** that are so important in the work place. This will further enhance an already excellent text."*
>
> —Marianne L. James, California State University, Los Angeles

> *"**[Applying Excel is] an excellent way for students to programmatically develop spreadsheet skills** without having to be taught spreadsheet techniques by the instructor. A significant associated benefit is that students gain more exposure to the dynamics of accounting information by working with what-if scenarios."*
>
> —Earl Godfrey, Gardner–Webb University

POWERFUL *NEW* PEDAGOGY

HELPFUL HINT

Helpful Hint boxes are found several times throughout each chapter and highlight a variety of common mistakes, key points, and "pulling it all together" insights for students.

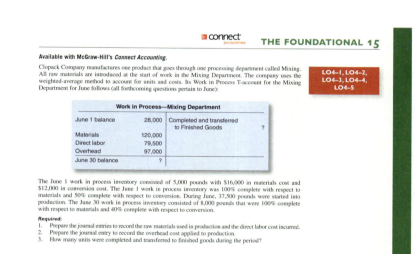

HELPFUL HINT

You need to perform separate equivalent units of production calculations for each manufacturing cost category, such as materials and conversion. When using the weighted-average method to compute equivalent units of production for a cost category you should ignore the completion percentage for the units in beginning inventory. The units transferred to the next department plus the units in ending work in process inventory multiplied by their percentage completion equals the equivalent units of production.

THE FOUNDATIONAL 15

Each chapter now contains one Foundational 15 exercise that includes 15 "building-block" questions related to one concise set of data. These exercises can be used for in-class discussion or as homework assignments. They are found before the Exercises and are available in *Connect Accounting*.

connect ACCOUNTING **THE FOUNDATIONAL 15**

Available with McGraw-Hill's *Connect Accounting*.

Clopack Company manufactures one product that goes through one processing department called Mixing. All raw materials are introduced at the start of work in the Mixing Department. The company uses the weighted-average method to account for units and costs. Its Work in Process T-account for the Mixing Department for June follows (all forthcoming questions pertain to June):

LO4–1, LO4–2, LO4–3, LO4–4, LO4–5

Work in Process—Mixing Department			
June 1 balance	28,000	Completed and transferred to Finished Goods	?
Materials	120,000		
Direct labor	79,500		
Overhead	97,000		
June 30 balance	?		

The June 1 work in process inventory consisted of 5,000 pounds with $16,000 in materials cost and $12,000 in conversion cost. The June 1 work in process inventory was 100% complete with respect to materials and 50% complete with respect to conversion. During June, 37,500 pounds were started into production. The June 30 work in process inventory consisted of 8,000 pounds that were 100% complete with respect to materials and 40% complete with respect to conversion.

Required:
1. Prepare the journal entries to record the raw materials used in production and the direct labor cost incurred.
2. Prepare the journal entry to record the overhead cost applied to production.
3. How many units were completed and transferred to finished goods during the period?

TAKE TWO

Take Two is a new end-of-chapter feature that provides a set of alternate numbers for selected exercises. These alternate numbers can be plugged into the exercise, thereby providing instructors an option to work out the same exercise more than once during class and students an option for additional practice when completing their homework. The Take Two alternate solutions can be found in the instructor's solutions manual.

TAKE TWO

Estimated direct labor-hours = 50,000

CHAPTER OUTLINE

Each chapter opens with an **outline** that provides direction to the student about the road they can expect to traverse throughout the chapter. The **A Look Back/A Look at This Chapter/A Look Ahead** feature reminds students what they have learned in previous chapters, what they can expect to learn in the current chapter, and how the topics will build on each other in chapters to come.

DECISION FEATURE

The **Decision Feature** at the beginning of each chapter provides a real-world example for students, allowing them to see how the chapter's information and insights apply to the world outside the classroom. **Learning Objectives** alert students to what they should expect as they progress through the chapter.

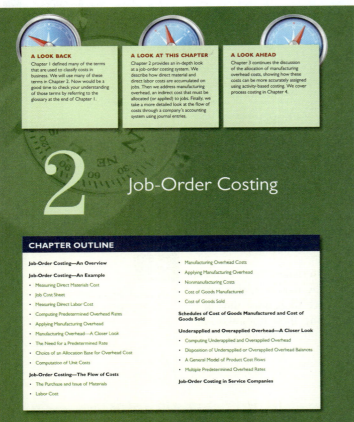

A LOOK BACK
Chapter 1 defined many of the terms that are used to classify costs in business. We will use many of these terms in Chapter 2. Now would be a good time to check your understanding of those terms by referring to the glossary at the end of Chapter 1.

A LOOK AT THIS CHAPTER
Chapter 2 provides an in-depth look at a job-order costing system. We describe how direct material and direct labor costs are accumulated on jobs. Then we address manufacturing overhead, an indirect cost that must be allocated (or applied) to jobs. Finally, we take a more detailed look at the flow of costs through a company's accounting system using journal entries.

A LOOK AHEAD
Chapter 3 continues the discussion of the allocation of manufacturing overhead costs, showing how these costs can be more accurately assigned using activity-based costing. We cover process costing in Chapter 4.

2 Job-Order Costing

CHAPTER OUTLINE

Job-Order Costing—An Overview

Job-Order Costing—An Example
- Measuring Direct Materials Cost
- Job Cost Sheet
- Measuring Direct Labor Cost
- Computing Predetermined Overhead Rates
- Applying Manufacturing Overhead
- Manufacturing Overhead—A Closer Look
- The Need for a Predetermined Rate
- Choice of an Allocation Base for Overhead Cost
- Computation of Unit Costs

Job-Order Costing—The Flow of Costs
- The Purchase and Issue of Materials
- Labor Cost

- Manufacturing Overhead Costs
- Applying Manufacturing Overhead
- Nonmanufacturing Costs
- Cost of Goods Manufactured
- Cost of Goods Sold

Schedules of Cost of Goods Manufactured and Cost of Goods Sold

Underapplied and Overapplied Overhead—A Closer Look
- Computing Underapplied and Overapplied Overhead
- Disposition of Underapplied or Overapplied Overhead Balances
- A General Model of Product Cost Flows
- Multiple Predetermined Overhead Rates

Job-Order Costing in Service Companies

DECISION FEATURE

University Tees: Serving Over 150 Campuses Nationwide

University Tees was founded in 2003 by two **Miami University** college students to provide screen-printing, embroidery, and promotional products for fraternities, sororities, and student organizations. Today, the company, which is headquartered in Cleveland, Ohio, employs as many as four Campus Managers on each of over 150 college campuses across America.

Accurately calculating the cost of each potential customer order is critically important to University Tees because the company needs to be sure that the sales price exceeds the cost associated with satisfying the order. The costs include the cost of the blank T-shirts themselves, printing costs (which vary depending on the quantity of shirts produced and the number of colors per shirt), screen costs (which also vary depending on the number of colors included in a design), shipping costs, and the artwork needed to create a design. The company also takes into account its competitors' pricing strategies when developing its own prices.

Given its success on college campuses, University Tees has introduced a sister company called **On Point Promos** to serve for-profit companies and nonprofit organizations.

Source: Conversation with Joe Haddad, cofounder of University Tees.

"I like . . . the 'A Look Back, A Look at This Chapter, A Look Ahead' and the Chapter Outline. I think **students will appreciate these tools.**"

—Cathy Larson, Middlesex Community College

IN BUSINESS BOXES

These helpful boxed features offer a glimpse into how real companies use the managerial accounting concepts discussed within the chapter. Every chapter contains these current examples.

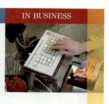

Cashiers Face the Stopwatch

IN BUSINESS

Operations Workforce Optimization (OWO) writes software that uses engineered labor standards to determine how long it should take a cashier to check out a customer. The software measures an employee's productivity by continuously comparing actual customer checkout times to pre-established labor efficiency standards. For example, the cashiers at **Meijer**, a regional retailer located in the Midwest, may be demoted or terminated if they do not meet or exceed labor efficiency standards for at least 95% of customers served. In addition to Meijer, OWO has attracted other clients such as **Gap, Limited Brands, Office Depot, Nike,** and **Toys "R" Us**, based on claims that its software can reduce labor costs by 5–15%. The software has also attracted the attention of the **United Food and Commercial Workers Union**, which represents 27,000 Meijer employees. The union has filed a grievance against Meijer related to its cashier monitoring system.

Source: Vanessa O'Connell, "Stores Count Seconds to Cut Labor Costs," *The Wall Street Journal*, November 17, 2008, pp. A1–A15.

The **DECISION POINT** feature fosters critical thinking and decision-making skills by providing real-world business scenarios that require the resolution of a business issue. The suggested solution is located at the end of the chapter.

Loan Officer

DECISION POINT

Steve Becker owns **Blue Ridge Brewery**, a microbrewery in Arden, North Carolina. He charges distributors $100 per case for his premium beer. The distributors tack on 25% when selling to retailers who in turn add a 30% markup before selling the beer to consumers. In the most recent year, Blue Ridge's revenue was $8 million and its net operating income was $700,000. Becker reports that the costs of making one case of his premium beer are $32 for raw ingredients, $20 for labor, $4 for bottling and packaging, and $12 for utilities.

Assume that Becker has approached your bank for a loan. As the loan officer, you should consider a variety of factors, including the company's margin of safety. Assuming that other information about the company is favorable, would you consider Blue Ridge's margin of safety to be comfortable enough to extend a loan?

CONCEPT CHECK

Concept Checks allow students to test their comprehension of topics and concepts covered at meaningful points throughout each chapter.

7. Which of the following statements is true? (You can select more than one answer.)
   a. A segment's contribution margin minus its traceable fixed expenses equals the segment margin.
   b. A company's common fixed costs should be evenly allocated to business segments when computing the dollar sales for a segment to break even.
   c. A segment's traceable fixed costs should include only those costs that would disappear over time if the segment disappeared.
   d. Fixed costs that are traceable to one segment may be a common cost of another segment.

CONCEPT CHECK

UTILIZING THE ICONS

To reflect our service-based economy, the text is replete with examples from service-based businesses. A helpful icon distinguishes service-related examples in the text.

Ethics assignments and examples serve as a reminder that good conduct is vital in business. Icons call out content that relates to ethical behavior for students.

The writing icon denotes problems that require students to use critical thinking as well as writing skills to explain their decisions.

An Excel© icon alerts students that spreadsheet templates are available for use with select problems and cases.

The IFRS icon highlights content that may be affected by the impending change to IFRS and possible convergence between U.S. GAAP and IFRS.

This new marginal end-of-chapter icon indicates the Take Two alternate number set for select exercises.

END-OF-CHAPTER MATERIAL

Introduction to Managerial Acounting has earned a reputation for the best end-of-chapter review and discussion material of any text on the market. Our problem and case material conforms to AICPA, AACSB, and Bloom's Taxonomy categories and makes a great starting point for class discussions and group projects. With review problems, discussion questions, Excel problems, the Foundational 15 set, exercises, problems, and cases, Brewer offers students practice material of varying complexity and depth. In order to provide even more practice opportunities, an **alternate problem set** is available on the text's website and in *Connect Accounting*, along with online quizzes and practice exams.

AUTHOR-WRITTEN SUPPLEMENTS

Unlike other managerial accounting texts, Brewer, Garrison, and Noreen write all of the text's major supplements, ensuring a perfect fit between text and supplements. For more information on *Introduction to Managerial Accounting*'s supplements package see pages xviii–xix.

"As Brewer, Garrison, and Noreen write most of the text's supplements, these materials really support the textbook material well. The **continuity/consistency between textbook and supporting materials** is not found with some other textbooks. All of the resources available with the Brewer book **help me to be a better teacher!**"

—Sheri Henson, Western Kentucky

New to the 7th edition

Faculty feedback helps us continue to improve *Introduction to Managerial Accounting*.
In response to reviewer suggestions we have implemented the following changes:

Overall:
- **In Business** boxes updated throughout.

All Chapters
- All chapters have additional Concept Check questions based on a review of the LearnSmart heat maps.

Prologue
- The prologue has a new section titled Managerial Accounting: Beyond the Numbers. It has expanded coverage of leadership skills and an expanded set of exercises.

Chapter 1
- The learning objective pertaining to direct and indirect costs has been moved to the front of the chapter to improve the students' ability to understand the material.

Chapter 2
- No significant changes except for two new In Business boxes.

Chapter 3
- No significant changes.

Chapter 4
- No significant changes except for one new In Business box.

Chapter 5
- The assumptions of CVP analysis have been moved from the end of the chapter to the beginning of the chapter. The target profit analysis and break-even analysis learning objectives have been reversed.

Chapter 6
- This chapter has added a new learning objective related to calculating companywide and segment break-even points for companies with traceable fixed costs.

Chapter 7
- Added new text and an exhibit to help students better understand how and why a master budget is created and how Microsoft Excel can be used to create a financial planning model that answers "what-if" questions. Added two new end-of-chapter exercises that enable students to use Microsoft Excel to answer "what-if" questions.

Chapter 8
- In response to customer feedback, we reversed the headings in the flexible budget performance report. The actual results are shown in the far-left column and the planning budget is shown in the far-right column. Similarly, we reversed the headings in the general model for standard cost variance analysis. The actual results (AQ × AP) are shown in the far-left column and the flexible budget (SQ × SP) is shown in the far-right column.

Chapter 9
- No significant changes beyond adding a new Business Focus feature and two new In Business boxes.

Chapter 10
- A section illustrating the meaning of a constraint has been added. Also, several new In Business boxes have been created.

Chapter 11
- Moved the learning objective pertaining to the payback period to the front of the chapter. Adopted a Microsoft Excel-based approach for depicting net present value calculations. Added a discussion of the behavioral implications of the simple rate of return method.

Chapter 12
- No significant changes except for new In Business boxes.

Chapter 13
- The learning objectives have all been redefined to emphasize an internal management perspective. Four new ratios have been added to the text to further enrich the students' learning opportunities.

*"This book provides in depth coverage of basic managerial accounting concepts and procedures in a **clear and concise** manner in logically sequenced topics. It's designed to help students use accounting information and make a decision. It's **very easy to read**."*
—Mehmet Kocakulah, University of Southern Indiana

*"An **excellent book** for an introductory Managerial Course **for all business students,** not just Accounting majors."*
—Tamara Phelan, Northern Illinois University

McGRAW-HILL CONNECT® ACCOUNTING

McGraw-Hill *Connect Accounting* is a digital teaching and learning environment that gives students the means to better connect with their coursework, with their instructors, and with the important concepts that they will need to know for success now and in the future. With *Connect Accounting*, instructors can deliver assignments, quizzes and tests easily online. Students can review course material and practice important skills. *Connect Accounting* provides the following features:

- SmartBook and LearnSmart
- SmartBook Achieve
- Auto-graded online homework
- Auto-graded Excel simulations
- Powerful learning resources including interactive presentations and guided examples

In short, *Connect Accounting* offers students powerful tools and features that optimize their time and energy, enabling them to focus on learning.

For more information about *Connect Accounting,* go to www.connect.mheducation.com, or contact your local McGraw-Hill Higher Education representative.

SmartBook, powered by LearnSmart

LearnSmart is the market-leading adaptive study resource that is proven to strengthen memory recall, increase class retention, and boost grades. LearnSmart allows students to study more efficiently because they are made aware of what they know and don't know.

SmartBook, which is powered by LearnSmart, is the first and only adaptive reading experience designed to change the way students read and learn. It creates a personalized reading experience by highlighting the most impactful concepts a student needs to learn at that moment in time. As a student engages with SmartBook, the reading experience continuously adapts by highlighting content based on what the student knows and doesn't know. This ensures that the focus is on the content he or she needs to learn, while simultaneously promoting long-term retention of material. Use SmartBook's real-time reports to quickly identify the concepts that require more attention from individual students–or the entire class. The end result? Students are more engaged with course content, can better prioritize their time, and come to class ready to participate.

MARKET-LEADING TECHNOLOGY

SmartBook Achieve

SmartBook Achieve™—a revolutionary study and learning experience—pinpoints an individual student's knowledge gaps and provides targeted, interactive learning help at the moment of need. The rich, dynamic learning resources delivered in that moment of need help students learn the material, retain more knowledge, and earn better grades. The program's continuously adaptive learning path ensures that every minute a student spends with Achieve is returned as the most value-added minute possible.

Online Assignments

Connect Accounting helps students learn more efficiently by providing feedback and practice material when they need it, where they need it. *Connect* grades homework automatically and gives immediate feedback on any questions students may have missed. Our assignable, gradable end-of-chapter content includes a general journal application that looks and feels more like what you would find in a general ledger software package. Also, select questions have been redesigned to test students' knowledge more fully. They now include tables for students to work through rather than requiring that all calculations be done offline.

Interactive Presentations

Interactive presentations provide engaging narratives of all chapter learning objectives in an assignable interactive online format. They follow the structure of the text and are organized to match the specific learning objectives within each chapter. While the interactive presentations are not meant to replace the textbook, they provide additional explanation and enhancement of material from the text chapter, allowing students to learn, study, and practice with instant feedback, at their own pace.

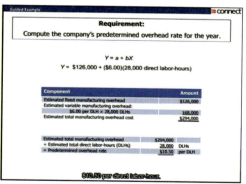

Guided Examples

The guided examples in *Connect Accounting* provide a narrated, animated step-by-step walkthrough of select exercises similar to those assigned. These short presentations, which can be turned on or off by instructors, provide reinforcement when students need it most.

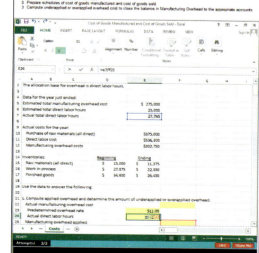

Auto-graded Excel Simulations

Simulated Excel questions, assignable within *Connect Accounting*, allow students to practice their Excel skills—such as basic formulas and formatting—within the context of managerial accounting. These questions feature animated, narrated Help and Show Me tutorials (when enabled), as well as automatic feedback and grading for both students and professors.

Student Resource Library

The *Connect Accounting* Student Resources give students access to additional resources such as recorded lectures, online practice materials, an eBook, and more.

McGraw-Hill *Connect*® *Accounting* Features

Connect Accounting offers powerful tools, resources, and features to make managing assignments easier, so faculty can spend more time teaching.

Simple Assignment Management and Smart Grading. With McGraw-Hill's *Connect Accounting,* creating assignments is easier than ever, so you can spend more time teaching and less time managing. *Connect Accounting* enables you to:

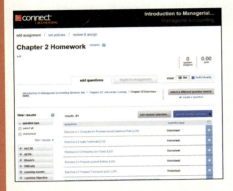

- Create and deliver assignments and assessments easily with selectable end-of-chapter questions and test bank items.
- Have assignments scored automatically, giving students immediate feedback on their work and comparisons with correct answers.
- Access and review each response; manually change grades or leave comments for students to review.
- Reinforce classroom concepts by assigning LearnSmart modules and Interactive Presentations.

Powerful Instructor and Student Reports

Connect Accounting keeps instructors informed about how each student, section, and class is performing, allowing for more productive use of lecture and office hours. The reports tab enables you to:

- View scored work immediately and track individual or group performance with assignment and grade reports.
- Access an instant view of student or class performance relative to learning objectives.
- Collect data and generate reports required by many accreditation organizations, such as AACSB and AICPA.

Connect Insight

The first and only analytics tool of its kind, Connect Insight™ is a series of visual data displays—each framed by an intuitive question—to provide at-a-glance information regarding how your class is doing. Connect Insight™ provides an at-a-glance analysis on five key insights, available at a moment's notice from your tablet device.

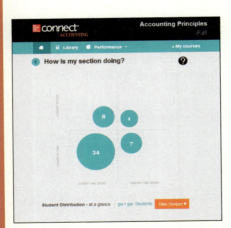

- How are my students doing?
- How is my section doing?
- How is this student doing?
- How are my assignments doing?
- How is this assignment going?

Instructor Library

The *Connect Accounting* Instructor Library is your repository for additional resources to improve student engagement in and out of class. You can select and use any asset that enhances your lecture. The *Connect Accounting* Instructor Library includes access to:

- Solutions manual
- Test bank
- Instructor PowerPoint® slides

- Instructor's Resource Guide—includes Assignment Topic Grids and Lecture Notes that correspond with the Instructor PowerPoints
- Applying Excel Solutions
- Sample Syllabus
- The eBook version of the text
- FIFO Supplement Chapter

TEGRITY CAMPUS: LECTURES 24/7

Tegrity Campus, is a service that makes class time available 24/7 by automatically capturing every lecture. With a simple one-click start-and-stop process, you capture all computer screens and corresponding audio in a format that is easily searchable, frame by frame. Students can replay any part of any class with easy-to-use browser-based viewing on a PC, Mac, or other mobile device.

Help turn your students' study time into learning moments immediately supported by your lecture. With Tegrity Campus, you also increase intent listening and class participation by easing students' concerns about note-taking. Lecture Capture will make it more likely you will see students' faces, not the tops of their heads.

To learn more about Tegrity, watch a 2-minute Flash demo at http://tegritycampus.mhhe.com.

McGRAW-HILL CAMPUS

McGraw-Hill Campus™ is a new one-stop teaching and learning experience available to users of any learning management system. This institutional service allows faculty and students to enjoy single sign-on (SSO) access to all McGraw-Hill Higher Education materials, including the award-winning McGraw-Hill *Connect* platform, from directly within the institution's website. To learn more about MH Campus, visit **http://mhcampus.mhhe.com.**

CUSTOM PUBLISHING THROUGH CREATE

McGraw-Hill Create is a new, self-service website that allows instructors to create custom course materials by drawing upon McGraw-Hill's comprehensive, cross-disciplinary content. Instructors can add their own content quickly and easily and tap into other rights-secured third–party sources as well, then arrange the content in a way that makes the most sense for their course. Instructors can even personalize their book with the course name and information and choose the best format for their students—color print, black-and-white print, or an eBook.

Through Create, instructors can

- Select and arrange the content in a way that makes the most sense for their course.
- Combine material from different sources and even upload their own content.
- Choose the best format for their students—print or eBook.
- Edit and update their course materials as often as they like.

Begin creating now at **www.mcgrawhillcreate.com**

McGRAW-HILL CUSTOMER EXPERIENCE GROUP CONTACT INFORMATION

At McGraw-Hill, we understand that getting the most from new technology can be challenging. That's why our services don't stop after you purchase our book. You can e-mail our product specialists 24 hours a day, get product training online, or search our knowledge bank of Frequently Asked Questions on our support Website. For Customer experience, call 800-331-5094 or visit www.mhhe.com/support. One of our Technical Support Analysts will assist you in a timely fashion.

Instructor Supplements

Assurance of Learning Ready

Many educational institutions today are focused on the notion of assurance of learning, an important element of some accreditation standards. *Introduction to Managerial Accounting,* 7e, is designed specifically to be support your assurance of learning initiatives with a simple, yet powerful, solution.

Each test bank question for *Introduction Managerial Accounting,* 7e maps to a specific chapter learning outcome/objective listed in the text. You can use our test bank software, EZ Test, and Connect to easily query for learning outcomes/objectives that directly relate to the learning objectives for your course. You can then use the reporting features of EZ Test and Connect to aggregate student results in similar fashion, making the collection and presentation of assurance of learning data simple and easy.

AACSB Statement

McGraw-Hill/Irwin is a proud corporate member of AACSB International. Recognizing the importance and value of AACSB accreditation, we have sought to recognize the curricula guidelines detailed in AACSB standards for business accreditation by connecting selected questions in Brewer 7e, with the general knowledge and skill guidelines found in the AACSB standards. The statements contained in Brewer 7e are provided only as a guide for the users of this text. The AACSB leaves content coverage and assessment clearly within the realm and control of individual schools, the mission of the school, and the faculty. The AACSB does also charge schools with the obligation of doing assessment against their own content and learning goals. While Brewer 7e and its teaching package make no claim of any specific AACSB qualification or evaluation, we have labeled selected questions according to the eight general knowledge and skills areas. The labels or tags within Brewer 7e are as indicated. There are, of course, many more within the test bank, the text, and the teaching package which might be used as a "standard" for your course. However, the labeled questions are suggested for your consideration.

McGraw-Hill *Connect*® *Accounting*

McGraw-Hill *Connect Accounting* offers a number of powerful tools and features to make managing your classroom easier. *Connect Accounting* with Brewer 7e offers enhanced features and technology to help both you and your students make the most of your time inside and outside the classroom.

EZ Test Online

This test bank in Word format contains multiple-choice questions, essay questions, and short problems. Each test item is coded for level of difficulty, learning objective, AACSB and AICPA skill area, and Bloom's Taxonomy level. McGraw-Hill's EZ Test Online is a flexible and easy-to-use electronic testing program that allows instructors to create tests from book-specific items. EZ Test Online accommodates a wide range of question types and allows instructors to add their own questions. Multiple versions of the test can be created and any test can be exported for use with course management systems such as BlackBoard/WebCT. EZ Test Online gives instructors a place to easily administer exams and quizzes online. The program is available for Windows and Macintosh environments.

Student **Supplements**

McGraw-Hill *Connect*® *Accounting*

McGraw-Hill *Connect Accounting* helps prepare you for your future by enabling faster learning, more efficient studying, and higher retention of knowledge. *Connect Accounting* includes access to a searchable, integrated online version of the text, and much more.

CourseSmart

CourseSmart is a way for faculty to find and review eTextbooks. It's also a great option for students who are interested in accessing their course materials digitally and saving money. CourseSmart offers thousands of the most commonly adopted textbooks across hundreds of courses from a wide variety of higher education publishers. With the CourseSmart eTextbook, students can save up to 45 percent off the cost of a print book, reduce their impact on the environment, and access powerful Web tools for learning. CourseSmart is an online eTextbook, which means users access and view their textbook online when connected to the Internet. Students can also print sections of the book for maximum portability. CourseSmart eTextbooks are available in one standard online reader with full text search, notes and highlighting, and e-mail tools for sharing notes between classmates. For more information on CourseSmart, go to **www.coursesmart.com.**

Applying Excel

Forms available in the *Connect* Student Library.

This feature has been added to Chapters 1-11 of the text. Applying Excel gives you the opportunity to build your own Excel worksheet using Excel formulas. You are then asked to answer "what if" questions, all of which illustrate the relationship among various pieces of accounting data. The Applying Excel feature links directly to the concepts introduced in the chapter, providing you with an invaluable opportunity to apply what you have learned utilizing an application you will use throughout your career.

Check Figures

Available with select problems in the end-of-chapter material, these provide key answers for selected problems and cases.

Acknowledgments

Suggestions have been received from many of our colleagues throughout the world who have used the prior edition of *Introduction to Managerial Accounting*. This is vital feedback that we rely on in each edition. Each of those who have offered comments and suggestions has our thanks.

The efforts of many people are needed to develop and improve a text. Among these people are the reviewers and consultants who point out areas of concern, cite areas of strength, and make recommendations for change. We thank current and past reviewers who have provided feedback that was enormously helpful in preparing *Introduction to Managerial Accounting*.

Seventh Edition Reviewers

Melanie Anderson, *Slippery Rock University*
Pat Carter, *Green River Community College*
Ru-Fang Chiang, *California State University—Chico*
Gene Elrod, *University of North Texas*
Daniel J. Gibbons, *Waubonsee Community College*
Olen L. Greer, *Missouri State University*
Tom Hrubec, *Franklin University*
Robert L. Hurt, *California State Polytechnic University—Pomona*
Frank Ilett, *Boise State University*
Daniel Law, *Gonzaga University*
Marisa Lester, *University at Albany*
Candace Leuck, *Clemson University*
Diane Marker, *University of Toledo*
Lawrence Metzger, *Loyola University Chicago*
Susan Minke, *Indiana Purdue University at Fort Wayne*
Samir Nissan, *California State University—Chico*
Marilyn Pipes, *Tarleton State University*
Ronald O. Reed, *University of Northern Colorado*
Anwar Salimi, *California State Polytechnic University—Pomona*
Rex A. Schildhouse, *Miramar College, San Diego Community College District*
Pat Seaton, *University of Northern Colorado*
Randy Serrett, *University of Houston—Downtown*
Meghna Singhvi, *Loyola Marymount University*
Mike Slaubaugh, *Indiana University Purdue University Fort Wayne*
Joel Sneed, *University of Oregon*
Stephen Strand, *Southern Maine Community College*
Gloria Stuart, *Georgia Southern University*
Dominique Svarc, *Harper College*
Dorothy A. Thompson, *University of North Texas*
Clark Wheatley, *Florida International University*
Blair Arthur William, *Slippery Rock University*
Jan Workman, *East Carolina University*
Weihong Xu, *State University of New York at Buffalo*
Minna Yu, *Monmouth University*
Ronald Zhao, *Monmouth University*

Previous Edition Reviewers

L. M. Abney, *LaSalle University*
Nas Ahadiat, *Cal Poly Pomona*
Sol Ahiarah, *SUNY College at Buffalo*
Markus Ahrens, *St. Louis Community College—Meramec*
Natalie Allen, *Texas A&M University*
William Ambrose, *DeVry University*
Elizabeth M. Ammann, *Lindenwood University*
Robert J. Angell, *North Carolina A&T State University*
Robert Appleton, *University of North Carolina-Wilmington*
Thomas Arcuri, *Florida Community College at Jacksonville*
Rowland Atiase, *University of Texas at Austin*
Steven Ault, *Montana State University*
Leonard Bacon, *California State University, Bakersfield*
Roderick Barclay, *Texas A&M University*
Linda Batiste, *Baton Rouge Community College*
Benjamin W. Bean, *Utah Valley State College*
Debbie Beard, *Southeast Missouri State University*
Sarah Bee, *Seattle University*
Stephen Benner, *Eastern Illinois University*
Ramesh C. Bhatia, *Millersville University*
Kristen Bigbee, *Texas Tech University*
Larry Bitner, *Hood College*
Jay Blazer, *Milwaukee Area Technical College*
Nancy Bledsoe, *Millsaps College*
William Blouch, *Loyola College*
Eugene Blue, *Governor State University*
Rick Blumenfeld, *Sierra Community College*
Linda Bolduc, *Mount Wachusett Community College*
William J. Bradberry, *New River Community and Technical College*
Casey Bradley, *Troy State University*
Jim Breyley, Jr., *University of New England*
Betty Jo Browning, *Bradley University*
Marley Brown, *Mt. Hood Community College*
Myra Bruegger, *Southeastern Community College*
Barry S. Buchoff, *Towson University*
Robert Burdette, *Salt Lake Community College*
Francis Bush, *Virginia Military Institute*
Rebecca Butler, *Gateway Community College*
Leah Cabaniss, *Holyoke Community College*
June Calahan, *Redlands Community College*
John Callister, *Cornell University*
Annhenrie Campbell, *California State University, Stanislaus*
David G. Campbell, *Sierra Community College*
Elizabeth Cannata, *Stonehill College*
Dennis Caplan, *Iowa State University*
Kay Carnes, *Gonzaga University*
Suzanne Cercone, *Keystone College*
Gayle Chaky, *Dutchess Community College*
John Chandler, *University of Illinois-Champaign*
Chiaho Chang, *Montclair State University*
Siew Chan, *University of Massachusetts, Boston*
Chak-Tong Chau, *University of Houston*
Julie Chenier, *Louisiana State University-Baton Rouge*
Lawrence Chin, *Golden Gate University*
Carolyn Clark, *St. Joseph's University*
Darlene Coarts, *University of Northern Iowa*
Jay Cohen, *Oakton Community College*
Joanne Collins, *California State University-Los Angeles*

Judith Cook, *Grossmont College*
Mark Cornman, *Youngstown State University*
Debra Cosgrove, *University Of Nebraska-Lincoln*
Charles Croxford, *Merced College*
Kathy Crusto-Way, *Tarrant County College*
Richard Cummings, *Benedictine College*
Jill Cunningham, *Santa Fe Community College*
Alan Czyzewski, *Indiana State University*
Paul E. Dascher, *Stetson University*
Betty David, *Francis Marion University*
Deborah Davis, *Hampton University*
Peggy Dejong, *Kirkwood Community College*
Sandra Devona, *Northern Illinois University*
G. DiLorenzo, *Gloucester County College*
Jan Duffy, *Iowa State University*
Keith Dusenbery, *Johnson State College*
Terry Elliott, *Morehead State University*
Robert S Ellison, *Texas State U–San Marcos*
Gene B. Elrod, *University of North Texas*
Emmanuel Emenyonu, *Southern Connecticut State University*
James Emig, *Villanova University*
Denise M. English, *Boise State University*
Martin L. Epstein, *Central New Mexico Community College*
Diane Eure, *Texas State University*
Michael Farina, *Cerritos College*
John Farlin, *Ohio Dominican University*
Amanda Farmer, *University of Georgia*
Harriet Farney, *University of Hartford*
M. A. Fekrat, *Georgetown University*
W. L. Ferrara, *Stetson University*
Jerry Ferry, *University of North Alabama*
Kathleen Fitzpatrick, *University of Toledo-Scott Park*
Benjamin Foster, *University of Louisville*
Joan Foster, *Collge Misericordia*
James Franklin, *Troy State University Montgomery*
Joseph Galante, *Millersville University of Pennsylvania*
Ananda Roop Ganguly, *Purdue University*
Frank Gersich, *Monmouth College*
David Gibson, *Hampden-Sydney College*
Jackson Gillespie, *University of Delaware*
Lisa Gillespie, *Loyola University-Chicago*
John Gill, *Jackson State University*
Joe Goetz, *Louisiana State University*
Art Goldman, *University of Kentucky*
David Gorton, *Eastern Washington University*
Suzanne Gradisher, *University Of Akron*
James Gravel, *Husson College*
Olen L. Greer, *Missouri State University*
Linda Hadley, *University of Dayton*
Joseph Hagan, *East Carolina University*
Laurie Hagberg, *Trident Technical College*
Ron Halsac, *Community College of Allegheny County*
Michael R. Hammond, *Missouri State University*
Heidi Hansel, *Kirkwood Community College*
Dan Hary, *Southwestern Oklahoma State University*
Susan Hass, *Simmons College*
Robert Hayes, *Tennessee State University*
Annette Hebble, *University of St. Thomas*
James Hendricks, *Northern Illinois University*
Sheri L. Henson, *Western Kentucky University*

Youngwon Her, *University of Missouri–St. Louis*
Nancy Thorley Hill, *DePaul University*
Joan Van Hise, *Fairfield University*
Mary Hollars, *Vincennes University*
Joan Hollister, *State University of New York–New Paltz*
Jay Holmen, *University of Wisconsin-Eau Claire*
Norma C. Holter, *Towson University*
Norma Holter, *Towson University*
Anita Hope, *Tarrant County College*
Kathy Ho, *Niagra University*
Tom Hrubec, *Franklin University*
Susan B Hughes, *University of Vermont*
Ronald Huntsman, *Texas Lutheran University*
Robert L. Hurt, *Cal Poly Pomona*
Wayne Ingalls, *University of Maine College*
David Jacobson, *Salem State College*
Martha Janis, *University of Wisconsin-Waukesha*
Robyn Dawn Jarnagin, *Montana State University*
Agatha E. Jeffers, *Montclair State University*
John Savash-*Elmira College*
Holly Johnston, *Boston University*
Sanford Kahn, *University of Cincinnati*
Jai S. Kang, *San Francisco State University*
Sushila Kedia, *University of Southern Indiana*
Debra Kerby, *Truman State University*
Marsha Kertz, *San Jose State University*
Raj Kiani, *California State University, Northridge*
Ethan Kinory, *Baruch College, CUNY*
Bonnie K. Klamm, *North Dakota State University*
Michael Klimesh, *Gustav Adolphus University*
Mehmet Kocakulah, *University of Southern Indiana*
Greg Kordecki, *Clayton College and State University*
Michael Kulper, *Santa Barbara City College*
Christoper Kwak, *Ohlone College*
Thomas Largay, *Thomas College*
Cathy Larson, *Middlesex Community College*
Robert Larson, *Penn State University*
Chor Lau, *California State University, Los Angeles*
Dan Law, *Gonzaga University*
Chuo-Hsuan Lee, *SUNY Plattsburgh*
Minwoo Lee, *Western Kentucky University*
Angela Letourneau, *Winthrop University*
Barry Lewis, *Southwest Missouri State University*
Roger P. Lewis, *Saint Cloud State University*
Harold T. Little Jr., *Western Kentucky University*
Joan Litton, *Ferrum College*
Rebecca Lohmann, *Southeast Missouri State University*
Dennis M. Lopez, *University of Texas-San Antonio*
G. D. Lorenzo, *Gloucester Community College*
Catherine Lumbattis, *Southern Illinois University-Carbondale*
Cathy Lumbattis, *Southern Illinois University*
Nace Magner, *Western Kentucky University*
Bob Mahan, *Milligan College*
Leland Mansuetti, *Sierra College*
Ariel Markelevich, *Bernard M. Baruch College*
Lisa Martin, *Western Michigan University*
Raj Mashruwala, *University of Illinois-Chicago*
Jayne Mass, *Towson University*

Allen Mcconnell, *University of Northern Colorado*
Britton A McKay, *Georgia Southern University*
Dawn McKinley, *William Rainey Harper College*
Laurie B. McWhorter, *Mississippi State University*
Michael J. Meyer, *Ohio University*
Pam Meyer, *University of Louisiana at Lafayette*
Lorie Milam, *University of Northern Colorado*
Robert Milbrath, *University of Houston*
Valerie Milliron, *California State University, Chico*
Earl Mitchell, *Santa Ana College*
Arabian Morgan, *Orange Coast College*
Laura Morgan, *University of New Hampshire*
Anthony Moses, *Saint Anselm College*
Daniel Mugavero, *Lake Superior State University*
Matthew Muller, *Adirondack Community College*
Muroki Mwaura, *William Patterson University*
Presha Neidermeyer, *Union College*
Joseph M. Nicassio, *Westmoreland County Community College*
Lee Nicholas, *University of Northern Iowa*
Tracie Nobles, *Austin Community College-Northridge*
Eizabeth Nolan, *Southwestern Oklahoma State University*
Michael O'Neill, *Seattle Central Community College*
Omneya Abd-Elsalam, *Aston University*
Aileen Ormiston, *Mesa Community College*
George Otto, *Truman College*
Chei Paik, *George Washington University*
Abbie Gail Parham, *Georgia Southern University*
George Scott Pate, *Robeson Community College*
Paige Paulsen, *Salt Lake Community College*
Nori Pearson, *Washington State University*
Tamara Phelan, *Northern Illinois University*
Eustace Phillip, *Emmanuel College*
Anthony Piltz, *Rocky Mountain College*
H. M. Pomroy, *Elizabethtown College*
Alan Porter, *Eastern New Mexico University*
Barbara Prince, *Cambridge Community College*
Grant Pritchard, *Dominican University of California*
Ahmad Rahman, *La Roche College*
Vasant Raval, *Creighton University–Omaha*
Ronald Reed, *University of Northern Colorado*
Joan Reicosky, *University of Minnesota-Morris*
Jacci Rodgers, *Oklahoma City University*
Leonardo Rodriguez, *Florida International University*
Rick Roscher, *University of North Carolina-Wilmington*
Gary Ross, *College of the Southwest*
Luther Ross, *Central Piedmont Community College*
Anwar Salimi, *California State Polytechnic University-Pomona*
Martha Sampsell, *Elmhurst College*
Angela H. Sandberg, *Jacksonville State University*
Eldon Schafer, *University of Arizona*
Roger Scherser, *Edison Community College*
Henry Schulman, *Grossmont College*
Henry Schwarzbach, *University of Colorado*
Randall Serrett, *University of Houston Downtown*
Deborah Shafer, *Temple College*
Meghna Singhvi, *Florida International University*
Michael Skaff, *College of the Sequoias*
Henry C. Smith, III, *Otterbein College*

We are grateful for the outstanding support from McGraw-Hill/Irwin. In particular, we would like to thank Tim Vertovec, Managing Director; Nichole Pullen, Brand Manager; Danielle Andries, Product Developer; Brad Parkins, Marketing Director; Pat Frederickson, Lead Content Project Manager; Debra Sylvester, Senior Buyer; Srdjan Savanovic, Senior Designer; Brian Nacik, Lead Content Project Manager; and Angela Norris, Content Project Manager.

Thank you to our Digital Contributor, Margaret Shackell-Dowell (Cornell University), for her many contributions to *Connect Accounting,* including Guided Example content and Interactive Presentation review. Thanks also to Patti Lopez (Valencia College), for her efforts as lead subject matter expert on LearnSmart.

Finally, we would like to thank Helen Roybark and Beth Woods for working so hard to ensure an error-free seventh edition.

We are grateful to the Institute of Certified Management Accountants for permission to use questions and/or unofficial answers from past Certificate in Management Accounting (CMA) examinations. Likewise, we thank the American Institute of Certified Public Accountants, the Society of Management Accountants of Canada, and the Chartered Institute of Management Accountants (United Kingdom) for permission to use (or to adapt) selected problems from their examinations. These problems bear the notations CMA, CPA, SMA, and CIMA, respectively.

Peter C. Brewer

Ray H. Garrison

Eric W. Noreen

BRIEF CONTENTS

CONTENTS

CHAPTER THREE
Activity-Based Costing   120

CHAPTER FOUR
Process Costing   160

CHAPTER SEVEN
Master Budgeting   292

CHAPTER EIGHT
Flexible Budgets, Standard Costs, and Variance Analysis   348

CHAPTER NINE
Performance Measurement in Decentralized Organizations   416

CHAPTER TEN
Differential Analysis: The Key to Decision Making   456

CHAPTER ELEVEN
Capital Budgeting Decisions   510

A LOOK AT THE PROLOGUE

The Prologue defines managerial accounting and explains why it is important to the future careers of all business students. It also explains how managerial accounting involves more than just quantitative calculations.

A LOOK AHEAD

Chapter 1 defines many of the cost terms that will be used throughout the textbook. It explains that in managerial accounting the term cost is used in many different ways depending on the immediate needs of management.

Managerial Accounting: An Overview

PROLOGUE OUTLINE

What Is Managerial Accounting?

- Planning
- Controlling
- Decision Making

Why Does Managerial Accounting Matter to Your Career?

- Business Majors
- Accounting Majors

Managerial Accounting: Beyond the Numbers

- An Ethics Perspective
- A Strategic Management Perspective
- An Enterprise Risk Management Perspective
- A Corporate Social Responsibility Perspective
- A Process Management Perspective
- A Leadership Perspective

This prologue explains why managerial accounting is important to the future careers of all business students. It begins by answering two questions: (1) What is managerial accounting? and (2) Why does managerial accounting matter to your career? It concludes by discussing six topics—ethics, strategic management, enterprise risk management, corporate social responsibility, process management, and leadership—that define the business context for applying the quantitative aspects of managerial accounting.

WHAT IS MANAGERIAL ACCOUNTING?

Many students enrolled in this course will have recently completed an introductory *financial accounting* course. **Financial accounting** is concerned with reporting financial information to external parties, such as stockholders, creditors, and regulators. **Managerial accounting** is concerned with providing information to managers for use within the organization. Exhibit P–1 summarizes seven key differences between financial and managerial accounting. It recognizes that the fundamental difference between financial and managerial accounting is that financial accounting serves the needs of those *outside* the organization, whereas managerial accounting serves the needs of managers employed *inside* the

EXHIBIT P–1   Comparison of Financial and Managerial Accounting

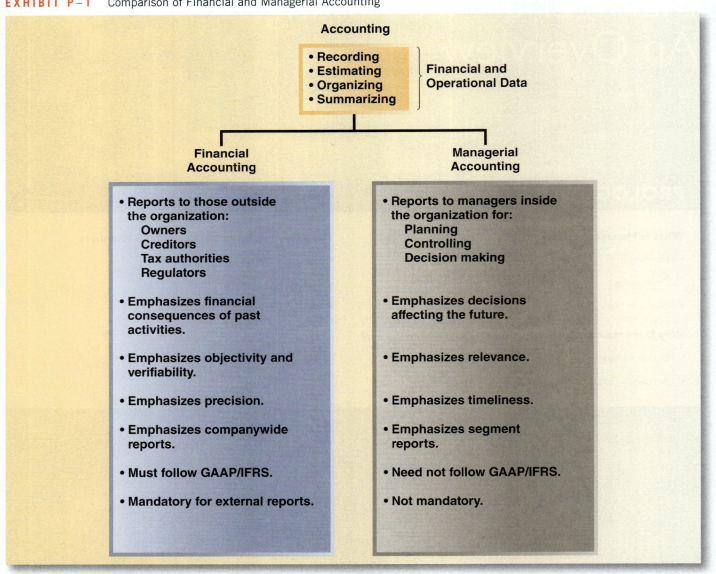

organization. Because of this fundamental difference in users, financial accounting empha-sizes the financial consequences of past activities, objectivity and verifiability, precision, and companywide performance, whereas managerial accounting emphasizes decisions affecting the future, relevance, timeliness, and *segment* performance. A **segment** is a part or activity of an organization about which managers would like cost, revenue, or profit data. Examples of business segments include product lines, customer groups (segmented by age, ethnicity, gender, volume of purchases, etc.), geographic territories, divisions, plants, and departments. Finally, financial accounting is mandatory for external reports and it needs to comply with rules, such as generally accepted accounting principles (GAAP) and international financial reporting standards (IFRS), whereas managerial accounting is not mandatory and it does not need to comply with externally imposed rules.

As mentioned in Exhibit P–1, managerial accounting helps managers perform three vital activities—*planning, controlling,* and *decision making.* **Planning** involves estab-lishing goals and specifying how to achieve them. **Controlling** involves gathering feed-back to ensure that the plan is being properly executed or modified as circumstances change. **Decision making** involves selecting a course of action from competing alterna-tives. Now let's take a closer look at these three pillars of managerial accounting.

Planning

Assume that you work for **Procter & Gamble (P&G)** and that you are in charge of the company's campus recruiting for all undergraduate business majors. In this example, your planning process would begin by establishing a goal such as: our goal is to recruit the "best and brightest" college graduates. The next stage of the planning process would require specifying how to achieve this goal by answering numerous questions such as:

- How many students do we need to hire in total and from each major?
- What schools do we plan to include in our recruiting efforts?
- Which of our employees will be involved in each school's recruiting activities?
- When will we conduct our interviews?
- How will we compare students to one another to decide who will be extended job offers?
- What salary will we offer our new hires? Will the salaries differ by major?
- How much money can we spend on our recruiting efforts?

As you can see, there are many questions that need to be answered as part of the plan-ning process. Plans are often accompanied by a *budget.* A **budget** is a detailed plan for the future that is usually expressed in formal quantitative terms. As the head of recruiting at P&G, your budget would include two key components. First, you would have to work with other senior managers inside the company to establish a budgeted amount of total salaries that can be offered to all new hires. Second, you would have to create a budget that quantifies how much you intend to spend on your campus recruiting activities.

Controlling

Once you established and started implementing P&G's recruiting plan, you would transi-tion to the control process. This process would involve gathering, evaluating, and respond-ing to feedback to ensure that this year's recruiting process meets expectations. It would also include evaluating the feedback in search of ways to run a more effective recruiting campaign next year. The control process would involve answering questions such as:

- Did we succeed in hiring the planned number of students within each major and at each school?
- Did we lose too many exceptional candidates to competitors?
- Did each of our employees involved in the recruiting process perform satisfactorily?

- Is our method of comparing students to one another working?
- Did the on-campus and office interviews run smoothly?
- Did we stay within our budget in terms of total salary commitments to new hires?
- Did we stay within our budget regarding spending on recruiting activities?

As you can see, there are many questions that need to be answered as part of the control process. When answering these questions your goal would be to go beyond simple yes or no answers in search of the underlying reasons why performance exceeded or failed to meet expectations. Part of the control process includes preparing *performance reports.* A **performance report** compares budgeted data to actual data in an effort to identify and learn from excellent performance and to identify and eliminate sources of unsatisfactory performance. Performance reports can also be used as one of many inputs to help evaluate and reward employees.

Although this example focused on P&G's campus recruiting efforts, we could have described how planning enables **FedEx** to deliver packages across the globe overnight, or how it helped **Apple** develop and market the iPad. We could have discussed how the control process helps **Pfizer**, **Eli Lilly**, and **Abbott Laboratories** ensure that their pharmaceutical drugs are produced in conformance with rigorous quality standards, or how **Kroger** relies on the control process to keep its grocery shelves stocked. We also could have looked at planning and control failures such as **BP**'s massive oil spill in the Gulf of Mexico. In short, all managers (and that probably includes you someday) perform planning and controlling activities.

Decision Making

Perhaps the most basic managerial skill is the ability to make intelligent, data-driven decisions. Broadly speaking, many of those decisions revolve around the following three questions. *What* should we be selling? *Who* should we be serving? *How* should we execute? Exhibit P–2 provides examples of decisions pertaining to each of these three categories.

The left-hand column of Exhibit P–2 suggests that every company must make decisions related to the products and services that it sells. For example, each year **Procter & Gamble** must decide how to allocate its marketing budget across numerous brands that each generates over $1 billion in sales as well as other brands that have promising growth potential. **Mattel** must decide what new toys to introduce to the market. **Southwest Airlines** must decide what ticket prices to establish for each of its thousands of flights per day. **General Motors** must decide whether to discontinue certain models of automobiles.

The middle column of Exhibit P–2 indicates that all companies must make decisions related to the customers that they serve. For example, **Sears** must decide how to allocate its marketing budget between products that tend to appeal to male versus female customers. **FedEx** must decide whether to expand its services into new markets across the globe. **Hewlett-Packard** must decide what price discounts to offer corporate clients that purchase large volumes of its products. A bank must decide whether to discontinue customers that may be unprofitable.

EXHIBIT P–2   Examples of Decisions

What should we be selling?	Who should we be serving?	How should we execute?
What products and services should be the focus of our marketing efforts?	Who should be the focus of our marketing efforts?	How should we supply our parts and services?
What new products and services should we offer?	Who should we start serving?	How should we expand our capacity?
What prices should we charge for our products and services?	Who should pay price premiums or receive price discounts?	How should we reduce our capacity?
What products and services should we discontinue?	Who should we stop serving?	How should we improve our efficiency and effectiveness?

The right-hand column of Exhibit P–2 shows that companies also make decisions related to how they execute. For example, **Boeing** must decide whether to rely on outside vendors such as **Goodrich**, **Saab**, and **Rolls-Royce** to manufacture many of the parts used to make its airplanes. **Cintas** must decide whether to expand its laundering and cleaning capacity in a given geographic region by adding square footage to an existing facility or by constructing an entirely new facility. In an economic downturn, a manufacturer might have to decide whether to eliminate one 8-hour shift at three plants or to close one plant. Finally, all companies have to decide among competing improvement opportunities. For example, a company may have to decide whether to implement a new software system, to upgrade a piece of equipment, or to provide extra training to its employees.

This portion of the prologue has explained that the three pillars of managerial accounting are planning, controlling, and decision making. This book helps prepare you to become an effective manager by explaining how to make intelligent data-driven decisions, how to create financial plans for the future, and how to continually make progress toward achieving goals by obtaining, evaluating, and responding to feedback.

WHY DOES MANAGERIAL ACCOUNTING MATTER TO YOUR CAREER?

Many students feel anxious about choosing a major because they are unsure if it will provide a fulfilling career. To reduce these anxieties, we recommend deemphasizing what you cannot control about the future; instead focusing on what you can control right now. More specifically, concentrate on answering the following question: What can you do now to prepare for success in an unknown future career? The best answer is to learn skills that will make it easier for you to adapt to an uncertain future. You need to become adaptable!

Whether you end up working in the United States or abroad, for a large corporation, a small entrepreneurial company, a nonprofit organization, or a governmental entity, you'll need to know how to plan for the future, how to make progress toward achieving goals, and how to make intelligent decisions. In other words, managerial accounting skills are useful in just about any career, organization, and industry. If you commit energy to this course, you'll be making a smart investment in your future—even though you cannot clearly envision it. Next, we will elaborate on this point by explaining how managerial accounting relates to the future careers of business majors and accounting majors.

Business Majors

Exhibit P–3 provides examples of how planning, controlling, and decision making affect three majors other than accounting—marketing, supply chain management, and human resource management.

The left-hand column of Exhibit P–3 describes some planning, controlling, and decision-making applications in the marketing profession. For example, marketing managers make planning decisions related to allocating advertising dollars across various communication mediums and to staffing new sales territories. From a control standpoint, they may closely track sales data to see if a budgeted price cut is generating an anticipated increase in unit sales, or they may study inventory levels during the holiday shopping season so that they can adjust prices as needed to optimize sales. Marketing managers also make many important decisions such as whether to bundle services together and sell them for one price or to sell each service separately. They may also decide whether to sell products directly to the customer or to sell to a distributor, who then sells to the end consumer.

The middle column of Exhibit P–3 states that supply chain managers have to plan how many units to produce to satisfy anticipated customer demand. They also need to budget for operating expenses such as utilities, supplies, and labor costs. In terms of control, they monitor actual spending relative to the budget, and closely watch operational measures such as the number of defects produced relative to the plan. Supply chain managers make

EXHIBIT P–3   Relating Managerial Accounting to Three Business Majors

	Marketing	Supply Chain Management	Human Resource Management
Planning	How much should we budget for TV, print, and Internet advertising?	How many units should we plan to produce next period?	How much should we plan to spend for occupational safety training?
	How many salespeople should we plan to hire to serve a new territory?	How much should we budget for next period's utility expense?	How much should we plan to spend on employee recruitment advertising?
Controlling	Is the budgeted price cut increasing unit sales as expected?	Did we spend more or less than expected for the units we actually produced?	Is our employee retention rate exceeding our goals?
	Are we accumulating too much inventory during the holiday shopping season?	Are we achieving our goal of reducing the number of defective units produced?	Are we meeting our goal of completing timely performance appraisals?
Decision Making	Should we sell our services as one bundle or sell them separately?	Should we transfer production of a component part to an overseas supplier?	Should we hire an on-site medical staff to lower our health care costs?
	Should we sell directly to customers or use a distributor?	Should we redesign our manufacturing process to lower inventory levels?	Should we hire temporary workers or full-time employees?

numerous decisions, such as deciding whether to transfer production of a component part to an overseas supplier. They also decide whether to invest in redesigning a manufacturing process to reduce inventory levels.

The right-hand column of Exhibit P–3 explains how human resource managers make a variety of planning decisions, such as budgeting how much to spend on occupational safety training and employee recruitment advertising. They monitor feedback related to numerous management concerns, such as employee retention rates and the timely completion of employee performance appraisals. They also help make many important decisions such as whether to hire on-site medical staff in an effort to lower health care costs, and whether to hire temporary workers or full-time employees in an uncertain economy.

For brevity, Exhibit P–3 does not include all business majors, such as finance, management information systems, and economics. Can you explain how planning, controlling, and decision-making activities would relate to these majors?

Accounting Majors

Many accounting graduates begin their careers working for public accounting firms that provide a variety of valuable services for their clients. Some of these graduates will build successful and fulfilling careers in the public accounting industry; however, most will leave public accounting at some point to work in other organizations. In fact, the **Institute of Management Accountants** (IMA) estimates that more than 80% of professional accountants in the United States work in nonpublic accounting environments (www.imanet.org/about_ima/our_mission.aspx).

The public accounting profession has a strong financial accounting orientation. Its most important function is to protect investors and other external parties by assuring them that companies are reporting historical financial results that comply with applicable accounting rules. Managerial accountants also have strong financial accounting skills. For example, they play an important role in helping their organizations design and

A Networking Opportunity   IN BUSINESS

The **Institute of Management Accountants** (IMA) is a network of more than 70,000 accounting and finance professionals from over 120 countries. Every year the IMA hosts a student leadership conference that attracts 300 students from over 50 colleges and universities. Guest speakers at past conferences have discussed topics such as leadership, advice for a successful career, how to market yourself in a difficult economy, and excelling in today's multigenerational workforce. One student who attended the conference said, "I liked that I was able to interact with professionals who are in fields that could be potential career paths for me." For more information on this worthwhile networking opportunity, contact the IMA at the phone number and website shown below.

Source: Conversation with Jodi Ryan, the Institute of Management Accountants' Director, Education/Corporate Partnerships. (201) 474-1556 or visit its website at www.imanet.org.

maintain financial reporting systems that generate reliable financial disclosures. However, the primary role of managerial accountants is to partner with their co-workers within the organization to improve performance.

Given the 80% figure mentioned above, if you are an accounting major there is a very high likelihood that your future will involve working for a nonpublic accounting employer. Your employer will expect you to have strong financial accounting skills, but more importantly, it will expect you to help improve organizational performance by applying the planning, controlling, and decision-making skills that are the foundation of managerial accounting.

Professional Certification—A Smart Investment   If you plan to become an accounting major, the Certified Management Accountant (CMA) designation is a globally respected credential (sponsored by the IMA) that will increase your credibility, upward mobility, and compensation. Exhibit P–4 summarizes the topics covered in the two-part CMA exam. For brevity, we are not going to define all the terms included in this exhibit. Its purpose is simply to emphasize that the CMA exam focuses on the planning, controlling, and decision-making skills that are critically important to nonpublic accounting employers. The CMA's internal management orientation is a complement to the highly respected Certified Public Accountant (CPA) exam that focuses on rule-based compliance—assurance standards, financial accounting standards, business law, and the tax code. Information about becoming a CMA is available on the IMA's website (www. imanet.org) or by calling 1-800-638-4427.

Part 1	*Financial Reporting, Planning, Performance, and Control*
	External financial reporting decisions
	Planning, budgeting, and forecasting
	Performance management
	Cost management
	Internal controls
Part 2	*Financial Decision Making*
	Financial statement analysis
	Corporate finance
	Decision analysis
	Risk management
	Investment decisions
	Professional ethics

EXHIBIT P–4
CMA Exam Content
Specifications

IN BUSINESS   How's the Pay?

The Institute of Management Accountants has created the following table that allows individuals to estimate what their salary would be as a management accountant.

			Your Calculation
Start with this base amount		$75,879	$75,879
If you are top-level management	ADD	$48,471	
OR, if you are senior-level management	ADD	$26,516	
OR, if you are entry-level management	SUBTRACT	$22,137	
Number of years in the field _____	TIMES	$7	
If you have an advanced degree......................	ADD	$14,662	
If you hold the CMA..	ADD	$19,992	
If you hold the CPA..	ADD	$15,837	_____
Your estimated salary level			======

For example, if you make it to top-level management in 10 years, have an advanced degree and a CMA, your estimated salary would be $159,074 [$75,879 + $48,471 + (10 × 7) + $14,662 + $19,992].

Source: Lee Schiffel, and Coleen Wilder, "IMA 2013 Salary Survey. Rainy Days Persist," *Strategic Finance* June 2014, pp. 23–39.

MANAGERIAL ACCOUNTING: BEYOND THE NUMBERS

Exhibit P–5 summarizes how each chapter of the book teaches measurement skills that managers use on the job every day. For example, Chapter 7 teaches you the measurement skills that managers use to answer the question—how should I create a financial plan for next year? Chapter 8 teaches you the measurement skills that managers use to answer the

EXHIBIT P–5   Measurement Skills: A Manager's Perspective

Chapter Number	The Key Question from a Manager's Perspective
Chapter 1	What cost classifications do I use for different management purposes?
Chapters 2 & 4	What is the value of our ending inventory and cost of goods sold for external reporting purposes?
Chapter 3	How profitable is each of our products, services, and customers?
Chapter 5	How will my profits change if I change my selling price, sales volume, or costs?
Chapter 6	How should the income statement be presented?
Chapter 7	How should I create a financial plan for next year?
Chapter 8	How well am I performing relative to my plan?
Chapter 9	What performance measures should we monitor to ensure that we achieve our strategic goals?
Chapter 10	How do I quantify the profit impact of pursuing one course of action versus another?
Chapter 11	How do I make long-term capital investment decisions?
Chapter 12	What cash inflows and outflows explain the change in our cash balance?
Chapter 13	How can we analyze our financial statements to better understand our performance?

question—how well am I performing relative to my plan? Chapter 3 teaches you measurement skills related to product, service, and customer profitability. However, it is vitally important that you also understand managerial accounting involves more than just "crunching numbers." To be successful, managers must complement their measurement skills with six business management perspectives that "go beyond the numbers" to enable intelligent planning, control, and decision making.

An Ethics Perspective

Ethical behavior is the lubricant that keeps the economy running. Without that lubricant, the economy would operate much less efficiently—less would be available to consumers, quality would be lower, and prices would be higher. In other words, without fundamental trust in the integrity of business, the economy would operate much less efficiently. Thus, for the good of everyone—including profit-making companies—it is vitally important that business be conducted within an ethical framework that builds and sustains trust.

Code of Conduct for Management Accountants　The **Institute of Management Accountants** (IMA) of the United States has adopted an ethical code called the *Statement of Ethical Professional Practice* that describes in some detail the ethical responsibilities of management accountants. Even though the standards were developed specifically for management accountants, they have much broader application. The standards consist of two parts that are presented in full in Exhibit P–6 (page 10). The first part provides general guidelines for ethical behavior. In a nutshell, a management accountant has ethical responsibilities in four broad areas: first, to maintain a high level of professional competence; second, to treat sensitive matters with confidentiality; third, to maintain personal integrity; and fourth, to disclose information in a credible fashion. The second part of the standards specifies what should be done if an individual finds evidence of ethical misconduct.

The ethical standards provide sound, practical advice for management accountants and managers. Most of the rules in the ethical standards are motivated by a very practical consideration—if these rules were not generally followed in business, then the economy and all of us would suffer. Consider the following specific examples of the consequences of not abiding by the standards:

- Suppose employees could not be trusted with confidential information. Then top managers would be reluctant to distribute such information within the company and, as a result, decisions would be based on incomplete information and operations would deteriorate.

- Suppose employees accepted bribes from suppliers. Then contracts would tend to go to the suppliers who pay the highest bribes rather than to the most competent suppliers. Would you like to fly in aircraft whose wings were made by the subcontractor who paid the highest bribe? Would you fly as often? What would happen to the airline industry if its safety record deteriorated due to shoddy workmanship on contracted parts and subassemblies?

- Suppose the presidents of companies routinely lied in their annual reports and financial statements. If investors could not rely on the basic integrity of a company's financial statements, they would have little basis for making informed decisions. Suspecting the worst, rational investors would pay less for securities issued by companies and may not be willing to invest at all. As a consequence, companies would have less money for productive investments—leading to slower economic growth, fewer goods and services, and higher prices.

Not only is ethical behavior the lubricant for our economy, it is the foundation of managerial accounting. The numbers that managers rely on for planning, control, and decision making are meaningless unless they have been competently, objectively, and honestly gathered, analyzed, and reported. As your career unfolds, you will inevitably face decisions with ethical implications. Before making such decisions, consider performing the following steps. First, define your alternative courses of action. Second, identify all of the parties that will be affected by your decision. Third, define how each course of action will favorably or unfavorably impact each affected party. Once you have a complete understanding of the decision context, seek guidance from external sources such as the IMA Statement of Ethical

EXHIBIT P–6   IMA Statement of Ethical Professional Practice

Members of IMA shall behave ethically. A commitment to ethical professional practice includes: overarching principles that express our values, and standards that guide our conduct.

PRINCIPLES

IMA's overarching ethical principles include: Honesty, Fairness, Objectivity, and Responsibility. Members shall act in accordance with these principles and shall encourage others within their organizations to adhere to them.

STANDARDS

A member's failure to comply with the following standards may result in disciplinary action.

I. COMPETENCE

Each member has a responsibility to:
1. Maintain an appropriate level of professional expertise by continually developing knowledge and skills.
2. Perform professional duties in accordance with relevant laws, regulations, and technical standards.
3. Provide decision support information and recommendations that are accurate, clear, concise, and timely.
4. Recognize and communicate professional limitations or other constraints that would preclude responsible judgment or successful performance of an activity.

II. CONFIDENTIALITY

Each member has a responsibility to:
1. Keep information confidential except when disclosure is authorized or legally required.
2. Inform all relevant parties regarding appropriate use of confidential information. Monitor subordinates' activities to ensure compliance.
3. Refrain from using confidential information for unethical or illegal advantage.

III. INTEGRITY

Each member has a responsibility to:
1. Mitigate actual conflicts of interest. Regularly communicate with business associates to avoid apparent conflicts of interest. Advise all parties of any potential conflicts.
2. Refrain from engaging in any conduct that would prejudice carrying out duties ethically.
3. Abstain from engaging in or supporting any activity that might discredit the profession.

IV. CREDIBILITY

Each member has a responsibility to:
1. Communicate information fairly and objectively.
2. Disclose all relevant information that could reasonably be expected to influence an intended user's understanding of the reports, analyses, or recommendations.
3. Disclose delays or deficiencies in information, timeliness, processing, or internal controls in conformance with organization policy and/or applicable law.

RESOLUTION OF ETHICAL CONFLICT

In applying the Standards of Ethical Professional Practice, you may encounter problems identifying unethical behavior or resolving an ethical conflict. When faced with ethical issues, you should follow your organization's established policies on the resolution of such conflict. If these policies do not resolve the ethical conflict, you should consider the following courses of action:
1. Discuss the issue with your immediate supervisor except when it appears that the supervisor is involved. In that case, present the issue to the next level. If you cannot achieve a satisfactory resolution, submit the issue to the next management level. If your immediate superior is the chief executive officer or equivalent, the acceptable reviewing authority may be a group such as the audit committee, executive committee, board of directors, board of trustees, or owners. Contact with levels above the immediate superior should be initiated only with your superior's knowledge, assuming he or she is not involved. Communication of such problems to authorities or individuals not employed or engaged by the organization is not considered appropriate, unless you believe there is a clear violation of the law.
2. Clarify relevant ethical issues by initiating a confidential discussion with an IMA Ethics Counselor or other impartial advisor to obtain a better understanding of possible courses of action.
3. Consult your own attorney as to legal obligations and rights concerning the ethical conflict.

Professional Practice, the IMA Ethics Helpline at (800) 245-1383, or a trusted confidant. Before executing your decision ask yourself one final question—would I be comfortable disclosing my chosen course of action on the front page of *The Wall Street Journal?*

Toyota Encounters Major Problems

IN BUSINESS

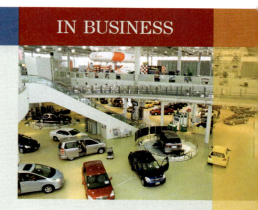

When **Toyota Motor Corporation** failed to meet its profit targets, the company set an aggressive goal of reducing the cost of its auto parts by 30%. The quality and safety of the company's automobiles eventually suffered mightily resulting in recalls, litigation, incentive campaigns, and marketing efforts that analysts estimate will cost the company more than $5 billion. The car maker's president, Akio Toyoda, blamed his company's massive quality lapses on an excessive focus on profits and market share. Similarly, Jim Press, Toyota's former top U.S. executive, said the problems were caused by "financially-oriented pirates who didn't have the character to maintain a customer-first focus."

Sources: Yoshio Takahashi, "Toyota Accelerates Its Cost-Cutting Efforts," *The Wall Street Journal*, December 23, 2009, p. B4; Mariko Sanchanta and Yoshio Takahashi, "Toyota's Recall May Top $5 Billion," *The Wall Street Journal*, March 10, 2010, p. B2; and Norihiko Shirouzu, "Toyoda Rues Excessive Profit Focus," *The Wall Street Journal*, March 2, 2010, p. B3.

A Strategic Management Perspective

Companies do not succeed by sheer luck; instead, they need to develop a *strategy* that defines how they intend to succeed in the marketplace. A **strategy** is a "game plan" that enables a company to attract customers by distinguishing itself from competitors. The focal point of a company's strategy should be its target customers. A company can only succeed if it creates a reason for its target customers to choose it over a competitor. These reasons, or what are more formally called *customer value propositions,* are the essence of strategy.

Customer value propositions tend to fall into three broad categories—*customer intimacy, operational excellence,* and *product leadership.* Companies that adopt a *customer intimacy* strategy are in essence saying to their customers, "You should choose us because we can customize our products and services to meet your individual needs better than our competitors." **Ritz-Carlton**, **Nordstrom**, and **Virtuoso** (a premium service travel agency) rely primarily on a customer intimacy value proposition for their success. Companies that pursue the second customer value proposition, called *operational excellence,* are saying to their target customers, "You should choose us because we deliver products and services faster, more conveniently, and at a lower price than our competitors." **Southwest Airlines**, **Walmart**, and **Google** are examples of companies that succeed first and foremost because of their operational excellence. Companies pursuing the third customer value proposition, called *product leadership,* are saying to their target customers, "You should choose us because we offer higher quality products than our competitors." **Apple**, **Cisco Systems**, and **W.L. Gore** (the creator of GORE-TEX® fabrics) are examples of companies that succeed because of their product leadership.[1]

The plans managers set forth, the variables they seek to control, and the decisions they make are all influenced by their company's strategy. For example, Walmart would not make plans to build ultra-expensive clothing boutiques because these plans would conflict with the company's strategy of operational excellence and "everyday low prices." Apple would not seek to control its operations by selecting performance measures that focus solely on cost-cutting because those measures would conflict with its product leadership customer value proposition. Finally, it is unlikely that **Rolex** would decide to

---

[1]These three customer value propositions were defined by Michael Treacy and Fred Wiersema in "Customer Intimacy and Other Value Disciplines," *Harvard Business Review,* Volume 71 Issue 1, pp. 84–93.

implement drastic price reductions for its watches even if a financial analysis indicated that establishing a lower price might boost short-run profits. Rolex would oppose this course of action because it would diminish the luxury brand that forms the foundation of the company's product leadership customer value proposition.

A Four-Year Waiting List at Vanilla Bicycles

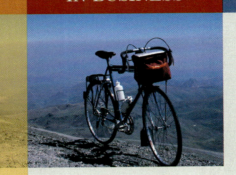

Sacha White started **Vanilla Bicycles** in Portland, Oregon, in 2001. After eight years in business, he had a four-year backlog of customer orders. He limits his annual production to 40–50 bikes per year that sell for an average of $7,000 each. He uses a silver alloy that costs 20 times as much as brass (which is the industry standard) to join titanium tubes together to form a bike frame. White spends three hours taking a buyer's measurements to determine the exact dimensions of the bike frame. He has resisted expanding production because it would undermine his strategy based on product leadership and customer intimacy. As White said, "If I ended up sacrificing what made Vanilla special just to make more bikes, that wouldn't be worth it to me."

Source: Christopher Steiner, "Heaven on Wheels," *Forbes,* April 13, 2009, p. 75.

An Enterprise Risk Management Perspective

Every strategy, plan, and decision involves risks. **Enterprise risk management** is a process used by a company to identify those risks and develop responses to them that enable it to be reasonably assured of meeting its goals. The left-hand column of Exhibit P–7 provides 12 examples of the types of business risks that companies face. They range from risks that relate to the weather to risks associated with computer hackers, complying with the law, employee theft, and products harming customers. The right-hand column of Exhibit P–7 provides an example of a control that could be implemented to help reduce each of the risks mentioned in the left-hand column of the exhibit.[2] Although these types of controls cannot completely eliminate risks, they enable companies to proactively manage their risks rather than passively reacting to unfortunate events that have already occurred.

In managerial accounting, companies use controls to reduce the risk that their plans will not be achieved. For example, if a company plans to build a new manufacturing facility within a predefined budget and time frame, it will establish and monitor control measures to ensure that the project is concluded on time and within the budget. Risk management is also a critically important aspect of decision making. For example, when a company quantifies the labor cost savings that it can realize by sending jobs overseas, it should complement its

---

Managing the Risk of a Power Outage

Between January and April of 2010, the United States had 35 major power outages. For business owners, these power outages can be costly. For example, a New York night club called the **Smoke Jazz and Supper Club** lost an estimated $1,500 in revenue when a power outage shut down its on-line reservation system for one night. George Pauli, the owner of **Great Embroidery LLC** in Mesa, Arizona, estimates that his company has an average of six power outages every year. Since Pauli's sewing machines cannot resume exactly where they leave off when abruptly shut down, each power outage costs him $120 in lost inventory. Pauli decided to buy $700 worth of batteries to keep his sewing machines running during power outages. The batteries paid for themselves in less than one year.

Source: Sarah E. Needleman, "Lights Out Means Lost Sales," *The Wall Street Journal,* July 22, 2010, p. B8.

---

[2]Besides using controls to reduce risks, companies can also choose other risk responses, such as accepting or avoiding a risk.

EXHIBIT P–7   Identifying and Controlling Business Risks

Examples of Business Risks	Examples of Controls to Reduce Business Risks
• Intellectual assets being stolen from computer files	• Create firewalls that prohibit computer hackers from corrupting or stealing intellectual property
• Products harming customers	• Develop a formal and rigorous new product testing program
• Losing market share due to the unforeseen actions of competitors	• Develop an approach for legally gathering information about competitors' plans and practices
• Poor weather conditions shutting down operations	• Develop contingency plans for overcoming weather-related disruptions
• A website malfunctioning	• Thoroughly test the website before going "live" on the Internet
• A supplier strike halting the flow of raw materials	• Establish a relationship with two companies capable of providing needed raw materials
• A poorly designed incentive compensation system causing employees to make bad decisions	• Create a balanced set of performance measures that motivates the desired behavior
• Financial statements inaccurately reporting the value of inventory	• Count the physical inventory on hand to make sure that it agrees with the accounting records
• An employee stealing assets	• Segregate duties so that the same employee does not have physical custody of an asset and the responsibility of accounting for it
• An employee accessing unauthorized information	• Create password-protected barriers that prohibit employees from obtaining information not needed to do their jobs
• Inaccurate budget estimates causing excessive or insufficient production	• Implement a rigorous budget review process
• Failing to comply with equal employment opportunity laws	• Create a report that tracks key metrics related to compliance with the laws

financial analysis with a prudent assessment of the accompanying risks. Will the overseas manufacturer use child labor? Will the product's quality decline, thereby leading to more warranty repairs, customer complaints, and lawsuits? Will the elapsed time from customer order to delivery dramatically increase? Will terminating domestic employees diminish morale within the company and harm perceptions within the community? These are the types of risks that managers should incorporate into their decision-making processes.

A Corporate Social Responsibility Perspective

Companies are responsible for creating strategies that produce financial results that satisfy stockholders. However, they also have a *corporate social responsibility* to serve other stakeholders—such as customers, employees, suppliers, communities, and environmental and human rights advocates—whose interests are tied to the company's performance. **Corporate social responsibility** (CSR) is a concept whereby organizations consider the needs of all stakeholders when making decisions. CSR extends beyond legal compliance to include voluntary actions that satisfy stakeholder expectations. Numerous companies, such as **Procter & Gamble**, **3M**, **Eli Lilly and Company**, **Starbucks**, **Microsoft**, **Genentech**, **Johnson & Johnson**, **Baxter International**, **Abbott Laboratories**, **KPMG**, **PNC Bank**, **Deloitte**, **Southwest Airlines**, and **Caterpillar**, prominently describe their corporate social performance on their websites.

EXHIBIT P–8   Examples of Corporate Social Responsibilities

Companies should provide *customers* with:
- Safe, high-quality products that are fairly priced.
- Competent, courteous, and rapid delivery of products and services.
- Full disclosure of product-related risks.
- Easy-to-use information systems for shopping and tracking orders.

Companies should provide *suppliers* with:
- Fair contract terms and prompt payments.
- Reasonable time to prepare orders.
- Hassle-free acceptance of timely and complete deliveries.
- Cooperative rather than unilateral actions.

Companies should provide *stockholders* with:
- Competent management.
- Easy access to complete and accurate financial information.
- Full disclosure of enterprise risks.
- Honest answers to knowledgeable questions.

Companies and their suppliers should provide *employees* with:
- Safe and humane working conditions.
- Nondiscriminatory treatment and the right to organize and file grievances.
- Fair compensation.
- Opportunities for training, promotion, and personal development.

Companies should provide *communities* with:
- Payment of fair taxes.
- Honest information about plans such as plant closings.
- Resources that support charities, schools, and civic activities.
- Reasonable access to media sources.

Companies should provide *environmental and human rights advocates* with:
- Greenhouse gas emissions data.
- Recycling and resource conservation data.
- Child labor transparency.
- Full disclosure of suppliers located in developing countries.

Exhibit P–8 presents examples of corporate social responsibilities that are of interest to six stakeholder groups.[3] If a company fails to meet the needs of these six stakeholder groups it can adversely affect its financial performance. For example, if a company pollutes the environment or fails to provide safe and humane working conditions for its employees, the negative publicity from environmental and human rights activists could cause the company's customers to defect and its "best and brightest" job candidates to apply elsewhere—both of which are likely to eventually harm financial performance. This explains why in managerial accounting a manager must establish plans, implement controls, and make decisions that consider impacts on all stakeholders.

A Process Management Perspective

Most companies organize themselves by functional departments, such as the Marketing Department, the Research and Development Department, and the Accounting Department. These departments tend to have a clearly defined "chain of command" that specifies superior and subordinate relationships. However, effective managers understand that *business processes,* more so than functional departments, serve the needs of a company's most important stakeholders—its customers. A **business process** is a series of steps that are followed in order to carry out some task in a business. These steps often span departmental boundaries, thereby requiring managers to cooperate across functional departments. The term *value chain* is often used to describe how an organization's functional

---

[3]Many of the examples in Exhibit P–8 were drawn from Terry Leap and Misty L. Loughry, "The Stakeholder-Friendly Firm," *Business Horizons,* March/April 2004, pp. 27–32.

EXHIBIT P–9   Business Functions Making Up the Value Chain

Research and Development	Product Design	Manufacturing	Marketing	Distribution	Customer Service

departments interact with one another to form business processes. A **value chain**, as shown in Exhibit P–9, consists of the major business functions that add value to a company's products and services.

Managers need to understand the value chain to be effective in terms of planning, control, and decision making. For example, if a company's engineers plan to design a new product, they must communicate with the Manufacturing Department to ensure that the product can actually be produced, the Marketing Department to ensure that customers will buy the product, the Distribution Department to ensure that large volumes of the product can be cost-effectively transported to customers, and the Accounting Department to ensure that the product will increase profits. From a control and decision-making standpoint, managers also need to focus on process excellence instead of functional performance. For example, if the Purchasing Department focuses solely on minimizing the cost of purchased materials, this narrowly focused attempt at cost reduction may lead to greater scrap and rework in the Manufacturing Department, more complaints in the Customer Service Department, and greater challenges in the Marketing Department because dissatisfied customers are turning their attention to competitors.

Managers frequently use a process management method known as *lean thinking,* or what is called *Lean Production* in the manufacturing sector. **Lean Production** is a management approach that organizes resources such as people and machines around the flow of business processes and that only produces units in response to customer orders. It is often called *just-in-time* production (or *JIT*) because products are only manufactured in response to customer orders and they are completed just-in-time to be shipped to customers. Lean thinking differs from traditional manufacturing methods, which organize work departmentally and encourage departments to maximize their output even if it exceeds customer demand and bloats inventories. Because lean thinking only allows production in response to customer orders, the number of units produced tends to equal the number of units sold, thereby resulting in minimal inventory. The lean approach also results in fewer defects, less wasted effort, and quicker customer response times than traditional production methods.

Greenpeace Leverages the Power of Social Media   IN BUSINESS

When **Nestlé** purchased palm oil from an Indonesian supplier to manufacture Kit-Kat candy bars **Greenpeace International** used social media to express its disapproval. Greenpeace claimed that the Indonesian company destroyed rainforest to create its palm oil plantation; therefore, Nestlé's actions were contributing to global warming and endangering orangutans. Greenpeace posted YouTube videos, added comments to Nestlé's Facebook page, and sent Twitter Tweets to communicate its message to supporters. At one point, the number of fans on Nestlé's Facebook page grew to 95,000, most of them being protesters. Nestlé terminated its relationship with the supplier, which provided 1.25% of Nestlé's palm oil needs. A Nestlé spokesperson says the difficulty in responding to social media is to "show that we are listening, which we obviously are, while not getting involved in a shouting match."

Source: Emily Steel, "Nestlé Takes a Beating on Social-Media Sites," *The Wall Street Journal,* March 29, 2010, p. B5.

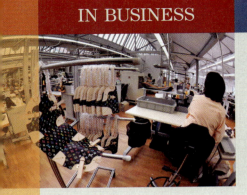

Louis Vuitton Implements Lean Production

Louis Vuitton, headquartered in Paris, France, used lean production to increase its manufacturing capacity without having to build a new factory. It created U-shaped work arrangements for teams of 10 workers, thereby freeing up 10% more floor space in its factories. The company was able to hire 300 more workers without adding any square footage. Louis Vuitton also uses robots and computer programs to reduce wasted leather and the time needed to perform certain tasks.

Source: Christina Passariello, "At Vuitton, Growth in Small Batches," *The Wall Street Journal,* June 27, 2011, pp. B1 and B10.

A Leadership Perspective

An organization's employees bring diverse needs, beliefs, and goals to the workplace. Therefore, an important role for organizational leaders is to unite the behaviors of their fellow employees around two common themes—pursuing strategic goals and making optimal decisions. To fulfill this responsibility, leaders need to understand how *intrinsic motivation, extrinsic incentives,* and *cognitive bias* influence human behavior.

Intrinsic Motivation   Intrinsic motivation refers to motivation that comes from within us. Stop for a moment and identify the greatest accomplishment of your life. Then ask yourself what motivated you to achieve this goal? In all likelihood, you achieved it because you wanted to, not because someone forced you to do it. In other words, you were intrinsically motivated. Similarly, an organization is more likely to prosper when its employees are intrinsically motivated to pursue its interests. A leader, who employees perceive as *credible* and *respectful* of their value to the organization, can increase the extent to which those employees are intrinsically motivated to pursue strategic goals. As your career evolves, to be perceived as a credible leader you'll need to possess three attributes— technical competence (that spans the value chain), personal integrity (in terms of work ethic and honesty), and strong communication skills (including oral presentation skills and writing skills). To be perceived as a leader who is respectful of your co-workers' value to the organization, you'll need to possess three more attributes—strong mentoring skills (to help others realize their potential), strong listening skills (to learn from your co-workers and be responsive to their needs), and personal humility (in terms of deferring recognition to all employees who contribute to the organization's success). If you possess these six traits, then you'll have the potential to become a leader who inspires others to readily and energetically channel their efforts toward achieving organizational goals.

Extrinsic Incentives   Many organizations use *extrinsic incentives* to highlight important goals and to motivate employees to achieve them. For example, assume a company establishes the goal of reducing the time needed to perform a task by 20%. In addition, assume the company agrees to pay bonus compensation to its employees if they achieve the goal within three months. In this example, the company is using a type of extrinsic incentive known as a bonus to highlight a particular goal and to presumably motivate employees to achieve it.

While proponents of extrinsic incentives rightly assert that these types of rewards can have a powerful influence on employee behavior, many critics warn that they can also produce dysfunctional consequences. For example, suppose the employees mentioned above earned their bonuses by achieving the 20% time reduction goal within three months. However, let's also assume that during those three months the quality of the employees' output plummeted, thereby causing a spike in the company's repair costs, product returns, and customer defections. In this instance, did the extrinsic incentive work properly? The answer is yes and no. The bonus system did motivate employees to attain the time reduction goal; however, it also had the unintended consequences of causing employees to neglect product quality, thereby increasing repair costs, product returns, and customer defections. In other words, what may have seemed like a well-intended extrinsic incentive actually produced dysfunctional results for the company. This example highlights an important leadership challenge that you are likely to face someday—designing financial compensation systems that fairly reward employees for their efforts without inadvertently creating extrinsic incentives that motivate them to take actions that harm the company.

Cognitive Bias Leaders need to be aware that all people (including themselves) possess *cognitive biases,* or distorted thought processes, that can adversely affect planning, controlling, and decision making. To illustrate how cognitive bias works, let's consider the scenario of a television "infomercial" where someone is selling a product with a proclaimed value of $200 for $19.99 if viewers call within the next 30 minutes. Why do you think the seller claims that the product has a $200 value? The seller is relying on a cognitive bias called *anchoring bias* in an effort to convince viewers that a $180 discount is simply too good to pass up. The "anchor" is the false assertion that the product is actually worth $200. If viewers erroneously attach credibility to this contrived piece of information, their distorted analysis of the situation may cause them to spend $19.99 on an item whose true economic value is much less than that amount.

While cognitive biases cannot be eliminated, effective leaders should take two steps to reduce their negative impacts. First, they should acknowledge their own susceptibility to cognitive bias. For example, a leader's judgment might be clouded by optimism bias (being overly optimistic in assessing the likelihood of future outcomes) or self-enhancement bias (overestimating ones strengths and underestimating ones weaknesses relative to others). Second, they should acknowledge the presence of cognitive bias in others and introduce techniques to minimize their adverse consequences. For example, to reduce the risks of confirmation bias (a bias where people pay greater attention to information that confirms their preconceived notions, while devaluing information that contradicts them) or groupthink bias (a bias where some group members support a course of action solely because other group members do), a leader may routinely appoint independent teams of employees to assess the credibility of recommendations set forth by other individuals and groups.

SUMMARY

This prologue defined managerial accounting and explained why it is relevant to business and accounting majors. It also discussed six topics—ethics, strategic management, enterprise risk management, corporate social responsibility, process management, and leadership—that define the context for applying the quantitative aspects of managerial accounting. The most important goal of the prologue was to help you understand that managerial accounting matters to your future career regardless of your major. Accounting is the language of business and you'll need to speak it to communicate effectively with and influence fellow managers.

GLOSSARY

At the end of each chapter, a list of key terms for review is given, along with the definition of each term. (These terms are printed in boldface where they are defined in the chapter.) Carefully study each term to be sure you understand its meaning. The list for the Prologue follows.

Budget A detailed plan for the future that is usually expressed in formal quantitative terms. (p. 3)

Business process A series of steps that are followed in order to carry out some task in a business. (p. 14)

Controlling The process of gathering feedback to ensure that a plan is being properly executed or modified as circumstances change. (p. 3)

Corporate social responsibility A concept whereby organizations consider the needs of all stakeholders when making decisions. (p. 13)

Decision making Selecting a course of action from competing alternatives. (p. 3)

Enterprise risk management A process used by a company to identify its risks and develop responses to them that enable it to be reasonably assured of meeting its goals. (p. 12)

Financial accounting The phase of accounting that is concerned with reporting historical financial information to external parties, such as stockholders, creditors, and regulators. (p. 2)

Lean Production A management approach that organizes resources such as people and machines around the flow of business processes and that only produces units in response to customer orders. (p. 15)

Managerial accounting The phase of accounting that is concerned with providing information to managers for use within the organization. (p. 2)

Performance report A report that compares budgeted data to actual data to highlight instances of excellent and unsatisfactory performance. (p. 4)

Planning The process of establishing goals and specifying how to achieve them. (p. 3)

Segment A part or activity of an organization about which managers would like cost, revenue, or profit data. (p. 3)

Strategy A company's "game plan" for attracting customers by distinguishing itself from competitors. (p. 11)

Value chain The major business functions that add value to a company's products and services, such as research and development, product design, manufacturing, marketing, distribution, and customer service. (p. 15)

QUESTIONS

P–1	How does managerial accounting differ from financial accounting?
P–2	Pick any major television network and describe some planning and control activities that its managers would engage in.
P–3	If you had to decide whether to continue making a component part or to begin buying the part from an overseas supplier, what quantitative and qualitative factors would influence your decision?
P–4	Why do companies prepare budgets?
P–5	Why is managerial accounting relevant to business majors and their future careers?
P–6	Why is managerial accounting relevant to accounting majors and their future careers?
P–7	Pick any large company and describe its strategy using the framework in the prologue.
P–8	Why do management accountants need to understand their company's strategy?
P–9	Pick any large company and describe three risks that it faces and how it responds to those risks.
P–10	Provide three examples of how a company's risks can influence its planning, controlling, and decision-making activities.
P–11	Pick any large company and explain three ways that it could segment its companywide performance.
P–12	Locate the website of any company that publishes a corporate social responsibility report (also referred to as a sustainability report). Describe three nonfinancial performance measures included in the report. Why do you think the company publishes this report?
P–13	Why do companies that implement Lean Production tend to have minimal inventories?
P–14	Why are leadership skills important to managers?
P–15	Why is ethical behavior important to business?

Multiple-choice questions are available in the *Connect Library*.

EXERCISES

Available with McGraw-Hill's *Connect Accounting*.

EXERCISE P–1   Planning and Control

Many companies use budgets for three purposes. First, they use them to plan how to deploy resources to best serve customers. Second, they use them to establish challenging goals, or stretch targets, to motivate employees to strive for exceptional results. Third, they use them to evaluate and reward employees.

Assume that you are a sales manager working with your boss to create a sales budget for next year. Once the sales budget is established, it will influence how other departments within the company plan to deploy their resources. For example, the manufacturing manager will plan to produce enough units to meet budgeted unit sales. The sales budget will also be instrumental in determining your pay raise, potential for promotion, and bonus. If actual sales exceed the sales budget, it bodes well for your career. If actual sales are less than budgeted sales, it will diminish your financial compensation and potential for promotion.

Required:

1. Do you think it would be appropriate for your boss to establish the sales budget without any input from you? Why?
2. Do you think the company would be comfortable with allowing you to establish the sales budget without any input from your boss? Why?

3. Assume the company uses its sales budget for only one purpose—planning to deploy resources in a manner that best serves customers. What thoughts would influence your estimate of future sales as well as your boss's estimate of future sales?

4. Assume the company uses its sales budget for only one purpose—motivating employees to strive for exceptional results. What thoughts would influence your estimate of future sales as well as your boss's estimate of future sales?

5. Assume the company uses its sales budget for only one purpose—to determine your pay raise, potential for promotion, and bonus. What thoughts would influence your estimate of future sales as well as your boss's estimate of future sales?

6. Assume the sales budget is used for all three purposes described in questions 3–5. Describe any conflicts or complications that might arise when using the sales budget for these three purposes.

EXERCISE P–2 Controlling

Assume that you work for an airline unloading luggage from airplanes. Your boss has said that, on average, each airplane contains 100 pieces of luggage. Furthermore, your boss has stated that you should be able to unload 100 pieces of luggage from an airplane in 10 minutes. Today an airplane arrived with 150 pieces of luggage and you unloaded all of it in 13 minutes. After finishing with the 150 pieces of luggage, your boss yelled at you for exceeding the 10 minute allowance for unloading luggage from an airplane.

Required:

How would you feel about being yelled at for taking 13 minutes to unload 150 pieces of luggage? How does this scenario relate to the larger issue of how companies design control systems?

EXERCISE P–3 Decision Making

Exhibit P–2 (see page 4) includes 12 questions related to 12 types of decisions that companies often face. In the prologue, these 12 decisions were discussed within the context of for-profit companies; however, they are also readily applicable to nonprofit organizations. To illustrate this point, assume that you are a senior leader, such as a president, provost, or dean, in a university setting.

Required:

For each of the 12 decisions in Exhibit P–2, provide an example of how that type of decision might be applicable to a university setting.

EXERCISE P–4 Ethics and the Manager

Richmond, Inc., operates a chain of 44 department stores. Two years ago, the board of directors of Richmond approved a large-scale remodeling of its stores to attract a more upscale clientele.

Before finalizing these plans, two stores were remodeled as a test. Linda Perlman, assistant controller, was asked to oversee the financial reporting for these test stores, and she and other management personnel were offered bonuses based on the sales growth and profitability of these stores. While completing the financial reports, Perlman discovered a sizable inventory of outdated goods that should have been discounted for sale or returned to the manufacturer. She discussed the situation with her management colleagues; the consensus was to ignore reporting this inventory as obsolete because reporting it would diminish the financial results and their bonuses.

Required:

1. According to the IMA's Statement of Ethical Professional Practice, would it be ethical for Perlman *not* to report the inventory as obsolete?

2. Would it be easy for Perlman to take the ethical action in this situation?

(CMA, adapted)

EXERCISE P–5 Strategy

The table below contains the names of six companies.

Required:

For each company, categorize its strategy as being focused on customer intimacy, operational excellence, or product leadership. If you wish to improve your understanding of each company's customer value proposition before completing the exercise, review its most recent annual report. To obtain electronic access to this information, perform an Internet search on each company's name followed by the words "annual report."

Company	Strategy
1. Deere	?
2. FedEx	?
3. State Farm Insurance	?
4. BMW	?
5. Amazon.com	?
6. Charles Schwab	?

EXERCISE P–6   Enterprise Risk Management

The table below refers to seven industries.

Required:

For each industry, identify one important risk faced by the companies that compete within that industry. Also, describe one control that companies could use to reduce the risk that you have identified.

Industry	Type of Risk	Control to Reduce the Risk
1. Airlines (e.g., Delta Airlines)		
2. Pharmaceutical drugs (e.g., Merck)		
3. Package delivery (e.g., United Parcel Service)		
4. Banking (e.g., Bank of America)		
5. Oil & gas (e.g., ExxonMobil)		
6. E-commerce (e.g., eBay)		
7. Automotive (e.g., Toyota)		

EXERCISE P–7   Ethics in Business

Consumers and attorney generals in more than 40 states accused a prominent nationwide chain of auto repair shops of misleading customers and selling them unnecessary parts and services, from brake jobs to front-end alignments. Lynn Sharpe Paine reported the situation as follows in "Managing for Organizational Integrity," *Harvard Business Review,* Volume 72 Issue 3:

> In the face of declining revenues, shrinking market share, and an increasingly competitive market . . . management attempted to spur performance of its auto centers. . . . The automotive service advisers were given product-specific sales quotas—sell so many springs, shock absorbers, alignments, or brake jobs per shift—and paid a commission based on sales. . . . [F]ailure to meet quotas could lead to a transfer or a reduction in work hours. Some employees spoke of the "pressure, pressure, pressure" to bring in sales.
>
> This pressure-cooker atmosphere created conditions under which employees felt that the only way to satisfy top management was by selling products and services to customers that they didn't really need.

Suppose all automotive repair businesses routinely followed the practice of attempting to sell customers unnecessary parts and services.

Required:

1. How would this behavior affect customers? How might customers attempt to protect themselves against this behavior?
2. How would this behavior probably affect profits and employment in the automotive service industry?

EXERCISE P–8   Cognitive Bias

In the 1970s, one million college-bound students were surveyed and asked to compare themselves to their peers. Some of the key findings of the survey were as follows:

a. 70% of the students rated themselves as above average in leadership ability, while only 2% rated themselves as below average in this regard.

b. With respect to athletic skills, 60% of the students rated their skills as above the median and only 6% of students rated themselves as below the median.

c. 60% of the students rated themselves in the top 10% in terms of their ability to get along with others, while 25% of the students felt that they were in the top 1% in terms of this interpersonal skill.

Required:

What type of cognitive bias reveals itself in the data mentioned above? How might this cognitive bias adversely influence a manager's planning, controlling, and decision-making activities? What steps could managers take to reduce the possibility that this cognitive bias would adversely influence their actions?

Source: Dan Lovallo and Daniel Kahneman, "Delusions of Success: How Optimism Undermines Executives' Decisions," *Harvard Business Review,* July 2003, pp. 56–63.

EXERCISE P–9   Ethics and Decision Making

Assume that you are the chairman of the Department of Accountancy at Mountain State University. One of the accounting professors in your department, Dr. Candler, has been consistently and uniformly regarded by students as an awful teacher for more than 10 years. Other accounting professors within your department have observed Dr. Candler's classroom teaching and they concur that his teaching skills are very poor. However, Dr. Candler was granted tenure 12 years ago, thereby ensuring him life-long job security at Mountain State University.

Much to your surprise, today you received a phone call from an accounting professor at Oregon Coastal University. During this phone call you are informed that Oregon Coastal University is on the verge of making a job offer to Dr. Candler. However, before extending the job offer, the faculty at Oregon Coastal wants your input regarding Dr. Candler's teaching effectiveness while at Mountain State University.

Required:

How would you respond to the professor from Oregon Coastal University? What would you say about Dr. Candler's teaching ability? Would you describe your answer to this inquiry as being ethical? Why?

EXERCISE P–10   Corporate Social Responsbility

In his book *Capitalism and Freedom,* economist Milton Friedman wrote on page 133: "There is one and only one social responsibility of business—to use its resources and engage in activities designed to increase its profits so long as it . . . engages in open and free competition, without deception or fraud."

Required:

Explain why you agree or disagree with this quote.

EXERCISE P–11   Intrinsic Motivation and Extrinsic Incentives

In a *Harvard Business Review* article titled "Why Incentive Plans Cannot Work," (Volume 71, Issue 5) author Alfie Kohn wrote: "Research suggests that, by and large, rewards succeed at securing one thing only: temporary compliance. When it comes to producing lasting change in attitudes and behavior, however, rewards, like punishment, are strikingly ineffective. Once the rewards run out, people revert to their old behaviors. . . . Incentives, a version of what psychologists call extrinsic motivators, do not alter the attitudes that underlie our behaviors. They do not create an enduring *commitment* to any value or action. Rather, incentives merely—and temporarily—change what we do."

Required:

1.   Do you agree with this quote? Why?
2.   As a manager, how would you seek to motivate your employees?
3.   As a manager, would you use financial incentives to compensate your employees? If so, what would be the keys to using them effectively? If not, then how would you compensate your employees?

EXERCISE P–12   Cognitive Bias and Decision Making

During World War II, the U.S. military was studying its combat-tested fighter planes to determine the parts of the plane that were most vulnerable to enemy fire. The purpose of the study was to identify the most vulnerable sections of each plane and then take steps to reinforce those sections to improve pilot safety and airplane durability. The data gathered by the U.S. military showed that certain sections of its combat-tested fighter planes were consistently hit more often with enemy fire than other sections of the plane.

Required:

1.   Would you recommend reinforcing the sections of the plane that were hit most often by enemy fire, or would you reinforce the sections that were hit less frequently by enemy fire? Why?
2.   Do you think cognitive bias had the potential to influence the U.S. military's decision-making process with respect to reinforcing its fighter planes?

Source: Jerker Denrell, "Selection Bias and the Perils of Benchmarking," *Harvard Business Review,* Volume 83, Issue 4, pp. 114–119.

EXERCISE P–13   Ethics and Decision Making

Assume that you just completed a December weekend vacation to a casino within the United States. During your trip you won $10,000 gambling. When the casino exchanged your chips for cash they did not record any personal information, such as your driver's license number or social security number. Four months later while preparing your tax returns for the prior year, you stop to contemplate the fact that the Internal Revenue Service requires taxpayers to report all gambling winnings on Form 1040.

Required:

Would you report your gambling winnings to the Internal Revenue Service so that you could pay federal income taxes on those winnings? Do you believe that your actions are ethical? Why?

A LOOK BACK

The Prologue defined managerial accounting and explained why it is important to the careers of all business students. It also explained how managerial accounting involves more than just quantitative calculations.

A LOOK AT THIS CHAPTER

This chapter defines many of the cost terms that will be used throughout the book. It explains that in managerial accounting the term *cost* is used in many different ways depending on the needs of management.

A LOOK AHEAD

Chapters 2, 3, and 4 describe costing systems that are used to compute product costs. Chapter 2 describes job-order costing. Chapter 3 describes activity-based costing, an elaboration of job-order costing. Chapter 4 covers process costing.

1

Managerial Accounting and Cost Concepts

After studying Chapter 1, you should be able to:

LO1–1 Understand cost classifications used for assigning costs to cost objects: direct costs and indirect costs.

LO1–2 Identify and give examples of each of the three basic manufacturing cost categories.

LO1–3 Understand cost classifications used to prepare financial statements: product costs and period costs.

LO1–4 Understand cost classifications used to predict cost behavior: variable costs, fixed costs, and mixed costs.

LO1–5 Analyze a mixed cost using a scattergraph plot and the high-low method.

LO1–6 Prepare income statements for a merchandising company using the traditional and contribution formats.

LO1–7 Understand cost classifications used in making decisions: differential costs, opportunity costs, and sunk costs.

Lowering Healthcare Costs and Improving Patient Care

Providence Regional Medical Center's (PRMC) "single stay" ward is lowering healthcare costs and increasing patient satisfaction. Rather than transporting post-surgical patients to stationary equipment throughout the hospital, a "single stay" ward brings all required equipment to stationary patients. For example, "after heart surgery, cardiac patients remain in one room throughout their recovery, only the gear and staff are in motion. As the patient's condition stabilizes, the beeping machines of intensive care are removed and physical therapy equipment is added." The results of this shift in orientation have been impressive. Patient satisfaction scores have skyrocketed and the average length of a patient's stay in the hospital has declined by more than a day.

Source: Catherine Arnst, "Radical Surgery," *Bloomberg Businessweek*, January 18, 2010, pp. 40–45.

This chapter explains that in managerial accounting the term *cost* is used in many different ways. The reason is that there are many types of costs, and these costs are classified differently according to the immediate needs of management. For example, managers may want cost data to prepare external financial reports, to prepare planning budgets, or to make decisions. Each different use of cost data demands a different classification and definition of costs. For example, the preparation of external financial reports requires the use of historical cost data, whereas decision making may require predictions about future costs. This notion of *different costs for different purposes* is a critically important aspect of managerial accounting.

Exhibit 1–1 summarizes the cost classifications that will be defined in this chapter, namely cost classifications (1) for assigning costs to cost objects, (2) for manufacturing companies, (3) for preparing financial statements, (4) for predicting cost behavior, and (5) for making decisions. As we begin defining the cost terminology related to each of these cost classifications, please refer back to this exhibit to help improve your understanding of the overall organization of the chapter.

COST CLASSIFICATIONS FOR ASSIGNING COSTS TO COST OBJECTS

LEARNING OBJECTIVE 1–1

Understand cost classifications used for assigning costs to cost objects: direct costs and indirect costs.

Costs are assigned to cost objects for a variety of purposes including pricing, preparing profitability studies, and controlling spending. A **cost object** is anything for which cost data are desired—including products, customers, jobs, and organizational subunits. For purposes of assigning costs to cost objects, costs are classified as either *direct* or *indirect*.

Direct Cost

A **direct cost** is a cost that can be easily and conveniently traced to a specified cost object. For example, if **Reebok** is assigning costs to its various regional and national sales offices, then the salary of the sales manager in its Tokyo office would be a direct cost of that office. If a printing company made 10,000 brochures for a specific customer, then the cost of the paper used to make the brochures would be a direct cost of that customer.

EXHIBIT 1–1
Summary of Cost Classifications

Purpose of Cost Classification	Cost Classifications
Assigning costs to cost objects	• Direct cost (can be easily traced) • Indirect cost (cannot be easily traced)

Accounting for costs in manufacturing companies	• Manufacturing costs
	  • Direct materials
	  • Direct labor
	  • Manufacturing overhead
	• Nonmanufacturing costs
	  • Selling costs
	  • Administrative costs

Preparing financial statements	• Product costs (inventoriable) • Period costs (expensed)
Predicting cost behavior in response to changes in activity	• Variable cost (proportional to activity) • Fixed cost (constant in total) • Mixed cost (has variable and fixed elements)
Making decisions	• Differential cost (differs between alternatives) • Sunk cost (should be ignored) • Opportunity cost (foregone benefit)

Indirect Cost

An **indirect cost** is a cost that cannot be easily and conveniently traced to a specified cost object. For example, a Campbell Soup factory may produce dozens of varieties of canned soups. The factory manager's salary would be an indirect cost of a particular variety such as chicken noodle soup. The reason is that the factory manager's salary is incurred as a consequence of running the entire factory—it is not incurred to produce any one soup variety. *To be traced to a cost object such as a particular product, the cost must be caused by the cost object.* The factory manager's salary is called a *common cost* of producing the various products of the factory. A **common cost** is a cost that is incurred to support a number of cost objects but cannot be traced to them individually. A common cost is a type of indirect cost.

A particular cost may be direct or indirect, depending on the cost object. While the Campbell Soup factory manager's salary is an *indirect* cost of manufacturing chicken noodle soup, it is a *direct* cost of the manufacturing division. In the first case, the cost object is chicken noodle soup. In the second case, the cost object is the entire manufacturing division.

COST CLASSIFICATIONS FOR MANUFACTURING COMPANIES

Manufacturing companies such as Texas Instruments, Ford, and DuPont separate their costs into two broad categories—manufacturing and nonmanufacturing costs.

Manufacturing Costs

Most manufacturing companies further separate their manufacturing costs into two direct cost categories, direct materials and direct labor, and one indirect cost category, manufacturing overhead. A discussion of each of these categories follows.

> **LEARNING OBJECTIVE 1–2**
>
> Identify and give examples of each of the three basic manufacturing cost categories.

Direct Materials   The materials that go into the final product are called **raw materials**. This term is somewhat misleading because it seems to imply unprocessed natural resources like wood pulp or iron ore. Actually, raw materials refer to any materials that are used in the final product; and the finished product of one company can become the raw materials of another company. For example, the plastics produced by Du Pont are a raw material used by Hewlett-Packard in its personal computers.

Raw materials may include both *direct* and *indirect materials*. **Direct materials** are those materials that become an integral part of the finished product and whose costs can be conveniently traced to the finished product. This would include, for example, the seats that Airbus purchases from subcontractors to install in its commercial aircraft and the electronic components that Apple uses in its iPhones.

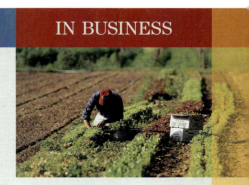

Food Prices Hit Record Highs for Restaurants   IN BUSINESS

Direct material costs are critically important to restaurants and fast-food chains. In recent years, some food costs have spiked to record highs. For example, unexpected freezing temperatures in the southwestern portion of the United States caused the cost of lettuce to increase 290%. Similarly, the costs of green peppers, tomatoes, and cucumbers jumped 145%, 85%, and 30%, respectively. A large chain such as Subway can withstand these price increases better than smaller competitors because of its buying power and long-term contracts.

Source: Anne VanderMey, "Food For Thought," *Fortune,* May 9, 2011, p. 12.

Sometimes it isn't worth the effort to trace the costs of relatively insignificant materials to end products. Such minor items would include the solder used to make electrical connections in a **Sony** HDTV or the glue used to assemble an **Ethan Allen** chair. Materials such as solder and glue are called **indirect materials** and are included as part of manufacturing overhead, which is discussed shortly.

Direct Labor   **Direct labor** consists of labor costs that can be easily (i.e., physically and conveniently) traced to individual units of product. Direct labor is sometimes called *touch labor* because direct labor workers typically touch the product while it is being made. Examples of direct labor include assembly-line workers at **Toyota**, carpenters at the home builder **KB Home**, and electricians who install equipment on aircraft at **Bombardier Learjet**.

Labor costs that cannot be physically traced to particular products, or that can be traced only at great cost and inconvenience, are termed **indirect labor**. Just like indirect materials, indirect labor is treated as part of manufacturing overhead. Indirect labor includes the labor costs of janitors, supervisors, materials handlers, and night security guards. Although the efforts of these workers are essential, it would be either impractical or impossible to accurately trace their costs to specific units of product. Hence, such labor costs are treated as indirect labor.

Manufacturing Overhead   **Manufacturing overhead**, the third manufacturing cost category, includes all manufacturing costs except direct materials and direct labor. Manufacturing overhead includes items such as indirect materials; indirect labor; maintenance and repairs on production equipment; and heat and light, property taxes, depreciation, and insurance on manufacturing facilities. A company also incurs costs for heat and light, property taxes, insurance, depreciation, and so forth, associated with its selling and administrative functions, but these costs are not included as part of manufacturing overhead. Only those costs associated with *operating the factory* are included in manufacturing overhead.

Various names are used for manufacturing overhead, such as *indirect manufacturing cost, factory overhead,* and *factory burden.* All of these terms are synonyms for *manufacturing overhead.*

Nonmanufacturing Costs

Nonmanufacturing costs are often divided into two categories: (1) *selling costs* and (2) *administrative costs.* **Selling costs** include all costs that are incurred to secure customer orders and get the finished product to the customer. These costs are sometimes called *order-getting* and *order-filling costs.* Examples of selling costs include advertising, shipping, sales travel, sales commissions, sales salaries, and costs of finished goods warehouses. Selling costs can be either direct or indirect costs. For example, the cost of an advertising campaign dedicated to one specific product is a direct cost of that product, whereas the salary of a marketing manager who oversees numerous products is an indirect cost with respect to individual products.

Administrative costs include all costs associated with the *general management* of an organization rather than with manufacturing or selling. Examples of administrative costs include executive compensation, general accounting, secretarial, public relations, and similar costs involved in the overall, general administration of the organization *as a whole.* Administrative costs can be either direct or indirect costs. For example, the salary of an accounting manager in charge of accounts receivable collections in the East region is a direct cost of that region, whereas the salary of a chief financial officer who oversees all of a company's regions is an indirect cost with respect to individual regions.

Nonmanufacturing costs are also often called selling, general, and administrative (SG&A) costs or just selling and administrative costs.

Walmart Looks to Reduce Its Shipping Costs

Walmart hopes to lower its shipping costs, thereby enabling it to reduce its "everyday low prices." In years past, suppliers would ship their merchandise to Walmart's distribution centers, and then Walmart would use its own fleet of trucks to ship goods from its distribution centers to its retail store locations. However, now Walmart wants to assume control of transporting merchandise from its suppliers' manufacturing facilities to its distribution centers. Walmart believes it can lower these shipping costs by carrying more merchandise per truck and by taking advantage of volume purchase price discounts for fuel. In exchange for assuming these shipping responsibilities, Walmart is seeking price reductions from suppliers that it can pass along, at least in part, to its customers.

Source: Chris Burritt, Carol Wolf, and Matthew Boyle, "Why Wal-Mart Wants to Take the Driver's Seat," *Bloomberg Businessweek,* May 31–June 6, 2010, pp. 17–18.

COST CLASSIFICATIONS FOR PREPARING FINANCIAL STATEMENTS

When preparing a balance sheet and an income statement, companies need to classify their costs as *product costs* or *period costs.* To understand the difference between product costs and period costs, we must first discuss the matching principle from financial accounting.

Generally, costs are recognized as expenses on the income statement in the period that benefits from the cost. For example, if a company pays for liability insurance in advance for two years, the entire amount is not considered an expense of the year in which the payment is made. Instead, one-half of the cost would be recognized as an expense each year. The reason is that both years—not just the first year—benefit from the insurance payment. The unexpensed portion of the insurance payment is carried on the balance sheet as an asset called prepaid insurance.

The *matching principle* is based on the *accrual* concept that *costs incurred to generate a particular revenue should be recognized as expenses in the same period that the revenue is recognized.* This means that if a cost is incurred to acquire or make something that will eventually be sold, then the cost should be recognized as an expense only when the sale takes place—that is, when the benefit occurs. Such costs are called *product costs.*

> **LEARNING OBJECTIVE 1–3**
>
> Understand cost classifications used to prepare financial statements: product costs and period costs.

Product Costs

For financial accounting purposes, **product costs** include all costs involved in acquiring or making a product. In the case of manufactured goods, these costs consist of direct materials, direct labor, and manufacturing overhead.[1] Product costs "attach" to units of product as the goods are purchased or manufactured, and they remain attached as the goods go into inventory awaiting sale. Product costs are initially assigned to an inventory account on the balance sheet. When the goods are sold, the costs are released from inventory as expenses (typically called cost of goods sold) and matched against sales revenue on the income statement. Because product costs are initially assigned to inventories, they are also known as **inventoriable costs**.

We want to emphasize that product costs are not necessarily recorded as expenses on the income statement in the period in which they are incurred. Rather, as explained above, they are recorded as expenses in the period in which the related products *are sold*.

---

[1]For internal management purposes, product costs may exclude some manufacturing costs. For example, see the discussion in Chapter 6.

Period Costs

Period costs are all the costs that are not product costs. *All selling and administrative expenses are treated as period costs.* For example, sales commissions, advertising, executive salaries, public relations, and the rental costs of administrative offices are all period costs. Period costs are not included as part of the cost of either purchased or manufactured goods; instead, period costs are expensed on the income statement in the period in which they are incurred using the usual rules of accrual accounting. Keep in mind that the period in which a cost is incurred is not necessarily the period in which cash changes hands. For example, as discussed earlier, the costs of liability insurance are spread across the periods that benefit from the insurance—regardless of the period in which the insurance premium is paid.

Prime Cost and Conversion Cost

Two more cost categories are often used in discussions of manufacturing costs—*prime cost* and *conversion cost*. **Prime cost** is the sum of direct materials cost and direct labor cost. **Conversion cost** is the sum of direct labor cost and manufacturing overhead cost. The term *conversion cost* is used to describe direct labor and manufacturing overhead because these costs are incurred to convert materials into the finished product.

To improve your understanding of these definitions, consider the following scenario: A company has reported the following costs and expenses for the most recent month:

Direct materials	$69,000
Direct labor	$35,000
Manufacturing overhead	$14,000
Selling expenses	$29,000
Administrative expenses	$50,000

These costs and expenses can be categorized in a number of ways, including product costs, period costs, conversion costs, and prime costs:

Product cost = Direct materials + Direct labor + Manufacturing overhead

= $69,000 + $35,000 + $14,000

= $118,000

Period cost = Selling expenses + Administrative expenses

= $29,000 + $50,000

= $79,000

Conversion cost = Direct labor + Manufacturing overhead

= $35,000 + $14,000

= $49,000

Prime cost = Direct materials + Direct labor

= $69,000 + $35,000

= $104,000

CONCEPT CHECK

COST CLASSIFICATIONS FOR PREDICTING COST BEHAVIOR

It is often necessary to predict how a certain cost will behave in response to a change in activity. For example, a manager at **Under Armour** may want to estimate the impact a 5 percent increase in sales would have on the company's total direct materials cost. **Cost behavior** refers to how a cost reacts to changes in the level of activity. As the activity level rises and falls, a particular cost may rise and fall as well—or it may remain constant. For planning purposes, a manager must be able to anticipate which of these will happen; and if a cost can be expected to change, the manager must be able to estimate how much it will change. To help make such distinctions, costs are often categorized as *variable, fixed,* or *mixed.* The relative proportion of each type of cost in an organization is known as its **cost structure.** For example, an organization might have many fixed costs but few variable or mixed costs. Alternatively, it might have many variable costs but few fixed or mixed costs.

> **LEARNING OBJECTIVE 1–4**
>
> Understand cost classifications used to predict cost behavior: variable costs, fixed costs, and mixed costs.

Variable Cost

A **variable cost** varies, in total, in direct proportion to changes in the level of activity. Common examples of variable costs include cost of goods sold for a merchandising company, direct materials, direct labor, variable elements of manufacturing overhead, such as indirect materials, supplies, and power, and variable elements of selling and administrative expenses, such as commissions and shipping costs.[2]

For a cost to be variable, it must be variable *with respect to something.* That "something" is its *activity base.* An **activity base** is a measure of whatever causes the incurrence of a variable cost. An activity base is sometimes referred to as a *cost driver.* Some of the most common activity bases are direct labor-hours, machine-hours, units produced, and units sold. Other examples of activity bases (cost drivers) include the number of miles driven by salespersons, the number of pounds of laundry cleaned by a hotel, the number of calls handled by technical support staff at a software company, and the number of beds occupied in a hospital. *While there are many activity bases within organizations, throughout this textbook, unless stated otherwise, you should assume that the activity base under consideration is the total volume of goods and services provided by the organization. We will specify the activity base only when it is something other than total output.*

---

[2]Direct labor costs often can be fixed instead of variable for a variety of reasons. For example, in some countries, such as France, Germany, and Japan, labor regulations and cultural norms may limit management's ability to adjust the labor force in response to changes in activity. In this textbook, always assume that direct labor is a variable cost unless you are explicitly told otherwise.

Food Costs at a Luxury Hotel

The **Sporthotel Theresa** (http://www.theresa.at/), owned and operated by the Egger family, is a four-star hotel located in Zell im Zillertal, Austria. The hotel features access to hiking, skiing, biking, and other activities in the Ziller alps as well as its own fitness facility and spa.

Three full meals a day are included in the hotel room charge. Breakfast and lunch are served buffet-style while dinner is a more formal affair with as many as six courses. The chef, Stefan Egger, believes that food costs are roughly proportional to the number of guests staying at the hotel; that is, they are a variable cost. He must order food from suppliers two or three days in advance, but he adjusts his purchases to the number of guests who are currently staying at the hotel and their consumption patterns. In addition, guests make their selections from the dinner menu early in the day, which helps Stefan plan which foodstuffs will be required for dinner. Consequently, he is able to prepare just enough food so that all guests are satisfied and yet waste is held to a minimum.

Source: Conversation with Stefan Egger, chef at the Sporthotel Theresa.

To provide an example of a variable cost, consider Nooksack Expeditions, a small company that provides daylong whitewater rafting excursions on rivers in the North Cascade Mountains. The company provides all of the necessary equipment and experienced guides, and it serves gourmet meals to its guests. The meals are purchased from a caterer for $30 a person for a daylong excursion. The behavior of this variable cost, on both a per unit and a total basis, is shown below:

Number of Guests	Cost of Meals per Guest	Total Cost of Meals
250	$30	$7,500
500	$30	$15,000
750	$30	$22,500
1,000	$30	$30,000

While total variable costs change as the activity level changes, it is important to note that a variable cost is constant if expressed on a *per unit* basis. For example, the per unit cost of the meals remains constant at $30 even though the total cost of the meals increases and decreases with activity. The graph on the left-hand side of Exhibit 1–2 illustrates that the total variable cost rises and falls as the activity level rises and falls. At an activity level of 250 guests, the total meal cost is $7,500. At an activity level of 1,000 guests, the total meal cost rises to $30,000.

Fixed Cost

A **fixed cost** is a cost that remains constant, in total, regardless of changes in the level of activity. Examples of fixed costs include straight-line depreciation, insurance, property taxes, rent, supervisory salaries, administrative salaries, and advertising. Unlike variable costs, fixed costs are not affected by changes in activity. Consequently, as the activity level rises and falls, total fixed costs remain constant unless influenced by some outside force, such as a landlord increasing your monthly rental expense. To continue the Nooksack Expeditions example, assume the company rents a building for $500 per month to store its equipment. The total amount of rent paid is the same regardless of the number of guests the company takes on its expeditions during any given month. The concept of a fixed cost is shown graphically on the right-hand side of Exhibit 1–2.

EXHIBIT 1–2   Variable and Fixed Cost Behavior

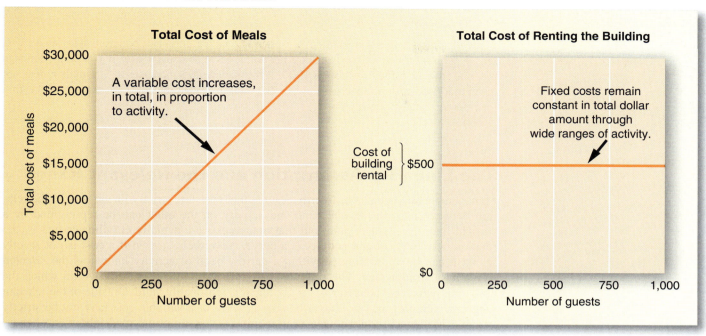

Because total fixed costs remain constant for large variations in the level of activity, the average fixed cost *per unit* becomes progressively smaller as the level of activity increases. If Nooksack Expeditions has only 250 guests in a month, the $500 fixed rental cost would amount to an average of $2 per guest. If there are 1,000 guests, the fixed rental cost would average only 50 cents per guest. The table below illustrates this aspect of the behavior of fixed costs. Note that as the number of guests increase, the average fixed cost per guest drops.

Monthly Rental Cost	Number of Guests	Average Cost per Guest
$500	250	$2.00
$500	500	$1.00
$500	750	$0.67
$500	1,000	$0.50

As a general rule, *we caution against expressing fixed costs on an average per unit basis in internal reports because it creates the false impression that fixed costs are like variable costs and that total fixed costs actually change as the level of activity changes.*

For planning purposes, fixed costs can be viewed as either *committed* or *discretionary*. **Committed fixed costs** represent organizational investments with a *multiyear* planning horizon that can't be significantly reduced even for short periods of time without making fundamental changes. Examples include investments in facilities and equipment, as well as real estate taxes, insurance expenses, and salaries of top management. Even if operations are interrupted or cut back, committed fixed costs remain largely unchanged in the short term because the costs of restoring them later are likely to be far greater than any short-run savings that might be realized. **Discretionary fixed costs** (often referred to as *managed fixed costs*) usually arise from *annual* decisions by management to spend on certain fixed cost items. Examples of discretionary fixed costs include advertising, research, public relations, management development programs, and internships for students. Discretionary fixed costs can be cut for short periods of time with minimal damage to the long-run goals of the organization.

HELPFUL HINT

Students often assume that fixed costs expressed on a per unit basis behave like variable costs. This is not true! If the average fixed cost per unit is $5 at an activity level of 100 units, it means the total amount of the fixed cost is $500. If the activity level increases to 101 units it does not mean that fixed costs will increase by $5. The total fixed cost remains constant at $500 within the relevant range of activity.

The Linearity Assumption and the Relevant Range

Management accountants ordinarily assume that costs are strictly linear; that is, the relation between cost on the one hand and activity on the other can be represented by a straight line. Economists point out that many costs are actually curvilinear; that is, the relation between cost and activity is a curve. Nevertheless, even if a cost is not strictly linear, it can be approximated within a narrow band of activity known as the *relevant range* by a straight line. The **relevant range** is the range of activity within which the assumption that cost behavior is strictly linear is reasonably valid. Outside of the relevant range, a fixed cost may no longer be strictly fixed or a variable cost may not be strictly variable. Managers should always keep in mind that assumptions made about cost behavior may be invalid if activity falls outside of the relevant range.

The concept of the relevant range is important in understanding fixed costs. For example, suppose the Mayo Clinic rents a machine for $20,000 per month that tests blood samples for the presence of leukemia cells. Furthermore, suppose that the capacity of the leukemia diagnostic machine is 3,000 tests per month. The assumption that the rent for the diagnostic machine is $20,000 per month is only valid within the relevant range of 0 to 3,000 tests per month. If the Mayo Clinic needed to test 5,000 blood samples per month, then it would need to rent another machine for an additional $20,000 per month. It would be difficult to rent half of a diagnostic machine; therefore, the step pattern depicted in Exhibit 1–3 is typical for such costs. This exhibit shows that the fixed rental expense is $20,000 for a relevant range of 0 to 3,000 tests. The fixed rental expense increases to $40,000 within the relevant range of 3,001 to 6,000 tests. The rental expense increases in discrete steps or increments of 3,000 tests, rather than increasing in a linear fashion per test.

EXHIBIT 1–3
Fixed Costs and the Relevant Range

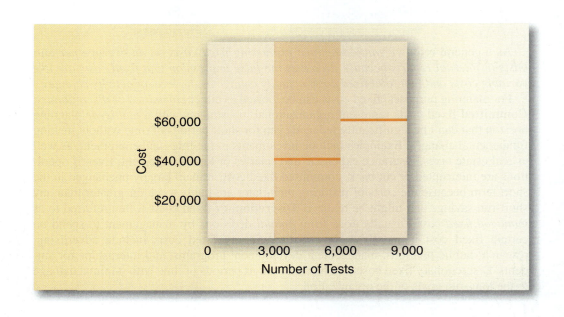

How Many Guides?

Majestic Ocean Kayaking, of Ucluelet, British Columbia, is owned and operated by Tracy Morben-Eeftink. The company offers a number of guided kayaking excursions ranging from three-hour tours of the Ucluelet harbor to six-day kayaking and camping trips in Clayoquot Sound. One of the company's excursions is a four-day kayaking and camping trip to The Broken Group Islands in the Pacific Rim National Park. Special regulations apply to trips in the park—including a requirement that one certified guide must be assigned for every five guests or fraction thereof. For example, a trip with 10 guests must have at least two certified guides. Guides are not salaried and are paid on a per-day basis. Therefore, the cost to the company of the guides for a trip is a step-variable cost rather than a fixed cost or a strictly variable cost. One guide is needed for 1 to 5 guests and two guides for 6 to 10 guests.

Sources: Tracy Morben-Eeftink, owner, Majestic Ocean Kayaking. For more information about the company, see www.oceankayaking.com.

This step-oriented cost behavior pattern can also be used to describe other costs, such as some labor costs. For example, salaried employee expenses can be characterized using a step pattern. Salaried employees are paid a fixed amount, such as $40,000 per year, for providing the capacity to work a prespecified amount of time, such as 40 hours per week for 50 weeks a year (= 2,000 hours per year). In this example, the total salaried employee expense is $40,000 within a relevant range of 0 to 2,000 hours of work. The total salaried employee expense increases to $80,000 (or two employees) if the organization's work requirements expand to a relevant range of 2,001 to 4,000 hours of work. Cost behavior patterns such as salaried employees are often called *step-variable costs*. Step-variable costs can often be adjusted quickly as conditions change. Furthermore, the width of the steps for step-variable costs is generally so narrow that these costs can be treated essentially as variable costs for most purposes. The width of the steps for fixed costs, on the other hand, is so wide that these costs should be treated as entirely fixed within the relevant range.

Exhibit 1–4 summarizes four key concepts related to variable and fixed costs. Study it carefully before reading further.

Mixed Costs

A **mixed cost** contains both variable and fixed cost elements. Mixed costs are also known as semivariable costs. To continue the Nooksack Expeditions example, the company incurs a mixed cost called fees paid to the state. It includes a license fee of $25,000 per year plus $3 per rafting party paid to the state's Department of Natural Resources. If the company runs 1,000 rafting parties this year, then the total fees paid to the state would be $28,000, made up of $25,000 in fixed cost plus $3,000 in variable cost. Exhibit 1–5 depicts the behavior of this mixed cost.

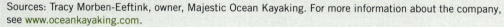

Cost	Behavior of the Cost (within the relevant range)	
	In Total	**Per Unit**
Variable cost	Total variable cost increases and decreases in proportion to changes in the activity level.	Variable cost per unit remains constant.
Fixed cost	Total fixed cost is not affected by changes in the activity level within the relevant range.	Fixed cost per unit decreases as the activity level rises and increases as the activity level falls.

EXHIBIT 1–4
Summary of Variable and Fixed Cost Behavior

EXHIBIT 1–5
Mixed Cost Behavior

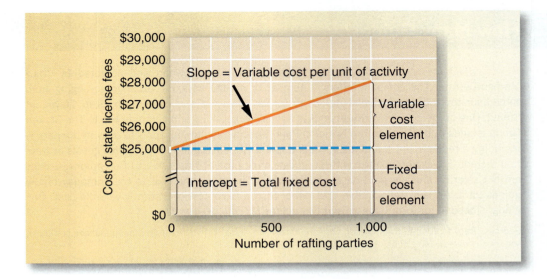

Even if Nooksack fails to attract any customers, the company will still have to pay the license fee of $25,000. This is why the cost line in Exhibit 1–5 intersects the vertical cost axis at the $25,000 point. For each rafting party the company organizes, the total cost of the state fees will increase by $3. Therefore, the total cost line slopes upward as the variable cost of $3 per party is added to the fixed cost of $25,000 per year.

Because the mixed cost in Exhibit 1–5 is represented by a straight line, the following equation for a straight line can be used to express the relationship between a mixed cost and the level of activity:

$$Y = a + bX$$

In this equation,

$Y =$ The total mixed cost

$a =$ The total fixed cost (the vertical intercept of the line)

$b =$ The variable cost per unit of activity (the slope of the line)

$X =$ The level of activity

Because the variable cost per unit equals the slope of the straight line, the steeper the slope, the higher the variable cost per unit.

In the case of the state fees paid by Nooksack Expeditions, the equation is written as follows:

$$Y = \$25,000 + \$3.00X$$

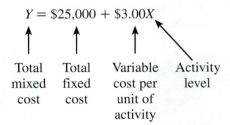

| Total mixed cost | Total fixed cost | Variable cost per unit of activity | Activity level |

This equation makes it easy to calculate the total mixed cost for any level of activity within the relevant range. For example, suppose that the company expects to organize 800 rafting parties in the next year. The total state fees would be calculated as follows:

$$Y = \$25,000 + (\$3.00 \text{ per rafting party} \times 800 \text{ rafting parties})$$

$$= \$27,400$$

3. Which of the following cost behavior assumptions is true? (You may select more than one answer.)
   a. Variable costs are constant if expressed on a per unit basis.
   b. Total variable costs increase as the level of activity increases.
   c. The average fixed cost per unit increases as the level of activity increases.
   d. Total fixed costs decrease as the level of activity decreases.
4. Assume the following: (1) three people go to a restaurant, (2) each person orders a soda for $2 and the group of three orders a large pizza to share for a price of $12, and (3) a fourth person joins the group and orders one soda and is invited to share in eating the pizza. Which of the following statements is false? (You may select more than one answer.)
   a. The cost of the fourth person's soda will be $2.
   b. The total cost of the four sodas consumed by the group is $8.
   c. When the fourth person joined the group the total cost of the large pizza increased to $16.
   d. When the fourth person joined the group the average "pizza cost" per person dropped to $3.

HELPFUL HINT

A mixed cost expressed on a per unit basis decreases as the activity level increases. Do you know why? Although the variable portion of a mixed cost stays constant on a per unit basis as the activity level increases, the fixed portion of a mixed cost decreases on a per unit basis as the activity level increases. This occurs because the fixed cost is being spread across more units.

THE ANALYSIS OF MIXED COSTS

Mixed costs are very common. For example, the overall cost of providing X-ray services to patients at the **Harvard Medical School Hospital** is a mixed cost. The costs of equipment depreciation and radiologists' and technicians' salaries are fixed, but the costs of X-ray film, power, and supplies are variable. At **Southwest Airlines**, maintenance costs are a mixed cost. The company incurs fixed costs for renting maintenance facilities and for keeping skilled mechanics on the payroll, but the costs of replacement parts, lubricating oils, tires, and so forth, are variable with respect to how often and how far the company's aircraft are flown.

The fixed portion of a mixed cost represents the minimum cost of having a service *ready and available* for use. The variable portion represents the cost incurred for *actual consumption* of the service, thus it varies in proportion to the amount of service actually consumed.

Managers can use a variety of methods to estimate the fixed and variable components of a mixed cost such as *account analysis,* the *engineering approach,* the *high-low method,* and *least-squares regression analysis.* In **account analysis**, an account is classified as either variable or fixed based on the analyst's prior knowledge of how the cost in the account behaves. For example, direct materials would be classified as variable and a building lease cost would be classified as fixed because of the nature of those costs. The **engineering approach** to cost analysis involves a detailed analysis of what cost behavior should be, based on an industrial engineer's evaluation of the production methods to be used, the materials specifications, labor requirements, equipment usage, production efficiency, power consumption, and so on.

The high-low and least-squares regression methods estimate the fixed and variable elements of a mixed cost by analyzing past records of cost and activity data. We will use an example from Brentline Hospital to illustrate the high-low method calculations and to compare the resulting high-low method cost estimates to those obtained using least-squares regression.

Diagnosing Cost Behavior with a Scattergraph Plot

LEARNING OBJECTIVE 1–5

Analyze a mixed cost using a scattergraph plot and the high-low method.

Assume that Brentline Hospital is interested in predicting future monthly maintenance costs for budgeting purposes. The senior management team believes that maintenance cost is a mixed cost and that the variable portion of this cost is driven by the number of patient-days. Each day a patient is in the hospital counts as one patient-day. The hospital's chief financial officer gathered the following data for the most recent seven-month period:

Month	Activity Level: Patient-Days	Maintenance Cost Incurred
January	5,600	$7,900
February	7,100	$8,500
March	5,000	$7,400
April	6,500	$8,200
May	7,300	$9,100
June	8,000	$9,800
July	6,200	$7,800

The first step in applying the high-low method or the least-squares regression method is to diagnose cost behavior with a scattergraph plot. The scattergraph plot of maintenance costs versus patient-days at Brentline Hospital is shown in Exhibit 1–6. Two things should be noted about this scattergraph:

EXHIBIT 1–6 Scattergraph Method of Cost Analysis

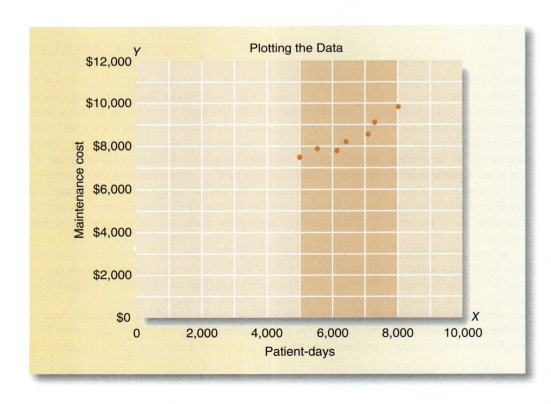

1. The total maintenance cost, Y, is plotted on the vertical axis. Cost is known as the **dependent variable** because the amount of cost incurred during a period depends on the level of activity for the period. (That is, as the level of activity increases, total cost will also ordinarily increase.)
2. The activity, X (patient-days in this case), is plotted on the horizontal axis. Activity is known as the **independent variable** because it causes variations in the cost.

From the scattergraph plot, it is evident that maintenance costs do increase with the number of patient-days in an approximately *linear* fashion. In other words, the points lie more or less along a straight line that slopes upward and to the right. Cost behavior is considered **linear** whenever a straight line is a reasonable approximation for the relation between cost and activity.

Plotting the data on a scattergraph is an essential diagnostic step that should be performed before performing the high-low method or least-squares regression calculations. If the scattergraph plot reveals linear cost behavior, then it makes sense to perform the high-low or least-squares regression calculations to separate the mixed cost into its variable and fixed components. If the scattergraph plot does not depict linear cost behavior, then it makes no sense to proceed any further in analyzing the data.

The High-Low Method

Assuming that the scattergraph plot indicates a linear relation between cost and activity, the fixed and variable cost elements of a mixed cost can be estimated using the *high-low method* or the *least-squares regression method*. The high-low method is based on the rise-over-run formula for the slope of a straight line. As previously discussed, if the relation between cost and activity can be represented by a straight line, then the slope of the straight line is equal to the variable cost per unit of activity. Consequently, the following formula can be used to estimate the variable cost:

$$\text{Variable cost} = \text{Slope of the line} = \frac{\text{Rise}}{\text{Run}} = \frac{Y_2 - Y_1}{X_2 - X_1}$$

To analyze mixed costs with the **high-low method**, begin by identifying the period with the lowest level of activity and the period with the highest level of activity. The period with the lowest activity is selected as the first point in the above formula and the period with the highest activity is selected as the second point. Consequently, the formula becomes

$$\text{Variable cost} = \frac{Y_2 - Y_1}{X_2 - X_1} = \frac{\text{Cost at the high activity level} - \text{Cost at the low activity level}}{\text{High activity level} - \text{Low activity level}}$$

or

$$\text{Variable cost} = \frac{\text{Change in cost}}{\text{Change in activity}}$$

Therefore, when the high-low method is used, the variable cost is estimated by dividing the difference in cost between the high and low levels of activity by the change in activity between those two points.

To return to the Brentline Hospital example, using the high-low method, we first identify the periods with the highest and lowest *activity*—in this case, June and March. We then use the activity and cost data from these two periods to estimate the variable cost component as follows:

	Patient-Days	Maintenance Cost Incurred
High activity level (June)	8,000	$9,800
Low activity level (March)	5,000	7,400
Change	3,000	$2,400

$$\text{Variable cost} = \frac{\text{Change in cost}}{\text{Change in activity}} = \frac{\$2,400}{3,000 \text{ patient-days}} = \$0.80 \text{ per patient-day}$$

Having determined that the variable maintenance cost is 80 cents per patient-day, we can now determine the amount of fixed cost. This is done by taking the total cost at *either* the high or the low activity level and deducting the variable cost element. In the computation below, total cost at the high activity level is used in computing the fixed cost element:

$$\text{Fixed cost element} = \text{Total cost} - \text{Variable cost element}$$
$$= \$9,800 - (\$0.80 \text{ per patient-day} \times 8,000 \text{ patient-days})$$
$$= \$3,400$$

Both the variable and fixed cost elements have now been isolated. The cost of maintenance can be expressed as $3,400 per month plus 80 cents per patient-day, or as

$$Y = \$3,400 + \$0.80X$$

Total maintenance cost   Total patient-days

The data used in this illustration are shown graphically in Exhibit 1–7. Notice that a straight line has been drawn through the points corresponding to the low and high levels of activity. In essence, that is what the high-low method does—it draws a straight line through those two points.

EXHIBIT 1–7   High-Low Method of Cost Analysis

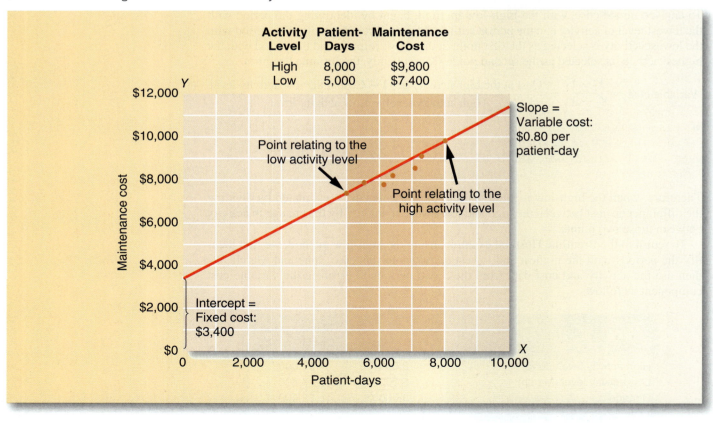

Activity Level	Patient-Days	Maintenance Cost
High	8,000	$9,800
Low	5,000	$7,400

Slope = Variable cost: $0.80 per patient-day

Point relating to the low activity level

Point relating to the high activity level

Intercept = Fixed cost: $3,400

Maintenance cost

Patient-days

Sometimes the high and low levels of activity don't coincide with the high and low amounts of cost. For example, the period that has the highest level of activity may not have the highest amount of cost. Nevertheless, the costs at the highest and lowest levels of *activity* are always used to analyze a mixed cost under the high-low method. The reason is that the analyst would like to use data that reflect the greatest possible variation in activity.

The high-low method is very simple to apply, but it suffers from a major (and sometimes critical) defect—it utilizes only two data points. Generally, two data points are not enough to produce accurate results. Additionally, the periods with the highest and lowest activity tend to be unusual. A cost formula that is estimated solely using data from these unusual periods may misrepresent the true cost behavior during normal periods. Such a distortion is evident in Exhibit 1–7. The straight line should probably be shifted down somewhat so that it is closer to more of the data points. For these reasons, least-squares regression will generally be more accurate than the high-low method.

HELPFUL HINT

Use the following five-step process to perform high-low method calculations:

Step 1: Select the two periods with the highest and lowest levels of activity.

Step 2: Compute the change in cost and the change in activity between the two periods.

Step 3: Divide the change in cost by the change in activity to derive your estimate of the variable cost per unit.

Step 4: Multiply the low (or high) level of activity by the variable cost per unit. Subtract this amount from the total cost at the low (or high) level of activity to derive the fixed portion of the mixed cost.

Step 5: Use the equation $Y = a + bx$ to estimate the total mixed cost for any level of activity within the relevant range.

The Least-Squares Regression Method

The **least-squares regression method**, unlike the high-low method, uses all of the data to separate a mixed cost into its fixed and variable components. A *regression line* of the form $Y = a + bX$ is fitted to the data, where a represents the total fixed cost and b represents the variable cost per unit of activity. The basic idea underlying the least-squares regression method is illustrated in Exhibit 1–8 using hypothetical data points. Notice from the exhibit that the deviations from the plotted points to the regression line are measured vertically on the graph. These vertical deviations are called the regression errors. There is nothing mysterious about the least-squares regression method. It simply computes the regression line that minimizes the sum of these squared errors. The formulas that accomplish this are fairly complex and involve numerous calculations, but the principle is simple.

Fortunately, computers are adept at carrying out the computations required by the least-squares regression formulas. The data—the observed values of X and Y—are entered into the computer, and software does the rest. In the case of the Brentline Hospital maintenance cost data, a statistical software package on a personal computer can calculate the following least-squares regression estimates of the total fixed cost (a) and the variable cost per unit of activity (b):

$$a = \$3,431$$

$$b = \$0.759$$

Therefore, using the least-squares regression method, the fixed element of the maintenance cost is $3,431 per month and the variable portion is 75.9 cents per patient-day.

EXHIBIT 1–8
The Concept of Least-Squares
Regression

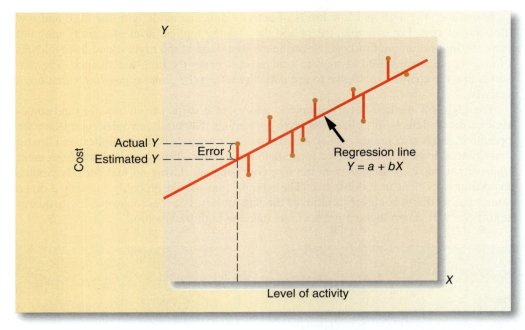

In terms of the linear equation $Y = a + bX$, the cost formula can be written as:

$$Y = \$3{,}431 + \$0.759X$$

where activity (X) is expressed in patient-days.

Least-squares regression analysis generally provides more accurate cost estimates than the high-low method because, rather than relying on just two data points, it uses all of the data points to fit a line that minimizes the sum of the squared errors. The table below compares Brentline Hospital's cost estimates using the high-low method and the least-squares regression method:

	High-Low Method	Least-Squares Regression Method
Variable cost estimate per patient-day	$0.800	$0.759
Fixed cost estimate per month	$3,400	$3,431

When Brentline uses the least-squares regression method to create a straight line that minimizes the sum of the squared errors, it results in estimated fixed costs that are $31 higher than the amount derived using the high-low method. It also decreases the slope of the straight line resulting in a lower variable cost estimate of $0.759 per patient-day rather than $0.80 per patient-day as derived using the high-low method.

IN BUSINESS

The Zipcar Comes to College Campuses

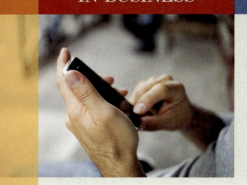

Zipcar is a car sharing service based in Cambridge, Massachusetts. The company serves 13 cities and 120 university campuses. Members pay a $50 annual fee plus $7 an hour to rent a car. They can use their iPhones to rent a car, locate it in the nearest Zipcar parking lot, unlock it using an access code, and drive it off the lot. This mixed cost arrangement is attractive to customers who need a car infrequently and wish to avoid the large cash outlay that comes with buying or leasing a vehicle.

Source: Jefferson Graham, "An iPhone Gets Zipcar Drivers on Their Way," *USA Today*, September 30, 2009, p. 3B.

5. In months 1 and 2, a company's total selling expense was $64,000 and $80,000, respectively, at sales volumes of 8,000 and 12,000 units, respectively. Using the high-low method, what is the company's estimated selling expense in month 3 if it plans to sell 11,000 units?

    a. $66,000
    b. $70,000
    c. $76,000
    d. $78,000

6. Which of the following statements is true with respect to the equation $Y = a + bX$? (You may select more than one answer.)

    a. Y equals the total amount of the mixed cost.
    b. a equals the total fixed cost included in the mixed cost.
    c. b equals the total variable cost included in the mixed cost.
    d. X equals the level of activity.

CONCEPT CHECK

TRADITIONAL AND CONTRIBUTION FORMAT INCOME STATEMENTS

In this section of the chapter, we discuss how to prepare traditional and contribution format income statements for a merchandising company.[3] Merchandising companies do not manufacture the products that they sell to customers. For example, **Lowe's** and **Home Depot** are merchandising companies because they buy finished products from manufacturers and then resell them to end consumers.

LEARNING OBJECTIVE 1–6

Prepare income statements for a merchandising company using the traditional and contribution formats.

The Traditional Format Income Statement

Traditional income statements are prepared primarily for external reporting purposes. The left-hand side of Exhibit 1–9 shows a traditional income statement format for merchandising companies. This type of income statement organizes costs into two categories—cost of goods sold and selling and administrative expenses. Sales minus cost of goods sold equals the *gross margin*. The gross margin minus selling and administrative expenses equals net operating income.

The cost of goods sold reports the *product costs* attached to the merchandise sold during the period. The selling and administrative expenses report all *period costs* that have

EXHIBIT 1–9 Comparing Traditional and Contribution Format Income Statements for Merchandising Companies (all numbers are given)

Traditional Format			Contribution Format		
Sales		$12,000	Sales		$12,000
Cost of goods sold*		6,000	Variable expenses:		
Gross margin		6,000	Cost of goods sold	$6,000	
Selling and administrative expenses:			Variable selling	600	
Selling	$3,100		Variable administrative	400	7,000
Administrative	1,900	5,000	Contribution margin		5,000
Net operating income		$ 1,000	Fixed expenses:		
			Fixed selling	2,500	
			Fixed administrative	1,500	4,000
			Net operating income		$ 1,000

*For a manufacturing company, the cost of goods sold would include some variable costs, such as direct materials, direct labor, and variable overhead, and some fixed costs, such as fixed manufacturing overhead. Income statement formats for manufacturing companies will be explored in greater detail in a subsequent chapter.

---

[3]Subsequent chapters compare the income statement formats for manufacturing companies.

been expensed as incurred. The cost of goods sold for a merchandising company can be computed directly by multiplying the number of units sold by their unit cost or indirectly using the equation below:

$$\text{Cost of goods sold} = \text{Beginning merchandise inventory} + \text{Purchases} - \text{Ending merchandise inventory}$$

For example, let's assume that the company depicted in Exhibit 1–9 purchased $3,000 of merchandise inventory during the period and had beginning and ending merchandise inventory balances of $7,000 and $4,000, respectively. The equation above could be used to compute the cost of goods sold as follows:

$$
\begin{aligned}
\text{Cost of goods sold} &= \text{Beginning merchandise inventory} + \text{Purchases} - \text{Ending merchandise inventory} \\
&= \$7,000 + \$3,000 - \$4,000 \\
&= \$6,000
\end{aligned}
$$

Although the traditional income statement is useful for external reporting purposes, it has serious limitations when used for internal purposes. It does not distinguish between fixed and variable costs. For example, under the heading "Selling and administrative expenses," both variable administrative costs ($400) and fixed administrative costs ($1,500) are lumped together ($1,900). Internally, managers need cost data organized by cost behavior to aid in planning, controlling, and decision making. The contribution format income statement has been developed in response to these needs.

The Contribution Format Income Statement

The crucial distinction between fixed and variable costs is at the heart of the **contribution approach** to constructing income statements. The unique thing about the contribution approach is that it provides managers with an income statement that clearly distinguishes between fixed and variable costs and therefore aids planning, controlling, and decision making. The right-hand side of Exhibit 1–9 shows a contribution format income statement for merchandising companies.

The contribution approach separates costs into fixed and variable categories, first deducting variable expenses from sales to obtain the *contribution margin*. For a merchandising company, cost of goods sold is a variable cost that gets included in the "Variable expenses" portion of the contribution format income statement. The **contribution margin** is the amount remaining from sales revenues after variable expenses have been deducted. This amount *contributes* toward covering fixed expenses and then toward profits for the period.

The contribution format income statement is used as an internal planning and decision-making tool. Its emphasis on cost behavior aids cost-volume-profit analysis (such as we

CONCEPT CHECK

7. Which of the following statements is true? (You may select more than one answer.)
    a. Traditional income statements include administrative expenses in the computation of gross margin.
    b. Contribution format income statements exclude variable selling expenses from the computation of contribution margin.
    c. Traditional income statements exclude fixed selling expenses from the computation of gross margin.
    d. Contribution format income statements exclude all fixed expenses from the computation of contribution margin.

shall be doing in a subsequent chapter), management performance appraisals, and budgeting. Moreover, the contribution approach helps managers organize data pertinent to numerous decisions such as product-line analysis, pricing, use of scarce resources, and make or buy analysis. All of these topics are covered in later chapters.

COST CLASSIFICATIONS FOR DECISION MAKING

Costs are an important feature of many business decisions. In making decisions, it is essential to have a firm grasp of the concepts *differential cost, opportunity cost,* and *sunk cost.*

LEARNING OBJECTIVE 1-7

Understand cost classifications used in making decisions: differential costs, opportunity costs, and sunk costs.

Differential Cost and Revenue

Decisions involve choosing between alternatives. In business decisions, each alternative will have costs and benefits that must be compared to the costs and benefits of the other available alternatives. A difference in costs between any two alternatives is known as a **differential cost**. A difference in revenues (usually just sales) between any two alternatives is known as **differential revenue**.

A differential cost is also known as an **incremental cost**, although technically an incremental cost should refer only to an increase in cost from one alternative to another; decreases in cost should be referred to as *decremental costs.* Differential cost is a broader term, encompassing both cost increases (incremental costs) and cost decreases (decremental costs) between alternatives.

The accountant's differential cost concept can be compared to the economist's marginal cost concept. In speaking of changes in cost and revenue, the economist uses the terms *marginal cost* and *marginal revenue.* The revenue that can be obtained from selling one more unit of product is called marginal revenue, and the cost involved in producing one more unit of product is called marginal cost. The economist's marginal concept is basically the same as the accountant's differential concept applied to a single unit of output.

Differential costs can be either fixed or variable. To illustrate, assume that Natural Cosmetics, Inc., is thinking about changing its marketing method from distribution through retailers to distribution by a network of neighborhood sales representatives. Present costs and revenues are compared to projected costs and revenues in the following table:

	Retailer Distribution (present)	Sales Representatives (proposed)	Differential Costs and Revenues
Sales (Variable)	$700,000	$800,000	$100,000
Cost of goods sold (Variable)	350,000	400,000	50,000
Advertising (Fixed)	80,000	45,000	(35,000)
Commissions (Variable)	0	40,000	40,000
Warehouse depreciation (Fixed)	50,000	80,000	30,000
Other expenses (Fixed)	60,000	60,000	0
Total expenses	540,000	625,000	85,000
Net operating income	$160,000	$175,000	$ 15,000

According to the above analysis, the differential revenue is $100,000 and the differential costs total $85,000, leaving a positive differential net operating income of $15,000 in favor of using sales representatives.

In general, only the differences between alternatives are relevant in decisions. Those items that are the same under all alternatives and that are not affected by the decision can be ignored. For example, in the Natural Cosmetics, Inc., example above, the "Other expenses" category, which is $60,000 under both alternatives, can be ignored because it has no effect on the decision. If it were removed from the calculations, the sales representatives would still be preferred by $15,000. This is an extremely important principle in management accounting that we will revisit in later chapters.

Opportunity Cost and Sunk Cost

Opportunity cost is the potential benefit that is given up when one alternative is selected over another. For example, assume that you have a part-time job while attending college that pays $200 per week. If you spend one week at the beach during spring break without pay, then the $200 in lost wages would be an opportunity cost of taking the week off to be at the beach. Opportunity costs are not usually found in accounting records, but they are costs that must be explicitly considered in every decision a manager makes. Virtually every alternative involves an opportunity cost.

A **sunk cost** is a cost *that has already been incurred* and that cannot be changed by any decision made now or in the future. Because sunk costs cannot be changed by any decision, they are not differential costs. And because only differential costs are relevant in a decision, sunk costs should always be ignored.

To illustrate a sunk cost, assume that a company paid $50,000 several years ago for a special-purpose machine. The machine was used to make a product that is now obsolete and is no longer being sold. Even though in hindsight purchasing the machine may have been unwise, the $50,000 cost has already been incurred and cannot be undone. And it would be folly to continue making the obsolete product in a misguided attempt to "recover" the original cost of the machine. In short, the $50,000 originally paid for the machine is a sunk cost that should be ignored in current decisions.

CONCEPT CHECK

8. Which of the following statements is true? (You may select more than one answer.)
   a. A common cost is one type of direct cost.
   b. A sunk cost is usually a differential cost.
   c. Opportunity costs are not usually recorded in the accounts of an organization.
   d. A particular cost may be direct or indirect depending on the cost object.

DECISION POINT

Your Decision to Attend Class

When you make the decision to attend class on a particular day, what are the opportunity costs that are inherent in that decision?

SUMMARY

LOI–I Understand cost classifications used for assigning costs to cost objects: direct costs and indirect costs.

A direct cost such as direct materials is a cost that can be easily and conveniently traced to a cost object. An indirect cost is a cost that cannot be easily and conveniently traced to a cost object. For example, the salary of the administrator of a hospital is an indirect cost of serving a particular patient.

LOI–2 Identify and give examples of each of the three basic manufacturing cost categories.

Manufacturing costs consist of two categories of costs that can be conveniently and directly traced to units of product—direct materials and direct labor—and one category that cannot be conveniently traced to units of product—manufacturing overhead.

LOI–3 Understand cost classifications used to prepare financial statements: product costs and period costs.

For purposes of valuing inventories and determining expenses for the balance sheet and income statement, costs are classified as either product costs or period costs. Product costs are assigned to inventories and are considered assets until the products are sold. A product cost becomes an expense—cost of goods sold—only when the product is sold. In contrast, period costs are taken directly to the income statement as expenses in the period in which they are incurred.

In a merchandising company, product cost is whatever the company paid for its merchandise. For external financial reports in a manufacturing company, product costs consist of all manufacturing costs. In both kinds of companies, selling and administrative costs are considered to be period costs and are expensed as incurred.

LOI–4 Understand cost classifications used to predict cost behavior: variable costs, fixed costs, and mixed costs.

For purposes of predicting how costs will react to changes in activity, costs are classified into three categories—variable, fixed, and mixed. Variable costs, in total, are strictly proportional to activity. The variable cost per unit is constant. Fixed costs, in total, remain the same as the activity level changes within the relevant range. The average fixed cost per unit decreases as the activity level increases. Mixed costs consist of variable and fixed elements and can be expressed in equation form as $Y = a + bX$, where X is the activity, Y is the total cost, a is the fixed cost element, and b is the variable cost per unit of activity.

LOI–5 Analyze a mixed cost using a scattergraph plot and the high-low method.

A scattergraph plots activity on the horizontal, X, axis and total cost on the vertical, Y, axis. If the relation between cost and activity appears to be linear, then the variable and fixed components of a mixed cost can be estimated using the high-low method or least-squares regression method.

To use the high-low method, first identify the periods with the highest and lowest levels of activity. Second, estimate the variable cost element by dividing the change in total cost by the change in activity for these two periods. Third, estimate the fixed cost element by subtracting the total variable cost from the total cost at either the highest or lowest level of activity.

The high-low method relies on only two, often unusual, data points rather than all of the available data and therefore may provide misleading estimates of variable and fixed costs.

LOI–6 Prepare income statements for a merchandising company using the traditional and contribution formats.

The traditional income statement format is used primarily for external reporting purposes. It organizes costs using product and period cost classifications. The contribution format income statement aids decision making because it organizes costs using variable and fixed cost classifications. The contribution margin is the amount remaining from sales revenues after variable expenses have been deducted. This amount contributes toward covering fixed expenses and then toward profits for the period.

LOI–7 Understand cost classifications used in making decisions: differential costs, opportunity costs, and sunk costs.

The concepts of differential cost and revenue, opportunity cost, and sunk cost are vitally important for purposes of making decisions. Differential costs and revenues refer to the costs and revenues that differ between alternatives. Opportunity cost is the benefit that is forgone when one alternative is selected over another. Sunk cost is a cost that occurred in the past and cannot be altered. Differential costs and opportunity costs are relevant in decisions and should be carefully considered. Sunk costs are always irrelevant in decisions and should be ignored.

The various cost classifications discussed in this chapter are different ways of looking at costs. A particular cost, such as the cost of cheese in a taco served at **Taco Bell**, can be a manufacturing cost, a product cost, a variable cost, a direct cost, and a differential cost—all at the same time. Taco Bell essentially manufactures fast food. Therefore the cost of the cheese in a taco would be considered a manufacturing cost as well as a product cost. In addition, the cost of cheese would be considered variable with respect to the number of tacos served and would be a direct cost of serving tacos. Finally, the cost of the cheese in a taco would be considered a differential cost of the taco.

GUIDANCE ANSWERS TO DECISION POINT

Your Decision to Attend Class (p. 44)

Every alternative involves an opportunity cost. Think about what you could be doing instead of attending class.

- You could have been working at a part-time job; you could quantify that cost by multiplying your pay rate by the time you spend preparing for and attending class.
- You could have spent the time studying for another class; the opportunity cost could be measured by the improvement in the grade that would result from spending more time on the other class.
- You could have slept in or taken a nap; depending on your level of sleep deprivation, this opportunity cost might be priceless.

GUIDANCE ANSWERS TO CONCEPT CHECKS

1. **Choices b and d.** Product costs attach to units of production and are expensed on the income statement when the units are sold. Conversion costs do not include direct materials.
2. **Choices a, b, and c.** Product costs (rather than period costs) are referred to as inventoriable costs.
3. **Choices a and b.** The average fixed cost per unit decreases, rather than increases, as the level of activity increases. Total fixed costs do not change as the level of activity decreases (within the relevant range).
4. **Choice c.** When the fourth person joined the group the total cost of the large pizza held constant at $12.
5. **Choice c.** The change in cost of $16,000 divided by the change in activity of 4,000 units provides an estimated variable cost of $4 per unit. Using the low-level of activity, $64,000 = a + ($4 per unit)(8,000 units). Solving for a provides an estimated fixed cost of $32,000. At an activity level of 11,000 units, Y = $32,000 + ($4 per unit)(11,000 units). Solving for Y provides an estimated selling expense of $76,000.
6. **Choices a, b, and d.** b equals the variable cost per unit, not the total amount of the variable cost.
7. **Choices c and d.** Traditional income statements exclude administrative expenses from the computation of gross margin. Contribution format income statements include variable selling expenses in the computation of contribution margin.
8. **Choices c and d.** A common cost is one type of indirect cost, rather than direct cost. A sunk cost is not a differential cost.

REVIEW PROBLEM 1: COST TERMS

Many new cost terms have been introduced in this chapter. It will take you some time to learn what each term means and how to properly classify costs in an organization. Consider the following example: Porter Company manufactures furniture, including tables. Selected costs are given below:

1. The tables are made of wood that costs $100 per table.
2. The tables are assembled by workers, at a wage cost of $40 per table.
3. Workers assembling the tables are supervised by a factory supervisor who is paid $38,000 per year.
4. Electrical costs are $2 per machine-hour. Four machine-hours are required to produce a table.
5. The depreciation on the machines used to make the tables totals $10,000 per year. The machines have no resale value and do not wear out through use.
6. The salary of the president of the company is $100,000 per year.
7. The company spends $250,000 per year to advertise its products.
8. Salespersons are paid a commission of $30 for each table sold.
9. Instead of producing the tables, the company could rent its factory space for $50,000 per year.

Required:

Classify these costs according to the various cost terms used in the chapter. *Carefully study the classification of each cost.* If you don't understand why a particular cost is classified the way it is, reread the section of the chapter discussing the particular cost term. The terms *variable cost* and *fixed cost* refer to how costs behave with respect to the number of tables produced in a year.

Solution to Review Problem 1

	Variable Cost	Fixed Cost	Period (Selling and Administrative) Cost	Product Cost			Sunk Cost	Opportunity Cost
				Direct Materials	Direct Labor	Manufacturing Overhead		
1. Wood used in a table ($100 per table)	X			X				
2. Labor cost to assemble a table ($40 per table)	X				X			
3. Salary of the factory supervisor ($38,000 per year)		X				X		
4. Cost of electricity to produce tables ($2 per machine-hour)	X					X		
5. Depreciation of machines used to produce tables ($10,000 per year)		X				X	X*	
6. Salary of the company president ($100,000 per year)		X	X					
7. Advertising expense ($250,000 per year)		X	X					
8. Commissions paid to salespersons ($30 per table sold)	X		X					
9. Rental income forgone on factory space								X†

*This is a sunk cost because the outlay for the equipment was made in a previous period.

†This is an opportunity cost because it represents the potential benefit that is lost or sacrificed as a result of using the factory space to produce tables. Opportunity cost is a special category of cost that is not ordinarily recorded in an organization's accounting records. To avoid possible confusion with other costs, we will not attempt to classify this cost in any other way except as an opportunity cost.

REVIEW PROBLEM 2: HIGH-LOW METHOD

The administrator of Azalea Hills Hospital would like a cost formula linking the administrative costs involved in admitting patients to the number of patients admitted during a month. The Admitting Department's costs and the number of patients admitted during the immediately preceding eight months are given in the following table:

Month	Number of Patients Admitted	Admitting Department Costs
May	1,800	$14,700
June	1,900	$15,200
July	1,700	$13,700
August	1,600	$14,000
September	1,500	$14,300
October	1,300	$13,100
November	1,100	$12,800
December	1,500	$14,600

Required:

1. Use the high-low method to estimate the fixed and variable components of admitting costs.
2. Express the fixed and variable components of admitting costs as a cost formula in the form $Y = a + bX$.

Solution to Review Problem 2

1. The first step in the high-low method is to identify the periods of the lowest and highest activity. Those periods are November (1,100 patients admitted) and June (1,900 patients admitted).

   The second step is to compute the variable cost per unit using those two data points:

Month	Number of Patients Admitted	Admitting Department Costs
High activity level (June)	1,900	$15,200
Low activity level (November)	1,100	12,800
Change	800	$ 2,400

   $$\text{Variable cost} = \frac{\text{Change in cost}}{\text{Change in activity}} = \frac{\$2,400}{800 \text{ patients admitted}} = \$3 \text{ per patient admitted}$$

   The third step is to compute the fixed cost element by deducting the variable cost element from the total cost at either the high or low activity. In the computation below, the high point of activity is used:

   $$\text{Fixed cost element} = \text{Total cost} - \text{Variable cost element}$$

   $$= \$15,200 - (\$3 \text{ per patient admitted} \times 1,900 \text{ patients admitted})$$

   $$= \$9,500$$

2. The cost formula is $Y = \$9,500 + \$3X$.

GLOSSARY

Account analysis A method for analyzing cost behavior in which an account is classified as either variable or fixed based on the analyst's prior knowledge of how the cost in the account behaves. (p. 35)

Activity base A measure of whatever causes the incurrence of a variable cost. For example, the total cost of X-ray film in a hospital will increase as the number of X-rays taken increases. Therefore, the number of X-rays is the activity base that explains the total cost of X-ray film. (p. 29)

Administrative costs All executive, organizational, and clerical costs associated with the general management of an organization rather than with manufacturing or selling. (p. 26)

Committed fixed costs Investments in facilities, equipment, and basic organizational structure that can't be significantly reduced even for short periods of time without making fundamental changes. (p. 31)

Common cost A cost that is incurred to support a number of cost objects but that cannot be traced to them individually. For example, the wage cost of the pilot of a 747 airliner is a common cost of all of the passengers on the aircraft. Without the pilot, there would be no flight and no passengers. But no part of the pilot's wage is caused by any one passenger taking the flight. (p. 25)

Contribution approach An income statement format that organizes costs by their behavior. Costs are separated into variable and fixed categories rather than being separated into product and period costs for external reporting purposes. (p. 42)

Contribution margin The amount remaining from sales revenues after all variable expenses have been deducted. (p. 42)

Conversion cost Direct labor cost plus manufacturing overhead cost. (p. 28)

Cost behavior The way in which a cost reacts to changes in the level of activity. (p. 29)

Cost object Anything for which cost data are desired. Examples of cost objects are products, customers, jobs, and parts of the organization such as departments or divisions. (p. 24)

Cost structure The relative proportion of fixed, variable, and mixed costs in an organization. (p. 29)

Dependent variable A variable that responds to some causal factor; total cost is the dependent variable, as represented by the letter Y, in the equation $Y = a + bX$. (p. 37)

Differential cost A difference in cost between two alternatives. Also see *Incremental cost*. (p. 43)

Differential revenue The difference in revenue between two alternatives. (p. 43)

Direct cost A cost that can be easily and conveniently traced to a specified cost object. (p. 24)

Direct labor   Factory labor costs that can be easily traced to individual units of product. Also called *touch labor*. (p. 26)

Direct materials   Materials that become an integral part of a finished product and whose costs can be conveniently traced to it. (p. 25)

Discretionary fixed costs   Those fixed costs that arise from annual decisions by management to spend on certain fixed cost items, such as advertising and research. (p. 31)

Engineering approach   A detailed analysis of cost behavior based on an industrial engineer's evaluation of the inputs that are required to carry out a particular activity and of the prices of those inputs. (p. 35)

Fixed cost   A cost that remains constant, in total, regardless of changes in the level of activity within the relevant range. If a fixed cost is expressed on a per unit basis, it varies inversely with the level of activity. (p. 30)

High-low method   A method of separating a mixed cost into its fixed and variable elements by analyzing the change in cost between the high and low activity levels. (p. 37)

Incremental cost   An increase in cost between two alternatives. Also see *Differential cost*. (p. 43)

Independent variable   A variable that acts as a causal factor; activity is the independent variable, as represented by the letter X, in the equation $Y = a + bX$. (p. 37)

Indirect cost   A cost that cannot be easily and conveniently traced to a specified cost object. (p. 25)

Indirect labor   The labor costs of janitors, supervisors, materials handlers, and other factory workers that cannot be conveniently traced to particular products. (p. 26)

Indirect materials   Small items of material such as glue and nails that may be an integral part of a finished product, but whose costs cannot be easily or conveniently traced to it. (p. 26)

Inventoriable costs   Synonym for product costs. (p. 27)

Least-squares regression method   A method of separating a mixed cost into its fixed and variable elements by fitting a regression line that minimizes the sum of the squared errors. (p. 39)

Linear cost behavior   Cost behavior is said to be linear whenever a straight line is a reasonable approximation for the relation between cost and activity. (p. 37)

Manufacturing overhead   All manufacturing costs except direct materials and direct labor. (p. 26)

Mixed cost   A cost that contains both variable and fixed cost elements. (p. 33)

Opportunity cost   The potential benefit that is given up when one alternative is selected over another. (p. 44)

Period costs   Costs that are taken directly to the income statement as expenses in the period in which they are incurred or accrued. (p. 28)

Prime cost   Direct materials cost plus direct labor cost. (p. 28)

Product costs   All costs that are involved in acquiring or making a product. In the case of manufactured goods, these costs consist of direct materials, direct labor, and manufacturing overhead. Also see *Inventoriable costs*. (p. 27)

Raw materials   Any materials that go into the final product. (p. 25)

Relevant range   The range of activity within which assumptions about variable and fixed cost behavior are valid. (p. 32)

Selling costs   All costs that are incurred to secure customer orders and get the finished product or service into the hands of the customer. (p. 26)

Sunk cost   A cost that has already been incurred and that cannot be changed by any decision made now or in the future. (p. 44)

Variable cost   A cost that varies, in total, in direct proportion to changes in the level of activity. A variable cost is constant per unit. (p. 29)

QUESTIONS

1–1   What are the three major elements of product costs in a manufacturing company?

1–2   Define the following: (*a*) direct materials, (*b*) indirect materials, (*c*) direct labor, (*d*) indirect labor, and (*e*) manufacturing overhead.

1–3   Explain the difference between a product cost and a period cost.

1–4   Distinguish between (*a*) a variable cost, (*b*) a fixed cost, and (*c*) a mixed cost.

1–5   What effect does an increase in volume have on—
   a.   Unit fixed costs?
   b.   Unit variable costs?
   c.   Total fixed costs?
   d.   Total variable costs?

1–6   Define the following terms: (*a*) cost behavior and (*b*) relevant range.

1–7   What is meant by an *activity base* when dealing with variable costs? Give several examples of activity bases.

1–8   Managers often assume a strictly linear relationship between cost and volume. How can this practice be defended in light of the fact that many costs are curvilinear?

1–9 Distinguish between discretionary fixed costs and committed fixed costs.

1–10 Does the concept of the relevant range apply to fixed costs? Explain.

1–11 What is the major disadvantage of the high-low method?

1–12 Give the general formula for a mixed cost. Which term represents the variable cost? The fixed cost?

1–13 What is meant by the term *least-squares regression?*

1–14 What is the difference between a contribution format income statement and a traditional format income statement?

1–15 What is the contribution margin?

1–16 Define the following terms: differential cost, opportunity cost, and sunk cost.

1–17 Only variable costs can be differential costs. Do you agree? Explain.

Multiple-choice questions are available in the *Connect Library*.

APPLYING EXCEL

_____

Available with McGraw-Hill's *Connect Accounting*.

LO1-6

The Excel worksheet form that appears below is to be used to recreate Exhibit 1–9 on page 42. Download the workbook containing this form in the *Connect Library. On the website you will also receive instructions about how to use this worksheet form.*

	A	B	C	D
1	**Chapter 1: Applying Excel**			
2				
3	**Data**			
4	Sales	$12,000		
5	Variable costs:			
6	Cost of goods sold	$6,000		
7	Variable selling	$600		
8	Variable administrative	$400		
9	Fixed costs:			
10	Fixed selling	$2,500		
11	Fixed administrative	$1,500		
12				
13	*Enter a formula into each of the cells marked with a ? below*			
14	**Exhibit 1–9**			
15				
16	**Traditional Format Income Statement**			
17	Sales		?	
18	Cost of goods sold		?	
19	Gross margin		?	
20	Selling and administrative expenses:			
21	Selling	?		
22	Administrative	?	?	
23	Net operating income		?	
24				
25	**Contribution Format Income Statement**			
26	Sales		?	
27	Variable expenses:			
28	Cost of goods sold	?		
29	Variable selling	?		
30	Variable administration	?	?	
31	Contribution margin		?	
32	Fixed expenses:			
33	Fixed selling	?		
34	Fixed administrative	?	?	
35	Net operating income		?	
36				

Chapter 1 Form   Filled in Chapter 1 Fo

Required:

1. Check your worksheet by changing the variable selling cost in the Data area to $900, keeping all of the other data the same as in Exhibit 1–9. If your worksheet is operating properly, the net operating income under the traditional format income statement and under the contribution format income statement should now be $700 and the contribution margin should now be $4,700. If you do not get these answers, find the errors in your worksheet and correct them.

   How much is the gross margin? Did it change? Why or why not?

2. Suppose that sales are 10% higher as shown below:

Sales	$13,200
Variable costs:	
Cost of goods sold	$6,600
Variable selling	$990
Variable administrative	$440
Fixed costs:	
Fixed selling	$2,500
Fixed administrative	$1,500

Enter this new data into your worksheet. Make sure that you change all of the data that are different—not just the sales. Print or copy the income statements from your worksheet.

What happened to the variable costs and to the fixed costs when sales increased by 10%? Why? Did the contribution margin increase by 10%? Why or why not? Did the net operating income increase by 10%? Why or why not?

THE FOUNDATIONAL 15

Available with McGraw-Hill's *Connect Accounting.*

Martinez Company's relevant range of production is 7,500 units to 12,500 units. When it produces and sells 10,000 units, its unit costs are as follows:

LO1–1, LO1–2, LO1–3, LO1–4, LO1–6, LO1–7

	Amount Per Unit
Direct materials	$6.00
Direct labor	$3.50
Variable manufacturing overhead	$1.50
Fixed manufacturing overhead	$4.00
Fixed selling expense	$3.00
Fixed administrative expense	$2.00
Sales commissions	$1.00
Variable administrative expense	$0.50

Required:

1. For financial accounting purposes, what is the total amount of product costs incurred to make 10,000 units?
2. For financial accounting purposes, what is the total amount of period costs incurred to sell 10,000 units?
3. If 8,000 units are sold, what is the variable cost per unit sold?
4. If 12,500 units are sold, what is the variable cost per unit sold?
5. If 8,000 units are sold, what is the total amount of variable costs related to the units sold?

6. If 12,500 units are sold, what is the total amount of variable costs related to the units sold?
7. If 8,000 units are produced, what is the average fixed manufacturing cost per unit produced?
8. If 12,500 units are produced, what is the average fixed manufacturing cost per unit produced?
9. If 8,000 units are produced, what is the total amount of fixed manufacturing cost incurred to support this level of production?
10. If 12,500 units are produced, what is the total amount of fixed manufacturing cost incurred to support this level of production?
11. If 8,000 units are produced, what is the total amount of manufacturing overhead cost incurred to support this level of production? What is this total amount expressed on a per unit basis?
12. If 12,500 units are produced, what is the total amount of manufacturing overhead cost incurred to support this level of production? What is this total amount expressed on a per unit basis?
13. If the selling price is $22 per unit, what is the contribution margin per unit sold?
14. If 11,000 units are produced, what are the total amounts of direct and indirect manufacturing costs incurred to support this level of production?
15. What total incremental cost will Martinez incur if it increases production from 10,000 to 10,001 units?

EXERCISES

All applicable exercises are available with McGraw-Hill's *Connect Accounting.*

EXERCISE 1–1   Identifying Direct and Indirect Costs [LO1–1]
Northwest Hospital is a full-service hospital that provides everything from major surgery and emergency room care to outpatient clinics.

Required:
For each cost incurred at Northwest Hospital, indicate whether it would most likely be a direct cost or an indirect cost of the specified cost object by placing an *X* in the appropriate column.

Cost	Cost Object	Direct Cost	Indirect Cost
Ex. Catered food served to patients	A particular patient	X	
1. The wages of pediatric nurses	The pediatric department		
2. Prescription drugs	A particular patient		
3. Heating the hospital	The pediatric department		
4. The salary of the head of pediatrics	The pediatric department		
5. The salary of the head of pediatrics	A particular pediatric patient		
6. Hospital chaplain's salary	A particular patient		
7. Lab tests by outside contractor	A particular patient		
8. Lab tests by outside contractor	A particular department		

EXERCISE 1–2   Classifying Manufacturing Costs [LO1–2]
The PC Works assembles custom computers from components supplied by various manufacturers. The company is very small and its assembly shop and retail sales store are housed in a single facility in a Redmond, Washington, industrial park. Listed below are some of the costs that are incurred at the company.

Required:
For each cost, indicate whether it would most likely be classified as direct labor, direct materials, manufacturing overhead, selling, or an administrative cost.
1. The cost of a hard drive installed in a computer.
2. The cost of advertising in the *Puget Sound Computer User* newspaper.
3. The wages of employees who assemble computers from components.
4. Sales commissions paid to the company's salespeople.

5. The wages of the assembly shop's supervisor.
6. The wages of the company's accountant.
7. Depreciation on equipment used to test assembled computers before release to customers.
8. Rent on the facility in the industrial park.

EXERCISE 1–3 Classification of Costs as Product or Period Cost [LO1–3]

Suppose that you have been given a summer job as an intern at Issac Aircams, a company that manufactures sophisticated spy cameras for remote-controlled military reconnaissance aircraft. The company, which is privately owned, has approached a bank for a loan to help it finance its growth. The bank requires financial statements before approving such a loan. You have been asked to help prepare the financial statements and were given the following list of costs:

1. Depreciation on salespersons' cars.
2. Rent on equipment used in the factory.
3. Lubricants used for machine maintenance.
4. Salaries of personnel who work in the finished goods warehouse.
5. Soap and paper towels used by factory workers at the end of a shift.
6. Factory supervisors' salaries.
7. Heat, water, and power consumed in the factory.
8. Materials used for boxing products for shipment overseas. (Units are not normally boxed.)
9. Advertising costs.
10. Workers' compensation insurance for factory employees.
11. Depreciation on chairs and tables in the factory lunchroom.
12. The wages of the receptionist in the administrative offices.
13. Cost of leasing the corporate jet used by the company's executives.
14. The cost of renting rooms at a Florida resort for the annual sales conference.
15. The cost of packaging the company's product.

Required:

Classify the above costs as either product costs or period costs for the purpose of preparing the financial statements for the bank.

EXERCISE 1–4 Fixed and Variable Cost Behavior [LO1–4]

Espresso Express operates a number of espresso coffee stands in busy suburban malls. The fixed weekly expense of a coffee stand is $1,200 and the variable cost per cup of coffee served is $0.22.

Required:

1. Fill in the following table with your estimates of total costs and cost per cup of coffee at the indicated levels of activity for a coffee stand. Round off the cost of a cup of coffee to the nearest tenth of a cent.

TAKE TWO

Fixed weekly
   expense = $1,000
Variable cost per
   cup = $0.30

	Cups of Coffee Served in a Week		
	2,000	**2,100**	**2,200**
Fixed cost . . .	?	?	?
Variable cost . . .	?	?	?
Total cost . . .	?	?	?
Average cost per cup of coffee served . .	?	?	?

2. Does the average cost per cup of coffee served increase, decrease, or remain the same as the number of cups of coffee served in a week increases? Explain.

EXERCISE 1–5 High-Low Method [LO1–5]

The Cheyenne Hotel in Big Sky, Montana, has accumulated records of the total electrical costs of the hotel and the number of occupancy-days over the last year. An occupancy-day represents a room rented out for one day. The hotel's business is highly seasonal, with peaks occurring during the ski season and in the summer.

October
    occupancy-days = 580
October electrical
    cost = $2,315

Month	Occupancy-Days	Electrical Costs
January	1,736	$4,127
February	1,904	$4,207
March	2,356	$5,083
April	960	$2,857
May	360	$1,871
June	744	$2,696
July	2,108	$4,670
August	2,406	$5,148
September	840	$2,691
October	124	$1,588
November	720	$2,454
December	1,364	$3,529

Required:
1. Using the high-low method, estimate the fixed cost of electricity per month and the variable cost of electricity per occupancy-day. Round off the fixed cost to the nearest whole dollar and the variable cost to the nearest whole cent.
2. What other factors other than occupancy-days are likely to affect the variation in electrical costs from month to month?

EXERCISE 1–6   Traditional and Contribution Format Income Statements [LO1–6]
Cherokee Inc. is a merchandiser that provided the following information:

Number of units
    sold = 24,000
Merchandise
    purchases = $212,000

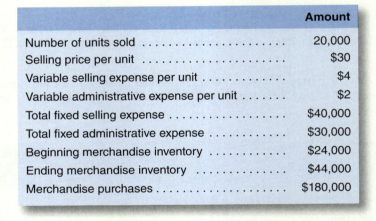

	Amount
Number of units sold	20,000
Selling price per unit	$30
Variable selling expense per unit	$4
Variable administrative expense per unit	$2
Total fixed selling expense	$40,000
Total fixed administrative expense	$30,000
Beginning merchandise inventory	$24,000
Ending merchandise inventory	$44,000
Merchandise purchases	$180,000

Required:
1. Prepare a traditional income statement.
2. Prepare a contribution format income statement.

EXERCISE 1–7   Differential, Opportunity, and Sunk Costs [LO1–7]

Northwest Hospital is a full-service hospital that provides everything from major surgery and emergency room care to outpatient clinics. The hospital's Radiology Department is considering replacing an old inefficient X-ray machine with a state-of-the-art digital X-ray machine. The new machine would provide higher quality X-rays in less time and at a lower cost per X-ray. It would also require less power and would use a color laser printer to produce easily readable X-ray images. Instead of investing the funds in the new X-ray machine, the Laboratory Department is lobbying the hospital's management to buy a new DNA analyzer.

Required:

For each of the items below, indicate by placing an X in the appropriate column whether it should be considered a differential cost, an opportunity cost, or a sunk cost in the decision to replace the old X-ray machine with a new machine. If none of the categories apply for a particular item, leave all columns blank.

Item	Differential Cost	Opportunity Cost	Sunk Cost
Ex. Cost of X-ray film used in the old machine	X		
1. Cost of the old X-ray machine			
2. The salary of the head of the Radiology Department ...			
3. The salary of the head of the Pediatrics Department			
4. Cost of the new color laser printer			
5. Rent on the space occupied by Radiology			
6. The cost of maintaining the old machine			
7. Benefits from a new DNA analyzer			
8. Cost of electricity to run the X-ray machines			

EXERCISE 1–8   Cost Behavior; High-Low Method [LO1–4, LO1–5]

Hoi Chong Transport, Ltd., operates a fleet of delivery trucks in Singapore. The company has determined that if a truck is driven 105,000 kilometers during a year, the average operating cost is 11.4 cents per kilometer. If a truck is driven only 70,000 kilometers during a year, the average operating cost increases to 13.4 cents per kilometer.

Required:
1. Using the high-low method, estimate the variable and fixed cost elements of the annual cost of the truck operation.
2. Express the variable and fixed costs in the form $Y = a + bX$.
3. If a truck were driven 80,000 kilometers during a year, what total cost would you expect to be incurred?

TAKE TWO

Average operating cost = 10.0 cents per mile at 105,000 miles

EXERCISE 1–9   Cost Terminology for Manufacturers [LO1–2, LO1–3]

Arden Company reported the following costs and expenses for the most recent month:

Direct materials	$80,000
Direct labor	$42,000
Manufacturing overhead	$19,000
Selling expenses	$22,000
Administrative expenses	$35,000

Required:
1. What is the total amount of product costs?
2. What is the total amount of period costs?
3. What is the total amount of conversion costs?
4. What is the total amount of prime costs?

EXERCISE 1–10   Cost Behavior; Contribution Format Income Statement [LO1–4, LO1–6]

Harris Company manufactures and sells a single product. A partially completed schedule of the company's total and per unit costs over the relevant range of 30,000 to 50,000 units produced and sold annually is given below:

	Units Produced and Sold		
	30,000	40,000	50,000
Total costs:			
Variable costs	$180,000	?	?
Fixed costs	300,000	?	?
Total costs	$480,000	?	?
Cost per unit:			
Variable cost	?	?	?
Fixed cost	?	?	?
Total cost per unit ...	?	?	?

Required:

1. Complete the schedule of the company's total and unit costs above.
2. Assume that the company produces and sells 45,000 units during the year at a selling price of $16 per unit. Prepare a contribution format income statement for the year.

EXERCISE 1–11   High-Low Method; Scattergraph Analysis [LO1–4, LO1–5]

The following data relating to units shipped and total shipping expense have been assembled by Archer Company, a wholesaler of large, custom-built air-conditioning units for commercial buildings:

Month	Units Shipped	Total Shipping Expense
January	3	$1,800
February	6	$2,300
March	4	$1,700
April	5	$2,000
May	7	$2,300
June	8	$2,700
July	2	$1,200

Required:

1. Prepare a scattergraph using the data given above. Plot cost on the vertical axis and activity on the horizontal axis. Is there an approximately linear relationship between shipping expense and the number of units shipped?
2. Using the high-low method, estimate the cost formula for shipping expense. Draw a straight line through the high and low data points shown in the scattergraph that you prepared in requirement 1. Make sure your line intersects the *Y* axis.
3. Comment on the accuracy of your high-low estimates assuming a least-squares regression analysis estimated the total fixed costs to be $910.71 per month and the variable cost to be $217.86 per unit. How would the straight line that you drew in requirement 2 differ from a straight line that minimizes the sum of the squared errors?
4. What factors, other than the number of units shipped, are likely to affect the company's shipping expense? Explain.

EXERCISE 1–12   Cost Classification [LO1–2, LO1–3, LO1–4, LO1–7]

Wollogong Group Ltd. of New South Wales, Australia, acquired its factory building about 10 years ago. For several years, the company has rented out a small annex attached to the rear of the building. The company has received a rental income of $30,000 per year on this space. The renter's lease will expire soon, and rather than renewing the lease, the company has decided to use the space itself to manufacture a new product.

Direct materials cost for the new product will total $80 per unit. To have a place to store finished units of product, the company will rent a small warehouse nearby. The rental cost will be $500 per month. In addition, the company must rent equipment for use in producing the new product; the rental cost will be $4,000 per month. Workers will be hired to manufacture the new product, with direct labor cost amounting to $60 per unit. The space in the annex will continue to be depreciated on a straight-line basis, as in prior years. This depreciation is $8,000 per year.

Advertising costs for the new product will total $50,000 per year. A supervisor will be hired to oversee production; her salary will be $1,500 per month. Electricity for operating machines will be $1.20 per unit. Costs of shipping the new product to customers will be $9 per unit.

To provide funds to purchase materials, meet payrolls, and so forth, the company will have to liquidate some temporary investments. These investments are presently yielding a return of about $3,000 per year.

Required:
Prepare an answer sheet with the following column headings:

Name of the Cost	Variable Cost	Fixed Cost	Product Cost			Period (Selling and Administrative) Cost	Opportunity Cost	Sunk Cost
			Direct Materials	Direct Labor	Manufacturing Overhead			

List the different costs associated with the new product decision down the extreme left column (under Name of the Cost). Then place an X under each heading that helps to describe the type of cost involved. There may be X's under several column headings for a single cost. (For example, a cost may be a fixed cost, a period cost, and a sunk cost; you would place an X under each of these column headings opposite the cost.)

EXERCISE 1–13   Traditional and Contribution Format Income Statements [LO1–6]
The Alpine House, Inc., is a large retailer of snow skis. The company assembled the information shown below for the quarter ended March 31:

	Amount
Total sales revenue	$150,000
Selling price per pair of skis	$750
Variable selling expense per pair of skis	$50
Variable administrative expense per pair of skis	$10
Total fixed selling expense	$20,000
Total fixed administrative expense	$20,000
Beginning merchandise inventory	$30,000
Ending merchandise inventory	$40,000
Merchandise purchases	$100,000

Total sales revenue
= $165,000
Merchandise purchases
= $135,000

Required:
1. Prepare a traditional income statement for the quarter ended March 31.
2. Prepare a contribution format income statement for the quarter ended March 31.
3. What was the contribution toward fixed expenses and profits for each pair of skis sold during the quarter? (State this figure in a single dollar amount per pair of skis.)

EXERCISE 1–14   High-Low Method; Predicting Cost [LO1–4, LO1–5]
The Lakeshore Hotel's guest-days of occupancy and custodial supplies expense over the last seven months were:

Month	Guest-Days of Occupancy	Custodial Supplies Expense
March	4,000	$7,500
April	6,500	$8,250
May	8,000	$10,500
June	10,500	$12,000
July	12,000	$13,500
August	9,000	$10,750
September	7,500	$9,750

Guest-days is a measure of the overall activity at the hotel. For example, a guest who stays at the hotel for three days is counted as three guest-days.

Required:
1. Using the high-low method, estimate a cost formula for custodial supplies expense.
2. Using the cost formula you derived above, what amount of custodial supplies expense would you expect to be incurred at an occupancy level of 11,000 guest-days?
3. Prepare a scattergraph using the data given above. Plot custodial supplies expense on the vertical axis and the number of guest-days occupied on the horizontal axis. Draw a straight line through the two data points that correspond to the high and low levels of activity. Make sure your line intersects the *Y*-axis.
4. Comment on the accuracy of your high-low estimates assuming a least-squares regression analysis estimated the total fixed costs to be $3,973.10 per month and the variable cost to be $0.77 per guest-day. How would the straight line that you drew in requirement 3 differ from a straight line that minimizes the sum of the squared errors?
5. Using the least-squares regression estimates given in requirement 4, what custodial supplies expense would you expect to be incurred at an occupancy level of 11,000 guest-days?

EXERCISE 1–15   Classification of Costs as Variable or Fixed and as Product or Period [LO1–3, LO1–4]
Below are listed various costs that are found in organizations.

1. Hamburger buns in a Wendy's outlet.
2. Advertising by a dental office.
3. Apples processed and canned by Del Monte.
4. Shipping canned apples from a Del Monte plant to customers.
5. Insurance on a Bausch & Lomb factory producing contact lenses.
6. Insurance on IBM's corporate headquarters.
7. Salary of a supervisor overseeing production of printers at Hewlett-Packard.
8. Commissions paid to automobile salespersons.
9. Depreciation of factory lunchroom facilities at a General Electric plant.
10. Steering wheels installed in BMWs.

Required:
Classify each cost as being either variable or fixed with respect to the number of units produced and sold. Also classify each cost as either a selling and administrative cost or a product cost. Prepare your answer sheet as shown below. Place an *X* in the appropriate columns to show the proper classification of each cost.

Cost Item	Cost Behavior		Period (Selling and Administrative) Cost	Product Cost
	Variable	Fixed		

PROBLEMS    **connect** |ACCOUNTING   Alternate problem set is available in the *Connect Library*.

All applicable problems are available with McGraw-Hill's *Connect Accounting*.

PROBLEM 1–16A   Cost Behavior; High-Low Method; Contribution Format Income Statement [LO1–4, LO1–5, LO1–6]
Morrisey & Brown, Ltd., of Sydney is a merchandising company that is the sole distributor of a product that is increasing in popularity among Australian consumers. The company's income statements for the three most recent months follow:

Morrisey & Brown, Ltd. Income Statements For the Three Months Ended September 30			
	July	August	September
Sales in units	4,000	4,500	5,000
Sales	$400,000	$450,000	$500,000
Cost of goods sold	240,000	270,000	300,000
Gross margin	160,000	180,000	200,000
Selling and administrative expenses:			
Advertising expense	21,000	21,000	21,000
Shipping expense	34,000	36,000	38,000
Salaries and commissions	78,000	84,000	90,000
Insurance expense	6,000	6,000	6,000
Depreciation expense	15,000	15,000	15,000
Total selling and administrative expenses	154,000	162,000	170,000
Net operating income	$ 6,000	$ 18,000	$ 30,000

Required:
1. Identify each of the company's expenses (including cost of goods sold) as either variable, fixed, or mixed.
2. Using the high-low method, separate each mixed expense into variable and fixed elements. State the cost formula for each mixed expense.
3. Redo the company's income statement at the 5,000-unit level of activity using the contribution format.

PROBLEM 1–17A High-Low Method; Predicting Cost [LO1–4, LO1–5]

Sawaya Co., Ltd., of Japan is a manufacturing company whose total factory overhead costs fluctuate considerably from year to year according to increases and decreases in the number of direct labor-hours worked in the factory. Total factory overhead costs at high and low levels of activity for recent years are given below:

	Level of Activity	
	Low	High
Direct labor-hours	50,000	75,000
Total factory overhead costs	$14,250,000	$17,625,000

The factory overhead costs above consist of indirect materials, rent, and maintenance. The company has analyzed these costs at the 50,000-hour level of activity as follows:

Indirect materials (variable)	$ 5,000,000
Rent (fixed)	6,000,000
Maintenance (mixed)	3,250,000
Total factory overhead costs	$14,250,000

To have data available for planning, the company wants to break down the maintenance cost into its variable and fixed cost elements.

Required:
1. Estimate how much of the $17,625,000 factory overhead cost at the high level of activity consists of maintenance cost. (*Hint:* To do this, it may be helpful to first determine how much of the $17,625,000 consists of indirect materials and rent. Think about the behavior of variable and fixed costs!)
2. Using the high-low method, estimate a cost formula for maintenance.
3. What total factory overhead costs would you expect the company to incur at an operating level of 70,000 direct labor-hours?

PROBLEM 1–18A Variable and Fixed Costs; Subtleties of Direct and Indirect Costs [LO1–1, LO1–4]

Madison Seniors Care Center is a nonprofit organization that provides a variety of health services to the elderly. The center is organized into a number of departments, one of which is the Meals-On-Wheels program that delivers hot meals to seniors in their homes on a daily basis. Below are listed a number of costs of the center and the Meals-On-Wheels program.

example   The cost of groceries used in meal preparation.

    a. The cost of leasing the Meals-On-Wheels van.

    b. The cost of incidental supplies such as salt, pepper, napkins, and so on.

    c. The cost of gasoline consumed by the Meals-On-Wheels van.

    d. The rent on the facility that houses Madison Seniors Care Center, including the Meals-On-Wheels program.

    e. The salary of the part-time manager of the Meals-On-Wheels program.

    f. Depreciation on the kitchen equipment used in the Meals-On-Wheels program.

    g. The hourly wages of the caregiver who drives the van and delivers the meals.

    h. The costs of complying with health safety regulations in the kitchen.

    i. The costs of mailing letters soliciting donations to the Meals-On-Wheels program.

Required:

For each cost listed above, indicate whether it is a direct or indirect cost of the Meals-On-Wheels program, whether it is a direct or indirect cost of particular seniors served by the program, and whether it is variable or fixed with respect to the number of seniors served. Use the form below for your answer.

		Direct or Indirect Cost of the Meals-on-Wheels Program		Direct or Indirect Cost of Particular Seniors Served by the Meals-on-Wheels Program		Variable or Fixed with Respect to the Number of Seniors Served by the Meals-on-Wheels Program	
Item	Description	Direct	Indirect	Direct	Indirect	Variable	Fixed
Example	The cost of groceries used in meal preparation...	X		X		X	

PROBLEM 1–19A Contribution Format versus Traditional Income Statement [LO1–6]

Marwick's Pianos, Inc., purchases pianos from a large manufacturer and sells them at the retail level. The pianos cost, on the average, $2,450 each from the manufacturer. Marwick's Pianos, Inc., sells the pianos to its customers at an average price of $3,125 each. The selling and administrative costs that the company incurs in a typical month are presented below:

Costs	Cost Formula
Selling:	
Advertising	$700 per month
Sales salaries and commissions	$950 per month, plus 8% of sales
Delivery of pianos to customers	$30 per piano sold
Utilities	$350 per month
Depreciation of sales facilities	$800 per month
Administrative:	
Executive salaries	$2,500 per month
Insurance	$400 per month
Clerical	$1,000 per month, plus $20 per piano sold
Depreciation of office equipment	$300 per month

During August, Marwick's Pianos, Inc., sold and delivered 40 pianos.

Required:
1. Prepare an income statement for Marwick's Pianos, Inc., for August. Use the traditional format, with costs organized by function.
2. Redo (1) above, this time using the contribution format, with costs organized by behavior. Show costs and revenues on both a total and a per unit basis down through contribution margin.
3. Refer to the income statement you prepared in (2) above. Why might it be misleading to show the fixed costs on a per unit basis?

PROBLEM 1–20A   High-Low Method; Predicting Cost [LO1–4, LO1–5]
Nova Company's total overhead cost at various levels of activity are presented below:

Month	Machine-Hours	Total Overhead Cost
April	70,000	$198,000
May	60,000	$174,000
June	80,000	$222,000
July	90,000	$246,000

Assume that the total overhead cost above consists of utilities, supervisory salaries, and maintenance. The breakdown of these costs at the 60,000 machine-hour level of activity is:

Utilities (variable)	$ 48,000
Supervisory salaries (fixed) ..	21,000
Maintenance (mixed)	105,000
Total overhead cost	$174,000

Nova Company's management wants to break down the maintenance cost into its variable and fixed cost elements.

Required:
1. Estimate how much of the $246,000 of overhead cost in July was maintenance cost. (*Hint:* to do this, it may be helpful to first determine how much of the $246,000 consisted of utilities and supervisory salaries. Think about the behavior of variable and fixed costs!)
2. Using the high-low method, estimate a cost formula for maintenance.
3. Express the company's *total* overhead cost in the linear equation form $Y = a + bX$.
4. What *total* overhead cost would you expect to be incurred at an activity level of 75,000 machine-hours?

PROBLEM 1–21A   Cost Classification [LO1–1, LO1–3, LO1–4]
Listed below are costs found in various organizations.
1. Property taxes, factory.
2. Boxes used for packaging detergent produced by the company.
3. Salespersons' commissions.
4. Supervisor's salary, factory.
5. Depreciation, executive autos.
6. Wages of workers assembling computers.
7. Insurance, finished goods warehouses.
8. Lubricants for production equipment.
9. Advertising costs.
10. Microchips used in producing calculators.
11. Shipping costs on merchandise sold.
12. Magazine subscriptions, factory lunchroom.
13. Thread in a garment factory.
14. Billing costs.
15. Executive life insurance.

16. Ink used in textbook production.
17. Fringe benefits, assembly-line workers.
18. Yarn used in sweater production.
19. Wages of receptionist, executive offices.

Required:
Prepare an answer sheet with column headings as shown below. For each cost item, indicate whether it would be variable or fixed with respect to the number of units produced and sold; and then whether it would be a selling cost, an administrative cost, or a manufacturing cost. If it is a manufacturing cost, indicate whether it would typically be treated as a direct cost or an indirect cost with respect to units of product. Three sample answers are provided for illustration.

Cost Item	Variable or Fixed	Selling Cost	Administrative Cost	Manufacturing (Product) Cost Direct	Manufacturing (Product) Cost Indirect
Direct labor	V			X	
Executive salaries	F		X		
Factory rent	F				X

PROBLEM 1–22A High-Low and Scattergraph Analysis [LO1–4, LO1–5]
Pleasant View Hospital of British Columbia has just hired a new chief administrator who is anxious to employ sound management and planning techniques in the business affairs of the hospital. Accordingly, she has directed her assistant to summarize the cost structure of the various departments so that data will be available for planning purposes.

The assistant is unsure how to classify the utilities costs in the Radiology Department because these costs do not exhibit either strictly variable or fixed cost behavior. Utilities costs are very high in the department due to a CAT scanner that draws a large amount of power and is kept running at all times. The scanner can't be turned off due to the long warm-up period required for its use. When the scanner is used to scan a patient, it consumes an additional burst of power. The assistant has accumulated the following data on utilities costs and use of the scanner since the first of the year.

Month	Number of Scans	Utilities Cost
January	60	$2,200
February	70	$2,600
March	90	$2,900
April	120	$3,300
May	100	$3,000
June	130	$3,600
July	150	$4,000
August	140	$3,600
September	110	$3,100
October	80	$2,500

The chief administrator has informed her assistant that the utilities cost is probably a mixed cost that will have to be broken down into its variable and fixed cost elements by use of a scattergraph. The assistant feels, however, that if an analysis of this type is necessary, then the high-low method should be used, since it is easier and quicker. The controller has suggested that there may be a better approach.

Required:
1. Using the high-low method, estimate a cost formula for utilities. Express the formula in the form $Y = a + bX$. (The variable rate should be stated in terms of cost per scan.)

2. Prepare a scattergraph by plotting the number of scans and utility cost on a graph. Draw a straight line through the two data points that correspond to the high and low levels of activity. Make sure your line intersects the *Y*-axis.

3. Comment on the accuracy of your high-low estimates assuming a least-squares regression analysis estimated the total fixed costs to be $1,170.90 per month and the variable cost to be $18.18 per scan. How would the straight line that you drew in requirement 2 differ from a straight line that minimizes the sum of the squared errors?

PROBLEM 1–23A High-Low Method; Contribution Format Income Statement [LO1–5, LO1–6]

Milden Company has an exclusive franchise to purchase a product from the manufacturer and distribute it on the retail level. As an aid in planning, the company has decided to start using a contribution format income statement. To have data to prepare such a statement, the company has analyzed its expenses and has developed the following cost formulas:

Cost	Cost Formula
Cost of good sold	$35 per unit sold
Advertising expense	$210,000 per quarter
Sales commissions	6% of sales
Shipping expense	?
Administrative salaries	$145,000 per quarter
Insurance expense	$9,000 per quarter
Depreciation expense	$76,000 per quarter

Management has concluded that shipping expense is a mixed cost, containing both variable and fixed cost elements. Units sold and the related shipping expense over the last eight quarters follow:

Quarter	Units Sold	Shipping Expense
Year 1:		
First	10,000	$119,000
Second	16,000	$175,000
Third	18,000	$190,000
Fourth	15,000	$164,000
Year 2:		
First	11,000	$130,000
Second	17,000	$185,000
Third	20,000	$210,000
Fourth	13,000	$147,000

Milden Company's president would like a cost formula derived for shipping expense so that a budgeted contribution format income statement can be prepared for the next quarter.

Required:

1. Using the high-low method, estimate a cost formula for shipping expense.
2. In the first quarter of Year 3, the company plans to sell 12,000 units at a selling price of $100 per unit. Prepare a contribution format income statement for the quarter.

PROBLEM 1–24A Cost Classification and Cost Behavior [LO1–1, LO1–2, LO1–3, LO1–4]

The Dorilane Company specializes in producing a set of wood patio furniture consisting of a table and four chairs. The set enjoys great popularity, and the company has ample orders to keep production going at its full capacity of 2,000 sets per year. Annual cost data at full capacity follow:

Direct labor	$118,000
Advertising	$50,000
Factory supervision	$40,000
Property taxes, factory building	$3,500
Sales commissions	$80,000
Insurance, factory	$2,500
Depreciation, administrative office equipment	$4,000
Lease cost, factory equipment	$12,000
Indirect materials, factory	$6,000
Depreciation, factory building	$10,000
Administrative office supplies (billing)	$3,000
Administrative office salaries	$60,000
Direct materials used (wood, bolts, etc.)	$94,000
Utilities, factory	$20,000

Required:

1. Prepare an answer sheet with the column headings shown below. Enter each cost item on your answer sheet, placing the dollar amount under the appropriate headings. As examples, this has been done already for the first two items in the list above. Note that each cost item is classified in two ways: first, as variable or fixed with respect to the number of units produced and sold; and second, as a selling and administrative cost or a product cost. (If the item is a product cost, it should also be classified as either direct or indirect as shown.)

	Cost Behavior		Period (Selling or Administrative) Cost	Product Cost	
Cost Item	**Variable**	**Fixed**		**Direct**	**Indirect***
Direct labor	$118,000			$118,000	
Advertising		$50,000	$50,000		

*To units of product.

2. Total the dollar amounts in each of the columns in (1) above. Compute the average product cost of one patio set.
3. Assume that production drops to only 1,000 sets annually. Would you expect the average product cost per set to increase, decrease, or remain unchanged? Explain. No computations are necessary.
4. Refer to the original data. The president's brother-in-law has considered making himself a patio set and has priced the necessary materials at a building supply store. The brother-in-law has asked the president if he could purchase a patio set from the Dorilane Company "at cost," and the president agreed to let him do so.
    a. Would you expect any disagreement between the two men over the price the brother-in-law should pay? Explain. What price does the president probably have in mind? The brother-in-law?
    b. Because the company is operating at full capacity, what cost term used in the chapter might be justification for the president to charge the full, regular price to the brother-in-law and still be selling "at cost"?

BUILDING YOUR SKILLS

ETHICS CHALLENGE [LO1–3]

M. K. Gallant is president of Kranbrack Corporation, a company whose stock is traded on a national exchange. In a meeting with investment analysts at the beginning of the year, Gallant had predicted that the company's earnings would grow by 20% this year. Unfortunately, sales have been less than expected for the year, and Gallant concluded within two weeks of the end of the fiscal year that it would be impossible to ultimately report an increase in earnings as large as predicted unless some drastic action was taken. Accordingly, Gallant has ordered that wherever possible, expenditures should be postponed to the new year—including canceling or postponing orders with suppliers, delaying planned maintenance and training, and cutting back on end-of-year advertising and travel. Additionally, Gallant ordered the company's controller to carefully scrutinize all costs that are currently classified as period costs and reclassify as many as possible as product costs. The company is expected to have substantial inventories at the end of the year.

Required:
1. Why would reclassifying period costs as product costs increase this period's reported earnings?
2. Do you believe Gallant's actions are ethical? Why or why not?

ANALYTICAL THINKING [LOI–5]

Angora Wraps of Pendleton, Oregon, makes fine sweaters out of pure angora wool. The business is seasonal, with the largest demand during the fall, the winter, and Christmas holidays. The company must increase production each summer to meet estimated demand.

The company has been analyzing its costs to determine which costs are fixed and variable for planning purposes. Below are data for the company's activity and direct labor costs over the last year.

Month	Thousands of Units Produced	Number of Paid Days	Direct Labor Cost
January	98	20	$14,162
February	76	20	$12,994
March	75	21	$15,184
April	80	22	$15,038
May	85	22	$15,768
June	102	21	$15,330
July	52	19	$13,724
August	136	21	$14,162
September	138	22	$15,476
October	132	23	$15,476
November	86	18	$12,972
December	56	21	$14,074

The number of workdays varies from month to month due to the number of weekdays, holidays, and days of vacation in the month. The paid days include paid vacations (in July) and paid holidays (in November and December). The number of units produced in a month varies depending on demand and the number of workdays in the month.

The company has eight workers who are classified as direct labor.

Required:
1. Plot the direct labor cost and units produced on a scattergraph. (Place cost on the vertical axis and units produced on the horizontal axis.)
2. Plot the direct labor cost and number of paid days on a scattergraph. (Place cost on the vertical axis and the number of paid days on the horizontal axis.)
3. Which measure of activity—number of units produced or paid days—should be used as the activity base for explaining direct labor cost? Explain.

TEAMWORK IN ACTION [LOI-4]

Understanding the nature of fixed and variable costs is extremely important to managers. This knowledge is used in planning, making strategic and tactical decisions, evaluating performance, and controlling operations.

Required:
Form a team consisting of three persons. Each team member will be responsible for one of the following businesses:

    a. Dental clinic
    b. Fast-food restaurant
    c. Auto repair shop

1. For each business, decide what single measure best reflects the overall level of activity in the business and give examples of costs that are fixed and variable with respect to small changes in the measure of activity you have chosen.
2. Explain the relationship between the level of activity in each business and each of the following: total fixed costs, fixed cost per unit of activity, total variable costs, variable cost per unit of activity, total costs, and average total cost per unit of activity.
3. Discuss and refine your answers to each of the above questions with your group. For example, which of the above businesses seems to have the lowest ratio of variable to fixed costs? Which of the businesses' profits would be most sensitive to changes in demand for its services? Why?

A LOOK BACK

Chapter 1 defined many of the terms that are used to classify costs in business. We will use many of these terms in Chapter 2. Now would be a good time to check your understanding of those terms by referring to the glossary at the end of Chapter 1.

A LOOK AT THIS CHAPTER

Chapter 2 provides an in-depth look at a job-order costing system. We describe how direct material and direct labor costs are accumulated on jobs. Then we address manufacturing overhead, an indirect cost that must be allocated (or applied) to jobs. Finally, we take a more detailed look at the flow of costs through a company's accounting system using journal entries.

A LOOK AHEAD

Chapter 3 continues the discussion of the allocation of manufacturing overhead costs, showing how these costs can be more accurately assigned using activity-based costing. We cover process costing in Chapter 4.

2 Job-Order Costing

CHAPTER OUTLINE

University Tees: Serving Over 150 Campuses Nationwide

University Tees was founded in 2003 by two **Miami University** college students to provide screen-printing, embroidery, and promotional products for fraternities, sororities, and student organizations. Today, the company, which is headquartered in Cleveland, Ohio, employs as many as four Campus Managers on each of over 150 college campuses across America.

Accurately calculating the cost of each potential customer order is critically important to University Tees because the company needs to be sure that the sales price exceeds the cost associated with satisfying the order. The costs include the cost of the blank T-shirts themselves, printing costs (which vary depending on the quantity of shirts produced and the number of colors per shirt), screen costs (which also vary depending on the number of colors included in a design), shipping costs, and the artwork needed to create a design. The company also takes into account its competitors' pricing strategies when developing its own prices.

Given its success on college campuses, University Tees has introduced a sister company called **On Point Promos** to serve for-profit companies and nonprofit organizations.

Source: Conversation with Joe Haddad, cofounder of University Tees.

LEARNING OBJECTIVES

After studying Chapter 2, you should be able to:

LO2–1 Compute a predetermined overhead rate.

LO2–2 Apply overhead cost to jobs using a predetermined overhead rate.

LO2–3 Compute the total cost and average cost per unit of a job.

LO2–4 Understand the flow of costs in a job-order costing system and prepare appropriate journal entries to record costs.

LO2–5 Use T-accounts to show the flow of costs in a job-order costing system.

LO2–6 Prepare schedules of cost of goods manufactured and cost of goods sold and an income statement.

LO2–7 Compute underapplied or overapplied overhead cost and prepare the journal entry to close the balance in Manufacturing Overhead to the appropriate account.

Understanding how products and services are costed is vital to managers because the way in which these costs are determined can have a substantial impact on reported profits, as well as on key management decisions.

A managerial costing system should provide cost data to help managers plan, control, and make decisions. Nevertheless, external financial reporting and tax reporting requirements often heavily influence how costs are accumulated and summarized on managerial reports. This is true of product costing. In this chapter we use *absorption costing* to determine product costs. In **absorption costing,** all manufacturing costs, both fixed and variable, are assigned to units of product—units are said to *fully absorb manufacturing costs.*

Most countries—including the United States—require some form of absorption costing for both external financial reports and for tax reports. In addition, the vast majority of companies throughout the world also use absorption costing in their management reports. Because absorption costing is the most common approach to product costing throughout the world, we discuss it first and then discuss the alternatives in subsequent chapters.

JOB-ORDER COSTING—AN OVERVIEW

Under absorption costing, product costs include all manufacturing costs. Some manufacturing costs, such as direct materials, can be directly traced to particular products. For example, the cost of the airbags installed in a **Toyota** Camry can be easily traced to that particular auto. But what about manufacturing costs like factory rent? Such costs do not change from month to month, whereas the number and variety of products made in the factory may vary dramatically from one month to the next. Because these costs remain unchanged from month to month regardless of what products are made, they are clearly not caused by—and cannot be directly traced to—any particular product. Therefore, these types of costs are assigned to products and services by averaging across time and across products. The type of production process influences how this averaging is done.

Job-order costing is used in situations where many *different* products, each with individual and unique features, are produced each period. For example, a **Levi Strauss** clothing factory would typically make many different types of jeans for both men and women during a month. A particular order might consist of 1,000 boot-cut men's blue denim jeans, style number A312. This order of 1,000 jeans is called a *job*. In a job-order costing system, costs are traced and allocated to jobs and then the costs of the job are divided by the number of units in the job to arrive at an average cost per unit.

Other examples of situations where job-order costing would be used include large-scale construction projects managed by **Bechtel International**, commercial aircraft produced by **Boeing**, greeting cards designed and printed by **Hallmark**, and airline meals prepared by **LSG SkyChefs**. All of these examples are characterized by diverse outputs. Each Bechtel project is unique and different from every other—the company may be simultaneously constructing a dam in Nigeria and a bridge in Indonesia. Likewise, each airline orders a different type of meal from LSG SkyChefs' catering service.

Job-order costing is also used extensively in service industries. For example, hospitals, law firms, movie studios, accounting firms, advertising agencies, and repair shops all use a variation of job-order costing to accumulate costs. Although the detailed example of job-order costing provided in the following section deals with a manufacturing company, the same basic concepts and procedures are used by many service organizations.

Is This Really a Job?

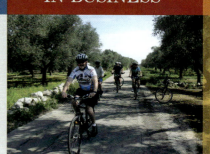

VBT Bicycling Vacations of Bristol, Vermont, offers deluxe bicycling vacations in the United States, Canada, Europe, and other locations throughout the world. For example, the company offers a 10-day tour of the Puglia region of Italy—the "heel of the boot." The tour price includes international airfare, 10 nights of lodging, most meals, use of a bicycle, and ground transportation as needed. Each tour is led by at least two local tour leaders, one of whom rides with the guests along the tour route. The other tour leader drives a "sag wagon" that carries extra water, snacks, and bicycle repair equipment and is available for a shuttle back to the hotel or up a hill. The sag wagon also transports guests' luggage from one hotel to another.

Each specific tour can be considered a job. For example, Giuliano Astore and Debora Trippetti, two natives of Puglia, led a VBT tour with 17 guests over 10 days in late April. At the end of the tour, Giuliano submitted a report, a sort of job cost sheet, to VBT headquarters. This report detailed the on the ground expenses incurred for this specific tour, including fuel and operating costs for the van, lodging costs for the guests, the costs of meals provided to guests, the costs of snacks, the cost of hiring additional ground transportation as needed, and the wages of the tour leaders. In addition to these costs, some costs are paid directly by VBT in Vermont to vendors. The total cost incurred for the tour is then compared to the total revenue collected from guests to determine the gross profit for the tour.

Sources: Giuliano Astore and Gregg Marston, President, VBT Bicycling Vacations. For more information about VBT, see www.vbt.com.

JOB-ORDER COSTING—AN EXAMPLE

To introduce job-order costing, we will follow a specific job as it progresses through the manufacturing process. This job consists of two experimental couplings that Yost Precision Machining has agreed to produce for Loops Unlimited, a manufacturer of roller coasters. Couplings connect the cars on the roller coaster and are a critical component in the performance and safety of the ride. Before we begin our discussion, recall from the previous chapter that companies generally classify manufacturing costs into three broad categories: (1) direct materials, (2) direct labor, and (3) manufacturing overhead. As we study the operation of a job-order costing system, we will see how each of these three types of costs is recorded and accumulated.

Yost Precision Machining is a small company in Michigan that specializes in fabricating precision metal parts that are used in a variety of applications ranging from deep-sea exploration vehicles to the inertial triggers in automobile air bags. The company's top managers gather every morning at 8:00 A.M. in the company's conference room for the daily planning meeting. Attending the meeting this morning are: Jean Yost, the company's president; David Cheung, the marketing manager; Debbie Turner, the production manager; and Marc White, the company controller. The president opened the meeting:

Jean: The production schedule indicates we'll be starting Job 2B47 today. Isn't that the special order for experimental couplings, David?

David: That's right. That's the order from Loops Unlimited for two couplings for their new roller coaster ride for Magic Mountain.

Debbie: Why only two couplings? Don't they need a coupling for every car?

David: Yes. But this is a completely new roller coaster. The cars will go faster and will be subjected to more twists, turns, drops, and loops than on any other existing roller coaster. To hold up under these stresses, Loops Unlimited's engineers completely

MANAGERIAL ACCOUNTING IN ACTION
The Issue

EXHIBIT 2–1
Materials Requisition Form

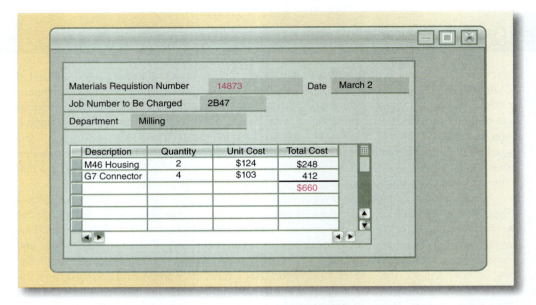

| Materials Requisition Number | 14873 | | Date | March 2 |

Job Number to Be Charged   2B47

Department   Milling

Description	Quantity	Unit Cost	Total Cost
M46 Housing	2	$124	$248
G7 Connector	4	$103	412
			$660

redesigned the cars and couplings. They want us to make just two of these new couplings for testing purposes. If the design works, then we'll have the inside track on the order to supply couplings for the whole ride.

Jean: We agreed to take on this initial order at our cost just to get our foot in the door. Marc, will there be any problem documenting our cost so we can get paid?

Marc: No problem. The contract with Loops stipulates that they will pay us an amount equal to our cost of goods sold. With our job-order costing system, I can tell you the cost on the day the job is completed.

Jean: Good. Is there anything else we should discuss about this job at this time? No? Well then let's move on to the next item of business.

Measuring Direct Materials Cost

The blueprints submitted by Loops Unlimited indicate that each experimental coupling will require three parts that are classified as direct materials: two G7 Connectors and one M46 Housing. Since each coupling requires two connectors and one housing, the production of two couplings requires four connectors and two housings. This is a custom product that is being made for the first time, but if this were one of the company's standard products, it would have an established *bill of materials*. A **bill of materials** is a document that lists the type and quantity of each type of direct material needed to complete a unit of product.

When an agreement has been reached with the customer concerning the quantities, prices, and shipment date for the order, a *production order* is issued. The Production Department then prepares a *materials requisition form* similar to the form in Exhibit 2–1. The **materials requisition form** is a document that specifies the type and quantity of materials to be drawn from the storeroom and identifies the job that will be charged for the cost of the materials. The form is used to control the flow of materials into production and also for making entries in the accounting records.

The Yost Precision Machining materials requisition form in Exhibit 2–1 shows that the company's Milling Department has requisitioned two M46 Housings and four G7 Connectors for the Loops Unlimited job, which has been designated as Job 2B47.

Job Cost Sheet

After a production order has been issued, the Accounting Department's job-order costing software system automatically generates a *job cost sheet* like the one presented in Exhibit 2–2. A **job cost sheet** records the materials, labor, and manufacturing overhead costs charged to that job.

EXHIBIT 2–2
Job Cost Sheet

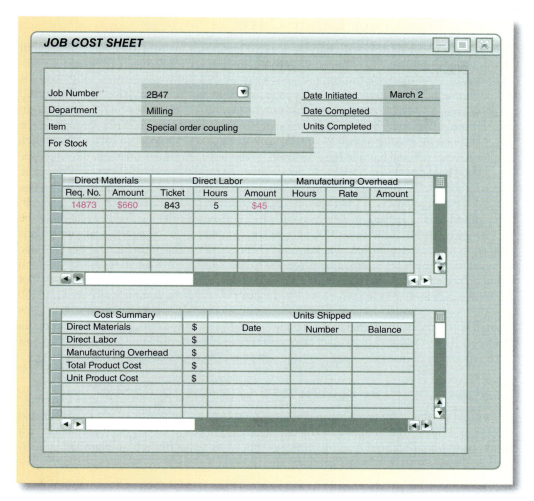

After direct materials are issued, the cost of these materials are automatically recorded on the job cost sheet. Note from Exhibit 2–2, for example, that the $660 cost for direct materials shown earlier on the materials requisition form has been charged to Job 2B47 on its job cost sheet. The requisition number 14873 from the materials requisition form appears on the job cost sheet to make it easier to identify the source document for the direct materials charge.

Supply and Demand Influence Lumber Prices   IN BUSINESS

When the housing market crumbled between 2005 and 2009, lumber mills responded by slashing output by 45%. However, in 2010 many home builders decided to expand speculative construction on the belief that an expiring federal tax credit would entice more customers to purchase new homes. The result of plummeting supply coupled with an uptick in demand was predictable—the price of lumber spiked to $279 per thousand board feet, thereby adding about $1,000 to the price of a typical new home. **Pulte Homes** told investors that it would attempt to offset the increase in direct materials cost by reducing its labor costs.

   Home builders use job-order costing systems to accumulate the costs incurred to build each new home. When materials and labor costs fluctuate, job-order costing systems can measure these impacts on each customer's new home construction costs.

Source: Liam Pleven and Lester Aldrich, "Builders Nailed by Lumber Prices," *The Wall Street Journal*, February 16, 2010, pp. C1 and C4.

Measuring Direct Labor Cost

Direct labor consists of labor charges that are easily traced to a particular job. Labor charges that cannot be easily traced directly to any job are treated as part of manufacturing overhead. As discussed in the previous chapter, this latter category of labor costs is called *indirect labor* and includes tasks such as maintenance, supervision, and cleanup.

Most companies rely on computerized systems to maintain employee *time tickets*. A completed **time ticket** is an hour-by-hour summary of the employee's activities throughout the day. One computerized approach to creating time tickets uses bar codes to capture data. Each employee and each job has a unique bar code. When beginning work on a job, the employee scans three bar codes using a handheld device much like the bar code readers at grocery store checkout stands. The first bar code indicates that a job is being started; the second is the unique bar code on the employee's identity badge; and the third is the unique bar code of the job itself. This information is fed automatically via an electronic network to a computer that notes the time and records all of the data. When the task is completed, the employee scans a bar code indicating the task is complete, the bar code on his or her identity badge, and the bar code attached to the job. This information is relayed to the computer that again notes the time, and a time ticket, such as the one shown in Exhibit 2–3, is automatically prepared. Because all of the source data is already in computer files, the labor costs can be automatically posted to job cost sheets. For example, Exhibit 2–3 shows $45 of direct labor cost related to Job 2B47. This amount is automatically posted to the job cost sheet shown in Exhibit 2–2. The time ticket in Exhibit 2–3 also shows $9 of indirect labor costs related to performing maintenance. This cost is treated as part of manufacturing overhead and does not get posted on a job cost sheet.

Computing Predetermined Overhead Rates

Recall that product costs include manufacturing overhead as well as direct materials and direct labor. Therefore, manufacturing overhead also needs to be recorded on the job cost sheet. However, assigning manufacturing overhead to a specific job involves some difficulties. There are three reasons for this:

1. Manufacturing overhead is an *indirect cost*. This means that it is either impossible or difficult to trace these costs to a particular product or job.
2. Manufacturing overhead consists of many different types of costs ranging from the grease used in machines to the annual salary of the production manager. Some of these costs are variable overhead costs because they vary in direct proportion to changes in the level of production (e.g., indirect materials, supplies, and power) and some are fixed overhead costs because they remain constant as the level of production fluctuates (e.g., heat and light, property taxes, and insurance).

EXHIBIT 2–3   Employee Time Ticket

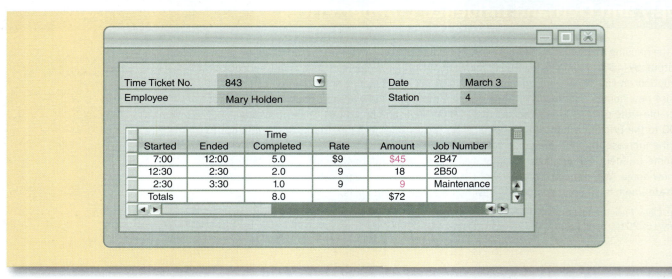

| Time Ticket No. | 843 | | | Date | March 3 |
| Employee | Mary Holden | | | Station | 4 |

Started	Ended	Time Completed	Rate	Amount	Job Number
7:00	12:00	5.0	$9	$45	2B47
12:30	2:30	2.0	9	18	2B50
2:30	3:30	1.0	9	9	Maintenance
Totals		8.0		$72	

3. Because of the fixed costs in manufacturing overhead, total manufacturing overhead costs tend to remain relatively constant from one period to the next even though the number of units produced can fluctuate widely. Consequently, the average cost per unit will vary from one period to the next.

Given these problems, allocation is used to assign overhead costs to products. Allocation is accomplished by selecting an *allocation base* that is common to all of the company's products and services. An **allocation base** is a measure such as direct labor-hours (DLH) or machine-hours (MH) that is used to assign overhead costs to products and services. The most widely used allocation bases in manufacturing are direct labor-hours, direct labor cost, machine-hours, and (where a company has only a single product) units of product.

Manufacturing overhead is commonly assigned to products using *a predetermined overhead rate.* The **predetermined overhead rate** is computed by dividing the total estimated manufacturing overhead cost for the period by the estimated total amount of the allocation base as follows:

$$\text{Predetermined overhead rate} = \frac{\text{Estimated total manufacturing overhead cost}}{\text{Estimated total amount of the allocation base}}$$

The predetermined overhead rate is computed before the period begins using a four-step process. The first step is to estimate the total amount of the allocation base (the denominator) that will be required for next period's estimated level of production. The second step is to estimate the total fixed manufacturing overhead cost for the coming period and the variable manufacturing overhead cost per unit of the allocation base. The third step is to use the cost formula shown below to estimate the total manufacturing overhead cost (the numerator) for the coming period:

$$Y = a + bX$$

where,

Y = The estimated total manufacturing overhead cost
a = The estimated total fixed manufacturing overhead cost
b = The estimated variable manufacturing overhead cost per unit of the allocation base
X = The estimated total amount of the allocation base

The fourth step is to compute the predetermined overhead rate. Notice, the estimated amount of the allocation base is determined before estimating the total manufacturing overhead cost. This needs to be done because total manufacturing overhead cost includes variable overhead costs that depend on the amount of the allocation base.

Applying Manufacturing Overhead

To repeat, the predetermined overhead rate is computed *before* the period begins. The predetermined overhead rate is then used to apply overhead cost to jobs throughout the period. The process of assigning overhead cost to jobs is called **overhead application**. The formula for determining the amount of overhead cost to apply to a particular job is

$$\text{Overhead applied to a particular job} = \text{Predetermined overhead rate} \times \text{Amount of the allocation base incurred by the job}$$

LEARNING OBJECTIVE 2–2
Apply overhead cost to jobs using a predetermined overhead rate.

For example, if the predetermined overhead rate is $8 per direct labor-hour, then $8 of overhead cost is *applied* to a job for each direct labor-hour incurred on the job. When the allocation base is direct labor-hours, the formula becomes

$$\text{Overhead applied to a particular job} = \text{Predetermined overhead rate} \times \text{Actual direct labor-hours charged to the job}$$

Manufacturing Overhead—A Closer Look

To illustrate the steps involved in computing and using a predetermined overhead rate, let's return to Yost Precision Machining and make the following assumptions. In step one, the company estimated that 40,000 direct labor-hours would be required to support the production planned for the year. In step two, it estimated $220,000 of total fixed manufacturing overhead cost for the coming year and $2.50 of variable manufacturing overhead cost per direct labor-hour. Given these assumptions, in step three the company used the cost formula shown below to estimate its total manufacturing overhead cost for the year:

$$Y = a + bX$$

$$Y = \$220,000 + (\$2.50 \text{ per direct labor-hour} \times 40,000 \text{ direct labor-hours})$$

$$Y = \$220,000 + \$100,000$$

$$Y = \$320,000$$

In step four, Yost Precision Machining computed its predetermined overhead rate for the year of $8 per direct labor-hour as shown below:

$$\text{Predetermined overhead rate} = \frac{\text{Estimated total manufacturing overhead cost}}{\text{Estimated total amount of the allocation base}}$$

$$= \frac{\$320,000}{40,000 \text{ direct labor-hours}}$$

$$= \$8 \text{ per direct labor-hour}$$

The job cost sheet in Exhibit 2–4 indicates that 27 direct labor-hours (i.e., DLHs) were charged to Job 2B47. Therefore, a total of $216 of manufacturing overhead cost would be applied to the job:

$$\begin{array}{c}\text{Overhead applied to} \\ \text{Job 2B47}\end{array} = \begin{array}{c}\text{Predetermined} \\ \text{overhead rate}\end{array} \times \begin{array}{c}\text{Actual direct labor-hours} \\ \text{charged to Job 2B47}\end{array}$$

$$= \$8 \text{ per DLH} \times 27 \text{ DLHs}$$

$$= \$216 \text{ of overhead applied to Job 2B47}$$

This amount of overhead has been entered on the job cost sheet in Exhibit 2–4. Note that this is *not* the actual amount of overhead caused by the job. Actual overhead costs are *not* assigned to jobs—if that could be done, the costs would be direct costs, not overhead. The overhead assigned to the job is simply a share of the total overhead that was estimated at the beginning of the year. A **normal cost system,** which we have been describing, applies overhead to jobs by multiplying a predetermined overhead rate by the actual amount of the allocation base incurred by the jobs.

HELPFUL HINT

This chapter is based on the concept of normal costing. A normal cost system assigns actual direct materials and direct labor costs to jobs; however, it does *not* assign actual overhead costs to jobs. Instead, a predetermined overhead rate is used to apply overhead cost to jobs. The predetermined overhead rate is multiplied by the actual quantity of the allocation base consumed by a job to apply overhead cost to that job. Many companies use normal cost systems; however, companies can also use other types of cost systems, such as actual costing and standard costing, that will be discussed in later chapters.

The Need for a Predetermined Rate

Instead of using a predetermined rate based on estimates, why not base the overhead rate on the *actual* total manufacturing overhead cost and the *actual* total amount of the allocation base incurred on a monthly, quarterly, or annual basis? If an actual rate is computed

EXHIBIT 2–4
A Completed Job Cost Sheet

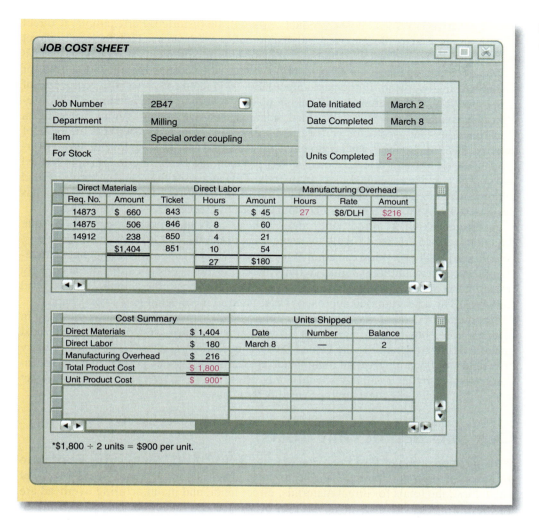

JOB COST SHEET

Job Number	2B47		Date Initiated	March 2
Department	Milling		Date Completed	March 8
Item	Special order coupling			
For Stock			Units Completed	2

Direct Materials		Direct Labor			Manufacturing Overhead		
Req. No.	Amount	Ticket	Hours	Amount	Hours	Rate	Amount
14873	$ 660	843	5	$ 45	27	$8/DLH	$216
14875	506	846	8	60			
14912	238	850	4	21			
	$1,404	851	10	54			
			27	$180			

Cost Summary		Units Shipped		
Direct Materials	$ 1,404	Date	Number	Balance
Direct Labor	$ 180	March 8	—	2
Manufacturing Overhead	$ 216			
Total Product Cost	$ 1,800			
Unit Product Cost	$ 900*			

*$1,800 ÷ 2 units = $900 per unit.

monthly or quarterly, seasonal factors in overhead costs or in the allocation base can produce fluctuations in the overhead rate. For example, the costs of heating and cooling a factory in Illinois will be highest in the winter and summer months and lowest in the spring and fall. If the overhead rate is recomputed at the end of each month or each quarter based on actual costs and activity, the overhead rate would go up in the winter and summer and down in the spring and fall. As a result, two identical jobs, one completed in the winter and one completed in the spring, would be assigned different manufacturing overhead costs. Many managers believe that such fluctuations in product costs serve no useful purpose. To avoid such fluctuations, actual overhead rates could be computed on an annual or less-frequent basis. However, if the overhead rate is computed annually based on the actual costs and activity for the year, the manufacturing overhead assigned to any particular job would not be known until the end of the year. For example, the cost of Job 2B47 at Yost Precision Machining would not be known until the end of the year, even though the job will be completed and shipped to the customer in March. For these reasons, most companies use predetermined overhead rates rather than actual overhead rates in their cost accounting systems.

Choice of an Allocation Base for Overhead Cost

Ideally, the allocation base in the predetermined overhead rate should *drive* the overhead cost. A **cost driver** is a factor, such as machine-hours, beds occupied, computer time, or flight-hours, that causes overhead costs. If the base in the predetermined overhead rate does not "drive" overhead costs, product costs will be distorted. For example, if direct labor-hours is used to allocate overhead, but in reality overhead has little to do with direct labor-hours, then products with high direct labor-hour requirements will be overcosted.

Most companies use direct labor-hours or direct labor cost as the allocation base for manufacturing overhead. In the past, direct labor accounted for up to 60% of the cost of many products, with overhead cost making up only a portion of the remainder. This situation has changed for two reasons. First, sophisticated automated equipment has taken over functions that used to be performed by direct labor workers. Because the costs of acquiring and maintaining such equipment are classified as overhead, this increases overhead while decreasing direct labor. Second, products are becoming more sophisticated and complex and are changed more frequently. This increases the need for highly skilled indirect workers such as engineers. As a result of these two trends, direct labor has decreased relative to overhead as a component of product costs.

In companies where direct labor and overhead costs have been moving in opposite directions, it would be difficult to argue that direct labor "drives" overhead costs. Accordingly, managers in some companies use *activity-based costing* principles to redesign their cost accounting systems. Activity-based costing is designed to more accurately reflect the demands that products, customers, and other cost objects make on overhead resources. The activity-based approach is discussed in more detail in the next chapter.

Although direct labor may not be an appropriate allocation base in some industries, in others it continues to be a significant driver of manufacturing overhead. Indeed, most manufacturing companies in the United States continue to use direct labor as the primary or secondary allocation base for manufacturing overhead. The key point is that the allocation base used by the company should really drive, or cause, overhead costs, and direct labor is not always the most appropriate allocation base.

Computation of Unit Costs

With the application of Yost Precision Machining's $216 of manufacturing overhead to the job cost sheet in Exhibit 2–4, the job cost sheet is complete except for two final steps. First, the totals for direct materials, direct labor, and manufacturing overhead are transferred to the Cost Summary section of the job cost sheet and added together to obtain the total cost for the job.[1] Then the total product cost ($1,800) is divided by the number of units (2) to obtain the unit product cost ($900). This unit product cost information is used for valuing unsold units in ending inventory and for determining cost of goods sold. As indicated earlier, *this unit product cost is an average cost and should not be interpreted as the cost that would actually be incurred if another unit were produced.* The incremental cost of an additional unit is something less than the average unit cost of $900 because much of the actual overhead costs would not change if another unit were produced.

In the 8:00 A.M. daily planning meeting on March 9, Jean Yost, the president of Yost Precision Machining, once again drew attention to Job 2B47, the experimental couplings:

Jean: I see Job 2B47 is completed. Let's get those couplings shipped immediately to Loops Unlimited so they can get their testing program under way. Marc, how much are we going to bill Loops for those two units?

Marc: Because we agreed to sell the experimental couplings at cost, we will be charging Loops Unlimited just $900 a unit.

Jean: Fine. Let's hope the couplings work out and we make some money on the big order later.

---

[1] Notice, we are assuming that Job 2B47 required direct materials and direct labor beyond the charges shown in Exhibit 2–1 and 2–3.

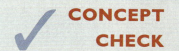

CONCEPT CHECK

1. Which of the following statements is false? (You may select more than one answer.)
   a. Absorption costing assigns fixed and variable manufacturing overhead costs to products.
   b. Job-order costing systems are used when companies produce many different types of products.
   c. A normal costing system assigns overhead costs to products by multiplying the actual overhead rate by the actual amount of the allocation base.
   d. A unit product cost represents the additional cost that would be incurred if another unit were produced.

2. Assume that a company's total estimated fixed overhead cost for the coming year is $100,000 and its estimated variable overhead cost is $3.00 per direct labor-hour. If the company estimates that it will work 50,000 direct labor-hours in the coming year, what is its predetermined overhead rate per direct labor-hour?
   a. $2.00
   b. $3.00
   c. $4.00
   d. $5.00

3. Which of the following statements is true? (You may select more than one answer.)
   a. Manufacturing overhead is an indirect cost.
   b. Because manufacturing overhead includes fixed costs, the predetermined overhead rate tends to remain stable from period to period.
   c. Ideally, the allocation base in a predetermined overhead rate should be a cost driver.
   d. A unit product cost includes three types of manufacturing costs—direct materials, direct labor, and manufacturing overhead.

One-of-a-Kind Masterpiece

IN BUSINESS

In a true job-order costing environment, every job is unique. For example, **Purdey** manufactures 80–90 shotguns per year with each gun being a specially commissioned one-of-a-kind masterpiece. The prices start at $110,000 because every detail is custom built, engraved, assembled, and polished by a skilled craftsman. The hand engraving can take months to complete and may add as much as $100,000 to the price. The guns are designed to shoot perfectly straight and their value increases over time even with heavy use. One Purdey gun collector said "when I shoot my Purdeys I feel like an orchestra conductor waving my baton."

Source: Eric Arnold, "Aim High," *Forbes,* December 28, 2009, p. 86.

JOB-ORDER COSTING—THE FLOW OF COSTS

We are now ready to discuss the flow of costs through a job-order costing system. Exhibit 2–5 provides a conceptual overview of these cost flows. It highlights the fact that *product costs* flow through inventories on the balance sheet and then on to cost of goods sold in the income statement. More specifically, raw materials purchases are recorded in the *Raw Materials* inventory account. **Raw materials** include any materials that go into the final product. When raw materials are used in production, their costs are transferred to the *Work in Process* inventory account as direct materials.[2] **Work in process** consists of units of product

LEARNING OBJECTIVE 2–4

Understand the flow of costs in a job-order costing system and prepare appropriate journal entries to record costs.

---

[2]Indirect material costs are accounted for as part of manufacturing overhead.

EXHIBIT 2–5   Cost Flows and Classifications in a Manufacturing Company

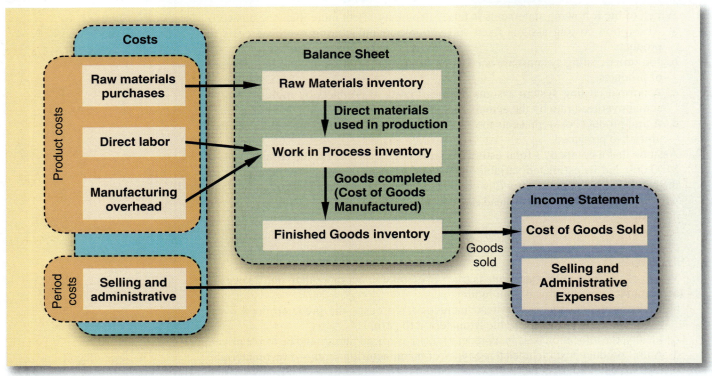

that are only partially complete and will require further work before they are ready for sale to the customer. Notice that direct labor costs are added directly to Work in Process—they do not flow through Raw Materials inventory. Manufacturing overhead costs are applied to Work in Process by multiplying the predetermined overhead rate by the actual quantity of the allocation base consumed by each job.[3] When goods are completed, their costs are transferred from Work in Process to *Finished Goods*. **Finished goods** consist of completed units of product that have not yet been sold to customers. The amount transferred from Work in Process to Finished Goods is referred to as the *cost of goods manufactured*. The **cost of goods manufactured** includes the manufacturing costs associated with the goods that were finished during the period. As goods are sold, their costs are transferred from Finished Goods to Cost of Goods Sold. At this point, the various costs required to make the product are finally recorded as an expense. Until that point, these costs are in inventory accounts on the balance sheet. Period costs (or selling and administrative expenses) do not flow through inventories on the balance sheet. They are recorded as expenses on the income statement in the period incurred.

To illustrate the cost flows through a company's general ledger, we will consider a single month's activity at Ruger Corporation, a producer of gold and silver commemorative medallions. Ruger Corporation has two jobs in process during April, the first month of its fiscal year. Job A, a special minting of 1,000 gold medallions commemorating the invention of motion pictures, was started during March. By the end of March, $30,000 in manufacturing costs had been recorded for the job. Job B, an order for 10,000 silver medallions commemorating the fall of the Berlin Wall, was started in April.

The Purchase and Issue of Materials

On April 1, Ruger Corporation had $7,000 in raw materials on hand. During the month, the company purchased on account an additional $60,000 in raw materials. The purchase is recorded in journal entry (1) below:

---

[3]For simplicity, Exhibit 2–5 assumes that Cost of Goods Sold does not need to be adjusted as discussed later in the chapter.

(1)			
Raw Materials	60,000		
Accounts Payable		60,000	

Remember that Raw Materials is an asset account. Thus, when raw materials are purchased, they are initially recorded as an asset—not as an expense.

Issue of Direct and Indirect Materials

During April, $52,000 in raw materials were requisitioned from the storeroom for use in production. These raw materials included $50,000 of direct and $2,000 of indirect materials. Entry (2) records issuing the materials to the production departments.

(2)			
Work in Process	50,000		
Manufacturing Overhead	2,000		
Raw Materials		52,000	

The materials charged to Work in Process represent direct materials for specific jobs. These costs are also recorded on the appropriate job cost sheets. This point is illustrated in Exhibit 2–6, where $28,000 of the $50,000 in direct materials is charged to Job A's cost sheet and the remaining $22,000 is charged to Job B's cost sheet. (In this example, all data are presented in summary form and the job cost sheet is abbreviated.)

The $2,000 charged to Manufacturing Overhead in entry (2) represents indirect materials. Observe that the Manufacturing Overhead account is separate from the Work in Process account. The purpose of the Manufacturing Overhead account is to accumulate all manufacturing overhead costs as they are incurred during a period.

Before leaving Exhibit 2–6, we need to point out one additional thing. Notice from the exhibit that the job cost sheet for Job A contains a beginning balance of $30,000. We stated earlier that this balance represents the cost of work done during March that has been carried forward to April. Also note that the Work in Process account contains the same $30,000 balance. Thus, the Work in Process account summarizes all of the costs appearing on the job cost sheets of the jobs that are in process. Job A was the only job in process at the beginning of April, so the beginning balance in the Work in Process account equals Job A's beginning balance of $30,000.

EXHIBIT 2–6　Raw Materials Cost Flows

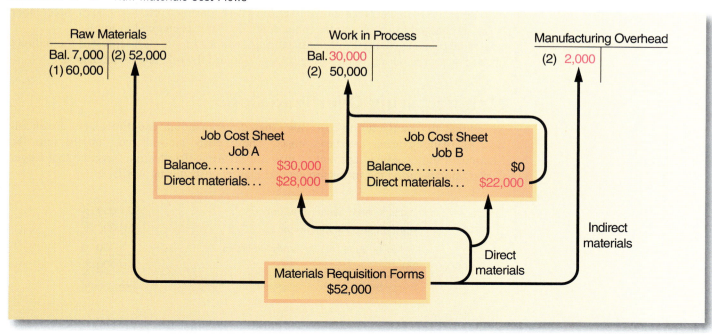

EXHIBIT 2–7   Labor Cost Flows

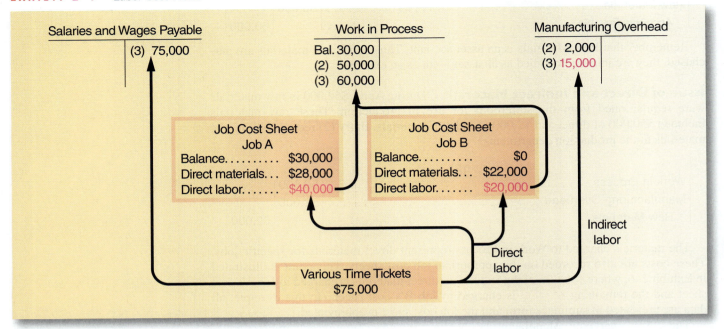

Labor Cost

In April, the employee time tickets included $60,000 recorded for direct labor and $15,000 for indirect labor. The following entry summarizes these costs:

	(3)		
Work in Process	60,000	
Manufacturing Overhead	15,000	
Salaries and Wages Payable		75,000

Only the direct labor cost of $60,000 is added to the Work in Process account. At the same time that direct labor costs are added to Work in Process, they are also added to the individual job cost sheets, as shown in Exhibit 2–7. During April, $40,000 of direct labor cost was charged to Job A and the remaining $20,000 was charged to Job B.

The labor costs charged to Manufacturing Overhead ($15,000) represent the indirect labor costs of the period, such as supervision, janitorial work, and maintenance.

Manufacturing Overhead Costs

Recall that all manufacturing costs other than direct materials and direct labor are classified as manufacturing overhead costs. These costs are entered directly into the Manufacturing Overhead account as they are incurred. To illustrate, assume that Ruger Corporation incurred the following general factory costs during April:

Utilities (heat, water, and power)	$21,000
Rent on factory equipment	16,000
Miscellaneous factory overhead costs	3,000
Total	$40,000

The following entry records the incurrence of these costs:

(4)

| Manufacturing Overhead.................................. | 40,000 | |
| Accounts Payable*.................................. | | 40,000 |

*Accounts such as Cash may also be credited

In addition, assume that during April, Ruger Corporation recognized $13,000 in accrued property taxes and that $7,000 in prepaid insurance expired on factory buildings and equipment. The following entry records these items:

(5)

Manufacturing Overhead..................................	20,000	
Property Taxes Payable		13,000
Prepaid Insurance		7,000

Finally, assume that the company recognized $18,000 in depreciation on factory equipment during April. The following entry records the accrual of this depreciation:

(6)

| Manufacturing Overhead .... | 18,000 | |
| Accumulated Depreciation .... | | 18,000 |

In short, all actual manufacturing overhead costs are debited to the Manufacturing Overhead account as they are incurred.

Applying Manufacturing Overhead

Because actual manufacturing costs are charged to the Manufacturing Overhead control account rather than to Work in Process, how are manufacturing overhead costs assigned to Work in Process? The answer is, by means of the predetermined overhead rate. Recall from our discussion earlier in the chapter that a predetermined overhead rate is established at the beginning of each year. The rate is calculated by dividing the estimated total manufacturing overhead cost for the year by the estimated total amount of the allocation base (measured in machine-hours, direct labor-hours, or some other base). The predetermined overhead rate is then used to apply overhead costs to jobs. For example, if machine-hours is the allocation base, overhead cost is applied to each job by multiplying the predetermined overhead rate by the number of machine-hours charged to the job.

To illustrate, assume that Ruger Corporation's predetermined overhead rate is $6 per machine-hour. Also assume that during April, 10,000 machine-hours were worked on Job A and 5,000 machine-hours were worked on Job B (a total of 15,000 machine-hours). Thus, $90,000 in overhead cost ($6 per machine-hour × 15,000 machine-hours = $90,000) would be applied to Work in Process. The following entry records the application of Manufacturing Overhead to Work in Process:

(7)

| Work in Process .... | 90,000 | |
| Manufacturing Overhead .... | | 90,000 |

The flow of costs through the Manufacturing Overhead account is shown in Exhibit 2–8. The actual overhead costs on the debit side in the Manufacturing Overhead account in Exhibit 2–8 are the costs that were added to the account in entries (2)–(6). Observe that recording these actual overhead costs [entries (2)–(6)] and the application of overhead to Work in Process [entry (7)] represent two separate and entirely distinct processes.

EXHIBIT 2–8   The Flow of Costs in Overhead Application

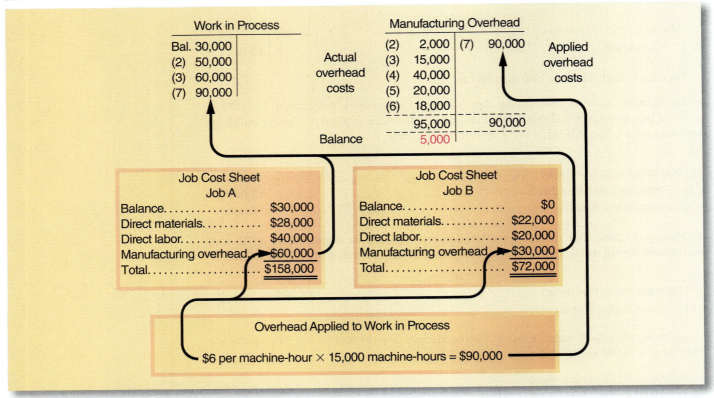

The Concept of a Clearing Account

The Manufacturing Overhead account operates as a clearing account. As we have noted, actual factory overhead costs are debited to the account as they are incurred throughout the year. When a job is completed (or at the end of an accounting period), overhead cost is applied to the job using the predetermined overhead rate, and Work in Process is debited and Manufacturing Overhead is credited. This sequence of events is illustrated below:

**Manufacturing Overhead
(a clearing account)**

Actual overhead costs are charged to this account as they are incurred throughout the period.	Overhead is applied to Work in Process using the predetermined overhead rate.

As we emphasized earlier, the predetermined overhead rate is based entirely on estimates of what the level of activity and overhead costs are *expected* to be, and it is established before the year begins. As a result, the overhead cost applied during a year will almost certainly turn out to be more or less than the actual overhead cost incurred. For example, notice from Exhibit 2–8 that Ruger Corporation's actual overhead costs for the period are $5,000 greater than the overhead cost that has been applied to Work in Process, resulting in a $5,000 debit balance in the Manufacturing Overhead account. We will reserve discussion of what to do with this $5,000 balance until later in the chapter.

For the moment, we can conclude from Exhibit 2–8 that the cost of a completed job consists of the actual direct materials cost of the job, the actual direct labor cost of the job, and the manufacturing overhead cost *applied* to the job. Pay particular attention to the following subtle but important point: *Actual overhead costs are not charged to jobs; actual overhead costs do not appear on the job cost sheet nor do they appear in the Work in Process account. Only the applied overhead cost, based on the predetermined overhead rate, appears on the job cost sheet and in the Work in Process account.*

Nonmanufacturing Costs

In addition to manufacturing costs, companies also incur selling and administrative costs. These costs should be treated as period expenses and charged directly to the income statement. *Nonmanufacturing costs should not go into the Manufacturing Overhead account.* To illustrate the correct treatment of nonmanufacturing costs, assume that Ruger Corporation incurred $30,000 in selling and administrative salary costs during April. The following entry summarizes the accrual of those salaries:

(8)

Salaries Expense	30,000	
Salaries and Wages Payable		30,000

Assume that depreciation on office equipment during April was $7,000. The entry is as follows:

(9)

Depreciation Expense	7,000	
Accumulated Depreciation		7,000

Pay particular attention to the difference between this entry and entry (6) where we recorded depreciation on factory equipment. In journal entry (6), depreciation on factory equipment was debited to Manufacturing Overhead and is therefore a product cost. In journal entry (9) above, depreciation on office equipment is debited to Depreciation Expense. Depreciation on office equipment is a period expense rather than a product cost.

Finally, assume that advertising was $42,000 and that other selling and administrative expenses in April totaled $8,000. The following entry records these items:

(10)

Advertising Expense	42,000	
Other Selling and Administrative Expense	8,000	
Accounts Payable*		50,000

*Other accounts, such as Cash may be credited.

The amounts in entries (8) through (10) are recorded directly into expense accounts—they have no effect on product costs. The same will be true of any other selling and administrative expenses incurred during April, including sales commissions, depreciation on sales equipment, rent on office facilities, insurance on office facilities, and related costs.

Cost of Goods Manufactured

When a job has been completed, the finished output is transferred from the production departments to the finished goods warehouse. By this time, the accounting department will have charged the job with direct materials and direct labor cost, and manufacturing overhead will have been applied using the predetermined overhead rate. A transfer of costs is made within the costing system that *parallels* the physical transfer of goods to the finished goods warehouse. The costs of the completed job are transferred out of the Work in Process account and into the Finished Goods account. The sum of all amounts transferred between these two accounts represents the cost of goods manufactured for the period.

In the case of Ruger Corporation, assume that Job A was completed during April. The following entry transfers the cost of Job A from Work in Process to Finished Goods:

(11)

Finished Goods	158,000	
Work in Process		158,000

The $158,000 represents the completed cost of Job A, as shown on the job cost sheet in Exhibit 2–8. Because Job A was the only job completed during April, the $158,000 also represents the cost of goods manufactured for the month.

Job B was not completed by the end of the month, so its cost will remain in the Work in Process account and carry over to the next month. If a balance sheet is prepared at the end of April, the cost accumulated thus far on Job B will appear as the asset "Work in Process inventory."

Cost of Goods Sold

As finished goods are shipped to customers, their accumulated costs are transferred from the Finished Goods account to the Cost of Goods Sold account. If an entire job is shipped at one time, then the entire cost appearing on the job cost sheet is transferred to the Cost of Goods Sold account. In most cases, however, only a portion of the units involved in a particular job will be immediately sold. In these situations, the unit product cost must be used to determine how much product cost should be removed from Finished Goods and charged to Cost of Goods Sold.

For Ruger Corporation, we will assume 750 of the 1,000 gold medallions in Job A were shipped to customers by the end of the month for total sales revenue of $225,000. Because 1,000 units were produced and the total cost of the job from the job cost sheet was $158,000, the unit product cost was $158. The following journal entries would record the sale (all sales were on account):

(12)

Accounts Receivable	225,000	
Sales		225,000

(13)

Cost of Goods Sold	118,500	
Finished Goods		118,500
(750 units × $158 per unit = $118,500)		

CONCEPT CHECK

4. Which of the following statements is true? (You may select more than one answer.)
    a. Direct labor costs are debited to Work in Process and indirect labor costs are debited to Manufacturing Overhead.
    b. Raw material purchases are immediately debited to the Raw Materials account and recorded as an expense on the income statement.
    c. Administrative expenses are debited to the Manufacturing Overhead clearing account.
    d. Assume a company sells finished goods to a customer for $200 on credit. To record this transaction, the company would debit Accounts Receivable for $200 and credit Finished Goods Inventory for $200.

5. Which of the following statements is true with respect to the Manufacturing Overhead clearing account? (You may select more than one answer.)
    a. Actual manufacturing overhead expenses are debited to Manufacturing Overhead.
    b. Applied manufacturing overhead costs are credited to Manufacturing Overhead.
    c. If the Manufacturing Overhead account has a debit balance at the end of an accounting period, it means that manufacturing overhead was overapplied.
    d. If the Manufacturing Overhead account has a debit balance at the end of an accounting period, the closing entry pertaining to this account will lower net operating income.

Entry (13) completes the flow of costs through the job-order costing system. To pull the entire Ruger Corporation example together, journal entries (1) through (13) are summarized in Exhibit 2–9. The flow of costs through the accounts is presented in T-account form in Exhibit 2–10.

EXHIBIT 2–9   Summary of Journal Entries—Ruger Corporation

(1)		
Raw Materials	60,000	
Accounts Payable		60,000
(2)		
Work in Process	50,000	
Manufacturing Overhead	2,000	
Raw Materials		52,000
(3)		
Work in Process	60,000	
Manufacturing Overhead	15,000	
Salaries and Wages Payable		75,000
(4)		
Manufacturing Overhead	40,000	
Accounts Payable		40,000
(5)		
Manufacturing Overhead.	20,000	
Property Taxes Payable		13,000
Prepaid Insurance		7,000
(6)		
Manufacturing Overhead	18,000	
Accumulated Depreciation		18,000
(7)		
Work in Process	90,000	
Manufacturing Overhead		90,000
(8)		
Salaries Expense	30,000	
Salaries and Wages Payable		30,000
(9)		
Depreciation Expense	7,000	
Accumulated Depreciation		7,000
(10)		
Advertising Expense	42,000	
Other Selling and Administrative Expense	8,000	
Accounts Payable		50,000
(11)		
Finished Goods	158,000	
Work in Process		158,000
(12)		
Accounts Receivable	225,000	
Sales		225,000
(13)		
Cost of Goods Sold	118,500	
Finished Goods		118,500

EXHIBIT 2–10 Summary of Cost Flows—Ruger Corporation

Accounts Receivable

Bal.	XX	
(12)	225,000	

Prepaid Insurance

Bal.	XX		
		(5)	7,000

Raw Materials

Bal.	7,000	(2)	52,000
(1)	60,000		
Bal.	15,000		

Work in Process

Bal.	30,000	(11)	158,000
(2)	50,000		
(3)	60,000		
(7)	90,000		
Bal.	72,000		

Finished Goods

Bal.	10,000	(13)	118,500
(11)	158,000		
Bal.	49,500		

Accumulated Depreciation

		Bal.	XX
		(6)	18,000
		(9)	7,000

Manufacturing Overhead

(2)	2,000	(7)	90,000
(3)	15,000		
(4)	40,000		
(5)	20,000		
(6)	18,000		
	95,000		90,000
Bal.	5,000		

Accounts Payable

		Bal.	XX
		(1)	60,000
		(4)	40,000
		(10)	50,000

Salaries and Wages Payable

		Bal.	XX
		(3)	75,000
		(8)	30,000

Property Taxes Payable

		Bal.	XX
		(5)	13,000

Sales

		(12)	225,000

Cost of Goods Sold

(13)	118,500	

Salaries Expense

(8)	30,000	

Depreciation Expense

(9)	7,000	

Advertising Expense

(10)	42,000	

Other Selling and Administrative Expense

(10)	8,000	

Explanation of entries:
 (1) Raw materials purchased.
 (2) Direct and indirect materials issued into production.
 (3) Direct and indirect factory labor cost incurred.
 (4) Utilities and other factory costs incurred.
 (5) Property taxes and insurance incurred on the factory.
 (6) Depreciation recorded on factory assets.
 (7) Overhead cost applied to Work in Process.
 (8) Administrative salaries expense incurred.
 (9) Depreciation recorded on office equipment.
 (10) Advertising and other selling and administrative expense incurred.
 (11) Cost of goods manufactured transferred to finished goods.
 (12) Sale of Job A recorded.
 (13) Cost of goods sold recorded for Job A.

SCHEDULES OF COST OF GOODS MANUFACTURED AND COST OF GOODS SOLD

This section uses the Ruger Corporation example to explain how to prepare schedules of cost of goods manufactured and cost of goods sold as well as an income statement. The **schedule of cost of goods manufactured** contains three elements of product costs—direct materials, direct labor, and manufacturing overhead—and it summarizes the portions of those costs that remain in ending Work in Process inventory and that are transferred out of Work in Process into Finished Goods. The **schedule of cost of goods sold** also contains three elements of product costs—direct materials, direct labor, and manufacturing overhead—and it summarizes the portions of those costs that remain in ending Finished Goods inventory and that are transferred out of Finished Goods into Cost of Goods Sold.

Exhibit 2–11 presents Ruger Corporation's schedules of cost of goods manufactured and cost of goods sold. We want to draw your attention to three equations that are embedded within the schedule of cost of goods manufactured. First, the *raw materials used in production* are computed using the following equation:

$$\text{Raw materials used in production} = \text{Beginning raw materials inventory} + \text{Purchases of raw materials} - \text{Ending raw materials inventory}$$

For Ruger Corporation, the beginning raw materials inventory of $7,000 plus the purchases of raw materials of $60,000 minus the ending raw materials inventory of $15,000

EXHIBIT 2–11 Schedules of Cost of Goods Manufactured and Cost of Goods Sold

Cost of Goods Manufactured

Direct materials:		
Beginning raw materials inventory	$ 7,000	
Add: Purchases of raw materials	60,000	
Total raw materials available	67,000	
Deduct: Ending raw materials inventory	15,000	
Raw materials used in production	52,000	
Deduct: Indirect materials included in manufacturing overhead	2,000	$ 50,000
Direct labor		60,000
Manufacturing overhead applied to work in process		90,000
Total manufacturing costs		200,000
Add: Beginning work in process inventory		30,000
		230,000
Deduct: Ending work in process inventory		72,000
Cost of goods manufactured		$158,000

Cost of Goods Sold

Beginning finished goods inventory	$ 10,000
Add: Cost of goods manufactured	158,000
Cost of goods available for sale	168,000
Deduct: Ending finished goods inventory	49,500
Unadjusted cost of goods sold	118,500
Add: Underapplied overhead	5,000
Adjusted cost of goods sold	$123,500

*Note that the underapplied overhead is added to cost of goods sold. If overhead were overapplied, it would be deducted from cost of goods sold.

equals the raw materials used in production of $52,000. Second, the *total manufacturing costs* are computed using the following equation:

$$
\begin{array}{ccccc}
\text{Total} & & & & \text{Manufacturing} \\
\text{manufacturing} & = & \text{Direct materials} + \text{Direct labor} + & \text{overhead applied to} \\
\text{costs} & & & & \text{work in process}
\end{array}
$$

For Ruger Corporation, the direct materials of $50,000 plus the direct labor of $60,000 plus the manufacturing overhead applied to work in process of $90,000 equals the total manufacturing costs of $200,000. Notice, the direct materials used in production ($50,000) is included in total manufacturing costs instead of raw materials purchases ($60,000). The direct materials used in production will usually differ from the amount of raw material purchases when the raw materials inventory balance changes or indirect materials are withdrawn from raw materials inventory. You should also make a note that *this equation includes manufacturing overhead applied to work in process rather than actual manufacturing overhead costs.* For Ruger Corporation, its manufacturing overhead applied to work in process of $90,000 is computed by multiplying the predetermined overhead rate of $6 per machine-hour by the actual amount of the allocation base recorded on all jobs, or 15,000 machine-hours. *The actual manufacturing overhead costs incurred during the period are not added to the Work in Process account.*

The third equation included in the schedule of cost of goods manufactured relates to computing the cost of goods manufactured:

$$
\begin{array}{ccccc}
\text{Cost of goods} & = & \text{Total} & + & \text{Beginning work in} & - & \text{Ending work in} \\
\text{manufactured} & & \text{manufacturing costs} & & \text{process inventory} & & \text{process inventory}
\end{array}
$$

For Ruger, the total manufacturing costs of $200,000 plus the beginning work in process inventory of $30,000 minus the ending work in process inventory of $72,000 equals the cost of goods manufactured of $158,000. The cost of goods manufactured represents the cost of the goods completed during the period and transferred from Work in Process to Finished Goods.

The schedule of cost of goods sold shown in Exhibit 2–11 relies on the following equation to compute the unadjusted cost of goods sold:

$$
\begin{array}{ccccc}
\text{Unadjusted cost} & = & \text{Beginning finished} & + & \text{Cost of goods} & - & \text{Ending finished} \\
\text{of goods sold} & & \text{goods inventory} & & \text{manufactured} & & \text{goods inventory}
\end{array}
$$

The beginning finished goods inventory ($10,000) plus the cost of goods manufactured ($158,000) equals the cost of goods available for sale ($168,000). The cost of goods available for sale ($168,000) minus the ending finished goods inventory ($49,500) equals the unadjusted cost of goods sold ($118,500). Finally, the unadjusted cost of goods sold ($118,500) plus the underapplied overhead ($5,000) equals adjusted cost of goods sold ($123,500). The next section of the chapter takes a closer look at why cost of goods sold needs to be adjusted for the amount of underapplied or overapplied overhead.

Exhibit 2–12 presents Ruger Corporation's income statement for April. Observe that the cost of goods sold on this statement is carried over from Exhibit 2–11. The selling and administrative expenses (which total $87,000) did not flow through the schedules of cost of goods manufactured and cost of goods sold. Journal entries 8–10 (pages 83–84) show that these items were immediately debited to expense accounts rather than being debited to inventory accounts.

Ruger Corporation Income Statement For the Month Ending April 30		
Sales		$225,000
Cost of goods sold ($118,500 + $5,000)		123,500
Gross margin		101,500
Selling and administrative expenses:		
Salaries expense	$30,000	
Depreciation expense	7,000	
Advertising expense	42,000	
Other expense	8,000	87,000
Net operating income		$ 14,500

EXHIBIT 2–12
Income Statement

> **CONCEPT CHECK**
>
> 6. Which of the following statements is false with respect to the schedule of cost of goods manufactured? (You may select more than one answer.)
>   a. The beginning raw materials inventory plus raw materials purchases minus ending raw materials inventory equals the raw materials used in production.
>   b. Direct labor costs and actual manufacturing overhead costs are included in the schedule of cost of goods manufactured.
>   c. The cost of goods manufactured represents the amount that will be debited to Cost of Goods Sold during an accounting period.
>   d. If the finished goods inventory increases during an accounting period, it will decrease the cost of goods manufactured.

UNDERAPPLIED AND OVERAPPLIED OVERHEAD—A CLOSER LOOK

This section explains how to compute underapplied and overapplied overhead and how to dispose of any balance remaining in the Manufacturing Overhead account at the end of a period.

LEARNING OBJECTIVE 2–7

Compute underapplied or overapplied overhead cost and prepare the journal entry to close the balance in Manufacturing Overhead to the appropriate accounts.

Computing Underapplied and Overapplied Overhead

Because the predetermined overhead rate is established before the period begins and is based entirely on estimated data, the overhead cost applied to Work in Process will generally differ from the amount of overhead cost actually incurred. In the case of Ruger Corporation, for example, the predetermined overhead rate of $6 per hour was used to apply $90,000 of overhead cost to Work in Process, whereas actual overhead costs for April proved to be $95,000 (see Exhibit 2–8). The difference between the overhead cost applied to Work in Process and the actual overhead costs of a period is called either **underapplied** or **overapplied overhead.** For Ruger Corporation, overhead was underapplied by $5,000 because the applied cost ($90,000) was $5,000 less than the actual cost ($95,000). If the situation had been reversed and the company had applied $95,000 in overhead cost to Work in Process while incurring actual overhead costs of only $90,000, then the overhead would have been overapplied.

What is the cause of underapplied or overapplied overhead? Basically, the method of applying overhead to jobs using a predetermined overhead rate assumes that actual overhead costs will be proportional to the actual amount of the allocation base incurred during the period. If, for example, the predetermined overhead rate is $6 per machine-hour, then it is assumed that actual overhead costs incurred will be $6 for every machine-hour that is actually worked. There are at least two reasons why this may not be true. First, much of the overhead often consists of fixed costs that do not change as the number of machine-hours incurred goes up or down. Second, spending on overhead items may or may not be under control. If individuals who are responsible for overhead costs do a good job, those costs should be less than were expected at the beginning of the period. If they do a poor job, those costs will be more than expected.

To illustrate these concepts, suppose that two companies—Turbo Crafters and Black & Howell—have prepared the following estimated data for the coming year:

	Turbo Crafters	Black & Howell
Allocation base	Machine-hours	Direct materials cost
Estimated manufacturing overhead cost (a)	$300,000	$120,000
Estimated total amount of the allocation base (b)	75,000 machine-hours	$80,000 direct materials cost
Predetermined overhead rate (a) ÷ (b)	$4 per machine-hour	150% of direct materials cost

Note that when the allocation base is dollars (such as direct materials cost in the case of Black & Howell) the predetermined overhead rate is expressed as a percentage of the allocation base. When dollars are divided by dollars, the result is a percentage.

Now assume that because of unexpected changes in overhead spending and in demand for the companies' products, the *actual* overhead cost and the actual activity recorded during the year in each company are as follows:

	Turbo Crafters	Black & Howell
Actual manufacturing overhead cost	$290,000	$130,000
Actual total amount of the allocation base	68,000 machine-hours	$90,000 direct materials cost

For each company, note that the actual data for both cost and the allocation base differ from the estimates used in computing the predetermined overhead rate. This results in underapplied and overapplied overhead as follows:

	Turbo Crafters	Black & Howell
Actual manufacturing overhead cost	$290,000	$130,000
Manufacturing overhead cost applied to Work in Process during the year:		
Predetermined overhead rate (a)	$4 per machine-hour	150% of direct materials cost
Actual total amount of the allocation base (b)	68,000 machine-hours	$90,000 direct materials cost
Manufacturing overhead applied (a) × (b)	$272,000	$135,000
Underapplied (overapplied) manufacturing overhead	$18,000	$(5,000)

For Turbo Crafters, the amount of overhead cost applied to Work in Process ($272,000) is less than the actual overhead cost for the year ($290,000). Therefore, overhead is underapplied.

For Black & Howell, the amount of overhead cost applied to Work in Process ($135,000) is greater than the actual overhead cost for the year ($130,000), so overhead is overapplied.

A summary of these concepts is presented in Exhibit 2–13.

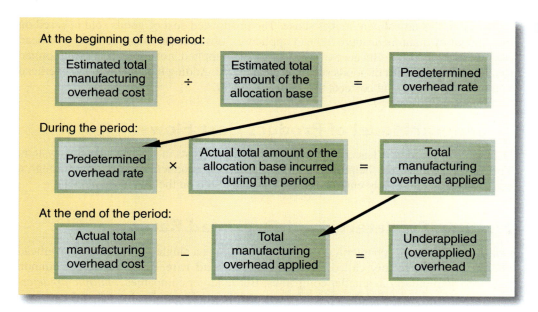

EXHIBIT 2–13
Summary of Overhead Concepts

Disposition of Underapplied or Overapplied Overhead Balances

If we return to the Ruger Corporation example and look at the Manufacturing Overhead T-account in Exhibit 2–10, you will see that there is a debit balance of $5,000. Remember that debit entries to the account represent actual overhead costs incurred, whereas credit entries represent overhead costs applied to jobs. In this case, the actual overhead costs incurred exceeded the overhead costs applied to jobs by $5,000—hence the debit balance of $5,000. This may sound familiar. We just discussed in the previous section the fact that the overhead costs incurred ($95,000) exceeded the overhead costs applied ($90,000), and that the difference is called underapplied overhead. These are just two ways of looking at the same thing. If there is a *debit* balance in the Manufacturing Overhead account of X dollars, then the overhead is *underapplied* by X dollars. On the other hand, if there is a *credit* balance in the Manufacturing Overhead account of Y dollars, then the overhead is *overapplied* by Y dollars.

What happens to any underapplied or overapplied balance remaining in the Manufacturing Overhead account at the end of a period? The simplest method is to close out the balance to Cost of Goods Sold. More complicated methods are sometimes used, but they are beyond the scope of this book. To illustrate the simplest method, recall that Ruger Corporation had underapplied overhead of $5,000. The entry to close this underapplied overhead to Cost of Goods Sold would be

(14)

Cost of Goods Sold.	5,000	
Manufacturing Overhead		5,000

Note that because the Manufacturing Overhead account has a debit balance, Manufacturing Overhead must be credited to close out the account. This has the effect of increasing Cost of Goods Sold for April to $123,500:

Unadjusted cost of goods sold [from entry (13)]	$118,500
Add underapplied overhead [from entry (14)]	5,000
Adjusted cost of goods sold	$123,500

After this adjustment has been made, Ruger Corporation's income statement for April will appear as shown earlier in Exhibit 2–12.

Note that this adjustment makes sense. The unadjusted cost of goods sold is based on the amount of manufacturing overhead applied to jobs, not the manufacturing overhead costs actually incurred. Because overhead was underapplied, not enough cost was applied to jobs. Hence, the cost of goods sold was understated. Adding the underapplied overhead to the cost of goods sold corrects this understatement.

A General Model of Product Cost Flows

Exhibit 2–14 presents a T-account model of the flow of costs in a product costing system. This model can be very helpful in understanding how production costs flow through a costing system and finally end up as Cost of Goods Sold on the income statement.

Multiple Predetermined Overhead Rates

Our discussion in this chapter has assumed that there is a single predetermined overhead rate for an entire factory called a **plantwide overhead rate.** This is a fairly common practice—particularly in smaller companies. But in larger companies, *multiple predetermined overhead rates* are often used. In a **multiple predetermined overhead rate** system each production department may have its own predetermined overhead rate. Such a system, while more complex, is more accurate because it can reflect differences across departments in how overhead costs are incurred. For example, in departments that are relatively labor intensive overhead might be allocated based on direct labor-hours and in departments that are relatively machine intensive overhead might be allocated based on

CONCEPT CHECK

7. The estimated total manufacturing overhead cost is $200,000. The estimated total amount of the allocation base is 40,000 direct labor-hours. The actual total manufacturing overhead cost for the period is $220,000 and the actual direct labor-hours worked on all jobs during the period is 41,000 hours. The total underapplied (overapplied) overhead for the period is:
   a. $20,000 underapplied
   b. $20,000 overapplied
   c. $15,000 underapplied
   d. $15,000 overapplied
8. The predetermined overhead rate is $50 per machine-hour, underapplied overhead is $5,000, and the actual amount of machine-hours is 2,000. What is the actual amount of total manufacturing overhead incurred during the period?
   a. $105,000
   b. $95,000
   c. $150,000
   d. $110,000

EXHIBIT 2-14   A General Model of Cost Flows

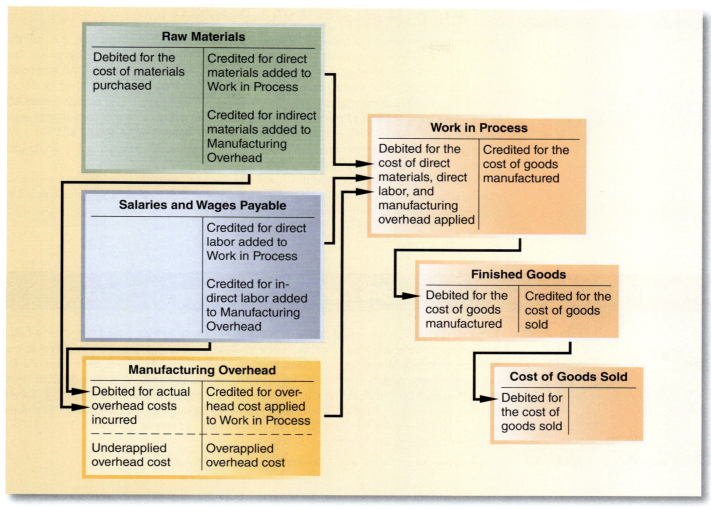

machine-hours. When multiple predetermined overhead rates are used, overhead is applied in each department according to its own overhead rate as jobs proceed through the department.

JOB-ORDER COSTING IN SERVICE COMPANIES

Job-order costing is used in service organizations such as law firms, movie studios, hospitals, and repair shops, as well as in manufacturing companies. In a law firm, for example, each client is a "job," and the costs of that job are accumulated day by day on a job cost sheet as the client's case is handled by the firm. Legal forms and similar inputs represent the direct materials for the job; the time expended by attorneys is like direct labor; and the costs of secretaries and legal aids, rent, depreciation, and so forth, represent the overhead.

In a movie studio such as **Columbia Pictures**, each film produced by the studio is a "job," and costs of direct materials (costumes, props, film, etc.) and direct labor (actors, directors, and extras) are charged to each film's job cost sheet. A share of the studio's overhead costs, such as utilities, depreciation of equipment, wages of maintenance workers, and so forth, is also charged to each film.

In sum, job-order costing is a versatile and widely used costing method that may be encountered in virtually any organization that provides diverse products or services.

DECISION POINT

Treasurer, Class Reunion Committee

You've agreed to handle the financial arrangements for your high school reunion. You call the restaurant where the reunion will be held and jot down the most important information. The meal cost (including beverages) will be $30 per person plus a 15% gratuity. An additional $200 will be charged for a banquet room with a dance floor. A band has been hired for $500. One of the members of the reunion committee informs you that there is just enough money left in the class bank account to cover the printing and mailing costs. He mentions that at least one-half of the class of 400 will attend the reunion and wonders if he should add the 15% gratuity to the $30 per person meal cost when he drafts the invitation, which will indicate that a check must be returned with the reply card.

How should you respond? How much will you need to charge to cover the various costs? After making your decision, label your answer with the managerial accounting terms covered in this chapter. Finally, identify any issues that should be investigated further.

IN BUSINESS

Computing Job Costs at Fast Wrap

In 2007, Michael Enos founded **Fast Wrap**, a company that shrink-wraps everything from jet skis and recreation vehicles (RVs) to entire buildings. Today, the company has 64 locations across America and generates more than $6 million in annual sales. The company's revenues far exceed its direct materials and direct labor costs. For example, Fast Wrap charges customers $400 to wrap a 20-foot boat that requires $25 worth of plastic and $30 worth of labor. Larger jobs are even more profitable. For example, Fast Wrap signed a $250,000 contract to shrink-wrap a 244,000-square-foot hospital under construction in Fontana, California. The materials and labor for this job cost Fast Wrap $44,000.

Source: Susan Adams, "It's a Wrap," *Forbes,* March 15, 2010, pp. 36–38.

SUMMARY

LO2–1 Compute a predetermined overhead rate.

Manufacturing overhead costs are assigned to jobs using a predetermined overhead rate. The rate is determined at the beginning of the period so that jobs can be costed throughout the period rather than waiting until the end of the period. The predetermined overhead rate is determined by dividing the estimated total manufacturing overhead cost for the period by the estimated total amount of the allocation base for the period.

LO2–2 Apply overhead cost to jobs using a predetermined overhead rate.

Overhead is applied to jobs by multiplying the predetermined overhead rate by the actual amount of the allocation base used by the job.

LO2–3 Compute the total cost and average cost per unit of a job.

The total cost of a job includes the actual direct materials and direct labor costs assigned to the job plus the applied overhead. The average cost per unit of a job is computed by dividing the total cost of a job by the number of units included in the job. Importantly, the average cost per unit does not represent the additional cost that would be incurred if another unit were produced.

LO2–4 Understand the flow of costs in a job-order costing system and prepare appropriate journal entries to record costs.
Direct materials costs are debited to Work in Process when they are released for use in production. Direct labor costs are debited to Work in Process as incurred. Actual manufacturing overhead costs are debited to the Manufacturing Overhead account as incurred. Manufacturing overhead costs are applied to Work in Process using the predetermined overhead rate. The journal entry that accomplishes this is a debit to Work in Process and a credit to Manufacturing Overhead.

LO2–5 Use T-accounts to show the flow of costs in a job-order costing system.
See Exhibits 2–10 and 2–14 for summaries of the cost flows through the T-accounts.

LO2–6 Prepare schedules of cost of goods manufactured and cost of goods sold and an income statement.
See Exhibits 2–11 and 2–12 for an example of these schedules and an income statement.

LO2–7 Compute underapplied or overapplied overhead cost and prepare the journal entry to close the balance in Manufacturing Overhead to the appropriate account.
The difference between the actual overhead cost incurred during a period and the amount of overhead cost applied to production is referred to as underapplied or overapplied overhead. Underapplied or overapplied overhead is closed out to Cost of Goods Sold. When overhead is underapplied, the balance in the Manufacturing Overhead account is debited to Cost of Goods Sold. This has the effect of increasing the Cost of Goods Sold and occurs because costs assigned to products have been understated. When overhead is overapplied, the balance in the Manufacturing Overhead account is credited to Cost of Goods Sold. This has the effect of decreasing the Cost of Goods Sold and occurs because costs assigned to products have been overstated.

GUIDANCE ANSWER TO DECISION POINT

Treasurer, Class Reunion Committee (p. 94)
You should charge $38.00 per person to cover the costs calculated as follows:

Meal cost	$30.00	Direct material cost
Gratuity ($30 × 0.15)	4.50	Direct labor cost
Room charge ($200 ÷ 200 expected attendees)	1.00	Overhead cost
Band cost ($500 ÷ 200 expected attendees)	2.50	Overhead cost
Total cost	$38.00	

If exactly 200 classmates attend the reunion, the $7,600 of receipts (200 × $38) will cover the expenditures of $7,600 [meal cost of $6,000 (or 200 × $30) plus gratuity cost of $900 (or $6,000 × 0.15) plus the $200 room charge plus the $500 band cost]. Unfortunately, if less than 200 attend, the Reunion Committee will come up short in an amount equal to the difference between the 200 estimated attendees and the actual number of attendees times $3.50 (the total per person overhead charge). As such, you should talk to the members of the Reunion Committee to ensure that (1) the estimate is as reasonable as possible, and (2) there is a plan to deal with any shortage. On the other hand, if more than 200 attend, the Reunion Committee will collect more money than it needs to disburse. The amount would be equal to the difference between the actual number of attendees and the 200 estimated attendees times $3.50.

GUIDANCE ANSWERS TO CONCEPT CHECKS

1. **Choices c and d.** A predetermined overhead rate rather than an actual overhead rate is used in a normal costing system. A unit product cost does not represent an incremental cost.
2. **Choice d.** At an activity level of 50,000 direct labor-hours, $Y = \$100,000 + (\$3$ per direct labor-hour)(50,000 direct labor-hours). Solving for Y provides an estimated total manufacturing overhead cost of $250,000. The total manufacturing overhead ($250,000) divided by the total estimated direct labor-hours (50,000) equals the predetermined overhead rate of $5 per direct labor-hour.
3. **Choices a, c, and d.** Because manufacturing overhead includes fixed costs, the predetermined overhead rate tends to fluctuate from period to period.
4. **Choice a.** Raw materals are not expensed when purchased. Administrative expenses are period costs; therefore, they are never recorded in the Manufacturing Overhead account. The debit to Accounts Receivable for $200 would be accompanied by a credit to Sales for $200.
5. **Choices a, b, and d.** If the Manufacturing Overhead account has a debit balance at the end of an accounting period, it means that manufacturing overhead was underapplied.
6. **Choices b, c, and d.** Applied manufacturing overhead costs are included in the schedule of cost of goods manufactured. The cost of goods manufactured represents the amount that will be debited to Finished Goods during an accounting period. A change in the finished goods inventory balance has no impact on the cost of goods manufactured.
7. **Choice c.** Actual overhead of $220,000 minus applied overhead of $205,000 ($200,000 ÷ 40,000 direct labor-hours × 41,000 actual hours worked) equals $15,000 underapplied.
8. **Choice a.** The amount of overhead applied to production is 2,000 hours multiplied by the $50 predetermined rate, or $100,000. If overhead is underapplied by $5,000, the actual amount of overhead is $100,000 + $5,000, or $105,000.

REVIEW PROBLEM: JOB-ORDER COSTING

Hogle Corporation is a manufacturer that uses job-order costing. On January 1, the beginning of its fiscal year, the company's inventory balances were as follows:

Raw materials	$20,000
Work in process	$15,000
Finished goods	$30,000

The company applies overhead cost to jobs on the basis of machine-hours worked. For the current year, the company's predetermined overhead rate was based on a cost formula that estimated $450,000 of total manufacturing overhead cost for an estimated activity level of 75,000 machine-hours. The following transactions were recorded for the year:

a. Raw materials were purchased on account, $410,000.
b. Raw materials were requisitioned for use in production, $380,000 ($360,000 direct materials and $20,000 indirect materials).
c. The following costs were accrued for employee services: direct labor, $75,000; indirect labor, $110,000; sales commissions, $90,000; and administrative salaries, $200,000.
d. Sales travel costs were $17,000.
e. Utility costs in the factory were $43,000.
f. Advertising costs were $180,000.
g. Depreciation was recorded for the year, $350,000 (80% relates to factory operations, and 20% relates to selling and administrative activities).
h. Insurance expired during the year, $10,000 (70% relates to factory operations, and the remaining 30% relates to selling and administrative activities).
i. Manufacturing overhead was applied to production. Due to greater than expected demand for its products, the company worked 80,000 machine-hours on all jobs during the year.

j. Goods costing $900,000 to manufacture according to their job cost sheets were completed during the year.

k. Goods were sold on account to customers during the year for a total of $1,500,000. The goods cost $870,000 to manufacture according to their job cost sheets.

Required:

1. Prepare journal entries to record the preceding transactions.
2. Post the entries in (1) above to T-accounts (don't forget to enter the beginning balances in the inventory accounts).
3. Is Manufacturing Overhead underapplied or overapplied for the year? Prepare a journal entry to close any balance in the Manufacturing Overhead account to Cost of Goods Sold.
4. Prepare an income statement for the year.

Solution to Review Problem

1.

a.	Raw Materials	410,000	
	Accounts Payable		410,000
b.	Work in Process	360,000	
	Manufacturing Overhead	20,000	
	Raw Materials		380,000
c.	Work in Process	75,000	
	Manufacturing Overhead	110,000	
	Sales Commissions Expense	90,000	
	Administrative Salaries Expense	200,000	
	Salaries and Wages Payable		475,000
d.	Sales Travel Expense	17,000	
	Accounts Payable		17,000
e.	Manufacturing Overhead	43,000	
	Accounts Payable		43,000
f.	Advertising Expense	180,000	
	Accounts Payable		180,000
g.	Manufacturing Overhead	280,000	
	Depreciation Expense	70,000	
	Accumulated Depreciation		350,000
h.	Manufacturing Overhead	7,000	
	Insurance Expense	3,000	
	Prepaid Insurance		10,000

i. The predetermined overhead rate for the year is computed as follows:

$$\text{Predetermined overhead rate} = \frac{\text{Estimated total manufacturing overhead cost}}{\text{Estimated total amount of the allocation base}}$$

$$= \frac{\$450,000}{75,000 \text{ machine-hours}}$$

$$= \$6 \text{ per machine-hour}$$

Based on the 80,000 machine-hours actually worked during the year, the company applied $480,000 in overhead cost to production: $6 per machine-hour × 80,000 machine-hours = $480,000. The following entry records this application of overhead cost:

	Work in Process	480,000	
	Manufacturing Overhead		480,000
j.	Finished Goods	900,000	
	Work in Process		900,000
k.	Accounts Receivable	1,500,000	
	Sales		1,500,000
	Cost of Goods Sold	870,000	
	Finished Goods		870,000

2.

Accounts Receivable		
(k)	1,500,000	

Prepaid Insurance		
		(h) 10,000

Raw Materials		
Bal.	20,000	(b) 380,000
(a)	410,000	
Bal.	50,000	

Work in Process		
Bal.	15,000	(j) 900,000
(b)	360,000	
(c)	75,000	
(i)	480,000	
Bal.	30,000	

Finished Goods		
Bal.	30,000	(k) 870,000
(j)	900,000	
Bal.	60,000	

Manufacturing Overhead		
(b)	20,000	(i) 480,000
(c)	110,000	
(e)	43,000	
(g)	280,000	
(h)	7,000	
	460,000	480,000
		Bal. 20,000

Accumulated Depreciation		
		(g) 350,000

Accounts Payable		
		(a) 410,000
		(d) 17,000
		(e) 43,000
		(f) 180,000

Salaries and Wages Payable		
		(c) 475,000

Sales		
		(k) 1,500,000

Cost of Goods Sold		
(k)	870,000	

Sales Commissions Expense		
(c)	90,000	

Administrative Salaries Expense		
(c)	200,000	

Sales Travel Expense		
(d)	17,000	

Advertising Expense		
(f)	180,000	

Depreciation Expense		
(g)	70,000	

Insurance Expense		
(h)	3,000	

3.   Manufacturing overhead is overapplied for the year. The entry to close it out to Cost of Goods Sold is as follows:

Manufacturing Overhead	20,000	
Cost of Goods Sold		20,000

4.

Hogle Corporation
Income Statement
For the Year Ended December 31

Sales		$1,500,000
Cost of goods sold ($870,000 − $20,000)		850,000
Gross margin		650,000
Selling and administrative expenses:		
Sales commissions expense	$ 90,000	
Administrative salaries expense	200,000	
Sales travel expense	17,000	
Advertising expense	180,000	
Depreciation expense	70,000	
Insurance expense	3,000	560,000
Net operating income		$ 90,000

GLOSSARY

Absorption costing   A costing method that includes all manufacturing costs—direct materials, direct labor, and both variable and fixed manufacturing overhead—in the cost of a product. (p. 68)

Allocation base   A measure of activity such as direct labor-hours or machine-hours that is used to assign costs to cost objects. (p. 73)

Bill of materials   A document that shows the quantity of each type of direct material required to make a product. (p. 70)

Cost driver   A factor, such as machine-hours, beds occupied, computer time, or flight-hours, that causes overhead costs. (p. 75)

Cost of goods manufactured   The manufacturing costs associated with the goods that were finished during the period. (p. 78)

Finished goods   Units of product that have been completed but not yet sold to customers. (p. 78)

Job cost sheet   A form that records the materials, labor, and manufacturing overhead costs charged to a job. (p. 70)

Job-order costing   A costing system used in situations where many different products, jobs, or services are produced each period. (p. 68)

Materials requisition form   A document that specifies the type and quantity of materials to be drawn from the storeroom and that identifies the job that will be charged for the cost of those materials. (p. 70)

Multiple predetermined overhead rates   A costing system with multiple overhead cost pools and a different predetermined overhead rate for each cost pool, rather than a single predetermined overhead rate for the entire company. Each production department may be treated as a separate overhead cost pool. (p. 92)

Normal cost system   A costing system in which overhead costs are applied to a job by multiplying a predetermined overhead rate by the actual amount of the allocation base incurred by the job. (p. 74)

Overapplied overhead   A credit balance in the Manufacturing Overhead account that occurs when the amount of overhead cost applied to Work in Process exceeds the amount of overhead cost actually incurred during a period. (p. 89)

Overhead application   The process of charging manufacturing overhead cost to job cost sheets and to the Work in Process account. (p. 73)

Plantwide overhead rate   A single predetermined overhead rate that is used throughout a plant. (p. 92)

Predetermined overhead rate   A rate used to charge manufacturing overhead cost to jobs that is established in advance for each period. It is computed by dividing the estimated total manufacturing overhead cost for the period by the estimated total amount of the allocation base for the period. (p. 92)

Raw materials   Any materials that go into the final product. (p. 77)

Schedule of cost of goods manufactured   A schedule that contains three elements of product costs—direct materials, direct labor, and manufacturing overhead—and that summarizes the portions of those costs that remain in ending Work in Process inventory and that are transferred out of Work in Process into Finished Goods. (p. 87)

Schedule of cost of goods sold   A schedule that contains three elements of product costs—direct materials, direct labor, and manufacturing overhead—and that summarizes the portions of those costs that remain in ending Finished Goods inventory and that are transferred out of Finished Goods into Cost of Goods Sold. (p. 87)

Time ticket   A document that is used to record the amount of time an employee spends on various activities. (p. 72)

Underapplied overhead   A debit balance in the Manufacturing Overhead account that occurs when the amount of overhead cost actually incurred exceeds the amount of overhead cost applied to Work in Process during a period. (p. 89)

Work in process   Units of product that are only partially complete and will require further work before they are ready for sale to the customer. (p. 77)

QUESTIONS

2–1   Why aren't actual manufacturing overhead costs traced to jobs just as direct materials and direct labor costs are traced to jobs?

2–2   Explain the four-step process used to compute a predetermined overhead rate.

2–3   What is the purpose of the job cost sheet in a job-order costing system?

2–4   Explain why some production costs must be assigned to products through an allocation process.

2–5   Why do companies use predetermined overhead rates rather than actual manufacturing overhead costs to apply overhead to jobs?

2–6   What factors should be considered in selecting a base to be used in computing the predetermined overhead rate?

2–7   If a company fully allocates all of its overhead costs to jobs, does this guarantee that a profit will be earned for the period?

2–8   What account is credited when overhead cost is applied to Work in Process? Would you expect the amount applied for a period to equal the actual overhead costs of the period? Why or why not?

2–9   What is underapplied overhead? Overapplied overhead? What disposition is made of these amounts at the end of the period?

2–10 Provide two reasons why overhead might be underapplied in a given year.

2–11 What adjustment is made for underapplied overhead on the schedule of cost of goods sold? What adjustment is made for overapplied overhead?

2–12 What is a plantwide overhead rate? Why are multiple overhead rates, rather than a plantwide overhead rate, used in some companies?

2–13 What happens to overhead rates based on direct labor when automated equipment replaces direct labor?

Multiple-choice questions are available in the *Connect Library*.

APPLYING EXCEL    connect
ACCOUNTING

Available with McGraw-Hill's *Connect Accounting*.

LO2–1, LO2–4, LO2–7

The Excel worksheet form that appears below is to be used to recreate part of the example on pages 90. Download the workbook containing this form in the *Connect Library. On the website you will also receive instructions about how to use this worksheet form.*

	A	B	C	D
1	Chapter 2: Applying Excel			
2				
3	Data			
4	Allocation base	Machine-hours		
5	Estimated manufacturing overhead cost	$300,000		
6	Estimated total amount of the allocation base	75,000	machine-hours	
7	Actual manufacturing overhead cost	$290,000		
8	Actual total amount of the allocation base	68,000	machine-hours	
9				
10	Enter a formula into each of the cells marked with a ? below			
11				
12	Computation of the predetermined overhead rate			
13	Estimated manufacturing overhead cost	?		
14	Estimated total amount of the allocation base	?	machine-hours	
15	Predetermined overhead rate	?	per machine-hour	
16				
17	Computation of underapplied or overapplied manufacturing overhead			
18	Actual manufacturing overhead cost	?		
19	Manufacturing overhead cost applied to Work in Process during the year:			
20	Predetermined overhead rate	?	per machine-hour	
21	Actual total amount of the allocation base	?	machine-hours	
22	Manufacturing overhead applied	?		
23	Underapplied (overapplied) manufacturing overhead	?		
24				

You should proceed to the requirements below only after completing your worksheet.

Required:

1. Check your worksheet by changing the estimated total amount of the allocation base in the Data area to 60,000 machine-hours, keeping all of the other data the same as in the original example. If your worksheet is operating properly, the predetermined overhead rate should now be $5.00 per machine-hour. If you do not get this answer, find the errors in your worksheet and correct them.

    How much is the underapplied (overapplied) manufacturing overhead? Did it change? Why or why not?

2. Determine the underapplied (overapplied) manufacturing overhead for a different company with the following data:

Allocation base	Machine-hours
Estimated manufacturing overhead cost	$100,000
Estimated total amount of the allocation base	50,000 machine-hours
Actual manufacturing overhead cost	$90,000
Actual total amount of the allocation base	40,000 machine-hours

3. What happens to the underapplied (overapplied) manufacturing overhead from part (2) if the estimated total amount of the allocation base is changed to 40,000 machine-hours and everything else remains the same? Why is the amount of underapplied (overapplied) manufacturing overhead different from part (2)?

4. Change the estimated total amount of the allocation base back to 50,000 machine-hours so that the data look exactly like they did in part (2). Now change the actual manufacturing overhead cost to $100,000. What is the underapplied (overapplied) manufacturing overhead now? Why is the amount of underapplied (overapplied) manufacturing overhead different from part (2)?

 **|ACCOUNTING**

THE FOUNDATIONAL 15

Available with McGraw-Hill's *Connect Accounting.*

Sweeten Company had no jobs in progress at the beginning of March and no beginning inventories. It started only two jobs during March—Job P and Job Q. Job P was completed and sold by the end of the March and Job Q was incomplete at the end of the March. The company uses a plantwide predetermined overhead rate based on direct labor-hours. The following additional information is available for the company as a whole and for Jobs P and Q (all data and questions relate to the month of March):

LO2–1, LO2–2, LO2–3, LO2–4, LO2–5, LO2–6, LO2–7

Estimated total fixed manufacturing overhead	$10,000
Estimated variable manufacturing overhead per direct labor-hour	$1.00
Estimated total direct labor-hours to be worked	2,000
Total actual manufacturing overhead costs incurred	$12,500

	Job P	Job Q
Direct materials	$13,000	$8,000
Direct labor cost	$21,000	$7,500
Actual direct labor-hours worked	1,400	500

1. What is the company's predetermined overhead rate?
2. How much manufacturing overhead was applied to Job P and Job Q?
3. What is the direct labor hourly wage rate?
4. If Job P includes 20 units, what is its unit product cost? What is the total amount of manufacturing cost assigned to Job Q as of the end of March (including applied overhead)?
5. Assume the ending raw materials inventory is $1,000 and the company does not use any indirect materials. Prepare the journal entries to record raw materials purchases and the issuance of direct materials for use in production.

6. Assume that the company does not use any indirect labor. Prepare the journal entry to record the direct labor costs added to production.
7. Prepare the journal entry to apply manufacturing overhead costs to production.
8. Assume the ending raw materials inventory is $1,000 and the company does not use any indirect materials. Prepare a schedule of cost of goods manufactured.
9. Prepare the journal entry to transfer costs from Work in Process to Finished Goods.
10. Prepare a completed Work in Process T-account including the beginning and ending balances and all debits and credits posted to the account.
11. Prepare a schedule of cost of goods sold. (Stop after computing the unadjusted cost of goods sold.)
12. Prepare the journal entry to transfer costs from Finished Goods to Cost of Goods Sold.
13. What is the amount of underapplied or overapplied overhead?
14. Prepare the journal entry to close the amount of underapplied or overapplied overhead to Cost of Goods Sold.
15. Assume that Job P includes 20 units that each sell for $3,000 and that the company's selling and administrative expenses in March were $14,000. Prepare an absorption costing income statement for March.

EXERCISES

All applicable exercises are available with McGraw-Hill's *Connect Accounting.*

Estimated direct labor-hours = 18,000

EXERCISE 2–1   Compute the Predetermined Overhead Rate [LO2–1]
Harris Fabrics computes its predetermined overhead rate annually on the basis of direct labor-hours. At the beginning of the year, it estimated that 20,000 direct labor-hours would be required for the period's estimated level of production. The company also estimated $94,000 of fixed manufacturing overhead expenses for the coming period and variable manufacturing overhead of $2.00 per direct labor-hour. Harris's actual manufacturing overhead for the year was $123,900 and its actual total direct labor was 21,000 hours.

Required:
Compute the company's predetermined overhead rate for the year.

Actual total manufacturing overhead costs = $270,000

EXERCISE 2–2   Apply Overhead [LO2–2]
Luthan Company uses a predetermined overhead rate of $23.40 per direct labor-hour. This predetermined rate was based on a cost formula that estimated $257,400 of total manufacturing overhead for an estimated activity level of 11,000 direct labor-hours.

The company incurred actual total manufacturing overhead costs of $249,000 and 10,800 total direct labor-hours during the period.

Required:
Determine the amount of manufacturing overhead that would have been applied to all jobs during the period.

Predetermined overhead rate = $24 per DLH

EXERCISE 2–3   Computing Job Costs [LO2–3]
Mickley Company's predetermined overhead rate is $14.00 per direct labor-hour and its direct labor wage rate is $12.00 per hour. The following information pertains to Job A-500:

Direct materials.	$230
Direct labor	$108

Required:
1. What is the total manufacturing cost assigned to Job A-500?
2. If Job A-500 consists of 40 units, what is the average cost assigned to each unit included in the job?

EXERCISE 2–4   Prepare Journal Entries [LO2–4]
Larned Corporation recorded the following transactions for the just completed month.
a. $80,000 in raw materials were purchased on account.
b. $71,000 in raw materials were requisitioned for use in production. Of this amount, $62,000 was for direct materials and the remainder was for indirect materials.

c.   Total labor wages of $112,000 were incurred. Of this amount, $101,000 was for direct labor and the remainder was for indirect labor.

d.   Additional manufacturing overhead costs of $175,000 were incurred.

Required:

Record the above transactions in journal entries.

EXERCISE 2–5   Prepare T-Accounts [LO2–5, LO2–7]

Jurvin Enterprises recorded the following transactions for the just completed month. The company had no beginning inventories.

a. $94,000 in raw materials were purchased for cash.

b. $89,000 in raw materials were requisitioned for use in production. Of this amount, $78,000 was for direct materials and the remainder was for indirect materials.

c.   Total labor wages of $132,000 were incurred and paid. Of this amount, $112,000 was for direct labor and the remainder was for indirect labor.

d.   Additional manufacturing overhead costs of $143,000 were incurred and paid.

e.   Manufacturing overhead costs of $152,000 were applied to jobs using the company's predetermined overhead rate.

f.   All of the jobs in progress at the end of the month were completed and shipped to customers.

g.   Any underapplied or overapplied overhead for the period was closed out to Cost of Goods Sold.

Required:

1.   Post the above transactions to T-accounts.

2.   Determine the cost of goods sold for the period.

EXERCISE 2–6   Schedules of Cost of Goods Manufactured and Cost of Goods Sold [LO2–6]

Primare Corporation has provided the following data concerning last month's manufacturing operations:

Purchases of raw materials	$30,000
Indirect materials included in manufacturing overhead	$5,000
Direct labor	$58,000
Manufacturing overhead applied to work in process	$87,000
Underapplied overhead	$4,000

Inventories	Beginning	Ending
Raw materials	$12,000	$18,000
Work in process	$56,000	$65,000
Finished goods	$35,000	$42,000

Ending raw material inventory = $25,000; Ending work in process inventory = $43,000

Required:

1.   Prepare a schedule of cost of goods manufactured for the month.

2.   Prepare a schedule of cost of goods sold for the month.

EXERCISE 2–7   Underapplied and Overapplied Overhead [LO2–7]

Osborn Manufacturing uses a predetermined overhead rate of $18.20 per direct labor-hour. This predetermined rate was based on a cost formula that estimates $218,400 of total manufacturing overhead for an estimated activity level of 12,000 direct labor-hours.

The company incurred actual total manufacturing overhead costs of $215,000 and 11,500 total direct labor-hours during the period.

Actual total manufacturing overhead costs = $198,000

Required:

1.   Determine the amount of underapplied or overapplied manufacturing overhead for the period.

2.   Assuming that the entire amount of the underapplied or overapplied overhead is closed out to Cost of Goods Sold, what would be the effect of the underapplied or overapplied overhead on the company's gross margin for the period?

EXERCISE 2–8   Applying Overhead; Computing Unit Product Cost [LO2–2, LO2–3]

A company assigns overhead cost to completed jobs on the basis of 125% of direct labor cost. The job cost sheet for Job 313 shows that $10,000 in direct materials has been used on the job and that $12,000 in direct labor cost has been incurred. A total of 1,000 units were produced in Job 313.

Direct labor charges for Job 313 = $10,000

Required:
What is the total manufacturing cost assigned to Job 313? What is the unit product cost for Job 313?

EXERCISE 2–9   Journal Entries and T-accounts [LO2–2, LO2–4, LO2–5]
The Polaris Company uses a job-order costing system. The following data relate to October, the first month of the company's fiscal year.

a.   Raw materials purchased on account, $210,000.
b.   Raw materials issued to production, $190,000 ($178,000 direct materials and $12,000 indirect materials).
c.   Direct labor cost incurred, $90,000; indirect labor cost incurred, $110,000.
d.   Depreciation recorded on factory equipment, $40,000.
e.   Other manufacturing overhead costs incurred during October, $70,000 (credit Accounts Payable).
f.   The company applies manufacturing overhead cost to production on the basis of $8 per machine-hour. A total of 30,000 machine-hours were recorded for October.
g.   Production orders costing $520,000 according to their job cost sheets were completed during October and transferred to Finished Goods.
h.   Production orders that had cost $480,000 to complete according to their job cost sheets were shipped to customers during the month. These goods were sold on account at 25% above cost.

Required:
1.   Prepare journal entries to record the information given above.
2.   Prepare T-accounts for Manufacturing Overhead and Work in Process. Post the relevant information above to each account. Compute the ending balance in each account, assuming that Work in Process has a beginning balance of $42,000.

EXERCISE 2–10   Applying Overhead to a Job [LO2–2]
Sigma Corporation applies overhead cost to jobs on the basis of direct labor cost. Job V, which was started and completed during the current period, shows charges of $5,000 for direct materials, $8,000 for direct labor, and $6,000 for overhead on its job cost sheet. Job W, which is still in process at year-end, shows charges of $2,500 for direct materials and $4,000 for direct labor.

Direct labor charges for Job V = $2,000

Required:
Should any overhead cost be added to Job W at year-end? If so, how much? Explain.

EXERCISE 2–11   Schedules of Cost of Goods Manufactured and Cost of Goods Sold; Income Statement [LO2–6]
The following data from the just completed year are taken from the accounting records of Mason Company:

Ending raw material inventory = $8,000; Ending work in process inventory = $16,000

Sales	$524,000
Direct labor cost	$70,000
Raw material purchases	$118,000
Selling expenses	$140,000
Administrative expenses	$63,000
Manufacturing overhead applied to work in process	$90,000
Actual manufacturing overhead costs	$80,000

Inventories	Beginning of Year	End of Year
Raw materials	$7,000	$15,000
Work in process	$10,000	$5,000
Finished goods	$20,000	$35,000

Required:
1.   Prepare a schedule of cost of goods manufactured. Assume all raw materials used in production were direct materials.
2.   Prepare a schedule of cost of goods sold.
3.   Prepare an income statement.

EXERCISE 2–12   Applying Overhead; Cost of Goods Manufactured [LO2–2, LO2–6, LO2–7]

The following cost data relate to the manufacturing activities of Chang Company during the just completed year:

TAKE TWO

Purchases of raw materials = $350,000

Manufacturing overhead costs incurred:	
Indirect materials	$ 15,000
Indirect labor	130,000
Property taxes, factory	8,000
Utilities, factory	70,000
Depreciation, factory	240,000
Insurance, factory	10,000
Total actual manufacturing overhead costs incurred	$473,000
Other costs incurred:	
Purchases of raw materials (both direct and indirect)	$400,000
Direct labor cost	$60,000
Inventories:	
Raw materials, beginning	$20,000
Raw materials, ending	$30,000
Work in process, beginning	$40,000
Work in process, ending	$70,000

The company uses a predetermined overhead rate to apply overhead cost to jobs. The rate for the year was $25 per machine-hour. A total of 19,400 machine-hours was recorded for the year.

Required:

1. Compute the amount of underapplied or overapplied overhead cost for the year.
2. Prepare a schedule of cost of goods manufactured for the year.

EXERCISE 2–13   Varying Predetermined Overhead Rates [LO2–1, LO2–2, LO2–3]

Kingsport Containers Company makes a single product that is subject to wide seasonal variations in demand. The company uses a job-order costing system and computes predetermined overhead rates on a quarterly basis using the number of units to be produced as the allocation base. Its estimated costs, by quarter, for the coming year are given below:

	Quarter			
	First	**Second**	**Third**	**Fourth**
Direct materials	$240,000	$120,000	$ 60,000	$180,000
Direct labor	128,000	64,000	32,000	96,000
Manufacturing overhead.................	300,000	220,000	180,000	?
Total manufacturing costs (a)	$668,000	$404,000	$272,000	$?
Number of units to be produced (b)	80,000	40,000	20,000	60,000
Estimated unit product cost (a) ÷ (b)	$8.35	$10.10	$13.60	?

Management finds the variation in quarterly unit product costs to be confusing and difficult to work with. It has been suggested that the problem lies with manufacturing overhead because it is the largest element of total manufacturing cost. Accordingly, you have been asked to find a more appropriate way of assigning manufacturing overhead cost to units of product.

Required:

1. Using the high-low method, estimate the fixed manufacturing overhead cost per quarter and the variable manufacturing overhead cost per unit. Create a cost formula to estimate the total manufacturing overhead cost for the fourth quarter. Compute the total manufacturing cost and unit product cost for the fourth quarter.
2. What is causing the estimated unit product cost to fluctuate from one quarter to the next?
3. How would you recommend stabilizing the company's unit product cost? Support your answer with computations that adapt the cost formula you created in requirement 1.

TAKE TWO

Machine-hours required to
support estimated
production = 120,000

EXERCISE 2–14   Computing Predetermined Overhead Rates and Job Costs [LO2–1, LO2–2, LO2–3, LO2–7]

Moody Corporation uses a job-order costing system with a plantwide overhead rate based on machine-hours. At the beginning of the year, the company made the following estimates:

Machine-hours required to support estimated production	100,000
Fixed manufacturing overhead cost	$650,000
Variable manufacturing overhead cost per machine-hour	$3.00

Required:

1. Compute the predetermined overhead rate.
2. During the year, Job 400 was started and completed. The following information was available with respect to this job:

Direct materials requisitioned	$450
Direct labor cost	$210
Machine-hours used	40

   Compute the total manufacturing cost assigned to Job 400.
3. During the year, the company worked a total of 146,000 machine-hours on all jobs and incurred actual manufacturing overhead costs of $1,350,000. What is the amount of underapplied or overapplied overhead for the year? If this amount were closed out entirely to Cost of Goods Sold would the journal entry increase or decrease net operating income?

EXERCISE 2–15   Departmental Overhead Rates [LO2–1, LO2–2, LO2–3]

White Company has two departments, Cutting and Finishing. The company uses a job-order costing system and computes a predetermined overhead rate in each department. The Cutting Department bases its rate on machine-hours, and the Finishing Department bases its rate on direct labor-hours. At the beginning of the year, the company made the following estimates:

	Department	
	Cutting	**Finishing**
Direct labor-hours	6,000	30,000
Machine-hours	48,000	5,000
Total fixed manufacturing overhead cost	$264,000	$366,000
Variable manufacturing overhead per machine-hour	$2.00	—
Variable manufacturing overhead per direct labor-hour	—	$4.00

Required:

1. Compute the predetermined overhead rate to be used in each department.
2. Assume that the overhead rates that you computed in (1) above are in effect. The job cost sheet for Job 203, which was started and completed during the year, showed the following:

	Department	
	Cutting	**Finishing**
Direct labor-hours	6	20
Machine-hours	80	4
Materials requisitioned	$500	$310
Direct labor cost	$70	$150

   Compute the total manufacturing cost assigned to Job 203.

3. Would you expect substantially different amounts of overhead cost to be assigned to some jobs if the company used a plantwide overhead rate based on direct labor-hours, rather than using departmental rates? Explain. No computations are necessary.

EXERCISE 2–16 Applying Overhead; Journal Entries; Disposition of Underapplied or Overapplied Overhead [LO2–4, LO2–5, LO2–7]

The following information is taken from the accounts of Latta Company. The entries in the T-accounts are summaries of the transactions that affected those accounts during the year.

Manufacturing Overhead				Work in Process			
(a)	460,000	(b)	390,000	Bal.	15,000	(c)	710,000
Bal.	70,000				260,000		
					85,000		
				(b)	390,000		
				Bal.	40,000		

Finished Goods				Cost of Goods Sold			
Bal.	50,000	(d)	640,000	(d)	640,000		
(c)	710,000						
Bal.	120,000						

Required:
1. Identify reasons for entries (a) through (d).
2. Assume that the company closes any balance in the Manufacturing Overhead account directly to Cost of Goods Sold. Prepare the necessary journal entry.

EXERCISE 2–17 Plantwide and Departmental Overhead Rates; Job Costs [LO2–1, LO2–2, LO2–3]

Delph Company uses a job-order costing system and has two manufacturing departments—Molding and Fabrication. The company provided the following estimates at the beginning of the year:

	Molding	Fabrication	Total
Machine-hours	20,000	30,000	50,000
Fixed manufacturing overhead costs	$700,000	$210,000	$910,000
Variable manufacturing overhead per machine-hour	$3.00	$3.00	

During the year, the company had no beginning or ending inventories and it started, completed, and sold only two jobs—Job D-70 and Job C-200. It provided the following information related to those two jobs:

Job D-70	Molding	Fabrication	Total
Direct materials cost	$375,000	$325,000	$700,000
Direct labor cost	$200,000	$160,000	$360,000
Machine-hours	14,000	6,000	20,000

Job C-200	Molding	Fabrication	Total
Direct materials cost	$300,000	$250,000	$550,000
Direct labor cost	$175,000	$225,000	$400,000
Machine-hours	6,000	24,000	30,000

Delph had no overapplied or underapplied manufacturing overhead during the year.

Required:

1. Assume Delph uses a plantwide overhead rate based on machine-hours.
   a. Compute the predetermined plantwide overhead rate.
   b. Compute the total manufacturing costs assigned to Job D-70 and Job C-200.
   c. If Delph establishes bid prices that are 150% of total manufacturing costs, what bid price would it have established for Job D-70 and Job C-200?
   d. What is Delph's cost of goods sold for the year?
2. Assume Delph uses departmental overhead rates based on machine-hours.
   a. Compute the predetermined departmental overhead rates.
   b. Compute the total manufacturing costs assigned to Job D-70 and Job C-200.
   c. If Delph establishes bid prices that are 150% of total manufacturing costs, what bid price would it have established for Job D-70 and Job C-200?
   d. What is Delph's cost of goods sold for the year?
3. What managerial insights are revealed by the computations that you performed in this problem? (*Hint:* Do the cost of goods sold amounts that you computed in requirements 1 and 2 differ from one another? Do the bid prices that you computed in requirements 1 and 2 differ from one another? Why?)

TAKE TWO

Estimated variable manufacturing overhead per machine-hour = $0.75

EXERCISE 2–18 Applying Overhead; T-accounts; Journal Entries [LO2–1, LO2–2, LO2–4, LO2–5, LO2–7]

Harwood Company uses a job-order costing system. Overhead costs are applied to jobs on the basis of machine-hours. At the beginning of the year, management estimated that 80,000 machine-hours would be required for the period's estimated level of production. The company also estimated $128,000 of fixed manufacturing overhead expenses for the coming period and variable manufacturing overhead of $0.80 per machine-hour.

Required:

1. Compute the company's predetermined overhead rate.
2. Assume that during the year the company works only 75,000 machine-hours and incurs the following costs in the Manufacturing Overhead and Work in Process accounts:

Manufacturing Overhead			Work in Process		
(Maintenance)	21,000	?	(Direct materials)	710,000	
(Indirect materials)	8,000		(Direct labor)	90,000	
(Indirect labor)	60,000		(Overhead)	?	
(Utilities)	32,000				
(Insurance)	7,000				
(Depreciation)	56,000				

Copy the data in the T-accounts above onto your answer sheet. Compute the amount of overhead cost that would be applied to Work in Process for the year and make the entry in your T-accounts.
3. Compute the amount of underapplied or overapplied overhead for the year and show the balance in your Manufacturing Overhead T-account. Prepare a journal entry to close out the balance in this account to Cost of Goods Sold.
4. Explain why the manufacturing overhead was underapplied or overapplied for the year.

EXERCISE 2–19 Applying Overhead in a Service Company [LO2–1, LO2–2, LO2–3]

Leeds Architectural Consultants began operations on January 2. The following activity was recorded in the company's Work in Process account for the first month of operations:

Work in Process			
Costs of subcontracted work	230,000	To completed projects	390,000
Direct staff costs	75,000		
Studio overhead	120,000		

Leeds Architectural Consultants is a service firm, so the names of the accounts it uses are different from the names used in manufacturing companies. Costs of Subcontracted Work is comparable to Direct Materials; Direct Staff Costs is the same as Direct Labor; Studio Overhead is the same as Manufacturing Overhead; and Completed Projects is the same as Finished Goods. Apart from the difference in terms, the accounting methods used by the company are identical to the methods used by manufacturing companies.

Leeds Architectural Consultants uses a job-order costing system and applies studio overhead to Work in Process on the basis of direct staff costs. At the end of January, only one job was still in process. This job (Lexington Gardens Project) had been charged with $6,500 in direct staff costs.

Required:
1. Compute the predetermined overhead rate that was in use during January.
2. Complete the following job cost sheet for the partially completed Lexington Gardens Project:

Job Cost Sheet—Lexington Gardens Project As of January 31	
Costs of subcontracted work	$?
Direct staff costs	?
Studio overhead	?
Total cost to January 31	$?

EXERCISE 2–20 Applying Overhead; Journal Entries; T-accounts [LO2–1, LO2–2, LO2–3, LO2–4, LO2–5]

Dillon Products manufactures various machined parts to customer specifications. The company uses a job-order costing system and applies overhead cost to jobs on the basis of machine-hours. At the beginning of the year, the company used a cost formula to estimate that it would incur $4,800,000 in manufacturing overhead costs at an activity level of 240,000 machine-hours.

The company spent the entire month of January working on a large order for 16,000 custommade machined parts. The company had no work in process at the beginning of January. Cost data relating to January follow:

a. Raw materials purchased on account, $325,000.
b. Raw materials requisitioned for production, $290,000 (80% direct materials and 20% indirect materials).
c. Labor cost incurred in the factory, $180,000 (one-third direct labor and two-thirds indirect labor).
d. Depreciation recorded on factory equipment, $75,000.
e. Other manufacturing overhead costs incurred, $62,000 (credit Accounts Payable).
f. Manufacturing overhead cost was applied to production on the basis of 15,000 machine-hours actually worked during the month.
g. The completed job was moved into the finished goods warehouse on January 31 to await delivery to the customer. (In computing the dollar amount for this entry, remember that the cost of a completed job consists of direct materials, direct labor, and *applied* overhead.)

Required:
1. Prepare journal entries to record items (a) through (f) above [ignore item (g) for the moment].
2. Prepare T-accounts for Manufacturing Overhead and Work in Process. Post the relevant items from your journal entries to these T-accounts.
3. Prepare a journal entry for item (g) above.
4. Compute the unit product cost that will appear on the job cost sheet.

PROBLEMS

Alternate problem set is available in the *Connect Library*.

All applicable problems are available with McGraw-Hill's *Connect Accounting*.

PROBLEM 2–21A   T-Account Analysis of Cost Flows [LO2–1, LO2–5, LO2–6, LO2–7]
Selected T-accounts of Moore Company are given below for the just completed year:

Raw Materials					Manufacturing Overhead			
Bal. 1/1	15,000	Credits	?		Debits	230,000	Credits	?
Debits	120,000							
Bal. 12/31	25,000							

Work in Process					Factory Wages Payable			
Bal. 1/1	20,000	Credits	470,000		Debits	185,000	Bal. 1/1	9,000
Direct materials	90,000						Credits	180,000
Direct labor	150,000						Bal. 12/31	4,000
Overhead	240,000							
Bal. 12/31	?							

Finished Goods					Cost of Goods Sold		
Bal. 1/1	40,000	Credits	?		Debits	?	
Debits	?						
Bal. 12/31	60,000						

Required:

1. What was the cost of raw materials put into production during the year?
2. How much of the materials in (1) above consisted of indirect materials?
3. How much of the factory labor cost for the year consisted of indirect labor?
4. What was the cost of goods manufactured for the year?
5. What was the cost of goods sold for the year (before considering underapplied or overapplied overhead)?
6. If overhead is applied to production on the basis of direct labor cost, what rate was in effect during the year?
7. Was manufacturing overhead underapplied or overapplied? By how much?
8. Compute the ending balance in the Work in Process inventory account. Assume that this balance consists entirely of goods started during the year. If $8,000 of this balance is direct labor cost, how much of it is direct materials cost? Manufacturing overhead cost?

PROBLEM 2–22A   Predetermined Overhead Rate; Disposition of Underapplied or Overapplied Overhead [LO2–1, LO2–7]
Luzadis Company makes furniture using the latest automated technology. The company uses a job-order costing system and applies manufacturing overhead cost to products on the basis of machine-hours. The following estimates were used in preparing the predetermined overhead rate at the beginning of the year:

Machine-hours	75,000
Fixed manufacturing overhead cost	$795,000
Variable manufacturing overhead per computer-hour	$1.40

During the year, a glut of furniture on the market resulted in cutting back production and a buildup of furniture in the company's warehouse. The company's cost records revealed the following actual cost and operating data for the year:

Machine-hours	60,000
Manufacturing overhead cost	$850,000

Required:
1. Compute the company's predetermined overhead rate.
2. Compute the underapplied or overapplied overhead.
3. Assume that the company closes any underapplied or overapplied overhead directly to Cost of Goods Sold. Prepare the appropriate journal entry.

PROBLEM 2–23A Schedules of Cost of Goods Manufactured and Cost of Goods Sold; Income Statement [LO2–6]

Superior Company provided the following account balances for the year ended December 31 (all raw materials are used in production as direct materials):

Selling expenses	$140,000
Purchases of raw materials	$290,000
Direct labor	?
Administrative expenses	$100,000
Manufacturing overhead applied to work in process	$285,000
Total actual manufacturing overhead costs	$270,000

Inventory balances at the beginning and end of the year were as follows:

	Beginning of Year	End of Year
Raw materials	$40,000	$10,000
Work in process	?	$35,000
Finished goods	$50,000	?

The total manufacturing costs for the year were $683,000; the cost of goods available for sale totaled $740,000; the unadjusted cost of goods sold totaled $660,000; and the net operating income was $30,000. The company's overapplied or underapplied overhead is closed entirely to Cost of Goods Sold.

Required:
Prepare schedules of cost of goods manufactured and cost of goods sold and an income statement. (*Hint:* Prepare the income statement and schedule of cost of goods sold first followed by the schedule of cost of goods manufactured.)

PROBLEM 2–24A Multiple Departments; Applying Overhead [LO2–1, LO2–2, LO2–3, LO2–7]

High Desert Potteryworks makes a variety of pottery products that it sells to retailers such as Home Depot. The company uses a job-order costing system in which predetermined overhead rates are used to apply manufacturing overhead cost to jobs. The predetermined overhead rate in the Molding Department is based on machine-hours, and the rate in the Painting Department is based on direct labor-hours. At the beginning of the year, the company's management made the following estimates:

	Department	
	Molding	**Painting**
Direct labor-hours	12,000	60,000
Machine-hours	70,000	8,000
Direct materials cost	$510,000	$650,000
Direct labor cost	$130,000	$420,000
Fixed manufacturing overhead cost	$497,000	$615,000
Variable manufacturing overhead per machine-hour	$1.50	–
Variable manufacturing overhead per direct labor-hour	–	$2.00

Job 205 was started on August 1 and completed on August 10. The company's cost records show the following information concerning the job:

	Department	
	Molding	**Painting**
Direct labor-hours	30	84
Machine-hours	110	20
Materials placed into production	$470	$332
Direct labor cost	$325	$588

Required:

1. Compute the predetermined overhead rate used during the year in the Molding Department. Compute the rate used in the Painting Department.
2. Compute the total overhead cost applied to Job 205.
3. What would be the total cost recorded for Job 205? If the job contained 50 units, what would be the unit product cost?
4. At the end of the year, the records of High Desert Potteryworks revealed the following *actual* cost and operating data for all jobs worked on during the year:

	Department	
	Molding	**Painting**
Direct labor-hours	10,000	62,000
Machine-hours	65,000	9,000
Direct materials cost	$430,000	$680,000
Direct labor cost	$108,000	$436,000
Manufacturing overhead cost	$570,000	$750,000

What was the amount of underapplied or overapplied overhead in each department at the end of the year?

PROBLEM 2–25A   Schedule of Cost of Goods Manufactured; Overhead Analysis [LO2–1, LO2–2, LO2–3, LO2–6, LO2–7]

Gitano Products operates a job-order costing system and applies overhead cost to jobs on the basis of direct materials *used in production* (*not* on the basis of raw materials purchased). Its predetermined overhead rate was based on a cost formula that estimated $800,000 of manufacturing overhead for an estimated allocation base of $500,000 direct material dollars to be used in production. The company has provided the following data for the just completed year:

Purchase of raw materials	$510,000
Direct labor cost	$90,000
Manufacturing overhead costs:	
Indirect labor	$170,000
Property taxes	$48,000
Depreciation of equipment	$260,000
Maintenance	$95,000
Insurance	$7,000
Rent, building	$180,000

	Beginning	**Ending**
Raw Materials	$20,000	$80,000
Work in Process	$150,000	$70,000
Finished Goods	$260,000	$400,000

Required:

1. a. Compute the predetermined overhead rate for the year.
   b. Compute the amount of underapplied or overapplied overhead for the year.
2. Prepare a schedule of cost of goods manufactured for the year. Assume all raw materials are used in production as direct materials.
3. Compute the unadjusted cost of goods sold for the year. (Do not include any underapplied or overapplied overhead in your cost of goods sold figure.)
4. Job 215 was started and completed during the year. What price would have been charged to the customer if the job required $8,500 in direct materials and $2,700 in direct labor cost and the company priced its jobs at 25% above the job's cost according to the accounting system?
5. Direct materials made up $24,000 of the $70,000 ending Work in Process inventory balance. Supply the information missing below:

Direct materials	$24,000
Direct labor	?
Manufacturing overhead	?
Work in process inventory	$70,000

PROBLEM 2–26A   Journal Entries; T-Accounts; Financial Statements [LO2–1, LO2–2, LO2–3, LO2–4, LO2–5, LO2–6, LO2–7]

Froya Fabrikker A/S of Bergen, Norway, is a small company that manufactures specialty heavy equipment for use in North Sea oil fields. The company uses a job-order costing system and applies manufacturing overhead cost to jobs on the basis of direct labor-hours. Its predetermined overhead rate was based on a cost formula that estimated $360,000 of manufacturing overhead for an estimated allocation base of 900 direct labor-hours. The following transactions took place during the year (all purchases and services were acquired on account):

a. Raw materials were purchased for use in production, $200,000.
b. Raw materials were requisitioned for use in production (all direct materials), $185,000.
c. Utility bills were incurred, $70,000 (90% related to factory operations, and the remainder related to selling and administrative activities).
d. Salary and wage costs were incurred:

Direct labor (975 hours)	$230,000
Indirect labor	$90,000
Selling and administrative salaries	$110,000

e. Maintenance costs were incurred in the factory, $54,000.
f. Advertising costs were incurred, $136,000.
g. Depreciation was recorded for the year, $95,000 (80% related to factory equipment, and the remainder related to selling and administrative equipment).
h. Rental cost incurred on buildings, $120,000 (85% related to factory operations, and the remainder related to selling and administrative facilities).
i. Manufacturing overhead cost was applied to jobs, $? .
j. Cost of goods manufactured for the year, $770,000.
k. Sales for the year (all on account) totaled $1,200,000. These goods cost $800,000 according to their job cost sheets.

The balances in the inventory accounts at the beginning of the year were as follows:

Raw Materials	$30,000
Work in Process	$21,000
Finished Goods	$60,000

Required:

1. Prepare journal entries to record the preceding data.
2. Post your entries to T-accounts. (Don't forget to enter the beginning inventory balances above.) Determine the ending balances in the inventory accounts and in the Manufacturing Overhead account.

3. Prepare a schedule of cost of goods manufactured.
4. Prepare a journal entry to close any balance in the Manufacturing Overhead account to Cost of Goods Sold. Prepare a schedule of cost of goods sold.
5. Prepare an income statement for the year.
6. Job 412 was one of the many jobs started and completed during the year. The job required $8,000 in direct materials and 39 hours of direct labor time at a total direct labor cost of $9,200. The job contained only four units. If the company bills at a price 60% above the unit product cost on the job cost sheet, what price per unit would have been charged to the customer?

PROBLEM 2–27A   Comprehensive Problem [LO2–1, LO2–2, LO2–4, LO2–5, LO2–7]

Gold Nest Company of Guandong, China, is a family-owned enterprise that makes birdcages for the South China market. The company sells its birdcages through an extensive network of street vendors who receive commissions on their sales. All of the company's transactions with customers, employees, and suppliers are conducted in cash; there is no credit.

The company uses a job-order costing system in which overhead is applied to jobs on the basis of direct labor cost. Its predetermined overhead rate is based on a cost formula that estimated $330,000 of manufacturing overhead for an estimated activity level of $200,000 direct labor dollars. At the beginning of the year, the inventory balances were as follows:

Raw materials	$25,000
Work in process	$10,000
Finished goods	$40,000

During the year, the following transactions were completed:

a. Raw materials purchased for cash, $275,000.
b. Raw materials requisitioned for use in production, $280,000 (materials costing $220,000 were charged directly to jobs; the remaining materials were indirect).
c. Costs for employee services were incurred as follows:

Direct labor	$180,000
Indirect labor	$72,000
Sales commissions	$63,000
Administrative salaries	$90,000

d. Rent for the year was $18,000 ($13,000 of this amount related to factory operations, and the remainder related to selling and administrative activities).
e. Utility costs incurred in the factory, $57,000.
f. Advertising costs incurred, $140,000.
g. Depreciation recorded on equipment, $100,000. ($88,000 of this amount was on equipment used in factory operations; the remaining $12,000 was on equipment used in selling and administrative activities.)
h. Manufacturing overhead cost was applied to jobs, $? .
i. Goods that had cost $675,000 to manufacture according to their job cost sheets were completed.
j. Sales for the year totaled $1,250,000. The total cost to manufacture these goods according to their job cost sheets was $700,000.

Required:
1. Prepare journal entries to record the transactions for the year.
2. Prepare T-accounts for inventories, Manufacturing Overhead, and Cost of Goods Sold. Post relevant data from your journal entries to these T-accounts (don't forget to enter the beginning balances in your inventory accounts). Compute an ending balance in each account.
3. Is Manufacturing Overhead underapplied or overapplied for the year? Prepare a journal entry to close any balance in the Manufacturing Overhead account to Cost of Goods Sold.
4. Prepare an income statement for the year. (Do not prepare a schedule of cost of goods manufactured; all of the information needed for the income statement is available in the journal entries and T-accounts you have prepared.)

PROBLEM 2–28A Cost Flows; T-Accounts; Income Statement [LO2–1, LO2–2, LO2–5, LO2–6, LO2–7]

Supreme Videos, Inc., produces short musical videos for sale to retail outlets. The company's balance sheet accounts as of January 1, the beginning of its fiscal year, are given below.

Supreme Videos, Inc.
Balance Sheet
January 1

Assets

Current assets:		
Cash		$ 63,000
Accounts receivable		102,000
Inventories:		
Raw materials (film, costumes)	$ 30,000	
Videos in process	45,000	
Finished videos awaiting sale	81,000	156,000
Prepaid insurance		9,000
Total current assets		330,000
Studio and equipment	730,000	
Less accumulated depreciation	210,000	520,000
Total assets		$850,000

Liabilities and Stockholders' Equity

Accounts payable		$160,000
Capital stock	$420,000	
Retained earnings	270,000	690,000
Total liabilities and stockholders' equity		$850,000

Because the videos differ in length and in complexity of production, the company uses a job-order costing system to determine the cost of each video produced. Studio (manufacturing) overhead is charged to videos on the basis of camera-hours of activity. The company's predetermined overhead rate for the year is based on a cost formula that estimated $280,000 in manufacturing overhead for an estimated allocation base of 7,000 camera-hours. The following transactions were recorded for the year:

a. Film, costumes, and similar raw materials purchased on account, $185,000.
b. Film, costumes, and other raw materials issued to production, $200,000 (85% of this material was considered direct to the videos in production, and the other 15% was considered indirect).
c. Utility costs incurred in the production studio, $72,000.
d. Depreciation recorded on the studio, cameras, and other equipment, $84,000. Three-fourths of this depreciation related to actual production of the videos, and the remainder related to equipment used in marketing and administration.
e. Advertising expense incurred, $130,000.
f. Costs for salaries and wages were incurred as follows:

Direct labor (actors and directors)	$82,000
Indirect labor (carpenters to build sets, costume designers, and so forth)	$110,000
Administrative salaries	$95,000

g. Prepaid insurance expired during the year, $7,000 (80% related to production of videos, and 20% related to marketing and administrative activities).
h. Miscellaneous marketing and administrative expenses incurred, $8,600.
i. Studio (manufacturing) overhead was applied to videos in production. The company recorded 7,250 camera-hours of activity during the year.
j. Videos that cost $550,000 to produce according to their job cost sheets were transferred to the finished videos warehouse to await sale and shipment.

k. Sales for the year totaled $925,000 and were all on account. The total cost to produce these videos according to their job cost sheets was $600,000.
l. Collections from customers during the year totaled $850,000.
m. Payments to suppliers on account during the year, $500,000; payments to employees for salaries and wages, $285,000.

Required:

1. Prepare a T-account for each account on the company's balance sheet and enter the beginning balances.
2. Record the transactions directly into the T-accounts. Prepare new T-accounts as needed. Key your entries to the letters (a) through (m) above. Compute the ending balance in each account.
3. Is the Studio (manufacturing) Overhead account underapplied or overapplied for the year? Make an entry in the T-accounts to close any balance in the Studio Overhead account to Cost of Goods Sold.
4. Prepare an income statement for the year. (Do not prepare a schedule of cost of goods manufactured; all of the information needed for the income statement is available in the T-accounts.)

BUILDING YOUR SKILLS

CASE [LO2–1, LO2–2, LO2–3, LO2–7]

"Blast it!" said David Wilson, president of Teledex Company. "We've just lost the bid on the Koopers job by $2,000. It seems we're either too high to get the job or too low to make any money on half the jobs we bid."

Teledex Company manufactures products to customers' specifications and operates a job-order costing system. Manufacturing overhead cost is applied to jobs on the basis of direct labor cost. The following estimates were made at the beginning of the year:

	Department			Total Plant
	Fabricating	Machining	Assembly	
Direct labor	$200,000	$100,000	$300,000	$600,000
Manufacturing overhead	$350,000	$400,000	$90,000	$840,000

Jobs require varying amounts of work in the three departments. The Koopers job, for example, would have required manufacturing costs in the three departments as follows:

	Department			Total Plant
	Fabricating	Machining	Assembly	
Direct materials	$3,000	$200	$1,400	$4,600
Direct labor	$2,800	$500	$6,200	$9,500
Manufacturing overhead	?	?	?	?

The company uses a plantwide overhead rate to apply manufacturing overhead cost to jobs.

Required:

1. Assuming use of a plantwide overhead rate:
    a. Compute the rate for the current year.
    b. Determine the amount of manufacturing overhead cost that would have been applied to the Koopers job.
2. Suppose that instead of using a plantwide overhead rate, the company had used a separate predetermined overhead rate in each department. Under these conditions:
    a. Compute the rate for each department for the current year.
    b. Determine the amount of manufacturing overhead cost that would have been applied to the Koopers job.

3. Explain the difference between the manufacturing overhead that would have been applied to the Koopers job using the plantwide rate in question 1 (b) and using the departmental rates in question 2 (b).

4. Assume that it is customary in the industry to bid jobs at 150% of total manufacturing cost (direct materials, direct labor, and applied overhead). What was the company's bid price on the Koopers job? What would the bid price have been if departmental overhead rates had been used to apply overhead cost?

5. At the end of the year, the company assembled the following *actual* cost data relating to all jobs worked on during the year:

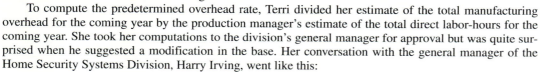

	Department			Total Plant
	Fabricating	Machining	Assembly	
Direct materials	$190,000	$16,000	$114,000	$320,000
Direct labor	$210,000	$108,000	$262,000	$580,000
Manufacturing overhead	$360,000	$420,000	$84,000	$864,000

Compute the underapplied or overapplied overhead for the year (a) assuming that a plantwide overhead rate is used, and (b) assuming that departmental overhead rates are used.

ETHICS CHALLENGE [LO2–1, LO2–2, LO2–7]

Terri Ronsin had recently been transferred to the Home Security Systems Division of National Home Products. Shortly after taking over her new position as divisional controller, she was asked to develop the division's predetermined overhead rate for the upcoming year. The accuracy of the rate is important because it is used throughout the year and any overapplied or underapplied overhead is closed out to Cost of Goods Sold at the end of the year. National Home Products uses direct labor-hours in all of its divisions as the allocation base for manufacturing overhead.

To compute the predetermined overhead rate, Terri divided her estimate of the total manufacturing overhead for the coming year by the production manager's estimate of the total direct labor-hours for the coming year. She took her computations to the division's general manager for approval but was quite surprised when he suggested a modification in the base. Her conversation with the general manager of the Home Security Systems Division, Harry Irving, went like this:

Ronsin: Here are my calculations for next year's predetermined overhead rate. If you approve, we can enter the rate into the computer on January 1 and be up and running in the job-order costing system right away this year.

Irving: Thanks for coming up with the calculations so quickly, and they look just fine. There is, however, one slight modification I would like to see. Your estimate of the total direct labor-hours for the year is 440,000 hours. How about cutting that to about 420,000 hours?

Ronsin: I don't know if I can do that. The production manager says she will need about 440,000 direct labor-hours to meet the sales projections for the year. Besides, there are going to be over 430,000 direct labor-hours during the current year and sales are projected to be higher next year.

Irving: Teri, I know all of that. I would still like to reduce the direct labor-hours in the base to something like 420,000 hours. You probably don't know that I had an agreement with your predecessor as divisional controller to shave 5% or so off the estimated direct labor-hours every year. That way, we kept a reserve that usually resulted in a big boost to net operating income at the end of the fiscal year in December. We called it our Christmas bonus. Corporate headquarters always seemed as pleased as punch that we could pull off such a miracle at the end of the year. This system has worked well for many years, and I don't want to change it now.

Required:

1. Explain how shaving 5% off the estimated direct labor-hours in the base for the predetermined overhead rate usually results in a big boost in net operating income at the end of the fiscal year.

2. Should Terri Ronsin go along with the general manager's request to reduce the direct labor-hours in the predetermined overhead rate computation to 420,000 direct labor-hours?

TEAMWORK IN ACTION [LO2–1, LO2–2, LO2–4, LO2–5, LO2–7]

After a dispute concerning wages, Orville Arson tossed an incendiary device into the Sparkle Company's record vault. Within moments, only a few charred fragments were readable from the company's factory ledger, as shown below:

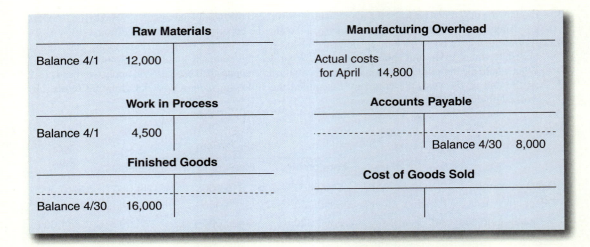

Sifting through ashes and interviewing selected employees has turned up the following additional information:

a.   The controller remembers clearly that the predetermined overhead rate was based on an estimated 60,000 direct labor-hours to be worked over the year and an estimated $180,000 in manufacturing overhead costs.

b.   The production superintendent's cost sheets showed only one job in process on April 30. Materials of $2,600 had been added to the job, and 300 direct labor-hours had been expended at $6 per hour.

c.   The accounts payable are for raw material purchases only, according to the accounts payable clerk. He clearly remembers that the balance in the account was $6,000 on April 1. An analysis of canceled checks (kept in the treasurer's office) shows that payments of $40,000 were made to suppliers during April. (All materials used during April were direct materials.)

d.   A charred piece of the payroll ledger shows that 5,200 direct labor-hours were recorded for the month. The personnel department has verified that there were no variations in pay rates among employees.

e.   Records maintained in the finished goods warehouse indicate that the finished goods inventory totaled $11,000 on April 1.

f.   From another charred piece in the vault, you are able to discern that the cost of goods manufactured for April was $89,000.

Required:

1.   Assign one of the following sets of accounts to each member of the team:
     a. Raw Materials and Accounts Payable.
     b. Work in Process and Manufacturing Overhead.
     c. Finished Goods and Cost of Goods Sold.
     Determine the types of transactions that would be posted to each account and present a summary to the other team members. When agreement is reached, the team should work together to complete steps 2 through 4.

2.   Determine the company's predetermined overhead rate and the total manufacturing overhead applied for the month.

3.   Determine the April 30 balance in the company's Work in Process account.

4.   Prepare the company's T-accounts for the month. (It is easiest to complete the T-accounts in the following order: Accounts Payable, Work in Process, Raw Materials, Manufacturing Overhead, Finished Goods, Cost of Goods Sold.)

COMMUNICATING IN PRACTICE [LO2–1, LO2–2]
Search the Internet or contact your local chamber of commerce or local chapter of the Institute of Management Accountants to find the names of manufacturing companies in your area. Call or make an appointment to meet with the controller or chief financial officer of one of these companies.

Required:

Ask the following questions and write a brief memorandum to your instructor that addresses what you found out.

1. What are the company's main products?
2. Does the company use job-order costing or some other method of determining product costs?
3. How is overhead applied to products? What is the overhead rate? What is the basis of allocation? Is more than one overhead rate used?
4. Has the company recently changed its cost system or is it considering changing its cost system? If so, why? What changes were made or what changes are being considered?

A LOOK BACK

Chapter 2 provided an overview of job-order costing. Direct materials and direct labor costs are traced directly to jobs. Manufacturing overhead is applied to jobs using a predetermined overhead rate.

A LOOK AT THIS CHAPTER

In Chapter 3, we continue the discussion of allocation of overhead in job-order costing. Activity-based costing is a technique that uses a number of allocation bases to assign overhead costs to products.

A LOOK AHEAD

After comparing job-order and process costing systems, we go into the details of a process costing system in Chapter 4.

3 Activity-Based Costing

CHAPTER OUTLINE

Assigning Overhead Costs to Products

- Plantwide Overhead Rate
- Departmental Overhead Rates
- Activity-Based Costing (ABC)

Designing an Activity-Based Costing System

- Hierarchy of Activities
- An Example of an Activity-Based Costing System Design

Using Activity-Based Costing

- Comtek Inc.'s Basic Data
- Direct Labor-Hours as a Base
- Computing Activity Rates
- Computing Product Costs
- Shifting of Overhead Cost

Targeting Process Improvements

Evaluation of Activity-Based Costing

- The Benefits of Activity-Based Costing
- Limitations of Activity-Based Costing
- Activity-Based Costing and Service Industries

Managing Product Complexity

Managers often understand that increasing the variety of raw material inputs used in their products increases costs. For example, **General Mills** studied its 50 varieties of Hamburger Helper and concluded that it could lower costs by discontinuing half of them without alienating customers. **Seagate** studied seven varieties of its computer hard drives and found that only 2% of their parts could be shared by more than one hard drive. The engineers fixed the problem by redesigning the hard drives so that they used more common component parts. Instead of using 61 types of screws to make the hard drives, the engineers reduced the number of screws needed to 19. Eventually all Seagate products were designed so that 75% of their component parts were shared with other product lines.

Activity-based costing systems quantify the increase in costs, such as procurement costs, material handling costs, and assembly costs that are caused by inefficient product designs and other factors.

Sources: Mina Kimes, "Cereal Cost Cutters," *Fortune,* November 10, 2008, p. 24; Erika Brown, "Drive Fast, Drive Hard," *Forbes,* January 9, 2006, pp. 92–96.

As discussed in earlier chapters, direct materials and direct labor costs can be directly traced to products. Overhead costs, on the other hand, cannot be easily traced to products. Some other means must be found for assigning them to products for financial reporting and other purposes. In the previous chapter, overhead costs were assigned to products using a plantwide predetermined overhead rate. This method is simpler than the methods of assigning overhead costs to products described in this chapter, but this simplicity has a cost. A plantwide predetermined overhead rate spreads overhead costs uniformly over products in proportion to whatever allocation base is used—most commonly, direct labor-hours. This procedure results in high overhead costs for products with a high direct labor-hour content and low overhead costs for products with a low direct labor-hour content. However, the real causes of overhead may have little to do with direct labor-hours and as a consequence, product costs may be distorted. Activity-based costing attempts to correct these distortions by more accurately assigning overhead costs to products.

ASSIGNING OVERHEAD COSTS TO PRODUCTS

LEARNING OBJECTIVE 3–1

Understand the basic approach in activity-based costing and how it differs from conventional costing.

Companies use three common approaches to assign overhead costs to products. The simplest method is to use a plantwide overhead rate. A slightly more refined approach is to use departmental overhead rates. The most complex method is activity-based costing, which is the most accurate of the three approaches to overhead cost assignment.

Plantwide Overhead Rate

The preceding chapter assumed that a single overhead rate, called a *plantwide overhead rate,* was used throughout an entire factory. This simple approach to overhead assignment can result in distorted unit product costs, as we shall see below.

When cost systems were developed in the 1800s, cost and activity data had to be collected by hand and all calculations were done with paper and pen. Consequently, the emphasis was on simplicity. Companies often established a single overhead cost pool for an entire facility or department as described in Chapter 2. Direct labor was the obvious choice as an allocation base for overhead costs. Direct labor-hours were already being recorded for purposes of determining wages. In the labor-intensive production processes of that time, direct labor was a large component of product costs—larger than it is today. Moreover, managers believed direct labor and overhead costs were highly correlated. (Two variables, such as direct labor and overhead costs, are highly correlated if they tend to move together.) And finally, most companies produced a very limited variety of similar products, so in fact there was probably little difference in the overhead costs attributable to different products. Under these conditions, it was not cost-effective to use a more elaborate costing system.

Conditions have changed. Many companies now sell a large variety of products that consume significantly different amounts of overhead resources. Consequently, a costing system that assigns essentially the same overhead cost to every product may no longer be adequate. Additionally, factors other than direct labor often drive overhead costs.

On an economywide basis, direct labor and overhead costs have been moving in opposite directions for a long time. As a percentage of total cost, direct labor has been declining, whereas overhead has been increasing. Many tasks previously done by hand are now done with largely automated equipment—a component of overhead. Furthermore, product diversity has increased. Companies are introducing new products and services at an ever-accelerating rate. Managing and sustaining this product diversity requires many more overhead resources such as production schedulers and product design engineers, and many of these overhead resources have no obvious connection with direct labor. Finally, computers, bar code readers, and other technology have dramatically reduced the costs of collecting and processing data—making more complex (and accurate) costing systems such as activity-based costing much less expensive to build and maintain.

Nevertheless, direct labor remains a viable base for applying overhead to products in some companies—particularly for external reports. Direct labor is an appropriate allocation base for overhead when overhead costs and direct labor are highly correlated. And indeed, most companies throughout the world continue to base overhead allocations on direct labor or machine-hours. However, if factorywide overhead costs do not move in tandem with factorywide direct labor or machine-hours, product costs will be distorted.

Departmental Overhead Rates

Rather than use a plantwide overhead rate, many companies use departmental overhead rates with a different predetermined overhead rate in each production department. The nature of the work performed in a department will determine the department's allocation base. For example, overhead costs in a machining department may be allocated on the basis of machine-hours. In contrast, the overhead costs in an assembly department may be allocated on the basis of direct labor-hours.

Unfortunately, even departmental overhead rates will not correctly assign overhead costs in situations where a company has a range of products and complex overhead costs. The reason is that the departmental approach usually relies on a single measure of activity as the base for allocating overhead cost to products. For example, if the machining department's overhead is applied to products on the basis of machine-hours, it is assumed that the department's overhead costs are caused by, and are directly proportional to, machine-hours. However, the department's overhead costs are probably more complex than this and are caused by a variety of factors, including the range of products processed in the department, the number of batch setups that are required, the complexity of the products, and so on. A more sophisticated method like *activity-based costing* is required to adequately account for these diverse factors.

HELPFUL HINT

Conventional cost systems that use plantwide or departmental overhead rates suffer from an important limitation. They tend to inaccurately assign too much overhead to high-volume products and too little overhead to low-volume products. This distortion occurs because conventional cost systems rely exclusively on allocation bases, such as direct labor-hours and machine-hours, that are highly correlated with (or move in tandem with) the volume of production. Make a point of noticing a recurring theme throughout this chapter—activity-based costing systems usually reveal that low-volume (high-volume) products cost more than (less than) reported by conventional cost systems.

Activity-Based Costing (ABC)

Activity-based costing (ABC) is a technique that attempts to assign overhead costs more accurately to products than the simpler methods discussed thus far. The basic idea underlying the activity-based costing approach is illustrated in Exhibit 3–1. A customer order triggers a number of activities. For example, if **Nordstrom** orders a line of women's skirts from **Calvin Klein**, a production order is generated, patterns are created, materials are ordered, textiles are cut to pattern and then sewn, and the finished products are packed for shipping. These activities consume resources. For example, ordering the appropriate materials consumes clerical time—a resource the company must pay for. In activity-based costing, an attempt is made to trace these costs directly to the products that cause them.

Rather than a single allocation base such as direct labor-hours or machine-hours, in activity-based costing a company uses a number of allocation bases for assigning costs to products. Each allocation base in an activity-based costing system represents a major

EXHIBIT 3–1
The Activity-Based Costing Model

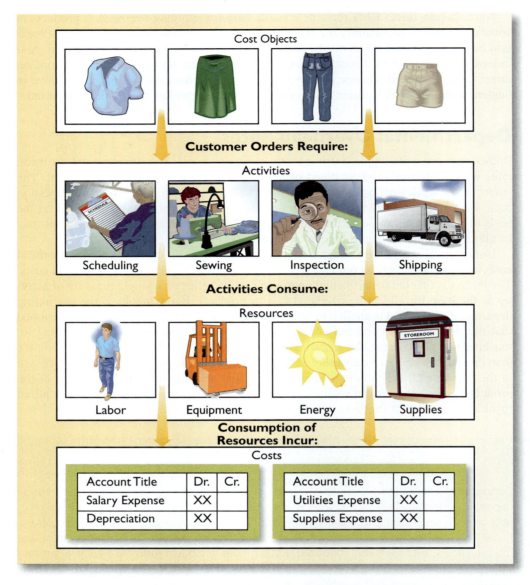

activity that causes overhead costs. An **activity** in activity-based costing is an event that causes the consumption of overhead resources. Examples of activities in various organizations include the following:

- Setting up machines.
- Admitting patients to a hospital.
- Scheduling production.
- Performing blood tests at a clinic.
- Billing customers.
- Maintaining equipment.
- Ordering materials or supplies.
- Stocking shelves at a store.
- Meeting with clients at a law firm.
- Preparing shipments.
- Inspecting materials for defects.
- Opening an account at a bank.

Activity-based costing focuses on these activities. Each major activity has its own overhead cost pool (also known as an *activity cost pool*), its own *activity measure,* and its own overhead rate (also known as an *activity rate*). An **activity cost pool** is a "cost bucket" in which costs related to a particular activity measure are accumulated. The **activity measure** expresses how much of the activity is carried out and it is used as the allocation base for assigning overhead costs to products and services. For example, *the number of patients admitted* is a natural choice of an activity measure for the activity *admitting patients to the hospital.* An **activity rate** is an overhead rate in an activity-based costing system. Each activity has its own activity rate that is used to assign overhead costs to cost objects.

For example, the activity *setting up machines to process a batch* would have its own activity cost pool. Products are ordinarily processed in batches. And because each product has its own machine settings, machines must be set up when changing over from a batch of one product to another. If the total cost in this activity cost pool is $150,000 and the total expected activity is 1,000 machine setups, the activity rate for this activity would be $150 per machine setup ($150,000 ÷ 1,000 machine setups = $150 per machine setup). Each product that requires a machine setup would be charged $150. Note that this charge does not depend on how many units are produced after the machine is set up. A small batch requiring a machine setup would be charged $150—just the same as a large batch.

Taking each activity in isolation, this system works exactly like the job-order costing system described in the last chapter. An activity rate is computed for each activity and then these rates are used to assign costs to jobs and products based on the amount of activity consumed by the job or product.

DESIGNING AN ACTIVITY-BASED COSTING SYSTEM

The most important decisions in designing an activity-based costing system concern what activities will be included in the system and how the activities will be measured. In most companies, hundreds or even thousands of different activities cause overhead costs. These activities range from taking a telephone order to training new employees. Setting up and maintaining a complex costing system that includes all of these activities would be prohibitively expensive. The challenge in designing an activity-based costing system is to identify a reasonably small number of activities that explain the bulk of the variation in overhead costs. This is usually done by interviewing a broad range of managers in the organization to find out what activities they think are important and that consume most of the resources they manage. This often results in a long list of potential activities that could be included in the activity-based costing system. This list is refined and pruned in consultation with top managers. Related activities are frequently combined to reduce the amount of detail and record-keeping cost. For example, several actions may be involved in handling and moving raw materials, but these may be combined into a single activity titled *material handling.* The end result of this stage of the design process is an *activity dictionary* that defines each of the activities that will be included in the activity-based costing system and how the activities will be measured.

Some of the activities commonly found in activity-based costing systems in manufacturing companies are listed in Exhibit 3–2. In the exhibit, activities have been grouped into a four-level hierarchy: *unit-level activities, batch-level activities, product-level activities,* and *facility-level activities.* This cost hierarchy is useful in understanding the difference between activity-based costing and conventional approaches. It also serves as a guide when simplifying an activity-based costing system. In general, activities and costs should be combined in the activity-based costing system only if they fall within the same level in the cost hierarchy.

Hierarchy of Activities

Unit-level activities are performed each time a unit is produced. The costs of unit-level activities should be proportional to the number of units produced. For example, providing power to run processing equipment is a unit-level activity because power tends to be consumed in proportion to the number of units produced.

Level	Activities	Activity Measures
Unit-level	Processing units on machines Processing units by hand Consuming factory supplies	Machine-hours Direct labor-hours Units produced
Batch-level	Processing purchase orders Processing production orders Setting up equipment Handling material	Purchase orders processed Production orders processed Number of setups; setup hours Pounds of material handled; number of times material moved
Product-level	Testing new products Administering parts inventories Designing products	Hours of testing time Number of part types Hours of design time
Facility-level	General factory administration Plant building and grounds	Direct labor-hours* Direct labor-hours*

*Facility-level costs cannot be traced on a cause-and-effect basis to individual products. Nevertheless, companies that choose to use activity-based absorption costing will allocate these costs to products using some arbitrary allocation base such as direct labor-hours.

Batch-level activities consist of tasks that are performed each time a batch is processed, such as processing purchase orders, setting up equipment, packing shipments to customers, and handling material. Costs at the batch level depend on *the number of batches processed* rather than on the number of units produced. For example, the cost of processing a purchase order is the same no matter how many units of an item are ordered.

Product-level activities (sometimes called *product-sustaining activities*) relate to specific products and typically must be carried out regardless of how many batches or units of the product are manufactured. Product-level activities include maintaining inventories of parts for a product, issuing engineering change notices to modify a product to meet a customer's specifications, and developing special test routines when a product is first placed into production.

Facility-level activities (also called *organization-sustaining activities*) are activities that are carried out regardless of which products are produced, how many batches are run, or how many units are made. Facility-level costs include items such as factory management salaries, insurance, property taxes, and building depreciation. These costs cannot be traced on a cause-and-effect basis to individual products. Therefore, companies that choose to implement an activity-based absorption costing system will be required to arbitrarily allocate facility-level cost to products. As we will see later in the book, these types of arbitrary allocations can lead to bad decisions.

HELPFUL HINT

Students often struggle to grasp the meaning of unit-level, batch-level, and product-level activities. Imagine a professor who teaches one section of managerial accounting that includes 35 students and one section of financial accounting that includes 25 students. In this example, the two courses represent two separate products. The activity "preparing a syllabus" would be a product-level activity because it needs to be performed once for each course regardless of the number of class meetings during the semester or the number of enrolled students per class. The activity "preparing a lesson plan" would be a batch-level activity because it needs to be performed once for each class session regardless of the number of enrolled students in each class. The activity "grading exams" would be a unit-level activity because it needs to be performed once for each student enrolled in each class.

Dining in the Canyon

Western River Expeditions (www.westernriver.com) runs river rafting trips on the Colorado, Green, and Salmon rivers. One of its most popular trips is a six-day trip down the Grand Canyon, which features famous rapids such as Crystal and Lava Falls as well as the awesome scenery accessible only from the bottom of the Grand Canyon. The company runs trips of one or two rafts, each of which carries two guides and up to 18 guests. The company provides all meals on the trip, which are prepared by the guides.

In terms of the hierarchy of activities, a guest can be considered as a unit and a raft as a batch. In that context, the wages paid to the guides are a batch-level cost because each raft requires two guides regardless of the number of guests in the raft. Each guest is given a mug to use during the trip and to take home at the end of the trip as a souvenir. The cost of the mug is a unit-level cost because the number of mugs given away is strictly proportional to the number of guests on a trip.

What about the costs of food served to guests and guides—is this a unit-level cost, a batch-level cost, a product-level cost, or an organization-sustaining cost? At first glance, it might be thought that food costs are a unit-level cost—the greater the number of guests, the higher the food costs. However, that is not quite correct. Standard menus have been created for each day of the trip. For example, the first night's menu might consist of shrimp cocktail, steak, cornbread, salad, and cheesecake. The day before a trip begins, all of the food needed for the trip is taken from the central warehouse and packed in modular containers. It isn't practical to finely adjust the amount of food for the actual number of guests planned to be on a trip—most of the food comes prepackaged in large lots. For example, the shrimp cocktail menu may call for two large bags of frozen shrimp per raft and that many bags will be packed regardless of how many guests are expected on the raft. Consequently, the costs of food are not a unit-level cost that varies with the number of guests actually on a trip. Instead, the costs of food are a batch-level cost.

Source: Conversations with Western River Expeditions personnel.

An Example of an Activity-Based Costing System Design

The complexity of an activity-based costing system will differ from company to company. In some companies, the activity-based costing system will be simple with only one or two activity cost pools at the unit, batch, and product levels. For other companies, the activity-based costing system will be much more complex.

Under activity-based costing, the manufacturing overhead costs at the top of Exhibit 3–3 are allocated to products via a two-stage process. In the first stage, overhead costs are assigned to the activity cost pools. In the second stage, the costs in the activity cost pools are allocated to products using activity rates and activity measures. For example, in the first-stage cost assignment, various manufacturing overhead costs are assigned to the production-order activity cost pool. These costs could include the salaries of engineers who modify products for individual orders, the costs of scheduling and monitoring orders, and other costs that are incurred as a consequence of the number of different orders received and processed by the company. We will not go into the details of how these first-stage cost assignments are made. In all of the examples and assignments in this book, the first-stage cost assignments have already been completed. Once the amount of cost in the production-order activity cost pool is known, the activity rate for the cost pool is computed by dividing the total cost in the production-order activity cost pool by the anticipated number of orders for the upcoming year. For example, the total cost in the production-order activity cost pool might be $450,000 and the company might expect to process a total of 1,200 orders. In that case, the activity rate would be $375 per order. Each order would be charged $375 for production-order costs. This is no different from the way overhead was assigned to products in Chapter 2 except that the number of orders is the allocation base rather than direct labor-hours.

EXHIBIT 3-3   Graphic Example of Activity-Based Costing

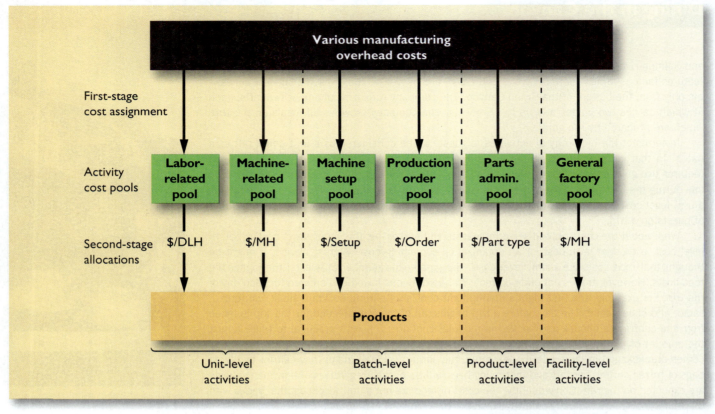

1. Which of the following statements is false? (You may select more than one answer.)
    a. In recent years, most companies have experienced increasing manufacturing overhead costs in relation to direct labor costs.
    b. Batch-level costs do not depend on the number of units produced in a batch.
    c. Facility-level costs are not caused by particular products.
    d. Product-level costs are larger for high-volume products than for low-volume products.
2. Which of the following statements is true? (You may select more than one answer.)
    a. The costs of a unit-level activity should be proportional to the number of units produced.
    b. Unit-level activities are performed each time a unit is produced.
    c. Setting up equipment is an example of a unit-level activity.
    d. Activity-based costing systems may use direct labor-hours and/or machine-hours to assign unit-level costs to products.

USING ACTIVITY-BASED COSTING

Different products place different demands on resources. This is not recognized by conventional costing systems, which assume that overhead resources are consumed in direct proportion to direct labor-hours or machine-hours. The following example illustrates the distortions in product costs that can result from using a traditional costing system.

Comtek Inc. makes two products, a GPS system and a Phone system, that are both sold to automobile manufacturers for installation in new vehicles. Recently, the company has been losing bids to supply GPS systems because competitors have been bidding less than Comtek has been willing to bid. At the same time, Comtek has been winning every bid it has submitted for its Phone system, which management regards as a secondary product. The marketing manager has been complaining that at the prices Comtek is willing to bid, competitors are taking the company's high-volume GPS business and leaving Comtek with just the low-volume Phone business. However, the prices competitors quote on the GPS systems are below Comtek's manufacturing cost for these units—at least according to Comtek's conventional accounting system that applies manufacturing overhead to products based on direct labor-hours. Production managers suspected that the conventional costing system might be distorting the relative costs of the GPS system and the Phone system—the Phone system takes more overhead resources to make than the GPS system and yet their manufacturing overhead costs are identical under the conventional costing system. With the enthusiastic cooperation of the company's accounting department, a cross-functional team was formed to develop an activity-based costing system to more accurately assign overhead costs to the two products.

Comtek Inc.'s Basic Data

The ABC team gathered basic information relating to the company's two products. A summary of some of this information follows. For the current year, the company's budget provides for selling 50,000 Phone systems and 200,000 GPS systems. Both products require two direct labor-hours to complete. Therefore, the company plans to work 500,000 direct labor-hours (DLHs) during the current year, computed as follows:

Phone: 50,000 units × 2 DLHs per unit 100,000
GPS: 200,000 units × 2 DLHs per unit 400,000
Total direct labor-hours 500,000

Costs for direct materials and direct labor for one unit of each product are given below:

	Phone	GPS
Direct materials	$90	$50
Direct labor (at $10 per DLH)	$20	$20

The company's estimated manufacturing overhead costs for the current year total $10,000,000. The ABC team discovered that although the same amount of direct labor time is required for each product, the more complex Phone system requires more machine time, more machine setups, and more testing than the GPS system. Also, the team found that it is necessary to manufacture the Phone systems in smaller batches; consequently, they require more production orders than the GPS systems.

The company has always used direct labor-hours as the base for assigning overhead costs to its products.

With these data in hand, the ABC team was prepared to begin the design of the new activity-based costing system. But first, they wanted to compute the cost of each product using the company's existing cost system.

HELPFUL HINT

As you continue to read through the Comtek Inc., example, keep the following "big picture" insight in mind. The company's existing cost system and the ABC system will both assign a total of $10 million in manufacturing overhead costs to the two products. In other words, the total amount of the "pie" being assigned to GPS systems and Phone systems will be the same in both cost systems. However, the two cost systems will assign different portions of the pie to each product. The existing cost system will assign $8,000,000 (= 200,000 units × $40 per unit) of manufacturing overhead cost to the high-volume GPS systems and $2,000,000 (= 50,000 units × $40 per unit) of overhead cost to the low-volume Phone systems. The ABC system will correct this inaccuracy by assigning $5,110,000 of overhead to GPS systems and $4,890,000 of overhead to Phone systems. Again, both cost systems will be assigning a total $10 million in manufacturing overhead to the GPS and Phone systems. They will simply apportion the pie differently.

Direct Labor-Hours as a Base

Under the company's existing costing system, the predetermined overhead rate would be $20 per direct labor-hour, computed as follows:

$$\text{Predetermined overhead rate} = \frac{\text{Estimated total manufacturing overhead}}{\text{Estimated total amount of the allocation base}}$$

$$= \frac{\$10,000,000}{500,000 \text{ DLHs}} = \$20 \text{ per DLH}$$

Using this rate, the ABC team computed the unit product costs as given below:

	Phone	GPS
Direct materials	$ 90	$ 50
Direct labor.	20	20
Manufacturing overhead (2 DLHs × $20 per DLH)	40	40
Unit product cost	$150	$110

The problem with this costing approach is that it relies entirely on direct labor-hours to assign overhead cost to products and does not consider the impact of other factors—such as setups and testing—on the overhead costs of the company. Even though these other factors suggest that the two products place different demands on overhead resources, under the company's conventional costing system, the two products are assigned the same overhead cost per unit because they require equal amounts of direct labor time.

While this method of computing costs is fast and simple, it is accurate only in those situations where other factors affecting overhead costs are not significant. These other factors *are* significant in the case of Comtek Inc.

Computing Activity Rates

LEARNING OBJECTIVE 3–2

Compute activity rates for an activity-based costing system.

The ABC team then analyzed Comtek Inc.'s operations and identified six major activities to include in the new activity-based costing system. Cost and other data relating to the activities are presented in Exhibit 3–4. That exhibit shows the amount of overhead cost for each activity cost pool, along with the expected amount of activity for the current year. The machine setups activity cost pool, for example, was assigned $1,600,000 in overhead cost. The company expects to complete 4,000 setups during the year, of which 3,000 will be for Phone systems and 1,000 will be for GPS systems. Data for other activities are also shown in the exhibit.

The ABC team then computed an activity rate for each activity. (See the middle panel in Exhibit 3–4.) The activity rate of $400 per machine setup, for example, was computed by dividing the total estimated overhead cost in the activity cost pool, $1,600,000, by the expected amount of activity, 4,000 setups. This process was repeated for each of the other activities in the activity-based costing system.

HELPFUL HINT

Students often make the mistake of trying to compute an activity rate for each product. This is incorrect because you should compute only one activity rate for each activity cost pool. The activity rate is then multiplied by the amount of the activity measure used by each product to assign overhead costs to that product.

EXHIBIT 3–4   Comtek's Activity-Based Costing System

Basic Data

Activity Cost Pools and Activity Measures	Estimated Overhead Cost	Expected Activity Phone	GPS	Total
Labor-related (direct labor-hours)	$ 800,000	100,000	400,000	500,000
Machine-related (machine-hours)	2,100,000	300,000	700,000	1,000,000
Machine setups (setups).	1,600,000	3,000	1,000	4,000
Production orders (orders).	3,150,000	800	400	1,200
Parts administration (part types).	350,000	400	300	700
General factory (machine-hours)	2,000,000	300,000	700,000	1,000,000
	$10,000,000			

Computation of Activity Rates

Activity Cost Pools	(a) Estimated Overhead Cost	(b) Total Expected Activity	(a) ÷ (b) Activity Rate
Labor-related.	$800,000	500,000 DLHs	$1.60 per DLH
Machine-related	$2,100,000	1,000,000 MHs	$2.10 per MH
Machine setups.	$1,600,000	4,000 setups	$400.00 per setup
Production orders	$3,150,000	1,200 orders	$2,625.00 per order
Parts administration	$350,000	700 part types	$500.00 per part type
General factory	$2,000,000	1,000,000 MHs	$2.00 per MH

Computation of the Overhead Cost per Unit of Product

Activity Cost Pools and Activity Rates	Phone Expected Activity	Amount	GPS Expected Activity	Amount
Labor-related, at $1.60 per DLH	100,000	$ 160,000	400,000	$ 640,000
Machine-related, at $2.10 per MH.	300,000	630,000	700,000	1,470,000
Machine setups, at $400 per setup.	3,000	1,200,000	1,000	400,000
Production orders, at $2,625 per order	800	2,100,000	400	1,050,000
Parts administration, at $500 per part type.	400	200,000	300	150,000
General factory, at $2.00 per MH	300,000	600,000	700,000	1,400,000
Total overhead costs assigned (a)		$4,890,000		$5,110,000
Number of units produced (b)		50,000		200,000
Overhead cost per unit (a) ÷ (b).		$97.80		$25.55

Computing Product Costs

Once the activity rates were calculated, it was easy to compute the overhead cost that would be allocated to each product. (See the bottom panel of Exhibit 3–4.) For example, the amount of machine setup cost allocated to Phone systems was determined by multiplying the activity rate of $400 per setup by the 3,000 expected setups for Phones during the year. This yielded a total of $1,200,000 in machine setup costs to be assigned to the Phone systems.

Note from the exhibit that the use of an activity approach has resulted in $97.80 in overhead cost being assigned to each Phone system and $25.55 to each GPS system. The ABC team then used these amounts to determine unit product costs under activity-based

LEARNING OBJECTIVE 3–3

Compute product costs using activity-based costing.

EXHIBIT 3–5
Comparison of Unit Product
Costs

	Activity-Based Costing		Direct-Labor-Based Costing	
	Phone	**GPS**	**Phone**	**GPS**
Direct materials	$ 90.00	$ 50.00	$ 90.00	$ 50.00
Direct labor	20.00	20.00	20.00	20.00
Manufacturing overhead	97.80	25.55	40.00	40.00
Unit product cost	$207.80	$ 95.55	$150.00	$110.00

costing, as presented in Exhibit 3–5. For comparison, the exhibit also shows the unit product costs derived earlier when direct labor-hours were used as the base for assigning overhead costs to the products.

The ABC team members summarized their findings as follows in the team's report:

> In the past, the company has been charging $40.00 in overhead cost to a unit of either product, whereas it should have been charging $97.80 in overhead cost to each Phone system and only $25.55 to each GPS system. Thus, unit costs have been badly distorted as a result of using direct labor-hours as the allocation base. The company may even have been suffering a loss on the Phone systems without knowing it because the cost of these units has been so vastly understated. Through activity-based costing, we have been able to more accurately assign overhead costs to each product.
>
> Although in the past we thought our competitors were pricing below their cost on the GPS systems, it turns out that we were overcharging for these units because our costs were overstated. Similarly, we always used to believe that our competitors were overpricing the Phone systems, but now we realize that our prices have been way too low because the cost of our Phone systems was being understated. It turns out that we, not our competitors, had everything backwards.

The pattern of cost distortion shown by the ABC team's findings is quite common. Such distortion can happen in any company that relies on direct labor-hours or machine-hours in assigning overhead cost to products and ignores other significant causes of overhead costs.

IN BUSINESS

How Much Does it Cost to Handle a Piece of Luggage?

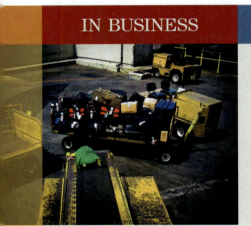

It costs an airline about $15 to carry a piece of checked luggage from one destination another. The activity "transporting luggage" consists of numerous subactivities such as tagging bags, sorting them, placing them on carts, transporting bags planeside, loading them into the airplane, and delivering them to carousels and connecting flights.

A variety of employees invest a portion of their labor hours "transporting luggage" including ground personnel, check-in agents, service clerks, baggage service managers, and maintenance workers. In total, labor costs comprise $9 per bag. Airlines also spend millions of dollars on baggage equipment, sorting systems, carts, tractors, and conveyors, as well as rental costs related to bag rooms, carousels, and offices. They also pay to deliver misplaced bags to customers' homes and to compensate customers for lost bags that are never found. These expenses add up to about $4 per bag. The final expense related to transporting luggage is fuel costs, which average about $2 per bag.

Many major airlines are now charging fees for checked luggage. In fact, United Airlines expects to collect $275 million annually for its first and second bag fees.

Source: Scott McCartney, "What It Costs an Airline to Fly Your Luggage," *The Wall Street Journal*, November 25, 2008, pp. D1 and D8.

Shifting of Overhead Cost

When a company implements activity-based costing, overhead cost often shifts from high-volume products to low-volume products, with a higher unit product cost resulting for the low-volume products. We saw this happen in the Comtek example, where the product cost of the low-volume Phone systems increased from $150.00 to $207.80 per unit. This increase in cost resulted from batch-level and product-level costs, which shifted from the high-volume product to the low-volume product. For example, consider the cost of issuing production orders, which is a batch-level activity. As shown in Exhibit 3–4, the average cost to Comtek to issue a single production order is $2,625. This cost is assigned to a production order regardless of how many units are processed in that order. The key here is to realize that fewer Phone systems (the low-volume product) are processed per production order than GPS systems.

LEARNING OBJECTIVE 3–4

Contrast the product costs computed under activity-based costing and conventional costing methods.

	Phone	GPS
Number of units produced per year (a)	50,000	200,000
Number of production orders issued per year (b)	800	400
Average number of units processed per production order (a) ÷ (b)	62.5	500

Spreading the $2,625 cost to issue a production order over the number of units processed per order results in the following average cost per unit:

	Phone	GPS
Cost to issue a production order (a)	$2,625	$2,625
Average number of units processed per production order (see above) (b)	62.5	500
Average production order cost per unit (a) ÷ (b)	$42.00	$5.25

Thus, the production order cost for a Phone system (the low-volume product) is $42, which is *eight times* the $5.25 cost for a GPS system.

Product-level costs—such as parts administration—have a similar impact. In a conventional costing system, these costs are spread more or less uniformly across all units that are produced. In an activity-based costing system, these costs are assigned more accurately to products. Because product-level costs are fixed with respect to the number of units processed, the average cost per unit of an activity such as parts administration will be higher for low-volume products than for high-volume products.

An ABC Application in the Construction Industry

IN BUSINESS

Researchers from the United States and the Republic of Korea studied how a Korean manufacturer assigned the indirect costs of supplying reinforced steel bars (also called *rebar*) to various construction projects. The company's traditional cost system assigned all indirect costs to projects using rebar tonnage as the allocation base. Its ABC system had 10 activities that assigned indirect costs to projects using activity measures such as number of orders, number of sheets, number of distributing runs, number of production runs, and number of inspections.

(continued)

The traditional and ABC systems assigned the following overhead costs to three construction projects called Commercial, High-Rise Condo, and Heavy Civil:

	Commercial	High-Rise Condo	Heavy Civil
Traditional cost system allocations	$ 64,587	$ 50,310	$91,102
ABC allocations	90,466	61,986	53,548
Difference	$(25,879)	$(11,676)	$37,554

Notice that the traditional cost system was undercosting the Commercial and High-Rise Condo projects relative to the ABC system. It was also overcosting the Heavy Civil project by $37,554 when compared to the ABC system.

Source: Yong-Woo Kim, Seungheon Han, Sungwon Shin, and Kunhee Choi, "A Case Study of Activity-Based Costing in Allocation Rebar Fabrication Costs to Projects," *Construction Management and Economics,* May 2010, pp. 449–461.

TARGETING PROCESS IMPROVEMENTS

Activity-based costing can be used to identify activities that would benefit from process improvements. When used in this way, activity-based costing is often called *activity-based management.* Basically, **activity-based management** involves focusing on activities to eliminate waste, decrease processing time, and reduce defects. Activity-based management is used in organizations as diverse as manufacturing companies, hospitals, and the U.S. Marine Corps.

The first step in any improvement program is to decide what to improve. The activity rates computed in activity-based costing can provide valuable clues concerning where there is waste and opportunity for improvement. For example, looking at the activity rates in Exhibit 3–4, Comtek's managers may conclude that $2,625 to process a production order is far too expensive for an activity that adds no value to the product. As a consequence, they may target production-order processing for a process improvement project.

Benchmarking is another way to leverage the information in activity rates. **Benchmarking** is a systematic approach to identifying the activities with the greatest room for improvement. It is based on comparing the performance in an organization with the performance of other, similar organizations known for their outstanding performance. If a particular part of the organization performs far below the world-class standard, managers will target that area for improvement.

EVALUATION OF ACTIVITY-BASED COSTING

Activity-based costing improves the accuracy of product costs, helps managers to understand the nature of overhead costs, and helps target areas for improvement through benchmarking and other techniques. These benefits are discussed in this section.

The Benefits of Activity-Based Costing

Activity-based costing improves the accuracy of product costs in three ways. First, activity-based costing usually increases the number of cost pools used to accumulate overhead costs. Rather than accumulating all overhead costs in a single, plantwide pool, or accumulating them in departmental pools, the company accumulates costs for each major activity. Second, the activity cost pools are more homogeneous than departmental cost pools. In principle, all of the costs in an activity cost pool pertain to a single activity. In contrast, departmental cost pools contain the costs of many different activities carried out in the department. Third, activity-based costing uses a variety of activity measures to assign overhead costs to products, some of which are correlated with volume and some of which are not. This differs from conventional approaches that rely exclusively on direct labor-hours or other measures of volume such as machine-hours to assign overhead costs to products.

Because conventional costing systems typically apply overhead costs to products using direct labor-hours, it may appear to managers that overhead costs are caused by direct labor-hours. Activity-based costing makes it clear that batch setups, engineering change orders, and other activities cause overhead costs rather than just direct labor. Managers thus have a better understanding of the causes of overhead costs, which should lead to better decisions and better cost control.

Finally, activity-based costing highlights the activities that could benefit most from process improvement initiatives. Thus, activity-based costing can be used as a part of programs to improve operations.

Is Activity-Based Costing Still Being Used?

IN BUSINESS

Researchers surveyed 348 managers to determine which costing methods their companies use. The table below shows the percentage of respondents whose companies use the various costing methods to assign departmental costs to cost objects such as products.

Costing Method	Research and Development	Product and Process Design	Production	Sales and Marketing	Distribution	Customer Service	Shared Services
	Departments						
Activity-based	13.0%	14.7%	18.3%	17.3%	17.2%	21.8%	23.0%
Standard[1]	17.6%	20.7%	42.0%	18.1%	28.4%	18.5%	23.0%
Normal[2]	4.6%	8.6%	9.9%	7.9%	6.0%	8.1%	5.6%
Actual[3]	23.1%	25.0%	23.7%	23.6%	26.7%	16.9%	15.9%
Other	1.9%	0.9%	0.0%	0.8%	0.9%	1.6%	2.4%
Not allocated	39.8%	30.2%	6.1%	32.3%	20.7%	33.1%	30.2%

[1]Standard costing is used for the variance computations in Chapter 8.
[2]Normal costing is used for the job-order costing computations in Chapter 2.
[3]Actual costing is used to create the absorption and variable costing income statements in Chapter 6.

The results show that 18.3% of respondents use ABC to allocate production costs to cost objects and 42% use standard costing for the same purpose. ABC is used by at least 13% of respondents within all functional departments across the value chain. Many companies do not allocate nonproduction costs to cost objects.

Source: William O. Stratton, Denis Desroches, Raef Lawson, and Toby Hatch, "Activity-Based Costing: Is It Still Relevant?" *Management Accounting Quarterly,* Spring 2009, pp. 31–40.

Limitations of Activity-Based Costing

Any discussion of activity-based costing is incomplete without some cautionary warnings. First, the cost of implementing and maintaining an activity-based costing system may outweigh the benefits. Second, it would be naïve to assume that product costs provided even by an activity-based costing system are always relevant when making decisions. These limitations are discussed below.

The Cost of Implementing Activity-Based Costing

Implementing ABC is a major project that requires substantial resources. First, the cost system must be designed—preferably by a cross-functional team. This requires taking valued employees away from other tasks for a major project. In addition, the data used in the activity-based costing system must be collected and verified. In some cases, this requires collecting data that has never been collected before. In short, implementing and maintaining an activity-based costing system can present a formidable challenge, and management may decide that the costs are too great to justify the expected benefits. Nevertheless, it should be kept in mind that the costs of collecting and processing data have dropped dramatically over the last several decades due to bar coding and other technologies, and these costs can be expected to continue to fall.

When are the benefits of activity-based costing most likely to be worth the cost? Companies that have some of the following characteristics are most likely to benefit from activity-based costing:

1. Products differ substantially in volume, batch size, and in the activities they require.
2. Conditions have changed substantially since the existing cost system was established.
3. Overhead costs are high and increasing and no one seems to understand why.
4. Management does not trust the existing cost system and ignores cost data from the system when making decisions.

Limitations of the ABC Model

The activity-based costing model relies on a number of critical assumptions.[1] Perhaps the most important of these assumptions is that the cost in each activity cost pool is strictly proportional to its activity measure. What little evidence we have on this issue suggests that overhead costs are less than proportional to activity.[2] Economists call this increasing returns to scale—as activity increases, the average cost drops. As a practical matter, this means that product costs computed by a traditional or activity-based costing system will be overstated for the purposes of making decisions. The product costs generated by activity-based costing are almost certainly more accurate than those generated by a conventional costing system, but they should nevertheless be viewed with caution. Managers should be particularly alert to product costs that contain allocations of facility-level costs. As we shall see later in the book, product costs that include facility-level or organization-sustaining costs can easily lead managers astray.

Modifying the ABC Model

The discussion in this chapter has assumed that companies use an absorption costing approach when they design an activity-based costing system. If the product costs are to be used by managers for internal decisions, some modifications should be made to the absorption approach. For example, for decision-making purposes, the distinction between manufacturing costs on the one hand and selling and administrative expenses on the other hand is unimportant. Managers need to know what costs a product causes, and it doesn't matter whether the costs are manufacturing costs or selling and administrative expenses. Consequently, for decision-making purposes, some selling and administrative expenses should be assigned to products as well as manufacturing costs. Moreover, as mentioned above, facility-level and organization-sustaining costs should be removed from product costs when making decisions. Nevertheless, the techniques covered in this chapter provide a good basis for

---

[1] Eric Noreen, "Conditions under Which Activity-Based Cost Systems Provide Relevant Costs," *Journal of Management Accounting Research,* Fall 1991, pp. 159–168.
[2] Eric Noreen and Naomi Soderstrom, "The Accuracy of Proportional Cost Models: Evidence from Hospital Service Departments," *Review of Accounting Studies* 2, 1997; and Eric Noreen and Naomi Soderstrom, "Are Overhead Costs Proportional to Activity? Evidence from Hospital Service Departments," *Journal of Accounting and Economics,* January 1994, pp. 253–278.

Bakery Owner

You are the owner of a bakery that makes a complete line of specialty breads, pastries, cakes, and pies for the retail and wholesale markets. A summer intern has just completed an activity-based costing study that concluded, among other things, that one of your largest recurring jobs is losing money. A local luxury hotel orders the same assortment of desserts every week for its Sunday brunch buffet for a fixed price of $975 per week. The hotel is quite happy with the quality of the desserts the bakery has been providing, but it would seek bids from other local bakeries if the price were increased.

The activity-based costing study conducted by the intern revealed that the cost to the bakery of providing these desserts is $1,034 per week, resulting in an apparent loss of $59 per week or over $3,000 per year. Scrutinizing the intern's report, you find that the weekly cost of $1,034 includes facility-level costs of $329. These facility-level costs include portions of the rent on the bakery's building, your salary, depreciation on the office personal computer, and so on. The facility-level costs were arbitrarily allocated to the Sunday brunch job on the basis of direct labor-hours.

Should you demand an increase in price from the luxury hotel for the Sunday brunch desserts to at least $1,034? If an increase is not forthcoming, should you withdraw from the agreement and discontinue providing the desserts?

understanding the mechanics of activity-based costing. For a more complete coverage of the use of activity-based costing in decisions, see more advanced texts.[3]

Activity-Based Costing and Service Industries

Although initially developed as a tool for manufacturing companies, activity-based costing is also being used in service industries. Successful implementation of an activity-based costing system depends on identifying the key activities that generate costs and tracking how many of those activities are performed for each service the organization provides. Activity-based costing has been implemented in a wide variety of service industries including railroads, hospitals, banks, and data services companies.

CONCEPT CHECK

3. Which of the following explain why activity-based costing improves product cost accuracy? (You may select more than one answer.)
   a. Activity-based costing typically uses more cost pools than traditional methods.
   b. Activity-based costing uses more homogeneous cost pools than traditional methods.
   c. Activity-based costing often uses a plantwide overhead rate, whereas traditional methods do not.
   d. Activity-based costing uses a variety of activity measures to assign overhead costs to products, some of which are correlated with volume and some of which are not.
4. Which of the following statements is false? (You may select more than one answer.)
   a. Activity-based costing systems usually shift costs from low-volume products to high-volume products.
   b. Benchmarking can be used to identify activities with the greatest potential for improvement.
   c. Activity-based costing is most valuable to companies that manufacture products that are similar in terms of their volume of production, batch size, and complexity.
   d. Activity-based costing systems are based on the assumption that the costs included in each activity cost pool are strictly proportional to the cost pool's activity measure.

[3]See, for example, Chapter 7 and its Appendix 7A in Ray Garrison, Eric Noreen, and Peter Brewer, *Managerial Accounting,* 15th edition, McGraw-Hill/Irwin © 2015.

IN BUSINESS

An ABC Implementation in Thailand

APS, a parawood furniture factory located in the Songkhla Province of Southern Thailand, employs over 250 workers to make more than 100 types of furniture. The company's traditional cost system assigns indirect manufacturing costs to products based on each product's total sales. Its ABC system relies on various volume-related and non-volume-related activity measures, such as direct labor-hours, number of setups, and number of trips, to assign overhead costs to products.

The company's traditional and ABC systems assigned per-unit overhead costs to its five best-selling products as follows:

	Tile Top Table	Side Chair	Telephone Table	Plant Tree with Grooves	Computer Desk
Traditional cost system allocations	$7.08	$2.21	$3.53	$3.65	$ 4.53
ABC allocations	2.18	1.13	1.32	1.80	6.07
Difference	$4.90	$1.08	$2.21	$1.85	$(1.54)

Given that all five of these products have high sales volumes, it is not surprising to see that the traditional cost system has overcosted four of them.

Source: Sakesun Suthummanon, Wanida Ratanamanee, Nirachara Boonyanuwat, and Pieanpon Saritprit, "Applying Activity-Based Costing (ABC) to a Parawood Furniture Factory," *The Engineering Economist*, Volume 56 (2011), pp. 80–93.

SUMMARY

LO3–1 Understand the basic approach in activity-based costing and how it differs from conventional costing.

Activity-based costing was developed to more accurately assign overhead costs to products. Activity-based costing differs from conventional costing as described in Chapter 2 in two major ways. First, in activity-based costing, each major activity that consumes overhead resources has its own cost pool and its own activity rate, whereas in Chapter 2 there was only a single overhead cost pool and a single predetermined overhead rate. Second, the allocation bases (or activity measures) in activity-based costing are diverse. They may include machine setups, purchase orders, engineering change orders, and so on, in addition to direct labor-hours or machine-hours.

LO3–2 Compute activity rates for an activity-based costing system.

Each activity in an activity-based costing system has its own cost pool and its own activity measure. The activity rate for a particular activity is computed by dividing the total cost in the activity's cost pool by the total amount of activity.

LO3–3 Compute product costs using activity-based costing.

Product costs in activity-based costing, as in conventional costing systems, consist of direct materials, direct labor, and overhead. In the case of an activity-based costing system, each activity has its own activity rate. The activities required by a product are multiplied by their respective activity rates to determine the amount of overhead that is assigned to the product.

LO3–4 Contrast the product costs computed under activity-based costing and conventional costing methods.
Under conventional costing methods, overhead costs are applied to products using some measure of volume such as direct labor-hours or machine-hours. This results in most of the overhead cost being applied to high-volume products. In contrast, under activity-based costing, some overhead costs are assigned on the basis of batch-level or product-level activities. This change in allocation bases shifts overhead costs from high-volume products to low-volume products. Accordingly, product costs for high-volume products are commonly lower under activity-based costing than under conventional costing methods, and product costs for low-volume products are higher.

GUIDANCE ANSWER TO DECISION POINT

Bakery Owner (p. 137)
The bakery really isn't losing money on the weekly order of desserts from the luxury hotel. By definition, facility-level costs are not affected by individual products and jobs—these costs would continue unchanged even if the weekly order were dropped. Recalling the discussion in Chapter 1 concerning decision making, only those costs and benefits that differ between alternatives in a decision are relevant. Because the facility-level costs would be the same whether the dessert order is kept or dropped, they are not relevant in this decision and should be ignored. Hence, the real cost of the job is $705 ($1,034 − $329), which reveals that the job actually yields a weekly profit of $270 ($975 − $705) rather than a loss.

No, the bakery owner should not press for a price increase—particularly if that would result in the hotel seeking bids from competitors. And no, the bakery owner certainly should not withdraw from the agreement to provide the desserts.

GUIDANCE ANSWERS TO CONCEPT CHECKS

1. **Choice d.** Product-level costs are unrelated to the amount of a product that is made.
2. **Choices a, b, and d.** Setting up equipment is an example of a batch-level activity.
3. **Choices a, b, and d.** Traditional methods rely on plantwide overhead allocation.
4. **Choices a and c.** Activity-based costing systems usually shift costs from high-volume products to low-volume products. Activity-based costing is most valuable for companies with highly diverse products rather than with similar products.

REVIEW PROBLEM: ACTIVITY-BASED COSTING

Aerodec, Inc., manufactures and sells two types of wooden deck chairs: Deluxe and Tourist. Annual sales in units, direct labor-hours (DLHs) per unit, and total direct labor-hours per year are provided below:

Deluxe deck chair: 2,000 units × 5 DLHs per unit	10,000
Tourist deck chair: 10,000 units × 4 DLHs per unit.	40,000
Total direct labor-hours	50,000

Costs for direct materials and direct labor for one unit of each product are given below:

	Deluxe	Tourist
Direct materials.	$25	$17
Direct labor (at $12 per DLH)	$60	$48

Manufacturing overhead costs total $800,000 each year. The breakdown of these costs among the company's six activity cost pools is given below. The activity measures are shown in parentheses.

Activity Cost Pools and Activity Measures	Estimated Overhead Cost	Expected Activity		
		Deluxe	Tourist	Total
Labor-related (direct labor-hours)	$ 80,000	10,000	40,000	50,000
Machine setups (number of setups)	150,000	3,000	2,000	5,000
Parts administration (number of parts) . . .	160,000	50	30	80
Production orders (number of orders)	70,000	100	300	400
Material receipts (number of receipts) . . .	90,000	150	600	750
General factory (machine-hours)	250,000	12,000	28,000	40,000
	$800,000			

Required:

1. Classify each of Aerodec's activities as either a unit-level, batch-level, product-level, or facility-level activity.
2. Assume that the company applies overhead cost to products on the basis of direct labor-hours.
   a. Compute the predetermined overhead rate.
   b. Determine the unit product cost of each product, using the predetermined overhead rate computed in (2)(a) above.
3. Assume that the company uses activity-based costing to compute overhead rates.
   a. Compute the activity rate for each of the six activities listed above.
   b. Using the rates developed in (3)(a) above, determine the amount of overhead cost that would be assigned to a unit of each product.
   c. Determine the unit product cost of each product and compare this cost to the cost computed in (2)(b) above.

Solution to Review Problem

1.

Activity Cost Pool	Type of Activity
Labor-related.	Unit-level
Machine setups	Batch-level
Parts administration	Product-level
Production orders	Batch-level
Material receipts	Batch-level
General factory.	Facility-level

2. a.

$$\text{Predetermined overhead rate} = \frac{\text{Estimated total manufacturing overhead}}{\text{Estimated total amount of the allocation base}}$$

$$= \frac{\$800,000}{50,000 \text{ DLHs}} = \$16 \text{ per DLH}$$

b.

	Deluxe	Tourist
Direct materials	$ 25	$ 17
Direct labor.	60	48
Manufacturing overhead applied:		
Deluxe: 5 DLHs × $16 per DLH	80	
Tourist: 4 DLHs × $16 per DLH.		64
Unit product cost	$165	$129

3. a.

Activity Cost Pools	(a) Estimated Overhead Cost	(b) Total Expected Activity	(a) ÷ (b) Activity Rate
Labor-related	$80,000	50,000 DLHs	$1.60 per DLH
Machine setups	$150,000	5,000 setups	$30.00 per setup
Parts administration	$160,000	80 parts	$2,000.00 per part
Production orders	$70,000	400 orders	$175.00 per order
Material receipts.	$90,000	750 receipts	$120.00 per receipt
General factory.	$250,000	40,000 MHs	$6.25 per MH

b.

Activity Cost Pools and Activity Rates	Deluxe Expected Activity	Deluxe Amount	Tourist Expected Activity	Tourist Amount
Labor-related, at $1.60 per DLH.	10,000	$ 16,000	40,000	$ 64,000
Machine setups, at $30 per setup	3,000	90,000	2,000	60,000
Parts administration, at $2,000 per part. . . .	50	100,000	30	60,000
Production orders, at $175 per order	100	17,500	300	52,500
Material receipts, at $120 per receipt.	150	18,000	600	72,000
General factory, at $6.25 per MH	12,000	75,000	28,000	175,000
Total overhead cost assigned (a)		$316,500		$483,500
Number of units produced (b)		2,000		10,000
Overhead cost per unit, (a) ÷ (b).		$158.25		$48.35

c.

	Deluxe	Tourist
Direct materials	$ 25.00	$ 17.00
Direct labor.	60.00	48.00
Manufacturing overhead (see above).	158.25	48.35
Unit product cost	$243.25	$113.35

Under activity-based costing, the unit product cost of the Deluxe deck chair is much greater than the cost computed in (2)(b), and the unit product cost of the Tourist deck chair is much less. Using volume (direct labor-hours) in (2)(b) to apply overhead cost to products results in too little overhead cost being applied to the Deluxe deck chair (the low-volume product) and too much overhead cost being applied to the Tourist deck chair (the high-volume product).

GLOSSARY

Activity   An event that causes the consumption of overhead resources. (p. 124)

Activity-based costing (ABC)   A two-stage costing method in which overhead costs are assigned to products on the basis of the activities they require. (p. 123)

Activity-based management   A management approach that focuses on managing activities as a way of eliminating waste and reducing delays and defects. (p. 134)

Activity cost pool   A "bucket" in which costs are accumulated that relate to a single activity measure in an activity-based costing system. (p. 125)

Activity measure   An allocation base in an activity-based costing system; ideally, a measure of whatever causes the costs in an activity cost pool. (p. 125)

Activity rate   An overhead rate in activity-based costing. Each activity cost pool has its own activity rate which is used to assign overhead to products and services. (p. 125)

Batch-level activities   Activities that are performed each time a batch of goods is handled or processed, regardless of how many units are in a batch. The amount of resources consumed depends on the number of batches run rather than on the number of units in the batch. (p. 126)

Benchmarking   A systematic approach to identifying the activities with the greatest room for improvement. It is based on comparing the performance in an organization with the performance of other, similar organizations known for their outstanding performance. (p. 134)

Facility-level activities   Activities that are carried out regardless of which products are produced, how many batches are run, or how many units are made. (p. 126)

Product-level activities   Activities that relate to specific products that must be carried out regardless of how many units are produced and sold or batches run. (p. 126)

Unit-level activities   Activities that arise as a result of the total volume of goods and services that are produced, and that are performed each time a unit is produced. (p. 125)

QUESTIONS

3–1   What are the three common approaches for assigning overhead costs to products?
3–2   Why does activity-based costing appeal to some companies?
3–3   Why do departmental overhead rates sometimes result in inaccurate product costs?
3–4   What are the four hierarchical levels of activity discussed in the chapter?
3–5   Why is activity-based costing described as a "two-stage" costing method?
3–6   Why do overhead costs often shift from high-volume products to low-volume products when a company switches from a conventional costing method to activity-based costing?
3–7   What are the three major ways in which activity-based costing improves the accuracy of product costs?
3–8   What are the major limitations of activity-based costing?

Multiple-choice questions are available in the *Connect Library*.

APPLYING EXCEL

LO3–1, LO3–2, LO3–3, LO3–4

Available with McGraw-Hill's *Connect Accounting*.

A form for using Excel to recreate the Review Problem on pages 139–141 appears on the following page. For simplicity, the form excludes the Parts Administration and Material Receipts activities that were included in the Review Problem. Download the workbook containing this form in the *Connect Library*. *On the website you will also receive instructions about how to use this worksheet form.*

	A	B	C	D	E	F	G
1	**Chapter 3: Applying Excel**						
2							
3	*Enter a formula into each of the cells marked with a ? below*						
4	**Review Problem: Activity-Based Costing**						
5							
6	**Data**						
7		*Deluxe*	*Tourist*				
8	Annual sales in units	2,000	10,000				
9	Direct materials per unit	$25	$17				
10	Direct labor-hours per unit	5	4				
11							
12	Direct labor rate	$12	per DLH				
13							
14		*Estimated*					
15		*Overhead*		*Expected Activity*			
16	*Activities and Activity Measures*	*Cost*	*Deluxe*	*Tourist*	*Total*		
17	Labor-related (direct labor-hours)	$ 80,000	?	?	?		
18	Machine setups (setups)	150,000	3,000	2,000	?		
19	Production orders (orders)	70,000	100	300	?		
20	General factory (machine-hours)	250,000	12,000	28,000	?		
21		?					
22							
23	**Compute the predetermined overhead rate**						
24	Estimated total manufacturing overhead (a)		?				
25	Estimated total amount of the allocation base (b)		? DLHs				
26	Predetermined overhead rate (a) ÷ (b)		? per DLH				
27							
28	**Compute the manufacturing overhead applied**		*Deluxe*		*Tourist*		
29	Direct labor-hours per unit (a)		? DLHs		? DLHs		
30	Predetermined overhead rate (b)		? per DLH		? per DLH		
31	Manufacturing overhead applied per unit (a) × (b)		?		?		
32							
33	**Compute traditional unit product costs**	*Deluxe*	*Tourist*				
34	Direct materials	?	?				
35	Direct labor	?	?				
36	Manufacturing overhead applied	?	?				
37	Traditonal unit product cost	?	?				
38							
39	**Compute activity rates**	*Estimated*					
40		*Overhead*					
41	*Activities*	*Cost*	*Total Expected Activity*		*Activity Rate*		
42	Labor-related	?	? DLHs		? per DLH		
43	Machine setups	?	? setups		? per setup		
44	Production orders	?	? orders		? per order		
45	General factory	?	? MHs		? per MH		
46							
47	**Compute the ABC overhead cost per unit**			*Deluxe*		*Tourist*	
48		*Activity*	*Expected*		*Expected*		
49	*Activities*	*Rate*	*Activity*	*Amount*	*Activity*	*Amount*	
50	Labor-related	?	?	?	?	?	
51	Machine setups	?	?	?	?	?	
52	Production orders	?	?	?	?	?	
53	General factory	?	?	?	?	?	
54	Total overhead cost assigned (a)			?		?	
55	Number of units produced (b)			?		?	
56	ABC overhead cost per unit (a) ÷ (b)			?		?	
57							
58	**Compute the ABC unit product costs**	*Deluxe*	*Tourist*				
59	Direct materials	?	?				
60	Direct labor	?	?				
61	ABC overhead cost per unit (see above)	?	?				
62	ABC unit product cost	?	?				
63							

Chapter 3 Form / Chapter 3 Master / Filled in Chapter 3 Form

Chapter 3

You should proceed to the requirements below only after completing your worksheet.

Required:
1. Check your worksheet by reducing the direct labor-hours per unit to 2 for the Deluxe model in cell B10. The Data area of the worksheet should look like this:

Data

	Deluxe	Tourist
Annual sales in units.	2,000	10,000
Direct materials per unit	$25	$17
Direct labor-hours per unit . . .	2	4
Direct labor rate	$12 per DLH	

Activity Cost Pools and Activity Measures	Estimated Overhead Cost	Expected Activity		
		Deluxe	Tourist	Total
Labor-related (direct labor-hours). . .	$ 80,000	4,000	40,000	44,000
Machine setups (setups)	150,000	3,000	2,000	5,000
Production orders (orders)	70,000	100	300	400
General factory (machine-hours) . . .	250,000	12,000	28,000	40,000
	$550,000			

The Deluxe model's unit product cost under traditional costing should now be $74.00 and the ABC unit product cost should be $143.89. If you do not get these results, find the errors in your worksheet and correct them.
   a. What happened to the predetermined overhead rate when the direct labor-hour requirement for the Deluxe model dropped from 5 hours to 2 hours? Explain.
   b. Compare the unit product costs for the *Tourist* model before and after changing the direct labor-hour requirements for the *Deluxe* model. The traditional unit product cost of the Tourist model increased from $109 to $115 when the direct labor-hour requirement for the Deluxe model changed from 5 to 2 hours per unit. In contrast, the ABC unit product cost of the Tourist model increased from $100.15 to $101.20. Which costing method do you trust more for making decisions? Explain.
2. Change the direct labor-hour requirement for the Deluxe model back to 5 hours in cell B10. Assume that the production orders change so that the Deluxe model will have 300 orders in cell C19 and the Tourist model will have 100 orders in cell D19. The Data area should now look like this:

Data

	Deluxe	Tourist
Annual sales in units.	2,000	10,000
Direct materials per unit	$25	$17
Direct labor-hours per unit . . .	5	4
Direct labor rate	$12 per DLH	

Activity Cost Pools and Activity Measures	Estimated Overhead Cost	Expected Activity		
		Deluxe	Tourist	Total
Labor-related (direct labor-hours). . . .	$ 80,000	10,000	40,000	50,000
Machine setups (setups)	150,000	3,000	2,000	5,000
Production orders (orders)	70,000	300	100	400
General factory (machine-hours)	250,000	12,000	28,000	40,000
	$550,000			

a. What effect does this change have on the traditional unit product costs? Explain.

b. What effect does this change have on the ABC unit product costs? Explain.

c. Which method, the traditional direct labor-based costing system or the ABC costing system, apparently provides more accurate costs? Explain.

3. Change the data in red so that the Data area looks like this:

Data

	Deluxe	Tourist
Annual sales in units.	1,000	9,000
Direct materials per unit	$20	$20
Direct labor-hours per unit . . .	1	1
Direct labor rate	$10 per DLH	

Activity Cost Pools and Activity Measures	Estimated Overhead Cost	Expected Activity		
		Deluxe	Tourist	Total
Labor-related (direct labor-hours) . . .	$ 33,000	1,000	9,000	10,000
Machine setups (setups)	120,000	20	80	100
Production orders (orders)	70,000	15	35	50
General factory (machine-hours) . . .	150,000	10,000	10,000	20,000
	$373,000			

a. Are the traditional unit product costs for the two products the same or different? Explain.

b. Are the ABC unit product costs for the two products the same or different? Explain.

c. Which method, the traditional direct labor-based costing system or the ABC costing system, apparently provides more accurate costs? Explain.

THE FOUNDATIONAL 15

Available with McGraw-Hill's *Connect Accounting*.

Greenwood Company manufactures two products—14,000 units of Product Y and 6,000 units of Product Z. The company uses a plantwide overhead rate based on direct labor-hours. It is considering implementing an activity-based costing (ABC) system that allocates all of its manufacturing overhead to four cost pools. The following additional information is available for the company as a whole and for Products Y and Z:

LO3–1, LO3–2, LO3–3, LO3–4

Activity Cost Pool	Activity Measure	Estimated Overhead Cost	Expected Activity
Machining.	Machine-hours	$200,000	10,000 MHs
Machine setups	Number of setups	$100,000	200 setups
Production design.	Number of products	$84,000	2 products
General factory.	Direct labor-hours	$300,000	12,000 DLHs

Activity Measure	Product Y	Product Z
Machining.	8,000	2,000
Number of setups.	40	160
Number of products	1	1
Direct labor-hours.	9,000	3,000

1. What is the company's plantwide overhead rate?

2. Using the plantwide overhead rate, how much manufacturing overhead cost is allocated to Product Y? How much is allocated to Product Z?

3. What is the activity rate for the Machining activity cost pool?
4. What is the activity rate for the Machine Setups activity cost pool?
5. What is the activity rate for the Product Design activity cost pool?
6. What is the activity rate for the General Factory activity cost pool?
7. Which of the four activities is a batch-level activity? Why?
8. Which of the four activities is a product-level activity? Why?
9. Using the ABC system, how much total manufacturing overhead cost would be assigned to Product Y?
10. Using the ABC system, how much total manufacturing overhead cost would be assigned to Product Z?
11. Using the plantwide overhead rate, what percentage of the total overhead cost is allocated to Product Y? What percentage is allocated to Product Z?
12. Using the ABC system, what percentage of the Machining costs is assigned to Product Y? What percentage is assigned to Product Z? Are these percentages similar to those obtained in question 11? Why?
13. Using the ABC system, what percentage of Machine Setups cost is assigned to Product Y? What percentage is assigned to Product Z? Are these percentages similar to those obtained in question 11? Why?
14. Using the ABC system, what percentage of the Product Design cost is assigned to Product Y? What percentage is assigned to Product Z? Are these percentages similar to those obtained in question 11? Why?
15. Using the ABC system, what percentage of the General Factory cost is assigned to Product Y? What percentage is assigned to Product Z? Are these percentages similar to those obtained in question 11? Why?

EXERCISES

All applicable exercises are available with McGraw-Hill's *Connect Accounting*.

EXERCISE 3–1   ABC Cost Hierarchy [LO3–1]
The following activities occur at Greenwich Corporation, a company that manufactures a variety of products:
a. Various individuals manage the parts inventories.
b. A clerk in the factory issues purchase orders for a job.
c. The personnel department trains new production workers.
d. The factory's general manager meets with other department heads to coordinate plans.
e. Direct labor workers assemble products.
f. Engineers design new products.
g. The materials storekeeper issues raw materials to be used in jobs.
h. The maintenance department performs periodic preventive maintenance on general-use equipment.

Required:
Classify each of the activities above as either a unit-level, batch-level, product-level, or facility-level activity.

EXERCISE 3–2   Compute Activity Rates [LO3–2]
Rustafson Corporation is a diversified manufacturer of consumer goods. The company's activity-based costing system has the following seven activity cost pools:

Estimated direct labor-hours = 10,000

Activity Cost Pool	Estimated Overhead Cost	Expected Activity
Labor-related	$52,000	8,000 direct labor-hours
Machine-related	$15,000	20,000 machine-hours
Machine setups	$42,000	1,000 setups
Production orders	$18,000	500 orders
Product testing	$48,000	2,000 tests
Packaging	$75,000	5,000 packages
General factory	$108,800	8,000 direct labor-hours

Required:
1. Compute the activity rate for each activity cost pool.
2. Compute the company's predetermined overhead rate, assuming that the company uses a single plantwide predetermined overhead rate based on direct labor-hours.

EXERCISE 3–3   Compute ABC Product Costs [LO3–3]

Larner Corporation is a diversified manufacturer of industrial goods. The company's activity-based costing system contains the following six activity cost pools and activity rates:

Activity Cost Pool	Activity Rates
Labor-related..........	$7.00 per direct labor-hour
Machine-related	$3.00 per machine-hour
Machine setups	$40.00 per setup
Production orders	$160.00 per order
Shipments.............	$120.00 per shipment
General factory...........	$4.00 per direct labor-hour

Number of units of J78 produced = 3,000

Cost and activity data have been supplied for the following products:

	J78	B52
Direct materials cost per unit	$6.50	$31.00
Direct labor cost per unit...........	$3.75	$6.00
Number of units produced per year ...	4,000	100

	Total Expected Activity	
	J78	B52
Direct labor-hours.............	1,000	40
Machine-hours	3,200	30
Machine setups	5	1
Production orders	5	1
Shipments..................	10	1

Required:
Compute the unit product cost of each product listed above.

EXERCISE 3–4   Contrast ABC and Conventional Product Costs [LO3–4]

Pacifica Industrial Products Corporation makes two products, Product H and Product L. Product H is expected to sell 40,000 units next year and Product L is expected to sell 8,000 units. A unit of either product requires 0.4 direct labor-hours.

The company's total manufacturing overhead for the year is expected to be $1,632,000.

Required:
1. The company currently applies manufacturing overhead to products using direct labor-hours as the allocation base. If this method is followed, how much overhead cost would be applied to each product? Compute both the overhead cost per unit and the total amount of overhead cost that would be applied to each product. (In other words, how much overhead cost is applied to a unit of Product H? Product L? How much overhead cost is applied in total to all the units of Product H? Product L?)
2. Management is considering an activity-based costing system and would like to know what impact this change might have on product costs. For purposes of discussion, it has been suggested that all of the manufacturing overhead be treated as a product-level cost. The total manufacturing overhead would be divided in half between the two products, with $816,000 assigned to Product H and $816,000 assigned to Product L.

Direct labor-hours per unit of either product = 0.5 hours

   If this suggestion is followed, how much overhead cost per unit would be assigned to each product?
3. Explain the impact on unit product costs of the switch in costing systems.

EXERCISE 3–5   Assigning Overhead to Products in ABC [LO3–2, LO3–3]

Sultan Company uses an activity-based costing system.

At the beginning of the year, the company made the following estimates of cost and activity for its five activity cost pools:

Activity Cost Pool	Activity Measure	Expected Overhead Cost	Expected Activity
Labor-related	Direct labor-hours	$156,000	26,000 DLHs
Purchase orders	Number of orders	$11,000	220 orders
Parts management	Number of part types	$80,000	100 part types
Board etching	Number of boards	$90,000	2,000 boards
General factory	Machine-hours	$180,000	20,000 MHs

Required:

1. Compute the activity rate for each of the activity cost pools.
2. The expected activity for the year was distributed among the company's four products as follows:

	Expected Activity			
Activity Cost Pool	Product A	Product B	Product C	Product D
Labor-related (DLHs)	6,000	11,000	4,000	5,000
Purchase orders (orders)	60	30	40	90
Parts management (part types)	30	15	40	15
Board etching (boards)	500	900	600	0
General factory (MHs)	3,000	8,000	3,000	6,000

Using the ABC data, determine the total amount of overhead cost assigned to each product.

EXERCISE 3–6   Cost Hierarchy and Activity Measures [LO3–1]

Various activities at Companhia de Textils, S.A., a manufacturing company located in Brazil, are listed below. The company makes a variety of products in its plant outside São Paulo.

a. Preventive maintenance is performed on general-purpose production equipment.
b. Products are assembled by hand.
c. A security guard patrols the company grounds after normal working hours.
d. Purchase orders are issued for materials to be used in production.
e. Modifications are made to product designs.
f. New employees are hired by the personnel office.
g. Machine settings are changed between batches of different products.
h. Parts inventories are maintained in the storeroom. (Each product requires its own unique parts.)
i. Insurance costs are incurred on the company's facilities.

Required:

1. Classify each of the activities as either a unit-level, batch-level, product-level, or facility-level activity.
2. Where possible, name one or more activity measures that could be used to assign costs generated by the activity to products or customers.

EXERCISE 3–7   Contrast ABC and Conventional Product Costs [LO3–2, LO3–3, LO3–4]

Kunkel Company makes two products and uses a conventional costing system in which a single plantwide predetermined overhead rate is computed based on direct labor-hours. Data for the two products for the upcoming year follow:

TAKE
TWO

Number of units of Wurcon
= 48,000

	Mercon	Wurcon
Direct materials cost per unit	$10.00	$8.00
Direct labor cost per unit	$3.00	$3.75
Direct labor-hours per unit	0.20	0.25
Number of units produced	10,000	40,000

These products are customized to some degree for specific customers.

Required:
1. The company's manufacturing overhead costs for the year are expected to be $336,000. Using the company's conventional costing system, compute the unit product costs for the two products.
2. Management is considering an activity-based costing system in which half of the overhead would continue to be allocated on the basis of direct labor-hours and half would be allocated on the basis of engineering design time. This time is expected to be distributed as follows during the upcoming year:

	Mercon	Wurcon	Total
Engineering design time (in hours)	4,000	4,000	8,000

Compute the unit product costs for the two products using the proposed ABC system.
3. Explain why the product costs differ between the two systems.

EXERCISE 3–8 Computing ABC Product Costs [LO3–2, LO3–3]

Performance Products Corporation makes two products, titanium Rims and Posts. Data regarding the two products follow:

	Direct Labor-Hours per Unit	Annual Production
Rims...................	0.40	20,000 units
Posts	0.20	80,000 units

Additional information about the company follows:
a. Rims require $17 in direct materials per unit, and Posts require $10.
b. The direct labor wage rate is $16 per hour.
c. Rims are more complex to manufacture than Posts and they require special equipment.
d. The ABC system has the following activity cost pools:

Activity Cost Pool	Activity Measure	Estimated Overhead Cost	Estimated Activity Rims	Posts	Total
Machine setups	Number of setups	$21,600	100	80	180
Special processing.................	Machine-hours	$180,000	4,000	0	4,000
General factory....................	Direct labor-hours	$288,000	8,000	16,000	24,000

Required:
1. Compute the activity rate for each activity cost pool.
2. Determine the unit product cost of each product according to the ABC system.

EXERCISE 3–9 Compute and Use Activity Rates to Determine the Costs of Serving Customers [LO3–2, LO3–3]

Med Max buys surgical supplies from a variety of manufacturers and then resells and delivers these supplies to dozens of hospitals. In the face of declining profits, Med Max decided to implement an activity-based costing system to improve its understanding of the costs incurred to serve each hospital. The company broke its selling and administrative expenses into four activities as shown below:

Total number of deliveries = 4,000

Activity Cost Pool	Activity Measure	Total Cost	Total Activity
Customer deliveries	Number of deliveries	$ 400,000	5,000 deliveries
Manual order processing	Number of manual orders	300,000	4,000 orders
Electronic order processing	Number of electronic orders	200,000	12,500 orders
Line item picking	Number of line items picked	500,000	400,000 line items
Total selling and administrative expenses		$1,400,000	

Med Max gathered the data below for two of the many hospitals that it serves—City General and County General:

Activity Measure	Activity	
	City General	County General
Number of deliveries.	10	20
Number of manual orders.	0	40
Number of electronic orders	10	0
Number of line items picked	100	260

Required:
1. Compute the activity rate for each activity cost pool.
2. Compute the total activity costs that would be assigned to City General and County General.
3. Describe the purchasing behaviors that are likely to increase Med Max's cost to serve its customers.

EXERCISE 3–10 Contrasting ABC and Conventional Product Costs [LO3–2, LO3–3, LO3–4]
Rocky Mountain Corporation makes two types of hiking boots—Xactive and Pathbreaker. Data concerning these two product lines appear below:

	Xactive	Pathbreaker
Direct materials per unit	$64.80	$51.00
Direct labor cost per unit	$18.20	$13.00
Direct labor-hours per unit	1.4 DLHs	1.0 DLHs
Estimated annual production and sales	25,000 units	75,000 units

The company has a conventional costing system in which manufacturing overhead is applied to units based on direct labor-hours. Data concerning manufacturing overhead and direct labor-hours for the upcoming year appear below:

Estimated total manufacturing overhead	$2,200,000
Estimated total direct labor-hours	110,000 DLHs

Required:
1. Compute the predetermined overhead rate based on direct labor-hours. Using this rate and other data from the problem, determine the unit product cost of each product.
2. The company is considering replacing its conventional costing system with an activity-based costing system that would assign its manufacturing overhead to the following four activity cost pools:

Activity Cost Pools and Activity Measures	Estimated Overhead Cost	Expected Activity		
		Xactive	Pathbreaker	Total
Supporting direct labor (direct labor-hours)	$ 797,500	35,000	75,000	110,000
Batch setups (setups).	680,000	250	150	400
Product sustaining (number of products)	650,000	1	1	2
General factory (machine-hours)	72,500	2,500	7,500	10,000
Total manufacturing overhead cost.	$2,200,000			

    Determine the activity rate for each of the four activity cost pools.
3. Using the activity rates and other data from the problem, determine the unit product cost of each product.
4. Explain why the conventional and activity-based cost assignments differ.

EXERCISE 3–11 Contrasting Activity-Based Costing and Conventional Product Costing [LO3–2, LO3–3, LO3–4]
Rusties Company recently implemented an activity-based costing system. At the beginning of the year, management made the following estimates of cost and activity in the company's five activity cost pools:

Activity Cost Pool	Activity Measure	Expected Overhead Cost	Expected Activity
Labor-related	Direct labor-hours	$18,000	2,000 DLHs
Purchase orders	Number of orders	$1,050	525 orders
Product testing	Number of tests	$3,500	350 tests
Template etching	Number of templates	$700	28 templates
General factory	Machine-hours	$50,000	10,000 MHs

Required:

1. Compute the activity rate for each of the activity cost pools.
2. The expected activity for the year was distributed among the company's four products as follows:

Activity Cost Pool	Expected Activity			
	Product A	Product B	Product C	Product D
Labor-related (DLHs)	500	100	700	700
Purchase orders (orders)	80	105	180	160
Product testing (tests)	200	60	0	90
Template etching (templates)	0	14	10	4
General factory (MHs)	3,400	2,200	1,800	2,600

    Using the ABC data, determine the total amount of overhead cost assigned to each product.

3. Assume that prior to implementing ABC, Rusties used a conventional cost system that applied all manufacturing overhead to products based on direct labor-hours. Explain how the conventional overhead cost assignments would differ from the activity-based cost assignments with respect to Product B.

Alternate problem set is available in the *Connect Library.*      **PROBLEMS**

All applicable problems are available with McGraw-Hill's *Connect Accounting.*

PROBLEM 3–12A   Contrasting ABC and Conventional Product Costs [LO3–2, LO3–3, LO3–4]

Precision Manufacturing Inc. (PMI) makes two types of industrial component parts—the EX300 and the TX500. It annually produces 60,000 units of EX300 and 12,500 units of TX500. The company's conventional cost system allocates manufacturing overhead to products using a plantwide overhead rate and direct labor dollars as the allocation base. Additional information relating to the company's two product lines is shown below:

	EX300	TX500	Total
Direct materials	$366,325	$162,550	$528,875
Direct labor	$120,000	$42,500	$162,500

The company is considering implementing an activity-based costing system that distributes all of its manufacturing overhead to four activities as shown below:

Activity Cost Pool (and Activity Measure)	Manufacturing Overhead	Activity		
		EX300	TX500	Total
Machining (machine-hours)	$198,250	90,000	62,500	152,500
Setups (setup hours)	150,000	75	300	375
Product-level (number of products)	100,250	1	1	2
General factory (direct labor dollars)	60,125	$120,000	$42,500	$162,500
Total manufacturing overhead cost	$508,625			

Required:
1. Compute the plantwide overhead rate that would be used in the company's conventional cost system. Using the plantwide rate, compute the unit product cost for each product.
2. Compute the activity rate for each activity cost pool. Using the activity rates, compute the unit product cost for each product.
3. Why do the conventional and activity-based cost assignments differ from one another?

PROBLEM 3–13A   ABC Cost Hierarchy [LO3–1]

Mitchell Corporation manufactures a variety of products in a single facility. Consultants hired by the company to do an activity-based costing analysis have identified the following activities carried out in the company on a routine basis:

a. Milling machines are used to make components for products.
b. A percentage of all completed goods are inspected on a random basis.
c. Production orders are issued for jobs.
d. The company's grounds crew maintains planted areas surrounding the factory.
e. Employees are trained in general procedures.
f. The human resources department screens and hires new employees.
g. Purchase orders are issued for materials required in production.
h. Material is received on the receiving dock and moved to the production area.
i. The plant controller prepares periodic accounting reports.
j. The engineering department makes modifications in the designs of products.
k. Machines are set up between batches of different products.
i. The maintenance crew does routine periodic maintenance on general-purpose equipment.

Required:
1. Classify each of the above activities as a unit-level, batch-level, product-level, or facility-level activity.
2. For each of the above activities, suggest an activity measure that could be used to allocate its costs to products.

PROBLEM 3–14A   Compute and Use Activity Rates to Determine the Costs of Serving Customers [LO3–2, LO3–3, LO3–4]

Gino's Restaurant is a popular restaurant in Boston, Massachusetts. The owner of the restaurant has been trying to better understand costs at the restaurant and has hired a student intern to conduct an activity-based costing study. The intern, in consultation with the owner, identified the following major activities:

Activity Cost Pool	Activity Measure
Serving a party of diners	Number of parties served
Serving a diner	Number of diners served
Serving drinks	Number of drinks ordered

A group of diners who ask to sit at the same table is counted as a party. Some costs, such as the costs of cleaning linen, are the same whether one person is at a table or the table is full. Other costs, such as washing dishes, depend on the number of diners served.

Data concerning these activities are shown below:

	Serving a Party	Serving a Diner	Serving Drinks	Total
Total cost	$32,800	$211,200	$69,600	$313,600
Total activity ...	8,000 parties	32,000 diners	58,000 drinks	

Prior to the activity-based costing study, the owner knew very little about the costs of the restaurant. She knew that the total cost for the month was $313,600 and that 32,000 diners had been served. Therefore, the average cost per diner was $9.80 ($313,600 ÷ 32,000 diners = $9.80 per diner).

Required:
1. Compute the activity rates for each of the three activities.
2. According to the activity-based costing system, what is the total cost of serving each of the following parties of diners?

a. A party of four diners who order three drinks in total.
b. A party of two diners who do not order any drinks.
c. A lone diner who orders two drinks.
3. Convert the total costs you computed in part (2) above to costs per diner. In other words, what is the average cost per diner for serving each of the following parties?
a. A party of four diners who order three drinks in total.
b. A party of two diners who do not order any drinks.
c. A lone diner who orders two drinks.
4. Why do the costs per diner for the three different parties differ from each other and from the overall average cost of $9.80 per diner?

PROBLEM 3–15A Contrasting ABC and Conventional Product Costs [LO3–2, LO3–3, LO3–4]

Marine, Inc., manufactures a product that is available in both a flexible and a rigid model. The company has made the rigid model for years; the flexible model was introduced several years ago to tap a new segment of the market. Since introduction of the flexible model, the company's profits have steadily declined, and management has become concerned about the accuracy of its costing system. Sales of the flexible model have been increasing rapidly.

Overhead is applied to products on the basis of direct labor-hours. At the beginning of the current year, management estimated that $600,000 in overhead costs would be incurred and the company would produce and sell 1,000 units of the flexible model and 10,000 units of the regular model. The flexible model requires 2.0 hours of direct labor time per unit, and the regular model requires 1.0 hours. Direct materials and labor costs per unit are given below:

	Flexible	Rigid
Direct materials cost per unit	$110.00	$80.00
Direct labor cost per unit	$30.00	$15.00

Required:
1. Compute the predetermined overhead rate using direct labor-hours as the basis for allocating overhead costs to products. Compute the unit product cost for one unit of each model.
2. An intern suggested that the company use activity-based costing to cost its products. A team was formed to investigate this idea. It came back with the recommendation that four activity cost pools be used. These cost pools and their associated activities are listed as follows:

Activity Cost Pool and Activity Measure	Estimated Overhead Cost	Expected Activity		
		Flexible	Rigid	Total
Purchase orders (number of orders).	$ 20,000	100	300	400
Rework requests (number of requests)	10,000	60	140	200
Product testing (number of tests)	210,000	900	1,200	2,100
Machine-related (machine-hours).	360,000	1,500	2,500	4,000
	$600,000			

Compute the activity rate for each of the activity cost pools.
3. Using activity-based costing, do the following:
a. Determine the total amount of overhead that would be assigned to each model for the year.
b. Compute the unit product cost for one unit of each model.
4. Can you identify a possible explanation for the company's declining profits? If so, what is it?

PROBLEM 3–16A Contrasting ABC and Conventional Product Costs [LO3–2, LO3–3, LO3–4]

For many years, Thomson Company manufactured a single product called LEC 40. Then three years ago, the company automated a portion of its plant and at the same time introduced a second product called LEC 90 that has become increasingly popular. The LEC 90 is a more complex product, requiring 0.80 hours of direct labor time per unit to manufacture and extensive machining in the automated portion of the plant. The LEC 40 requires only 0.40 hours of direct labor time per unit and only a small amount of machining. Manufacturing overhead costs are currently assigned to products on the basis of direct labor-hours.

Despite the growing popularity of the company's new LEC 90, profits have been declining steadily. Management is beginning to believe that there may be a problem with the company's costing system. Direct material and direct labor costs per unit are as follows:

	LEC 40	LEC 90
Direct materials	$30.00	$50.00
Direct labor (0.40 hours and 0.80 hours @ $15.00 per hour).	$6.00	$12.00

Management estimates that the company will incur $912,000 in manufacturing overhead costs during the current year and 60,000 units of the LEC 40 and 20,000 units of the LEC 90 will be produced and sold.

Required:
1. Compute the predetermined overhead rate assuming that the company continues to apply manufacturing overhead cost on the basis of direct labor-hours. Using this rate and other data from the problem, determine the unit product cost of each product.
2. Management is considering using activity-based costing to assign manufacturing overhead cost to products. The activity-based costing system would have the following four activity cost pools:

Activity Cost Pool	Activity Measure	Estimated Overhead Cost
Maintaining parts inventory	Number of part types	$225,000
Processing purchase orders.	Number of purchase orders	182,000
Quality control	Number of tests run	45,000
Machine-related	Machine-hours	460,000
		$912,000

		Expected Activity	
Activity Measure	LEC 40	LEC 90	Total
Number of part types	600	900	1,500
Number of purchase orders	2,000	800	2,800
Number of tests run	500	1,750	2,250
Machine-hours	1,600	8,400	10,000

Determine the activity rate for each of the four activity cost pools.
3. Using the activity rates you computed in part (2) above, do the following:
   a. Determine the total amount of manufacturing overhead cost that would be assigned to each product using the activity-based costing system. After these totals have been computed, determine the amount of manufacturing overhead cost per unit of each product.
   b. Compute the unit product cost of each product.
4. From the data you have developed in parts (1) through (3) above, identify factors that may account for the company's declining profits.

PROBLEM 3–17A   Contrast Activity-Based Costing and Conventional Product Costing [LO3–2, LO3–3, LO3–4]
Puget World, Inc., manufactures two models of television sets, the N 800 XL model and the N 500 model. Data regarding the two products follow:

	Direct Labor-Hours per Unit	Annual Production	Total Direct Labor-Hours
Model N 800 XL	3.0	3,000 units	9,000
Model N 500.	1.0	12,000 units	12,000
			21,000

Additional information about the company follows:
a. Model N 800 XL requires $75 in direct materials per unit, and Model N 500 requires $25.
b. The direct labor wage rate is $18 per hour.
c. The company has always used direct labor-hours as the base for applying manufacturing overhead cost to products.
d. Model N 800 XL is more complex to manufacture than Model N 500 and requires the use of special equipment. Consequently, the company is considering the use of activity-based costing to assign manufacturing overhead cost to products. Three activity cost pools have been identified as follows:

Activity Cost Pool	Activity Measure	Estimated Overhead Cost
Machine setups	Number of setups	$ 360,000
Special processing.	Machine-hours	165,000
General factory.	Direct labor-hours	1,260,000
		$1,785,000

Activity Measure	Expected Activity		
	Model N 800 XL	Model N 500	Total
Number of setups	100	200	300
Machine-hours	16,500	0	16,500
Direct labor-hours	9,000	12,000	21,000

Required:
1. Assume that the company continues to use direct labor-hours as the base for applying overhead cost to products.
   a. Compute the predetermined overhead rate.
   b. Compute the unit product cost of each model.
2. Assume that the company decides to use activity-based costing to assign manufacturing overhead cost to products.
   a. Compute the activity rate for each activity cost pool and determine the amount of overhead cost that would be assigned to each model using the activity-based costing system.
   b. Compute the unit product cost of each model.
3. Explain why manufacturing overhead cost shifts from Model N 500 to Model N 800 XL under activity-based costing.

PROBLEM 3–18A   Contrasting Activity-Based Costing and Conventional Product Costing [LO3–2, LO3–3, LO3–4]

Adria Company recently implemented an activity-based costing system. At the beginning of the year, management made the following estimates of cost and activity in the company's five activity cost pools:

Activity Cost Pool	Activity Measure	Expected Overhead Cost	Expected Activity
Labor-related.	Direct labor-hours	$35,000	7,000 DLHs
Purchase orders	Number of orders	$4,000	2,000 orders
Material receipts	Number of receipts	$10,450	950 receipts
Relay assembly	Number of relays	$7,000	1,000 relays
General factory.	Machine-hours	$240,000	40,000 MHs

Required:
1. Compute the activity rate for each of the activity cost pools.
2. The expected activity for the year was distributed among the company's four products as follows:

Activity Cost Pool	Expected Activity			
	Product A	Product B	Product C	Product D
Labor-related (DLHs)	2,400	500	3,500	600
Production orders (orders)	100	350	800	750
Materials receipts (receipts)	400	208	342	0
Relay assembly (relays)	170	170	300	360
General factory (MHs)	12,000	7,000	8,000	13,000

Using the ABC data, determine the total amount of overhead cost assigned to each product.
3. Assume that prior to implementing ABC, Adria used a conventional cost system that applied all manufacturing overhead to products based on machine-hours. Explain how the conventional cost assignments would differ from the activity-based cost assignments with respect to Product C.

BUILDING YOUR SKILLS

COMMUNICATING IN PRACTICE [LO3–1]

You often provide advice to Maria Graham, a client who is interested in diversifying her company. Maria is considering the purchase of a small manufacturing company that assembles and packages its many products by hand. She plans to automate the factory and her projections indicate that the company will once again be profitable within two to three years. During her review of the company's records, she discovered that the company currently uses direct labor-hours to allocate overhead to its products. Because of its simplicity, Maria hopes that this approach can continue to be used.

Required:
Write a memorandum to Maria that addresses whether or not direct labor should continue to be used as an allocation base for overhead.

TEAMWORK IN ACTION [LO3–1]

Your team should visit and closely observe the operations at a fast-food restaurant.

Required:
Identify activities and costs at the restaurant that fall into each of the following categories:
a. Unit-level activities and costs.
b. Customer-level activities and costs. (This is like a batch-level activity at a manufacturing company.)
c. Product-level activities and costs.
d. Facility-level activities and costs.

ETHICS CHALLENGE [LO3–1]

You and your friends go to a restaurant as a group. At the end of the meal, the issue arises of how the bill for the group should be shared. One alternative is to figure out the cost of what each individual consumed and divide up the bill accordingly. Another alternative is to split the bill equally among the individuals.

Required:
Which system for dividing the bill is more equitable? Which system is easier to use? How does this issue relate to the material covered in this chapter?

CASE [LO3–2, LO3–3, LO3–4]

Coffee Bean, Inc. (CBI), is a processor and distributor of a variety of blends of coffee. The company buys coffee beans from around the world and roasts, blends, and packages them for resale. CBI offers a large variety of different coffees that it sells to gourmet shops in one-pound bags. The major cost of the coffee is raw materials. However, the company's predominantly automated roasting, blending, and packing processes require a substantial amount of manufacturing overhead. The company uses relatively little direct labor. Some of CBI's coffees are very popular and sell in large volumes, while a few of the newer blends sell in very low volumes.

For the coming year, CBI's budget includes estimated manufacturing overhead cost of $3,000,000. CBI assigns manufacturing overhead to products on the basis of direct labor-hours. The expected direct labor cost totals $600,000, which represents 50,000 hours of direct labor time.

The expected costs for direct materials and direct labor for one-pound bags of two of the company's coffee products appear below.

	Mona Loa	Malaysian
Direct materials	$4.20	$3.20
Direct labor (0.025 hours per bag)	$0.30	$0.30

CBI's controller believes that the company's traditional costing system may be providing misleading cost information. To determine whether or not this is correct, the controller has prepared an analysis of the year's expected manufacturing overhead costs, as shown in the following table:

Activity Cost Pool	Activity Measure	Expected Activity for the Year	Expected Cost for the Year
Purchasing	Purchase orders	1,710 orders	$ 513,000
Material handling	Number of setups	1,800 setups	720,000
Quality control	Number of batches	600 batches	144,000
Roasting	Roasting hours	96,100 roasting hours	961,000
Blending	Blending hours	33,500 blending hours	402,000
Packaging	Packaging hours	26,000 packaging hours	260,000
Total manufacturing overhead cost			$3,000,000

Data regarding the expected production of Mona Loa and Malaysian coffee are presented below. There will be no raw materials inventory for either of these coffees at the beginning of the year.

	Mona Loa	Malaysian
Expected sales	100,000 pounds	2,000 pounds
Batch size	10,000 pounds	500 pounds
Setups	3 per batch	3 per batch
Purchase order size	20,000 pounds	500 pounds
Roasting time per 100 pounds	1.0 roasting hours	1.0 roasting hours
Blending time per 100 pounds	0.5 blending hours	0.5 blending hours
Packaging time per 100 pounds	0.1 packaging hours	0.1 packaging hours

Required:

1. Using direct labor-hours as the base for assigning manufacturing overhead cost to products, do the following:
   a. Determine the predetermined overhead rate that will be used during the year.
   b. Determine the unit product cost of one pound of the Mona Loa coffee and one pound of the Malaysian coffee.
2. Using activity-based costing as the basis for assigning manufacturing overhead cost to products, do the following:
   a. Determine the total amount of manufacturing overhead cost assigned to the Mona Loa coffee and to the Malaysian coffee for the year.
   b. Using the data developed in part (2a) above, compute the amount of manufacturing overhead cost per pound of the Mona Loa coffee and the Malaysian coffee. Round all computations to the nearest whole cent.
   c. Determine the unit product cost of one pound of the Mona Loa coffee and one pound of the Malaysian coffee.
3. Write a brief memo to the president of CBI explaining what you have found in parts (1) and (2) above and discussing the implications to the company of using direct labor as the base for assigning manufacturing overhead cost to products.

(CMA, adapted)

ANALYTICAL THINKING* [LO3–2, LO3–3, LO3–4]

"Two dollars of gross margin per briefcase? That's ridiculous!" roared Roy Thurmond, president of First-Line Cases, Inc. "Why do we go on producing those standard briefcases when we're able to make over $11 per unit on our specialty items? Maybe it's time to get out of the standard line and focus the whole plant on specialty work."

Mr. Thurmond was referring to a summary of unit costs and revenues that he had just received from the company's accounting department:

	Standard Briefcases	Specialty Briefcases
Selling price per unit.	$26.25	$42.50
Unit product cost	24.25	31.40
Gross margin per unit.	$ 2.00	$11.10

FirstLine Cases produces briefcases from leather, fabric, and synthetic materials in a single plant. The basic product is a standard briefcase that is made from leather lined with fabric. The standard briefcase is a high-quality item and has sold well for many years.

Last year, the company decided to expand its product line and produce specialty briefcases for special orders. These briefcases differ from the standard in that they vary in size, they contain the finest leather and synthetic materials, and they are imprinted with the buyer's name. To reduce labor costs on the specialty briefcases, automated machines do most of the cutting and stitching. These machines are used to a much lesser degree in the production of standard briefcases.

"I agree that the specialty business is looking better and better," replied Beth Mersey, the company's marketing manager. "And there seems to be plenty of demand out there, particularly because the competition hasn't been able to touch our price. Did you know that Velsun Company, our biggest competitor, charges over $50 a unit for its specialty items? Now that's what I call gouging the customer!"

A breakdown of the manufacturing cost for each of FirstLine Cases' products is given below:

	Standard Briefcases	Specialty Briefcases
Units produced each month	10,000	2,500
Direct materials:		
Leather	$ 8.00	$12.00
Fabric	2.00	1.00
Synthetic	0	7.00
Total materials	10.00	20.00
Direct labor (0.5 DLH and 0.40 DLH @ $12.00 per DLH) . . .	6.00	4.80
Manufacturing overhead (0.5 DLH and 0.4 DLH @ $16.50 per DLH)	8.25	6.60
Total cost per unit	$24.25	$31.40

Manufacturing overhead is applied to products on the basis of direct labor-hours. The rate of $16.50 per hour was determined by dividing the total manufacturing overhead cost for a month by the direct labor-hours:

$$\text{Predetermined overhead rate} = \frac{\text{Manufacturing overhead}}{\text{Direct labor-hours}} = \frac{\$99,000}{6,000 \text{ DLHs}} = \$16.50 \text{ per DLH}$$

---

*Adapted from Harold P. Roth and Imogene Posey, "Management Accounting Case Study: Carry All Company," *Management Accounting Campus Report,* Institute of Management Accountants, Fall 1991, p. 9. Used by permission from the IMA, Montvale, NJ, USA, www.imanet.org.

The following additional information is available about the company and its products:

a. Standard briefcases are produced in batches of 1,000 units, and specialty briefcases are produced in batches of 100 units. Thus, the company does 10 setups for the standard items each month and 25 setups for the specialty items. A setup for the standard items requires one hour, whereas a setup for the specialty items requires two hours.

b. All briefcases are inspected to ensure that quality standards are met. Each month a total of 200 hours is spent inspecting the standard briefcases and 400 hours is spent inspecting the specialty briefcases.

c. A standard briefcase requires 0.5 hours of machine time, and a specialty briefcase requires 1.2 hours of machine time.

d. The company is considering the use of activity-based costing as an alternative to its traditional costing system for computing unit product costs. The activity-based costing system has already been designed and costs have been allocated to the activity cost pools. The activity cost pools and activity measures are detailed below:

Activity Cost Pool	Activity Measure	Estimated Overhead Cost
Purchasing	Number of orders	$15,000
Material handling	Number of receipts	16,000
Production orders and setups.	Setup-hours	6,000
Inspection.	Inspection-hours	18,000
Frame assembly.	Assembly-hours	12,000
Machine-related	Machine-hours	32,000
		$99,000

	Expected Activity		
Activity Measure	Standard Briefcases	Specialty Briefcases	Total
Number of orders:			
Leather	50	10	60
Fabric	70	20	90
Synthetic material	0	150	150
Number of receipts:			
Leather	70	10	80
Fabric	85	20	105
Synthetic material	0	215	215
Setup-hours	?	?	?
Inspection-hours.	200	400	600
Assembly-hours	700	800	1,500
Machine-hours	?	?	?

Required:

1. Using activity-based costing, determine the amount of manufacturing overhead cost that would be assigned to each standard briefcase and each specialty briefcase.

2. Using the data computed in part (1) above and other data from the case as needed, determine the unit product cost of each product line from the perspective of the activity-based costing system.

3. Within the limitations of the data that have been provided, evaluate the president's concern about the profitability of the two product lines. Would you recommend that the company shift its resources entirely to the production of specialty briefcases? Explain.

4. Beth Mersey stated that "the competition hasn't been able to touch our price on specialty business." Why do you suppose the competition hasn't been able to touch FirstLine Cases' price?

A LOOK BACK

We described a basic job-order costing system in Chapter 2 that used a single plantwide overhead rate. Then, in Chapter 3, we looked at activity-based costing, a more sophisticated technique that uses a variety of allocation bases to assign overhead costs to products.

A LOOK AT THIS CHAPTER

Chapter 4 covers process costing, which is an important alternative to job-order costing. In process costing, departmental costs are applied uniformly to the products processed through the department during the period.

A LOOK AHEAD

Chapter 5 describes the basics of cost-volume-profit analysis, a tool that helps managers understand the interrelationships among cost, volume, and profit.

4

Process Costing

CHAPTER OUTLINE

Comparison of Job-Order and Process Costing

- Similarities between Job-Order and Process Costing

- Differences between Job-Order and Process Costing

Cost Flows in Process Costing

- Processing Departments

- The Flow of Materials, Labor, and Overhead Costs

- Materials, Labor, and Overhead Cost Entries

Equivalent Units of Production

- Weighted-Average Method

Compute and Apply Costs

- Cost per Equivalent Unit—Weighted-Average Method

- Applying Costs—Weighted-Average Method

- Cost Reconciliation Report

SUPPLEMENT: PROCESS COSTING USING THE FIFO METHOD
(available in the *Connect Library*)

Equivalent Units—FIFO Method

Comparison of Equivalent Units of Production under the Weighted-Average and FIFO Methods

Cost per Equivalent Unit—FIFO Method

Applying Costs—FIFO Method

Cost Reconciliation Report—FIFO Method

A Comparison of Costing Methods

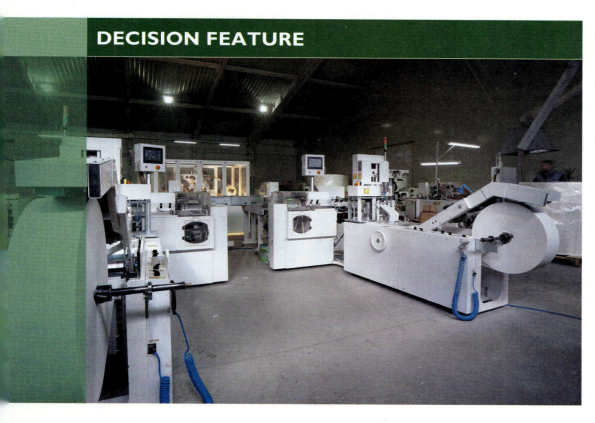

Costing the "Quicker-Picker-Upper"

If you have ever spilled milk, there is a good chance that you used Bounty paper towels to clean up the mess. **Procter & Gamble (P&G)** manufactures Bounty in two main processing departments—Paper Making and Paper Converting. In the Paper Making Department, wood pulp is converted into paper and then spooled into 2,000-pound rolls that are inventoried and retrieved as needed to supply the paper converting process. In the Paper Converting Department, two 2,000-pound rolls of paper are simultaneously unwound into a machine that creates a two-ply paper towel that is decorated, perforated, and embossed to create texture. The large sheets of paper towels that emerge from this process are wrapped around a cylinder-shaped cardboard core measuring eight feet in length. Once enough sheets wrap around the core, the eight-foot roll is cut into individual rolls of Bounty that are sent down a conveyor to be wrapped, packed, and shipped.

In this type of manufacturing environment, costs cannot be readily traced to individual rolls of Bounty; however, given the homogeneous nature of the product, the total costs incurred in the Paper Making Department can be spread uniformly across its output of 2,000-pound rolls of paper. Similarly, the total costs incurred to produce a particular style of Bounty in the Paper Converting Department (including the cost of the 2,000-pound rolls that are transferred in from the Paper Making Department) can be spread uniformly across the number of cases produced of that style.

P&G uses a similar costing approach for many of its products such as Tide, Crest toothpaste, and Dawn dishwashing liquid.

Source: Conversation with Brad Bays, retired financial executive from Procter & Gamble.

Job-order costing and process costing are two common methods for determining unit product costs. As explained in Chapter 2, job-order costing is used when many different jobs or products are worked on each period. Examples of industries that use job-order costing include furniture manufacturing, special-order printing, shipbuilding, and many types of service organizations.

By contrast, **process costing** is used most commonly in industries that convert raw materials into homogeneous (i.e., uniform) products, such as bricks, soda, or paper, on a continuous basis. Examples of companies that would use process costing include **Reynolds Consumer Products** (aluminum ingots), **Scott Paper** (paper towels), **General Mills** (flour), **ExxonMobil** (gasoline and lubricating oils), **Coppertone** (sunscreens), and **Kellogg's** (breakfast cereals). In addition, process costing is sometimes used in companies with assembly operations. A form of process costing may also be used in utilities that produce gas, water, and electricity.

Our purpose in this chapter is to explain how product costing works in a process costing system.

COMPARISON OF JOB-ORDER AND PROCESS COSTING

In some ways process costing is very similar to job-order costing, and in some ways it is very different. In this section, we focus on these similarities and differences to provide a foundation for the detailed discussion of process costing that follows.

Similarities between Job-Order and Process Costing

Much of what you learned in the job-order costing chapter about costing and cost flows applies equally well to process costing in this chapter. We are not throwing out all that we have learned about costing and starting from "scratch" with a whole new system. The similarities between job-order and process costing can be summarized as follows:

1. Both systems have the same basic purposes—to assign material, labor, and manufacturing overhead costs to products and to provide a mechanism for computing unit product costs.
2. Both systems use the same basic manufacturing accounts, including Manufacturing Overhead, Raw Materials, Work in Process, and Finished Goods.
3. The flow of costs through the manufacturing accounts is basically the same in both systems.

As can be seen from this comparison, much of the knowledge that you have already acquired about costing is applicable to a process costing system. Our task now is to refine and extend your knowledge to process costing.

Differences between Job-Order and Process Costing

There are three differences between job-order and process costing. First, process costing is used when a company produces a continuous flow of units that are indistinguishable from one another. Job-order costing is used when a company produces many different jobs that have unique production requirements. Second, under process costing, it makes no sense to try to identify materials, labor, and overhead costs with a particular customer order (as we did with job-order costing) because each order is just one of many that are filled from a continuous flow of virtually identical units from the production line. Accordingly, process costing accumulates costs by department (rather than by order) and assigns these costs uniformly to all units that pass through the department during a period. Job cost sheets (which we used for job-order costing) are not used to accumulate costs. Third, process costing systems compute unit costs by department. This differs from job-order costing where unit costs are computed by job on the job cost sheet. Exhibit 4–1 summarizes the differences just described.

EXHIBIT 4–1
Differences between Job-Order
and Process Costing

Job-Order Costing	Process Costing
1. Many different jobs are worked on during each period, with each job having different production requirements.	1. A single product is produced either on a continuous basis or for long periods of time. All units of product are identical.
2. Costs are accumulated by individual job.	2. Costs are accumulated by department.
3. Unit costs are computed *by job* on the job cost sheet.	3. Unit costs are computed *by department.*

COST FLOWS IN PROCESS COSTING

Before going through a detailed example of process costing, it will be helpful to see how, in a general way, manufacturing costs flow through a process costing system.

Processing Departments

A **processing department** is an organizational unit where work is performed on a product and where materials, labor, or overhead costs are added to the product. For example, a **Nalley's** potato chip factory might have three processing departments—one for preparing potatoes, one for cooking, and one for inspecting and packaging. A brick factory might have two processing departments—one for mixing and molding clay into brick form and one for firing the molded brick. Some products and services may go through a number of processing departments, while others may go through only one or two. Regardless of the number of processing departments, they all have two essential features. First, the activity in the processing department is performed uniformly on all of the units passing through it. Second, the output of the processing department is homogeneous; in other words, all of the units produced are identical.

Products in a process costing environment, such as bricks or potato chips, typically flow in sequence from one department to another as in Exhibit 4–2.

The Flow of Materials, Labor, and Overhead Costs

Cost accumulation is simpler in a process costing system than in a job-order costing system. In a process costing system, instead of having to trace costs to hundreds of different jobs, costs are traced to only a few processing departments.

EXHIBIT 4–2   Sequential Processing Departments

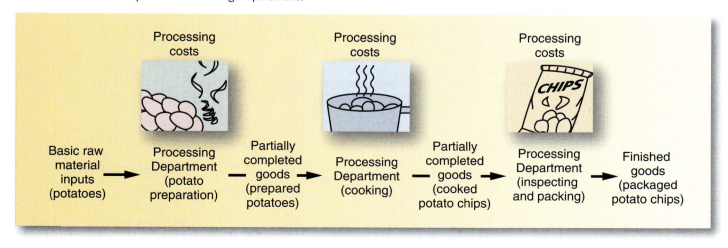

IN BUSINESS

Monks Make a Living Selling Beer

The Trappist monks of St. Sixtus monastery in Belgium have been brewing beer since 1839. Customers must make an appointment with the monastery to buy a maximum of two 24-bottle cases per month. The scarce and highly prized beer sells for more than $15 per 11-ounce bottle.

The monk's brewing ingredients include water, malt, hops, sugar, and yeast. The sequential steps of the beer-making process include grinding and crushing the malt grain, brewing by adding water to the crushed malt, filtering to separate a liquid called wort from undissolved grain particles, boiling to sterilize the wort (including adding sugar to increase the density of the wort), fermentation by adding yeast to convert sugar into alcohol and carbon dioxide, storage where the beer is aged for at least three weeks, and bottling where more sugar and yeast are added to enable two weeks of additional fermentation in the bottle.

Unlike growth-oriented for-profit companies, the monastery has not expanded its production capacity since 1946, seeking instead to sell just enough beer to sustain the monks' modest lifestyle.

Source: John W. Miller, "Trappist Command: Thou Shalt Not Buy Too Much of Our Beer," *The Wall Street Journal*, November 29, 2007, pp. A1 and A14.

A T-account model of materials, labor, and overhead cost flows in a process costing system is shown in Exhibit 4–3. Several key points should be noted from this exhibit. First, note that a separate Work in Process account is maintained for *each processing department*. In contrast, in a job-order costing system the entire company may have only one Work in Process account. Second, note that the completed production of the first processing department (Department A in the exhibit) is transferred to the Work in Process account of the second processing department (Department B). After further work in

EXHIBIT 4–3   T-Account Model of Process Costing Flows

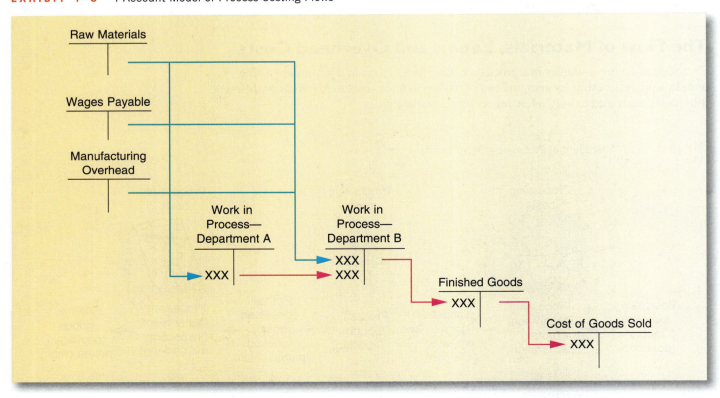

Department B, the completed units are then transferred to Finished Goods. (In Exhibit 4–3, we show only two processing departments, but a company can have many processing departments.)

Finally, note that materials, labor, and overhead costs can be added in *any* processing department—not just the first. Costs in Department B's Work in Process account consist of the materials, labor, and overhead costs incurred in Department B plus the costs attached to partially completed units transferred in from Department A (called transferred-in costs).

Materials, Labor, and Overhead Cost Entries

To complete our discussion of cost flows in a process costing system, in this section we show journal entries relating to materials, labor, and overhead costs at Megan's Classic Cream Soda, a company that has two processing departments—Formulating and Bottling. In the Formulating Department, ingredients are checked for quality and then mixed and injected with carbon dioxide to create bulk cream soda. In the Bottling Department, bottles are checked for defects, filled with cream soda, capped, visually inspected again for defects, and then packed for shipping.

LEARNING OBJECTIVE 4–1

Record the flow of materials, labor, and overhead through a process costing system.

Materials Costs   As in job-order costing, materials are drawn from the storeroom using a materials requisition form. Materials can be added in any processing department, although it is not unusual for materials to be added only in the first processing department, with subsequent departments adding only labor and overhead costs.

At Megan's Classic Cream Soda, some materials (i.e., water, flavors, sugar, and carbon dioxide) are added in the Formulating Department and some materials (i.e., bottles, caps, and packing materials) are added in the Bottling Department. The journal entry to record the materials used in the first processing department, the Formulating Department, is as follows:

| Work in Process—Formulating .... | XXX | |
| Raw Materials .... | | XXX |

The journal entry to record the materials used in the second processing department, the Bottling Department, is as follows:

| Work in Process—Bottling .... | XXX | |
| Raw Materials .... | | XXX |

Labor Costs   In process costing, labor costs are traced to departments—not to individual jobs. The following journal entry records the labor costs in the Formulating Department at Megan's Classic Cream Soda:

| Work in Process—Formulating .... | XXX | |
| Salaries and Wages Payable .... | | XXX |

A similar entry would be made to record labor costs in the Bottling Department.

Overhead Costs   In process costing, as in job-order costing, predetermined overhead rates are usually used. Manufacturing overhead cost is applied according to the amount of the allocation base that is incurred in the department. The following journal entry records the overhead cost applied in the Formulating Department:

| Work in Process—Formulating .... | XXX | |
| Manufacturing Overhead .... | | XXX |

A similar entry would be made to apply manufacturing overhead costs in the Bottling Department.

Completing the Cost Flows   Once processing has been completed in a department, the units are transferred to the next department for further processing, as illustrated in the T-accounts in Exhibit 4–3. The following journal entry transfers the cost of partially completed units from the Formulating Department to the Bottling Department:

Work in Process—Bottling.	XXX	
Work in Process—Formulating.		XXX

After processing has been completed in the Bottling Department, the costs of the completed units are transferred to the Finished Goods inventory account:

Finished Goods	XXX	
Work in Process—Bottling		XXX

Finally, when a customer's order is filled and units are sold, the cost of the units is transferred to Cost of Goods Sold:

Cost of Goods Sold.	XXX	
Finished Goods		XXX

To summarize, the cost flows between accounts are basically the same in a process costing system as they are in a job-order costing system. The only difference at this point is that in a process costing system each department has a separate Work in Process account.

We now turn our attention to Double Diamond Skis, a company that manufactures a high-performance deep-powder ski, and that uses process costing to determine its unit product costs. The company's production process is illustrated in Exhibit 4–4. Skis go through a sequence of five processing departments, starting with the Shaping and Milling Department and ending with the Finishing and Pairing Department. The basic idea in process costing is to add together all of the costs incurred in a department during a period and then to spread those costs uniformly across the units processed in that department during that period. As we shall see, applying this simple idea involves a few complications.

CONCEPT CHECK

1. Which of the following statements is true? (You may select more than one answer.)
    a. Job-order costing and process costing systems both use the same basic manufacturing accounts, including Manufacturing Overhead, Raw Materials, Work in Process, and Finished Goods.
    b. Process costing is used when a company produces a continuous flow of units that are indistinguishable from one another.
    c. Process costing systems accumulate costs by customer order rather than by department.
    d. Job-order costing and process costing systems both provide a mechanism for computing unit product costs.

EQUIVALENT UNITS OF PRODUCTION

After materials, labor, and overhead costs have been accumulated in a department, the department's output must be determined so that unit product costs can be computed. The difficulty is that a department usually has some partially completed units in its ending inventory. It does not seem reasonable to count these partially completed units as

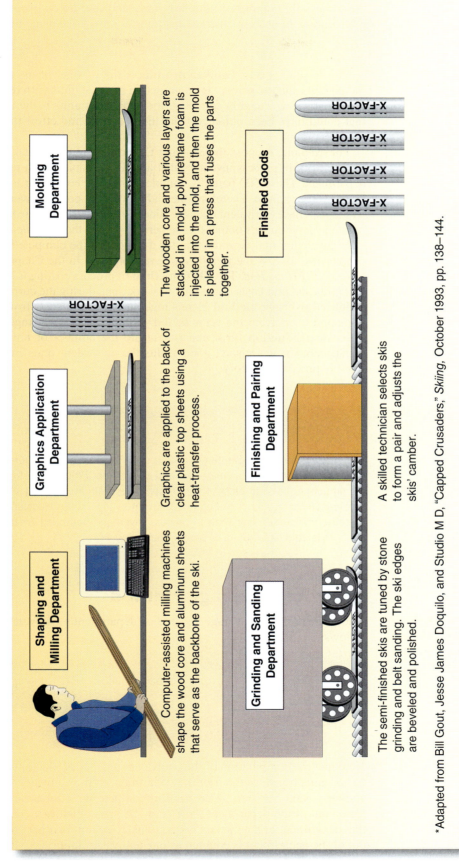

Shaping and Milling Department

Computer-assisted milling machines shape the wood core and aluminum sheets that serve as the backbone of the ski.

Graphics Application Department

Graphics are applied to the back of clear plastic top sheets using a heat-transfer process.

Molding Department

The wooden core and various layers are stacked in a mold, polyurethane foam is injected into the mold, and then the mold is placed in a press that fuses the parts together.

Grinding and Sanding Department

The semi-finished skis are tuned by stone grinding and belt sanding. The ski edges are beveled and polished.

Finishing and Pairing Department

A skilled technician selects skis to form a pair and adjusts the skis' camber.

Finished Goods

EXHIBIT 4–4   The Production Process at Double Diamond Skis*

*Adapted from Bill Gout, Jesse James Doquilo, and Studio M D, "Capped Crusaders," *Skiing*, October 1993, pp. 138–144.

equivalent to fully completed units when counting the department's output. Therefore, these partially completed units are translated into an *equivalent* number of fully completed units. In process costing, this translation is done using the following formula:

$$\text{Equivalent units} = \text{Number of partially completed units} \times \text{Percentage completion}$$

As the formula states, **equivalent units** is the product of the number of partially completed units and the percentage completion of those units with respect to the processing in the department. Roughly speaking, the equivalent units is the number of complete units that could have been obtained from the materials and effort that went into the partially complete units.

For example, suppose the Molding Department at Double Diamond has 500 units in its ending work in process inventory that are 60% complete with respect to processing in the department. These 500 partially complete units are equivalent to 300 fully complete units ($500 \times 60\% = 300$). Therefore, the ending work in process inventory contains 300 equivalent units. These equivalent units are added to any units completed during the period to determine the department's output for the period—called the *equivalent units of production*.

Equivalent units of production for a period can be computed in different ways. In this chapter, we discuss the *weighted-average method*. In the Chapter 4 Supplement, we discuss the *FIFO method*. The **FIFO method** of process costing is a method in which equivalent units and unit costs relate only to work done during the current period. In contrast, the **weighted-average method** blends together units and costs from the current period with units and costs from the prior period. In the weighted-average method, the **equivalent units of production** for a department are the number of units transferred to the next department (or to finished goods) plus the equivalent units in the department's ending work in process inventory.

HELPFUL HINT

You need to perform separate equivalent units of production calculations for each manufacturing cost category, such as materials and conversion. When using the weighted-average method to compute equivalent units of production for a cost category you should ignore the completion percentage for the units in beginning inventory. The units transferred to the next department plus the units in ending work in process inventory multiplied by their percentage completion equals the equivalent units of production.

Weighted-Average Method

LEARNING OBJECTIVE 4–2

Compute the equivalent units of production using the weighted-average method.

Under the weighted-average method, a department's equivalent units are computed as follows:

> **WEIGHTED-AVERAGE METHOD**
> (a separate calculation is made for each cost category in each processing department)
>
> $$\frac{\text{Equivalent units}}{\text{of production}} = \frac{\text{Units transferred to the next}}{\text{department or to finished goods}} + \frac{\text{Equivalent units in ending}}{\text{work in process inventory}}$$

Note that the computation of the equivalent units of production involves adding the number of units transferred out of the department to the equivalent units in the department's ending inventory. There is no need to compute the equivalent units for the units transferred out of the department—they are 100% complete with respect to the work done in that department or they would not be transferred out. In other words, each unit transferred out of the department is counted as one equivalent unit.

| Shaping and Milling Department | Units | Percent Complete | |
		Materials	Conversion
Beginning work in process inventory.	200	55%	30%
Units started into production during May	5,000		
Units completed during May and transferred to the next department.	4,800	100%*	100%*
Ending work in process inventory.	400	40%	25%

*We always assume that units transferred out of a department are 100% complete with respect to the processing done in that department.

Consider the Shaping and Milling Department at Double Diamond. This department uses computerized milling machines to precisely shape the wooden core and metal sheets that will be used to form the backbone of the ski. (See Exhibit 4–4 for an overview of the production process at Double Diamond.) The activity shown above took place in the department in May.

The first thing to note about the activity in the Shaping and Milling Department is the flow of units through the department. The department started with 200 units in beginning work in process inventory. During May, 5,000 units were started into production. This made a total of 5,200 units. Of this total, 4,800 units were completed and transferred to the next department during May and 400 units were still in the department at the end of the month as ending work in process inventory. In general, the units in beginning work in process inventory plus the units started into production must equal the units in ending work in process inventory plus the units completed and transferred out. In equation form, this is:

Units in beginning work in process inventory + Units started into production or transferred in = Units in ending work in process inventory + Units completed and transferred out

Note the use of the term *conversion* in the table above. **Conversion cost,** as defined in an earlier chapter, is direct labor cost plus manufacturing overhead cost. In process costing, conversion cost is often treated as a single element of product cost.

Note that the beginning work in process inventory was 55% complete with respect to materials costs and 30% complete with respect to conversion costs. This means that 55% of the materials costs required to complete the units in the department had already been incurred. Likewise, 30% of the conversion costs required to complete the units had already been incurred.

Two equivalent unit figures must be computed—one for materials and one for conversion. These computations are shown in Exhibit 4–5.

Note that the computations in Exhibit 4–5 ignore the fact that the units in the beginning work in process inventory were partially complete. For example, the 200 units in beginning inventory were already 30% complete with respect to conversion costs. Nevertheless, the weighted-average method is concerned only with the 4,900 equivalent

Shaping and Milling Department	Materials	Conversion
Units transferred to the next department	4,800	4,800
Ending work in process inventory:		
Materials: 400 units × 40% complete	160	
Conversion: 400 units × 25% complete		100
Equivalent units of production.	4,960	4,900

EXHIBIT 4–5
Equivalent Units of Production: Weighted-Average Method

units that are in ending inventories and in units transferred to the next department; it is not concerned with the fact that the beginning inventory was already partially complete. In other words, the 4,900 equivalent units computed using the weighted-average method include work that was accomplished in prior periods. This is a key point concerning the weighted-average method and it is easy to overlook.

IN BUSINESS

Getting Less for the Same Price

When the prices of raw materials such as sugar and cotton increase during an economic downturn, companies realize that they cannot pass these cost increases on to customers in the form of higher prices. Instead, companies often respond to these circumstances by holding their prices constant while giving customers less for their money. For example, when the price of cotton increased **Georgia-Pacific** responded by decreasing the width of its Angel Soft Double Roll toilet paper from 4.27 inches to 4.00 inches. The company also reduced the number of sheets per roll from 352 to 300. Similarly, **Procter & Gamble** decreased the number of sheets in a roll of Charmin Ultra Soft Big Roll from 200 to 176.

These product size reductions not only lower raw material costs, but they also reduce shipping costs. Georgia-Pacific estimates that its smaller rolls of toilet paper enable it to transport 12–17% more units per truck, thereby saving 345,000 gallons of gasoline per year.

Source: Beth Kowitt, "When Less is . . . Less?" *Fortune,* November 15, 2010, p. 21.

DECISION POINT

Writing Term Papers

Assume your professors assigned four separate five-page papers that were all due on the same day. You turned in two complete papers and two incomplete papers—one of which was two pages long and the other was three pages long. Assuming that each page requires the same time and effort, how many complete papers could you have turned in with the same expenditure of time and effort?

Exhibit 4–6 provides another way of looking at the computation of equivalent units of production. This exhibit depicts the equivalent units computation for conversion costs. Study it carefully before going on.

EXHIBIT 4–6   Visual Perspective of Equivalent Units of Production

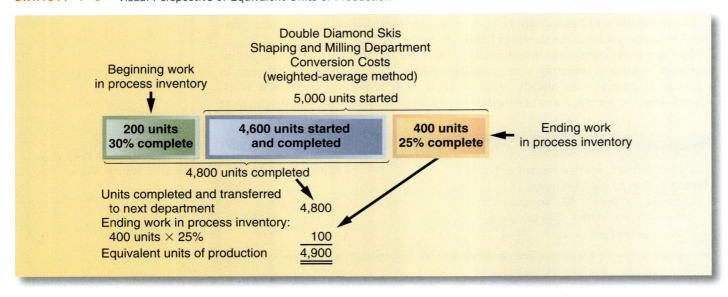

COMPUTE AND APPLY COSTS

In the last section, we computed the equivalent units of production for materials and for conversion at Double Diamond Skis. In this section we will compute the cost per equivalent unit for materials and for conversion. We will then use these costs to value ending work in process and finished goods inventories. Exhibit 4–7 displays all of the data concerning May's operations in the Shaping and Milling Department that we will need to complete these tasks.

EXHIBIT 4–7
Shaping and Milling Department Data for May Operations

Beginning work in process inventory:	
Units in process	200
Completion with respect to materials.	55%
Completion with respect to conversion	30%
Costs in beginning work in process inventory:	
Materials cost	$ 9,600
Conversion cost.	5,575
Total cost in beginning work in process inventory	$15,175
Units started into production during the period	5,000
Units completed and transferred out	4,800
Costs added during the period:	
Materials cost	$368,600
Conversion cost	350,900
Total cost added during the period	$719,500
Ending work in process inventory:	
Units in process	400
Completion with respect to materials	40%
Completion with respect to conversion	25%

Cost per Equivalent Unit—Weighted-Average Method

In the weighted-average method, the cost per equivalent unit is computed as follows:

$$\text{WEIGHTED-AVERAGE METHOD}$$
(a separate calculation is made for each cost category in each processing department)

$$\text{Cost per equivalent unit} = \frac{\begin{array}{c}\text{Cost of beginning} \\ \text{work in process inventory}\end{array} + \begin{array}{c}\text{Cost added} \\ \text{during the period}\end{array}}{\text{Equivalent units of production}}$$

Note that the numerator is the sum of the cost of beginning work in process inventory and of the cost added during the period. Thus, the weighted-average method blends together costs from the prior and current periods. That is why it is called the weighted-average method; it averages together units and costs from both the prior and current periods.

The costs per equivalent unit for materials and for conversion are computed below for the Shaping and Milling Department for May:

Shaping and Milling Department Costs per Equivalent Unit	Materials	Conversion
Cost of beginning work in process inventory	$ 9,600	$ 5,575
Costs added during the period	368,600	350,900
Total cost (a)	$378,200	$356,475
Equivalent units of production (see Exhibit 4–5) (b)	4,960	4,900
Cost per equivalent unit (a) ÷ (b)	$76.25	$72.75

Applying Costs—Weighted-Average Method

The costs per equivalent unit are used to value units in ending inventory and units that are transferred to the next department. For example, each unit transferred out of Double Diamond's Shaping and Milling Department to the Graphics Application Department, as depicted in Exhibit 4–4, will carry with it a cost of $149.00 ($76.25 for materials cost and $72.75 for conversion cost). Because 4,800 units were transferred out in May to the next department, the total cost assigned to those units would be $715,200 (= 4,800 units × $149.00 per unit).

A complete accounting of the costs of both ending work in process inventory and the units transferred out appears below:

Shaping and Milling Department Costs of Ending Work in Process Inventory and the Units Transferred Out	Materials	Conversion	Total
Ending work in process inventory:			
Equivalent units of production (materials:			
400 units × 40% complete; conversion:			
400 units × 25% complete) (a)	160	100	
Cost per equivalent unit (see above) (b)	$76.25	$72.75	
Cost of ending work in process inventory (a) × (b)	$12,200	$7,275	$19,475
Units completed and transferred out:			
Units transferred to the next department (a)	4,800	4,800	
Cost per equivalent unit (see above) (b)	$76.25	$72.75	
Cost of units transferred out (a) × (b)	$366,000	$349,200	$715,200

In each case, the equivalent units are multiplied by the cost per equivalent unit to determine the cost assigned to the units. This is done for each cost category—in this case, materials and conversion. The equivalent units for the units completed and transferred out are simply the number of units transferred to the next department because they would not have been transferred unless they were complete.

CONCEPT CHECK

2. Which of the following statements is false? (You may select more than one answer.)
   a. The activity in a processing department is performed uniformly on all units passing through the department.
   b. The output of a processing department is heterogeneous; in other words, all of the units produced are distinct from one another.
   c. Equivalent units are calculated by taking the number of partially completed units on hand and multiplying those units by their percentage of completion.
   d. The weighted-average method of computing the cost per equivalent unit averages together units and costs from the current and prior periods.

Cost Reconciliation Report

The costs assigned to ending work in process inventory and to the units transferred out reconcile with the costs we started with in Exhibit 4–7 as shown below:

LEARNING OBJECTIVE 4–5

Prepare a cost reconciliation report.

Shaping and Milling Department Cost Reconciliation	
Costs to be accounted for:	
Cost of beginning work in process inventory (Exhibit 4–7)	$ 15,175
Costs added to production during the period (Exhibit 4–7).............	719,500
Total cost to be accounted for	$734,675
Costs accounted for as follows:	
Cost of ending work in process inventory (see page 172)	$ 19,475
Cost of units transferred out (see page 172)......................	715,200
Total cost accounted for	$734,675

The $715,200 cost of the units transferred to the next department, Graphics Application, will be accounted for in that department as "costs transferred in." It will be treated in the process costing system as just another category of costs like materials or conversion costs. The only difference is that the costs transferred in will always be 100% complete with respect to the work done in the Shaping and Milling Department. Costs are passed on from one department to the next in this fashion, until they reach the last processing department, Finishing and Pairing. When the products are completed in this last department, their costs are transferred to finished goods.

HELPFUL HINT

To help you understand the logic of a cost reconciliation report, imagine that you have a non-interest bearing checking account with a balance on March 1 of $200. Also, assume that during March you earned paychecks totaling $1,000. On March 31, you would have $1,200 to be accounted for. At the end of the month, your $1,200 dollars must be accounted for in one of two ways. Either it remains in your checking account as of March 31 or it has been transferred out during the month (perhaps to your landlord, to the supermarket, or to your savings account). The ending balance in your checking account plus the total amount of cash transferred out during the month must equal $1,200.

The same concepts apply to the cost reconciliation report in this chapter. The cost of beginning work in process inventory plus the costs added to production during the period equals the total cost to be accounted for. The cost of ending work in process inventory plus the cost of units transferred out equals the total cost accounted for.

3. Beginning work in process includes 400 units that are 20% complete with respect to conversion and 30% complete with respect to materials. Ending work in process includes 200 units that are 40% complete with respect to conversion and 50% complete with respect to materials. If 2,000 units were started during the period, what are the equivalent units of production for the period according to the weighted-average method?
   a. Conversion equivalent units = 2,280 units; Material equivalent units = 2,100 units
   b. Conversion equivalent units = 1,980 units; Material equivalent units = 2,080 units
   c. Conversion equivalent units = 2,480 units; Material equivalent units = 1,980 units
   d. Conversion equivalent units = 2,280 units; Material equivalent units = 2,300 units

4. Assume the same facts as above in Concept Check 3. Also, assume that $9,900 of material costs and $14,880 of conversion costs were in the beginning inventory and $180,080 of materials and $409,200 of conversion costs were added to production during the period. What is the total cost per equivalent unit using the weighted-average method?
   a. $268.60   c. $280.00
   b. $267.85   d. $265.00

CONCEPT CHECK

SUMMARY

LO4–1 Record the flow of materials, labor, and overhead through a process costing system.

The journal entries to record the flow of costs in process costing are basically the same as in job-order costing. Direct materials costs are debited to Work in Process when the materials are released for use in production. Direct labor costs are debited to Work in Process as incurred. Manufacturing overhead costs are applied to Work in Process by debiting Work in Process. Costs are accumulated by department in process costing and by job in job-order costing.

LO4–2 Compute the equivalent units of production using the weighted-average method.

To compute unit costs for a department, the department's output in terms of equivalent units must be determined. In the weighted-average method, the equivalent units for a period are the sum of the units transferred out of the department during the period and the equivalent units in ending work in process inventory at the end of the period.

LO4–3 Compute the cost per equivalent unit using the weighted-average method.

The cost per equivalent unit for a particular cost category in a department is computed by dividing the sum of the cost of beginning work in process inventory and the cost added during the period by the equivalent units of production for the period.

LO4–4 Assign costs to units using the weighted-average method.

The cost per equivalent unit is used to value units in ending inventory and units transferred to the next department. The cost assigned to ending inventory is determined by multiplying the cost per equivalent unit by the equivalent units in ending inventory. The cost assigned to the units transferred to the next department is determined by multiplying the cost per equivalent unit by the number of units transferred.

LO4–5 Prepare a cost reconciliation report.

The costs to be accounted for consist of beginning work in process inventory plus the cost added to work in process. These costs must equal the cost of ending work in process inventory plus the cost of the units transferred out.

GUIDANCE ANSWERS TO DECISION POINT

Writing Term Papers (p. 170)

Each complete paper is five pages long and, by assumption, each page requires the same time and effort to write. Therefore, the time and effort that went into writing one incomplete two-page paper and one incomplete three-page paper could have been used to write one complete five-page paper. Added to the two complete papers that were turned in, this would have resulted in three complete papers.

GUIDANCE ANSWERS TO CONCEPT CHECKS

1. **Choices a, b, and d.** Process costing systems accumulate costs by department.
2. **Choice b.** The output of a processing department is homogeneous, meaning that all of the units are indistinguishable from one another.
3. **Choice d.** Material equivalent units are 2,200 units completed and transferred to the next department plus 100 equivalent units in ending work in process inventory (200 units × 50%). Conversion equivalent units are 2,200 units completed and transferred to the next department plus 80 equivalent units in ending work in process inventory (200 units × 40%).
4. **Choice a.** ($189,980 ÷ 2,300 equivalent units) + ($424,080 ÷ 2,280 equivalent units) = $268.60.

REVIEW PROBLEM: PROCESS COST FLOWS AND COSTING UNITS

Luxguard Home Paint Company produces exterior latex paint, which it sells in one-gallon containers. The company has two processing departments—Base Fab and Finishing. White paint, which is used as a base for all the company's paints, is mixed from raw ingredients in the Base Fab Department. Pigments are then added to the basic white paint, the pigmented paint is squirted under pressure into one-gallon containers, and the containers are labeled and packed for shipping in the Finishing Department. Information relating to the company's operations for April follows:

a. Issued raw materials for use in production: Base Fab Department, $851,000; and Finishing Department, $629,000.
b. Incurred direct labor costs: Base Fab Department, $330,000; and Finishing Department, $270,000.
c. Applied manufacturing overhead cost: Base Fab Department, $665,000; and Finishing Department, $405,000.
d. Transferred basic white paint from the Base Fab Department to the Finishing Department, $1,850,000.
e. Transferred paint that had been prepared for shipping from the Finishing Department to Finished Goods, $3,200,000.

Required:

1. Prepare journal entries to record items (a) through (e) above.
2. Post the journal entries from (1) above to T-accounts. The balance in the Base Fab Department's Work in Process account on April 1 was $150,000; the balance in the Finishing Department's Work in Process account was $70,000. After posting entries to the T-accounts, find the ending balance in each department's Work in Process account.
3. Determine the cost of ending work in process inventories and of units transferred out of the Base Fab Department in April. The following additional information is available regarding production in the Base Fab Department during April:

Production data:	
Units (gallons) in process, April 1: materials 100% complete;	
labor and overhead 60% complete	30,000
Units (gallons) started into production during April	420,000
Units (gallons) completed and transferred to the	
Finishing Department	370,000
Units (gallons) in process, April 30: materials 50% complete;	
labor and overhead 25% complete	80,000
Cost data:	
Work in process inventory, April 1:	
Materials	$ 92,000
Labor	21,000
Overhead.	37,000
Total cost of work in process inventory	$150,000
Cost added during April:	
Materials	$ 851,000
Labor	330,000
Overhead	665,000
Total cost added during April	$1,846,000

4. Prepare a cost reconciliation report for April.

Solution to Review Problem

1.

a.	Work in Process—Base Fab Department		851,000	
	Work in Process—Finishing Department		629,000	
	Raw Materials			1,480,000
b.	Work in Process—Base Fab Department		330,000	
	Work in Process—Finishing Department		270,000	
	Salaries and Wages Payable			600,000
c.	Work in Process—Base Fab Department		665,000	
	Work in Process—Finishing Department		405,000	
	Manufacturing Overhead			1,070,000
d.	Work in Process—Finishing Department		1,850,000	
	Work in Process—Base Fab Department			1,850,000
e.	Finished Goods		3,200,000	
	Work in Process—Finishing Department			3,200,000

2.

Raw Materials		
Bal. XXX	(a)	1,480,000

Salaries and Wages Payable		
	(b)	600,000

Work in Process— Base Fab Department

Bal. 150,000	(d)	1,850,000
(a) 851,000		
(b) 330,000		
(c) 665,000		
Bal. 146,000		

Manufacturing Overhead

(Various actual costs)	(c)	1,070,000

Work in Process—Finishing Department

Bal. 70,000	(e)	3,200,000
(a) 629,000		
(b) 270,000		
(c) 405,000		
(d) 1,850,000		
Bal. 24,000		

Finished Goods

Bal. XXX		
(e) 3,200,000		

3.   First, we must compute the equivalent units of production for each cost category:

Base Fab Department Equivalent Units of Production			
	Materials	Labor	Overhead
Units transferred to the next department	370,000	370,000	370,000
Ending work in process inventory (materials: 80,000 units × 50% complete; labor: 80,000 units × 25% complete; overhead: 80,000 units × 25% complete)	40,000	20,000	20,000
Equivalent units of production	410,000	390,000	390,000

Then we must compute the cost per equivalent unit for each cost category:

Base Fab Department Costs per Equivalent Unit			
	Materials	Labor	Overhead
Costs:			
Cost of beginning work in process inventory	$ 92,000	$ 21,000	$ 37,000
Costs added during the period	851,000	330,000	665,000
Total cost (a)	$943,000	$351,000	$702,000
Equivalent units of production (b)	410,000	390,000	390,000
Cost per equivalent unit (a) ÷ (b)	$2.30	$0.90	$1.80

The costs per equivalent unit can then be applied to the units in ending work in process inventory and the units transferred out as follows:

Base Fab Department Costs of Ending Work in Process Inventory and the Units Transferred Out				
	Materials	Labor	Overhead	Total
Ending work in process inventory:				
Equivalent units of production	40,000	20,000	20,000	
Cost per equivalent unit	$2.30	$0.90	$1.80	
Cost of ending work in process inventory	$92,000	$18,000	$36,000	$146,000
Units completed and transferred out:				
Units transferred to the next department	370,000	370,000	370,000	
Cost per equivalent unit	$2.30	$0.90	$1.80	
Cost of units completed and transferred out ...	$851,000	$333,000	$666,000	$1,850,000

4.

Base Fab Department Cost Reconciliation	
Costs to be accounted for:	
Cost of beginning work in process inventory	$ 150,000
Costs added to production during the period	1,846,000
Total cost to be accounted for	$1,996,000
Costs accounted for as follows:	
Cost of ending work in process inventory	$ 146,000
Cost of units transferred out	1,850,000
Total cost accounted for	$1,996,000

GLOSSARY

Conversion cost   Direct labor cost plus manufacturing overhead cost. (p. 169)

Equivalent units   The product of the number of partially completed units and their percentage of completion with respect to a particular cost. Equivalent units are the number of complete whole units that could be obtained from the materials and effort contained in partially completed units. (p. 168)

Equivalent units of production (weighted-average method)   The units transferred to the next department (or to finished goods) during the period plus the equivalent units in the department's ending work in process inventory. (p. 168)

FIFO method   A process costing method in which equivalent units and unit costs relate only to work done during the current period. (p. 168)

Process costing   A costing method used when essentially homogeneous products are produced on a continuous basis. (p. 162)

Processing department   An organizational unit where work is performed on a product and where materials, labor, or overhead costs are added to the product. (p. 163)

Weighted-average method   A process costing method that blends together units and costs from both the current and prior periods. (p. 168)

QUESTIONS

4–1   Under what conditions would it be appropriate to use a process costing system?

4–2   In what ways are job-order and process costing similar?

4–3   Why is cost accumulation simpler in a process costing system than it is in a job-order costing system?

4–4   How many Work in Process accounts are maintained in a company that uses process costing?

4–5   Assume that a company has two processing departments—Mixing followed by Firing. Prepare a journal entry to show a transfer of work in process from the Mixing Department to the Firing Department.

4–6   Assume that a company has two processing departments—Mixing followed by Firing. Explain what costs might be added to the Firing Department's Work in Process account during a period.

4–7   What is meant by the term *equivalent units of production* when the weighted-average method is used?

4–8   Watkins Trophies, Inc., produces thousands of medallions made of bronze, silver, and gold. The medallions are identical except for the materials used in their manufacture. What costing system would you advise the company to use?

Multiple-choice questions are available in the *Connect Library.*

APPLYING EXCEL

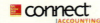

LO4–2, LO4–3,
LO4–4, LO4–5

Available with McGraw-Hill's *Connect Accounting.*

The Excel worksheet form that appears below is to be used to recreate the extended example on pages 171–173. Download the workbook containing this form in the *Connect Library*. On the website you will also receive instructions about how to use this worksheet form.

	A	B	C	D	E
1	Chapter 4: Applying Excel				
2					
3	Data				
4	Work in process, beginning:				
5	Units in process	200			
6	Completion with respect to materials	55%			
7	Completion with respect to conversion	30%			
8	Costs in the beginning inventory:				
9	Materials cost	$9,600			
10	Conversion cost	$5,575			
11	Units started into production during the period	5,000			
12	Costs added to production during the period:				
13	Materials cost	$368,600			
14	Conversion cost	$350,900			
15	Work in process, ending:				
16	Units in process	400			
17	Completion with respect to materials	40%			
18	Completion with respect to conversion	25%			
19					
20	Enter a formula into each of the cells marked with a ? below				
21					
22	Weighted–average method:				
23					
24	Equivalent Units of Production				
25		Materials	Conversion		
26	Units transferred to the next department	?	?		
27	Ending work in process				
28	Materials	?			
29	Conversion		?		
30	Equivalent units of production	?	?		
31					
32	Costs per Equivalent Unit				
33		Materials	Conversion		
34	Cost of beginning work in process inventory	?	?		
35	Costs added during the period	?	?		
36	Total cost	?	?		
37	Equivalent units of production	?	?		
38	Cost per equivalent unit	?	?		
39					
40	Costs of Ending Work in Process Inventory and the Units Transferred Out				
41		Materials	Conversion	Total	
42	Ending work in process inventory:				
43	Equivalent units of production	?	?		
44	Cost per equivalent unit	?	?		
45	Cost of ending work in process inventory	?	?	?	
46					
47	Units completed and transferred out:				
48	Units transferred to the next department	?	?		
49	Cost per equivalent unit	?	?		
50	Cost of units transferred out	?	?	?	
51					
52	Cost Reconciliation				
53	Costs to be accounted for:				
54	Cost of beginning work in process inventory	?			
55	Costs added to production during the period	?			
56	Total cost to be accounted for	?			
57	Costs to be accounted for as follows:				
58	Cost of ending work in process inventory	?			
59	Cost of units transferred out	?			
60	Total cost accounted for	?			
61					

Chapter 4 Form | Filled in Chapter 4 Form | Chapt

You should proceed to the requirements below only after completing your worksheet.

Required:

1. Check your worksheet by changing the beginning work in process inventory to 100 units, the units started into production during the period to 2,500 units, and the units in ending work in process inventory to 200 units, keeping all of the other data the same as in the original example. If your worksheet is operating properly, the cost per equivalent unit for materials should now be $152.50 and

the cost per equivalent unit for conversion should be $145.50. If you do not get these answers, find the errors in your worksheet and correct them.

How much is the total cost of the units transferred out? Did it change? Why or why not?

2.   Enter the following data from a different company into your worksheet:

> Beginning work in process inventory:
>
> Units in process 200
>
> Completion with respect to materials 100%
>
> Completion with respect to conversion 20%
>
> Costs in the beginning work in process inventory:
>
>   Materials cost $2,000
>
>   Conversion cost $800
>
> Units started into production during the period 1,800
>
> Costs added during the period:
>
>   Materials cost $18,400
>
>   Conversion cost $38,765
>
> Ending work in process inventory:
>
> Units in process 100
>
> Completion with respect to materials 100%
>
> Completion with respect to conversion 30%

What is the cost of the units transferred out?

3.   What happens to the cost of the units transferred out in part (2) above if the percentage completion with respect to conversion for the beginning inventory is changed from 20% to 40% and everything else remains the same? What happens to the cost per equivalent unit for conversion? Explain.

THE FOUNDATIONAL 15

Available with McGraw-Hill's *Connect Accounting*.

Clopack Company manufactures one product that goes through one processing department called Mixing. All raw materials are introduced at the start of work in the Mixing Department. The company uses the weighted-average method to account for units and costs. Its Work in Process T-account for the Mixing Department for June follows (all forthcoming questions pertain to June):

LO4–1, LO4–2, LO4–3, LO4–4, LO4–5

Work in Process—Mixing Department		
June 1 balance	28,000	Completed and transferred to Finished Goods ?
Materials	120,000	
Direct labor	79,500	
Overhead	97,000	
June 30 balance	?	

The June 1 work in process inventory consisted of 5,000 pounds with $16,000 in materials cost and $12,000 in conversion cost. The June 1 work in process inventory was 100% complete with respect to materials and 50% complete with respect to conversion. During June, 37,500 pounds were started into production. The June 30 work in process inventory consisted of 8,000 pounds that were 100% complete with respect to materials and 40% complete with respect to conversion.

Required:

1.   Prepare the journal entries to record the raw materials used in production and the direct labor cost incurred.

2.   Prepare the journal entry to record the overhead cost applied to production.

3.   How many units were completed and transferred to finished goods during the period?

4. Compute the equivalent units of production for materials.
5. Compute the equivalent units of production for conversion.
6. What is the amount of the cost of beginning work in process inventory plus the cost added during the period for materials?
7. What is the amount of the cost of beginning work in process inventory plus the cost added during the period for conversion?
8. What is the cost per equivalent unit for materials?
9. What is the cost per equivalent unit for conversion?
10. What is the cost of ending work in process inventory for materials?
11. What is the cost of ending work in process inventory for conversion?
12. What is the cost of materials transferred to finished goods?
13. What is the amount of conversion cost transferred to finished goods?
14. Prepare the journal entry to record the transfer of costs from Work in Process to Finished Goods.
15. What is the total cost to be accounted for? What is the total cost accounted for?

EXERCISES

All applicable exercises are available with McGraw-Hill's *Connect Accounting*.

EXERCISE 4–1   Process Costing Journal Entries [LO4–1]

Quality Brick Company produces bricks in two processing departments—Molding and Firing. Information relating to the company's operations in March follows:

a. Raw materials were issued for use in production: Molding Department, $23,000; and Firing Department, $8,000.
b. Direct labor costs were incurred: Molding Department, $12,000; and Firing Department, $7,000.
c. Manufacturing overhead was applied: Molding Department, $25,000; and Firing Department, $37,000.
d. Unfired, molded bricks were transferred from the Molding Department to the Firing Department. According to the company's process costing system, the cost of the unfired, molded bricks was $57,000.
e. Finished bricks were transferred from the Firing Department to the finished goods warehouse. According to the company's process costing system, the cost of the finished bricks was $103,000.
f. Finished bricks were sold to customers. According to the company's process costing system, the cost of the finished bricks sold was $101,000.

Required:
Prepare journal entries to record items (a) through (f) above.

EXERCISE 4–2   Computation of Equivalent Units—Weighted-Average Method [LO4–2]

Clonex Labs, Inc., uses a process costing system. The following data are available for one department for October:

Work in process, October 1: materials 20% complete

		Percent Completed	
	Units	Materials	Conversion
Work in process, October 1	30,000	65%	30%
Work in process, October 31	15,000	80%	40%

The department started 175,000 units into production during the month and transferred 190,000 completed units to the next department.

Required:
Compute the equivalent units of production for October assuming that the company uses the weighted-average method of accounting for units and costs.

EXERCISE 4–3 Cost per Equivalent Unit—Weighted-Average Method [LO4–3]
Superior Micro Products uses the weighted-average method in its process costing system. Data for the Assembly Department for May appear below:

TAKE TWO

Cost added during May, labor: $81,950

	Materials	Labor	Overhead
Work in process, May 1	$18,000	$5,500	$27,500
Cost added during May	$238,900	$80,300	$401,500
Equivalent units of production	35,000	33,000	33,000

Required:
1. Compute the cost per equivalent unit for materials, for labor, and for overhead.
2. Compute the total cost per equivalent whole unit.

EXERCISE 4–4 Applying Costs to Units—Weighted-Average Method [LO4–4]
Data concerning a recent period's activity in the Prep Department, the first processing department in a company that uses process costing, appear below:

TAKE TWO

Cost per equivalent unit, conversion: $5.00

	Materials	Conversion
Equivalent units of production in ending work in process	2,000	800
Cost per equivalent unit	$13.86	$4.43

A total of 20,100 units were completed and transferred to the next processing department during the period.

Required:
Compute the cost of the units transferred to the next department during the period and the cost of ending work in process inventory.

EXERCISE 4–5 Cost Reconciliation Report—Weighted-Average Method [LO4–5]
Maria Am Corporation uses a process costing system. The Baking Department is one of the processing departments in its strudel manufacturing facility. In June in the Baking Department, the cost of beginning work in process inventory was $3,570, the cost of ending work in process inventory was $2,860, and the cost added to production was $43,120.

TAKE TWO

Cost of ending work in process inventory: $1,300

Required:
Prepare a cost reconciliation report for the Baking Department for June.

EXERCISE 4–6 Equivalent Units—Weighted-Average Method [LO4–2]
Hielta Oy, a Finnish company, processes wood pulp for various manufacturers of paper products. Data relating to tons of pulp processed during June are provided below:

TAKE TWO

Started into production during June: 270,000

		Percent Completed	
	Tons of Pulp	Materials	Labor and Overhead
Work in process, June 1	20,000	90%	80%
Work in process, June 30	30,000	60%	40%
Started into production during June ..	190,000		

Required:
1. Compute the number of tons of pulp completed and transferred out during June.
2. Compute the equivalent units of production for materials and for labor and overhead for June.

EXERCISE 4–7 Process Costing Journal Entries [LO4–1]
Chocolaterie de Geneve, SA, is located in a French-speaking canton in Switzerland. The company makes chocolate truffles that are sold in popular embossed tins. The company has two processing departments—Cooking and Molding. In the Cooking Department, the raw ingredients for the truffles are mixed and then cooked in special candy-making vats. In the Molding Department, the melted chocolate and other ingredients from the Cooking Department are carefully poured into molds and decorative flourishes are applied

by hand. After cooling, the truffles are packed for sale. The company uses a process costing system. The T-accounts below show the flow of costs through the two departments in April:

Work in Process—Cooking

Balance 4/1	8,000	Transferred out	160,000
Direct materials	42,000		
Direct labor	50,000		
Overhead	75,000		

Work in Process—Molding

Balance 4/1	4,000	Transferred out	240,000
Transferred in	160,000		
Direct labor	36,000		
Overhead	45,000		

Required:
Prepare journal entries showing the flow of costs through the two processing departments during April.

EXERCISE 4–8 Equivalent Units and Cost per Equivalent Unit—Weighted-Average Method [LO4–2, LO4–3, LO4–4]
Helix Corporation produces prefabricated flooring in a series of steps carried out in production departments. All of the material that is used in the first production department is added at the beginning of processing in that department. Data for May for the first production department follow:

		Percent Complete	
	Units	Materials	Conversion
Work in process inventory, May 1..............	5,000	100%	40%
Work in process inventory, May 31.............	10,000	100%	30%
Materials cost in work in process inventory, May 1		$1,500	
Conversion cost in work in process inventory, May 1		$4,000	
Units started into production		180,000	
Units transferred to the next production department		175,000	
Materials cost added during May		$54,000	
Conversion cost added during May		$352,000	

Required:
1. Assume that the company uses the weighted-average method of accounting for units and costs. Determine the equivalent units for May for the first process.
2. Compute the costs per equivalent unit for May for the first process.
3. Determine the total cost of ending work in process inventory and the total cost of units transferred to the next process in May.

EXERCISE 4–9 Equivalent Units and Cost per Equivalent Unit—Weighted-Average Method [LO4–2, LO4–3]
Pureform, Inc., manufactures a product that passes through two departments. Data for a recent month for the first department follow:

Work in process, Beginning: 4,000 units; units transferred out: 41,000

	Units	Materials	Labor	Overhead
Work in process inventory, beginning......	5,000	$4,320	$1,040	$1,790
Units started in process	45,000			
Units transferred out	42,000			
Work in process inventory, ending	8,000			
Cost added during the month............		$52,800	$21,500	$32,250

The beginning work in process inventory was 80% complete with respect to materials and 60% complete with respect to labor and overhead. The ending work in process inventory was 75% complete with respect to materials and 50% complete with respect to labor and overhead.

Required:
Assume that the company uses the weighted-average method of accounting for units and costs.
1. Compute the equivalent units for the month for the first department.
2. Determine the costs per equivalent unit for the month.

EXERCISE 4–10 Equivalent Units—Weighted-Average Method [LO4–2]

Alaskan Fisheries, Inc., processes salmon for various distributors. Two departments are involved—Cleaning and Packing. Data relating to pounds of salmon processed in the Cleaning Department during July are presented below:

Work in process, July 1: 22,000 pounds of salmon

		Percent Completed	
	Pounds of Salmon	Materials	Labor and Overhead
Work in process inventory, July 1	20,000	100%	30%
Work in process inventory, July 31	25,000	100%	60%

A total of 380,000 pounds of salmon were started into processing during July. All materials are added at the beginning of processing in the Cleaning Department.

Required:
Compute the equivalent units for July for both materials and labor and overhead assuming that the company uses the weighted-average method of accounting for units.

EXERCISE 4–11 Comprehensive Exercise; Second Production Department—Weighted-Average Method [LO4–2, LO4–3, LO4–4, LO4–5]

Scribners Corporation produces fine papers in three production departments—Pulping, Drying, and Finishing. In the Pulping Department, raw materials such as wood fiber and rag cotton are mechanically and chemically treated to separate their fibers. The result is a thick slurry of fibers. In the Drying Department, the wet fibers transferred from the Pulping Department are laid down on porous webs, pressed to remove excess liquid, and dried in ovens. In the Finishing Department, the dried paper is coated, cut, and spooled onto reels. The company uses the weighted-average method in its process costing system. Data for March for the Drying Department follow:

		Percent Completed	
	Units	Pulping	Conversion
Work in process inventory, March 1	5,000	100%	20%
Work in process inventory, March 31	8,000	100%	25%
Pulping cost in work in process inventory, March 1		$4,800	
Conversion cost in work in process inventory, March 1		$500	
Units transferred to the next production department		157,000	
Pulping cost added during March		$102,450	
Conversion cost added during March		$31,300	

No materials are added in the Drying Department. Pulping cost represents the costs of the wet fibers transferred in from the Pulping Department. Wet fiber is processed in the Drying Department in batches; each unit in the above table is a batch and one batch of wet fibers produces a set amount of dried paper that is passed on to the Finishing Department.

Required:
1. Determine the equivalent units for March for pulping and conversion.
2. Compute the costs per equivalent unit for March for pulping and conversion.
3. Determine the total cost of ending work in process inventory and the total cost of units transferred to the Finishing Department in March.
4. Prepare a cost reconciliation report for the Drying Department for March.

TAKE
TWO

Cost per equivalent unit of
materials: $14.00; Total
cost to be accounted for
$640,880

EXERCISE 4–12 Cost Assignment; Cost Reconciliation—Weighted-Average Method [LO4–2, LO4–4, LO4–5]

Superior Micro Products uses the weighted-average method in its process costing system. During January, the Delta Assembly Department completed its processing of 25,000 units and transferred them to the next department. The cost of beginning inventory and the costs added during January amounted to $599,780 in total. The ending inventory in January consisted of 3,000 units, which were 80% complete with respect to materials and 60% complete with respect to labor and overhead. The costs per equivalent unit for the month were as follows:

	Materials	Labor	Overhead
Cost per equivalent unit	$12.50	$3.20	$6.40

Required:
1. Compute the equivalent units of materials, labor, and overhead in the ending inventory for the month.
2. Compute the cost of ending inventory and of the units transferred to the next department for January.
3. Prepare a cost reconciliation for January. (Note: You will not be able to break the cost to be accounted for into the cost of beginning inventory and costs added during the month.)

PROBLEMS

 Alternate problem set is available in the *Connect Library*.

All applicable problems are available with McGraw-Hill's *Connect Accounting*.

PROBLEM 4–13A Comprehensive Problem; Second Production Department—Weighted-Average Method [LO4–2, LO4–3, LO4–4, LO4–5]

Old Country Links Inc. produces sausages in three production departments—Mixing, Casing and Curing, and Packaging. In the Mixing Department, meats are prepared and ground and then mixed with spices. The spiced meat mixture is then transferred to the Casing and Curing Department, where the mixture is force-fed into casings and then hung and cured in climate-controlled smoking chambers. In the Packaging Department, the cured sausages are sorted, packed, and labeled. The company uses the weighted-average method in its process costing system. Data for September for the Casing and Curing Department follow:

		Percent Completed		
	Units	Mixing	Materials	Conversion
Work in process inventory, September 1	1	100%	90%	80%
Work in process inventory, September 30	1	100%	80%	70%

	Mixing	Materials	Conversion
Work in process inventory, September 1	$1,670	$90	$605
Cost added during September	$81,460	$6,006	$42,490

Mixing cost represents the costs of the spiced meat mixture transferred in from the Mixing Department. The spiced meat mixture is processed in the Casing and Curing Department in batches; each unit in the above table is a batch and one batch of spiced meat mixture produces a set amount of sausages that are passed on to the Packaging Department. During September, 50 batches (i.e., units) were completed and transferred to the Packaging Department.

Required:
1. Determine the equivalent units for September for mixing, materials, and conversion. Do not round off your computations.
2. Compute the costs per equivalent unit for September for mixing, materials, and conversion.

3. Determine the total cost of ending work in process inventory and the total cost of units transferred to the Packaging Department in September.
4. Prepare a cost reconciliation report for the Casing and Curing Department for September.

PROBLEM 4–14A Analysis of Work in Process T-account—Weighted-Average Method [LO4–1, LO4–2, LO4–3, LO4–4]

Weston Products manufactures an industrial cleaning compound that goes through three processing departments—Grinding, Mixing, and Cooking. All raw materials are introduced at the start of work in the Grinding Department. The Work in Process T-account for the Grinding Department for May is given below:

Work in Process—Grinding Department			
Inventory, May 1	21,800	Completed and transferred to the Mixing Department	?
Materials	133,400		
Conversion	225,500		
Inventory, May 31	?		

The May 1 work in process inventory consisted of 18,000 pounds with $14,600 in materials cost and $7,200 in conversion cost. The May 1 work in process inventory was 100% complete with respect to materials and 30% complete with respect to conversion. During May, 167,000 pounds were started into production. The May 31 inventory consisted of 15,000 pounds that were 100% complete with respect to materials and 60% complete with respect to conversion. The company uses the weighted-average method to account for units and costs.

Required:
1. Determine the equivalent units of production for May.
2. Determine the costs per equivalent unit for May.
3. Determine the cost of the units completed and transferred to the Mixing Department during May.

PROBLEM 4–15A Comprehensive Problem—Weighted-Average Method [LO4–2, LO4–3, LO4–4, LO4–5]

Sunspot Beverages, Ltd., of Fiji makes blended tropical fruit drinks in two stages. Fruit juices are extracted from fresh fruits and then blended in the Blending Department. The blended juices are then bottled and packed for shipping in the Bottling Department. The following information pertains to the operations of the Blending Department for June.

		Percent Completed	
	Units	Materials	Conversion
Work in process, beginning	20,000	100%	75%
Started into production	180,000		
Completed and transferred out	160,000		
Work in process, ending	40,000	100%	25%

	Materials	Conversion
Work in process, beginning	$25,200	$24,800
Cost added during June	$334,800	$238,700

Required:
Assume that the company uses the weighted-average method.
1. Determine the equivalent units for June for the Blending Department.
2. Compute the costs per equivalent unit for the Blending Department.
3. Determine the total cost of ending work in process inventory and the total cost of units transferred to the Bottling Department.
4. Prepare a cost reconciliation report for the Blending Department for June.

PROBLEM 4–16A   Comprehensive Problem—Weighted-Average Method [LO4–2, LO4–3, LO4–4, LO4–5]

Builder Products, Inc., manufactures a caulking compound that goes through three processing stages prior to completion. Information on work in the first department, Cooking, is given below for May:

Production data:	
Pounds in process, May 1; materials 100% complete;	
conversion 80% complete	10,000
Pounds started into production during May	100,000
Pounds completed and transferred out	?
Pounds in process, May 31; materials 60% complete;	
conversion 20% complete	15,000
Cost data:	
Work in process inventory, May 1:	
Materials cost	$1,500
Conversion cost	$7,200
Cost added during May:	
Materials cost	$154,500
Conversion cost	$90,800

The company uses the weighted-average method.

Required:
1.   Compute the equivalent units of production.
2.   Compute the costs per equivalent unit for the month.
3.   Determine the cost of ending work in process inventory and of the units transferred out to the next department.
4.   Prepare a cost reconciliation report for the month.

PROBLEM 4–17A   Cost Flows [LO4–1]

Lubricants, Inc., produces a special kind of grease that is widely used by race car drivers. The grease is produced in two processing departments: Refining and Blending.

The following incomplete Work in Process account is available for the Refining Department for March:

Work in Process—Refining Department			
March 1 balance	38,000	Completed and transferred to Blending	?
Materials	495,000		
Direct labor	72,000		
Overhead	181,000		
March 31 balance	?		

The March 1 work in process inventory in the Refining Department consists of the following elements: materials, $25,000; direct labor, $4,000; and overhead, $9,000.

Costs incurred during March in the Blending Department were: materials used, $115,000; direct labor, $18,000; and overhead cost applied to production, $42,000.

Required:
1.   Prepare journal entries to record the costs incurred in both the Refining Department and Blending Department during March. Key your entries to the items (a) through (g) below.
   a.   Raw materials were issued for use in production.
   b.   Direct labor costs were incurred.
   c.   Manufacturing overhead costs for the entire factory were incurred, $225,000. (Credit Accounts Payable.)
   d.   Manufacturing overhead cost was applied to production using a predetermined overhead rate.
   e.   Units that were complete with respect to processing in the Refining Department were transferred to the Blending Department, $740,000.

f.   Units that were complete with respect to processing in the Blending Department were transferred to Finished Goods, $950,000.

g.   Completed units were sold on account, $1,500,000. The Cost of Goods Sold was $900,000.

2.   Post the journal entries from (1) above to T-accounts. The following account balances existed at the beginning of March. (The beginning balance in the Refining Department's Work in Process account is given on the prior page.)

Raw Materials	$618,000
Work in Process—Blending Department	$65,000
Finished Goods	$20,000

After posting the entries to the T-accounts, find the ending balance in the inventory accounts and the manufacturing overhead account.

PROBLEM 4–18A   Interpreting a Report—Weighted-Average Method [LO4–2, LO4–3, LO4–4]

Cooperative San José of southern Sonora state in Mexico makes a unique syrup using cane sugar and local herbs. The syrup is sold in small bottles and is prized as a flavoring for drinks and for use in desserts. The bottles are sold for $12 each. The first stage in the production process is carried out in the Mixing Department, which removes foreign matter from the raw materials and mixes them in the proper proportions in large vats. The company uses the weighted-average method in its process costing system.

A hastily prepared report for the Mixing Department for April appears below:

Units to be accounted for:	
Work in process, April 1 (materials 90% complete; conversion 80% complete)	30,000
Started into production	200,000
Total units to be accounted for	230,000
Units accounted for as follows:	
Transferred to next department	190,000
Work in process, April 30 (materials 75% complete; conversion 60% complete)	40,000
Total units accounted for	230,000
Cost Reconciliation	
Cost to be accounted for:	
Work in process, April 1	$ 98,000
Cost added during the month	827,000
Total cost to be accounted for	$925,000
Cost accounted for as follows:	
Work in process, April 30	$119,400
Transferred to next department	805,600
Total cost accounted for	$925,000

Management would like some additional information about Cooperative San José's operations.

Required:

1.   What were the equivalent units for the month?

2.   What were the costs per equivalent unit for the month? The beginning inventory consisted of the following costs: materials, $67,800; and conversion cost, $30,200. The costs added during the month consisted of: materials, $579,000; and conversion cost, $248,000.

3.   How many of the units transferred to the next department were started and completed during the month?

4.   The manager of the Mixing Department stated, "Materials prices jumped from about $2.50 per unit in March to $3 per unit in April, but due to good cost control I was able to hold our materials cost to less than $3 per unit for the month." Should this manager be rewarded for good cost control? Explain.

BUILDING YOUR SKILLS

ANALYTICAL THINKING [LO4–2, LO4–3, LO4–4]

"I think we goofed when we hired that new assistant controller," said Ruth Scarpino, president of Provost Industries. "Just look at this report that he prepared for last month for the Finishing Department. I can't understand it."

Finishing Department costs:	
Work in process inventory, April 1, 450 units; materials 100% complete; conversion 60% complete	$ 8,208*
Costs transferred in during the month from the preceding department, 1,950 units	17,940
Materials cost added during the month	6,210
Conversion costs incurred during the month	13,920
Total departmental costs	$46,278
Finishing Department costs assigned to:	
Units completed and transferred to finished goods, 1,800 units at $25.71 per unit	$46,278
Work in process inventory, April 30, 600 units; materials 0% complete; conversion 35% complete	0
Total departmental costs assigned	$46,278

*Consists of cost transferred in, $4,068; materials cost, $1,980; and conversion cost, $2,160.

"He's struggling to learn our system," replied Frank Harrop, the operations manager. "The problem is that he's been away from process costing for a long time, and it's coming back slowly."

"It's not just the format of his report that I'm concerned about. Look at that $25.71 unit cost that he's come up with for April. Doesn't that seem high to you?" said Ms. Scarpino.

"Yes, it does seem high; but on the other hand, I know we had an increase in materials prices during April, and that may be the explanation," replied Mr. Harrop. "I'll get someone else to redo this report and then we may be able to see what's going on."

Provost Industries manufactures a ceramic product that goes through two processing departments—Molding and Finishing. The company uses the weighted-average method in its process costing.

Required:

1. Prepare a report for the Finishing Department showing how much cost should have been assigned to the units completed and transferred to finished goods, and how much cost should have been assigned to ending work in process inventory in the Finishing Department.
2. Explain to the president why the unit cost on the new assistant controller's report is so high.

ETHICS CHALLENGE [LO4–2, LO4–3, LO4–4]

Gary Stevens and Mary James are production managers in the Consumer Electronics Division of General Electronics Company, which has several dozen plants scattered in locations throughout the world. Mary manages the plant located in Des Moines, Iowa, while Gary manages the plant in El Segundo, California. Production managers are paid a salary and get an additional bonus equal to 5% of their base salary if the entire division meets or exceeds its target profits for the year. The bonus is determined in March after the company's annual report has been prepared and issued to stockholders.

Shortly after the beginning of the new year, Mary received a phone call from Gary that went like this:

Gary: How's it going, Mary?

Mary: Fine, Gary. How's it going with you?

Gary: Great! I just got the preliminary profit figures for the division for last year and we are within $200,000 of making the year's target profits. All we have to do is pull a few strings, and we'll be over the top!

Mary: What do you mean?

Gary: Well, one thing that would be easy to change is your estimate of the percentage completion of your ending work in process inventories.

Mary: I don't know if I can do that, Gary. Those percentage completion figures are supplied by Tom Winthrop, my lead supervisor, who I have always trusted to provide us with good estimates. Besides, I have already sent the percentage completion figures to corporate headquarters.

Gary: You can always tell them there was a mistake. Think about it, Mary. All of us managers are doing as much as we can to pull this bonus out of the hat. You may not want the bonus check, but the rest of us sure could use it.

The final processing department in Mary's production facility began the year with no work in process inventories. During the year, 210,000 units were transferred in from the prior processing department and 200,000 units were completed and sold. Costs transferred in from the prior department totaled $39,375,000. No materials are added in the final processing department. A total of $20,807,500 of conversion cost was incurred in the final processing department during the year.

Required:

1. Tom Winthrop estimated that the units in ending inventory in the final processing department were 30% complete with respect to the conversion costs of the final processing department. If this estimate of the percentage completion is used, what would be the Cost of Goods Sold for the year?

2. Does Gary Stevens want the estimated percentage completion to be increased or decreased? Explain why.

3. What percentage completion would result in increasing reported net operating income by $200,000 over the net operating income that would be reported if the 30% figure were used?

4. Do you think Mary James should go along with the request to alter estimates of the percentage completion? Why or why not?

A LOOK BACK

We provided overviews of the systems that are used to accumulate product costs in Chapters 2 (job-order costing), 3 (activity-based costing), and 4 (process costing).

A LOOK AT THIS CHAPTER

Chapter 5 describes the basics of cost-volume-profit analysis, an essential tool for decision making. Cost-volume-profit analysis helps managers understand the interrelationships among cost, volume, and profit.

A LOOK AHEAD

Chapter 6 contrasts variable costing and absorption costing income statements for manufacturers and it explains how the contribution format can be used to measure the profitability of business segments.

5 Cost-Volume-Profit Relationships

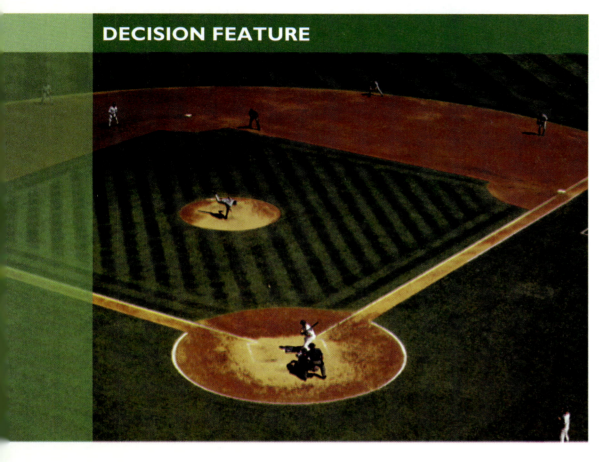

DECISION FEATURE

LEARNING OBJECTIVES

After studying Chapter 5, you should be able to:

LO5–1 Explain how changes in activity affect contribution margin and net operating income.

LO5–2 Prepare and interpret a cost-volume-profit (CVP) graph and a profit graph.

LO5–3 Use the contribution margin ratio (CM ratio) to compute changes in contribution margin and net operating income resulting from changes in sales volume.

LO5–4 Show the effects on net operating income of changes in variable costs, fixed costs, selling price, and volume.

LO5–5 Determine the break-even point.

LO5–6 Determine the level of sales needed to achieve a desired target profit.

LO5–7 Compute the margin of safety and explain its significance.

LO5–8 Compute the degree of operating leverage at a particular level of sales and explain how it can be used to predict changes in net operating income.

LO5–9 Compute the break-even point for a multiproduct company and explain the effects of shifts in the sales mix on contribution margin and the break-even point.

Moreno Turns Around the Los Angeles Angels

When Arturo Moreno bought Major League Baseball's **Los Angeles Angels** in 2003, the team was drawing 2.3 million fans and losing $5.5 million per year. Moreno immediately cut prices to attract more fans and increase profits. In his first spring training game, he reduced the price of selected tickets from $12 to $6. By increasing attendance, Moreno understood that he would sell more food and souvenirs. He dropped the price of draft beer by $2 and cut the price of baseball caps from $20 to $7.

The Angels now consistently draw about 3.4 million fans per year. This growth in attendance helped double stadium sponsorship revenue to $26 million, and it motivated the Fox Sports Network to pay the Angels $500 million to broadcast all of its games for the next ten years. Since Moreno bought the Angels, annual revenues have jumped from $127 million to $212 million, and the team's operating loss of $5.5 million has been transformed to a profit of $10.3 million.

Source: Matthew Craft, "Moreno's Math," Forbes, May 11, 2009, pp. 84–87.

Cost-volume-profit (CVP) analysis helps managers make many important decisions such as what products and services to offer, what prices to charge, what marketing strategy to use, and what cost structure to maintain. Its primary purpose is to estimate how profits are affected by the following five factors:

1. Selling prices.
2. Sales volume.
3. Unit variable costs.
4. Total fixed costs.
5. Mix of products sold.

To simplify CVP calculations, managers typically adopt the following assumptions with respect to these factors[1]:

1. Selling price is constant. The price of a product or service will not change as volume changes.
2. Costs are linear and can be accurately divided into variable and fixed elements. The variable element is constant per unit. The fixed element is constant in total over the entire relevant range.
3. In multiproduct companies, the mix of products sold remains constant.

While these assumptions may be violated in practice, the results of CVP analysis are often "good enough" to be quite useful. Perhaps the greatest danger lies in relying on simple CVP analysis when a manager is contemplating a large change in sales volume that lies outside the relevant range. However, even in these situations the CVP model can be adjusted to take into account anticipated changes in selling prices, variable costs per unit, total fixed costs, and the sales mix that arise when the estimated sales volume falls outside the relevant range.

To help explain the role of CVP analysis in business decisions, we'll now turn our attention to the case of Acoustic Concepts, Inc., a company founded by Prem Narayan.

**MANAGERIAL
ACCOUNTING IN ACTION**
The Issue

Prem, who was a graduate student in engineering at the time, started Acoustic Concepts to market a radical new speaker he had designed for automobile sound systems. The speaker, called the Sonic Blaster, uses an advanced microprocessor and proprietary software to boost amplification to awesome levels. Prem contracted with a Taiwanese electronics manufacturer to produce the speaker. With seed money provided by his family, Prem placed an order with the manufacturer and ran advertisements in auto magazines.

The Sonic Blaster was an immediate success, and sales grew to the point that Prem moved the company's headquarters out of his apartment and into rented quarters in a nearby industrial park. He also hired a receptionist, an accountant, a sales manager, and a small sales staff to sell the speakers to retail stores. The accountant, Bob Luchinni, had worked for several small companies where he had acted as a business advisor as well as accountant and bookkeeper. The following discussion occurred soon after Bob was hired:

Prem: Bob, I've got a lot of questions about the company's finances that I hope you can help answer.

Bob: We're in great shape. The loan from your family will be paid off within a few months.

Prem: I know, but I am worried about the risks I've taken on by expanding operations. What would happen if a competitor entered the market and our sales slipped? How far could sales drop without putting us into the red? Another question I've been trying to resolve is how much our sales would have to increase to justify the big marketing campaign the sales staff is pushing for.

Bob: Marketing always wants more money for advertising.

---

[1]One additional assumption often used in manufacturing companies is that inventories do not change. The number of units produced equals the number of units sold.

Prem: And they are always pushing me to drop the selling price on the speaker. I agree with them that a lower price will boost our sales volume, but I'm not sure the increased volume will offset the loss in revenue from the lower price.

Bob: It sounds like these questions are all related in some way to the relationships among our selling prices, our costs, and our volume. I shouldn't have a problem coming up with some answers.

Prem: Can we meet again in a couple of days to see what you have come up with?

Bob: Sounds good. By then I'll have some preliminary answers for you as well as a model you can use for answering similar questions in the future.

THE BASICS OF COST-VOLUME-PROFIT (CVP) ANALYSIS

Bob Luchinni's preparation for his forthcoming meeting with Prem begins with the contribution income statement. The contribution income statement emphasizes the behavior of costs and therefore is extremely helpful to managers in judging the impact on profits of changes in selling price, cost, or volume. Bob will base his analysis on the following contribution income statement he prepared last month:

Acoustic Concepts, Inc.
Contribution Income Statement
For the Month of June

	Total	Per Unit
Sales (400 speakers)	$100,000	$250
Variable expenses	60,000	150
Contribution margin	40,000	$100
Fixed expenses.	35,000	
Net operating income	$ 5,000	

Notice that sales, variable expenses, and contribution margin are expressed on a per unit basis as well as in total on this contribution income statement. The per unit figures will be very helpful to Bob in some of his calculations. Note that this contribution income statement has been prepared for management's use inside the company and would not ordinarily be made available to those outside the company.

HELPFUL HINT

Students often struggle to derive the selling price per unit and the variable expense per unit when they are not explicitly stated in a problem. Therefore, remember that the total sales and total variable expenses can each be divided by the quantity of units sold to derive the selling price per unit and the variable expense per unit.

Contribution Margin

Contribution margin is the amount remaining from sales revenue after variable expenses have been deducted. Thus, it is the amount available to cover fixed expenses and then to provide profits for the period. Notice the sequence here—contribution margin is used *first* to cover the fixed expenses, and then whatever remains goes toward profits. If the contribution margin is not sufficient to cover the fixed expenses, then a loss occurs for

LEARNING OBJECTIVE 5–1

Explain how changes in activity affect contribution margin and net operating income.

the period. To illustrate with an extreme example, assume that Acoustic Concepts sells only one speaker during a particular month. The company's income statement would appear as follows:

Contribution Income Statement
Sales of 1 Speaker

	Total	Per Unit
Sales (1 speaker)	$ 250	$250
Variable expenses	150	150
Contribution margin	100	$100
Fixed expenses.	35,000	
Net operating loss.	$(34,900)	

For each additional speaker the company sells during the month, $100 more in contribution margin becomes available to help cover the fixed expenses. If a second speaker is sold, for example, then the total contribution margin will increase by $100 (to a total of $200) and the company's loss will decrease by $100, to $34,800:

Contribution Income Statement
Sales of 2 Speakers

	Total	Per Unit
Sales (2 speakers)	$ 500	$250
Variable expenses	300	150
Contribution margin	200	$100
Fixed expenses.	35,000	
Net operating loss.	$(34,800)	

If enough speakers can be sold to generate $35,000 in contribution margin, then all of the fixed expenses will be covered and the company will *break even* for the month—that is, it will show neither profit nor loss but just cover all of its costs. To reach the break-even point, the company will have to sell 350 speakers in a month because each speaker sold yields $100 in contribution margin:

Contribution Income Statement
Sales of 350 Speakers

	Total	Per Unit
Sales (350 speakers)	$87,500	$250
Variable expenses	52,500	150
Contribution margin	35,000	$100
Fixed expenses.	35,000	
Net operating income	$ 0	

Computation of the break-even point is discussed in detail later in the chapter; for the moment, note that the **break-even point** is the level of sales at which profit is zero.

Once the break-even point has been reached, net operating income will increase by the amount of the unit contribution margin for each additional unit sold. For example, if

351 speakers are sold in a month, then the net operating income for the month will be $100 because the company will have sold 1 speaker more than the number needed to break even:

Contribution Income Statement **Sales of 351 Speakers**	Total	Per Unit
Sales (351 speakers)	$87,750	$250
Variable expenses	52,650	150
Contribution margin	35,100	$100
Fixed expenses.	35,000	
Net operating income	$ 100	

If 352 speakers are sold (2 speakers above the break-even point), the net operating income for the month will be $200. If 353 speakers are sold (3 speakers above the break-even point), the net operating income for the month will be $300, and so forth. To estimate the profit at any sales volume above the break-even point, multiply the number of units sold in excess of the break-even point by the unit contribution margin. The result represents the anticipated profits for the period. Or, to estimate the effect of a planned increase in sales on profits, simply multiply the increase in units sold by the unit contribution margin. The result will be the expected increase in profits. To illustrate, if Acoustic Concepts is currently selling 400 speakers per month and plans to increase sales to 425 speakers per month, the anticipated impact on profits can be computed as follows:

Increased number of speakers to be sold	25
Contribution margin per speaker	× $100
Increase in net operating income	$2,500

These calculations can be verified as follows:

	Sales Volume			
	400 Speakers	425 Speakers	Difference (25 Speakers)	Per Unit
Sales (@ $250 per speaker).	$100,000	$106,250	$6,250	$250
Variable expenses (@ $150 per speaker).	60,000	63,750	3,750	150
Contribution margin.	40,000	42,500	2,500	$100
Fixed expenses.	35,000	35,000	0	
Net operating income.	$ 5,000	$ 7,500	$2,500	

To summarize, if sales are zero, the company's loss would equal its fixed expenses. Each unit that is sold reduces the loss by the amount of the unit contribution margin. Once the break-even point has been reached, each additional unit sold increases the company's profit by the amount of the unit contribution margin.

1. Which of the following statements is a common assumption underlying cost-volume-profit analysis? (You may select more than one answer.)
   a. The variable cost per unit remains constant.
   b. The selling price per unit remains constant.
   c. Total fixed costs are constant within the relevant range.
   d. The total variable costs remain constant as the level of sales fluctuates.
2. Once a company hits its break-even point, net operating income will
   a. Increase by an amount equal to the selling price per unit multiplied by the number of units sold above the break-even point.
   b. Increase by an amount equal to the contribution margin ratio multiplied by the number of units sold above the break-even point.
   c. Increase by an amount equal to the contribution margin per unit multiplied by the number of units sold above the break-even point.
   d. Increase by an amount equal to the variable cost per unit multiplied by the number of units sold above the break-even point.

CVP Relationships in Equation Form

The contribution format income statement can be expressed in equation form as follows:

$$\text{Profit} = (\text{Sales} - \text{Variable expenses}) - \text{Fixed expenses}$$

For brevity, we use the term *profit* to stand for net operating income in equations.

When a company has only a *single* product, as at Acoustic Concepts, we can further refine the equation as follows:

$$\text{Sales} = \text{Selling price per unit} \times \text{Quantity sold} = P \times Q$$

$$\text{Variable expenses} = \text{Variable expenses per unit} \times \text{Quantity sold} = V \times Q$$

$$\text{Profit} = (P \times Q - V \times Q) - \text{Fixed expenses}$$

We can do all of the calculations of the previous section using this simple equation. For example, on the previous page we computed that the net operating income (profit) at sales of 351 speakers would be $100. We can arrive at the same conclusion using the above equation as follows:

$$\text{Profit} = (P \times Q - V \times Q) - \text{Fixed expenses}$$
$$\text{Profit} = (\$250 \times 351 - \$150 \times 351) - \$35,000$$
$$= (\$250 - \$150) \times 351 - \$35,000$$
$$= (\$100) \times 351 - \$35,000$$
$$= \$35,100 - \$35,000 = \$100$$

It is often useful to express the simple profit equation in terms of the unit contribution margin (Unit CM) as follows:

$$\text{Unit CM} = \text{Selling price per unit} - \text{Variable expenses per unit} = P - V$$
$$\text{Profit} = (P \times Q - V \times Q) - \text{Fixed expenses}$$
$$\text{Profit} = (P - V) \times Q - \text{Fixed expenses}$$

$$\text{Profit} = \text{Unit CM} \times Q - \text{Fixed expenses}$$

We could also have used this equation to determine the profit at sales of 351 speakers as follows:

$$\text{Profit} = \text{Unit CM} \times Q - \text{Fixed expenses}$$

$$= \$100 \times 351 - \$35,000$$

$$= \$35,100 - \$35,000 = \$100$$

For those who are comfortable with algebra, the quickest and easiest approach to solving the problems in this chapter may be to use the simple profit equation in one of its forms.

CVP Relationships in Graphic Form

The relationships among revenue, cost, profit, and volume are illustrated on a **cost-volume-profit (CVP) graph.** A CVP graph highlights CVP relationships over wide ranges of activity. To help explain his analysis to Prem Narayan, Bob Luchinni prepared a CVP graph for Acoustic Concepts.

Preparing the CVP Graph   In a CVP graph (sometimes called a *break-even chart*), unit volume is represented on the horizontal (*X*) axis and dollars on the vertical (*Y*) axis. Preparing a CVP graph involves the three steps depicted in Exhibit 5–1:

1. Draw a line parallel to the volume axis to represent total fixed expense. For Acoustic Concepts, total fixed expenses are $35,000.
2. Choose some volume of unit sales and plot the point representing total expense (fixed and variable) at the sales volume you have selected. In Exhibit 5–1, Bob Luchinni chose a volume of 600 speakers. Total expense at that sales volume is

Fixed expense	$ 35,000
Variable expense (600 speakers × $150 per speaker)	90,000
Total expense	$125,000

After the point has been plotted, draw a line through it back to the point where the fixed expense line intersects the dollars axis.
3. Again choose some sales volume and plot the point representing total sales dollars at the activity level you have selected. In Exhibit 5–1, Bob Luchinni again chose a volume of 600 speakers. Sales at that volume total $150,000 (600 speakers × $250 per speaker). Draw a line through this point back to the origin.

The interpretation of the completed CVP graph is given in Exhibit 5–2. The anticipated profit or loss at any given level of sales is measured by the vertical distance between the total revenue line (sales) and the total expense line (variable expense plus fixed expense).

The break-even point is where the total revenue and total expense lines cross. The break-even point of 350 speakers in Exhibit 5–2 agrees with the break-even point computed earlier.

As discussed earlier, when sales are below the break-even point—in this case, 350 units—the company suffers a loss. Note that the loss (represented by the vertical distance between the total expense and total revenue lines) gets bigger as sales decline. When sales are above the break-even point, the company earns a profit and the size of the profit (represented by the vertical distance between the total revenue and total expense lines) increases as sales increase.

EXHIBIT 5–1
Preparing the CVP Graph

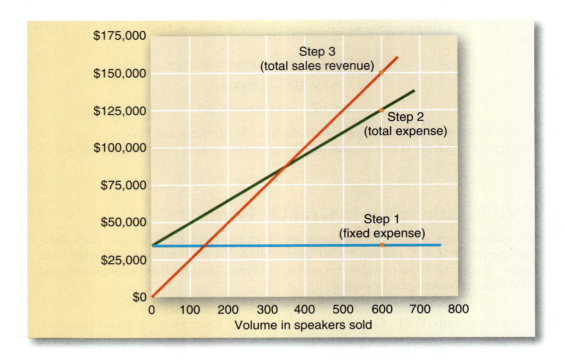

EXHIBIT 5–2
The Completed CVP Graph

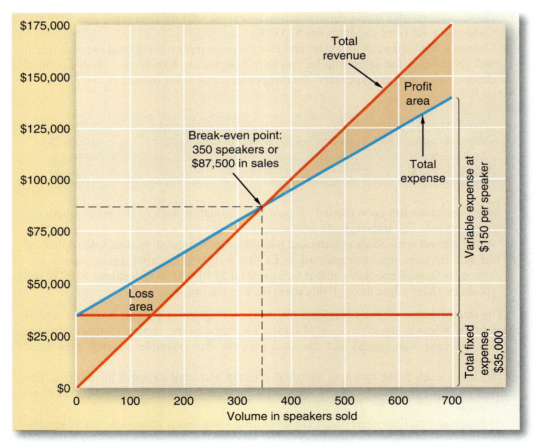

An even simpler form of the CVP graph, which we call a profit graph, is presented in Exhibit 5–3. That graph is based on the following equation:

$$\text{Profit} = \text{Unit CM} \times Q - \text{Fixed expenses}$$

In the case of Acoustic Concepts, the equation can be expressed as

$$\text{Profit} = \$100 \times Q - \$35,000$$

EXHIBIT 5–3   The Profit Graph

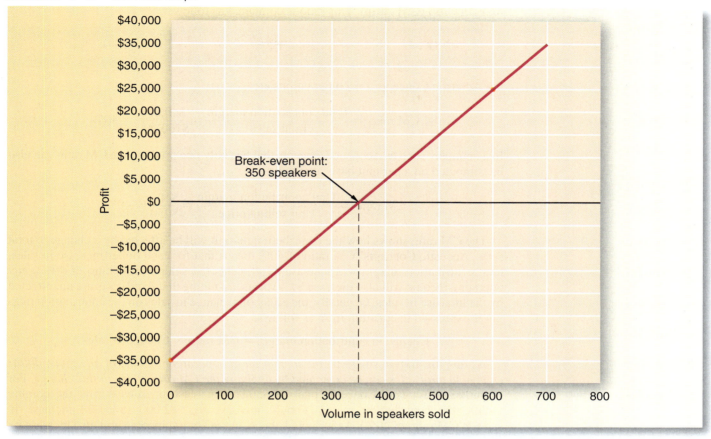

Because this is a linear equation, it plots as a single straight line. To plot the line, compute the profit at two different sales volumes, plot the points, and then connect them with a straight line. For example, when the sales volume is zero (i.e., $Q = 0$), the profit is − $35,000 (= $100 × 0 − $35,000). When Q is 600, the profit is $25,000 (= $100 × 600 − $35,000). These two points are plotted in Exhibit 5–3 and a straight line has been drawn through them.

The break-even point on the profit graph is the volume of sales at which profit is zero and is indicated by the dashed line on the graph. Note that the profit steadily increases to the right of the break-even point as the sales volume increases and that the loss becomes steadily worse to the left of the break-even point as the sales volume decreases.

Contribution Margin Ratio (CM Ratio)

In the previous section, we explored how cost-volume-profit relationships can be visualized. In this section, we show how the *contribution margin ratio* can be used in cost-volume-profit calculations. As the first step, we have added a column to Acoustic Concepts' contribution format income statement in which sales revenues, variable expenses, and contribution margin are expressed as a percentage of sales:

	Total	Per Unit	Percent of Sales
Sales (400 speakers).........	$100,000	$250	100%
Variable expenses............	60,000	150	60%
Contribution margin...........	40,000	$100	40%
Fixed expenses..............	35,000		
Net operating income.........	$ 5,000		

The contribution margin as a percentage of sales is referred to as the **contribution margin ratio (CM ratio).** This ratio is computed as follows:

$$\text{CM ratio} = \frac{\text{Contribution margin}}{\text{Sales}}$$

For Acoustic Concepts, the computations are

$$\text{CM ratio} = \frac{\text{Total contribution margin}}{\text{Total sales}} = \frac{\$40,000}{\$100,000} = 40\%$$

In a company such as Acoustic Concepts that has only one product, the CM ratio can also be computed on a per unit basis as follows:

$$\text{CM ratio} = \frac{\text{Unit contribution margin}}{\text{Unit selling price}} = \frac{\$100}{\$250} = 40\%$$

The CM ratio shows how the contribution margin will be affected by a change in total sales. Acoustic Concepts' CM ratio of 40% means that for each dollar increase in sales, total contribution margin will increase by 40 cents ($1 sales × CM ratio of 40%). Net operating income will also increase by 40 cents, assuming that fixed costs are not affected by the increase in sales. Generally, the effect of a change in sales on the contribution margin is expressed in equation form as follows:

$$\text{Change in contribution margin} = \text{CM ratio} \times \text{Change in sales}$$

As this illustration suggests, *the impact on net operating income of any given dollar change in total sales can be computed by applying the CM ratio to the dollar change.* For example, if Acoustic Concepts plans a $30,000 increase in sales during the coming month, the contribution margin should increase by $12,000 ($30,000 increase in sales × CM ratio of 40%). As we noted above, net operating income will also increase by $12,000 if fixed costs do not change. This is verified by the following table:

	Sales Volume			Percent of Sales
	Present	Expected	Increase	
Sales	$100,000	$130,000	$30,000	100%
Variable expenses	60,000	78,000*	18,000	60%
Contribution margin	40,000	52,000	12,000	40%
Fixed expenses	35,000	35,000	0	
Net operating income	$ 5,000	$ 17,000	$12,000	

*$130,000 expected sales ÷ $250 per unit = 520 units. 520 units × $150 per unit = $78,000.

The relation between profit and the CM ratio can also be expressed using the following equations:

$$\text{Profit} = \text{CM ratio} \times \text{Sales} - \text{Fixed expenses}^2$$

———————

[2]This equation can be derived using the basic profit equation and the definition of the CM ratio as follows:

Profit = (Sales − Variable expenses) − Fixed expenses

Profit = Contribution margin − Fixed expenses

$$\text{Profit} = \frac{\text{Contribution margin}}{\text{Sales}} \times \text{Sales} - \text{Fixed expenses}$$

Profit = CM ratio × Sales − Fixed expenses

or, in terms of changes,

Change in profit = CM ratio × Change in sales − Change in fixed expenses

For example, at sales of $130,000, the profit is expected to be $17,000 as shown below:

$$\text{Profit} = \text{CM ratio} \times \text{Sales} - \text{Fixed expenses}$$
$$= 0.40 \times \$130,000 - \$35,000$$
$$= \$52,000 - \$35,000 = \$17,000$$

Again, if you are comfortable with algebra, this approach will often be quicker and easier than constructing contribution format income statements.

The CM ratio is particularly valuable in situations where the dollar sales of one product must be traded off against the dollar sales of another product. In this situation, products that yield the greatest amount of contribution margin per dollar of sales should be emphasized.

3. The contribution margin ratio always increases when (you may select more than one answer):
    a. Sales increase.
    b. Fixed costs decrease.
    c. Total variable costs decrease.
    d. Variable costs as a percent of sales decrease.

CONCEPT CHECK

Some Applications of CVP Concepts

Bob Luchinni, the accountant at Acoustic Concepts, wanted to demonstrate to the company's president Prem Narayan how the concepts developed on the preceding pages can be used in planning and decision making. Bob gathered the following basic data:

LEARNING OBJECTIVE 5–4

Show the effects on net operating income of changes in variable costs, fixed costs, selling price, and volume.

	Per Unit	Percent of Sales
Selling price	$250	100%
Variable expenses	150	60%
Contribution margin	$100	40%

Recall that fixed expenses are $35,000 per month. Bob Luchinni will use these data to show the effects of changes in variable costs, fixed costs, sales price, and sales volume on the company's profitability in a variety of situations.

Before proceeding further, however, we need to introduce another concept—the *variable expense ratio*. The **variable expense ratio** is the ratio of variable expenses to sales. It can be computed by dividing the total variable expenses by the total sales, or in a single product analysis, it can be computed by dividing the variable expenses per unit by the unit selling price. In the case of Acoustic Concepts, the variable expense ratio is 0.60; that is, variable expense is 60% of sales. Expressed as an equation, the definition of the variable expense ratio is

$$\text{Variable expense ratio} = \frac{\text{Variable expenses}}{\text{Sales}}$$

This leads to a useful equation that relates the CM ratio to the variable expense ratio as follows:

$$\text{CM ratio} = \frac{\text{Contribution margin}}{\text{Sales}}$$

$$\text{CM ratio} = \frac{\text{Sales} - \text{Variable expenses}}{\text{Sales}}$$

$$\text{CM ratio} = 1 - \text{Variable expense ratio}$$

HELPFUL HINT

The picture below may improve your understanding of Learning Objective 5–4. It highlights the four variables that impact net operating income—the number of units sold (also called sales volume), the selling price per unit, the variable expense per unit, and total fixed expenses. Once you input the proper amounts for each of these variables in the tan boxes shown below, follow four steps to compute the new net operating income. First, multiply the number of units sold by the selling price per unit to derive total sales. The second step is to multiply the number of units sold by the variable expense per unit to derive total variable expenses. The third step is to subtract the total variable expenses from total sales to derive the contribution margin. The fourth step is to subtract total fixed expenses from the contribution margin to derive the new net operating income.

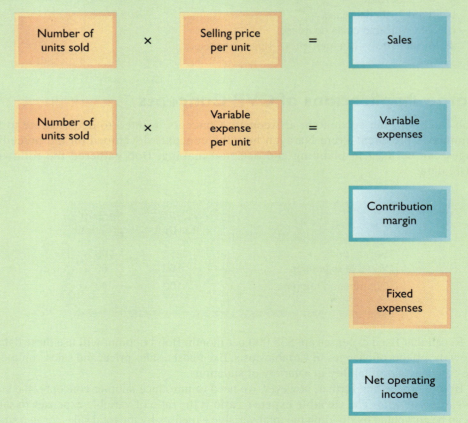

Change in Fixed Cost and Sales Volume

Acoustic Concepts is currently selling 400 speakers per month at $250 per speaker for total monthly sales of $100,000. The sales manager feels that a $10,000 increase in the monthly advertising budget would increase monthly sales by $30,000 to a total of 520 units. Should the advertising budget be increased? The table below shows the financial impact of the proposed change in the monthly advertising budget.

	Current Sales	Sales with Additional Advertising Budget	Difference	Percent of Sales
Sales	$100,000	$130,000	$30,000	100%
Variable expenses	60,000	78,000*	18,000	60%
Contribution margin	40,000	52,000	12,000	40%
Fixed expenses.	35,000	45,000†	10,000	
Net operating income	$ 5,000	$ 7,000	$ 2,000	

*520 units × $150 per unit = $78,000.
†$35,000 + additional $10,000 monthly advertising budget = $45,000.

Assuming no other factors need to be considered, the increase in the advertising budget should be approved because it would increase net operating income by $2,000. There are two shorter ways to arrive at this solution. The first alternative solution follows:

Alternative Solution 1

Expected total contribution margin:	
$130,000 × 40% CM ratio	$52,000
Present total contribution margin:	
$100,000 × 40% CM ratio	40,000
Increase in total contribution margin.	12,000
Change in fixed expenses:	
Less incremental advertising expense	10,000
Increased net operating income	$ 2,000

Because in this case only the fixed costs and the sales volume change, the solution can also be quickly derived as follows:

Alternative Solution 2

Incremental contribution margin:	
$30,000 × 40% CM ratio	$12,000
Less incremental advertising expense.	10,000
Increased net operating income	$ 2,000

Notice that this approach does not depend on knowledge of previous sales. Also note that it is unnecessary under either shorter approach to prepare an income statement. Both of the alternative solutions involve **incremental analysis**—they consider only the costs and revenues that will change if the new program is implemented. Although in each case a new income statement could have been prepared, the incremental approach is simpler and more direct and focuses attention on the specific changes that would occur as a result of the decision.

Change in Variable Costs and Sales Volume   Refer to the original data. Recall that Acoustic Concepts is currently selling 400 speakers per month. Prem is considering the use of higher-quality components, which would increase variable costs (and thereby reduce the contribution margin) by $10 per speaker. However, the sales manager predicts that using higher-quality components would increase sales to 480 speakers per month. Should the higher-quality components be used?

The $10 increase in variable costs would decrease the unit contribution margin by $10—from $100 down to $90.

Solution

Expected total contribution margin with higher-quality components:	
480 speakers × $90 per speaker	$43,200
Present total contribution margin:	
400 speakers × $100 per speaker	40,000
Increase in total contribution margin.	$ 3,200

According to this analysis, the higher-quality components should be used. Because fixed costs would not change, the $3,200 increase in contribution margin shown above should result in a $3,200 increase in net operating income.

Change in Fixed Cost, Selling Price, and Sales Volume   Refer to the original data and recall again that Acoustic Concepts is currently selling 400 speakers per month. To increase sales, the sales manager would like to cut the selling price by $20 per speaker and increase the advertising budget by $15,000 per month. The sales manager believes that if these two steps are taken, unit sales will increase by 50% to 600 speakers per month. Should the changes be made?

A decrease in the selling price of $20 per speaker would decrease the unit contribution margin by $20 down to $80.

Solution

Expected total contribution margin with lower selling price:	
600 speakers × $80 per speaker	$48,000
Present total contribution margin:	
400 speakers × $100 per speaker	40,000
Incremental contribution margin	8,000
Change in fixed expenses:	
Less incremental advertising expense	15,000
Reduction in net operating income.	$ (7,000)

According to this analysis, the changes should not be made. The $7,000 reduction in net operating income that is shown above can be verified by preparing comparative income statements as shown below.

	Present 400 Speakers per Month Total	Present 400 Speakers per Month Per Unit	Expected 600 Speakers per Month Total	Expected 600 Speakers per Month Per Unit	Difference
Sales	$100,000	$250	$138,000	$230	$38,000
Variable expenses	60,000	150	90,000	150	30,000
Contribution margin	40,000	$100	48,000	$ 80	8,000
Fixed expenses	35,000		50,000*		15,000
Net operating income (loss)	$ 5,000		$ (2,000)		$ (7,000)

*35,000 + Additional monthly advertising budget of $15,000 = $50,000.

Change in Variable Cost, Fixed Cost, and Sales Volume   Refer to Acoustic Concepts' original data. As before, the company is currently selling 400 speakers per month. The sales manager would like to pay salespersons a sales commission of $15 per speaker sold, rather than the flat salaries that now total $6,000 per month. The sales manager is confident that the change would increase monthly sales by 15% to 460 speakers per month. Should the change be made?

Solution   Changing the sales staff's compensation from salaries to commissions would affect both fixed and variable expenses. Fixed expenses would decrease by $6,000, from $35,000 to $29,000. Variable expenses per unit would increase by $15, from $150 to $165, and the unit contribution margin would decrease from $100 to $85.

Expected total contribution margin with sales staff on commissions:	
460 speakers × $85 per speaker	$39,100
Present total contribution margin:	
400 speakers × $100 per speaker	40,000
Decrease in total contribution margin	(900)
Change in fixed expenses:	
Add salaries avoided if a commission is paid	6,000
Increase in net operating income	$ 5,100

According to this analysis, the changes should be made. Again, the same answer can be obtained by preparing comparative income statements:

	Present 400 Speakers per Month		Expected 460 Speakers per Month		
	Total	Per Unit	Total	Per Unit	Difference
Sales	$100,000	$250	$115,000	$250	$15,000
Variable expenses	60,000	150	75,900	165	15,900
Contribution margin	40,000	$100	39,100	$ 85	900
Fixed expenses	35,000		29,000		(6,000)*
Net operating income	$ 5,000		$ 10,100		$ 5,100

*Note: A *reduction* in fixed expenses has the effect of *increasing* net operating income.

Change in Selling Price   Refer to the original data where Acoustic Concepts is currently selling 400 speakers per month. The company has an opportunity to make a bulk sale of 150 speakers to a wholesaler if an acceptable price can be negotiated. This sale would not alter the company's regular sales and would not affect the company's total fixed expenses. What price per speaker should be quoted to the wholesaler if Acoustic Concepts is seeking a profit of $3,000 on the bulk sale?

Solution

Variable cost per speaker	$150
Desired profit per speaker:	
$3,000 ÷ 150 speakers	20
Quoted price per speaker	$170

Notice that fixed expenses are not included in the computation. This is because fixed expenses are not affected by the bulk sale, so all of the additional contribution margin increases the company's profits.

BREAK-EVEN AND TARGET PROFIT ANALYSIS

Managers use break-even and target profit analysis to answer questions such as how much would we have to sell to avoid incurring a loss or how much would we have to sell to make a profit of $10,000 per month? We'll discuss break-even analysis first followed by target profit analysis.

Break-Even Analysis

LEARNING OBJECTIVE 5–5

Determine the break-even point.

Earlier in the chapter we defined the break-even point as *the level of sales at which the company's profit is zero.* To calculate the break-even point (in unit sales and dollar sales), managers can use either of two approaches, the equation method or the formula method. We'll demonstrate both approaches using the data from Acoustic Concepts.

The Equation Method   The equation method relies on the basic profit equation introduced earlier in the chapter. Since Acoustic Concepts has only one product, we'll use the contribution margin form of this equation to perform the break-even calculations. Remembering that Acoustic Concepts' unit contribution margin is $100, and its fixed expenses are $35,000, the company's break-even point is computed as follows:

$$\text{Profit} = \text{Unit CM} \times Q - \text{Fixed expense}$$
$$\$0 = \$100 \times Q - \$35,000$$
$$\$100 \times Q = \$0 + \$35,000$$
$$Q = \$35,000 \div \$100$$
$$Q = 350$$

Thus, as we determined earlier in the chapter, Acoustic Concepts will break even (or earn zero profit) at a sales volume of 350 speakers per month.

The Formula Method The formula method is a shortcut version of the equation method. It centers on the idea discussed earlier in the chapter that each unit sold provides a certain amount of contribution margin that goes toward covering fixed expenses. In a single product situation, the formula for computing the unit sales to break even is

$$\text{Unit sales to break even} = \frac{\text{Fixed expenses}^3}{\text{Unit CM}}$$

In the case of Acoustic Concepts, the unit sales needed to break even is computed as follows:

$$\text{Units sales to break even} = \frac{\text{Fixed expenses}}{\text{Unit CM}}$$

$$= \frac{\$35,000}{\$100}$$

$$= 350$$

Notice that 350 units is the same answer that we got when using the equation method. This will always be the case because the formula method and equation method are mathematically equivalent. The formula method simply skips a few steps in the equation method.

4. Assume the selling price per unit is $30, the contribution margin ratio is 40%, and the total fixed cost is $60,000. What is the break-even point in unit sales?
    a. 2,000
    b. 3,000
    c. 4,000
    d. 5,000

CONCEPT CHECK

Break-Even in Dollar Sales In addition to finding the break-even point in unit sales, we can also find the break-even point in dollar sales using three methods. First, we could solve for the break-even point in *unit* sales using the equation method or formula method and then simply multiply the result by the selling price. In the case of Acoustic Concepts, the break-even point in dollar sales using this approach would be computed as 350 speakers × $250 per speaker, or $87,500 in total sales.

Second, we can use the equation method to compute the break-even point in dollar sales. Remembering that Acoustic Concepts' contribution margin ratio is 40% and its fixed expenses are $35,000, the equation method calculates the break-even point in dollar sales as follows:

$$\text{Profit} = \text{CM ratio} \times \text{Sales} - \text{Fixed expenses}$$

$$\$0 = 0.40 \times \text{Sales} - \$35,000$$

$$0.40 \times \text{Sales} = \$0 + \$35,000$$

$$\text{Sales} = \$35,000 \div 0.40$$

$$\text{Sales} = \$87,500$$

---

[3]This formula can be derived as follows:

$$\text{Profit} = \text{Unit CM} \times Q - \text{Fixed expenses}$$

$$\$0 = \text{Unit CM} \times Q - \text{Fixed expenses}$$

$$\text{Unit CM} \times Q = \$0 + \text{Fixed expenses}$$

$$Q = \text{Fixed expenses} \div \text{Unit CM}$$

Third, we can use the formula method to compute the dollar sales needed to break even as shown below:

$$\text{Dollar sales to break even} = \frac{\text{Fixed expenses}[4]}{\text{CM ratio}}$$

In the case of Acoustic Concepts, the computations are performed as follows:

$$\text{Dollar sales to break even} = \frac{\text{Fixed expenses}}{\text{CM ratio}}$$

$$= \frac{\$35,000}{0.40}$$

$$= \$87,500$$

Again, you'll notice that the break-even point in dollar sales ($87,500) is the same under all three methods. This will always be the case because these methods are mathematically equivalent.

Target Profit Analysis

Target profit analysis is one of the key uses of CVP analysis. In **target profit analysis,** we estimate what sales volume is needed to achieve a specific target profit. For example, suppose Prem Narayan of Acoustic Concepts would like to estimate the sales needed to attain a target profit of $40,000 per month. To determine the unit sales and dollar sales needed to achieve a target profit, we can rely on the same two approaches that we have been discussing thus far, the equation method or the formula method.

The Equation Method   To compute the unit sales required to achieve a target profit of $40,000 per month, Acoustic Concepts can use the same profit equation that was used for its break-even analysis. Remembering that the company's contribution margin per unit is $100 and its total fixed expenses are $35,000, the equation method could be applied as follows:

$$\text{Profit} = \text{Unit CM} \times Q - \text{Fixed expense}$$

$$\$40,000 = \$100 \times Q - \$35,000$$

$$\$100 \times Q = \$40,000 + \$35,000$$

$$Q = \$75,000 \div \$100$$

$$Q = 750$$

Thus, the target profit can be achieved by selling 750 speakers per month. Notice that the only difference between this equation and the equation used for Acoustic Concepts' break-even calculation is the profit figure. In the break-even scenario, the profit is $0, whereas in the target profit scenario the profit is $40,000.

---

[4]This formula can be derived as follows:

$$\text{Profit} = \text{CM ratio} \times \text{Sales} - \text{Fixed expenses}$$

$$\$0 = \text{CM ratio} \times \text{Sales} - \text{Fixed expenses}$$

$$\text{CM ratio} \times \text{Sales} = \$0 + \text{Fixed expenses}$$

$$\text{Sales} = \text{Fixed expenses} \div \text{CM ratio}$$

The Formula Method In general, in a single product situation, we can compute the sales volume required to attain a specific target profit using the following formula:

$$\text{Unit sales to attain the target profit} = \frac{\text{Target profit} + \text{Fixed expenses}}{\text{Unit CM}}$$

In the case of Acoustic Concepts, the unit sales needed to attain a target profit of 40,000 is computed as follows:

$$\text{Unit sales to attain the target profit} = \frac{\text{Target profit} + \text{Fixed expenses}}{\text{Unit CM}}$$

$$= \frac{\$40,000 + \$35,000}{\$100}$$

$$= 750$$

Target Profit Analysis in Terms of Dollar Sales When quantifying the dollar sales needed to attain a target profit we can apply the same three methods that we used for calculating the dollar sales needed to break even. First, we can solve for the *unit* sales needed to attain the target profit using the equation method or formula method and then simply multiply the result by the selling price. In the case of Acoustic Concepts, the dollar sales to attain its target profit would be computed as 750 speakers × $250 per speaker, or $187,500 in total sales.

Second, we can use the equation method to compute the dollar sales needed to attain the target profit. Remembering that Acoustic Concepts' target profit is $40,000, its contribution margin ratio is 40%, and its fixed expenses are $35,000, the equation method calculates the answer as follows:

$$\text{Profit} = \text{CM ratio} \times \text{Sales} - \text{Fixed expenses}$$

$$\$40,000 = 0.40 \times \text{Sales} - \$35,000$$

$$0.40 \times \text{Sales} = \$40,000 + \$35,000$$

$$\text{Sales} = \$75,000 \div 0.40$$

$$\text{Sales} = \$187,500$$

Third, we can use the formula method to compute the dollar sales needed to attain the target profit as shown below:

$$\text{Dollar sales to attain the target profit} = \frac{\text{Target profit} + \text{Fixed expenses}}{\text{CM ratio}}$$

In the case of Acoustic Concepts, the computations would be as follows:

$$\text{Dollar sales to attain the target profit} = \frac{\text{Target profit} + \text{Fixed expenses}}{\text{CM ratio}}$$

$$= \frac{\$40,000 + \$35,000}{\$0.40}$$

$$= \$187,500$$

Again, you'll notice that the answers are the same regardless of which method we use. This is because all of the methods discussed are simply different roads to the same destination.

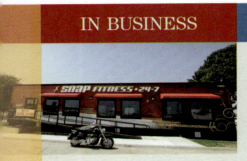
Snap Fitness Grows in a Weak Economy

When **Bally's Total Fitness** was filing for bankruptcy, **Snap Fitness** was expanding to more than 900 clubs in the United States with 400,000 members. The secret to Snap Fitness' success is its "no frills" approach to exercise. Each club typically has five treadmills, two stationary bikes, five elliptical machines, and weight equipment while bypassing amenities such as on-site child care, juice bars, and showers. Each club is usually staffed only 25–40 hours per week and it charges a membership fee of $35 per month.

To open a new Snap Fitness location, each franchise owner has an initial capital outlay of $120,000 for various types of equipment and a one-time licensing fee of $15,000. The franchisee also pays Snap (the parent company) a royalty fee of $400 per month plus $0.50 for each membership. Snap also collects one-time fees of $5 for each new member's "billing setup" and $5 for each security card issued. If a new club attracts 275 members, it can break even in as little as three months. Can you estimate the underlying calculations related to this break-even point?

Source: Nicole Perlroth, "Survival of the Fittest," *Forbes*, January 12, 2009, pp. 54–55.

The Margin of Safety

The **margin of safety** is the excess of budgeted or actual sales dollars over the break-even volume of sales dollars. It is the amount by which sales can drop before losses are incurred. The higher the margin of safety, the lower the risk of not breaking even and incurring a loss. The formula for the margin of safety is shown below:

$$\text{Margin of safety in dollars} = \text{Total budgeted (or actual) sales} - \text{Break-even sales}$$

The margin of safety can also be expressed in percentage form by dividing the margin of safety in dollars by total dollar sales:

$$\text{Margin of safety percentage} = \frac{\text{Margin of safety in dollars}}{\text{Total budgeted (or actual) sales in dollars}}$$

The calculation of the margin of safety for Acoustic Concepts is as follows:

Sales (at the current volume of 400 speakers) (a)	$100,000
Break-even sales (at 350 speakers)	87,500
Margin of safety in dollars (b)	$ 12,500
Margin of safety percentage, (b) ÷ (a)	12.5%

This margin of safety means that at the current level of sales and with the company's current prices and cost structure, a reduction in sales of $12,500, or 12.5%, would result in just breaking even.

In a single-product company like Acoustic Concepts, the margin of safety can also be expressed in terms of the number of units sold by dividing the margin of safety in dollars by the selling price per unit. In this case, the margin of safety is 50 speakers ($12,500 ÷ $250 per speaker = 50 speakers).

Loan Officer

Steve Becker owns **Blue Ridge Brewery**, a microbrewery in Arden, North Carolina. He charges distributors $100 per case for his premium beer. The distributors tack on 25% when selling to retailers who in turn add a 30% markup before selling the beer to consumers. In the most recent year, Blue Ridge's revenue was $8 million and its net operating income was $700,000. Becker reports that the costs of making one case of his premium beer are $32 for raw ingredients, $20 for labor, $4 for bottling and packaging, and $12 for utilities.

Assume that Becker has approached your bank for a loan. As the loan officer, you should consider a variety of factors, including the company's margin of safety. Assuming that other information about the company is favorable, would you consider Blue Ridge's margin of safety to be comfortable enough to extend a loan?

Prem Narayan and Bob Luchinni met to discuss the results of Bob's analysis.

Prem: Bob, everything you have shown me is pretty clear. I can see what impact the sales manager's suggestions would have on our profits. Some of those suggestions are quite good and others are not so good. I am concerned that our margin of safety is only 50 speakers. What can we do to increase this number?

Bob: Well, we have to increase total sales or decrease the break-even point or both.

Prem: And to decrease the break-even point, we have to either decrease our fixed expenses or increase our unit contribution margin?

Bob: Exactly.

Prem: And to increase our unit contribution margin, we must either increase our selling price or decrease the variable cost per unit?

Bob: Correct.

Prem: So what do you suggest?

Bob: Well, the analysis doesn't tell us which of these to do, but it does indicate we have a potential problem here.

Prem: If you don't have any immediate suggestions, I would like to call a general meeting next week to discuss ways we can work on increasing the margin of safety. I think everyone will be concerned about how vulnerable we are to even small downturns in sales.

ACOUSTIC
concepts

5. Assume a company produces one product that sells for $55, has a variable cost per unit of $35, and has fixed costs of $100,000. How many units must the company sell to earn a target profit of $50,000?
   a. 7,500 units   c. 12,500 units
   b. 10,000 units   d. 15,000 units
6. Given the same facts as in question 5 above, if the company exactly meets its target profit, what will be its margin of safety in sales dollars?
   a. $110,000   c. $137,500
   b. $127,500   d. $150,000
7. Which of the following statements is false with respect to the margin of safety? (You may select more than one answer.)
   a. The total budgeted (or actual) sales minus sales at the break-even point equals the margin of safety in dollars.
   b. The margin of safety in dollars divided by the total budgeted (or actual) sales in dollars equals the margin of safety percentage.
   c. In a single product company, the margin of safety in dollars divided by the variable cost per unit equals the margin of safety in units.
   d. The margin of safety in dollars can be a negative number.

CVP CONSIDERATIONS IN CHOOSING A COST STRUCTURE

Cost structure refers to the relative proportion of fixed and variable costs in an organization. Managers often have some latitude in trading off between these two types of costs. For example, fixed investments in automated equipment can reduce variable labor costs. In this section, we discuss the choice of a cost structure. We also introduce the concept of *operating leverage*.

Cost Structure and Profit Stability

Which cost structure is better—high variable costs and low fixed costs, or the opposite? No single answer to this question is possible; each approach has its advantages. To show what we mean, refer to the following contribution format income statements for two blueberry farms. Bogside Farm depends on migrant workers to pick its berries by hand, whereas Sterling Farm has invested in expensive berry-picking machines. Consequently, Bogside Farm has higher variable costs, but Sterling Farm has higher fixed costs:

	Bogside Farm		Sterling Farm	
	Amount	Percent	Amount	Percent
Sales	$100,000	100%	$100,000	100%
Variable expenses	60,000	60%	30,000	30%
Contribution margin	40,000	40%	70,000	70%
Fixed expenses	30,000		60,000	
Net operating income	$ 10,000		$ 10,000	

Which farm has the better cost structure? The answer depends on many factors, including the long-run trend in sales, year-to-year fluctuations in the level of sales, and the attitude of the owners toward risk. If sales are expected to exceed $100,000 in the future, then Sterling Farm probably has the better cost structure. The reason is that its CM ratio is higher, and its profits will therefore increase more rapidly as sales increase. To illustrate, assume that each farm experiences a 10% increase in sales without any increase in fixed costs. The new income statements would be as follows:

	Bogside Farm		Sterling Farm	
	Amount	Percent	Amount	Percent
Sales	$110,000	100%	$110,000	100%
Variable expenses	66,000	60%	33,000	30%
Contribution margin	44,000	40%	77,000	70%
Fixed expenses	30,000		60,000	
Net operating income	$ 14,000		$ 17,000	

Sterling Farm has experienced a greater increase in net operating income due to its higher CM ratio even though the increase in sales was the same for both farms.

What if sales drop below $100,000? What are the farms' break-even points? What are their margins of safety? The computations needed to answer these questions are shown on the next page using the formula method:

	Bogside Farm	Sterling Farm
Fixed expenses	$ 30,000	$ 60,000
Contribution margin ratio	÷ 0.40	÷ 0.70
Dollar sales to break even	$ 75,000	$ 85,714
Total current sales (a)	$100,000	$100,000
Break-even sales	75,000	85,714
Margin of safety in sales dollars (b)	$ 25,000	$ 14,286
Margin of safety percentage (b) ÷ (a)	25.0%	14.3%

Bogside Farm's margin of safety is greater and its contribution margin ratio is lower than Sterling Farm. Therefore, Bogside Farm is less vulnerable to downturns than Sterling Farm. Due to its lower contribution margin ratio, Bogside Farm will not lose contribution margin as rapidly as Sterling Farm when sales decline. Thus, Bogside Farm's profit will be less volatile. We saw earlier that this is a drawback when sales increase, but it provides more protection when sales drop. And because its break-even point is lower, Bogside Farm can suffer a larger sales decline before losses emerge.

To summarize, without knowing the future, it is not obvious which cost structure is better. Both have advantages and disadvantages. Sterling Farm, with its higher fixed costs and lower variable costs, will experience wider swings in net operating income as sales fluctuate, with greater profits in good years and greater losses in bad years. Bogside Farm, with its lower fixed costs and higher variable costs, will enjoy greater profit stability and will be more protected from losses during bad years, but at the cost of lower net operating income in good years.

Operating Leverage

A lever is a tool for multiplying force. Using a lever, a massive object can be moved with only a modest amount of force. In business, *operating leverage* serves a similar purpose. **Operating leverage** is a measure of how sensitive net operating income is to a given percentage change in dollar sales. Operating leverage acts as a multiplier. If operating leverage is high, a small percentage increase in sales can produce a much larger percentage increase in net operating income.

Operating leverage can be illustrated by returning to the data for the two blueberry farms. We previously showed that a 10% increase in sales (from $100,000 to $110,000 in each farm) results in a 70% increase in the net operating income of Sterling Farm (from $10,000 to $17,000) and only a 40% increase in the net operating income of Bogside Farm (from $10,000 to $14,000). Thus, for a 10% increase in sales, Sterling Farm experiences a much greater percentage increase in profits than does Bogside Farm. Therefore, Sterling Farm has greater operating leverage than Bogside Farm.

The **degree of operating leverage** at a given level of sales is computed by the following formula:

LEARNING OBJECTIVE 5–8

Compute the degree of operating leverage at a particular level of sales and explain how it can be used to predict changes in net operating income.

$$\text{Degree of operating leverage} = \frac{\text{Contribution margin}}{\text{Net operating income}}$$

The degree of operating leverage is a measure, at a given level of sales, of how a percentage change in sales volume will affect profits. To illustrate, the degree of operating leverage for the two farms at $100,000 sales would be computed as follows:

$$\text{Bogside Farm: } \frac{\$40,000}{\$10,000} = 4$$

$$\text{Sterling Farm: } \frac{\$70,000}{\$10,000} = 7$$

Because the degree of operating leverage for Bogside Farm is 4, the farm's net operating income grows four times as fast as its sales. In contrast, Sterling Farm's net operating income grows seven times as fast as its sales. Thus, if sales increase by 10%, then we can expect the net operating income of Bogside Farm to increase by four times this amount, or by 40%, and the net operating income of Sterling Farm to increase by seven times this amount, or by 70%. In general, this relation between the percentage change in sales and the percentage change in net operating income is given by the following formula:

$$\text{Percentage change in net operating income} = \text{Degree of operating leverage} \times \text{Percentage change in sales}$$

Bogside Farm: Percentage change in net operating income $= 4 \times 10\% = 40\%$

Sterling Farm: Percentage change in net operating income $= 7 \times 10\% = 70\%$

What is responsible for the higher operating leverage at Sterling Farm? The only difference between the two farms is their cost structure. If two companies have the same total revenue and same total expense but different cost structures, then the company with the higher proportion of fixed costs in its cost structure will have higher operating leverage. Referring back to the original example on page 212, when both farms have sales of $100,000 and total expenses of $90,000, one-third of Bogside Farm's costs are fixed but two-thirds of Sterling Farm's costs are fixed. As a consequence, Sterling's degree of operating leverage is higher than Bogside's.

The degree of operating leverage is not a constant; it is greatest at sales levels near the break-even point and decreases as sales and profits rise. The following table shows the degree of operating leverage for Bogside Farm at various sales levels. (Data used earlier for Bogside Farm are shown in color.)

Sales	$75,000	$80,000	$100,000	$150,000	$225,000
Variable expenses	45,000	48,000	60,000	90,000	135,000
Contribution margin (a).	30,000	32,000	40,000	60,000	90,000
Fixed expenses	30,000	30,000	30,000	30,000	30,000
Net operating income (b)	$ 0	$ 2,000	$ 10,000	$ 30,000	$ 60,000
Degree of operating leverage, (a) ÷ (b)	∞	16	4	2	1.5

Thus, a 10% increase in sales would increase profits by only 15% (10% × 1.5) if sales were previously $225,000, as compared to the 40% increase we computed earlier at the $100,000 sales level. The degree of operating leverage will continue to decrease the farther the company moves from its break-even point. At the break-even point, the degree of operating leverage is infinitely large ($30,000 contribution margin ÷ $0 net operating income = ∞).

The degree of operating leverage can be used to quickly estimate what impact various percentage changes in sales will have on profits, without the necessity of preparing detailed income statements. As shown by our examples, the effects of operating leverage can be dramatic. If a company is near its break-even point, then even small percentage increases in sales can yield large percentage increases in profits. *This explains why management will often work very hard for only a small increase in sales volume.* If the degree of operating leverage is 5, then a 6% increase in sales would translate into a 30% increase in profits.

The Dangers of a High Degree of Operating Leverage

IN BUSINESS

In recent years, computer chip manufacturers have poured more than $75 billion into constructing new manufacturing facilities to meet the growing demand for digital devices such as iPhones and Blackberrys. Because 70% of the costs of running these facilities are fixed, a sharp drop in customer demand forces these companies to choose between two undesirable options. They can slash production levels and absorb large amounts of unused capacity costs, or they can continue producing large volumes of output in spite of shrinking demand, thereby flooding the market with excess supply and lowering prices. Either choice distresses investors who tend to shy away from computer chip makers in economic downturns.

Source: Bruce Einhorn, "Chipmakers on the Edge," *BusinessWeek,* January 5, 2009, pp. 30–31.

STRUCTURING SALES COMMISSIONS

Companies usually compensate salespeople by paying them a commission based on sales, a salary, or a combination of the two. Commissions based on sales dollars can lead to lower profits. To illustrate, consider Pipeline Unlimited, a producer of surfing equipment. Salespersons sell the company's products to retail sporting goods stores throughout North America and the Pacific Basin. Data for two of the company's surfboards, the XR7 and Turbo models, appear below:

	Model	
	XR7	**Turbo**
Selling price	$695	$749
Variable expenses	344	410
Contribution margin	$351	$339

Which model will salespeople push hardest if they are paid a commission of 10% of sales revenue? The answer is the Turbo because it has the higher selling price and hence the larger commission. On the other hand, from the standpoint of the company, profits will be greater if salespeople steer customers toward the XR7 model because it has the higher contribution margin.

To eliminate such conflicts, commissions can be based on contribution margin rather than on selling price. If this is done, the salespersons will want to sell the mix of products that maximizes contribution margin. Providing that fixed costs are not affected by the sales mix, maximizing the contribution margin will also maximize the company's profit.[5] In effect, by maximizing their own compensation, salespersons will also maximize the company's profit.

---

[5]This also assumes the company has no production constraint. If it does, the sales commissions should be modified.

SALES MIX

LEARNING OBJECTIVE 5–9

Compute the break-even point for a multiproduct company and explain the effects of shifts in the sales mix on contribution margin and the break-even point.

Before concluding our discussion of CVP concepts, we need to consider the impact of changes in *sales mix* on a company's profit.

The Definition of Sales Mix

The term **sales mix** refers to the relative proportions in which a company's products are sold. The idea is to achieve the combination, or mix, that will yield the greatest profits. Most companies have many products, and often these products are not equally profitable. Hence, profits will depend to some extent on the company's sales mix. Profits will be greater if high-margin rather than low-margin items make up a relatively large proportion of total sales.

Changes in the sales mix can cause perplexing variations in a company's profits. A shift in the sales mix from high-margin items to low-margin items can cause total profits to decrease even though total sales may increase. Conversely, a shift in the sales mix from low-margin items to high-margin items can cause the reverse effect—total profits may increase even though total sales decrease. It is one thing to achieve a particular sales volume; it is quite another to sell the most profitable mix of products.

IN BUSINESS | **Netbook Sales Cannibalize PC Sales**

When computer manufacturers introduced the "netbook," they expected it to serve as a consumer's third computer—complementing home and office personal computers (PCs) rather than replacing them. However, when the economy soured many customers decided to buy lower-priced netbooks instead of PCs, which in turn adversely affected the financial performance of many companies. For example, when **Microsoft** failed to achieve its sales goals, the company partially blamed growing netbook sales and declining PC sales for its troubles. Microsoft's Windows operating system for netbooks sells for $15–$25 per device, which is less than half the cost of the company's least expensive Windows operating system for PCs.

Source: Olga Kharif, "Small, Cheap—and Frighteningly Popular," *BusinessWeek*, December 8, 2008, p. 64.

Sales Mix and Break-Even Analysis

If a company sells more than one product, break-even analysis is more complex than discussed to this point. The reason is that different products will have different selling prices, different costs, and different contribution margins. Consequently, the break-even point depends on the mix in which the various products are sold. To illustrate, consider Virtual Journeys Unlimited, a small company that sells two DVDs: the Monuments DVD, a tour of the United States' most popular National Monuments; and the Parks DVD, which tours the United States' National Parks. The company's September sales, expenses, and break-even point are shown in Exhibit 5–4.

As shown in the exhibit, the break-even point is $60,000 in sales, which was computed by dividing the company's fixed expenses of $27,000 by its overall CM ratio of 45%. However, this is the break-even only if the company's sales mix does not change. Currently, the Monuments DVD is responsible for 20% and the Parks DVD for 80% of the company's dollar sales. Assuming this sales mix does not change, if total sales are $60,000, the sales of the Monuments DVD would be $12,000 (20% of $60,000) and the sales of the Parks DVD would be $48,000 (80% of $60,000). As shown in Exhibit 5–4, at these levels of sales, the company would indeed break even. But $60,000 in sales represents the break-even point for the company only if the sales mix does not change. *If the*

EXHIBIT 5–4 Multiproduct Break-Even Analysis

Virtual Journeys Unlimited
Contribution Income Statement
For the Month of September

	Monuments DVD Amount	Percent	Parks DVD Amount	Percent	Total Amount	Percent
Sales.	$20,000	100%	$80,000	100%	$100,000	100%
Variable expenses	15,000	75%	40,000	50%	55,000	55%
Contribution margin	$ 5,000	25%	$40,000	50%	45,000	45%
Fixed expenses.					27,000	
Net operating income					$ 18,000	

Computation of the break-even point:

$$\frac{\text{Fixed expenses}}{\text{Overall CM ratio}} = \frac{\$27,000}{0.45} = \$60,000$$

Verification of the break-even point:

	Monuments DVD	Parks DVD	Total
Current dollar sales	$20,000	$80,000	$100,000
Percentage of total dollar sales.	20%	80%	100%
Sales at the break-even point	$12,000	$48,000	$60,000

	Monuments DVD Amount	Percent	Parks DVD Amount	Percent	Total Amount	Percent
Sales.	$12,000	100%	$48,000	100%	$60,000	100%
Variable expenses	9,000	75%	24,000	50%	33,000	55%
Contribution margin	$ 3,000	25%	$24,000	50%	27,000	45%
Fixed expenses.					27,000	
Net operating income					$ 0	

sales mix changes, then the break-even point will also usually change. This is illustrated by the results for October in which the sales mix shifted away from the more profitable Parks DVD (which has a 50% CM ratio) toward the less profitable Monuments DVD (which has a 25% CM ratio). These results appear in Exhibit 5–5.

Although sales have remained unchanged at $100,000, the sales mix is exactly the reverse of what it was in Exhibit 5–4, with the bulk of the sales now coming from the less profitable Monuments DVD. Notice that this shift in the sales mix has caused both the overall CM ratio and total profits to drop sharply from the prior month even though total sales are the same. The overall CM ratio has dropped from 45% in September to only 30% in October, and net operating income has dropped from $18,000 to only $3,000. In addition, with the drop in the overall CM ratio, the company's break-even point is no longer $60,000 in sales. Because the company is now realizing less average contribution margin per dollar of sales, it takes more sales to cover the same amount of fixed costs. Thus, the break-even point has increased from $60,000 to $90,000 in sales per year.

In preparing a break-even analysis, an assumption must be made concerning the sales mix. Usually the assumption is that it will not change. However, if the sales mix is expected to change, then this must be explicitly considered in any CVP computations.

EXHIBIT 5–5 Multiproduct Break-Even Analysis: A Shift in Sales Mix (see Exhibit 5–4)

Virtual Journeys Unlimited
Contribution Income Statement
For the Month of October

	Monuments DVD		Parks DVD		Total	
	Amount	Percent	Amount	Percent	Amount	Percent
Sales................................	$80,000	100%	$20,000	100%	$100,000	100%
Variable expenses	60,000	75%	10,000	50%	70,000	70%
Contribution margin	$20,000	25%	$10,000	50%	30,000	30%
Fixed expenses.....................					27,000	
Net operating income...............					$ 3,000	

Computation of the break-even point:

$$\frac{\text{Fixed expenses}}{\text{Overall CM ratio}} = \frac{\$27,000}{0.30} = \$90,000$$

CONCEPT CHECK

8. Which of the following statements is true? (You may select more than one answer.)
    a. One minus the contribution margin ratio equals the variable expense ratio.
    b. Incremental analysis focuses only on the costs and revenues that change as a result of a decision.
    c. Sales commissions based on sales dollars can lead to lower profits than commissions based on contribution margin.
    d. If a company's total sales remain constant, then its net operating income must remain constant even if the sales mix fluctuates.

SUMMARY

LO5–1 Explain how changes in activity affect contribution margin and net operating income.

The unit contribution margin, which is the difference between a unit's selling price and its variable cost, indicates how net operating income will change as the result of selling one more or one less unit. For example, if a product's unit contribution margin is $10, then selling one more unit will add $10 to the company's profit.

LO5–2 Prepare and interpret a cost-volume-profit (CVP) graph and a profit graph.

A cost-volume-profit graph displays sales revenues and expenses as a function of unit sales. The break-even point on the graph is the point at which the total sales revenue and total expense lines intersect. A profit graph displays profit as a function of unit sales. The break-even point on the profit graph is the point at which profit is zero.

LO5–3 Use the contribution margin ratio (CM ratio) to compute changes in contribution margin and net operating income resulting from changes in sales volume.

The contribution margin ratio is computed by dividing the unit contribution margin by the unit selling price, or by dividing the total contribution margin by the total sales.

The contribution margin shows how much a dollar increase in sales affects the total contribution margin and net operating income. For example, if a product has a 40% contribution margin ratio, then a $100 increase in sales should result in a $40 increase in contribution margin and in net operating income.

LO5–4 Show the effects on net operating income of changes in variable costs, fixed costs, selling price, and volume.
Contribution margin concepts can be used to estimate the effects of changes in various parameters such as variable costs, fixed costs, selling prices, and volume on net operating income.

LO5–5 Determine the break-even point.
The break-even point is the level of sales at which profit is zero. This is just a special case of solving for the level of sales needed to achieve a desired target profit—in this special case the target profit is zero.

LO5–6 Determine the level of sales needed to achieve a desired target profit.
The level of sales needed to achieve a desired target profit can be computed using several methods. The answer can be derived using the fundamental profit equation and simple algebra or formulas can be used. In either approach, the unit sales required to attain a desired target profit is ultimately determined by summing the desired target profit and the fixed expenses and then dividing the result by the unit contribution margin.

LO5–7 Compute the margin of safety and explain its significance.
The margin of safety is the difference between the total budgeted (or actual) sales dollars of a period and the break-even sales dollars. It expresses how much cushion there is in the current level of sales above the break-even point.

LO5–8 Compute the degree of operating leverage at a particular level of sales and explain how it can be used to predict changes in net operating income.
The degree of operating leverage is computed by dividing the total contribution margin by net operating income. The degree of operating leverage can be used to determine the impact a given percentage change in sales would have on net operating income. For example, if a company's degree of operating leverage is 2.5, then a 10% increase in sales from the current level of sales should result in a 25% increase in net operating income.

LO5–9 Compute the break-even point for a multiproduct company and explain the effects of shifts in the sales mix on contribution margin and the break-even point.
The break-even point for a multiproduct company can be computed by dividing the company's total fixed expenses by the overall contribution margin ratio.

 This method for computing the break-even point assumes that the sales mix is constant. If the sales mix shifts toward products with a lower contribution margin ratio, then more total sales are required to attain any given level of profits.

GUIDANCE ANSWER TO DECISION POINT

Loan Officer (p. 211)
To determine the company's margin of safety, you need to determine its break-even point. Start by estimating the company's variable expense ratio:

$$\text{Variable cost per unit} \div \text{Selling price per unit} = \text{Variable expense ratio}$$

$$\$68 \div \$100 = 68\%$$

Then, estimate the company's variable expenses:

$$\text{Sales} \times \text{Variable expense ratio} = \text{Estimated amount of variable expenses}$$

$$\$8,000,000 \times 0.68 = \$5,440,000$$

Next, estimate the company's current level of fixed expenses as follows:

$$\text{Sales} = \text{Variable expenses} + \text{Fixed expenses} + \text{Profits}$$

$$\$8,000,000 = \$5,440,000 + X + \$700,000$$

$$X = \$8,000,000 - \$5,440,000 - \$700,000$$

$$X = \$1,860,000$$

Use the equation approach to estimate the company's break-even point:

$$\text{Sales} = \text{Variable expenses} + \text{Fixed expenses} + \text{Profits}$$

$$X = 0.68X + \$1,860,000 + \$0$$

$$0.32X = \$1,860,000$$

$$X = \$5,812,500$$

Finally, compute the company's margin of safety:

$$\text{Margin of safety} = (\text{Sales} - \text{Break-even sales}) \div \text{Sales}$$

$$= (\$8,000,000 - \$5,812,500) \div \$8,000,000$$

$$= 27.3\%$$

The margin of safety appears to be adequate, so if the other information about the company is favorable, a loan would seem to be justified.

GUIDANCE ANSWERS TO CONCEPT CHECKS

1. **Choices a, b, and c.** The total variable costs will change as the level of sales fluctuates.
2. **Choice c.** Choice *a* fails to consider variable costs. Choice *b* is invalid because it is not stated in terms of dollars. Choice *d* excludes the selling price per unit.
3. **Choice d.** The contribution margin ratio equals 1.0 − Variable costs as a percent of sales.
4. **Choice d.** The contribution margin per unit is $12 (40% of $30). Therefore, the break-even point in units sold = $60,000 ÷ $12 = 5,000.
5. **Choice a.** ($100,000 + $50,000) ÷ $20 contribution margin per unit = 7,500 units.
6. **Choice c.** 7,500 units is 2,500 units above the break-even point. Therefore, the margin of safety is 2,500 units × $55 per unit = $137,500.
7. **Choice c.** The margin of safety in dollars divided by the selling price per unit equals the margin of safety in units.
8. **Choices a, b, and c.** If a company's total sales remain constant, its net operating income may change if the sales mix fluctuates.

REVIEW PROBLEM: CVP RELATIONSHIPS

Voltar Company manufactures and sells a specialized cordless telephone for high electromagnetic radiation environments. The company's contribution format income statement for the most recent year is given below:

	Total	Per Unit	Percent of Sales
Sales (20,000 units)	$1,200,000	$60	100%
Variable expenses	900,000	45	? %
Contribution margin	300,000	$15	? %
Fixed expenses.	240,000		
Net operating income	$ 60,000		

Management is anxious to increase the company's profit and has asked for an analysis of a number of items.

Required:

1. Compute the company's CM ratio and variable expense ratio.
2. Compute the company's break-even point in both unit sales and dollar sales. Use the equation method.
3. Assume that sales increase by $400,000 next year. If cost behavior patterns remain unchanged, by how much will the company's net operating income increase? Use the CM ratio to compute your answer.
4. Refer to the original data. Assume that next year management wants the company to earn a profit of at least $90,000. How many units will have to be sold to meet this target profit?

5. Refer to the original data. Compute the company's margin of safety in both dollar and percentage form.
6. a. Compute the company's degree of operating leverage at the present level of sales.
   b. Assume that through a more intense effort by the sales staff, the company's sales increase by 8% next year. By what percentage would you expect net operating income to increase? Use the degree of operating leverage to obtain your answer.
   c. Verify your answer to (b) by preparing a new contribution format income statement showing an 8% increase in sales.
7. In an effort to increase sales and profits, management is considering the use of a higher-quality speaker. The higher-quality speaker would increase variable costs by $3 per unit, but management could eliminate one quality inspector who is paid a salary of $30,000 per year. The sales manager estimates that the higher-quality speaker would increase annual sales by at least 20%.
   a. Assuming that changes are made as described above, prepare a projected contribution format income statement for next year. Show data on a total, per unit, and percentage basis.
   b. Compute the company's new break-even point in both unit sales and dollar sales. Use the formula method.
   c. Would you recommend that the changes be made?

Solution to Review Problem

1.
$$\text{CM ratio} = \frac{\text{Unit contribution margin}}{\text{Unit selling price}} = \frac{\$15}{\$60} = 25\%$$

$$\text{Variable expense ratio} = \frac{\text{Variable expense}}{\text{Selling price}} = \frac{\$45}{\$60} = 75\%$$

2.
$$\text{Profit} = \text{Unit CM} \times Q - \text{Fixed expenses}$$

$$\$0 = (\$60 - \$45) \times Q - \$240,000$$

$$\$15Q = \$240,000$$

$$Q = \$240,000 \div \$15$$

$$Q = 16,000 \text{ units; or, at } \$60 \text{ per unit, } \$960,000$$

3.

Increase in sales..........................	$400,000
Multiply by the CM ratio	× 25%
Expected increase in contribution margin........	$100,000

Because the fixed expenses are not expected to change, net operating income will increase by the entire $100,000 increase in contribution margin computed above.

4. Equation method:

$$\text{Profit} = \text{Unit CM} \times Q - \text{Fixed expenses}$$

$$\$90,000 = (\$60 - \$45) \times Q - \$240,000$$

$$\$15Q = \$90,000 + \$240,000$$

$$Q = \$330,000 \div \$15$$

$$Q = 22,000 \text{ units}$$

Formula method:

$$\frac{\text{Unit sales to attain}}{\text{the target profit}} = \frac{\text{Target profit} + \text{Fixed expenses}}{\text{Contribution margin per unit}} = \frac{\$90,000 + \$240,000}{\$15 \text{ per unit}} = 22,000 \text{ units}$$

5.
$$\text{Margin of safety in dollars} = \text{Total sales} - \text{Break-even sales}$$

$$= \$1,200,000 - \$960,000 = \$240,000$$

$$\text{Margin of safety percentage} = \frac{\text{Margin of safety in dollars}}{\text{Total sales}} = \frac{\$240,000}{\$1,200,000} = 20\%$$

6. a.
$$\text{Degree of operating leverage} = \frac{\text{Contribution margin}}{\text{Net operating income}} = \frac{\$300,000}{\$60,000} = 5$$

b.

Expected increase in sales.	8%
Degree of operating leverage	× 5
Expected increase in net operating income	40%

c. If sales increase by 8%, then 21,600 units (20,000 × 1.08 = 21,600) will be sold next year. The new contribution format income statement would be as follows:

	Total	Per Unit	Percent of Sales
Sales (21,600 units)	$1,296,000	$60	100%
Variable expenses	972,000	45	75%
Contribution margin	324,000	$15	25%
Fixed expenses.	240,000		
Net operating income	$ 84,000		

Thus, the $84,000 expected net operating income for next year represents a 40% increase over the $60,000 net operating income earned during the current year:

$$\frac{\$84,000 - \$60,000}{\$60,000} = \frac{\$24,000}{\$60,000} = 40\% \text{ increase}$$

Note that the increase in sales from 20,000 to 21,600 units has increased *both* total sales and total variable expenses.

7.   a. A 20% increase in sales would result in 24,000 units being sold next year: 20,000 units × 1.20 = 24,000 units.

	Total	Per Unit	Percent of Sales
Sales (24,000 units)	$1,440,000	$60	100%
Variable expenses	1,152,000	48*	80%
Contribution margin	288,000	$12	20%
Fixed expenses.	210,000†		
Net operating income	$ 78,000		

*$45 + $3 = $48; $48 ÷ $60 = 80%.
†$240,000 − $30,000 = $210,000.

Note that the change in per unit variable expenses results in a change in both the per unit contribution margin and the CM ratio.

b. $$\text{Unit sales to break even} = \frac{\text{Fixed expenses}}{\text{Unit contribution margin}}$$

$$= \frac{\$210,000}{\$12 \text{ per unit}} = 17,500 \text{ units}$$

$$\text{Dollar sales to break even} = \frac{\text{Fixed expenses}}{\text{CM ratio}}$$

$$= \frac{\$210,000}{0.20} = \$1,050,000$$

c. Yes, based on these data, the changes should be made. The changes increase the company's net operating income from the present $60,000 to $78,000 per year. Although the changes also result in a higher break-even point (17,500 units as compared to the present 16,000 units), the company's margin of safety actually becomes greater than before:

$$\text{Margin of safety in dollars} = \text{Total sales} - \text{Break-even sales}$$

$$= \$1,440,000 - \$1,050,000 = \$390,000$$

As shown in (5) on the prior page, the company's present margin of safety is only $240,000. Thus, several benefits will result from the proposed changes.

Break-even point   The level of sales at which profit is zero. (p. 194)

Contribution margin ratio (CM ratio)   A ratio computed by dividing contribution margin by dollar sales. (p. 200)

Cost-volume-profit (CVP) graph   A graphical representation of the relationships between an organization's revenues, costs, and profits on the one hand and its sales volume on the other hand. (p. 197)

Degree of operating leverage   A measure, at a given level of sales, of how a percentage change in sales will affect profits. The degree of operating leverage is computed by dividing contribution margin by net operating income. (p. 213)

Incremental analysis   An analytical approach that focuses only on those costs and revenues that change as a result of a decision. (p. 203)

Margin of safety   The excess of budgeted or actual dollar sales over the break-even dollar sales. (p. 210)

Operating leverage   A measure of how sensitive net operating income is to a given percentage change in dollar sales. (p. 213)

Sales mix   The relative proportions in which a company's products are sold. Sales mix is computed by expressing the sales of each product as a percentage of total sales. (p. 216)

Target profit analysis   Estimating what sales volume is needed to achieve a specific target profit. (p. 208)

Variable expense ratio   A ratio computed by dividing variable expenses by dollar sales. (p. 201)

QUESTIONS

5–1   What is meant by a product's contribution margin ratio? How is this ratio useful in planning business operations?

5–2   Often the most direct route to a business decision is an incremental analysis. What is meant by an *incremental analysis?*

5–3   In all respects, Company A and Company B are identical except that Company A's costs are mostly variable, whereas Company B's costs are mostly fixed. When sales increase, which company will tend to realize the greatest increase in profits? Explain.

5–4   What is meant by the term *operating leverage?*

5–5   What is meant by the term *break-even point?*

5–6   In response to a request from your immediate supervisor, you have prepared a CVP graph portraying the cost and revenue characteristics of your company's product and operations. Explain how the lines on the graph and the break-even point would change if (*a*) the selling price per unit decreased, (*b*) fixed cost increased throughout the entire range of activity portrayed on the graph, and (*c*) variable cost per unit increased.

5–7   What is meant by the margin of safety?

5–8   What is meant by the term *sales mix?* What assumption is usually made concerning sales mix in CVP analysis?

5–9   Explain how a shift in the sales mix could result in both a higher break-even point and a lower net income.

Multiple-choice questions are available in the *Connect Library*.

APPLYING EXCEL

Available with McGraw-Hill's *Connect Accounting*.

The Excel worksheet form that appears on the next page is to be used to recreate portions of the Review Problem on pages 220–222. Download the workbook containing this form in the *Connect Library*. On the website you will also receive instructions about how to use this worksheet form.

LO5–6, LO5–7, LO5–8

	A	B	C	D
1	**Chapter 5: Applying Excel**			
2				
3	**Data**			
4	Unit sales	20,000	units	
5	Selling price per unit	$60	per unit	
6	Variable expenses per unit	$45	per unit	
7	Fixed expenses	$240,000		
8				
9	*Enter a formula into each of the cells marked with a ? below*			
10	**Review Problem: CVP Relationships**			
11				
12	*Compute the CM ratio and variable expense ratio*			
13	Selling price per unit	?	per unit	
14	Variable expenses per unit	?	per unit	
15	Contribution margin per unit	?	per unit	
16				
17	CM ratio	?		
18	Variable expense ratio	?		
19				
20	*Compute the break-even*			
21	Break-even in unit sales	?	units	
22	Break-even in dollar sales	?		
23				
24	*Compute the margin of safety*			
25	Margin of safety in dollars	?		
26	Margin of safety percentage	?		
27				
28	*Compute the degree of operating leverage*			
29	Sales	?		
30	Variable expenses	?		
31	Contribution margin	?		
32	Fixed expenses	?		
33	Net operating income	?		
34				
35	Degree of operating leverage	?		
36				

Chapter 5 Form   Filled in Chapter 5 Form

You should proceed to the requirements below only after completing your worksheet.

Required:
1. Check your worksheet by changing the fixed expenses to $270,000. If your worksheet is operating properly, the degree of operating leverage should be 10. If you do not get this answer, find the errors in your worksheet and correct them. How much is the margin of safety percentage? Did it change? Why or why not?
2. Enter the following data from a different company into your worksheet:

Unit sales	10,000 units
Selling price per unit.	$120 per unit
Variable expenses per unit	$72 per unit
Fixed expenses.	$420,000

What is the margin of safety percentage? What is the degree of operating leverage?
3. Using the degree of operating leverage and without changing anything in your worksheet, calculate the percentage change in net operating income if unit sales increase by 15%.

4. Confirm the calculations you made in part (3) above by increasing the unit sales in your worksheet by 15%. What is the new net operating income and by what percentage did it increase?
5. Thad Morgan, a motorcycle enthusiast, has been exploring the possibility of relaunching the Western Hombre brand of cycle that was popular in the 1930s. The retro-look cycle would be sold for $10,000 and at that price, Thad estimates 600 units would be sold each year. The variable cost to produce and sell the cycles would be $7,500 per unit. The annual fixed cost would be $1,200,000.
    a. Using your worksheet, what would be the break-even unit sales, the margin of safety in dollars, and the degree of operating leverage?
    b. Thad is worried about the selling price. Rumors are circulating that other retro brands of cycles may be revived. If so, the selling price for the Western Hombre would have to be reduced to $9,000 to compete effectively. In that event, Thad would also reduce fixed expenses by $300,000 by reducing advertising expenses, but he still hopes to sell 600 units per year. Do you think this is a good plan? Explain. Also, explain the degree of operating leverage that appears on your worksheet.

 **connect** |ACCOUNTING

THE FOUNDATIONAL 15

Available with McGraw-Hill's *Connect Accounting*.

Oslo Company prepared the following contribution format income statement based on a sales volume of 1,000 units (the relevant range of production is 500 units to 1,500 units):

> LO5–1, LO5–3,
> LO5–4, LO5–5,
> LO5–6, LO5–7,
> LO5–8

Sales.	$20,000
Variable expenses	12,000
Contribution margin	8,000
Fixed expenses.	6,000
Net operating income	$ 2,000

Required:
(Answer each question independently and always refer to the original data unless instructed otherwise.)
1. What is the contribution margin per unit?
2. What is the contribution margin ratio?
3. What is the variable expense ratio?
4. If sales increase to 1,001 units, what would be the increase in net operating income?
5. If sales decline to 900 units, what would be the net operating income?
6. If the selling price increases by $2 per unit and the sales volume decreases by 100 units, what would be the net operating income?
7. If the variable cost per unit increases by $1, spending on advertising increases by $1,500, and unit sales increase by 250 units, what would be the net operating income?
8. What is the break-even point in unit sales?
9. What is the break-even point in dollar sales?
10. How many units must be sold to achieve a target profit of $5,000?
11. What is the margin of safety in dollars? What is the margin of safety percentage?
12. What is the degree of operating leverage?
13. Using the degree of operating leverage, what is the estimated percent increase in net operating income of a 5% increase in sales?
14. Assume that the amounts of the company's total variable expenses and total fixed expenses were reversed. In other words, assume that the total variable expenses are $6,000 and the total fixed expenses are $12,000. Under this scenario and assuming that total sales remain the same, what is the degree of operating leverage?
15. Using the degree of operating leverage that you computed in the previous question, what is the estimated percent increase in net operating income of a 5% increase in sales?

EXERCISES

All applicable exercises are available with McGraw-Hill's *Connect Accounting*.

EXERCISE 5–1   Preparing a Contribution Format Income Statement [LO5–1]

Whirly Corporation's most recent income statement is shown below:

	Total	Per Unit
Sales (10,000 units)	$350,000	$35.00
Variable expenses	200,000	20.00
Contribution margin	150,000	$15.00
Fixed expenses.	135,000	
Net operating income	$ 15,000	

Required:

Prepare a new contribution format income statement under each of the following conditions (consider each case independently):

1. The sales volume increases by 100 units.
2. The sales volume decreases by 100 units.
3. The sales volume is 9,000 units.

EXERCISE 5–2   Prepare a Cost-Volume-Profit (CVP) Graph [LO5–2]

Karlik Enterprises distributes a single product whose selling price is $24 and whose variable expense is $18 per unit. The company's monthly fixed expense is $24,000.

Required:

1. Prepare a cost-volume-profit graph for the company up to a sales level of 8,000 units.
2. Estimate the company's break-even point in unit sales using your cost-volume-profit graph.

EXERCISE 5–3   Prepare a Profit Graph [LO5–2]

Jaffre Enterprises distributes a single product whose selling price is $16 and whose variable expense is $11 per unit. The company's fixed expense is $16,000 per month.

Required:

1. Prepare a profit graph for the company up to a sales level of 4,000 units.
2. Estimate the company's break-even point in unit sales using your profit graph.

EXERCISE 5–4   Computing and Using the CM Ratio [LO5–3]

Last month when Holiday Creations, Inc., sold 50,000 units, total sales were $200,000, total variable expenses were $120,000, and fixed expenses were $65,000.

Total variable expenses = $110,000

Required:

1. What is the company's contribution margin (CM) ratio?
2. Estimate the change in the company's net operating income if it were to increase its total sales by $1,000.

EXERCISE 5–5   Changes in Variable Costs, Fixed Costs, Selling Price, and Volume [LO5–4]

Data for Hermann Corporation are shown below:

Selling price = $100;
Variable expenses per unit = $40

	Per Unit	Percent of Sales
Selling price	$90	100%
Variable expenses	63	70
Contribution margin	$27	30%

Fixed expenses are $30,000 per month and the company is selling 2,000 units per month.

Required:
1. The marketing manager argues that a $5,000 increase in the monthly advertising budget would increase monthly sales by $9,000. Should the advertising budget be increased?
2. Refer to the original data. Management is considering using higher-quality components that would increase the variable expense by $2 per unit. The marketing manager believes that the higher-quality product would increase sales by 10% per month. Should the higher-quality components be used?

EXERCISE 5–6 Compute the Break-Even Point [LO5–5]

Mauro Products distributes a single product, a woven basket whose selling price is $15 and whose variable expense is $12 per unit. The company's monthly fixed expense is $4,200.

Monthly fixed expense = $6,000

Required:
1. Solve for the company's break-even point in unit sales using the equation method.
2. Solve for the company's break-even point in dollar sales using the equation method and the CM ratio.
3. Solve for the company's break-even point in unit sales using the formula method.
4. Solve for the company's break-even point in dollar sales using the formula method and the CM ratio.

EXERCISE 5–7 Compute the Level of Sales Required to Attain a Target Profit [LO5–6]

Lin Corporation has a single product whose selling price is $120 and whose variable expense is $80 per unit. The company's monthly fixed expense is $50,000.

Selling price = $160

Required:
1. Using the equation method, solve for the unit sales that are required to earn a target profit of $10,000.
2. Using the formula method, solve for the unit sales that are required to earn a target profit of $15,000.

EXERCISE 5–8 Compute the Margin of Safety [LO5–7]

Molander Corporation is a distributor of a sun umbrella used at resort hotels. Data concerning the next month's budget appear below:

Unit sales = 900 units per month

Selling price	$30 per unit
Variable expenses	$20 per unit
Fixed expenses.	$7,500 per month
Unit sales	1,000 units per month

Required:
1. Compute the company's margin of safety.
2. Compute the company's margin of safety as a percentage of its sales.

EXERCISE 5–9 Compute and Use the Degree of Operating Leverage [LO5–8]

Engberg Company installs lawn sod in home yards. The company's most recent monthly contribution format income statement follows:

Sales = $90,000; Variable expenses = $36,000

	Amount	Percent of Sales
Sales.	$80,000	100%
Variable expenses	32,000	40%
Contribution margin	48,000	60%
Fixed expenses.	38,000	
Net operating income	$10,000	

Required:
1. Compute the company's degree of operating leverage.
2. Using the degree of operating leverage, estimate the impact on net operating income of a 5% increase in sales.
3. Verify your estimate from part (2) above by constructing a new contribution format income statement for the company assuming a 5% increase in sales.

Claimjumper variable
expenses = $25,000

TAKE TWO

EXERCISE 5–10 Compute the Break-Even Point for a Multiproduct Company [LO5–9]
Lucido Products markets two computer games: Claimjumper and Makeover. A contribution format income statement for a recent month for the two games appears below:

	Claimjumper	Makeover	Total
Sales.	$30,000	$70,000	$100,000
Variable expenses	20,000	50,000	70,000
Contribution margin	$10,000	$20,000	30,000
Fixed expenses.			24,000
Net operating income			$ 6,000

Required:
1. Compute the overall contribution margin (CM) ratio for the company.
2. Compute the overall break-even point for the company in dollar sales.
3. Verify the overall break-even point for the company by constructing a contribution format income statement showing the appropriate levels of sales for the two products.

EXERCISE 5–11 Missing Data; Basic CVP Concepts [LO5–1, LO5–9]
Fill in the missing amounts in each of the eight case situations below. Each case is independent of the others. (*Hint:* One way to find the missing amounts would be to prepare a contribution format income statement for each case, enter the known data, and then compute the missing items.)
a. Assume that only one product is being sold in each of the four following case situations:

Case	Units Sold	Sales	Variable Expenses	Contribution Margin per Unit	Fixed Expenses	Net Operating Income (Loss)
1	15,000	$180,000	$120,000	?	$50,000	?
2	?	$100,000	?	$10	$32,000	$8,000
3	10,000	?	$70,000	$13	?	$12,000
4	6,000	$300,000	?	?	$100,000	$(10,000)

b. Assume that more than one product is being sold in each of the four following case situations:

Case	Sales	Variable Expenses	Average Contribution Margin Ratio	Fixed Expenses	Net Operating Income (Loss)
1	$500,000	?	20%	?	$7,000
2	$400,000	$260,000	?	$100,000	?
3	?	?	60%	$130,000	$20,000
4	$600,000	$420,000	?	?	$(5,000)

EXERCISE 5–12 Multiproduct Break-Even Analysis [LO5–9]
Olongapo Sports Corporation distributes two premium golf balls—the Flight Dynamic and the Sure Shot. Monthly sales and the contribution margin ratios for the two products follow:

	Flight Dynamic	Sure Shot	Total
Sales.	$150,000	$250,000	$400,000
CM ratio	80%	36%	?

Fixed expenses total $183,750 per month.

Required:
1. Prepare a contribution format income statement for the company as a whole. Carry computations to one decimal place.
2. Compute the break-even point for the company based on the current sales mix.
3. If sales increase by $100,000 a month, by how much would you expect net operating income to increase? What are your assumptions?

EXERCISE 5–13 Using a Contribution Format Income Statement [LO5–1, LO5–4]

Miller Company's most recent contribution format income statement is shown below:

	Total	Per Unit
Sales (20,000 units)	$300,000	$15.00
Variable expenses	180,000	9.00
Contribution margin	120,000	$ 6.00
Fixed expenses.	70,000	
Net operating income	$ 50,000	

Required:
Prepare a new contribution format income statement under each of the following conditions (consider each case independently):
1. The number of units sold increases by 15%.
2. The selling price decreases by $1.50 per unit, and the number of units sold increases by 25%.
3. The selling price increases by $1.50 per unit, fixed expenses increase by $20,000, and the number of units sold decreases by 5%.
4. The selling price increases by 12%, variable expenses increase by 60 cents per unit, and the number of units sold decreases by 10%.

EXERCISE 5–14 Break-Even and Target Profit Analysis [LO5–3, LO5–4, LO5–5, LO5–6]

Lindon Company is the exclusive distributor for an automotive product that sells for $40 per unit and has a CM ratio of 30%. The company's fixed expenses are $180,000 per year. The company plans to sell 16,000 units this year.

Required:
1. What are the variable expenses per unit?
2. Using the equation method:
   a. What is the break-even point in unit sales and in dollar sales?
   b. What amount of unit sales and dollar sales is required to earn an annual profit of $60,000?
   c. Assume that by using a more efficient shipper, the company is able to reduce its variable expenses by $4 per unit. What is the company's new break-even point in unit sales and in dollar sales?
3. Repeat (2) above using the formula method.

EXERCISE 5–15 Operating Leverage [LO5–4, LO5–8]

Magic Realm, Inc., has developed a new fantasy board game. The company sold 15,000 games last year at a selling price of $20 per game. Fixed expenses associated with the game total $182,000 per year, and variable expenses are $6 per game. Production of the game is entrusted to a printing contractor. Variable expenses consist mostly of payments to this contractor.

Fixed costs = $189,000

Required:
1. Prepare a contribution format income statement for the game last year and compute the degree of operating leverage.
2. Management is confident that the company can sell 18,000 games next year (an increase of 3,000 games, or 20%, over last year). Compute:
   a. The expected percentage increase in net operating income for next year.
   b. The expected total dollar net operating income for next year. (Do not prepare an income statement; use the degree of operating leverage to compute your answer.)

EXERCISE 5–16 Break-Even Analysis and CVP Graphing [LO5–2, LO5–4, LO5–5]
The Hartford Symphony Guild is planning its annual dinner-dance. The dinner-dance committee has assembled the following expected costs for the event:

Dinner (per person)	$18
Favors and program (per person)	$2
Band	$2,800
Rental of ballroom	$900
Professional entertainment during intermission	$1,000
Tickets and advertising	$1,300

The committee members would like to charge $35 per person for the evening's activities.

Required:
1. Compute the break-even point for the dinner-dance (in terms of the number of persons who must attend).
2. Assume that last year only 300 persons attended the dinner-dance. If the same number attend this year, what price per ticket must be charged in order to break even?
3. Refer to the original data ($35 ticket price per person). Prepare a CVP graph for the dinner-dance from zero tickets up to 600 tickets sold.

EXERCISE 5–17 Break-Even and Target Profit Analysis [LO5–4, LO5–5, LO5–6]
Outback Outfitters sells recreational equipment. One of the company's products, a small camp stove, sells for $50 per unit. Variable expenses are $32 per stove, and fixed expenses associated with the stove total $108,000 per month.

Required:
1. Compute the break-even point in unit sales and in dollar sales.
2. If the variable expenses per stove increase as a percentage of the selling price, will it result in a higher or a lower break-even point? Why? (Assume that the fixed expenses remain unchanged.)
3. At present, the company is selling 8,000 stoves per month. The sales manager is convinced that a 10% reduction in the selling price would result in a 25% increase in monthly sales of stoves. Prepare two contribution format income statements, one under present operating conditions, and one as operations would appear after the proposed changes. Show both total and per unit data on your statements.
4. Refer to the data in (3) above. How many stoves would have to be sold at the new selling price to yield a minimum net operating income of $35,000 per month?

Variable expenses
= $45 per stove

EXERCISE 5–18 Break-Even and Target Profit Analysis; Margin of Safety;
CM Ratio [LO5–1, LO5–3, LO5–5, LO5–6, LO5–7]
Menlo Company distributes a single product. The company's sales and expenses for last month follow:

	Total	Per Unit
Sales	$450,000	$30
Variable expenses	180,000	12
Contribution margin	270,000	$18
Fixed expenses	216,000	
Net operating income	$ 54,000	

Required:
1. What is the monthly break-even point in unit sales and in dollar sales?
2. Without resorting to computations, what is the total contribution margin at the break-even point?
3. How many units would have to be sold each month to earn a target profit of $90,000? Use the formula method. Verify your answer by preparing a contribution format income statement at the target sales level.
4. Refer to the original data. Compute the company's margin of safety in both dollar and percentage terms.
5. What is the company's CM ratio? If sales increase by $50,000 per month and there is no change in fixed expenses, by how much would you expect monthly net operating income to increase?

Alternate problem set is available in the *Connect Library*.

PROBLEMS

All applicable problems are available with McGraw-Hill's *Connect Accounting*.

PROBLEM 5–19A   Break-Even Analysis; Pricing [LO5–1, LO5–4, LO5–5]

Minden Company introduced a new product last year for which it is trying to find an optimal selling price. Marketing studies suggest that the company can increase sales by 5,000 units for each $2 reduction in the selling price. The company's present selling price is $70 per unit, and variable expenses are $40 per unit. Fixed expenses are $540,000 per year. The present annual sales volume (at the $70 selling price) is 15,000 units.

Required:
1. What is the present yearly net operating income or loss?
2. What is the present break-even point in unit sales and in dollar sales?
3. Assuming that the marketing studies are correct, what is the maximum annual profit that the company can earn? At how many units and at what selling price per unit would the company generate this profit?
4. What would be the break-even point in unit sales and in dollar sales using the selling price you determined in (3) above (e.g., the selling price at the level of maximum profits)? Why is this break-even point different from the break-even point you computed in (2) above?

PROBLEM 5–20A   Various CVP Questions: Break-Even Point; Cost Structure;
Target Sales [LO5–1, LO5–3, LO5–4, LO5–5, LO5–6, LO5–8]

Northwood Company manufactures basketballs. The company has a ball that sells for $25. At present, the ball is manufactured in a small plant that relies heavily on direct labor workers. Thus, variable expenses are high, totaling $15 per ball, of which 60% is direct labor cost.

Last year, the company sold 30,000 of these balls, with the following results:

Sales (30,000 balls)	$750,000
Variable expenses	450,000
Contribution margin	300,000
Fixed expenses	210,000
Net operating income	$ 90,000

Required:
1. Compute (a) the CM ratio and the break-even point in balls, and (b) the degree of operating leverage at last year's sales level.
2. Due to an increase in labor rates, the company estimates that variable expenses will increase by $3 per ball next year. If this change takes place and the selling price per ball remains constant at $25, what will be the new CM ratio and break-even point in balls?
3. Refer to the data in (2) above. If the expected change in variable expenses takes place, how many balls will have to be sold next year to earn the same net operating income, $90,000, as last year?
4. Refer again to the data in (2) above. The president feels that the company must raise the selling price of its basketballs. If Northwood Company wants to maintain the same CM ratio as last year, what selling price per ball must it charge next year to cover the increased labor costs?
5. Refer to the original data. The company is discussing the construction of a new, automated manufacturing plant. The new plant would slash variable expenses per ball by 40%, but it would cause fixed expenses per year to double. If the new plant is built, what would be the company's new CM ratio and new break-even point in balls?
6. Refer to the data in (5) above.
   a. If the new plant is built, how many balls will have to be sold next year to earn the same net operating income, $90,000, as last year?
   b. Assume the new plant is built and that next year the company manufactures and sells 30,000 balls (the same number as sold last year). Prepare a contribution format income statement and compute the degree of operating leverage.
   c. If you were a member of top management, would you have been in favor of constructing the new plant? Explain.

PROBLEM 5–21A Sales Mix; Multiproduct Break-Even Analysis [LO5–9]
Gold Star Rice, Ltd., of Thailand exports Thai rice throughout Asia. The company grows three varieties of rice—Fragrant, White, and Loonzain. Budgeted sales by product and in total for the coming month are shown below:

	Product							
	White		Fragrant		Loonzain		Total	
Percentage of total sales	20%		52%		28%		100%	
Sales.	$150,000	100%	$390,000	100%	$210,000	100%	$750,000	100%
Variable expenses	108,000	72%	78,000	20%	84,000	40%	270,000	36%
Contribution margin	$ 42,000	28%	$312,000	80%	$126,000	60%	480,000	64%
Fixed expenses.							449,280	
Net operating income							$ 30,720	

$$\frac{\text{Dollar sales to}}{\text{break even}} = \frac{\text{Fixed expenses}}{\text{CM ratio}} = \frac{\$449{,}280}{0.64} = \$702{,}000$$

As shown by these data, net operating income is budgeted at $30,720 for the month and break-even sales at $702,000.

Assume that actual sales for the month total $750,000 as planned. Actual sales by product are: White, $300,000; Fragrant, $180,000; and Loonzain, $270,000.

Required:
1. Prepare a contribution format income statement for the month based on actual sales data. Present the income statement in the format shown above.
2. Compute the break-even point in dollar sales for the month based on your actual data.
3. Considering the fact that the company met its $750,000 sales budget for the month, the president is shocked at the results shown on your income statement in (1) above. Prepare a brief memo for the president explaining why both the operating results and the break-even point in dollar sales are different from what was budgeted.

PROBLEM 5–22A Basics of CVP Analysis; Cost Structure [LO5–1, LO5–3, LO5–4, LO5–5, LO5–6]
Due to erratic sales of its sole product—a high-capacity battery for laptop computers—PEM, Inc., has been experiencing difficulty for some time. The company's contribution format income statement for the most recent month is given below:

Sales (19,500 units × $30 per unit)	$585,000
Variable expenses	409,500
Contribution margin	175,500
Fixed expenses.	180,000
Net operating loss.	$ (4,500)

Required:
1. Compute the company's CM ratio and its break-even point in both unit sales and dollar sales.
2. The president believes that a $16,000 increase in the monthly advertising budget, combined with an intensified effort by the sales staff, will result in an $80,000 increase in monthly sales. If the president is right, what will be the effect on the company's monthly net operating income or loss? (Use the incremental approach in preparing your answer.)
3. Refer to the original data. The sales manager is convinced that a 10% reduction in the selling price, combined with an increase of $60,000 in the monthly advertising budget, will double unit sales. What will the new contribution format income statement look like if these changes are adopted?
4. Refer to the original data. The Marketing Department thinks that a fancy new package for the laptop computer battery would help sales. The new package would increase packaging costs by 75 cents per unit. Assuming no other changes, how many units would have to be sold each month to earn a profit of $9,750?

5. Refer to the original data. By automating, the company could reduce variable expenses by $3 per unit. However, fixed expenses would increase by $72,000 each month.
    a. Compute the new CM ratio and the new break-even point in both unit sales and dollar sales.
    b. Assume that the company expects to sell 26,000 units next month. Prepare two contribution format income statements, one assuming that operations are not automated and one assuming that they are. (Show data on a per unit and percentage basis, as well as in total, for each alternative.)
    c. Would you recommend that the company automate its operations? Explain.

PROBLEM 5–23A   Basics of CVP Analysis [LO5–1, LO5–3, LO5–4, LO5–5, LO5–8]

Feather Friends, Inc., distributes a high-quality wooden birdhouse that sells for $20 per unit. Variable expenses are $8 per unit, and fixed expenses total $180,000 per year.

Required:
Answer the following independent questions:
1. What is the product's CM ratio?
2. Use the CM ratio to determine the break-even point in dollar sales.
3. Due to an increase in demand, the company estimates that sales will increase by $75,000 during the next year. By how much should net operating income increase (or net loss decrease) assuming that fixed expenses do not change?
4. Assume that the operating results for last year were as follows:

Sales.	$400,000
Variable expenses	160,000
Contribution margin	240,000
Fixed expenses.	180,000
Net operating income	$ 60,000

   a. Compute the degree of operating leverage at the current level of sales.
   b. The president expects sales to increase by 20% next year. By what percentage should net operating income increase?
5. Refer to the original data. Assume that the company sold 18,000 units last year. The sales manager is convinced that a 10% reduction in the selling price, combined with a $30,000 increase in advertising, would increase annual unit sales by one-third. Prepare two contribution format income statements, one showing the results of last year's operations and one showing the results of operations if these changes are made. Would you recommend that the company do as the sales manager suggests?
6. Refer to the original data. Assume again that the company sold 18,000 units last year. The president does not want to change the selling price. Instead, he wants to increase the sales commission by $1 per unit. He thinks that this move, combined with some increase in advertising, would increase annual sales by 25%. By how much could advertising be increased with profits remaining unchanged? Do not prepare an income statement; use the incremental analysis approach.

PROBLEM 5–24A   Break-Even and Target Profit Analysis [LO5–5, LO5–6]

The Shirt Works sells a large variety of tee shirts and sweatshirts. Steve Hooper, the owner, is thinking of expanding his sales by hiring high school students, on a commission basis, to sell sweatshirts bearing the name and mascot of the local high school.

These sweatshirts would have to be ordered from the manufacturer six weeks in advance, and they could not be returned because of the unique printing required. The sweatshirts would cost Hooper $8 each with a minimum order of 75 sweatshirts. Any additional sweatshirts would have to be ordered in increments of 75.

Since Hooper's plan would not require any additional facilities, the only costs associated with the project would be the costs of the sweatshirts and the costs of the sales commissions. The selling price of the sweatshirts would be $13.50 each. Hooper would pay the students a commission of $1.50 for each shirt sold.

Required:
1. To make the project worthwhile, Hooper would require a $1,200 profit for the first three months of the venture. What level of unit sales and dollar sales would be required to reach this target net operating income? Show all computations.
2. Assume that the venture is undertaken and an order is placed for 75 sweatshirts. What would be Hooper's break-even point in unit sales and in dollar sales? Show computations and explain the reasoning behind your answer.

**PROBLEM 5–25A   Changes in Fixed and Variable Expenses; Break-Even
and Target Profit Analysis [LO5–4, LO5–5, LO5–6]**

Neptune Company produces toys and other items for use in beach and resort areas. A small, inflatable toy has come onto the market that the company is anxious to produce and sell. The new toy will sell for $3 per unit. Enough capacity exists in the company's plant to produce 16,000 units of the toy each month. Variable expenses to manufacture and sell one unit would be $1.25, and fixed expenses associated with the toy would total $35,000 per month.

The company's Marketing Department predicts that demand for the new toy will exceed the 16,000 units that the company is able to produce. Additional manufacturing space can be rented from another company at a fixed expense of $1,000 per month. Variable expenses in the rented facility would total $1.40 per unit, due to somewhat less efficient operations than in the main plant.

Required:
1.   Compute the monthly break-even point for the new toy in unit sales and in dollar sales.
2.   How many units must be sold each month to make a monthly profit of $12,000?
3.   If the sales manager receives a bonus of 10 cents for each unit sold in excess of the break-even point, how many units must be sold each month to earn a return of 25% on the monthly investment in fixed expenses?

PROBLEM 5–26A   Basic CVP Analysis; Graphing [LO5–1, LO5–2, LO5–4, LO5–5]

The Fashion Shoe Company operates a chain of women's shoe shops that carry many styles of shoes that are all sold at the same price. Sales personnel in the shops are paid a substantial commission on each pair of shoes sold (in addition to a small base salary) in order to encourage them to be aggressive in their sales efforts.

The following worksheet contains cost and revenue data for Shop 48 and is typical of the company's many outlets:

	Per Pair of Shoes
Selling price	$30.00
Variable expenses:	
Invoice cost.	$13.50
Sales commission.	4.50
Total variable expenses	$18.00

	Annual
Fixed expenses:	
Advertising	$ 30,000
Rent	20,000
Salaries.	100,000
Total fixed expenses	$150,000

Required:
1.   Calculate the annual break-even point in unit sales and in dollar sales for Shop 48.
2.   Prepare a CVP graph showing cost and revenue data for Shop 48 from zero shoes up to 17,000 pairs of shoes sold each year. Clearly indicate the break-even point on the graph.
3.   If 12,000 pairs of shoes are sold in a year, what would be Shop 48's net operating income or loss?
4.   The company is considering paying the store manager of Shop 48 an incentive commission of 75 cents per pair of shoes (in addition to the salesperson's commission). If this change is made, what will be the new break-even point in unit sales and in dollar sales?
5.   Refer to the original data. As an alternative to (4) above, the company is considering paying the store manager 50 cents commission on each pair of shoes sold in excess of the break-even point. If this change is made, what will be the shop's net operating income or loss if 15,000 pairs of shoes are sold?

6. Refer to the original data. The company is considering eliminating sales commissions entirely in its shops and increasing fixed salaries by $31,500 annually. If this change is made, what will be the new break-even point in unit sales and in dollar sales for Shop 48? Would you recommend that the change be made? Explain.

PROBLEM 5–27A Sales Mix; Break-Even Analysis; Margin of Safety [LO5–7, LO5–9]

Island Novelties, Inc., of Palau makes two products, Hawaiian Fantasy and Tahitian Joy. Present revenue, cost, and sales data for the two products follow:

	Hawaiian Fantasy	Tahitian Joy
Selling price per unit..................	$15	$100
Variable expenses per unit.............	$9	$20
Number of units sold annually	20,000	5,000

Fixed expenses total $475,800 per year.

Required:

1. Assuming the sales mix given above, do the following:
    a. Prepare a contribution format income statement showing both dollar and percent columns for each product and for the company as a whole.
    b. Compute the break-even point in dollar sales for the company as a whole and the margin of safety in both dollars and percent.
2. The company has developed a new product to be called Samoan Delight. Assume that the company could sell 10,000 units at $45 each. The variable expenses would be $36 each. The company's fixed expenses would not change.
    a. Prepare another contribution format income statement, including sales of the Samoan Delight (sales of the other two products would not change).
    b. Compute the company's new break-even point in dollar sales and the new margin of safety in both dollars and percent.
3. The president of the company examines your figures and says, "There's something strange here. Our fixed expenses haven't changed and you show greater total contribution margin if we add the new product, but you also show our break-even point going up. With greater contribution margin, the break-even point should go down, not up. You've made a mistake somewhere." Explain to the president what has happened.

PROBLEM 5–28A Sales Mix; Commission Structure; Multiproduct Break-Even Analysis [LO5–9]

Carbex, Inc., produces cutlery sets out of high-quality wood and steel. The company makes a standard cutlery set and a deluxe set and sells them to retail department stores throughout the country. The standard set sells for $60, and the deluxe set sells for $75. The variable expenses associated with each set are given below.

	Standard	Deluxe
Production costs..............................	$15.00	$30.00
Sales commissions (15% of sales price)	$9.00	$11.25

The company's fixed expenses each month are shown below:

Advertising	$105,000
Depreciation	$21,700
Administrative...............	$63,000

Salespersons are paid on a commission basis to encourage them to be aggressive in their sales efforts. Mary Parsons, the financial vice president, watches sales commissions carefully and has noted that they have risen steadily over the last year. For this reason, she was shocked to find that even though sales have increased, profits for the current month—May—are down substantially from April. Sales, in sets, for the last two months are given below:

	Standard	Deluxe	Total
April	4,000	2,000	6,000
May.	1,000	5,000	6,000

Required:
1. Prepare contribution format income statements for April and May. Use the following headings:

	Standard		Deluxe		Total	
	Amount	Percent	Amount	Percent	Amount	Percent
Sales.						
Etc						

Place the fixed expenses only in the Total column. Do not show percentages for the fixed expenses.
2. Explain the difference in net operating incomes between the two months, even though the same total number of sets was sold in each month.
3. What can be done to the sales commissions to improve the sales mix?
   a. Using April's sales mix, what is the break-even point in dollar sales?
   b. Without doing any calculations, explain whether the break-even points would be higher or lower with May's sales mix than April's sales mix.

PROBLEM 5–29A   Changes in Cost Structure; Break-Even Analysis; Operating Leverage; Margin of Safety [LO5–4, LO5–5, LO5–7, LO5–8]
Morton Company's contribution format income statement for last month is given below:

Sales (15,000 units × $30 per unit)	$450,000
Variable expenses	315,000
Contribution margin	135,000
Fixed expenses.	90,000
Net operating income	$ 45,000

The industry in which Morton Company operates is quite sensitive to cyclical movements in the economy. Thus, profits vary considerably from year to year according to general economic conditions. The company has a large amount of unused capacity and is studying ways of improving profits.

Required:
1. New equipment has come onto the market that would allow Morton Company to automate a portion of its operations. Variable expenses would be reduced by $9 per unit. However, fixed expenses would increase to a total of $225,000 each month. Prepare two contribution format income statements, one showing present operations and one showing how operations would appear if the new equipment is purchased. Show an Amount column, a Per Unit column, and a Percent column on each statement. Do not show percentages for the fixed expenses.
2. Refer to the income statements in (1) above. For both present operations and the proposed new operations, compute (a) the degree of operating leverage, (b) the break-even point in dollar sales, and (c) the margin of safety in both dollar and percentage terms.

3. Refer again to the data in (1) above. As a manager, what factor would be paramount in your mind in deciding whether to purchase the new equipment? (Assume that enough funds are available to make the purchase.)

4. Refer to the original data. Rather than purchase new equipment, the marketing manager argues that the company's marketing strategy should be changed. Rather than pay sales commissions, which are currently included in variable expenses, the company would pay salespersons fixed salaries and would invest heavily in advertising. The marketing manager claims this new approach would increase unit sales by 30% without any change in selling price; the company's new monthly fixed expenses would be $180,000; and its net operating income would increase by 20%. Compute the break-even point in dollar sales for the company under the new marketing strategy. Do you agree with the marketing manager's proposal?

PROBLEM 5–30A   Graphing; Incremental Analysis; Operating Leverage
[LO5–2, LO5–4, LO5–5, LO5–6, LO5–8]

Angie Silva has recently opened The Sandal Shop in Brisbane, Australia, a store that specializes in fashionable sandals. Angie has just received a degree in business and she is anxious to apply the principles she has learned to her business. In time, she hopes to open a chain of sandal shops. As a first step, she has prepared the following analysis for her new store:

Sales price per pair of sandals..............	$40
Variable expenses per pair of sandals	16
Contribution margin per pair of sandals	$24
Fixed expenses per year:	
Building rental.........................	$15,000
Equipment depreciation	7,000
Selling...............................	20,000
Administrative	18,000
Total fixed expenses......................	$60,000

Required:

1. How many pairs of sandals must be sold each year to break even? What does this represent in total sales dollars?

2. Prepare a CVP graph or a profit graph for the store from zero pairs up to 4,000 pairs of sandals sold each year. Indicate the break-even point on your graph.

3. Angie has decided that she must earn at least $18,000 the first year to justify her time and effort. How many pairs of sandals must be sold to reach this target profit?

4. Angie now has two salespersons working in the store—one full time and one part time. It will cost her an additional $8,000 per year to convert the part-time position to a full-time position. Angie believes that the change would bring in an additional $25,000 in sales each year. Should she convert the position? Use the incremental approach. (Do not prepare an income statement.)

5. Refer to the original data. During the first year, the store sold only 3,000 pairs of sandals and reported the following operating results:

Sales (3,000 pairs).............	$120,000
Variable expenses	48,000
Contribution margin	72,000
Fixed expenses................	60,000
Net operating income...........	$ 12,000

a. What is the store's degree of operating leverage?

b. Angie is confident that with a more intense sales effort and with a more creative advertising program she can increase sales by 50% next year. What would be the expected percentage increase in net operating income? Use the degree of operating leverage to compute your answer.

PROBLEM 5–31A   Interpretive Questions on the CVP Graph [LO5–2, LO5–5]
A CVP graph such as the one shown below is a useful technique for showing relationships among an organization's costs, volume, and profits.

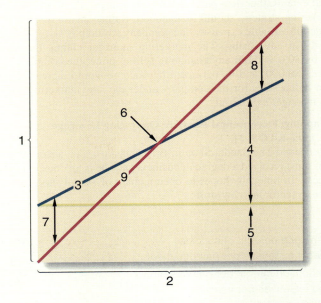

Required:
1.   Identify the numbered components in the CVP graph.
2.   State the effect of each of the following actions on line 3, line 9, and the break-even point. For line 3 and line 9, state whether the action will cause the line to

    Remain unchanged.
    Shift upward.
    Shift downward.
    Have a steeper slope (i.e., rotate upward).
    Have a flatter slope (i.e., rotate downward).
    Shift upward *and* have a steeper slope.
    Shift upward *and* have a flatter slope.
    Shift downward *and* have a steeper slope.
    Shift downward *and* have a flatter slope.

In the case of the break-even point, state whether the action will cause the break-even point to
    Remain unchanged.
    Increase.
    Decrease.
    Probably change, but the direction is uncertain.

Treat each case independently.

   x. Example.   Fixed expenses are reduced by $5,000 per period.
      Answer (see choices above):   Line 3:   Shift downward.
                               Line 9:   Remain unchanged.
                               Break-even point: Decrease.

   a.   The unit selling price is increased from $18 to $20.
   b.   Unit variable expenses are decreased from $12 to $10.
   c.   Fixed expenses are increased by $3,000 per period.
   d.   Two thousand more units are sold during the period than were budgeted.
   e.   Due to paying salespersons a commission rather than a flat salary, fixed expenses are reduced by $8,000 per period and unit variable expenses are increased by $3.
   f.   Due to an increase in the cost of materials, both unit variable expenses and the selling price are increased by $2.
   g.   Advertising costs are increased by $10,000 per period, resulting in a 10% increase in the number of units sold.
   h.   Due to automating an operation previously done by workers, fixed expenses are increased by $12,000 per period and unit variable expenses are reduced by $4.

BUILDING YOUR SKILLS

CASE [LO5–4, LO5–5, LO5–6]

Pittman Company is a small but growing manufacturer of telecommunications equipment. The company has no sales force of its own; rather, it relies completely on independent sales agents to market its products. These agents are paid a sales commission of 15% for all items sold.

Barbara Cheney, Pittman's controller, has just prepared the company's budgeted income statement for next year. The statement follows:

Pittman Company Budgeted Income Statement For the Year Ended December 31		
Sales.		$16,000,000
Manufacturing expenses:		
Variable	$7,200,000	
Fixed overhead	2,340,000	9,540,000
Gross margin		6,460,000
Selling and administrative expenses:		
Commissions to agents.	2,400,000	
Fixed marketing expenses	120,000*	
Fixed administrative expenses	1,800,000	4,320,000
Net operating income		2,140,000
Fixed interest expenses		540,000
Income before income taxes.		1,600,000
Income taxes (30%)		480,000
Net income		$ 1,120,000

*Primarily depreciation on storage facilities.

As Barbara handed the statement to Karl Vecci, Pittman's president, she commented, "I went ahead and used the agents' 15% commission rate in completing these statements, but we've just learned that they refuse to handle our products next year unless we increase the commission rate to 20%."

"That's the last straw," Karl replied angrily. "Those agents have been demanding more and more, and this time they've gone too far. How can they possibly defend a 20% commission rate?"

"They claim that after paying for advertising, travel, and the other costs of promotion, there's nothing left over for profit," replied Barbara.

"I say it's just plain robbery," retorted Karl. "And I also say it's time we dumped those guys and got our own sales force. Can you get your people to work up some cost figures for us to look at?"

"We've already worked them up," said Barbara. "Several companies we know about pay a 7.5% commission to their own salespeople, along with a small salary. Of course, we would have to handle all promotion costs, too. We figure our fixed expenses would increase by $2,400,000 per year, but that would be more than offset by the $3,200,000 (20% × $16,000,000) that we would avoid on agents' commissions."

The breakdown of the $2,400,000 cost follows:

Salaries:	
Sales manager	$ 100,000
Salespersons	600,000
Travel and entertainment	400,000
Advertising	1,300,000
Total	$2,400,000

"Super," replied Karl. "And I noticed that the $2,400,000 is just what we're paying the agents under the old 15% commission rate."

"It's even better than that," explained Barbara. "We can actually save $75,000 a year because that's what we're having to pay the auditing firm now to check out the agents' reports. So our overall administrative expenses would be less."

"Pull all of these numbers together and we'll show them to the executive committee tomorrow," said Karl. "With the approval of the committee, we can move on the matter immediately."

Required:

1. Compute Pittman Company's break-even point in dollar sales for next year assuming
   a. The agents' commission rate remains unchanged at 15%.
   b. The agents' commission rate is increased to 20%.
   c. The company employs its own sales force.
2. Assume that Pittman Company decides to continue selling through agents and pays the 20% commission rate. Determine the volume of sales that would be required to generate the same net income as contained in the budgeted income statement for next year.
3. Determine the volume of sales at which net income would be equal regardless of whether Pittman Company sells through agents (at a 20% commission rate) or employs its own sales force.
4. Compute the degree of operating leverage that the company would expect to have on December 31 at the end of next year assuming
   a. The agents' commission rate remains unchanged at 15%.
   b. The agents' commission rate is increased to 20%.
   c. The company employs its own sales force.
   Use income *before* income taxes in your operating leverage computation.
5. Based on the data in (1) through (4) above, make a recommendation as to whether the company should continue to use sales agents (at a 20% commission rate) or employ its own sales force. Give reasons for your answer.

(CMA, adapted)

ANALYTICAL THINKING [LO5–5, LO5–9]

Cheryl Montoya picked up the phone and called her boss, Wes Chan, the vice president of marketing at Piedmont Fasteners Corporation: "Wes, I'm not sure how to go about answering the questions that came up at the meeting with the president yesterday."

"What's the problem?"

"The president wanted to know the break-even point for each of the company's products, but I am having trouble figuring them out."

"I'm sure you can handle it, Cheryl. And, by the way, I need your analysis on my desk tomorrow morning at 8:00 sharp in time for the follow-up meeting at 9:00."

Piedmont Fasteners Corporation makes three different clothing fasteners in its manufacturing facility in North Carolina. Data concerning these products appear below:

	Velcro	Metal	Nylon
Normal annual sales volume	100,000	200,000	400,000
Unit selling price	$1.65	$1.50	$0.85
Variable expense per unit	$1.25	$0.70	$0.25

Total fixed expenses are $400,000 per year.

All three products are sold in highly competitive markets, so the company is unable to raise its prices without losing unacceptable numbers of customers.

The company has an extremely effective lean production system, so there are no beginning or ending work in process or finished goods inventories.

Required:

1. What is the company's over-all break-even point in dollar sales?
2. Of the total fixed expenses of $400,000, $20,000 could be avoided if the Velcro product is dropped, $80,000 if the Metal product is dropped, and $60,000 if the Nylon product is dropped. The remaining fixed expenses of $240,000 consist of common fixed expenses such as administrative salaries and rent on the factory building that could be avoided only by going out of business entirely.
   a. What is the break-even point in unit sales for each product?
   b. If the company sells exactly the break-even quantity of each product, what will be the overall profit of the company? Explain this result.

TEAMWORK IN ACTION [LO5–1, LO5–4]

Revenue from major intercollegiate sports is an important source of funds for many colleges. Most of the costs of putting on a football or basketball game may be fixed and may increase very little as the size of the crowd increases. Thus, the revenue from every extra ticket sold may be almost pure profit.

Choose a sport played at your college or university, such as football or basketball, that generates significant revenue. Talk with the business manager of your college's sports programs before answering the following questions:

Required:

1. What is the maximum seating capacity of the stadium or arena in which the sport is played? During the past year, what was the average attendance at the games? On average, what percentage of the stadium or arena capacity was filled?

2. The number of seats sold often depends on the opponent. The attendance for a game with a traditional rival (e.g., Nebraska vs. Colorado, University of Washington vs. Washington State, or Texas vs. Texas A&M) is usually substantially above the average. Also, games against conference foes may draw larger crowds than other games. As a consequence, the number of tickets sold for a game is somewhat predictable. What implications does this have for the nature of the costs of putting on a game? Are most of the costs really fixed with respect to the number of tickets sold?

3. Estimate the variable cost per ticket sold.

4. Estimate the total additional revenue that would be generated in an average game if all of the tickets were sold at their normal prices. Estimate how much profit is lost because these tickets are not sold.

5. Estimate the ancillary revenue (parking and concessions) per ticket sold. Estimate how much profit is lost in an average game from these sources of revenue as a consequence of not having a sold-out game.

6. Estimate how much additional profit would be generated for your college if every game were sold out for the entire season.

A LOOK BACK

Chapter 5 explained how to compute a break-even point and how to determine the sales needed to achieve a desired profit. We also described how to compute and use the margin of safety and operating leverage.

A LOOK AT THIS CHAPTER

This chapter explains how to use the contribution format to create variable costing income statements for manufacturers and segmented income statements. It also contrasts variable costing income statements and absorption income statements.

A LOOK AHEAD

Chapter 7 describes the budgeting process.

6

Variable Costing and Segment Reporting: Tools for Management

CHAPTER OUTLINE

Overview of Variable and Absorption Costing

- Variable Costing
- Absorption Costing
- Selling and Administrative Expenses

Variable and Absorption Costing—An Example

- Variable Costing Contribution Format Income Statement
- Absorption Costing Income Statement

Reconciliation of Variable Costing with Absorption Costing Income

Advantages of Variable Costing and the Contribution Approach

- Enabling CVP Analysis
- Explaining Changes in Net Operating Income
- Supporting Decision Making

Segmented Income Statements and the Contribution Approach

- Traceable and Common Fixed Costs and the Segment Margin

- Identifying Traceable Fixed Costs
- Traceable Costs Can Become Common Costs

Segmented Income Statements—An Example

- Levels of Segmented Income Statements

Segmented Income Statements—Decision Making and Break-Even Analysis

- Decision Making
- Break-Even Analysis

Segmented Income Statements—Common Mistakes

- Omission of Costs
- Inappropriate Methods for Assigning Traceable Costs among Segments
- Arbitrarily Dividing Common Costs among Segments

Income Statements—An External Reporting Perspective

- Companywide Income Statements
- Segmented Financial Information

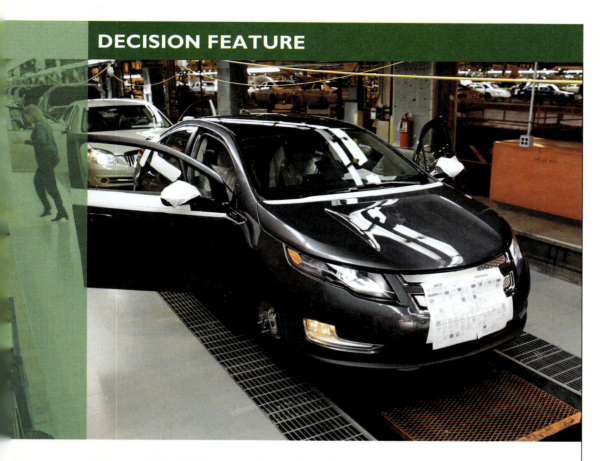

LEARNING OBJECTIVES

After studying Chapter 6, you should be able to:

LO6–1 Explain how variable costing differs from absorption costing and compute unit product costs under each method.

LO6–2 Prepare income statements using both variable and absorption costing.

LO6–3 Reconcile variable costing and absorption costing net operating incomes and explain why the two amounts differ.

LO6–4 Prepare a segmented income statement that differentiates traceable fixed costs from common fixed costs and use it to make decisions.

LO6–5 Compute companywide and segment break-even points for a company with traceable fixed costs.

Misguided Incentives in the Auto Industry

When the economy tanks, automakers, such as **General Motors** and **Chrysler**, often "flood the market" with a supply of vehicles that far exceeds customer demand. They pursue this course of action even though it tarnishes their brand image and increases their auto storage costs, tire replacement costs, customer rebate costs, and advertising costs. This begs the question why would managers knowingly produce more vehicles than are demanded by customers?

In the auto industry, a manager's bonus is often influenced by her company's reported profits; thus, there is a strong incentive to boost profits by producing more units. How can this be done you ask? It would seem logical that producing more units would have no impact on profits unless the units were sold, right? Wrong! As we will discover in this chapter, absorption costing—the most widely used method of determining product costs—can artificially increase profits when managers choose to increase the quantity of units produced.

Source: Marielle Segarra, "Lots of Trouble," CFO, March 2012, pp. 29–30.

This chapter describes two applications of the contribution format income statements that were introduced in earlier chapters. First, it explains how manufacturing companies can prepare *variable costing* income statements, which rely on the contribution format, for internal decision making purposes. The variable costing approach will be contrasted with *absorption costing* income statements, which are generally used for external reports. Ordinarily, variable costing and absorption costing produce different net operating income figures, and the difference can be quite large. In addition to showing how these two methods differ, we will describe the advantages of variable costing for internal reporting purposes and we will show how management decisions can be affected by the costing method chosen.

Second, the chapter explains how the contribution format can be used to prepare segmented income statements. In addition to companywide income statements, managers need to measure the profitability of individual *segments* of their organizations. A **segment** is a part or activity of an organization about which managers would like cost, revenue, or profit data. This chapter explains how to create contribution format income statements that report profit data for business segments, such as divisions, individual stores, geographic regions, customers, and product lines.

OVERVIEW OF VARIABLE AND ABSORPTION COSTING

As you begin to read about variable and absorption costing income statements in the coming pages, focus your attention on three key concepts. First, both income statement formats include product costs and period costs, although they define these cost classifications differently. Second, variable costing income statements are grounded in the contribution format. They categorize expenses based on cost behavior—variable expenses are reported separately from fixed expenses. Absorption costing income statements ignore variable and fixed cost distinctions. Third, as mentioned in the paragraph above, variable and absorption costing net operating income figures often differ from one another. The reason for these differences always relates to the fact the variable costing and absorption costing income statements account for fixed manufacturing overhead differently. *Pay very close attention to the two different ways that variable costing and absorption costing account for fixed manufacturing overhead.*

Variable Costing

Under **variable costing**, only those manufacturing costs that vary with output are treated as product costs. This would usually include direct materials, direct labor, and the variable portion of manufacturing overhead. Fixed manufacturing overhead is not treated as a product cost under this method. Rather, fixed manufacturing overhead is treated as a period cost and, like selling and administrative expenses, it is expensed in its entirety each period. Consequently, the cost of a unit of product in inventory or in cost of goods sold under the variable costing method does not contain any fixed manufacturing overhead cost. Variable costing is sometimes referred to as *direct costing* or *marginal costing*.

Absorption Costing

As discussed in Chapter 2, **absorption costing** treats *all* manufacturing costs as product costs, regardless of whether they are variable or fixed. The cost of a unit of product under the absorption costing method consists of direct materials, direct labor, and *both* variable and fixed manufacturing overhead. Thus, absorption costing allocates a portion of fixed manufacturing overhead cost to each unit of product, along with the variable manufacturing costs. Because absorption costing includes all manufacturing costs in product costs, it is frequently referred to as the *full cost* method.

EXHIBIT 6–1   Variable Costing versus Absorption Costing

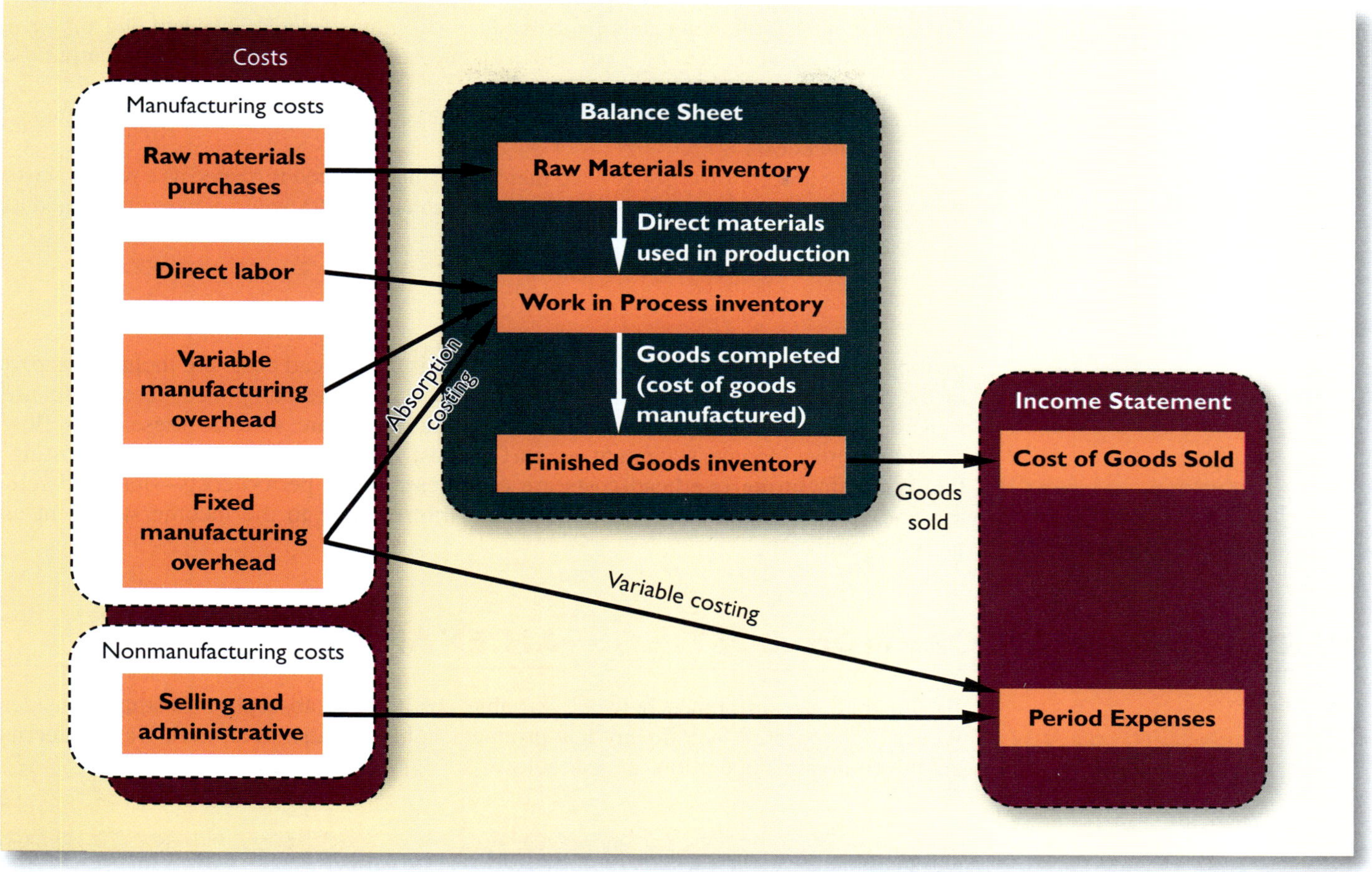

Selling and Administrative Expenses

Selling and administrative expenses are never treated as product costs, regardless of the costing method. Thus, under absorption and variable costing, variable and fixed selling and administrative expenses are always treated as period costs and are expensed as incurred.

Summary of Differences   The essential difference between variable costing and absorption costing, as illustrated in Exhibit 6–1, is how each method accounts for fixed manufacturing overhead costs—all other costs are treated the same under the two

HELPFUL HINT

In this chapter all differences in net operating income between variable costing and absorption costing will be caused by the accounting for fixed manufacturing overhead. Variable costing treats fixed manufacturing overhead as a period cost. This means that the entire amount of fixed manufacturing overhead incurred each period is recorded as an expense on the income statement within that period. Fixed manufacturing overhead is not attached to units of production. Absorption costing treats fixed manufacturing overhead as a product cost. This means that the entire amount of fixed manufacturing overhead incurred each period is attached to the units produced during that period. The fixed manufacturing overhead attached to units of production is recorded as an expense on the income statement only when the units are sold.

CONCEPT CHECK

1. Which of the following statements is false? (You may select more than one answer.)
   a. Under variable costing, only those manufacturing costs that vary with output are treated as product costs.
   b. Under variable costing, variable selling and administrative expenses are treated as product costs.
   c. Under absorption costing, fixed manufacturing overhead is treated as a product cost.
   d. Under absorption costing, fixed selling and administrative expenses are treated as period costs.

methods. In absorption costing, fixed manufacturing overhead costs are included as part of the costs of work in process inventories. When units are completed, these costs are transferred to finished goods and only when the units are sold do these costs flow through to the income statement as part of cost of goods sold. In variable costing, fixed manufacturing overhead costs are considered to be period costs—just like selling and administrative costs—and are taken immediately to the income statement as period expenses.

VARIABLE AND ABSORPTION COSTING—AN EXAMPLE

To illustrate the difference between variable costing and absorption costing, consider Weber Light Aircraft, a company that produces light recreational aircraft. Data concerning the company's operations appear below:

	Per Aircraft	Per Month
Selling price	$100,000	
Direct materials	$19,000	
Direct labor	$5,000	
Variable manufacturing overhead	$1,000	
Fixed manufacturing overhead		$70,000
Variable selling and administrative expenses	$10,000	
Fixed selling and administrative expenses		$20,000

	January	February	March
Beginning inventory	0	0	1
Units produced	1	2	4
Units sold	1	1	5
Ending inventory	0	1	0

As you review the data above, it is important to realize that for the months of January, February, and March, the selling price per aircraft, variable cost per aircraft, and total monthly fixed expenses never change. The only variables that change in this example are the number of units produced (January = 1 unit produced; February = 2 units produced; March = 4 units produced) and the number of units sold (January = 1 unit sold; February = 1 unit sold; March = 5 units sold).

We will first construct the company's variable costing income statements for January, February, and March. Then we will show how the company's net operating income would be determined for the same months using absorption costing.

Variable Costing Contribution Format Income Statement

LEARNING OBJECTIVE 6–2

Prepare income statements using both variable and absorption costing.

To prepare the company's variable costing income statements for January, February, and March we begin by computing the unit product cost. Under variable costing, product costs consist solely of variable production costs. At Weber Light Aircraft, the variable production cost per unit is $25,000, determined as follows:

Variable Costing Unit Product Cost	
Direct materials	$19,000
Direct labor	5,000
Variable manufacturing overhead	1,000
Variable costing unit product cost	$25,000

Since each month's variable production cost is $25,000 per aircraft, the variable costing cost of goods sold for all three months can be easily computed as follows:

Variable Costing Cost of Goods Sold	January	February	March
Variable production cost (a)	$25,000	$25,000	$ 25,000
Units sold (b)	1	1	5
Variable cost of goods sold (a) × (b)	$25,000	$25,000	$125,000

And the company's total selling and administrative expense would be derived as follows:

Selling and Administrative Expenses	January	February	March
Variable selling and administrative expense (@ $10,000 per unit sold)	$10,000	$10,000	$50,000
Fixed selling and administrative expense	20,000	20,000	20,000
Total selling and administrative expense	$30,000	$30,000	$70,000

Putting it all together, the variable costing income statements would appear as shown in Exhibit 6–2. Notice, the contribution format has been used in these income statements. Also, the monthly fixed manufacturing overhead costs ($70,000) have been recorded as a period expense in the month incurred.

Variable Costing Contribution Format Income Statements	January	February	March
Sales	$100,000	$100,000	$500,000
Variable expenses:			
Variable cost of goods sold	25,000	25,000	125,000
Variable selling and administrative expense	10,000	10,000	50,000
Total variable expenses	35,000	35,000	175,000
Contribution margin	65,000	65,000	325,000
Fixed expenses:			
Fixed manufacturing overhead	70,000	70,000	70,000
Fixed selling and administrative expense	20,000	20,000	20,000
Total fixed expenses	90,000	90,000	90,000
Net operating income (loss)	$ (25,000)	$ (25,000)	$235,000

EXHIBIT 6–2
Variable Costing Income Statements

A simple method for understanding how Weber Light Aircraft computed its variable costing net operating income figures is to focus on the contribution margin per aircraft sold, which is computed as follows:

Contribution Margin per Aircraft Sold		
Selling price per aircraft		$100,000
Variable production cost per aircraft	$25,000	
Variable selling and administrative expense per aircraft	10,000	35,000
Contribution margin per aircraft		$ 65,000

The variable costing net operating income for each period can always be computed by multiplying the number of units sold by the contribution margin per unit and then subtracting total fixed costs. For Weber Light Aircraft these computations would appear as follows:

	January	February	March
Number of aircraft sold	1	1	5
Contribution margin per aircraft	× $65,000	× $65,000	× $65,000
Total contribution margin	$65,000	$65,000	$325,000
Total fixed expenses	90,000	90,000	90,000
Net operating income (loss)	$(25,000)	$(25,000)	$235,000

Notice, January and February have the same net operating loss. This occurs because one aircraft was sold in each month and, as previously mentioned, the selling price per aircraft, variable cost per aircraft, and total monthly fixed expenses remain constant.

HELPFUL HINT

When students prepare variable costing income statements they often mistakenly assume that variable selling and administrative expense is a product cost. The confusion arises because variable selling and administrative expense *is* included in the calculation of contribution margin; however, it *is not* a product cost. Variable selling and administrative expense is always a period cost and the total amount of this expense included in the income statement is always derived by multiplying the variable selling and administrative expense per unit by the number of units sold—not the number of units produced.

CONCEPT CHECK

2. Smith Company produces and sells one product for $40 per unit. The company has no beginning inventories. Its variable manufacturing cost per unit is $18 and the variable selling and administrative expense per unit is $4. The fixed manufacturing overhead and fixed selling and administrative expense total $80,000 and $20,000, respectively. If Smith Company produces 8,000 units and sells 7,500 units during the year, then its net operating income under variable costing would be
    a. $65,000
    b. $41,250
    c. $40,000
    d. $35,000

Absorption Costing Income Statement

As we begin the absorption costing portion of the example, remember that the only reason absorption costing income differs from variable costing is that the methods account for fixed manufacturing overhead differently. Under absorption costing, fixed manufacturing overhead is included in product costs. In variable costing, fixed manufacturing overhead is not included in product costs and instead is treated as a period expense just like selling and administrative expenses.

The first step in preparing Weber's absorption costing income statements for January, February, and March is to determine the company's unit product costs for each month as follows[1]:

Absorption Costing Unit Product Cost			
	January	February	March
Direct materials	$19,000	$19,000	$19,000
Direct labor.....................................	5,000	5,000	5,000
Variable manufacturing overhead.................	1,000	1,000	1,000
Fixed manufacturing overhead ($70,000 ÷ 1 unit produced in January; $70,000 ÷ 2 units produced in February; $70,000 ÷ 4 units produced in March)...	70,000	35,000	17,500
Absorption costing unit product cost	$95,000	$60,000	$42,500

Compute the unit product cost for each period mentioned in a problem before attempting to create the income statements. To compute absorption costing unit product costs, always take the fixed manufacturing overhead incurred in each period and divide it by the number of units *produced* during that period. Do not use the number of units sold to calculate unit product costs. The number of units sold is used to calculate the cost of goods sold for an income statement; however, the number of units produced is used to compute unit product costs.

Notice that in each month, Weber's fixed manufacturing overhead cost of $70,000 is divided by the number of units produced to determine the fixed manufacturing overhead cost per unit.

Given these unit product costs, the company's absorption costing net operating income in each month would be determined as shown in Exhibit 6–3.

The sales for all three months in Exhibit 6–3 are the same as the sales shown in the variable costing income statements. The January cost of goods sold consists of one unit produced during January at a cost of $95,000 according to the absorption costing system. The February cost of goods sold consists of one unit produced during February at a cost of $60,000 according to the absorption costing system. The March cost of goods sold ($230,000) consists of one unit produced during February at an absorption cost of $60,000 plus four units produced in March with a total absorption cost of $170,000 (= 4 units produced × $42,500 per unit). The selling and administrative expenses equal the amounts reported in the variable costing income statements; however, they are reported as one amount rather than being separated into variable and fixed components.

Note that even though sales were exactly the same in January and February and the cost structure did not change, net operating income was $35,000 higher in February than in January under absorption costing. This occurs because one aircraft produced in

---

[1]For simplicity, we assume in this section that an actual costing system is used in which actual costs are spread over the units produced during the period. If a predetermined overhead rate were used, the analysis would be similar, but more complex.

EXHIBIT 6–3
Absorption Costing Income
Statements

Absorption Costing Income Statements	January	February	March
Sales	$100,000	$100,000	$500,000
Cost of goods sold ($95,000 × 1 unit; $60,000 × 1 unit; $60,000 × 1 unit + $42,500 × 4 units)	95,000	60,000	230,000
Gross margin	5,000	40,000	270,000
Selling and administrative expenses	30,000	30,000	70,000
Net operating income (loss)	$ (25,000)	$ 10,000	$200,000

February is not sold until March. This aircraft has $35,000 of fixed manufacturing over-head attached to it that was incurred in February, but will not be recorded as part of cost of goods sold until March.

Contrasting the variable costing and absorption costing income statements in Exhibits 6–2 and 6–3, note that net operating income is the same in January under variable costing and absorption costing, but differs in the other two months. We will discuss this in some depth shortly. Also note that the format of the variable costing income statement differs from the absorption costing income statement. An absorption costing income statement categorizes costs by function—manufacturing versus selling and administrative. All of the manufacturing costs flow through the absorption costing cost of goods sold and all of the selling and administrative expenses are listed separately as period expenses. In contrast, in the contribution approach, costs are categorized according to how they behave. All of the variable expenses are listed together and all of the fixed expenses are listed together. The variable expenses category includes manufacturing costs (i.e., variable cost of goods sold) as well as selling and administrative expenses. The fixed expenses category also includes both manufacturing costs and selling and administrative expenses.

HELPFUL HINT

Be careful computing the cost of goods sold under absorption costing when the units that have been sold were produced in *more than one period*. For example, if a company produces 8,000 units and sells 10,000 units in year 2, it is wrong to compute the cost of goods sold for year 2 by multiplying 10,000 units by the unit product cost for units produced in year 2. Logically speaking, it is impossible for this solution to be correct because only 8,000 units were produced in year 2. Assuming there is no ending inventory at the end of year 2, the correct cost of goods sold figure would include 8,000 units multiplied by the unit product cost for units produced in year 2 plus 2,000 units multiplied by the unit product cost for units produced in year 1.

CONCEPT CHECK

3. Smith Company produces and sells one product for $40 per unit. The company has no beginning inventories. Its variable manufacturing cost per unit is $18 and the variable selling and administrative expense per unit is $4. The fixed manufacturing overhead and fixed selling and administrative expense total $80,000 and $20,000, respectively. If Smith Company produces 8,000 units and sells 7,500 units during the year, then its net operating income under absorption costing would be
   a. $65,000
   b. $41,250
   c. $40,000
   d. $35,000

RECONCILIATION OF VARIABLE COSTING WITH ABSORPTION COSTING INCOME

As noted earlier, variable costing and absorption costing net operating incomes may not be the same. In the case of Weber Light Aircraft, the net operating incomes are the same in January, but differ in the other two months. These differences occur because under absorption costing some fixed manufacturing overhead is capitalized in inventories (i.e., included in product costs) rather than being immediately expensed on the income statement. If inventories increase during a period, under absorption costing some of the fixed manufacturing overhead of the current period will be *deferred* in ending inventories. For example, in February two aircraft were produced and each carried with it $35,000 (= $70,000 ÷ 2 aircraft produced) in fixed manufacturing overhead. Since only one aircraft was sold, $35,000 of this fixed manufacturing overhead was on February's absorption costing income statement as part of cost of goods sold, but $35,000 would have been on the balance sheet as part of finished goods inventories. In contrast, under variable costing *all* of the $70,000 of fixed manufacturing overhead appeared on the February income statement as a period expense. Consequently, net operating income was higher under absorption costing than under variable costing by $35,000 in February. This was reversed in March when four units were produced, but five were sold. In March, under absorption costing $105,000 of fixed manufacturing overhead was included in cost of goods sold ($35,000 for the unit produced in February and sold in March plus $17,500 for each of the four units produced and sold in March), but only $70,000 was recognized as a period expense under variable costing. Hence, the net operating income in March was $35,000 lower under absorption costing than under variable costing.

In general, when the units produced exceed unit sales and hence inventories increase, net operating income is higher under absorption costing than under variable costing. This occurs because some of the fixed manufacturing overhead of the period is *deferred* in inventories under absorption costing. In contrast, when unit sales exceed the units produced and hence inventories decrease, net operating income is lower under absorption costing than under variable costing. This occurs because some of the fixed manufacturing overhead of previous periods is *released* from inventories under absorption costing. When the units produced and unit sales are equal, no change in inventories occurs and absorption costing and variable costing net operating incomes are the same.[2]

Variable costing and absorption costing net operating incomes can be reconciled by determining how much fixed manufacturing overhead was deferred in, or released from, inventories during the period:

LEARNING OBJECTIVE 6–3

Reconcile variable costing and absorption costing net operating incomes and explain why the two amounts differ.

Fixed Manufacturing Overhead Deferred in, or Released from, Inventories under Absorption Costing	January	February	March
Fixed manufacturing overhead in ending inventories.	$0	$35,000	$ 0
Fixed manufacturing overhead in beginning inventories	0	0	35,000
Fixed manufacturing overhead deferred in (released from) inventories	$0	$35,000	$(35,000)

[2]These general statements about the relation between variable costing and absorption costing net operating income assume LIFO is used to value inventories. Even when LIFO is not used, the general statements tend to be correct. Although U.S. GAAP allows LIFO and FIFO inventory flow assumptions, International Financial Reporting Standards do not allow a LIFO inventory flow assumption.

In equation form, the fixed manufacturing overhead that is deferred in or released from inventories can be determined as follows:

$$
\begin{array}{ccc}
\text{Manufacturing overhead} & & \text{Fixed manufacturing} & & \text{Fixed manufacturing} \\
\text{deferred in} & = & \text{overhead in} & - & \text{overhead in} \\
\text{(released from) inventory} & & \text{ending inventories} & & \text{beginning inventories}
\end{array}
$$

The reconciliation would then be reported as shown in Exhibit 6–4:

EXHIBIT 6–4
Reconciliation of Variable Costing and Absorption Costing Net Operating Incomes

Reconciliation of Variable Costing and Absorption Costing Net Operating Incomes	January	February	March
Variable costing net operating income (loss)	$(25,000)	$(25,000)	$235,000
Add (deduct) fixed manufacturing overhead deferred in (released from) inventory under absorption costing	0	35,000	(35,000)
Absorption costing net operating income (loss)	$(25,000)	$ 10,000	$200,000

Again note that the difference between variable costing net operating income and absorption costing net operating income is entirely due to the amount of fixed manufacturing overhead that is deferred in, or released from, inventories during the period under absorption costing. Changes in inventories affect absorption costing net operating income—they do not affect variable costing net operating income, providing that variable manufacturing costs per unit are stable.

The reasons for differences between variable and absorption costing net operating incomes are summarized in Exhibit 6–5. When the units produced equal the units sold, as in January for Weber Light Aircraft, absorption costing net operating income will equal variable costing net operating income. This occurs because when production equals sales, all of the fixed manufacturing overhead incurred in the current period flows through to the income statement under both methods. For companies that use Lean Production, the number of units produced tends to equal the number of units sold. This occurs because goods are produced in response to customer orders, thereby eliminating finished goods inventories and reducing work in process inventory to almost nothing. So, when a company uses Lean Production differences in variable costing and absorption costing net operating income will largely disappear.

When the units produced exceed the units sold, absorption costing net operating income will exceed variable costing net operating income. This occurs because inventories have increased; therefore, under absorption costing some of the fixed manufacturing overhead incurred in the current period is deferred in ending inventories on the balance sheet, whereas under variable costing all of the fixed manufacturing overhead incurred in the current period flows through to the income statement. In contrast, when the units produced are less than the units sold, absorption costing net operating income will be less than variable costing net operating income. This occurs because inventories have decreased; therefore, under absorption costing fixed manufacturing overhead that had been deferred in inventories during a prior period flows through to the current period's income statement together with all of the fixed manufacturing overhead incurred during the current period. Under variable costing, just the fixed manufacturing overhead of the current period flows through to the income statement.

EXHIBIT 6–5   Comparative Income Effects—Absorption and Variable Costing

Relation between Production and Sales for the Period	Effect on Inventories	Relation between Absorption and Variable Costing Net Operating Incomes
Units produced = Units sold	No change in inventories	Absorption costing net operating income = Variable costing net operating income
Units produced > Units sold	Inventories increase	Absorption costing net operating income > Variable costing net operating income*
Units produced < Units sold	Inventories decrease	Absorption costing net operating income < Variable costing net operating income†

*Net operating income is higher under absorption costing because fixed manufacturing overhead cost is *deferred* in inventory under absorption costing as inventories increase.
†Net operating income is lower under absorption costing because fixed manufacturing overhead cost is *released* from inventory under absorption costing as inventories decrease.

Lean Manufacturing Shrinks Inventories

IN BUSINESS

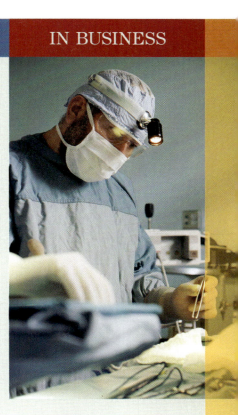

Conmed, a surgical device maker in Utica, New York, switched to lean manufacturing by replacing its assembly lines with U-shaped production cells. It also started producing only enough units to satisfy customer demand rather than producing as many units as possible and storing them in warehouses. The company calculated that its customers use one of its disposable surgical devices every 90 seconds, so that is precisely how often it produces a new unit. Its assembly area for fluid-injection devices used to occupy 3,300 square feet of space and contained $93,000 worth of parts. Now the company produces its fluid-injection devices in 660 square feet of space while maintaining only $6,000 of parts inventory.

When Conmed adopted lean manufacturing, it substantially reduced its finished goods inventories. What impact do you think this initial reduction in inventories may have had on net operating income? Why?

Source: Pete Engardio, "Lean and Mean Gets Extreme," *BusinessWeek*, March 23 and 30, 2009, pp. 60–62.

CONCEPT CHECK

In its first year of operations, Kelley Company produced 10,000 units and sold 7,000 units. Its direct materials, direct labor, variable manufacturing overhead, and variable selling and administrative unit costs were $12, $8, $2, and $1, respectively. Its total fixed manufacturing overhead for the year was $50,000.

4. What is the amount of cost of goods sold under variable costing?
    a. $220,000.
    b. $161,000.
    c. $154,000.
    d. $230,000.
5. What is the amount of cost of goods sold under absorption costing?
    a. $189,000.
    b. $196,000.
    c. $179,000.
    d. $186,000.
6. When comparing Kelley's absorption costing net operating income to its variable costing net operating income, which of the following will be true?
    a. Its absorption costing net operating income will be $35,000 lower than its variable costing net operating income.
    b. Its absorption costing net operating income will be $35,000 higher than its variable costing net operating income.
    c. Its absorption costing net operating income will be $15,000 lower than its variable costing net operating income.
    d. Its absorption costing net operating income will be $15,000 higher than its variable costing net operating income.

ADVANTAGES OF VARIABLE COSTING AND THE CONTRIBUTION APPROACH

Variable costing, together with the contribution approach, offers appealing advantages for internal reports. This section discusses three of those advantages.

Enabling CVP Analysis

CVP analysis requires that we break costs down into their fixed and variable components. Because variable costing income statements categorize costs as fixed and variable, it is much easier to use this income statement format to perform CVP analysis than attempting to use the absorption costing format, which mixes together fixed and variable costs.

Moreover, absorption costing net operating income may or may not agree with the results of CVP analysis. For example, let's suppose that you are interested in computing the sales that would be necessary to generate a target profit of $235,000 at Weber Light Aircraft. A CVP analysis based on the January variable costing income statement from Exhibit 6–2 would proceed as follows:

Sales (a)	$100,000
Contribution margin (b)	$ 65,000
Contribution margin ratio (b) ÷ (a)	65%
Total fixed expenses	$ 90,000

$$\text{Dollar sales to attain the target profit} = \frac{\text{Target profit} + \text{Fixed expenses}}{\text{CM ratio}}$$

$$= \frac{\$235,000 + \$90,000}{0.65} = \$500,000$$

Thus, a CVP analysis based on the January variable costing income statement predicts that the net operating income would be $235,000 when sales are $500,000. And indeed, the net operating income under variable costing *is* $235,000 when the sales are $500,000 in March. However, the net operating income under absorption costing is *not* $235,000 in March, even though the sales are $500,000. Why is this? The reason is that under absorption costing, net operating income can be distorted by changes in inventories. In March, inventories decreased, so some of the fixed manufacturing overhead that had been deferred in February's ending inventories was released to the March income statement, resulting in a net operating income that is $35,000 lower than the $235,000 predicted by CVP analysis. If inventories had increased in March, the opposite would have occurred— the absorption costing net operating income would have been higher than the $235,000 predicted by CVP analysis.

Explaining Changes in Net Operating Income

The variable costing income statements in Exhibit 6–2 are clear and easy to understand. All other things the same, when sales go up, net operating income goes up. When sales go down, net operating income goes down. When sales are constant, net operating income is constant. The number of units produced does not affect net operating income.

Absorption costing income statements can be confusing and are easily misinterpreted. Look again at the absorption costing income statements in Exhibit 6–3; a manager might wonder why net operating income went up from January to February even though sales were exactly the same. Was it a result of lower selling costs, more efficient operations, or was it some other factor? In fact, it was simply because the number of units produced exceeded the number of units sold in February and so some of the fixed manufacturing overhead costs were deferred in inventories in that month. These costs have not gone away— they will eventually flow through to the income statement in a later period when inventories go down. There is no way to tell this from the absorption costing income statements.

To avoid mistakes when absorption costing is used, readers of financial statements should be alert to changes in inventory levels. Under absorption costing, if inventories increase, fixed manufacturing overhead costs are deferred in inventories, which in turn increases net operating income. If inventories decrease, fixed manufacturing overhead costs are released from inventories, which in turn decreases net operating income. Thus, when absorption costing is used, fluctuations in net operating income can be caused by changes in inventories as well as changes in sales.

Supporting Decision Making

The variable costing method correctly identifies the additional variable costs that will be incurred to make one more unit. It also emphasizes the impact of fixed costs on profits. The total amount of fixed manufacturing costs appears explicitly on the income statement, highlighting that the whole amount of fixed manufacturing costs must be covered for the company to be truly profitable. In the Weber Light Aircraft example, the variable costing income statements correctly report that the cost of producing another unit is $25,000 and they explicitly recognize that $70,000 of fixed manufactured overhead must be covered to earn a profit.

Under absorption costing, fixed manufacturing overhead costs appear to be variable with respect to the number of units sold, but they are not. For example, in January, the absorption unit product cost at Weber Light Aircraft is $95,000, but the variable portion of this cost is only $25,000. The fixed overhead costs of $70,000 are commingled with variable production costs, thereby obscuring the impact of fixed overhead costs on profits. Because absorption unit product costs are stated on a per unit basis, managers may mistakenly believe that if another unit is produced, it will cost the company $95,000. But of course it would not. The cost of producing another unit would be only $25,000. Misinterpreting absorption unit product costs as variable can lead to many problems, including inappropriate pricing decisions and decisions to drop products that are in fact profitable.

DECISION POINT

The Pricing Decision

Each year Webb Company produces and sells 20,000 units of its only product. The selling price for this product is $100 per unit and its direct materials, direct labor, and variable manufacturing overhead costs per unit are $25, $15, and $10, respectively. Webb's annual fixed manufacturing overhead expenses and fixed selling and administrative expenses are $400,000 and $150,000, respectively. It does not have any variable selling and administrative expenses.

The company's marketing manager believes a 10% price increase would lead to a 20% decline in the number of units sold. He claims that if the level of production stays at 20,000 units his price hike will increase gross margins and net operating income by $40,000. Would you support the price increase? Do you think it will increase profits?

SEGMENTED INCOME STATEMENTS AND THE CONTRIBUTION APPROACH

LEARNING OBJECTIVE 6–4

Prepare a segmented income statement that differentiates traceable fixed costs from common fixed costs and use it to make decisions.

In the remainder of the chapter, we'll learn how to use the contribution approach to construct income statements for business segments. These segmented income statements are useful for analyzing the profitability of segments, making decisions, and measuring the performance of segment managers.

Traceable and Common Fixed Costs and the Segment Margin

You need to understand three new terms to prepare segmented income statements using the contribution approach—*traceable fixed cost, common fixed cost,* and *segment margin.*

A **traceable fixed cost** of a segment is a fixed cost that is incurred because of the existence of the segment—if the segment had never existed, the fixed cost would not have been incurred; and if the segment were eliminated, the fixed cost would disappear. Examples of traceable fixed costs include the following:

- The salary of the Fritos product manager at **PepsiCo** is a *traceable* fixed cost of the Fritos business segment of PepsiCo.
- The maintenance cost for the building in which Boeing 747s are assembled is a *traceable* fixed cost of the 747 business segment of **Boeing**.
- The liability insurance at **Disney World** is a *traceable* fixed cost of the Disney World business segment of **The Walt Disney Corporation**.

A **common fixed cost** is a fixed cost that supports the operations of more than one segment, but is not traceable in whole or in part to any one segment. Even if a segment were entirely eliminated, there would be no change in a true common fixed cost. For example:

- The salary of the CEO of **General Motors** is a *common* fixed cost of the various divisions of General Motors.
- The cost of heating a **Safeway** or **Kroger** grocery store is a *common* fixed cost of the store's various departments—groceries, produce, bakery, meat, and so forth.
- The cost of the receptionist's salary at an office shared by a number of doctors is a *common* fixed cost of the doctors. The cost is traceable to the office, but not to individual doctors.

To prepare a segmented income statement, variable expenses are deducted from sales to yield the contribution margin for the segment. The contribution margin tells us what happens to profits as volume changes—holding a segment's capacity and fixed costs constant. The contribution margin is especially useful in decisions involving temporary uses

Has the Internet Killed Catalogs?

IN BUSINESS

Smith & Hawken, an outdoor-accessories retailer, has experienced growing Internet sales and declining catalog sales. These trends seem consistent with conventional wisdom, which suggests that the Internet will make catalogs obsolete. Yet, Smith & Hawken, like many retailers with growing Internet sales, has no plans to discontinue its catalogs. In fact, the total number of catalogs mailed in the United States by all companies has jumped from 16.6 billion in 2002 to 19.2 billion in 2005. Why?

Catalog shoppers and Internet shoppers are not independent customer segments. Catalog shoppers frequently choose to complete their sales transactions online rather than placing telephone orders. This explains why catalogs remain a compelling marketing medium even though catalog sales are declining for many companies. If retailers separately analyze catalog sales and Internet sales, they may discontinue the catalogs segment while overlooking the adverse impact of this decision on Internet segment margins.

Source: Louise Lee, "Catalogs, Catalogs, Everywhere," *BusinessWeek*, December 4, 2006, pp. 32–34.

of capacity such as special orders. These types of decisions often involve only variable costs and revenues—the two components of contribution margin.

The **segment margin** is obtained by deducting the traceable fixed costs of a segment from the segment's contribution margin. It represents the margin available after a segment has covered all of its own costs. *The segment margin is the best gauge of the long-run profitability of a segment* because it includes only those costs that are caused by the segment. If a segment can't cover its own costs, then that segment probably should be dropped (unless it has important side effects on other segments). Notice, common fixed costs are not allocated to segments.

From a decision-making point of view, the segment margin is most useful in major decisions that affect capacity such as dropping a segment. By contrast, as we noted earlier, the contribution margin is most useful in decisions involving short-run changes in volume, such as pricing special orders that involve temporary use of existing capacity.

Identifying Traceable Fixed Costs

The distinction between traceable and common fixed costs is crucial in segment reporting because traceable fixed costs are charged to segments and common fixed costs are not. In an actual situation, it is sometimes hard to determine whether a cost should be classified as traceable or common.

The general guideline is to treat as traceable costs *only those costs that would disappear over time if the segment itself disappeared.* For example, if one division within a company were sold or discontinued, it would no longer be necessary to pay that division manager's salary. Therefore, the division manager's salary would be classified as a traceable fixed cost of the division. On the other hand, the president of the company undoubtedly would continue to be paid even if one of many divisions was dropped. In fact, he or she might even be paid more if dropping the division was a good idea. Therefore, the president's salary is common to the company's divisions and should not be charged to them.

When assigning costs to segments, the key point is to resist the temptation to allocate costs (such as depreciation of corporate facilities) that are clearly common and that will continue regardless of whether the segment exists or not. *Any allocation of common costs to segments reduces the value of the segment margin as a measure of long-run segment profitability and segment performance.*

IN BUSINESS   Segment Reporting at the Vilar Performing Arts Center

VILAR PERFORMING ARTS CENTER
BEAVER CREEK

The Vilar Performing Arts Center is a 535-seat theater located in Beaver Creek, Colorado, that presents an unusually wide variety of performances categorized into six business segments—Family Series, Broadway Series, Theatre/Comedy Series, Dance Series, Classical Series, and Concert Series. The executive director of the Vilar, Kris Sabel, must decide which shows to book, what financial terms to offer to the artists, what contributions are likely from underwriters (i.e., donors), and what prices to charge for tickets. He evaluates the profitability of the segments using segmented income statements that include traceable costs (such as the costs of transporting, lodging, and feeding the artists) and exclude common costs (such as the salaries of Kris and his staff, depreciation on the theater, and general marketing expenses).

Data concerning the Classical Series segment for one season appears below:

Number of shows	4
Number of seats budgeted	863
Number of seats sold	655
Average seats sold per show	164
Ticket sales	$ 46,800
Underwriting (donors)	65,000
Total revenue	$111,800
Artists fees	78,870
Other traceable expenses	11,231
Classical Series segment margin	$ 21,699

Although the Classical Series sold an average of only 164 seats per show, its overall segment margin ($21,699) is positive thanks to $65,000 of underwriting revenues from donors. Had common costs been allocated to the Classical Series, it may have appeared unprofitable and been discontinued—resulting in fewer shows during the season; less diverse programming; disappointment among a small, but dedicated, number of fans; and lower overall income for the Vilar due to the loss of its Classical Series segment margin.

Traceable Costs Can Become Common Costs

Fixed costs that are traceable to one segment may be a common cost of another segment. For example, **United Airlines** might want a segmented income statement that shows the segment margin for a particular flight from Chicago to Paris further broken down into first-class, business-class, and economy-class segment margins. The airline must pay a substantial landing fee at Charles DeGaulle airport in Paris. This fixed landing fee is a traceable cost of the flight, but it is a common cost of the first-class, business-class, and economy-class segments. Even if the first-class cabin is empty, the entire landing fee must be paid. So the landing fee is not a traceable cost of the first-class cabin. But on the other hand, paying the fee is necessary in order to have any first-class, business-class, or economy-class passengers. So the landing fee is a common cost of these three classes.

SEGMENTED INCOME STATEMENTS—AN EXAMPLE

ProphetMax, Inc., is a rapidly growing computer software company. Exhibit 6–6 shows its variable costing income statement for the most recent month. As the company has grown, its senior managers have asked for segmented income statements that could be used to make decisions and evaluate managerial performance. ProphetMax's controller responded by creating examples of contribution format income statements segmented by

ProphetMax, Inc. Variable Costing Income Statement	
Sales.	$500,000
Variable expenses:	
Variable cost of goods sold	180,000
Other variable expenses	50,000
Total variable expenses	230,000
Contribution margin	270,000
Fixed expenses.	256,500
Net operating income	$ 13,500

EXHIBIT 6–6
ProphetMax, Inc. Variable Costing Income Statement

the company's divisions, product lines, and sales channels. She created Exhibit 6–7 to explain that ProphetMax's profits can be segmented into its two divisions—the Business Products Division and the Consumer Products Division. The Consumer Products Division's profits can be further segmented into the Clip Art and Computer Games product lines. Finally, the Computer Games product line's profits (within the Consumer Products Division) can be segmented into the Online and Retail Stores sales channels.

Levels of Segmented Income Statements

Exhibit 6–8, on page 260, contains the controller's segmented income statements for the segments depicted in Exhibit 6–7. The contribution format income statement for the entire company appears at the very top of the exhibit under the column labeled Total Company.

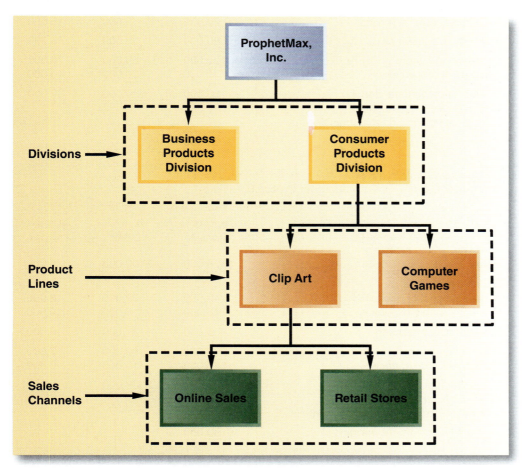

EXHIBIT 6–7
ProphetMax, Inc.: Examples of Business Segments

EXHIBIT 6–8
ProphetMax, Inc.—Segmented
Income Statements in the
Contribution Format

Segments Defined as Divisions

	Total Company	Divisions — Business Products Division	Divisions — Consumer Products Division
Sales	$500,000	$300,000	$200,000
Variable expenses:			
Variable cost of goods sold	180,000	120,000	60,000
Other variable expenses	50,000	30,000	20,000
Total variable expenses	230,000	150,000	80,000
Contribution margin	270,000	150,000	120,000
Traceable fixed expenses	171,000	90,000	81,000
Divisional segment margin	99,000	$ 60,000	$ 39,000
Common fixed expenses not traceable to individual divisions	85,500		
Net operating income	$ 13,500		

Segments Defined as Product Lines of the Consumer Products Division

	Consumer Products Division	Product Line — Clip Art	Product Line — Computer Games
Sales	$200,000	$75,000	$125,000
Variable expenses:			
Variable cost of goods sold	60,000	20,000	40,000
Other variable expenses	20,000	5,000	15,000
Total variable expenses	80,000	25,000	55,000
Contribution margin	120,000	50,000	70,000
Traceable fixed expenses	70,000	30,000	40,000
Product-line segment margin	50,000	$20,000	$ 30,000
Common fixed expenses not traceable to individual product lines	11,000		
Divisional segment margin	$ 39,000		

Segments Defined as Sales Channels for One Product Line, Computer Games, of the Consumer Products Division

	Computer Games	Sales Channels — Online Sales	Sales Channels — Retail Stores
Sales	$125,000	$100,000	$25,000
Variable expenses:			
Variable cost of goods sold	40,000	32,000	8,000
Other variable expenses	15,000	5,000	10,000
Total variable expenses	55,000	37,000	18,000
Contribution margin	70,000	63,000	7,000
Traceable fixed expenses	25,000	15,000	10,000
Sales-channel segment margin	45,000	$ 48,000	$ (3,000)
Common fixed expenses not traceable to individual sales channels	15,000		
Product-line segment margin	$ 30,000		

Notice, the net operating income shown in this column ($13,500) is the same as the net operating income shown in Exhibit 6–6. Immediately to the right of the Total Company column are two columns—one for each of the two divisions. We can see that the Business Products Division's traceable fixed expenses are $90,000 and the Consumer Products Division's are $81,000. These $171,000 of traceable fixed expenses (as shown in the Total Company column) plus the $85,500 of common fixed expenses not traceable to individual divisions equals ProphetMax's total fixed expenses ($256,500) as shown in Exhibit 6–6. We can also see that the Business Products Division's segment margin is $60,000 and the Consumer Products Division's is $39,000. These segment margins show the company's divisional managers how much each of their divisions is contributing to the company's profits.

The middle portion of Exhibit 6–8 further segments the Consumer Products Division into its two product lines, Clip Art and Computer Games. The dual nature of some fixed costs can be seen in this portion of the exhibit. Notice, in the top portion of Exhibit 6–8 when segments are defined as divisions, the Consumer Products Division has $81,000 in traceable fixed expenses. However, when we drill down to the product lines (in the middle portion of the exhibit), only $70,000 of the $81,000 cost that was traceable to the Consumer Products Division is traceable to the product lines. The other $11,000 becomes a common fixed cost of the two product lines of the Consumer Products Division.

Why would $11,000 of traceable fixed costs become a common fixed cost when the division is divided into product lines? The $11,000 is the monthly depreciation expense on a machine that is used to encase products in tamper-proof packages for the consumer market. The depreciation expense is a traceable cost of the Consumer Products Division as a whole, but it is a common cost of the division's two product lines. Even if one of the product lines were discontinued entirely, the machine would still be used to wrap the remaining products. Therefore, none of the depreciation expense can really be traced to individual products. Conversely, the $70,000 traceable fixed cost can be traced to the individual product lines because it consists of the costs of product-specific advertising. A total of $30,000 was spent on advertising clip art and $40,000 was spent on advertising computer programs.

The bottom portion of Exhibit 6–8 further segments the Computer Games product line into two sales channels, Online Sales and Retail Stores. The dual nature of some fixed costs can also be seen in this portion of the exhibit. In the middle portion of Exhibit 6–8 when segments are defined as product lines, the Computer Games product line has $40,000 in traceable fixed expenses. However, when we look at the sales channels in the bottom portion of the exhibit, only $25,000 of the $40,000 that was traceable to Computer Games is traceable to the sales channels. The other $15,000 becomes a common fixed cost of the two sales channels for the Computer Games product line.

SEGMENTED INCOME STATEMENTS—DECISION MAKING AND BREAK-EVEN ANALYSIS

Once a company prepares contribution format segmented income statements, it can use those statements to make decisions and perform break-even analysis.

Decision Making

Let's refer again to the bottom portion of Exhibit 6–8 to illustrate how segmented income statements support decision making. Notice that the Online Sales segment has a segment margin of $48,000 and the Retail Stores segment has a segment margin of $(3,000). Let's assume that ProphetMax wants to know the profit impact of discontinuing the sale of computer games through its Retail Stores sales channel. The company believes that online sales of its computer games will increase 10% if it discontinues the Retail Stores sales channel. It also believes that the Business Products Division and Clip Art product line will be unaffected by this decision. How would you compute the profit impact of this decision?

The first step is to calculate the profit impact of the Retail Stores sales channel disappearing. If this sales channel disappears, we assume its sales, variable expenses, and traceable fixed expenses would all disappear. The quickest way to summarize these financial impacts is to focus on the Retail Stores' segment margin. In other words, if the Retail Stores sales channel disappears, then its negative segment margin of $3,000 would also disappear. This would increase ProphetMax's net operating income by $3,000. The second step is to calculate the profit impact of increasing online sales of computer games by 10%. To perform this calculation, we assume that the Online Sales total traceable fixed expenses ($15,000) remain constant and its contribution margin ratio remains constant at 63% (= $63,000 ÷ $100,000). If online sales increase $10,000 (= $100,000 × 10%), then the Online Sales segment's contribution margin will increase by $6,300 (= $10,000 × 63%). The overall profit impact of discontinuing the Retail Stores sales channel can be summarized as follows:

Avoidance of the retail segment's loss	$3,000
Online Sales additional contribution margin	6,300
Increase in ProphetMax's net operating income	$9,300

LEARNING OBJECTIVE 6–5

Compute companywide and segment break-even points for a company with traceable fixed costs.

Break-Even Analysis

In Chapter 5, we learned how to compute a companywide break-even point for a multiproduct company with no traceable fixed expenses. Now we are going to use the ProphetMax, Inc., data in Exhibit 6–8 to explain how to compute companywide and segment break-even points for a company with traceable fixed expenses. The formula for computing a companywide break-even point is as follows:

$$\frac{\text{Dollar sales for company}}{\text{to break even}} = \frac{\text{Traceable fixed expenses + Common fixed expenses}}{\text{Overall CM ratio}}$$

In the case of ProphetMax, we should begin by reviewing the information in the Total Company column in the top portion of Exhibit 6–8. This column of data indicates that ProphetMax's total traceable fixed expenses are $171,000 and its total common fixed expenses are $85,500. Furthermore, the company's overall contribution margin of $270,000 divided by its total sales of $500,000 equals its overall CM ratio of 0.54. Given this information, ProphetMax's companywide break-even point is computed as follows:

$$\begin{aligned}
\text{Dollar sales for company} \atop \text{to break even} &= \frac{\text{Traceable fixed expenses + Common fixed expenses}}{\text{Overall CM ratio}}\\[6pt]
&= \frac{\$171,000 + \$85,500}{0.54}\\[6pt]
&= \frac{\$256,500}{0.54}\\[6pt]
&= \$475,000
\end{aligned}$$

It is important to emphasize that this computation assumes a constant sales mix. In other words, in the ProphetMax example, it assumes that 60% of the total sales ($300,000 ÷ $500,000) will always come from the Business Products Division and 40% of the total sales ($200,000 ÷ $500,000) will always come from the Consumer Products Division.

To compute the break-even point for a business segment, the formula is as follows:

$$\frac{\text{Dollar sales for a segment}}{\text{to break even}} = \frac{\text{Segment traceable fixed expenses}}{\text{Segment CM ratio}}$$

In the case of ProphetMax's Business Products Division, we should begin by reviewing the information in the Business Products Division column in the top portion of Exhibit 6–8. This column of data indicates that the Business Products Division's traceable fixed expenses are $90,000 and its CM ratio is 0.50 ($150,000 ÷ $300,000). Given this information, the Business Products Division's break-even point is computed as follows:

$$\text{Dollar sales for a segment to break even} = \frac{\text{Segment traceable fixed expenses}}{\text{Segment CM ratio}}$$

$$= \frac{\$90,000}{0.50}$$

$$= \$180,000$$

The same calculation can be performed for the Consumer Products Division using data from the Consumer Products Division column in the top portion of Exhibit 6–8. Given that the Consumer Products Division's traceable fixed expenses are $81,000 and its CM ratio is 0.60 ($120,000 ÷ $200,000), its break-even point is computed as follows:

$$\text{Dollar sales for a segment to break even} = \frac{\text{Segment traceable fixed expenses}}{\text{Segment CM ratio}}$$

$$= \frac{\$81,000}{0.60}$$

$$= \$135,000$$

Notice that the sum of the segment break-even sales figures of $315,000 ($180,000 + $135,000) is less than the companywide break-even point of $475,000. This occurs because the segment break-even calculations *do not include the company's common fixed expenses.* The exclusion of the company's common fixed expenses can be verified by preparing income statements based on each segment's break-even dollar sales as follows:

	Total Company	Business Products Division	Consumer Products Division
Sales	$315,000	$180,000	$135,000
Variable expenses	144,000	90,000	54,000
Contribution margin	171,000	90,000	81,000
Traceable fixed expenses	171,000	90,000	81,000
Segment margin	0	$ 0	$ 0
Common fixed expenses	85,500		
Net operating loss	$ (85,500)		

When each segment achieves its break-even point, the company's overall net operating loss of $85,500 equals its common fixed expenses of $85,500. This reality can often lead managers astray when making decisions. In an attempt to "cover the company's common fixed expenses," managers will often allocate common fixed expenses to business segments when performing break-even calculations and making decisions. *This is a mistake!* Allocating common fixed expenses to business segments artificially inflates each segment's break-even point. This may cause managers to erroneously discontinue business segments where the inflated break-even point appears unobtainable. The decision to retain or discontinue a business segment should be based on the sales and expenses that would disappear if the segment were dropped. Because common fixed expenses *will persist even if a business segment is dropped,* they should not be allocated to business segments when making decisions.

SEGMENTED INCOME STATEMENTS—COMMON MISTAKES

All of the costs attributable to a segment—and only those costs—should be assigned to the segment. Unfortunately, companies often make mistakes when assigning costs to segments. They omit some costs, inappropriately assign traceable fixed costs, and arbitrarily allocate common fixed costs.

Omission of Costs

The costs assigned to a segment should include all costs attributable to that segment from the company's entire value chain. All of these functions, from research and development, through product design, manufacturing, marketing, distribution, and customer service, are required to bring a product or service to the customer and generate revenues.

However, only manufacturing costs are included in product costs under absorption costing, which is widely regarded as required for external financial reporting. To avoid having to maintain two costing systems and to provide consistency between internal and external reports, many companies also use absorption costing for their internal reports such as segmented income statements. As a result, such companies omit from their profitability analysis part or all of the "upstream" costs in the value chain, which consist of research and development and product design, and the "downstream" costs, which consist of marketing, distribution, and customer service. Yet these nonmanufacturing costs are just as essential in determining product profitability as are the manufacturing costs. These upstream and downstream costs, which are usually included in selling and administrative expenses on absorption costing income statements, can represent half or more of the total costs of an organization. If either the upstream or downstream costs are omitted in profitability analysis, then the product is undercosted and management may unwittingly develop and maintain products that in the long run result in losses.

Inappropriate Methods for Assigning Traceable Costs among Segments

In addition to omitting costs, many companies do not correctly handle traceable fixed expenses on segmented income statements. First, they do not trace fixed expenses to segments even when it is feasible to do so. Second, they use inappropriate allocation bases to allocate traceable fixed expenses to segments.

Failure to Trace Costs Directly   Costs that can be traced directly to a specific segment should be charged directly to that segment and should not be allocated to other segments. For example, the rent for a branch office of an insurance company should be charged directly to the branch office rather than included in a companywide overhead pool and then spread throughout the company.

Inappropriate Allocation Base   Some companies use arbitrary allocation bases to allocate costs to segments. For example, some companies allocate selling and administrative expenses on the basis of sales revenues. Thus, if a segment generates 20% of total company sales, it would be allocated 20% of the company's selling and administrative expenses as its "fair share." This same basic procedure is followed if cost of goods sold or some other measure is used as the allocation base.

Costs should be allocated to segments for internal decision-making purposes only when the allocation base actually drives the cost being allocated (or is very highly correlated with the real cost driver). For example, sales should be used to allocate selling and administrative expenses only if a 10% increase in sales will result in a 10% increase in selling and administrative expenses. To the extent that selling and administrative expenses are not driven by sales volume, these expenses will be improperly allocated—with a disproportionately high percentage of the selling and administrative expenses assigned to the segments with the largest sales.

Arbitrarily Dividing Common Costs among Segments

The third business practice that leads to distorted segment costs is the practice of assigning nontraceable costs to segments. For example, some companies allocate the common costs of the corporate headquarters building to products on segment reports. However, in a multiproduct company, no single product is likely to be responsible for any significant amount of this cost. Even if a product were eliminated entirely, there would usually be no significant effect on any of the costs of the corporate headquarters building. In short, there is no cause-and-effect relation between the cost of the corporate headquarters building and the existence of any one product. As a consequence, any allocation of the cost of the corporate headquarters building to the products must be arbitrary.

Common costs like the costs of the corporate headquarters building are necessary, of course, to have a functioning organization. The practice of arbitrarily allocating common costs to segments is often justified on the grounds that "someone" has to "cover the common costs." While it is undeniably true that a company must cover its common costs to earn a profit, arbitrarily allocating common costs to segments does not ensure that this will happen. In fact, adding a share of common costs to the real costs of a segment may make an otherwise profitable segment appear to be unprofitable. If a manager eliminates the apparently unprofitable segment, the real traceable costs of the segment will be saved, but its revenues will be lost. And what happens to the common fixed costs that were allocated to the segment? They don't disappear; they are reallocated to the remaining segments of the company. That makes all of the remaining segments appear to be less profitable—possibly resulting in dropping other segments. The net effect will be to reduce the overall profits of the company and make it even more difficult to "cover the common costs."

Additionally, common fixed costs are not manageable by the manager to whom they are arbitrarily allocated; they are the responsibility of higher-level managers. When common fixed costs are allocated to managers, they are held responsible for those costs even though they cannot control them.

7. Which of the following statements is true? (You can select more than one answer.)
    a. A segment's contribution margin minus its traceable fixed expenses equals the segment margin.
    b. A company's common fixed costs should be evenly allocated to business segments when computing the dollar sales for a segment to break even.
    c. A segment's traceable fixed costs should include only those costs that would disappear over time if the segment disappeared.
    d. Fixed costs that are traceable to one segment may be a common cost of another segment.

CONCEPT CHECK

INCOME STATEMENTS—AN EXTERNAL REPORTING PERSPECTIVE

Companywide Income Statements

Practically speaking, absorption costing is required for external reports according to U.S. generally accepted accounting principles (GAAP).[3] Furthermore, International Financial Reporting Standards (IFRS) explicitly require companies to use absorption costing.

---

[3]The Financial Accounting Standards Board (FASB) has created a single source of authoritative nongovernmental U.S. generally accepted accounting principles (GAAP) called the FASB Accounting Standards Codification (FASB codification). Although the FASB codification does not explicitly disallow variable costing, it does explicitly prohibit companies from excluding all manufacturing overhead costs from product costs. It also provides an in-depth discussion of fixed overhead allocation to products, thereby implying that absorption costing is required for external reports. Although some companies expense significant elements of fixed manufacturing costs on their external reports, practically speaking, U.S. GAAP requires absorption costing for external reports.

Probably because of the cost and possible confusion of maintaining two separate costing systems—one for external reporting and one for internal reporting—most companies use absorption costing for their external and internal reports.

With all of the advantages of the contribution approach, you may wonder why the absorption approach is used at all. While the answer is partly due to adhering to tradition, absorption costing is also attractive to many accountants and managers because they believe it better matches costs with revenues. Advocates of absorption costing argue that *all* manufacturing costs must be assigned to products in order to properly match the costs of producing units of product with their revenues when they are sold. The fixed costs of depreciation, taxes, insurance, supervisory salaries, and so on, are just as essential to manufacturing products as are the variable costs.

Advocates of variable costing argue that fixed manufacturing costs are not really the costs of any particular unit of product. These costs are incurred to have the *capacity* to make products during a particular period and will be incurred even if nothing is made during the period. Moreover, whether a unit is made or not, the fixed manufacturing costs will be exactly the same. Therefore, variable costing advocates argue that fixed manufacturing costs are not part of the costs of producing a particular unit of product, and thus, the matching principle dictates that fixed manufacturing costs should be charged to the current period.

Segmented Financial Information

U.S. GAAP and IFRS require that publicly traded companies include segmented financial and other data in their annual reports and that the segmented reports prepared for external users *must use the same methods and definitions that the companies use in internal segmented reports that are prepared to aid in making operating decisions.* This is a very unusual stipulation because companies are not ordinarily required to report the same data to external users that are used for internal decision-making purposes. This requirement creates incentives for publicly traded companies to avoid using the contribution format for internal segmented reports. Segmented contribution format income statements contain vital information that companies are often very reluctant to release to the public (and hence competitors). In addition, this requirement creates problems in reconciling internal and external reports.

IN BUSINESS

3M Reports Segmented Profitability to Shareholders

In 2009, 3M Company reported segmented profitability to its shareholders by product lines and geographic areas. A portion of the company's segmented information is summarized below (all numbers are in millions):

	Net Sales	Net Operating Income
Product Lines:		
Industrial and transportation.	$7,116	$1,238
Health care.	$4,294	$1,350
Consumer and office.	$3,471	$748
Safety, security, and protection services. . . .	$3,180	$745
Display and graphics	$3,132	$590
Electro and communications	$2,276	$322
Geographic Areas:		
United States	$8,509	$1,640
Asia Pacific.	$6,120	$1,528
Europe, Middle East and Africa	$5,972	$1,003
Latin America and Canada.	$2,516	$631

3M's annual report does not report the gross margins or contribution margins for its business segments. Why do you think this is the case?

Source: 3M Company, 2009 Annual Report.

LO6–1 Explain how variable costing differs from absorption costing and compute unit product costs under each method.

Variable and absorption costing are alternative methods of determining unit product costs. Under variable costing, only variable manufacturing costs (direct materials, direct labor, and variable manufacturing overhead) are treated as product costs. Fixed manufacturing overhead is treated as a period cost and it is expensed on the income statement as incurred. By contrast, absorption costing treats fixed manufacturing overhead as a product cost, along with direct materials, direct labor, and variable overhead.

LO6–2 Prepare income statements using both variable and absorption costing.

The unit product costs under the two methods are different and so the cost of goods sold are different on the income statement. Additionally, fixed manufacturing overhead is expensed on the income statement under variable costing, but is included in unit product costs under absorption costing. Under both costing methods, selling and administrative expenses are treated as period costs and are expensed on the income statement as incurred.

LO6–3 Reconcile variable costing and absorption costing net operating incomes and explain why the two amounts differ.

Because absorption costing treats fixed manufacturing overhead as a product cost, a portion of fixed manufacturing overhead is assigned to each unit as it is produced. If units of product are unsold at the end of a period, then the fixed manufacturing overhead cost attached to those units is carried with them into the inventory account and deferred to a future period. When these units are later sold, the fixed manufacturing overhead cost attached to them is released from the inventory account and charged against income as part of cost of goods sold. Thus, under absorption costing, it is possible to defer a portion of the fixed manufacturing overhead cost from one period to a future period through the inventory account.

LO6–4 Prepare a segmented income statement that differentiates traceable fixed costs from common fixed costs and use it to make decisions.

Segmented income statements provide information for evaluating the profitability and performance of divisions, product lines, sales territories, and other segments of a company. Under the contribution approach, variable costs and fixed costs are clearly distinguished from each other and only those costs that are traceable to a segment are assigned to the segment. A cost is considered traceable to a segment only if the cost is caused by the segment and could be avoided by eliminating the segment. Fixed common costs are not allocated to segments. The segment margin consists of revenues, less variable expenses, less traceable fixed expenses of the segment.

LO6–5 Compute companywide and segment break-even points for a company with traceable fixed costs.

The dollar sales required for a segment to break even is computed by dividing the segment's traceable fixed expenses by its contribution margin ratio. A company's common fixed expenses should not be allocated to segments when performing break-even calculations because they will not change in response to segment-level decisions. Conversely, a company's common fixed expenses should be included when performing company wide break-even calculations.

GUIDANCE ANSWER TO DECISION POINT

The Pricing Decision (p. 256)

Under absorption costing, the fixed manufacturing overhead cost per unit is $20 ($400,000 ÷ 20,000 units). The absorption costing unit product cost is $70 ($25 + $15 + $10 + $20) and the gross margin per unit is $30 ($100 − $70). The variable costing unit product cost is $50 ($25 + $15 + $10) and the contribution margin per unit is $50 ($100 − $50). When the company produces and sells 20,000 units at a price of $100, it earns a total gross margin of $600,000 (20,000 units × $30) and a total contribution margin of $1,000,000 (20,000 units × $50).

A 10% price increase would raise the selling price to $110 per unit, whereas a 20% decline in unit sales would drop the sales volume to 16,000 units. In this scenario, the total gross margin earned is $640,000 (16,000 units × $40), which is $40,000 higher than the gross margin from the original scenario. This explains why the marketing manager thinks the price increase is a good idea. However, if the price increase is implemented the total contribution margin earned would become $960,000 (16,000 units × $60), which is $40,000 lower than the contribution margin from the original scenario. The price increase will lower profits by $40,000.

GUIDANCE ANSWERS TO CONCEPT CHECKS

1. **Choice b.** Under variable costing, variable selling and administrative expenses are treated as period costs.

2. **Choice d.** The contribution margin per unit equals $18 ($40 − $18 − $4). The number of units sold (7,500 units) multiplied by the contribution margin per unit ($18 per unit) minus the total fixed costs ($100,000) equals the net operating income ($35,000).

3. **Choice c.** The unit product cost of $28 includes $18 of variable manufacturing costs and $10 of fixed manufacturing overhead ($80,000 ÷ 8,000 = $10 per unit). The gross margin per unit is $12 ($40 − $28) and the total gross margin is $90,000 (7,500 units × $12 = $90,000). The gross margin of $90,000 minus variable selling and administrative expense of $30,000 (7,500 units × $4 per unit = $30,000) and fixed selling and adminstrative expense of $20,000 equals net operating income of $40,000.

4. **Choice c.** The variable costing unit product cost is $22 ($12 + $8 + $2). The cost of goods sold is $154,000 (7,000 units sold × $22 per unit). The variable selling and administrative expense is a period cost, not a product cost.

5. **Choice a.** The absorption costing fixed manufacturing overhead cost per unit is $5 ($50,000 ÷ 10,000 units). The absorption costing unit product cost is $27 ($12 + $8 + $2 + 5). The cost of goods sold is $189,000 (7,000 units sold × $27 per unit).

6. **Choice d.** Absorption costing income is $15,000 higher because it defers $15,000 (3,000 units × $5 per unit) of fixed manufacturing overhead in inventory, whereas variable costing expenses the entire $50,000 of fixed manufacturing overhead during the current period.

7. **Choices a, c, and d.** Common fixed costs should not be allocated to business segments.

REVIEW PROBLEM 1: CONTRASTING VARIABLE AND ABSORPTION COSTING

Dexter Corporation produces and sells a single product, a wooden hand loom for weaving small items such as scarves. Selected cost and operating data relating to the product for two years are given below:

Selling price per unit	$50
Manufacturing costs:	
Variable per unit produced:	
Direct materials.	$11
Direct labor	$6
Variable manufacturing overhead	$3
Fixed manufacturing overhead per year. . . .	$120,000
Selling and administrative expenses:	
Variable per unit sold	$4
Fixed per year	$70,000

	Year 1	Year 2
Units in beginning inventory	0	2,000
Units produced during the year	10,000	6,000
Units sold during the year	8,000	8,000
Units in ending inventory	2,000	0

Required:
1. Assume the company uses absorption costing.
   a. Compute the unit product cost in each year.
   b. Prepare an income statement for each year.
2. Assume the company uses variable costing.
   a. Compute the unit product cost in each year.
   b. Prepare an income statement for each year.
3. Reconcile the variable costing and absorption costing net operating incomes.

Solution to Review Problem 1

1.   a.   Under absorption costing, all manufacturing costs, variable and fixed, are included in unit product costs:

	Year 1	Year 2
Direct materials	$11	$11
Direct labor	6	6
Variable manufacturing overhead	3	3
Fixed manufacturing overhead		
($120,000 ÷ 10,000 units)	12	
($120,000 ÷ 6,000 units)		20
Absorption costing unit product cost	$32	$40

b.   The absorption costing income statements follow:

	Year 1	Year 2
Sales (8,000 units × $50 per unit)	$400,000	$400,000
Cost of goods sold (8,000 units × $32 per unit);		
(2,000 units × $32 per unit) +		
(6,000 units × $40 per unit).	256,000	304,000
Gross margin	144,000	96,000
Selling and administrative expenses		
(8,000 units × $4 per unit + $70,000)	102,000	102,000
Net operating income (loss)	$ 42,000	$ (6,000)

2.   a.   Under variable costing, only the variable manufacturing costs are included in unit product costs:

	Year 1	Year 2
Direct materials.	$11	$11
Direct labor.	6	6
Variable manufacturing overhead	3	3
Variable costing unit product cost	$20	$20

b.   The variable costing income statements follow:

	Year 1		Year 2	
Sales (8,000 units × $50 per unit).		$400,000		$400,000
Variable expenses:				
Variable cost of goods sold				
(8,000 units × $20 per unit)	$160,000		$160,000	
Variable selling and administrative				
expenses (8,000 units × $4 per unit) . . .	32,000	192,000	32,000	192,000
Contribution margin		208,000		208,000
Fixed expenses:				
Fixed manufacturing overhead.	120,000		120,000	
Fixed selling and administrative				
expenses	70,000	190,000	70,000	190,000
Net operating income		$ 18,000		$ 18,000

3. The reconciliation of the variable and absorption costing net operating incomes follows:

	Year 1	Year 2
Fixed manufacturing overhead in ending inventories	$24,000	$ 0
Fixed manufacturing overhead in beginning inventories . . .	0	24,000
Fixed manufacturing overhead deferred in (released from) inventories	$24,000	$(24,000)

	Year 1	Year 2
Variable costing net operating income.	$18,000	$18,000
Add fixed manufacturing overhead costs deferred in inventory under absorption costing (2,000 units × $12 per unit)	24,000	
Deduct fixed manufacturing overhead costs released from inventory under absorption costing (2,000 units × $12 per unit)		(24,000)
Absorption costing net operating income (loss)	$42,000	$ (6,000)

REVIEW PROBLEM 2: SEGMENTED INCOME STATEMENTS

The business staff of the law firm Frampton, Davis & Smythe has constructed the following report that breaks down the firm's overall results for last month into two business segments—family law and commercial law:

	Company Total	Family Law	Commercial Law
Revenues from clients	$1,000,000	$400,000	$600,000
Variable expenses	220,000	100,000	120,000
Contribution margin	780,000	300,000	480,000
Traceable fixed expenses	670,000	280,000	390,000
Segment margin	110,000	20,000	90,000
Common fixed expenses	60,000	24,000	36,000
Net operating income (loss) . . .	$ 50,000	$ (4,000)	$ 54,000

However, this report is not quite correct. The common fixed expenses such as the managing partner's salary, general administrative expenses, and general firm advertising have been allocated to the two segments based on revenues from clients.

Required:
1. Redo the segment report, eliminating the allocation of common fixed expenses. Would the firm be better off financially if the family law segment were dropped? (Note: Many of the firm's commercial law clients also use the firm for their family law requirements such as drawing up wills.)
2. The firm's advertising agency has proposed an ad campaign targeted at boosting the revenues of the family law segment. The ad campaign would cost $20,000, and the advertising agency claims that it would increase family law revenues by $100,000. The managing partner of Frampton, Davis & Smythe believes this increase in business could be accommodated without any increase in fixed expenses. Estimate the effect this ad campaign would have on the family law segment margin and on the firm's overall net operating income.
3. Compute the companywide break-even point in dollar sales and the dollar sales required for each business segment to break even.

Solution to Review Problem 2

1. The corrected segmented income statement appears below:

	Company Total	Family Law	Commercial Law
Revenues from clients	$1,000,000	$400,000	$600,000
Variable expenses	220,000	100,000	120,000
Contribution margin	780,000	300,000	480,000
Traceable fixed expenses	670,000	280,000	390,000
Segment margin	110,000	$ 20,000	$ 90,000
Common fixed expenses	60,000		
Net operating income	$ 50,000		

No, the firm would not be financially better off if the family law practice were dropped. The family law segment is covering all of its own costs and is contributing $20,000 per month to covering the common fixed expenses of the firm. While the segment margin for family law is much lower than for commercial law, it is still profitable. Moreover, family law may be a service that the firm must provide to its commercial clients in order to remain competitive.

2. The ad campaign would increase the family law segment margin by $55,000 as follows:

Increased revenues from clients	$100,000
Family law contribution margin ratio ($300,000 ÷ $400,000) . .	× 75%
Increased contribution margin	$ 75,000
Less cost of the ad campaign	20,000
Increased segment margin	$ 55,000

Because there would be no increase in fixed expenses (including common fixed expenses), the increase in overall net operating income is also $55,000.

3. The companywide break-even point is computed as follows:

$$\text{Dollar sales for company to break even} = \frac{\text{Traceable fixed expenses} + \text{Common fixed expenses}}{\text{Overall CM ratio}}$$

$$= \frac{\$670,000 + \$60,000}{0.78}$$

$$= \frac{\$730,000}{0.78}$$

$$= \$935,897 \text{ (rounded)}$$

The break-even point for the family law segment is computed as follows:

$$\text{Dollar sales for a segment to break even} = \frac{\text{Segment traceable fixed expenses}}{\text{Segment CM ratio}}$$

$$= \frac{\$280,000}{0.75}$$

$$= \$373,333 \text{ (rounded)}$$

The break-even point for the commercial law segment is computed as follows:

$$\text{Dollar sales for a segment to break even} = \frac{\text{Segment traceable fixed expenses}}{\text{Segment CM ratio}}$$

$$= \frac{\$390,000}{0.80}$$

$$= \$487,500$$

GLOSSARY

Absorption costing   A costing method that includes all manufacturing costs—direct materials, direct labor, and both variable and fixed manufacturing overhead—in unit product costs. (p. 244)

Common fixed cost   A fixed cost that supports more than one business segment, but is not traceable in whole or in part to any one of the business segments. (p. 256)

Segment   Any part or activity of an organization about which managers seek cost, revenue, or profit data. (p. 244)

Segment margin   A segment's contribution margin less its traceable fixed costs. It represents the margin available after a segment has covered all of its own traceable costs. (p. 257)

Traceable fixed cost   A fixed cost that is incurred because of the existence of a particular business segment and that would be eliminated if the segment were eliminated. (p. 256)

Variable costing   A costing method that includes only variable manufacturing costs—direct materials, direct labor, and variable manufacturing overhead—in unit product costs. (p. 244)

QUESTIONS

6–1   What is the basic difference between absorption costing and variable costing?

6–2   Are selling and administrative expenses treated as product costs or as period costs under variable costing?

6–3   Explain how fixed manufacturing overhead costs are shifted from one period to another under absorption costing.

6–4   What are the arguments in favor of treating fixed manufacturing overhead costs as product costs?

6–5   What are the arguments in favor of treating fixed manufacturing overhead costs as period costs?

6–6   If the units produced and unit sales are equal, which method would you expect to show the higher net operating income, variable costing or absorption costing? Why?

6–7   If the units produced exceed unit sales, which method would you expect to show the higher net operating income, variable costing or absorption costing? Why?

6–8   If fixed manufacturing overhead costs are released from inventory under absorption costing, what does this tell you about the level of production in relation to the level of sales?

6–9   Under absorption costing, how is it possible to increase net operating income without increasing sales?

6–10   How does Lean Production reduce or eliminate the difference in reported net operating income between absorption and variable costing?

6–11   What is a segment of an organization? Give several examples of segments.

6–12   What costs are assigned to a segment under the contribution approach?

6–13   Distinguish between a traceable cost and a common cost. Give several examples of each.

6–14   Explain how the segment margin differs from the contribution margin.

6–15   Why aren't common costs allocated to segments under the contribution approach?

6–16   How is it possible for a cost that is traceable to a segment to become a common cost if the segment is divided into further segments?

6–17   Should a company allocate its common fixed expenses to business segments when computing the break-even point for those segments? Why?

Multiple-choice questions are available in the *Connect Library*.

APPLYING EXCEL

Available with McGraw-Hill's *Connect Accounting*.

LO6–2

The Excel worksheet form that appears on the next page is to be used to recreate portions of Review Problem 1 on pages 268–270. Download the workbook containing this form in the *Connect Library*. On *the website you will also receive instructions about how to use this worksheet form.*

	A	B	C	D	E	F
1	Chapter 6: Applying Excel					
2						
3	Data					
4	Selling price per unit	$50				
5	Manufacturing costs:					
6	Variable per unit produced:					
7	Direct materials	$11				
8	Direct labor	$6				
9	Variable manufacturing overhead	$3				
10	Fixed manufacturing overhead per year	$120,000				
11	Selling and administrative expenses:					
12	Variable per unit sold	$4				
13	Fixed per year	$70,000				
14						
15		Year 1	Year 2			
16	Units in beginning inventory	0				
17	Units produced during the year	10,000	6,000			
18	Units sold during the year	8,000	8,000			
19						
20	Enter a formula into each of the cells marked with a ? below					
21	Review Problem 1: Contrasting Variable and Absorption Costing					
22						
23	Compute the Ending Inventory					
24		Year 1	Year 2			
25	Units in beginning inventory	0	?			
26	Units produced during the year	?	?			
27	Units sold during the year	?	?			
28	Units in ending inventory	?	?			
29						
30	Compute the Absorption Costing Unit Product Cost					
31		Year 1	Year 2			
32	Direct materials	?	?			
33	Direct labor	?	?			
34	Variable manufacturing overhead	?	?			
35	Fixed manufacturing overhead	?	?			
36	Absorption costing unit product cost	?	?			
37						
38	Construct the Absorption Costing Income Statement					
39		Year 1	Year 2			
40	Sales	?	?			
41	Cost of goods sold	?	?			
42	Gross margin	?	?			
43	Selling and administrative expenses	?	?			
44	Net operating income	?	?			
45						
46	Compute the Variable Costing Unit Product Cost					
47		Year 1	Year 2			
48	Direct materials	?	?			
49	Direct labor	?	?			
50	Variable manufacturing overhead	?	?			
51	Variable costing unit product cost	?	?			
52						
53	Construct the Variable Costing Income Statement					
54			Year 1		Year 2	
55	Sales		?		?	
56	Variable expenses:					
57	Variable cost of goods sold	?		?		
58	Variable selling and administrative expenses	?	?	?	?	
59	Contribution margin		?		?	
60	Fixed expenses:					
61	Fixed manufacturing overhead	?		?		
62	Fixed selling and administrative expenses	?	?	?	?	
63	Net operating income		?		?	
64						

Chapter 6 Form   Filled in Chapter 6 Form   Chapter 6

You should proceed to the requirements below only after completing your worksheet. The LIFO inventory flow assumption is used throughout this problem.

Required:
1. Check your worksheet by changing the units sold in the Data to 6,000 for Year 2. The cost of goods sold under absorption costing for Year 2 should now be $240,000. If it isn't, check cell C41. The formula in this cell should be =IF(C26 < C27,C26*C36 + (C27 - C26)*B36,C27*C36). If your worksheet is operating properly, the net operating income under both absorption costing and variable costing should be $(34,000) for Year 2. That is, the loss in Year 2 is $34,000 under both systems. If you do not get these answers, find the errors in your worksheet and correct them.

Why is the absorption costing net operating income now equal to the variable costing net operating income in Year 2?

2. Enter the following data from a different company into your worksheet:

Data	
Selling price per unit.	$75
Manufacturing costs:	
Variable per unit produced:	
Direct materials	$12
Direct labor	$5
Variable manufacturing overhead	$7
Fixed manufacturing overhead per year . . .	$150,000
Selling and administrative expenses:	
Variable per unit sold.	$1
Fixed per year	$60,000

	Year 1	Year 2
Units in beginning inventory	0	
Units produced during the year	15,000	10,000
Units sold during the year.	12,000	12,000

Is the net operating income under variable costing different in Year 1 and Year 2? Why or why not? Explain the relation between the net operating income under absorption costing and variable costing in Year 1. Explain the relation between the net operating income under absorption costing and variable costing in Year 2.

3. At the end of Year 1, the company's board of directors set a target for Year 2 of net operating income of $500,000 under absorption costing. If this target is met, a hefty bonus would be paid to the CEO of the company. Keeping everything else the same from part (2) above, change the units produced in Year 2 to 50,000 units. Would this change result in a bonus being paid to the CEO? Do you think this change would be in the best interests of the company? What is likely to happen in Year 3 to the absorption costing net operating income if sales remain constant at 12,000 units per year?

THE FOUNDATIONAL 15

LO6–1, LO6–2, LO6–3, LO6–4

Available with McGraw-Hill's *Connect Accounting*.

Diego Company manufactures one product that is sold for $80 per unit in two geographic regions—the East and West regions. The following information pertains to the company's first year of operations in which it produced 40,000 units and sold 35,000 units.

Variable costs per unit:	
Manufacturing:	
Direct materials	$24
Direct labor	$14
Variable manufacturing overhead	$2
Variable selling and administrative.	$4
Fixed costs per year:	
Fixed manufacturing overhead.	$800,000
Fixed selling and administrative expenses	$496,000

The company sold 25,000 units in the East region and 10,000 units in the West region. It determined that $250,000 of its fixed selling and administrative expenses is traceable to the West region, $150,000 is traceable to the East region, and the remaining $96,000 is a common fixed cost. The company will continue to incur the total amount of its fixed manufacturing overhead costs as long as it continues to produce any amount of its only product.

Required:

Answer each question independently based on the original data unless instructed otherwise. You do not need to prepare a segmented income statement until question 13.

1. What is the unit product cost under variable costing?
2. What is the unit product cost under absorption costing?
3. What is the company's total contribution margin under variable costing?
4. What is the company's net operating income under variable costing?
5. What is the company's total gross margin under absorption costing?
6. What is the company's net operating income under absorption costing?
7. What is the amount of the difference between the variable costing and absorption costing net operating incomes? What is the cause of this difference?
8. What is the company's break-even point in unit sales? Is it above or below the actual sales volume? Compare the break-even sales volume to your answer for question 6 and comment.
9. If the sales volumes in the East and West regions had been reversed, what would be the company's overall break-even point in unit sales?
10. What would have been the company's variable costing net operating income if it had produced and sold 35,000 units? You do not need to perform any calculations to answer this question.
11. What would have been the company's absorption costing net operating income if it had produced and sold 35,000 units? You do not need to perform any calculations to answer this question.
12. If the company produces 5,000 fewer units than it sells in its second year of operations, will absorption costing net operating income be higher or lower than variable costing net operating income in Year 2? Why? No calculations are necessary.
13. Prepare a contribution format segmented income statement that includes a Total column and columns for the East and West regions.
14. Diego is considering eliminating the West region because an internally generated report suggests the region's total *gross margin* in the first year of operations was $50,000 less than its traceable fixed selling and administrative expenses. Diego believes that if it drops the West region, the East region's sales will grow by 5% in Year 2. Using the contribution approach for analyzing segment profitability and assuming all else remains constant in Year 2, what would be the profit impact of dropping the West region in Year 2?
15. Assume the West region invests $30,000 in a new advertising campaign in Year 2 that increases its unit sales by 20%. If all else remains constant, what would be the profit impact of pursuing the advertising campaign?

EXERCISES

All applicable exercises are available with McGraw-Hill's *Connect Accounting.*

EXERCISE 6–1   Variable and Absorption Costing Unit Product Costs [LO6–1]

Ida Sidha Karya Company is a family-owned company located in the village of Gianyar on the island of Bali in Indonesia. The company produces a handcrafted Balinese musical instrument called a gamelan that is similar to a xylophone. The gamelans are sold for $850. Selected data for the company's operations last year follow:

Units sold = 200; Units in ending inventory = 50

Units in beginning inventory	0
Units produced	250
Units sold	225
Units in ending inventory	25
Variable costs per unit:	
Direct materials	$100
Direct labor	$320
Variable manufacturing overhead	$40
Variable selling and administrative	$20
Fixed costs:	
Fixed manufacturing overhead	$60,000
Fixed selling and administrative	$20,000

Required:

1. Assume that the company uses absorption costing. Compute the unit product cost for one gamelan.
2. Assume that the company uses variable costing. Compute the unit product cost for one gamelan.

EXERCISE 6–2   Variable Costing Income Statement; Explanation of Difference in Net Operating Income [LO6–2]

Refer to the data in Exercise 6–1 for Ida Sidha Karya Company. The absorption costing income statement prepared by the company's accountant for last year appears below:

Sales	$191,250
Cost of goods sold	157,500
Gross margin	33,750
Selling and administrative expense	24,500
Net operating income	$ 9,250

Required:

1. Determine how much of the ending inventory consists of fixed manufacturing overhead cost deferred in inventory to the next period.
2. Prepare an income statement for the year using variable costing. Explain the difference in net operating income between the two costing methods.

EXERCISE 6–3   Reconciliation of Absorption and Variable Costing Net Operating Incomes [LO6–3]

Jorgansen Lighting, Inc., manufactures heavy-duty street lighting systems for municipalities. The company uses variable costing for internal management reports and absorption costing for external reports to shareholders, creditors, and the government. The company has provided the following data:

Year 1 ending inventory = 140 units

	Year 1	Year 2	Year 3
Inventories:			
Beginning (units)	200	170	180
Ending (units)	170	180	220
Variable costing net operating income	$1,080,400	$1,032,400	$996,400

The company's fixed manufacturing overhead per unit was constant at $560 for all three years.

Required:

1. Determine each year's absorption costing net operating income. Present your answer in the form of a reconciliation report.
2. In Year 4, the company's variable costing net operating income was $984,400 and its absorption costing net operating income was $1,012,400. Did inventories increase or decrease during Year 4? How much fixed manufacturing overhead cost was deferred or released from inventory during Year 4?

EXERCISE 6–4   Basic Segmented Income Statement [LO6–4]

Royal Lawncare Company produces and sells two packaged products, Weedban and Greengrow. Revenue and cost information relating to the products follow:

Unit sales of Weedban = 16,000; Unit sales of Greengrow = 30,000

	Product	
	Weedban	Greengrow
Selling price per unit	$6.00	$7.50
Variable expenses per unit	$2.40	$5.25
Traceable fixed expenses per year	$45,000	$21,000

Common fixed expenses in the company total $33,000 annually. Last year the company produced and sold 15,000 units of Weedban and 28,000 units of Greengrow.

Required:

Prepare a contribution format income statement segmented by product lines.

EXERCISE 6–5   Companywide and Segment Break-Even Analysis [LO6–5]

Piedmont Company segments its business into two regions—North and South. The company prepared the contribution format segmented income statement shown below:

	Total Company	North	South
Sales	$600,000	$400,000	$200,000
Variable expenses	360,000	280,000	80,000
Contribution margin	240,000	120,000	120,000
Traceable fixed expenses	120,000	60,000	60,000
Segment margin	120,000	$ 60,000	$ 60,000
Common fixed expenses	50,000		
Net operating income	$ 70,000		

Required:
1. Compute the companywide break-even point in dollar sales.
2. Compute the break-even point in dollar sales for the North region.
3. Compute the break-even point in dollar sales for the South region.

EXERCISE 6–6   Variable and Absorption Costing Unit Product Costs and Income Statements [LO6–1, LO6–2]

Lynch Company manufactures and sells a single product. The following costs were incurred during the company's first year of operations:

Variable costs per unit:	
Manufacturing:	
Direct materials	$6
Direct labor	$9
Variable manufacturing overhead	$3
Variable selling and administrative	$4
Fixed costs per year:	
Fixed manufacturing overhead	$300,000
Fixed selling and administrative	$190,000

During the year, the company produced 25,000 units and sold 20,000 units. The selling price of the company's product is $50 per unit.

Required:
1. Assume that the company uses absorption costing:
   a. Compute the unit product cost.
   b. Prepare an income statement for the year.
2. Assume that the company uses variable costing:
   a. Compute the unit product cost.
   b. Prepare an income statement for the year.

EXERCISE 6–7   Segmented Income Statement [LO6–4]

Shannon Company segments its income statement into its North and South Divisions. The company's overall sales, contribution margin ratio, and net operating income are $500,000, 46%, and $10,000, respectively. The North Division's contribution margin and contribution margin ratio are $150,000 and 50%, respectively. The South Division's segment margin is $30,000. The company has $90,000 of common fixed expenses that cannot be traced to either division.

Required:
Prepare an income statement for Shannon Company that uses the contribution format and is segmented by divisions. In addition, for the company as a whole and for each segment, show each item on the segmented income statements as a percent of sales.

EXERCISE 6–8 Deducing Changes in Inventories [LO6–3]
Parker Products Inc, a manufacturer, reported $123 million in sales and a loss of $18 million in its annual report to shareholders. According to a CVP analysis prepared for management, the company's break-even point is $115 million in sales.

Sales = $110 million; absorption income = $10 million

Required:
Assuming that the CVP analysis is correct, is it likely that the company's inventory level increased, decreased, or remained unchanged during the year? Explain.

EXERCISE 6–9 Variable and Absorption Costing Unit Product Costs and Income Statements [LO6–1, LO6–2, LO6–3]
Walsh Company manufactures and sells one product. The following information pertains to each of the company's first two years of operations:

Fixed manufacturing overhead = $400,000

Variable costs per unit:	
Manufacturing:	
Direct materials	$25
Direct labor	$15
Variable manufacturing overhead	$5
Variable selling and administrative	$2
Fixed costs per year:	
Fixed manufacturing overhead	$250,000
Fixed selling and administrative expenses	$80,000

During its first year of operations, Walsh produced 50,000 units and sold 40,000 units. During its second year of operations, it produced 40,000 units and sold 50,000 units. The selling price of the company's product is $60 per unit.

Required:
1. Assume the company uses variable costing:
   a. Compute the unit product cost for Year 1 and Year 2.
   b. Prepare an income statement for Year 1 and Year 2.
2. Assume the company uses absorption costing:
   a. Compute the unit product cost for Year 1 and Year 2.
   b. Prepare an income statement for Year 1 and Year 2.
3. Explain the difference between variable costing and absorption costing net operating income in Year 1. Also, explain why the two net operating income figures differ in Year 2.

EXERCISE 6–10 Companywide and Segment Break-Even Analysis [LO6–5]
Crossfire Company segments its business into two regions—East and West. The company prepared the contribution format segmented income statement shown below:

	Total Company	East	West
Sales	$900,000	$600,000	$300,000
Variable expenses	675,000	480,000	195,000
Contribution margin	225,000	120,000	105,000
Traceable fixed expenses	141,000	50,000	91,000
Segment margin	84,000	$ 70,000	$ 14,000
Common fixed expenses	59,000		
Net operating income	$ 25,000		

Required:
1. Compute the companywide break-even point dollar in sales.
2. Compute the break-even point in dollar sales for the East region.
3. Compute the break-even point in dollar sales for the West region.

4. Prepare a new segmented income statement based on the break-even dollar sales that you computed in requirements 2 and 3. Use the same format as shown above. What is Crossfire's net operating income in your new segmented income statement?
5. Do you think that Crossfire should allocate its common fixed expenses to the East and West regions when computing the break-even points for each region? Why?

EXERCISE 6–11   Segmented Income Statement [LO6–4]

Wingate Company, a wholesale distributor of electronic equipment, has been experiencing losses for some time, as shown by its most recent monthly contribution format income statement, which follows:

Variable expense percentage for Central = 40%

Sales	$1,000,000
Variable expenses	390,000
Contribution margin	610,000
Fixed expenses	625,000
Net operating income (loss)	$ (15,000)

In an effort to isolate the problem, the president has asked for an income statement segmented by division. Accordingly, the Accounting Department has developed the following information:

		Division	
	East	**Central**	**West**
Sales	$250,000	$400,000	$350,000
Variable expenses as a percentage of sales	52%	30%	40%
Traceable fixed expenses	$160,000	$200,000	$175,000

Required:
1. Prepare a contribution format income statement segmented by divisions, as desired by the president.
2. As a result of a marketing study, the president believes that sales in the West Division could be increased by 20% if monthly advertising in that division were increased by $15,000. Would you recommend the increased advertising? Show computations to support your answer.

EXERCISE 6–12   Variable Costing Income Statement; Reconciliation [LO6–2, LO6–3]

Whitman Company has just completed its first year of operations. The company's absorption costing income statement for the year appears below:

Whitman Company Income Statement	
Sales (35,000 units × $25 per unit)	$875,000
Cost of goods sold (35,000 units × $16 per unit)	560,000
Gross margin	315,000
Selling and administrative expenses	280,000
Net operating income	$ 35,000

The company's selling and administrative expenses consist of $210,000 per year in fixed expenses and $2 per unit sold in variable expenses. The $16 per unit product cost given above is computed as follows:

Direct materials	$ 5
Direct labor	6
Variable manufacturing overhead	1
Fixed manufacturing overhead ($160,000 ÷ 40,000 units)	4
Absorption costing unit product cost	$16

Required:
1. Redo the company's income statement in the contribution format using variable costing.
2. Reconcile any difference between the net operating income on your variable costing income statement and the net operating income on the absorption costing income statement above.

TAKE TWO

Fixed manufacturing
overhead = $125,000

EXERCISE 6–13   Inferring Costing Method; Unit Product Cost [LO6–1]

Sierra Company incurs the following costs to produce and sell a single product.

Variable costs per unit:	
Direct materials	$9
Direct labor	$10
Variable manufacturing overhead	$5
Variable selling and administrative expenses	$3
Fixed costs per year:	
Fixed manufacturing overhead	$150,000
Fixed selling and administrative expenses	$400,000

During the last year, 25,000 units were produced and 22,000 units were sold. The Finished Goods inventory account at the end of the year shows a balance of $72,000 for the 3,000 unsold units.

Required:

1. Is the company using absorption costing or variable costing to cost units in the Finished Goods inventory account? Show computations to support your answer.
2. Assume that the company wishes to prepare financial statements for the year to issue to its stockholders.
   a. Is the $72,000 figure for Finished Goods inventory the correct amount to use on these statements for external reporting purposes? Explain.
   b. At what dollar amount *should* the 3,000 units be carried in the inventory for external reporting purposes?

EXERCISE 6–14   Variable Costing Unit Product Cost and Income Statement; Break-Even [LO6–1, LO6–2]

TAKE TWO

Fixed manufacturing
overhead = $740,000

Chuck Wagon Grills, Inc., makes a single product—a handmade specialty barbecue grill that it sells for $210. Data for last year's operations follow:

Units in beginning inventory	0
Units produced	20,000
Units sold	19,000
Units in ending inventory	1,000
Variable costs per unit:	
Direct materials	$ 50
Direct labor	80
Variable manufacturing overhead	20
Variable selling and administrative	10
Total variable cost per unit	$160
Fixed costs:	
Fixed manufacturing overhead	$700,000
Fixed selling and administrative	285,000
Total fixed costs	$985,000

Required:

1. Assume that the company uses variable costing. Compute the unit product cost for one barbecue grill.
2. Assume that the company uses variable costing. Prepare a contribution format income statement for the year.
3. What is the company's break-even point in terms of the number of barbecue grills sold?

EXERCISE 6–15   Absorption Costing Unit Product Cost and Income Statement [LO6–1, LO6–2]

TAKE TWO

See Exercise 6–14

Refer to the data in Exercise 6–14 for Chuck Wagon Grills. Assume in this exercise that the company uses absorption costing.

Required:

1. Compute the unit product cost for one barbecue grill.
2. Prepare an income statement.

EXERCISE 6–16 Working with a Segmented Income Statement; Break-Even Analysis [LO6–4, LO6–5]

Raner, Harris, & Chan is a consulting firm that specializes in information systems for medical and dental clinics. The firm has two offices—one in Chicago and one in Minneapolis. The firm classifies the direct costs of consulting jobs as variable costs. A contribution format segmented income statement for the company's most recent year is given below:

				Office		
	Total Company		Chicago		Minneapolis	
Sales	$450,000	100%	$150,000	100%	$300,000	100%
Variable expenses	225,000	50%	45,000	30%	180,000	60%
Contribution margin	225,000	50%	105,000	70%	120,000	40%
Traceable fixed expenses	126,000	28%	78,000	52%	48,000	16%
Office segment margin	99,000	22%	$ 27,000	18%	$ 72,000	24%
Common fixed expenses not traceable to offices	63,000	14%				
Net operating income	$ 36,000	8%				

Required:

1. Compute the companywide break-even point in dollar sales. Also, compute the break-even point for the Chicago office and for the Minneapolis office. Is the companywide break-even point greater than, less than, or equal to the sum of the Chicago and Minneapolis break-even points? Why?
2. By how much would the company's net operating income increase if Minneapolis increased its sales by $75,000 per year? Assume no change in cost behavior patterns.
3. Refer to the original data. Assume that sales in Chicago increase by $50,000 next year and that sales in Minneapolis remain unchanged. Assume no change in fixed costs.
   a. Prepare a new segmented income statement for the company using the above format. Show both amounts and percentages.
   b. Observe from the income statement you have prepared that the contribution margin ratio for Chicago has remained unchanged at 70% (the same as in the above data) but that the segment margin ratio has changed. How do you explain the change in the segment margin ratio?

EXERCISE 6–17 Working with a Segmented Income Statement [LO6–4]

Refer to the data in Exercise 6–16. Assume that Minneapolis' sales by major market are as follows:

				Market		
	Minneapolis		Medical		Dental	
Sales	$300,000	100%	$200,000	100%	$100,000	100%
Variable expenses	180,000	60%	128,000	64%	52,000	52%
Contribution margin	120,000	40%	72,000	36%	48,000	48%
Traceable fixed expenses	33,000	11%	12,000	6%	21,000	21%
Market segment margin	87,000	29%	$ 60,000	30%	$ 27,000	27%
Common fixed expenses not traceable to markets	15,000	5%				
Office segment margin	$ 72,000	24%				

The company would like to initiate an intensive advertising campaign in one of the two market segments during the next month. The campaign would cost $5,000. Marketing studies indicate that such a campaign would increase sales in the Medical market by $40,000 or increase sales in the Dental market by $35,000.

Required:

1. In which of the markets would you recommend that the company focus its advertising campaign? Show computations to support your answer.
2. In Exercise 6–16, Minneapolis shows $48,000 in traceable fixed expenses. What happened to the $48,000 in this exercise?

PROBLEMS

All applicable problems are available with McGraw-Hill's *Connect Accounting*.

PROBLEM 6–18A   Variable and Absorption Costing Unit Product Costs and Income Statements [LO6–1, LO6–2]

Haas Company manufactures and sells one product. The following information pertains to each of the company's first three years of operations:

Variable costs per unit:	
Manufacturing:	
Direct materials	$20
Direct labor	$12
Variable manufacturing overhead	$4
Variable selling and administrative	$2
Fixed costs per year:	
Fixed manufacturing overhead	$960,000
Fixed selling and administrative expenses	$240,000

During its first year of operations, Haas produced 60,000 units and sold 60,000 units. During its second year of operations, it produced 75,000 units and sold 50,000 units. In its third year, Haas produced 40,000 units and sold 65,000 units. The selling price of the company's product is $58 per unit.

Required:
1. Compute the company's break-even point in units sold.
2. Assume the company uses variable costing:
   a. Compute the unit product cost for Year 1, Year 2, and Year 3.
   b. Prepare an income statement for Year 1, Year 2, and Year 3.
3. Assume the company uses absorption costing:
   a. Compute the unit product cost for Year 1, Year 2, and Year 3.
   b. Prepare an income statement for Year 1, Year 2, and Year 3.
4. Compare the net operating income figures that you computed in requirements 2 and 3 to the break-even point that you computed in requirement 1. Which net operating income figures seem counterintuitive? Why?

PROBLEM 6–19A   Variable Costing Income Statement; Reconciliation [LO6–2, LO6–3]

During Heaton Company's first two years of operations, the company reported absorption costing net operating income as follows:

	Year 1	Year 2
Sales (@ $25 per unit)	$1,000,000	$1,250,000
Cost of goods sold (@ $18 per unit)	720,000	900,000
Gross margin	280,000	350,000
Selling and administrative expenses*	210,000	230,000
Net operating income	$ 70,000	$ 120,000

*$2 per unit variable; $130,000 fixed each year.

The company's $18 unit product cost is computed as follows:

Direct materials	$ 4
Direct labor	7
Variable manufacturing overhead	1
Fixed manufacturing overhead ($270,000 ÷ 45,000 units)	6
Absorption costing unit product cost	$18

Forty percent of fixed manufacturing overhead consists of wages and salaries; the remainder consists of depreciation charges on production equipment and buildings.

Production and cost data for the two years are

	Year 1	Year 2
Units produced	45,000	45,000
Units sold	40,000	50,000

Required:
1. Prepare a variable costing contribution format income statement for each year.
2. Reconcile the absorption costing and the variable costing net operating income figures for each year.

PROBLEM 6–20A Variable and Absorption Costing Unit Product Costs and Income Statements; Explanation of Difference in Net Operating Income [LO6–1, LO6–2, LO6–3]

High Country, Inc., produces and sells many recreational products. The company has just opened a new plant to produce a folding camp cot that will be marketed throughout the United States. The following cost and revenue data relate to May, the first month of the plant's operation:

Beginning inventory	0
Units produced	10,000
Units sold	8,000
Selling price per unit	$75
Selling and administrative expenses:	
Variable per unit	$6
Fixed (per month)	$200,000
Manufacturing costs:	
Direct materials cost per unit	$20
Direct labor cost per unit	$8
Variable manufacturing overhead cost per unit	$2
Fixed manufacturing overhead cost (per month)	$100,000

Management is anxious to see how profitable the new camp cot will be and has asked that an income statement be prepared for May.

Required:
1. Assume that the company uses absorption costing.
   a. Determine the unit product cost.
   b. Prepare an income statement for May.
2. Assume that the company uses variable costing.
   a. Determine the unit product cost.
   b. Prepare a contribution format income statement for May.
3. Explain the reason for any difference in the ending inventory balances under the two costing methods and the impact of this difference on reported net operating income.

PROBLEM 6–21A Segment Reporting and Decision-Making [LO6–4]

Vulcan Company's contribution format income statement for June is given below:

Vulcan Company Income Statement For the Month Ended June 30	
Sales	$750,000
Variable expenses	336,000
Contribution margin	414,000
Fixed expenses	378,000
Net operating income	$ 36,000

Management is disappointed with the company's performance and is wondering what can be done to improve profits. By examining sales and cost records, you have determined the following:

a. The company is divided into two sales territories—Northern and Southern. The Northern territory recorded $300,000 in sales and $156,000 in variable expenses during June; the remaining sales and variable expenses were recorded in the Southern territory. Fixed expenses of $120,000 and $108,000 are traceable to the Northern and Southern territories, respectively. The rest of the fixed expenses are common to the two territories.

b. The company is the exclusive distributor for two products—Paks and Tibs. Sales of Paks and Tibs totaled $50,000 and $250,000, respectively, in the Northern territory during June. Variable expenses are 22% of the selling price for Paks and 58% for Tibs. Cost records show that $30,000 of the Northern territory's fixed expenses are traceable to Paks and $40,000 to Tibs, with the remainder common to the two products.

Required:

1. Prepare contribution format segmented income statements first showing the total company broken down between sales territories and then showing the Northern territory broken down by product line. In addition, for the company as a whole and for each segment, show each item on the segmented income statements as a percent of sales.

2. Look at the statement you have prepared showing the total company segmented by sales territory. What insights revealed by this statement should be brought to the attention of management?

3. Look at the statement you have prepared showing the Northern territory segmented by product lines. What insights revealed by this statement should be brought to the attention of management?

PROBLEM 6–22A   Prepare and Reconcile Variable Costing Statements [LO6–1, LO6–2, LO6–3]
Denton Company manufactures and sells a single product. Cost data for the product are given below:

Variable costs per unit:	
Direct materials	$ 7
Direct labor	10
Variable manufacturing overhead	5
Variable selling and administrative	3
Total variable cost per unit	$25
Fixed costs per month:	
Fixed manufacturing overhead	$315,000
Fixed selling and administrative	245,000
Total fixed cost per month	$560,000

The product sells for $60 per unit. Production and sales data for July and August, the first two months of operations, follow:

	Units Produced	Units Sold
July	17,500	15,000
August	17,500	20,000

The company's Accounting Department has prepared absorption costing income statements for July and August as presented below:

	July	August
Sales	$900,000	$1,200,000
Cost of goods sold	600,000	800,000
Gross margin	300,000	400,000
Selling and administrative expenses	290,000	305,000
Net operating income	$ 10,000	$ 95,000

Required:
1. Determine the unit product cost under:
   a. Absorption costing.
   b. Variable costing.
2. Prepare contribution format variable costing income statements for July and August.
3. Reconcile the variable costing and absorption costing net operating income figures.
4. The company's Accounting Department has determined the company's break-even point to be 16,000 units per month, computed as follows:

$$\frac{\text{Fixed cost per month}}{\text{Unit contribution margin}} = \frac{\$560,000}{\$35 \text{ per unit}} = 16,000 \text{ units}$$

"I'm confused," said the president. "The accounting people say that our break-even point is 16,000 units per month, but we sold only 15,000 units in July, and the income statement they prepared shows a $10,000 profit for that month. Either the income statement is wrong or the break-even point is wrong." Prepare a brief memo for the president, explaining what happened on the July absorption costing income statement.

PROBLEM 6–23A Absorption and Variable Costing; Production Constant, Sales Fluctuate [LO6–1, LO6–2, LO6–3]

Tami Tyler opened Tami's Creations, Inc., a small manufacturing company, at the beginning of the year. Getting the company through its first quarter of operations placed a considerable strain on Ms. Tyler's personal finances. The following income statement for the first quarter was prepared by a friend who has just completed a course in managerial accounting at State University.

Tami's Creations, Inc.
Income Statement
For the Quarter Ended March 31

Sales (28,000 units)		$1,120,000
Variable expenses:		
Variable cost of goods sold	$462,000	
Variable selling and administrative	168,000	630,000
Contribution margin		490,000
Fixed expenses:		
Fixed manufacturing overhead	300,000	
Fixed selling and administrative	200,000	500,000
Net operating loss		$ (10,000)

Ms. Tyler is discouraged over the loss shown for the quarter, particularly because she had planned to use the statement as support for a bank loan. Another friend, a CPA, insists that the company should be using absorption costing rather than variable costing and argues that if absorption costing had been used the company probably would have reported at least some profit for the quarter.

At this point, Ms. Tyler is manufacturing only one product, a swimsuit. Production and cost data relating to the swimsuit for the first quarter follow:

Units produced	30,000
Units sold	28,000
Variable costs per unit:	
Direct materials	$3.50
Direct labor	$12.00
Variable manufacturing overhead	$1.00
Variable selling and administrative	$6.00

Required:
1. Complete the following:
   a. Compute the unit product cost under absorption costing.
   b. Redo the company's income statement for the quarter using absorption costing.
   c. Reconcile the variable and absorption costing net operating income (loss) figures.

2. Was the CPA correct in suggesting that the company really earned a "profit" for the quarter? Explain.
3. During the second quarter of operations, the company again produced 30,000 units but sold 32,000 units. (Assume no change in total fixed costs.)
   a. Prepare a contribution format income statement for the quarter using variable costing.
   b. Prepare an income statement for the quarter using absorption costing.
   c. Reconcile the variable costing and absorption costing net operating incomes.

PROBLEM 6–24A Companywide and Segment Break-Even Analysis; Decision Making [LO6–4, LO6–5]
Toxaway Company is a merchandiser that segments its business into two divisions—Commercial and Residential. The company's accounting intern was asked to prepare segmented income statements that the company's divisional managers could use to calculate their break-even points and make decisions. She took the prior month's companywide income statement and prepared the absorption format segmented income statement shown below:

	Total Company	Commercial	Residential
Sales	$750,000	$250,000	$500,000
Cost of goods sold	500,000	140,000	360,000
Gross margin	250,000	110,000	140,000
Selling and administrative expenses	240,000	104,000	136,000
Net operating income	$ 10,000	$ 6,000	$ 4,000

In preparing these statements, the intern determined that Toxaway's only variable selling and administrative expense is a 10% sales commission on all sales. The company's total fixed expenses include $72,000 of common fixed expenses that would continue to be incurred even if the Commercial or Residential segments are discontinued, $38,000 of fixed expenses that would be avoided if the Residential segment is dropped, and $55,000 of fixed expenses that would be avoided if the Commericial segment is dropped.

Required:
1. Do you agree with the intern's decision to use an absorption format for her segmented income statement? Why?
2. Based on the intern's segmented income statement, can you determine how she allocated the company's common fixed expenses to the Commercial and Residential segments? Do you agree with her decision to allocate the common fixed expenses to the Commercial and Residential segments?
3. Redo the intern's segmented income statement using the contribution format.
4. Compute the companywide break-even point in dollar sales.
5. Compute the break-even point in dollar sales for the Commercial Division and for the Residential Division.
6. Assume the company decided to pay its sales representatives in the Commercial and Residential Divisions a total monthly salary of $15,000 and $30,000, respectively, and to lower its companywide sales commission percentage from 10% to 5%. Calculate the new break-even point in dollar sales for the Commercial Division and the Residential Division.

PROBLEM 6–25A Prepare and Interpret Income Statements; Changes in Both Sales and Production; Lean Production [LO6–1, LO6–2, LO6–3]
Starfax, Inc., manufactures a small part that is widely used in various electronic products such as home computers. Operating results for the first three years of activity were as follows (absorption costing basis):

	Year 1	Year 2	Year 3
Sales	$800,000	$640,000	$800,000
Cost of goods sold	580,000	400,000	620,000
Gross margin	220,000	240,000	180,000
Selling and administrative expenses	190,000	180,000	190,000
Net operating income (loss)	$ 30,000	$ 60,000	$ (10,000)

In the latter part of Year 2, a competitor went out of business and in the process dumped a large number of units on the market. As a result, Starfax's sales dropped by 20% during Year 2 even though production increased during the year. Management had expected sales to remain constant at 50,000 units; the increased production was designed to provide the company with a buffer of protection against unexpected spurts in demand. By the start of Year 3, management could see that inventory was excessive and that spurts in demand were unlikely. To reduce the excessive inventories, Starfax cut back production during Year 3, as shown below:

	Year 1	Year 2	Year 3
Production in units	50,000	60,000	40,000
Sales in units	50,000	40,000	50,000

Additional information about the company follows:

a. The company's plant is highly automated. Variable manufacturing expenses (direct materials, direct labor, and variable manufacturing overhead) total only $2 per unit, and fixed manufacturing overhead expenses total $480,000 per year.

b. Fixed manufacturing overhead costs are applied to units of product on the basis of each year's production. That is, a new fixed manufacturing overhead rate is computed each year.

c. Variable selling and administrative expenses were $1 per unit sold in each year. Fixed selling and administrative expenses totaled $140,000 per year.

d. The company uses a FIFO inventory flow assumption.

Starfax's management can't understand why profits doubled during Year 2 when sales dropped by 20% and why a loss was incurred during Year 3 when sales recovered to previous levels.

Required:

1. Prepare a contribution format variable costing income statement for each year.
2. Refer to the absorption costing income statements on the previous page.
   a. Compute the unit product cost in each year under absorption costing. (Show how much of this cost is variable and how much is fixed.)
   b. Reconcile the variable costing and absorption costing net operating income figures for each year.
3. Refer again to the absorption costing income statements. Explain why net operating income was higher in Year 2 than it was in Year 1 under the absorption approach, in light of the fact that fewer units were sold in Year 2 than in Year 1.
4. Refer again to the absorption costing income statements. Explain why the company suffered a loss in Year 3 but reported a profit in Year 1 although the same number of units was sold in each year.
5. a. Explain how operations would have differed in Year 2 and Year 3 if the company had been using Lean Production, with the result that ending inventory was zero.
   b. If Lean Production had been used during Year 2 and Year 3 and the predetermined overhead rate is based on 50,000 units per year, what would the company's net operating income (or loss) have been in each year under absorption costing? Explain the reason for any differences between these income figures and the figures reported by the company in the statements above.

PROBLEM 6–26A   Restructuring a Segmented Income Statement [LO6–4]
Losses have been incurred at Millard Corporation for some time. In an effort to isolate the problem and improve the company's performance, management has requested that the monthly income statement be segmented by sales region. The company's first effort at preparing a segmented statement is given below. This statement is for May, the most recent month of activity.

	Sales Region		
	West	**Central**	**East**
Sales	$450,000	$800,000	$ 750,000
Regional expenses (traceable):			
Cost of goods sold	162,900	280,000	376,500
Advertising	108,000	200,000	210,000
Salaries	90,000	88,000	135,000
Utilities	13,500	12,000	15,000
Depreciation	27,000	28,000	30,000
Shipping expense	17,100	32,000	28,500
Total regional expenses	418,500	640,000	795,000
Regional income (loss) before corporate expenses ...	31,500	160,000	(45,000)
Corporate expenses:			
Advertising (general)	18,000	32,000	30,000
General administrative expense ..	50,000	50,000	50,000
Total corporate expenses	68,000	82,000	80,000
Net operating income (loss)	$ (36,500)	$ 78,000	$(125,000)

Cost of goods sold and shipping expense are both variable; other costs are all fixed.

Millard Corporation is a wholesale distributor of office products. It purchases office products from manufacturers and distributes them in the three regions given above. The three regions are about the same size, and each has its own manager and sales staff. The products that the company distributes vary widely in profitability.

Required:
1. List any disadvantages or weaknesses that you see to the statement format illustrated on the previous page.
2. Explain the basis that is apparently being used to allocate the corporate expenses to the regions. Do you agree with these allocations? Explain.
3. Prepare a new contribution format segmented income statement for May. Show a Total column as well as data for each region. In addition, for the company as a whole and for each sales region, show each item on the segmented income statement as a percent of sales.
4. Analyze the statement that you prepared in part (3) above. What points that might help to improve the company's performance would you bring to management's attention?

BUILDING YOUR SKILLS

ETHICS CHALLENGE [LO6–2]

Carlos Cavalas, the manager of Echo Products' Brazilian Division, is trying to set the production schedule for the last quarter of the year. The Brazilian Division had planned to sell 3,600 units during the year, but by September 30 only the following activity had been reported:

	Units
Inventory, January 1	0
Production	2,400
Sales	2,000
Inventory, September 30	400

The division can rent warehouse space to store up to 1,000 units. The minimum inventory level that the division should carry is 50 units. Mr. Cavalas is aware that production must be at least 200 units per quarter in order to retain a nucleus of key employees. Maximum production capacity is 1,500 units per quarter.

Demand has been soft, and the sales forecast for the last quarter is only 600 units. Due to the nature of the division's operations, fixed manufacturing overhead is a major element of product cost.

Required:
1. Assume that the division is using variable costing. How many units should be scheduled for production during the last quarter of the year? (The basic formula for computing the required production for a period in a company is Expected sales + Desired ending inventory − Beginning inventory = Required production.) Show computations and explain your answer. Will the number of units scheduled for production affect the division's reported income or loss for the year? Explain.
2. Assume that the division is using absorption costing and that the divisional manager is given an annual bonus based on divisional operating income. If Mr. Cavalas wants to maximize his division's operating income for the year, how many units should be scheduled for production during the last quarter? [See the formula in (1) above.] Explain.
3. Identify the ethical issues involved in the decision Mr. Cavalas must make about the level of production for the last quarter of the year.

ANALYTICAL THINKING [LO6–4]

Diversified Products, Inc., has recently acquired a small publishing company that offers three books for sale—a cookbook, a travel guide, and a handy speller. Each book sells for $10. The publishing company's most recent monthly income statement is given on the next page:

			Product Line	
	Total Company	Cookbook	Travel Guide	Handy Speller
Sales	$300,000	$90,000	$150,000	$60,000
Expenses:				
Printing costs	102,000	27,000	63,000	12,000
Advertising	36,000	13,500	19,500	3,000
General sales	18,000	5,400	9,000	3,600
Salaries	33,000	18,000	9,000	6,000
Equipment depreciation	9,000	3,000	3,000	3,000
Sales commissions	30,000	9,000	15,000	6,000
General administration	42,000	14,000	14,000	14,000
Warehouse rent	12,000	3,600	6,000	2,400
Depreciation—office facilities	3,000	1,000	1,000	1,000
Total expenses	285,000	94,500	139,500	51,000
Net operating income (loss)	$ 15,000	$ (4,500)	$ 10,500	$ 9,000

The following additional information is available about the company:

a. Only printing costs and sales commissions are variable; all other costs are fixed. The printing costs (which include materials, labor, and variable overhead) are traceable to the three product lines as shown in the statement above. Sales commissions are 10% of sales for any product.

b. The same equipment is used to produce all three books, so the equipment depreciation cost has been allocated equally among the three product lines. An analysis of the company's activities indicates that the equipment is used 30% of the time to produce cookbooks, 50% of the time to produce travel guides, and 20% of the time to produce handy spellers.

c. The warehouse is used to store finished units of product, so the rental cost has been allocated to the product lines on the basis of sales dollars. The warehouse rental cost is $3 per square foot per year. The warehouse contains 48,000 square feet of space, of which 7,200 square feet is used by the cookbook line, 24,000 square feet by the travel guide line, and 16,800 square feet by the handy speller line.

d. The general sales cost above includes the salary of the sales manager and other sales costs not traceable to any specific product line. This cost has been allocated to the product lines on the basis of sales dollars.

e. The general administration cost and depreciation of office facilities both relate to administration of the company as a whole. These costs have been allocated equally to the three product lines.

f. All other costs are traceable to the three product lines in the amounts shown on the statement above.

The management of Diversified Products, Inc., is anxious to improve the publishing company's 5% return on sales.

Required:

1. Prepare a new contribution format segmented income statement for the month. Adjust allocations of equipment depreciation and of warehouse rent as indicated by the additional information provided.

2. After seeing the income statement in the main body of the problem, management has decided to eliminate the cookbook because it is not returning a profit, and to focus all available resources on promoting the travel guide.

   a. Based on the statement you have prepared, do you agree with the decision to eliminate the cookbook? Explain.

   b. Based on the statement you have prepared, do you agree with the decision to focus all available resources on promoting the travel guide? Assume that an ample market is available for all three product lines. (*Hint:* Compute the contribution margin ratio for each product.)

CASE [LO6–4]

Music Teachers, Inc., is an educational association for music teachers that has 20,000 members. The association operates from a central headquarters but has local membership chapters throughout the United States. Monthly meetings are held by the local chapters to discuss recent developments on topics of interest to music teachers. The association's journal, Teachers' Forum, is issued monthly with features about recent developments in the field. The association publishes books and reports and also sponsors professional courses that qualify for continuing professional education credit. The association's statement of revenues and expenses for the current year is presented below.

Music Teachers, Inc. Statement of Revenues and Expenses For the Year Ended November 30	
Revenues	$3,275,000
Expenses:	
Salaries	920,000
Personnel costs	230,000
Occupancy costs	280,000
Reimbursement of member costs to local chapters	600,000
Other membership services	500,000
Printing and paper	320,000
Postage and shipping	176,000
Instructors' fees	80,000
General and administrative	38,000
Total expenses	3,144,000
Excess of revenues over expenses	$ 131,000

The board of directors of Music Teachers, Inc., has requested that a segmented income statement be prepared showing the contribution of each segment to the association. The association has four segments: Membership Division, Magazine Subscriptions Division, Books and Reports Division, and Continuing Education Division. Mike Doyle has been assigned responsibility for preparing the segmented income statement, and he has gathered the following data prior to its preparation.

a. Membership dues are $100 per year, of which $20 is considered to cover a one-year subscription to the association's journal. Other benefits include membership in the association and chapter affiliation. The portion of the dues covering the magazine subscription ($20) should be assigned to the Magazine Subscription Division.

b. One-year subscriptions to Teachers' Forum were sold to nonmembers and libraries at $30 per subscription. A total of 2,500 of these subscriptions were sold last year. In addition to subscriptions, the magazine generated $100,000 in advertising revenues. The costs per magazine subscription were $7 for printing and paper and $4 for postage and shipping.

c. A total of 28,000 technical reports and professional texts were sold by the Books and Reports Division at an average unit selling price of $25. Average costs per publication were $4 for printing and paper and $2 for postage and shipping.

d. The association offers a variety of continuing education courses to both members and nonmembers. The one-day courses had a tuition cost of $75 each and were attended by 2,400 students. A total of 1,760 students took two-day courses at a tuition cost of $125 for each student. Outside instructors were paid to teach some courses.

e. Salary costs and space occupied by division follow:

	Salaries	Space Occupied (square feet)
Membership	$210,000	2,000
Magazine Subscriptions	150,000	2,000
Books and Reports	300,000	3,000
Continuing Education	180,000	2,000
Corporate staff	80,000	1,000
Total	$920,000	10,000

Personnel costs are 25% of salaries in the separate divisions as well as for the corporate staff. The $280,000 in occupancy costs includes $50,000 in rental cost for a warehouse used by the Books and Reports Division for storage purposes.

f.   Printing and paper costs other than for magazine subscriptions and for books and reports relate to the Continuing Education Division.

g.   General and administrative expenses include costs relating to overall administration of the association as a whole. The company's corporate staff does some mailing of materials for general administrative purposes.

The expenses that can be traced or assigned to the corporate staff, as well as any other expenses that are not traceable to the segments, will be treated as common costs. It is not necessary to distinguish between variable and fixed costs.

Required:

1.   Prepare a contribution format segmented income statement for Music Teachers, Inc. This statement should show the segment margin for each division as well as results for the association as a whole.

2.   Give arguments for and against allocating all costs of the association to the four divisions.

(CMA, adapted)

A LOOK BACK

Chapter 6 explained how the contribution format can be used to create variable costing income statements for manufacturers and segmented income statements that distinguish between traceable fixed costs and common fixed costs. It also contrasted variable costing with the absorption format.

A LOOK AT THIS CHAPTER

After discussing why organizations prepare budgets and the process they use to create a budget, Chapter 7 overviews each of the parts of a master budget including the cash budget, the budgeted income statement, and the budgeted balance sheet.

A LOOK AHEAD

In Chapter 8, we turn our attention from the planning process to management control, focusing on the use of flexible budgets and variance analysis.

7 Master Budgeting

CHAPTER OUTLINE

What Is a Budget?

- Advantages of Budgeting
- Responsibility Accounting
- Choosing a Budget Period
- The Self-Imposed Budget
- Human Factors in Budgeting

The Master Budget: An Overview

- Seeing the Big Picture

Preparing the Master Budget

- The Beginning Balance Sheet
- The Budgeting Assumptions

- The Sales Budget
- The Production Budget
- Inventory Purchases—Merchandising Company
- The Direct Materials Budget
- The Direct Labor Budget
- The Manufacturing Overhead Budget
- The Ending Finished Goods Inventory Budget
- The Selling and Administrative Expense Budget
- The Cash Budget
- The Budgeted Income Statement
- The Budgeted Balance Sheet

Planning for a Crisis—Civil War Trust

The **Civil War Trust** (CWT) is a private, nonprofit organization with 70,000 members that works to preserve the nation's remaining Civil War battlefields—many of which are threatened by commercial development such as shopping centers, houses, industrial parks, and casinos. To forestall development, the CWT typically purchases the land or development rights to the land. The CWT has saved over 25,000 acres from development, including, for example, 698 acres of battlefield at Gettysburg.

CWT's management team was particularly concerned about the budget proposal for 2009, which was to be presented to the board of directors in the fall of 2008. The CWT is wholly supported by contributions from its members and many of those members had been adversely affected by the ongoing financial crisis that followed the collapse of the subprime mortgage market. Consequently, the funds that would be available for operations in 2009 were particularly difficult to predict. Accordingly, the budget for 2009 contained three variations based on progressively pessimistic economic assumptions. The more pessimistic budgets were called contingent budgets. As 2008 progressed and member contributions declined somewhat from previous levels, CWT switched to the first contingent budget. This contingent budget required a number of actions to reduce costs including a hiring freeze and a salary freeze, but maintained an aggressive program of protecting battlefield acreage through purchases of land and development rights. Fortunately, the CWT did not have to switch to the most pessimistic budget—which would have involved layoffs and other extraordinary cost-saving measures.

Instead of reacting in a panic mode to unfavorable developments, CWT used the budgeting process to carefully plan in advance for a number of possible contingencies.

Sources: Communications with James Lighthizer, president, and David Duncan, director of membership and development, Civil War Trust; and the CWT website, civilwar.org.

In this chapter, we describe how organizations strive to achieve their financial goals by preparing a number of budgets that together form an integrated business plan known as the *master budget*. The master budget is an essential management tool that communicates management's plans throughout the organization, allocates resources, and coordinates activities.

WHAT IS A BUDGET?

A **budget** is a detailed plan for the future that is usually expressed in formal quantitative terms. Individuals sometimes create household budgets that balance their income and expenditures for food, clothing, housing, and so on while providing for some savings. Once the budget is established, actual spending is compared to the budget to make sure the plan is being followed. Companies use budgets in a similar way, although the amount of work and underlying details far exceed a personal budget.

Budgets are used for two distinct purposes—*planning* and *control*. **Planning** involves developing goals and preparing various budgets to achieve those goals. **Control** involves gathering feedback to ensure that the plan is being properly executed or modified as circumstances change. To be effective, a good budgeting system must provide for both planning and control. Good planning without effective control is a waste of time and effort.

Advantages of Budgeting

Organizations realize many benefits from budgeting, including:

1. Budgets *communicate* management's plans throughout the organization.
2. Budgets force managers to *think about* and *plan* for the future. In the absence of the necessity to prepare a budget, many managers would spend all of their time dealing with day-to-day emergencies.
3. The budgeting process provides a means of *allocating resources* to those parts of the organization where they can be used most effectively.
4. The budgeting process can uncover potential *bottlenecks* before they occur.
5. Budgets *coordinate* the activities of the entire organization by *integrating* the plans of its various parts. Budgeting helps to ensure that everyone in the organization is pulling in the same direction.
6. Budgets define goals and objectives that can serve as *benchmarks* for evaluating subsequent performance.

IN BUSINESS   Executing Strategy with Budgets

Robert DeMartini, the CEO of **New Balance**, set a goal of tripling his company's revenues to $3 billion in four years. He tripled the company's annual advertising budget and doubled its consumer research budget in an effort to attract more young customers. These decisions represented a strategic shift for New Balance, which usually spends less than $20 million per year in advertising compared to competitors such as **Nike** and **Adidas**, which annually invest $184 million and $80 million, respectively.

One reason companies prepare budgets is to allocate resources across departments in a manner that supports strategic priorities. DeMartini used the budget to send a clear signal that his marketing department was expected to play a huge role in achieving the company's revenue growth targets.

Source: Stephanie Kang, "New Balance Steps up Marketing Drive," *The Wall Street Journal*, March 21, 2008, p. B3.

Responsibility Accounting

Most of what we say in this chapter and in the next three chapters is concerned with *responsibility accounting*. The basic idea underlying **responsibility accounting** is that a manager should be held responsible for those items—and *only* those items—that the manager can actually control to a significant extent. Each line item (i.e., revenue or cost) in the budget is the responsibility of a manager who is held responsible for subsequent deviations between budgeted goals and actual results. In effect, responsibility accounting *personalizes* accounting information by holding individuals responsible for revenues and costs. This concept is central to any effective planning and control system. Someone must be held responsible for each cost or else no one will be responsible and the cost will inevitably grow out of control.

What happens if actual results do not measure up to the budgeted goals? The manager is not necessarily penalized. However, the manager should take the initiative to understand the sources of significant favorable or unfavorable discrepancies, should take steps to correct unfavorable discrepancies and to exploit and replicate favorable discrepancies, and should be prepared to explain discrepancies and the steps taken to correct or exploit them to higher management. The point of an effective responsibility accounting system is to make sure that nothing "falls through the cracks," that the organization reacts quickly and appropriately to deviations from its plans, and that the organization learns from the feedback it gets by comparing budgeted goals to actual results. The point is *not* to penalize individuals for missing targets.

Small Businesses Are Cutting the Number of Employees

IN BUSINESS

Costume Specialists had to decrease its workforce by 20% when the economy tanked. However, when sales began to surge the company did not budget for a workforce expansion because it had learned to function more efficiently with fewer employees. Many other small businesses have also "tightened their budgeting belts" by choosing to operate with fewer employees. In some cases, these companies have used methods such as cross-training their employees to improve efficiency. However, in other cases they are using contract workers instead of hiring full-time employees to avoid the cost of providing full-time employees with fringe benefits such as health insurance.

Source: Sarah E. Needleman, "Entrepreneurs Prefer to Keep Staffs Lean," *The Wall Street Journal*, March 2, 2010, p. B5.

Choosing a Budget Period

Operating budgets ordinarily cover a one-year period corresponding to the company's fiscal year. Many companies divide their budget year into four quarters. The first quarter is then subdivided into months, and monthly budgets are developed. The last three quarters may be carried in the budget as quarterly totals only. As the year progresses, the figures for the second quarter are broken down into monthly amounts, then the third-quarter figures are broken down, and so forth. This approach has the advantage of requiring periodic review and reappraisal of budget data throughout the year.

Continuous or *perpetual budgets* are sometimes used. A **continuous** or **perpetual budget** is a 12-month budget that rolls forward one month (or quarter) as the current month (or quarter) is completed. In other words, one month (or quarter) is added to the end of the budget as each month (or quarter) comes to a close. This approach keeps managers focused at least one year ahead so that they do not become too narrowly focused on short-term results.

In this chapter, we will look at one-year operating budgets. However, using basically the same techniques, operating budgets can be prepared for periods that extend over many years. It may be difficult to accurately forecast sales and other data much beyond a year, but even rough estimates can be invaluable in uncovering potential problems and opportunities that would otherwise be overlooked.

The Self-Imposed Budget

The success of a budget program is largely determined by the way a budget is developed. Oftentimes, the budget is imposed from above, with little participation by lower-level managers. However, in the most successful budget programs, managers actively participate in preparing their own budgets. Imposing expectations from above and then penalizing employees who do not meet those expectations will generate resentment rather than cooperation and commitment. In fact, many managers believe that being empowered to create their own *self-imposed budgets* is the most effective method of budget preparation. A **self-imposed budget** or **participative budget** is a budget that is prepared with the full cooperation and participation of managers at all levels.

Self-imposed budgets have a number of advantages:

1. Individuals at all levels of the organization are recognized as members of the team whose views and judgments are valued by top management.
2. Budget estimates prepared by front-line managers are often more accurate and reliable than estimates prepared by top managers who have less intimate knowledge of markets and day-to-day operations.
3. Motivation is generally higher when individuals participate in setting their own goals than when the goals are imposed from above. Self-imposed budgets create commitment.
4. A manager who is not able to meet a budget that has been imposed from above can always say that the budget was unrealistic and impossible to meet. With a self-imposed budget, this claim cannot be made.

Self-imposed budgeting has two important limitations. First, lower-level managers may make suboptimal budgeting recommendations if they lack the broad strategic perspective possessed by top managers. Second, self-imposed budgeting may allow lower-level managers to create too much *budgetary slack*. Because the manager who creates the budget will be held accountable for actual results that deviate from the budget, the manager will have a natural tendency to submit a budget that is easy to attain (i.e., the manager will build slack into the budget). For this reason, budgets prepared by lower-level managers should be scrutinized by higher levels of management. Questionable items should be discussed and modified as appropriate. Without such a review, self-imposed budgets may fail to support the organization's strategy or may be too slack, resulting in suboptimal performance.

Unfortunately, many companies do not use self-imposed budgeting. Instead, top managers often initiate the budgeting process by issuing profit targets. Lower-level managers are directed to prepare budgets that meet those targets. The difficulty is that the targets set by top managers may be unrealistically high or may allow too much slack. If the targets are too high and employees know they are unrealistic, motivation will suffer. If the targets allow too much slack, waste will occur. Unfortunately, top managers are often not in a position to know whether the targets are appropriate. Admittedly, a self-imposed budgeting system may lack sufficient strategic direction and lower-level managers may be tempted to build slack into their budgets. Nevertheless, because of the motivational advantages of self-imposed budgets, top managers should be cautious about imposing inflexible targets from above.

Human Factors in Budgeting

The success of a budget program also depends on whether top management uses the budget to pressure or blame employees. Using budgets to blame employees breeds hostility, tension, and mistrust rather than cooperation and productivity. Unfortunately, the budget is too often used as a pressure device and excessive emphasis is placed on "meeting the budget" under all circumstances. Rather than being used as a weapon, the budget should be used as a positive instrument to assist in establishing goals, measuring operating results, and isolating areas that need attention.

The budgeting process is also influenced by the fact that bonuses are often based on meeting and exceeding budgets. Typically, no bonus is paid unless the budget is met. The bonus often increases when the budget target is exceeded, but the bonus is usually capped out at some level. For obvious reasons, managers who have such a bonus plan or whose performance is evaluated based on meeting budget targets usually prefer to be evaluated based on highly achievable budgets. Moreover, highly achievable budgets may help build a manager's confidence and generate greater commitment to the budget while also reducing the likelihood that a manager will engage in undesirable behavior at the end of budgetary periods to secure bonus compensation. So, while some experts argue that budget targets should be very challenging and should require managers to stretch to meet their goals, in practice, most companies set their budget targets at "highly achievable" levels.

CONCEPT CHECK

1. Which of the following statements is false? (You may select more than one answer.)
   a. Control involves gathering feedback to ensure that the plan is being properly executed or modified as circumstances change.
   b. Responsibility accounting is based on the belief that all managers should be held accountable for achieving the company's overall goals, even if this requires holding some managers responsible for items that are beyond their control.
   c. A self-imposed budget is prepared with the full cooperation and participation of managers at all levels of the organization.
   d. One limitation of self-imposed budgets is that lower-level managers may allow too much budgetary slack.

THE MASTER BUDGET: AN OVERVIEW

The **master budget** consists of a number of separate but interdependent budgets that formally lay out the company's sales, production, and financial goals. The master budget culminates in a cash budget, a budgeted income statement, and a budgeted balance sheet. Exhibit 7–1 provides an overview of the various parts of the master budget and how they are related.

The first step in the budgeting process is the preparation of the **sales budget**, which is a detailed schedule showing the expected sales for the budget period. An accurate sales budget is the key to the entire budgeting process. As illustrated in Exhibit 7–1, all other parts of the master budget depend on the sales budget. If the sales budget is inaccurate, the rest of the budget will be inaccurate. The sales budget is based on the company's sales forecast, which may require the use of sophisticated mathematical models and statistical tools that are beyond the scope of this course.

The sales budget influences the variable portion of the selling and administrative expense budget and it feeds into the production budget, which defines how many units need to be produced during the budget period. The production budget in turn is used to determine the direct materials, direct labor, and manufacturing overhead budgets. Once a company has prepared these three manufacturing cost budgets, it can prepare the ending finished goods inventory budget.

The master budget concludes with the preparation of a cash budget, income statement, and balance sheet. Information from the sales budget, selling and administrative expense budget, and the manufacturing cost budgets all influence the preparation of the *cash budget*. A **cash budget** is a detailed plan showing how cash resources will be acquired and used. The budgeted income statement provides an estimate of net income for the budget period and it relies on information from the sales budget, ending finished goods inventory budget, selling and administrative expense budget, and the cash budget. The final schedule of the master budget is the balance sheet, which estimates a company's assets, liabilities, and stockholders' equity at the end of a budget period.

EXHIBIT 7–1
The Master Budget
Interrelationships

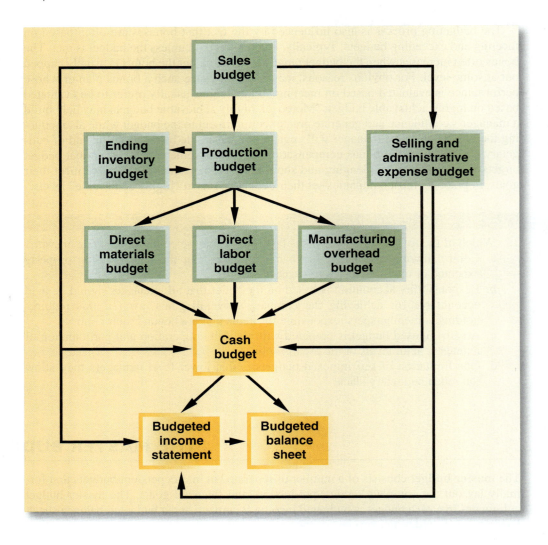

Seeing the Big Picture

The 10 schedules contained in a master budget can be overwhelming; therefore, it is important to see the big picture in two respects. First, a master budget for a manufacturing company is designed to answer 10 key questions as follows:

1. How much sales revenue will we earn?
2. How much cash will we collect from customers?
3. How much raw material will we need to purchase?
4. How much manufacturing cost (including direct materials, direct labor, and manufacturing overhead) will we incur?
5. How much cash will we pay to our suppliers and our direct laborers, and how much will we pay for manufacturing overhead resources?
6. What is the total cost that will be transferred from finished goods inventory to cost of goods sold?
7. How much selling and administrative expense will we incur and how much cash will we pay related to those expenses?
8. How much money will we borrow from or repay to lenders—including interest?
9. How much net operating income will we earn?
10. What will our balance sheet look like at the end of the budget period?

Second, it is important to understand that many of the schedules in a master budget hinge on a variety of estimates and assumptions that managers must make when preparing

EXHIBIT 7–2
Estimates and Assumptions
for a Master Budget

Sales budget:
1. What are the budgeted unit sales?
2. What is the budgeted selling price per unit?
3. What percentage of accounts receivable will be collected in the current and subsequent periods?

Production budget:
1. What percentage of next period's unit sales needs to be maintained in ending finished goods inventory?

Direct materials budget:
1. How many units of raw material are needed to make one unit of finished goods?
2. What is the budgeted cost for one unit of raw material?
3. What percentage of next period's production needs should be maintained in ending raw materials inventory?
4. What percentage of raw material purchases will be paid in the current and subsequent periods?

Direct labor budget:
1. How many direct labor-hours are required per unit of finished goods?
2. What is the budgeted direct labor wage rate per hour?

Manufacturing overhead budget:
1. What is the budgeted variable overhead cost per unit of the allocation base?
2. What is the total budgeted fixed overhead cost per period?
3. What is the budgeted depreciation expense on factory assets per period?

Selling and administrative expense budget:
1. What is the budgeted variable selling and administrative expense per unit sold?
2. What is the total budgeted fixed selling and administrative expense per period?
3. What is the budgeted depreciation expense on non-factory assets per period?

Cash budget:
1. What is the budgeted minimum cash balance?
2. What are our estimated expenditures for noncurrent asset purchases and dividends?
3. What is the estimated interest rate on borrowed funds?

those schedules. Exhibit 7–2 summarizes the questions that underlie these estimates and assumptions for seven of the schedules included in a master budget. As you study the forthcoming budget schedules, keep these two "big picture" insights in mind—that the budget is designed to answer 10 key questions and that it is based on various estimates and assumptions—because they will help you understand *why* and *how* a master budget is created.

PREPARING THE MASTER BUDGET

**MANAGERIAL
ACCOUNTING IN ACTION**
The Issue

Tom Wills is the majority stockholder and chief executive officer of Hampton Freeze, Inc., a company he started in 2013. The company makes premium popsicles using only natural ingredients and featuring exotic flavors such as tangy tangerine and minty mango. The company's business is highly seasonal, with most of the sales occurring in spring and summer.

In 2014, the company's second year of operations, a major cash crunch in the first and second quarters almost forced the company into bankruptcy. In spite of this cash crunch, 2014 turned out to be a very successful year in terms of both cash flow and net income. Partly as a result of that harrowing experience, Tom decided toward the end of 2014 to hire a professional financial manager. Tom interviewed several promising candidates for the job and settled on Larry Giano, who had considerable experience in the packaged foods industry. In the job interview, Tom questioned Larry about the steps he would take to prevent a recurrence of the 2014 cash crunch:

Tom: As I mentioned earlier, we are going to end 2014 with a very nice profit. What you may not know is that we had some very big financial problems this year.

Larry: Let me guess. You ran out of cash sometime in the first or second quarter.

Tom: How did you know?

Larry: Most of your sales are in the second and third quarter, right?

Tom: Sure, everyone wants to buy popsicles in the spring and summer, but nobody wants them when the weather turns cold.

Larry: So you don't have many sales in the first quarter?

Tom: Right.

Larry: And in the second quarter, which is the spring, you are producing like crazy to fill orders?

Tom: Sure.

Larry: Do your customers, the grocery stores, pay you the day you make your deliveries?

Tom: Are you kidding? Of course not.

Larry: So in the first quarter, you don't have many sales. In the second quarter, you are producing like crazy, which eats up cash, but you aren't paid by your customers until long after you have paid your employees and suppliers. No wonder you had a cash problem. I see this pattern all the time in food processing because of the seasonality of the business.

Tom: So what can we do about it?

Larry: The first step is to predict the magnitude of the problem before it occurs. If we can predict early in the year what the cash shortfall is going to be, we can go to the bank and arrange for credit before we really need it. Bankers tend to be leery of panicky people who show up begging for emergency loans. They are much more likely to make the loan if you look like you are in control of the situation.

Tom: How can we predict the cash shortfall?

Larry: You can put together a cash budget. In fact, while you're at it, you might as well do a master budget. You'll find it well worth the effort because we can use a master budget to estimate the financial statement implications of numerous "what-if" questions. For example, with the click of a mouse we can answer questions such as: What-if unit sales are 10% less than our original forecast, what will be the impact on profits? Or, what if we increase our selling price by 15% and unit sales drop by 5%, what will be the impact on profits?

Tom: That sounds great Larry! Not only do we need a cash budget, but I would love to have a master budget that could quickly answer the types of "what-if" questions that you just described. As far as I'm concerned, the sooner you get started, the better.

With the full backing of Tom Wills, Larry Giano set out to create a master budget for the company for the year 2015. In his planning for the budgeting process, Larry drew up the following list of documents that would be a part of the master budget:

1. A sales budget, including a schedule of expected cash collections.
2. A production budget (a merchandise purchases budget would be used in a merchandising company).
3. A direct materials budget, including a schedule of expected cash disbursements for purchases of materials.
4. A direct labor budget.
5. A manufacturing overhead budget.
6. An ending finished goods inventory budget.
7. A selling and administrative expense budget.

8. A cash budget.
9. A budgeted income statement.
10. A budgeted balance sheet.

Larry felt it was important to have everyone's cooperation in the budgeting process, so he asked Tom to call a companywide meeting to explain the budgeting process. At the meeting there was initially some grumbling, but Tom was able to convince nearly everyone of the necessity for planning and getting better control over spending. It helped that the cash crisis earlier in the year was still fresh in everyone's minds. As much as some people disliked the idea of budgets, they liked their jobs more.

In the months that followed, Larry worked closely with all of the managers involved in the master budget, gathering data from them and making sure that they understood and fully supported the parts of the master budget that would affect them.

The interdependent documents that Larry Giano prepared for Hampton Freeze are Schedules 1 through 10 of the company's master budget. In this section, we will study these schedules as well as the beginning balance sheet and the budgeting assumptions that Larry included in his master budget to help answer the types of "what-if" questions that he discussed with Tom Wills.

The Beginning Balance Sheet

Exhibit 7–3 shows the first tab included in Larry's Microsoft Excel master budget file. It contains Hampton Freeze's beginning balance sheet as of December 31, 2014. Larry included this balance sheet in his master budget file so that he could link some of this data

EXHIBIT 7–3
Hampton Freeze: The Beginning Balance Sheet

	A	B	C
1	**Hampton Freeze, Inc.**		
2	**Balance Sheet**		
3	**December 31, 2014**		
4			
5	**Assets**		
6	Current assets:		
7	Cash	$ 42,500	
8	Accounts receivable	90,000	
9	Raw materials inventory (21,000 pounds)	4,200	
10	Finished goods inventory (2,000 cases)	26,000	
11	Total current assets		$162,700
12	Plant and equipment:		
13	Land	80,000	
14	Buildings and equipment	700,000	
15	Accumulated depreciation	(292,000)	
16	Plant and equipment, net		488,000
17	Total assets		$650,700
18			
19	**Liabilities and Stockholders' Equity**		
20	Current liabilities:		
21	Accounts payable		$ 25,800
22	Stockholders' equity:		
23	Common stock	$ 175,000	
24	Retained earnings	449,900	
25	Total stockholders' equity		624,900
26	Total liabilities and stockholders' equity		$650,700
27			

Beginning Balance Sheet / Budgeting Assump

to subsequent schedules. For example, as you'll eventually see, he used cell references within Excel to link the beginning accounts receivable balance of $90,000 to the schedule of expected cash collections. He also used cell references to link the beginning cash balance of $42,500 to the cash budget.

The Budgeting Assumptions

Exhibit 7–4 shows the second tab included in Larry's master budget file. It is labeled Budgeting Assumptions and it contains all of Hampton Freeze's answers to the questions summarized in Exhibit 7–2. The data included in Exhibit 7–4 summarize the estimates and assumptions that provide the foundation for Hampton Freeze's entire master budget, so it is important to familiarize yourself with this information now. Beginning with the estimates underlying the sales budget, Exhibit 7–4 shows that Hampton Freeze's budgeted quarterly unit sales are 10,000, 30,000, 40,000, and 20,000 cases. Its budgeted selling price

EXHIBIT 7–4   Hampton Freeze: Budgeting Assumptions

	A	B	C	D	E	F
1		Hampton Freeze, Inc.				
2		Budgeting Assumptions				
3		For the Year Ended December 31, 2015				
4						
5			All 4 Quarters		Quarter	
				1	2	3	4
6	Sales Budget						
7	Budgeted sales in cases		10,000	30,000	40,000	20,000
8	Selling price per case	$ 20.00				
9	Percentage of sales collected in the quarter of sale	70%				
10	Percentage of sales collected in the quarter after sale	30%				
11						
12	Production Budget					
13	Percentage of next quarter's sales in ending finished goods inventory	20%				
14						
15	Direct Materials Budget					
16	Pounds of sugar per case	15				
17	Cost per pound of sugar	$ 0.20				
18	Percentage of next quarter's production needs in ending inventory	10%				
19	Percentage of purchases paid in the quarter purchased	50%				
20	Percentage of purchases paid in the quarter after purchase	50%				
21						
22	Direct Labor Budget					
23	Direct labor-hours required per case	0.40				
24	Direct labor cost per hour	$ 15.00				
25						
26	Manufacturing Overhead Budget					
27	Variable manufacturing overhead per direct labor-hour	$ 4.00				
28	Fixed manufacturing overhead per quarter	$ 60,600				
29	Depreciation per quarter	$ 15,000				
30						
31						
32	Selling and Administrative Expense Budget					
33	Variable selling and administrative expense per case	$ 1.80				
34	Fixed selling and administrative expense per quarter:					
35	Advertising	$ 20,000				
36	Executive salaries	$ 55,000				
37	Insurance	$ 10,000				
38	Property tax	$ 4,000				
39	Depreciation	$ 10,000				
40						
41	Cash Budget					
42	Minimum cash balance	$ 30,000				
43	Equipment purchases		$ 50,000	$ 40,000	$ 20,000	$ 20,000
44	Dividends	$ 8,000				
45	Simple interest rate per quarter	3%				
46						

Beginning Balance Sheet / Budgeting Assumptions / Schedule 1 / Schedule 2 / Sche

*For simplicity, we assume that all quarterly estimates, except quarterly unit sales and equipment purchases, will be the same for all four quarters.

is $20 per case. The company expects to collect 70% of its credit sales in the quarter of sale, and the remaining 30% of credit sales will be collected in the quarter after sale.

Exhibit 7–4 also shows that the production budget is based on the assumption that Hampton Freeze will maintain ending finished goods inventory equal to 20% of the next quarter's unit sales. In terms of the company's only direct material, high fructose sugar, it budgets 15 pounds of sugar per case of popsicles at a cost of $0.20 per pound.[1] It expects to maintain ending raw materials inventory equal to 10% of the raw materials needed to satisfy the following quarter's production. In addition, the company plans to pay for 50% of its material purchases within the month of purchase and the remaining 50% in the following month.

Continuing with a summary of Exhibit 7–4, the two key assumptions underlying the direct labor budget are that 0.40 direct labor-hours are required per case of popsicles and the direct labor cost per hour is $15. The manufacturing overhead budget is based on three underlying assumptions—the variable overhead cost per direct labor-hour is $4.00, the total fixed overhead per quarter is $60,600, and the quarterly depreciation on factory assets is $15,000. Exhibit 7–4 also shows that the budgeted variable selling and administrative expense per case of popsicles is $1.80 and the fixed selling and administrative expenses per quarter include advertising ($20,000), executive salaries ($55,000), insurance ($10,000), property tax ($4,000), and depreciation expense ($10,000). The remaining budget assumptions depicted in Exhibit 7–4 pertain to the cash budget. The company expects to maintain a minimum cash balance each quarter of $30,000; it plans to make quarterly equipment purchases of $50,000, $40,000, $20,000, and $20,000;[2] it plans to pay quarterly dividends of $8,000; and it expects to pay simple interest on borrowed money of 3% per quarter.

Before reading further, it is important to understand why Larry created the Budgeting Assumptions tab shown in Exhibit 7–4. He did it because it simplifies the process of using a master budget to answer "what-if" questions. For example, assume that Larry wanted to answer the question: What-if we increase the selling price per unit by $2 and expect sales to drop by 1,000 units per quarter, what would be the impact on profits? With a properly constructed Budgeting Assumptions tab, Larry would only need to make a few adjustments to the data within this tab and the formulas embedded in each of the budget schedules would automatically update the projected financial results. This is much simpler than attempting to adjust data inputs within each of the master budget schedules.

The Sales Budget

Schedule 1 contains Hampton Freeze's sales budget for 2015. As you study this schedule, keep in mind that all of its numbers are derived from cell references to the Budgeting Assumptions tab and formulas—none of the numbers appearing in the schedule were actually keyed into their respective cells. Furthermore, it bears emphasizing that all remaining schedules in the master budget are prepared in the same fashion—they rely almost exclusively on cell references and formulas.

For the year, Hampton Freeze expects to sell 100,000 cases of popsicles at a price of $20 per case for total budgeted sales of $2,000,000. The budgeted unit sales for each quarter (10,000, 30,000, 40,000, and 20,000) come from cells C7 through F7 in the Budgeting Assumptions tab shown in Exhibit 7–4, and the selling price per case ($20.00) comes from cell B8 in the Budgeting Assumptions tab. Schedule 1 also shows that the company's expected cash collections for 2015 are $1,970,000. The accounts receivable balance of $90,000 that is collected in the first quarter comes from cell B8 of the beginning balance sheet shown in Exhibit 7–3. All other cash collections rely on the estimated cash collection percentages from cells B9 and B10 of the Budgeting Assumptions tab. For example, Schedule 1 shows that the budgeted sales for the first quarter equal

> **LEARNING OBJECTIVE 7–2**
>
> Prepare a sales budget, including a schedule of expected cash collections.

---

[1]While popsicle manufacturing is likely to involve other raw materials, such as popsicle sticks and packaging materials, for simplicity, we have limited our scope to high fructose sugar.

[2]For simplicity, we assume that depreciation on these newly acquired assets is included in the quarterly depreciation estimates included in the Budgeting Assumptions tab.

SCHEDULE 1

	A	B	C	D	E	F
1		**Hampton Freeze, Inc.**				
2		**Sales Budget**				
3		**For the Year Ended December 31, 2015**				
4						
5				*Quarter*		
6		*1*	*2*	*3*	*4*	*Year*
7	Budgeted unit sales (in cases)	10,000	30,000	40,000	20,000	100,000
8	Selling price per unit	$ 20.00	$ 20.00	$ 20.00	$ 20.00	$ 20.00
9	Total sales	$200,000	$600,000	$800,000	$400,000	$2,000,000
10						
11		70%	30%			
12		**Schedule of Expected Cash Collections**				
13	Beginning accounts receivable[1]	$ 90,000				$ 90,000
14	First-quarter sales[2]	140,000	$ 60,000			200,000
15	Second-quarter sales[3]		420,000	$180,000		600,000
16	Third-quarter sales[4]			560,000	$240,000	800,000
17	Fourth-quarter sales[5]	-	-	-	280,000	280,000
18	Total cash collections[6]	$230,000	$480,000	$740,000	$520,000	$1,970,000

Budgeting Assumptions / Schedule 1 / Schedule 2 / Schedule 3 / Sc

[1]Cash collections from last year's fourth-quarter sales. See the beginning balance sheet in Exhibit 7–3.

[2]$200,000 × 70%; $200,000 × 30%.

[3]$600,000 × 70%; $600,000 × 30%.

[4]$800,000 × 70%; $800,000 × 30%.

[5]$400,000 × 70%.

[6]Uncollected fourth-quarter sales ($120,000) appear as accounts receivable on the company's end-of-year budgeted balance sheet (see Schedule 10 on page 319).

$200,000. In the first quarter, Hampton Freeze expects to collect 70% of this amount, or $140,000. In the second quarter, the company expects to collect the remaining 30% of this amount, or $60,000.

CONCEPT CHECK ✓

2. March, April, and May sales are $100,000, $120,000, and $125,000, respectively. A total of 80% of all sales are credit sales and 20% are cash sales. A total of 60% of credit sales are collected in the month of the sale and 40% are collected in the next month. There are no bad debt expenses. What is the amount of cash collections for April?
   a. $89,600
   b. $111,600
   c. $113,600
   d. $132,600

3. Referring to the facts in question 2 above, what is the accounts receivable balance at the end of May?
   a. $40,000
   b. $50,000
   c. $72,000
   d. $80,000

The Production Budget

The production budget is prepared after the sales budget. The **production budget** lists the number of units that must be produced to satisfy sales needs and to provide for the desired ending finished goods inventory. Production needs can be determined as follows:

Budgeted unit sales	XXXX
Add desired units of ending finished goods inventory	XXXX
Total needs	XXXX
Less units of beginning finished goods inventory	XXXX
Required production in units	XXXX

Note the production requirements are influenced by the desired level of the ending finished goods inventory. Inventories should be carefully planned. Excessive inventories tie up funds and create storage problems. Insufficient inventories can lead to lost sales or last-minute, high-cost production efforts.

Schedule 2 contains the production budget for Hampton Freeze. The budgeted sales data come from cells B7 through E7 of the sales budget. The desired ending finished goods inventory for the first quarter of 6,000 cases is computed by multiplying budgeted sales from the second quarter (30,000 cases) by the desired ending finished goods inventory percentage (20%) shown in cell B13 of the Budgeting Assumptions tab. The total needs for the first quarter (16,000 cases) are determined by adding together the budgeted sales of 10,000 cases for the quarter and the desired ending inventory of 6,000 cases. As

SCHEDULE 2

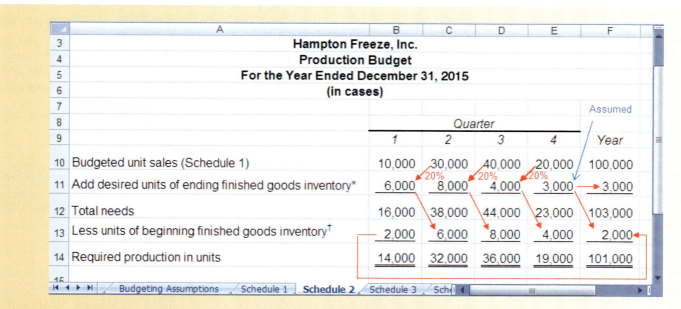

	A	B	C	D	E	F
3		Hampton Freeze, Inc.				
4		Production Budget				
5		For the Year Ended December 31, 2015				
6		(in cases)				
7						Assumed
8				Quarter		
9		1	2	3	4	Year
10	Budgeted unit sales (Schedule 1)	10,000	30,000	40,000	20,000	100,000
11	Add desired units of ending finished goods inventory*	6,000	8,000	4,000	3,000	3,000
12	Total needs	16,000	38,000	44,000	23,000	103,000
13	Less units of beginning finished goods inventory†	2,000	6,000	8,000	4,000	2,000
14	Required production in units	14,000	32,000	36,000	19,000	101,000

Budgeting Assumptions   Schedule 1   **Schedule 2**   Schedule 3   Sch

*Twenty percent of next quarter's sales. For example, the second-quarter sales are 30,000 cases. Therefore, the desired ending inventory of finished goods for the first quarter would be 20% × 30,000 cases = 6,000 cases.

†The beginning inventory in each quarter is the same as the prior quarter's ending inventory.

discussed above, the ending inventory is intended to provide some cushion in the event that problems develop in production or sales increase unexpectedly. Because the company already has 2,000 cases in beginning finished goods inventory (as shown in the beginning balance sheet in Exhibit 7–3), only 14,000 cases need to be produced in the first quarter.

Pay particular attention to the Year column to the right of the production budget in Schedule 2. In some cases (e.g., budgeted sales, total needs, and required production), the amount listed for the year is the sum of the quarterly amounts for the item. In other cases, (e.g., desired units of ending finished goods inventory and units of beginning finished goods inventory), the amount listed for the year is not simply the sum of the quarterly amounts. From the standpoint of the entire year, the beginning finished goods inventory is the same as the beginning finished goods inventory for the first quarter—it is *not* the sum of the beginning finished goods inventories for all four quarters. Similarly, from the standpoint of the entire year, the ending finished goods inventory, which Larry Giano assumed to be 3,000 units, is the same as the ending finished goods inventory for the fourth quarter—it is *not* the sum of the ending finished goods inventories for all four quarters. It is important to pay attention to such distinctions in all schedules that follow.

Inventory Purchases—Merchandising Company

Hampton Freeze prepares a production budget because it is a *manufacturing* company. If it were a *merchandising* company, instead it would prepare a **merchandise purchases budget** showing the amount of goods to be purchased from suppliers during the period. The format of the merchandise purchases budget is shown below:

Budgeted cost of goods sold	XXXX
Add desired ending merchandise inventory	XXXX
Total needs	XXXX
Less beginning merchandise inventory	XXXX
Required purchases	XXXX

A merchandising company would prepare a merchandise purchases budget, such as the one above, for each item carried in stock. The merchandise purchases budget can be expressed in dollars (as shown above) or in units. The top line of a merchandise purchases budget based on units would say Budgeted unit sales instead of Budgeted cost of goods sold.

A merchandise purchases budget is usually accompanied by a schedule of expected cash disbursements for merchandise purchases. The format of this schedule mirrors the approach used for the schedule of expected cash disbursements for purchases of materials that is illustrated at the bottom of Schedule 3 on page 307.

CONCEPT CHECK ✓

4. If a company has a beginning merchandise inventory of $50,000, a desired ending merchandise inventory of $30,000, and a budgeted cost of goods sold of $300,000, what is the amount of required inventory purchases?
   a. $320,000
   b. $280,000
   c. $380,000
   d. $300,000

5. Budgeted unit sales for March, April, and May are 75,000, 80,000, and 90,000 units. Management desires to maintain an ending inventory equal to 30% of the next month's unit sales. How many units should be produced in April?
   a. 80,000 units
   b. 83,000 units
   c. 77,000 units
   d. 85,000 units

The Direct Materials Budget

A *direct materials budget* is prepared after the production requirements have been computed. The **direct materials budget** details the raw materials that must be purchased to fulfill the production budget and to provide for adequate inventories. The required purchases of raw materials are computed as follows:

LEARNING OBJECTIVE 7–4

Prepare a direct materials budget, including a schedule of expected cash disbursements for purchases of materials.

Required production in units of finished goods	XXXX
Units of raw materials needed per unit of finished goods	XXXX
Units of raw materials needed to meet production	XXXX
Add desired units of ending raw materials inventory	XXXX
Total units of raw materials needed	XXXX
Less units of beginning raw materials inventory	XXXX
Units of raw materials to be purchased	XXXX
Unit cost of raw materials	XXXX
Cost of raw materials to be purchased	XXXX

Schedule 3 contains the direct materials budget for Hampton Freeze. The first line of this budget contains the required production for each quarter, which is taken directly from cells B14 through E14 of the production budget (Schedule 2). The second line of the direct materials budget recognizes that 15 pounds of sugar (see cell B16 from the Budgeting Assumptions

SCHEDULE 3

Hampton Freeze, Inc.
Direct Materials Budget
For the Year Ended December 31, 2015

	Quarter				Assumed
	1	2	3	4	Year
9 Required production in cases (Schedule 2)	14,000	32,000	36,000	19,000	101,000
10 Units of raw materials needed per case	15	15	15	15	15
11 Units of raw materials needed to meet production	210,000	480,000	540,000	285,000	1,515,000
12 Add desired units of ending raw materials inventory[1]	48,000 (10%)	54,000 (10%)	28,500 (10%)	22,500 (10%)	22,500
13 Total units of raw materials needed	258,000	534,000	568,500	307,500	1,537,500
14 Less units of beginning raw materials inventory	21,000	48,000	54,000	28,500	21,000
15 Units of raw materials to be purchased	237,000	486,000	514,500	279,000	1,516,500
16 Cost of raw materials per pound	$ 0.20	$ 0.20	$ 0.20	$ 0.20	$ 0.20
17 Cost of raw materials to be purchased	$47,400	$97,200	$102,900	$55,800	$ 303,300

Schedule of Expected Cash Disbursements for Purchases of Materials

	50%	50%			
22 Beginning accounts payable[2]	$25,800				$ 25,800
23 First-quarter purchases[3]	23,700	$23,700			47,400
24 Second-quarter purchases[4]		48,600	$ 48,600		97,200
25 Third-quarter purchases[5]			51,450	$51,450	102,900
26 Fourth-quarter purchases[6]	-	-	-	27,900	27,900
27 Total cash disbursements for materials	$49,500	$72,300	$100,050	$79,350	$ 301,200

Schedule 3 / Schedule 4 / Schedule 5 / Schedule 6 / Schedule 7 / S

[1] Ten percent of the next quarter's production needs. For example, the second-quarter production needs are 480,000 pounds. Therefore, the desired ending inventory for the first quarter would be 10% × 480,000 pounds = 48,000 pounds.

[2] Cash payments for last year's fourth-quarter purchases. See the beginning-of-year balance sheet in Exhibit 7–3 on page 301.

[3] $47,400 × 50%; $47,400 × 50%.

[4] $97,200 × 50%; $97,200 × 50%.

[5] $102,900 × 50%; $102,900 × 50%.

[6] $55,800 × 50%. Unpaid fourth-quarter purchases ($27,900) appear as accounts payable on the company's end-of-year budgeted balance sheet (see Schedule 10 on page 319).

tab) are required to make one case of popsicles. The third line of the budget presents the raw materials needed to meet production. For example, in the first quarter, the required production of 14,000 cases is multiplied by 15 pounds to equal 210,000 pounds of sugar needed to meet production. The fourth line shows the desired units of ending raw materials inventory. For the first quarter this amount is computed by multiplying the raw materials needed to meet production in the second quarter of 480,000 pounds by the desired ending inventory percentage of 10% as shown in cell B18 of the Budgeting Assumptions tab. The desired units of ending raw materials inventory of 48,000 pounds is added to 210,000 pounds to provide the total units of raw materials needed of 258,000 pounds. However, because the company already has 21,000 pounds of sugar in beginning inventory (as shown in cell A9 in the beginning balance sheet in Exhibit 7–3), only 237,000 pounds of sugar need to be purchased in the first quarter. Because the budgeted cost of raw materials per pound is $0.20 (see cell B17 from the Budgeting Assumptions tab), the cost of raw material to be purchased in the first quarter is $47,400. For the entire year, the company plans to purchase $303,300 of raw materials.

Schedule 3 also shows that the company's expected cash disbursements for material purchases for 2015 are $301,200. The accounts payable balance of $25,800 that is paid in the first quarter comes from cell C21 of the beginning balance sheet shown in Exhibit 7–3. All other cash disbursement computations rely on the estimated cash payment percentages (both of which are 50%) from cells B19 and B20 of the Budgeting Assumptions tab. For example, Schedule 3 shows that the budgeted raw material purchases for the first quarter equal $47,400. In the first quarter, Hampton Freeze expects to pay 50% of this amount, or $23,700. In the second quarter, the company expects to pay the remaining 50% of this amount, or $23,700.

HELPFUL HINT

The direct materials budget includes three different units of measure. It begins by defining the number of *units of finished goods* that need to be produced each period. It then defines the *quantity of raw material inputs* (measured in terms such as pounds or ounces) that need to be purchased to support production. It concludes by translating the quantity of raw materials to be purchased into the *cost of raw materials* to be purchased.

The Direct Labor Budget

LEARNING OBJECTIVE 7–5

Prepare a direct labor budget.

The **direct labor budget** shows the direct labor-hours required to satisfy the production budget. By knowing in advance how much labor time will be needed throughout the budget year, the company can develop plans to adjust the labor force as the situation requires. Companies that neglect the budgeting process run the risk of facing labor shortages or

SCHEDULE 4

	A	B	C	D	E	F	G
1		Hampton Freeze, Inc.					
2		Direct Labor Budget					
3		For the Year Ended December 31, 2015					
4							
5				Quarter			
6		1	2	3	4	Year	
7	Required production in cases (Schedule 2)	14,000	32,000	36,000	19,000	101,000	
8	Direct labor-hours per case	0.40	0.40	0.40	0.40	0.40	
9	Total direct labor-hours needed	5,600	12,800	14,400	7,600	40,400	
10	Direct labor cost per hour	$ 15.00	$ 15.00	$ 15.00	$ 15.00	$ 15.00	
11	Total direct labor cost	$ 84,000	$ 192,000	$ 216,000	$ 114,000	$ 606,000	
12							

Schedule 1 / Schedule 2 / Schedule 3 / **Schedule 4** / Schedule 5 / Schedule

*This schedule assumes that the direct labor workforce will be fully adjusted to the total direct labor-hours needed each quarter.

having to hire and lay off workers at awkward times. Erratic labor policies lead to insecurity, low morale, and inefficiency.

   The direct labor budget for Hampton Freeze is shown in Schedule 4. The first line in the direct labor budget consists of the required production for each quarter, which is taken directly from cells B14 through E14 of the production budget (Schedule 2). The direct labor requirement for each quarter is computed by multiplying the number of units to be produced in each quarter by the 0.40 direct labor-hours required to make one unit (see cell B23 from the Budgeting Assumptions tab). For example, 14,000 cases are to be produced in the first quarter and each case requires 0.40 direct labor-hours, so a total of 5,600 direct labor-hours (14,000 cases × 0.40 direct labor-hours per case) will be required in the first quarter. The direct labor requirements are then translated into budgeted direct labor costs. How this is done will depend on the company's labor policy. In Schedule 4, Hampton Freeze has assumed that the direct labor force will be adjusted as the work requirements change from quarter to quarter. In that case, the direct labor cost is computed by simply multiplying the direct labor-hour requirements by the direct labor rate of $15 per hour (see cell B24 from the Budgeting Assumptions tab). For example, the direct labor cost in the first quarter is $84,000 (5,600 direct labor-hours × $15 per direct labor-hour).

   However, many companies have employment policies or contracts that prevent them from laying off and rehiring workers as needed. Suppose, for example, that Hampton Freeze has 25 workers who are classified as direct labor, but each of them is guaranteed at least 480 hours of pay each quarter at a rate of $15 per hour. In that case, the minimum direct labor cost for a quarter would be computed as follows:

$$25 \text{ workers} \times 480 \text{ hours per worker} \times \$15 \text{ per hour} = \$180,000$$

Note that in this case the direct costs shown in the first and fourth quarters of Schedule 4 would have to be increased to $180,000.

The Manufacturing Overhead Budget

LEARNING OBJECTIVE 7–6

Prepare a manufacturing overhead budget.

The **manufacturing overhead budget** lists all costs of production other than direct materials and direct labor. Schedule 5 shows the manufacturing overhead budget for Hampton Freeze. At Hampton Freeze, manufacturing overhead is separated into variable and fixed components. As shown in the Budgeting Assumptions tab (Exhibit 7–4), the variable component is $4 per direct labor-hour and the fixed component is $60,600 per quarter. Because the variable component of manufacturing overhead depends on direct labor, the first line in the manufacturing overhead budget consists of the budgeted direct labor-hours from cells B9 through E9 of the direct labor budget (Schedule 4). The budgeted direct labor-hours in each quarter are multiplied by the variable overhead rate to determine the variable component of manufacturing overhead. For example, the variable manufacturing overhead for the first quarter is $22,400 (5,600 direct labor-hours × $4.00 per

SCHEDULE 5

	A	B	C	D	E	F
1		Hampton Freeze, Inc.				
2		Manufacturing Overhead Budget				
3		For the Year Ended December 31, 2015				
4						
5		Quarter				
6		1	2	3	4	Year
7	Budgeted direct labor-hours (Schedule 4)	5,600	12,800	14,400	7,600	40,400
8	Variable manufacturing overhead rate	$ 4.00	$ 4.00	$ 4.00	$ 4.00	$ 4.00
9	Variable manufacturing overhead	$ 22,400	$ 51,200	$ 57,600	$ 30,400	$ 161,600
10	Fixed manufacturing overhead	60,600	60,600	60,600	60,600	242,400
11	Total manufacturing overhead	83,000	111,800	118,200	91,000	404,000
12	Less depreciation	15,000	15,000	15,000	15,000	60,000
13	Cash disbursements for manufacturing overhead	$ 68,000	$ 96,800	$ 103,200	$ 76,000	$ 344,000
14						
15	Total manufacturing overhead (a)					$ 404,000
16	Budgeted direct labor-hours (b)					40,400
17	Predetermined overhead rate for the year (a)÷(b)					$10.00
18						
19						

Schedule 3 / Schedule 4 / **Schedule 5** / Schedule 6 / Schedule 7 / Schedule 8

direct labor-hour). This is added to the fixed manufacturing overhead for the quarter to determine the total manufacturing overhead for the quarter of $83,000 ($22,400 + $60,600).

A few words about fixed costs and the budgeting process are in order. In most cases, fixed costs are the costs of supplying capacity to make products, process purchase orders, handle customer calls, and so on. The amount of capacity that will be required depends on the expected level of activity for the period. If the expected level of activity is greater than the company's current capacity, then fixed costs may have to be increased. Or, if the expected level is appreciably below the company's current capacity, then it may be desirable to decrease fixed costs if possible. However, once the level of the fixed costs has been determined in the budget, the costs really are fixed. The time to adjust fixed costs is during the budgeting process. An activity-based costing system can help to determine the appropriate level of fixed costs at budget time by answering questions like, "How many clerks will we need to process the anticipated number of purchase orders next year?" For simplicity, all of the budgeting examples in this book assume that the appropriate levels of fixed costs have already been determined.

The last line of Schedule 5 for Hampton Freeze shows the budgeted cash disbursements for manufacturing overhead. Because some of the overhead costs are not cash outflows, the total budgeted manufacturing overhead costs must be adjusted to determine the cash disbursements for manufacturing overhead. At Hampton Freeze, the only significant noncash manufacturing overhead cost is depreciation, which is $15,000 per quarter (see cell B29 in the Budgeting Assumptions tab). These noncash depreciation charges are deducted from the total budgeted manufacturing overhead to determine the expected cash disbursements. Hampton Freeze pays all overhead costs involving cash disbursements in the quarter incurred. Note that the company's predetermined overhead rate for the year is $10 per direct labor-hour, which is determined by dividing the total budgeted manufacturing overhead for the year by the total budgeted direct labor-hours for the year.

The Ending Finished Goods Inventory Budget

After completing Schedules 1–5, Larry Giano had all of the data he needed to compute the unit product cost for the units produced during the budget year. This computation was needed for two reasons: first, to help determine cost of goods sold on the budgeted income

SCHEDULE 6

	Item	Quantity		Cost		Total	
				Hampton Freeze, Inc.			
				Ending Finished Goods Inventory Budget			
				(absorption costing basis)			
				For the Year Ended December 31, 2015			
	Item	*Quantity*		*Cost*		*Total*	
	Production cost per case:						
	Direct materials	15.00	pounds	$ 0.20	per pound	$	3.00
	Direct labor	0.40	hours	$15.00	per hour		6.00
	Manufacturing overhead	0.40	hours	$10.00	per hour		4.00
	Unit product cost					$	13.00
	Budgeted finished goods inventory:						
	Ending finished goods inventory in cases (Schedule 2)						3,000
	Unit product cost (see above)					$	13.00
	Ending finished goods inventory in dollars					$	39,000

Tabs: Schedule 3 | Schedule 4 | Schedule 5 | **Schedule 6** | Sch

statement; and second, to value ending inventories on the budgeted balance sheet. The cost of unsold units is computed on the **ending finished goods inventory budget**.[3]

Larry Giano considered using variable costing to prepare Hampton Freeze's budget statements, but he decided to use absorption costing instead because the bank would very likely require absorption costing. He also knew that it would be easy to convert the absorption costing financial statements to a variable costing basis later. At this point, the primary concern was to determine what financing, if any, would be required in 2015 and then to arrange for that financing from the bank.

The unit product cost computations are shown in Schedule 6. For Hampton Freeze, the absorption costing unit product cost is $13 per case of popsicles—consisting of $3 of direct materials, $6 of direct labor, and $4 of manufacturing overhead. The manufacturing overhead is applied to units of product at the rate of $10 per direct labor-hour. The budgeted carrying cost of the ending inventory is $39,000.

The Selling and Administrative Expense Budget

The **selling and administrative expense budget** lists the budgeted expenses for areas other than manufacturing. In large organizations, this budget would be a compilation of many smaller, individual budgets submitted by department heads and other persons responsible for selling and administrative expenses. For example, the marketing manager would submit a budget detailing the advertising expenses for each budget period.

Schedule 7 contains the selling and administrative expense budget for Hampton Freeze. Like the manufacturing overhead budget, the selling and administrative expense

LEARNING OBJECTIVE 7–7

Prepare a selling and administrative expense budget.

---

[3]For simplicity, the beginning balance sheet and the ending finished goods inventory budget both report a unit product cost of $13. For purposes of answering "what-if" questions, this schedule would assume a FIFO inventory flow. In other words, the ending inventory would consist solely of units that are produced during the budget year.

SCHEDULE 7

	B	C	D	E	F
Hampton Freeze, Inc.					
Selling and Administrative Expense Budget					
For the Year Ended December 31, 2015					
			Quarter		
	1	*2*	*3*	*4*	*Year*
Budgeted units sales (Schedule 1)	10,000	30,000	40,000	20,000	100,000
Variable selling and administrative expense per case	$ 1.80	$ 1.80	$ 1.80	$ 1.80	$ 1.80
Variable selling and administrative expense	$ 18,000	$ 54,000	$ 72,000	$ 36,000	$180,000
Fixed selling and administrative expenses:					
Advertising	20,000	20,000	20,000	20,000	80,000
Executive salaries	55,000	55,000	55,000	55,000	220,000
Insurance	10,000	10,000	10,000	10,000	40,000
Property taxes	4,000	4,000	4,000	4,000	16,000
Depreciation	10,000	10,000	10,000	10,000	40,000
Total fixed selling and administrative expenses	99,000	99,000	99,000	99,000	396,000
Total selling and administrative expenses	117,000	153,000	171,000	135,000	576,000
Less depreciation	10,000	10,000	10,000	10,000	40,000
Cash disbursements for selling and administrative expenses	$107,000	$143,000	$161,000	$125,000	$536,000

*Schedule 5 — Schedule 6 — **Schedule 7** — Schedule 8 — Schedule 9 — Schedule 10*

budget is divided into variable and fixed cost components. Consequently, budgeted sales in cases for each quarter are entered at the top of the schedule. These data are taken from cells B7 through E7 of the sales budget (Schedule 1). The budgeted variable selling and administrative expenses are determined by multiplying the budgeted cases sold by the variable selling and administrative expense of $1.80 per case (see cell B33 from the Budgeting Assumptions tab). For example, the budgeted variable selling and administrative expense for the first quarter is $18,000 (10,000 cases × $1.80 per case). The fixed selling and administrative expenses of $99,000 per quarter (see cells B35 through B39 from the Budgeting Assumptions tab) are then added to the variable selling and administrative expenses to arrive at the total budgeted selling and administrative expenses. Finally, to determine the cash disbursements for selling and administrative items, the total budgeted selling and administrative expense is adjusted by subtracting any noncash selling and administrative expenses (in this case, just depreciation).[4]

DECISION POINT

Budget Analyst

You have been hired as a budget analyst by a regional chain of Italian restaurants with attached bars. Management has had difficulty in the past predicting some of its costs; the assumption has always been that all operating costs are variable with respect to gross restaurant sales. What would you suggest doing to improve the accuracy of the budget forecasts?

---

[4]Other adjustments might need to be made for differences between cash flows on the one hand and revenues and expenses on the other hand. For example, if property taxes are paid twice a year in installments of $8,000 each, the expense for property tax would have to be "backed out" of the total budgeted selling and administrative expenses and the cash installment payments added to the appropriate quarters to determine the cash disbursements. Similar adjustments might also need to be made in the manufacturing overhead budget. We generally ignore these complications in this chapter.

6. Which of the following statements is true? (You may select more than one answer.)
   a. The manufacturing overhead budget includes depreciation related to assets that support a company's selling and administrative functions.
   b. The cash disbursements for selling and administrative expenses are reported in the budgeted income statement.
   c. The selling and administrative expense budget includes depreciation related to manufacturing assets.
   d. The total variable and fixed selling and administrative expenses incurred during a period are reported in the budgeted income statement.

CONCEPT CHECK

The Cash Budget

LEARNING OBJECTIVE 7–8

Prepare a cash budget.

The cash budget is composed of four major sections:

1. The receipts section.
2. The disbursements section.
3. The cash excess or deficiency section.
4. The financing section.

The receipts section lists all of the cash inflows, except from financing, expected during the budget period. Generally, the major source of receipts is from sales. The disbursements section summarizes all cash payments that are planned for the budget period. These payments include raw materials purchases, direct labor payments, manufacturing overhead costs, and so on, as contained in their respective budgets. In addition, other cash disbursements such as equipment purchases and dividends are listed.

The cash excess or deficiency section is computed as follows:

Beginning cash balance	XXXX
Add cash receipts	XXXX
Total cash available	XXXX
Less cash disbursements	XXXX
Excess (deficiency) of cash available over disbursements	XXXX

If a cash deficiency exists during any budget period or if there is a cash excess during any budget period that is less than the minimum required cash balance, the company will need to borrow money. Conversely, if there is a cash excess during any budget period that is greater than the minimum required cash balance, the company can invest the excess funds or repay principal and interest to lenders.

Mismatched Cash Flows—Climbing the Hills and Valleys

IN BUSINESS

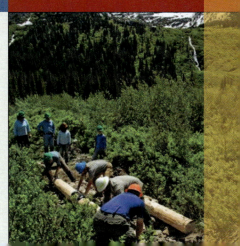

The Washington Trails Association (WTA) is a private, nonprofit organization primarily concerned with protecting and maintaining hiking trails in the state of Washington. Some 2,000 WTA volunteer workers donate more than 80,000 hours per year maintaining trails in rugged landscapes on federal, state, and private lands. The organization is supported by membership dues, voluntary contributions, grants, and some contract work for government.

The organization's income and expenses are erratic—although somewhat predictable—over the course of the year as shown in the chart on the following page. Expenses tend to be highest in the spring and summer when most of the trail maintenance work is done. However, income spikes in December well after the expenses have been incurred. With cash outflows running ahead of cash inflows for much of the year, it is very important for the WTA to carefully plan its cash budget and to maintain adequate cash reserves to be able to pay its bills.

IN BUSINESS

(continued)

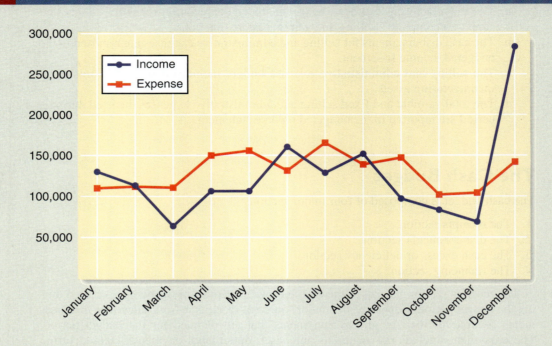

Note: Total income and total expense are approximately equal over the course of the year.

Sources: Conversation with Elizabeth Lunney, President of the Washington Trails Association; WTA documents; and the WTA website www.wta.org.

The financing section of the cash budget details the borrowings and principal and interest repayments projected to take place during the budget period. *In this chapter, we'll always assume that all borrowings take place on the first day of the borrowing period and all repayments take place on the last day of the final period included in the cash budget.* To calculate borrowings and interest payments, you'll need to pay attention to the company's desired minimum cash balance and to the terms of the company's loan agreement with the bank. For example, Hampton Freeze's desired minimum cash balance is $30,000 (see cell B42 in the Budgeting Assumptions tab). Furthermore, *we are going to assume that Hampton Freeze's loan agreement stipulates that it must borrow money in increments of $10,000* and that it must pay simple interest of 3% per quarter (as shown in cell B43 of the Budgeting Assumptions tab).[5]

The cash balances at both the beginning and end of the year may be adequate even though a serious cash deficit occurs at some point during the year. Consequently, the cash budget should be broken down into time periods that are short enough to capture major fluctuations in cash balances. While a monthly cash budget is most common, some organizations budget cash on a weekly or even daily basis. At Hampton Freeze, Larry Giano has prepared a quarterly cash budget that can be further refined as necessary. This budget appears in Schedule 8.[6]

The beginning cash balance in the first quarter of $42,500 agrees with cell B7 of the beginning balance sheet in Exhibit 7–3. Each quarter's collections from customers come from cells B18 through E18 of the schedule of expected cash collections in Schedule 1.

---

[5]We use simple interest rather than compound interest throughout the chapter for simplicity.
[6]The format for the statement of cash flows, which is discussed in a later chapter, may also be used for the cash budget.

SCHEDULE 8

	A	B	C	D	E	F	G	H
1			Hampton Freeze, Inc.					
2			Cash Budget					
3			For the Year Ended December 31, 2015					
4								
5					Quarter			
6		Schedule	1	2	3	4	Year	
7	Beginning cash balance		$ 42,500	$ 36,000	$ 33,900	$ 165,650	$ 42,500	
8	Add cash receipts:							
9	Collections from customers	1	230,000	480,000	740,000	520,000	1,970,000	
10	Total cash available		272,500	516,000	773,900	685,650	2,012,500	
11	Less cash disbursements:							
12	Direct materials	3	49,500	72,300	100,050	79,350	301,200	
13	Direct labor	4	84,000	192,000	216,000	114,000	606,000	
14	Manufacturing overhead	5	68,000	96,800	103,200	76,000	344,000	
15	Selling and administrative	7	107,000	143,000	161,000	125,000	536,000	
16	Equipment purchases		50,000	40,000	20,000	20,000	130,000	
17	Dividends		8,000	8,000	8,000	8,000	32,000	
18	Total cash disbursements		366,500	552,100	608,250	422,350	1,949,200	
19	Excess (deficiency) of cash available over disbursements		(94,000)	(36,100)	165,650	263,300	63,300	
20	Financing:							
21	Borrowings (at the beginnings of quarters)		130,000	70,000	-	-	200,000	
22	Repayments (at end of the year)		-	-	-	(200,000)	(200,000)	
23	Interest		-	-	-	(21,900)	(21,900)	
24	Total financing		130,000	70,000	-	(221,900)	(21,900)	
25	Ending cash balance		$ 36,000	$ 33,900	$ 165,650	$ 41,400	$ 41,400	
26								
27								

Schedule 5 / Schedule 6 / Schedule 7 / **Schedule 8** / Schedule 9 / Schedule 10

Each quarter's beginning cash balance plus the collections from customers equals the total cash available. For example, in the first quarter, the beginning cash balance of $42,500 plus the collections from customers of $230,000 equals the total cash available of $272,500.

The disbursements section of the cash budget includes six types of cash disbursements. Each quarter's cash disbursements for direct materials come from cells B27 through E27 of the schedule of expected cash disbursements for materials (see Schedule 3). The quarterly cash payments for direct labor were calculated in cells B11 through E11 of the direct labor budget (see Schedule 4), whereas the quarterly cash payments related to manufacturing overhead were calculated in cells B13 through E13 of the manufacturing overhead budget (see Schedule 5). The quarterly cash payments for selling and administrative expenses come from cells B19 through E19 of the selling and administrative expense budget (see Schedule 7). So putting it all together, in the first quarter, the cash disbursements for direct materials ($49,500), direct labor ($84,000), manufacturing overhead ($68,000), and selling and administrative expenses ($107,000), plus equipment purchases of $50,000 and a dividend of $8,000 (see cells C43 and B44 from the Budgeting Assumptions tab) equals the total cash disbursements of $366,500.

Each quarter's total cash available minus its total disbursements equals the excess (deficiency) of cash available over disbursements. For example, in the first quarter the total cash available of $272,500 minus the total disbursements of $366,500 results in a cash deficiency of $94,000. The excess or deficiency of cash directly influences whether Hampton Freeze will need to borrow money as shown in the Financing section of the cash budget.

The first row in the financing section of the cash budget relates to projected borrowings. In any period where a company's excess of cash available over disbursements is greater than its desired minimum cash balance, the company will not need to borrow money during that period. In the case of Hampton Freeze, the company wants to maintain a minimum cash balance of $30,000; therefore, it will not need to borrow money in any quarter where its excess of cash available over disbursements is greater than $30,000. However, in the first quarter of 2015 Hampton Freeze estimates that it will have a cash deficiency of $94,000; consequently, the company's minimum required borrowings at the beginning of the first quarter would be computed as follows:

Required Borrowings at the Beginning of the First Quarter	
Desired ending cash balance	$ 30,000
Plus deficiency of cash available over disbursements	94,000
Minimum required borrowings	$124,000

Recall that the bank requires that loans be made in increments of $10,000. Because Hampton Freeze needs to borrow at least $124,000, it will have to borrow $130,000.

In the second quarter of 2015 Hampton Freeze estimates that it will have another cash deficiency of $36,100; therefore, the company's minimum required borrowings at the beginning of the second quarter would be computed as follows:

Required Borrowings at the Beginning of the Second Quarter	
Desired ending cash balance	$30,000
Plus deficiency of cash available over disbursements	36,100
Minimum required borrowings	$66,100

Again, recall that the bank requires that loans be made in increments of $10,000. Because Hampton Freeze needs to borrow at least $66,100 at the beginning of the second quarter, the company will have to borrow $70,000 from the bank.

In the third and fourth quarters, Hampton Freeze has an excess of cash available over disbursements that is greater than $30,000, so it will not need to borrow money in these two quarters. Notice that in the third quarter Hampton Freeze has excess cash of $165,650, yet the cash budget does not include any principal or interest repayments during this quarter. This occurs because in this chapter, we always assume that the company will, as far as it is able, repay the loan plus accumulated interest on the *last day of the final period* included in the cash budget. Because Hampton Freeze has excess cash of $263,300 in the fourth quarter, on the last day of the fourth quarter, it would be able to repay the $200,000 that it borrowed from the lender plus $21,900 of interest computed as follows:

Interest on the $130,000 borrowed at the beginning of the first quarter:	
$130,000 × 0.01 per month × 12 months*	$15,600
Interest on the $70,000 borrowed at the beginning of the second quarter:	
$70,000 × 0.01 per month × 9 months*	6,300
Total interest accrued to the end of the fourth quarter	$21,900
*Simple, rather than compounded, interest is assume for simplicity	

The ending cash balance for each period is computed by taking the excess (deficiency) of cash available over disbursements plus the total financing. For example, in the first quarter, Hampton Freeze's cash deficiency of $(94,000) plus its total financing of $130,000 equals its ending cash balance of $36,000. The ending cash balance for each quarter then becomes the beginning cash balance for the next quarter. Also notice that the amounts under the Year column in the cash budget are not always the sum of the amounts for the four quarters. In particular, the beginning cash balance for the year is the same as the beginning cash balance for the first quarter and the ending cash balance for the year is the same as the ending cash balance for the fourth quarter.

The Budgeted Income Statement

Schedule 9 contains the budgeted income statement for Hampton Freeze. All of the revenues and expenses shown on the budgeted income statement come from the data in the beginning balance sheet and the data developed in Schedules 1–8. The sales of $2,000,000 come from cell F9 of the sales budget (Schedule 1). The cost of goods sold of $1,300,000 is computed in two steps. First, cost of goods sold includes the 2,000 units of finished goods inventory from the beginning balance sheet, which have a total cost of $26,000 (see Exhibit 7–3). Second, it includes 98,000 units produced and sold in 2014 multiplied by $13 per unit (see Schedule 6), for a total of $1,274,000. Combining these two steps, the total cost of the 100,000 units sold (see Schedule 1) is $1,300,000 ($26,000 + $1,274,000).[7] The selling and administrative expenses of $576,000 come from cell F17 of the selling and administrative expenses budget (Schedule 7). Finally, the interest expense of $21,900 comes from cell G23 of the cash budget (Schedule 8).

The budgeted income statement is one of the key schedules in the budget process. It shows the company's planned profit and serves as a benchmark against which subsequent company performance can be measured. Because Larry Giano created a Budgeting

LEARNING OBJECTIVE 7–9

Prepare a budgeted income statement.

SCHEDULE 9

	A	B	C
1	Hampton Freeze, Inc.		
2	Budgeted Income Statement		
3	For the Year Ended December 31, 2015		
4			
5		*Schedules*	
6	Sales	1	$ 2,000,000
7	Cost of goods sold	1, 6	1,300,000
8	Gross margin		700,000
9	Selling and administrative expenses	7	576,000
10	Net operating Income		124,000
11	Interest expense	8	21,900
12	Net Income		$ 102,100
13			

◄ ◄ ► ►◄   Schedule 8   **Schedule 9**   Schedule 10

---

[7]This explanation assumes a FIFO inventory flow assumption.

Assumptions tab in his Excel file and linked all of his budget schedules together using properly constructed Excel formulas, he can make changes to his underlying budgeting assumptions and instantly see the impact of the change on all of the schedules and on net income. For example, if Larry wanted to estimate the profit impact if fourth quarter sales are 18,000 cases instead of 20,000 cases, he would simply change the 20,000 cases shown in cell F7 of his Budgeting Assumptions worksheet to 18,000 cases. The revised net income of $87,045 would instantly appear in cell C12 of the budgeted income statement.

The Budgeted Balance Sheet

LEARNING OBJECTIVE 7–10

Prepare a budgeted balance sheet.

The budgeted balance sheet is developed using data from the balance sheet from the beginning of the budget period (see Exhibit 7–3) and data contained in the various schedules. Hampton Freeze's budgeted balance sheet accompanied by explanations of how the numbers were derived is presented in Schedule 10.

MANAGERIAL ACCOUNTING IN ACTION
The Wrap-Up

After completing the master budget, Larry Giano took the documents to Tom Wills, chief executive officer of Hampton Freeze, for his review.

Larry: Here's the budget. Overall, the income is excellent, and the net cash flow for the entire year is positive.

Tom: Yes, but I see on this cash budget that we have the same problem with negative cash flows in the first and second quarters that we had last year.

Larry: That's true. I don't see any way around that problem. However, there is no doubt in my mind that if you take this budget to the bank today, they'll approve an open line of credit that will allow you to borrow enough money to make it through the first two quarters without any problem.

Tom: Are you sure? They didn't seem very happy to see me last year when I came in for an emergency loan.

Larry: Did you repay the loan on time?

Tom: Sure.

Larry: I don't see any problem. You won't be asking for an emergency loan this time. The bank will have plenty of warning. And with this budget, you have a solid plan that shows when and how you are going to pay off the loan. Trust me, they'll go for it. Also, keep in mind that the master budget contains all the embedded formulas you'll need to answer the types of "what-if" questions that we discussed earlier. If you want to calculate the financial impact of changing any of your master budget's underlying estimates or assumptions, you can do it with the click of a mouse!

Tom: This sounds fabulous Larry. Thanks for all of your work on this project.

HELPFUL HINT

One of the most important equations that you should learn while studying accounting is shown in item (j) of Schedule 10. The beginning balance in Retained Earnings plus net income minus dividends equals the ending balance in Retained Earnings. This equation highlights how the income statement and the balance sheet connect to one another. The net income from the income statement plugs into Retained Earnings on the balance sheet. This concept, which is formally referred to as articulated financial statements, is something that all business students must understand.

SCHEDULE 10

	A	B	C	D	E
1		Hampton Freeze, Inc.			
2		Budgeted Balance Sheet			
3		December 31, 2015			
4					
5		*Assets*			
6	Current assets:				
7	Cash	$ 41,400	(a)		
8	Accounts receivable	120,000	(b)		
9	Raw materials inventory	4,500	(c)		
10	Finished goods inventory	39,000	(d)		
11	Total current assets			$ 204,900	
12	Plant and equipment:				
13	Land	80,000	(e)		
14	Buildings and equipment	830,000	(f)		
15	Accumulated depreciation	(392,000)	(g)		
16	Plant and equipment, net			518,000	
17	Total assets			$ 722,900	
18					
19		*Liabilities and Stockholders' Equity*			
20	Current liabilities:				
21	Accounts payable (raw materials)			$ 27,900	(h)
22	Stockholders' equity:				
23	Common stock, no par	$ 175,000	(i)		
24	Retained earnings	520,000	(j)		
25	Total stockholders' equity			695,000	
26	Total liabilities and stockholders' equity			$ 722,900	
27					

Schedule 8 | Schedule 9 | **Schedule 10**

Explanations of December 31, 2015, balance sheet figures:

(a) From cell G25 of the cash budget (Schedule 8).

(b) Thirty percent of fourth-quarter sales, from Schedule 1 ($400,000 × 30% = $120,000).

(c) From the direct materials budget (Schedule 3). Cell E12 multiplied by cell E16. In other words, 22,500 pounds × $0.20 per pound = $4,500.

(d) From cell H16 of the ending finished goods inventory budget (Schedule 6).

(e) From cell B13 of the beginning balance sheet (Exhibit 7–3).

(f) Cell B14 of the beginning balance sheet (Exhibit 7–3) plus cell G16 from the cash budget (Schedule 8). In other words, $700,000 + $130,000 = $830,000.

(g) The beginning balance of $292,000 (from cell B15 of the beginning balance sheet in Exhibit 7–3) plus the depreciation of $60,000 included in cell F12 of the manufacturing overhead budget (Schedule 5) plus depreciation expense of $40,000 included in cell F18 in the selling and administrative expense budget (Schedule 7). In other words, $292,000 + $60,000 + $40,000 = $392,000.

(h) One-half of fourth-quarter raw materials purchases, from Schedule 3.

(i) From cell B23 of the beginning balance sheet (Exhibit 7–3).

(j)

December 31, 2014, balance	$449,900
Add net income, from cell C12 of Schedule 9	102,100
	552,000
Deduct dividends paid, from cell G17 of Schedule 8	32,000
December 31, 2015, balance	$520,000

Local Municipalities Close Budget Deficits

Municipalities across the Unites States face a combined budget deficit of $56 to $86 billion. Many cities are responding to their budget shortfalls by outsourcing services to avoid the crushing cost of providing employee benefits. For example, **San Jose**, **California**, decided to put a dent in its $118 million budget deficit by outsourcing its janitorial services. The town of **Lakewood**, **California**, contracts 40% of its municipal services to outside vendors. **Maywood**, **California**, took the drastic step of outsourcing all of its public services to outside contractors. This small town of 40,000 residents terminated all municipal employees and hired the Los Angeles County Sheriff to oversee public safety.

Sources: Tamara Audi, "Cities Rent Police, Janitors to Save Cash," *The Wall Street Journal,* July 19, 2010, p. A3.

SUMMARY

LO7–1　Understand why organizations budget and the processes they use to create budgets.

Organizations budget for a variety of reasons, including to communicate management's plans throughout the organization, to force managers to think about and plan for the future, to allocate resources within the organization, to identify bottlenecks before they occur, to coordinate activities, and to provide benchmarks for evaluating subsequent performance.

Budgets should be developed with the full participation of all managers who will be subject to budgetary controls.

LO7–2　Prepare a sales budget, including a schedule of expected cash collections.

The sales budget forms the foundation for the master budget. It provides details concerning the anticipated unit and dollar sales.

The schedule of expected cash collections is based on the sales budget, the expected breakdown between cash and credit sales, and the expected pattern of collections on credit sales.

LO7–3　Prepare a production budget.

The production budget details how many units must be produced each budget period to satisfy expected sales and to provide for adequate levels of finished goods inventories.

LO7–4　Prepare a direct materials budget, including a schedule of expected cash disbursements for purchases of materials.

The direct materials budget shows the materials that must be purchased each budget period to meet anticipated production requirements and to provide for adequate levels of materials inventories.

Cash disbursements for purchases of materials will depend on the amount of materials purchased in each budget period and the company's policies concerning payments to suppliers for materials bought on credit.

LO7–5　Prepare a direct labor budget.

The direct labor budget shows the direct labor-hours that are required to meet the production schedule as detailed in the production budget. The direct labor-hour requirements are used to determine the direct labor cost in each budget period.

LO7–6　Prepare a manufacturing overhead budget.

Manufacturing overhead consists of both variable and fixed manufacturing overhead. The variable manufacturing overhead depends on the number of units produced from the production budget. The variable and fixed manufacturing overhead costs are combined to determine the total manufacturing overhead. Any noncash manufacturing overhead such as depreciation is deducted from the total manufacturing overhead to determine the cash disbursements for manufacturing overhead.

LO7–7 Prepare a selling and administrative expense budget.

Like manufacturing overhead, selling and administrative expenses consist of both variable and fixed expenses. The variable expenses depend on the number of units sold or some other measure of activity. The variable and fixed expenses are combined to determine the total selling and administrative expense. Any noncash selling and administrative expenses such as depreciation are deducted from the total to determine the cash disbursements for selling and administrative expenses.

LO7–8 Prepare a cash budget.

The cash budget is a critical piece of the master budget. It permits managers to anticipate and plan for cash shortfalls.

The cash budget is organized into a receipts section, a disbursements section, a cash excess or deficiency section, and a financing section. The cash budget draws on information taken from nearly all of the other budgets and schedules including the schedule of cash collections, the schedule of cash disbursements for purchases of materials, the direct labor budget, the manufacturing overhead budget, and the selling and administrative expense budget.

LO7–9 Prepare a budgeted income statement.

The budgeted income statement is constructed using data from the sales budget, the ending finished goods inventory budget, the manufacturing overhead budget, the selling and administrative budget, and the cash budget.

LO7–10 Prepare a budgeted balance sheet.

The budgeted balance sheet is constructed using data from virtually all other parts of the master budget.

GUIDANCE ANSWER TO DECISION POINT

Budget Analyst (p. 312)
Not all costs are variable with respect to gross restaurant sales. For example, assuming no change in the number of restaurant sites, rental costs are probably fixed. To more accurately forecast costs for the budget, costs should be separated into variable and fixed components. Furthermore, more appropriate activity measures should be selected for the variable costs. For example, gross restaurant sales may be divided into food sales and bar sales—each of which could serve as an activity measure for some costs. In addition, some costs (such as the costs of free dinner rolls) may be variable with respect to the number of diners rather than with respect to food or bar sales. Other activity measures may permit even more accurate cost predictions.

GUIDANCE ANSWERS TO CONCEPT CHECKS

1. **Choice b.** Responsibility accounting focuses on holding managers accountable for only those items that they can control.
2. **Choice c.** Cash collections for April are calculated as follows: ($100,000 × 80% × 40%) + ($120,000 × 20%) + ($120,000 × 80% × 60%) = $113,600.
3. **Choice a.** The May 31 accounts receivable balance is $125,000 × 80% × 40% = $40,000.
4. **Choice b.** Required inventory purchases are calculated as follows: Cost of goods sold of $300,000 + Ending inventory of $30,000 − Beginning inventory of $50,000 = $280,000.
5. **Choice b.** 80,000 units sold in April + 27,000 units of desired ending inventory − 24,000 units of beginning inventory = 83,000 units.
6. **Choice d.** The manufacturing overhead budget includes depreciation on manufacturing assets. Cash disbursements for selling and administrative expenses are reported in the cash budget. The selling and administrative expense budget included depreciation related to assets that support a company's selling and administrative functions.

REVIEW PROBLEM: BUDGET SCHEDULES

Mynor Corporation manufactures and sells a seasonal product that has peak sales in the third quarter. The following information concerns operations for Year 2—the coming year—and for the first two quarters of Year 3:

a. The company's single product sells for $8 per unit. Budgeted unit sales for the next six quarters are as follows (all sales are on credit):

	Year 2 Quarter				Year 3 Quarter	
	1	2	3	4	1	2
Budgeted unit sales	40,000	60,000	100,000	50,000	70,000	80,000

b. Sales are collected in the following pattern: 75% in the quarter the sales are made, and the remaining 25% in the following quarter. On January 1, Year 2, the company's balance sheet showed $65,000 in accounts receivable, all of which will be collected in the first quarter of the year. Bad debts are negligible and can be ignored.

c. The company desires an ending finished goods inventory at the end of each quarter equal to 30% of the budgeted unit sales for the next quarter. On December 31, Year 1, the company had 12,000 units on hand.

d. Five pounds of raw materials are required to complete one unit of product. The company requires ending raw materials inventory at the end of each quarter equal to 10% of the following quarter's production needs. On December 31, Year 1, the company had 23,000 pounds of raw materials on hand.

e. The raw material costs $0.80 per pound. Raw material purchases are paid for in the following pattern: 60% paid in the quarter the purchases are made, and the remaining 40% paid in the following quarter. On January 1, Year 2, the company's balance sheet showed $81,500 in accounts payable for raw material purchases, all of which will be paid for in the first quarter of the year.

Required:

Prepare the following budgets and schedules for the year, showing both quarterly and total figures:

1. A sales budget and a schedule of expected cash collections.
2. A production budget.
3. A direct materials budget and a schedule of expected cash payments for purchases of materials.

Solution to Review Problem

1. The sales budget is prepared as follows:

	Year 2 Quarter				
	1	2	3	4	Year
Budgeted unit sales	40,000	60,000	100,000	50,000	250,000
Selling price per unit	× $8	× $8	× $8	× $8	× $8
Total sales	$320,000	$480,000	$800,000	$400,000	$2,000,000

Based on the budgeted sales above, the schedule of expected cash collections is prepared as follows:

	Year 2 Quarter				
	1	2	3	4	Year
Beginning accounts receivable	$ 65,000				$ 65,000
First-quarter sales ($320,000 × 75%, 25%)	240,000	$ 80,000			320,000
Second-quarter sales ($480,000 × 75%, 25%)		360,000	$120,000		480,000
Third-quarter sales ($800,000 × 75%, 25%)			600,000	$200,000	800,000
Fourth-quarter sales ($400,000 × 75%)				300,000	300,000
Total cash collections	$305,000	$440,000	$720,000	$500,000	$1,965,000

2. Based on the sales budget in units, the production budget is prepared as follows:

	Year 2 Quarter					Year 3 Quarter	
	1	2	3	4	Year	1	2
Budgeted unit sales	40,000	60,000	100,000	50,000	250,000	70,000	80,000
Add desired ending finished goods inventory* ...	18,000	30,000	15,000	21,000†	21,000	24,000	
Total needs	58,000	90,000	115,000	71,000	271,000	94,000	
Less beginning finished goods inventory	12,000	18,000	30,000	15,000	12,000	21,000	
Required production	46,000	72,000	85,000	56,000	259,000	73,000	

*30% of the following quarter's budgeted unit sales.
†30% of the budgeted Year 3 first-quarter sales.

3. Based on the production budget, raw materials will need to be purchased during the year as follows:

	Year 2 Quarter					Year 3 Quarter
	1	2	3	4	Year 2	1
Required production in units of finished goods	46,000	72,000	85,000	56,000	259,000	73,000
Units of raw materials needed per unit of finished goods	× 5	× 5	× 5	× 5	× 5	× 5
Units of raw materials needed to meet production	230,000	360,000	425,000	280,000	1,295,000	365,000
Add desired units of ending raw materials inventory*	36,000	42,500	28,000	36,500†	36,500	
Total units of raw materials needed ...	266,000	402,500	453,000	316,500	1,331,500	
Less units of beginning raw materials inventory	23,000	36,000	42,500	28,000	23,000	
Units of raw materials to be purchased	243,000	366,500	410,500	288,500	1,308,500	
Unit cost of raw materials	× $0.80	× $0.80	× $0.80	× $0.80	× $0.80	
Cost of raw materials to be purchased	$194,400	$293,200	$328,400	$230,800	$1,046,800	

*10% of the following quarter's production needs in pounds.
†10% of the Year 3 first-quarter production needs in pounds.

Based on the raw material purchases above, expected cash payments are computed as follows:

	Year 2 Quarter				
	1	2	3	4	Year 2
Beginning accounts payable	$ 81,500				$ 81,500
First-quarter purchases ($194,400 × 60%, 40%)	116,640	$ 77,760			194,400
Second-quarter purchases ($293,200 × 60%, 40%)		175,920	$117,280		293,200
Third-quarter purchases ($328,400 × 60%, 40%)			197,040	$131,360	328,400
Fourth-quarter purchases ($230,800 × 60%)				138,480	138,480
Total cash disbursements	$198,140	$253,680	$314,320	$269,840	$1,035,980

GLOSSARY

Budget A detailed plan for the future that is usually expressed in formal quantitative terms. (p. 294)

Cash budget A detailed plan showing how cash resources will be acquired and used over a specific time period. (p. 297)

Continuous budget A 12-month budget that rolls forward one month as the current month is completed. (p. 295)

Control   The process of gathering feedback to ensure that a plan is being properly executed or modified as circumstances change. (p. 294)

Direct labor budget   A detailed plan that shows the direct labor-hours required to fulfill the production budget. (p. 308)

Direct materials budget   A detailed plan showing the amount of raw materials that must be purchased to fulfill the production budget and to provide for adequate inventories. (p. 307)

Ending finished goods inventory budget   A budget showing the dollar amount of unsold finished goods inventory that will appear on the ending balance sheet. (p. 311)

Manufacturing overhead budget   A detailed plan showing the production costs, other than direct materials and direct labor, that will be incurred over a specified time period. (p. 309)

Master budget   A number of separate but interdependent budgets that formally lay out the company's sales, production, and financial goals and that culminates in a cash budget, budgeted income statement, and budgeted balance sheet. (p. 297)

Merchandise purchases budget   A detailed plan used by a merchandising company that shows the amount of goods that must be purchased from suppliers during the period. (p. 306)

Participative budget   See *Self-imposed budget*. (p. 296)

Perpetual budget   See *Continuous budget*. (p. 295)

Planning   Developing goals and preparing budgets to achieve those goals. (p. 294)

Production budget   A detailed plan showing the number of units that must be produced during a period in order to satisfy both sales and inventory needs. (p. 305)

Responsibility accounting   A system of accountability in which managers are held responsible for those items of revenue and cost—and only those items—over which they can exert significant control. The managers are held responsible for differences between budgeted and actual results. (p. 295)

Sales budget   A detailed schedule showing expected sales expressed in both dollars and units. (p. 297)

Self-imposed budget   A method of preparing budgets in which managers prepare their own budgets. These budgets are then reviewed by higher-level managers, and any issues are resolved by mutual agreement. (p. 296)

Selling and administrative expense budget   A detailed schedule of planned expenses that will be incurred in areas other than manufacturing during a budget period. (p. 311)

QUESTIONS

7–1   What is a budget? What is budgetary control?

7–2   Discuss some of the major benefits to be gained from budgeting.

7–3   What is meant by the term *responsibility accounting?*

7–4   What is a master budget? Briefly describe its contents.

7–5   Why is the sales forecast the starting point in budgeting?

7–6   "As a practical matter, planning and control mean exactly the same thing." Do you agree? Explain.

7–7   Why is it a good idea to create a "Budgeting Assumptions" tab when creating a master budget in Microsoft Excel?

7–8   What is a self-imposed budget? What are the major advantages of self-imposed budgets? What caution must be exercised in their use?

7–9   How can budgeting assist a company in planning its workforce staffing levels?

7–10   "The principal purpose of the cash budget is to see how much cash the company will have in the bank at the end of the year." Do you agree? Explain.

Multiple-choice questions are available in the *Connect Library*.

APPLYING EXCEL    | ACCOUNTING

LO7–2, LO7–3, LO7–4

Available with McGraw-Hill's *Connect Accounting*.

The Excel worksheet form that appears on the next page is to be used to recreate the Review Problem on pages 322–323. Download the workbook containing this form in the *Connect Library*. On the website you will also receive instructions about how to use this worksheet form.

The worksheet image:

	A	B	C	D	E	F	G	H	I
1	Chapter 7: Applying Excel								
2									
3	Data			Year 2 Quarter			Year 3 Quarter		
4			1	2	3	4	1	2	
5	Budgeted unit sales		40,000	60,000	100,000	50,000	70,000	80,000	
6									
7	• Selling price per unit		$8 per unit						
8	• Accounts receivable, beginning balance	$65,000							
9	• Sales collected in the quarter sales are made	75%							
10	• Sales collected in the quarter after sales are made	25%							
11	• Desired ending finished goods inventory is	30% of the budgeted unit sales of the next quarter							
12	• Finished goods inventory, beginning	12,000 units							
13	• Raw materials required to produce one unit	5 pounds							
14	• Desired ending inventory of raw materials is	10% of the next quarter's production needs							
15	• Raw materials inventory, beginning	23,000 pounds							
16	• Raw material costs	$0.80 per pound							
17	• Raw materials purchases are paid	60% in the quarter the purchases are made							
18	and	40% in the quarter following purchase							
19	• Accounts payable for raw materials, beginning balance	$81,500							
20									
21	Enter a formula into each of the cells marked with a ? below								
22	Review Problem: Budget Schedules								

(Schedule rows 24–66 contain "?" placeholders for sales budget, cash collections, production budget, raw materials purchases budget, and cash payments schedules.)

Tabs: Chapter 7 Form | Filled in Chapter 7 Form | Chapter 7 Formulas | Chapter 7 Requirement

You should proceed to the requirements below only after completing your worksheet.

Required:

1. Check your worksheet by changing the budgeted unit sales in Quarter 2 of Year 2 in cell C5 to 75,000 units. The total expected cash collections for the year should now be $2,085,000. If you do not get this answer, find the errors in your worksheet and correct them. Have the total cash disbursements for the year changed? Why or why not?

2. The company has just hired a new marketing manager who insists that unit sales can be dramatically increased by dropping the selling price from $8 to $7. The marketing manager would like to use the following projections in the budget:

Data		Year 2 Quarter			Year 3 Quarter	
	1	2	3	4	1	2
Budgeted unit sales	50,000	70,000	120,000	80,000	90,000	100,000
Selling price per unit ...	$7					

a. What are the total expected cash collections for the year under this revised budget?
b. What is the total required production for the year under this revised budget?
c. What is the total cost of raw materials to be purchased for the year under this revised budget?
d. What are the total expected cash disbursements for raw materials for the year under this revised budget?
e. After seeing this revised budget, the production manager cautioned that due to the limited availability of a complex milling machine, the plant can produce no more than 90,000 units in any one quarter. Is this a potential problem? If so, what can be done about it?

THE FOUNDATIONAL 15

LO7–2, LO7–3, LO7–4, LO7–5, LO7–7, LO7–9, LO7–10

Available with McGraw-Hill's *Connect Accounting*.

Morganton Company makes one product and it provided the following information to help prepare the master budget for its first four months of operations:

a. The budgeted selling price per unit is $70. Budgeted unit sales for June, July, August, and September are 8,400, 10,000, 12,000, and 13,000 units, respectively. All sales are on credit.
b. Forty percent of credit sales are collected in the month of the sale and 60% in the following month.
c. The ending finished goods inventory equals 20% of the following month's unit sales.
d. The ending raw materials inventory equals 10% of the following month's raw materials production needs. Each unit of finished goods requires 5 pounds of raw materials. The raw materials cost $2.00 per pound.
e. Thirty percent of raw materials purchases are paid for in the month of purchase and 70% in the following month.
f. The direct labor wage rate is $15 per hour. Each unit of finished goods requires two direct labor-hours.
g. The variable selling and administrative expense per unit sold is $1.80. The fixed selling and administrative expense per month is $60,000.

Required:
1. What are the budgeted sales for July?
2. What are the expected cash collections for July?
3. What is the accounts receivable balance at the end of July?
4. According to the production budget, how many units should be produced in July?
5. If 61,000 pounds of raw materials are needed to meet production in August, how many pounds of raw materials should be purchased in July?
6. What is the estimated cost of raw materials purchases for July?
7. If the cost of raw material purchases in June is $88,880, what are the estimated cash disbursements for raw materials purchases in July?
8. What is the estimated accounts payable balance at the end of July?
9. What is the estimated raw materials inventory balance at the end of July?
10. What is the total estimated direct labor cost for July assuming the direct labor workforce is adjusted to match the hours required to produce the forecasted number of units produced?
11. If the company always uses an estimated predetermined plantwide overhead rate of $10 per direct labor-hour, what is the estimated unit product cost?
12. What is the estimated finished goods inventory balance at the end of July?
13. What is the estimated cost of goods sold and gross margin for July?
14. What is the estimated total selling and administrative expense for July?
15. What is the estimated net operating income for July?

EXERCISES

All applicable exercises are available with McGraw-Hill's *Connect Accounting*.

EXERCISE 7–1 Schedule of Expected Cash Collections [LO7–2]
Silver Company makes a product that is very popular as a Mother's Day gift. Thus, peak sales occur in May of each year, as shown in the company's sales budget for the second quarter given below:

Budgeted sales in
  June = $250,000

	April	May	June	Total
Budgeted sales (all on account)	$300,000	$500,000	$200,000	$1,000,000

From past experience, the company has learned that 20% of a month's sales are collected in the month of sale, another 70% are collected in the month following sale, and the remaining 10% are collected in the second month following sale. Bad debts are negligible and can be ignored. February sales totaled $230,000, and March sales totaled $260,000.

Required:
1. Prepare a schedule of expected cash collections from sales, by month and in total, for the second quarter.
2. Assume that the company will prepare a budgeted balance sheet as of June 30. Compute the accounts receivable as of that date.

EXERCISE 7–2   Production Budget [LO7–3]

Down Under Products, Ltd., of Australia has budgeted sales of its popular boomerang for the next four months as follows:

	Sales in Units
April	50,000
May	75,000
June	90,000
July	80,000

The company is now in the process of preparing a production budget for the second quarter. Past experience has shown that end-of-month inventory levels must equal 10% of the following month's sales. The inventory at the end of March was 5,000 units.

TAKE TWO

Ending finished goods inventory = 20% of next month's sales; The inventory at March 31 = 10,000 units

Required:
Prepare a production budget for the second quarter; in your budget, show the number of units to be produced each month and for the quarter in total.

EXERCISE 7–3   Direct Materials Budget [LO7–4]

Three grams of musk oil are required for each bottle of Mink Caress, a very popular perfume made by a small company in western Siberia. The cost of the musk oil is $1.50 per gram. Budgeted production of Mink Caress is given below by quarters for Year 2 and for the first quarter of Year 3:

TAKE TWO

	Year 2				Year 3
	First	Second	Third	Fourth	First
Budgeted production, in bottles	60,000	90,000	150,000	100,000	70,000

Each unit requires four grams of musk oil; Inventory at beginning of Year 2 = 48,000 grams of musk oil

Musk oil has become so popular as a perfume ingredient that it has become necessary to carry large inventories as a precaution against stock-outs. For this reason, the inventory of musk oil at the end of a quarter must be equal to 20% of the following quarter's production needs. Some 36,000 grams of musk oil will be on hand to start the first quarter of Year 2.

Required:
Prepare a direct materials budget for musk oil, by quarter and in total, for Year 2. At the bottom of your budget, show the amount of purchases for each quarter and for the year in total.

EXERCISE 7–4   Direct Labor Budget [LO7–5]

The production manager of Rordan Corporation has submitted the following forecast of units to be produced by quarter for the upcoming fiscal year:

TAKE TWO

	1st Quarter	2nd Quarter	3rd Quarter	4th Quarter
Units to be produced	8,000	6,500	7,000	7,500

Each unit requires 0.3 direct labor-hours

Each unit requires 0.35 direct labor-hours, and direct laborers are paid $12.00 per hour.

Required:
1. Construct the company's direct labor budget for the upcoming fiscal year, assuming that the direct labor workforce is adjusted each quarter to match the number of hours required to produce the forecasted number of units produced.

2. Construct the company's direct labor budget for the upcoming fiscal year, assuming that the direct labor workforce is not adjusted each quarter. Instead, assume that the company's direct labor workforce consists of permanent employees who are guaranteed to be paid for at least 2,600 hours of work each quarter. If the number of required direct labor-hours is less than this number, the workers are paid for 2,600 hours anyway. Any hours worked in excess of 2,600 hours in a quarter are paid at the rate of 1.5 times the normal hourly rate for direct labor.

EXERCISE 7–5   Manufacturing Overhead Budget [LO7–6]
The direct labor budget of Yuvwell Corporation for the upcoming fiscal year contains the following details concerning budgeted direct labor-hours:

Variable overhead rate = $2.00 per direct labor-hour

	1st Quarter	2nd Quarter	3rd Quarter	4th Quarter
Budgeted direct labor-hours	8,000	8,200	8,500	7,800

The company's variable manufacturing overhead rate is $3.25 per direct labor-hour and the company's fixed manufacturing overhead is $48,000 per quarter. The only noncash item included in fixed manufacturing overhead is depreciation, which is $16,000 per quarter.

Required:
1. Construct the company's manufacturing overhead budget for the upcoming fiscal year.
2. Compute the company's manufacturing overhead rate (including both variable and fixed manufacturing overhead) for the upcoming fiscal year. Round off to the nearest whole cent.

EXERCISE 7–6   Selling and Administrative Expense Budget [LO7–7]
The budgeted unit sales of Weller Company for the upcoming fiscal year are provided below:

	1st Quarter	2nd Quarter	3rd Quarter	4th Quarter
Budgeted unit sales	15,000	16,000	14,000	13,000

The company's variable selling and administrative expense per unit is $2.50. Fixed selling and administrative expenses include advertising expenses of $8,000 per quarter, executive salaries of $35,000 per quarter, and depreciation of $20,000 per quarter. In addition, the company will make insurance payments of $5,000 in the first quarter and $5,000 in the third quarter. Finally, property taxes of $8,000 will be paid in the second quarter.

Required:
Prepare the company's selling and administrative expense budget for the upcoming fiscal year.

EXERCISE 7–7   Cash Budget [LO7–8]
Garden Depot is a retailer that is preparing its budget for the upcoming fiscal year. Management has prepared the following summary of its budgeted cash flows:

Minimum cash balance = $15,000

	1st Quarter	2nd Quarter	3rd Quarter	4th Quarter
Total cash receipts	$180,000	$330,000	$210,000	$230,000
Total cash disbursements	$260,000	$230,000	$220,000	$240,000

The company's beginning cash balance for the upcoming fiscal year will be $20,000. The company requires a minimum cash balance of $10,000 and may borrow any amount needed from a local bank at a quarterly interest rate of 3%. The company may borrow any amount at the beginning of any quarter and may repay its loans, or any part of its loans, at the end of any quarter. Interest payments are due on any principal at the time it is repaid. For simplicity, assume that interest is not compounded.

Required:
Prepare the company's cash budget for the upcoming fiscal year.

EXERCISE 7–8 Budgeted Income Statement [LO7–9]

Gig Harbor Boating is the wholesale distributor of a small recreational catamaran sailboat. Management has prepared the following summary data to use in its annual budgeting process:

Budgeted unit sales	460
Selling price per unit	$1,950
Cost per unit	$1,575
Variable selling and administrative expenses (per unit)	$75
Fixed selling and administrative expenses (per year)	$105,000
Interest expense for the year	$14,000

TAKE TWO

Budgeted unit sales = 400

Required:

Prepare the company's budgeted income statement. Use the absorption costing income statement format shown in Schedule 9.

EXERCISE 7–9 Budgeted Balance Sheet [LO7–10]

The management of Mecca Copy, a photocopying center located on University Avenue, has compiled the following data to use in preparing its budgeted balance sheet for next year:

	Ending Balances
Cash	?
Accounts receivable	$8,100
Supplies inventory	$3,200
Equipment	$34,000
Accumulated depreciation	$16,000
Accounts payable	$1,800
Common stock	$5,000
Retained earnings	?

TAKE TWO

Net income = $10,000

The beginning balance of retained earnings was $28,000, net income is budgeted to be $11,500, and dividends are budgeted to be $4,800.

Required:

Prepare the company's budgeted balance sheet.

EXERCISE 7–10 Production and Direct Materials Budgets [LO7–3, LO7–4]

Pearl Products Limited of Shenzhen, China, manufactures and distributes toys throughout South East Asia. Three cubic centimeters (cc) of solvent H300 are required to manufacture each unit of Supermix, one of the company's products. The company is now planning raw materials needs for the third quarter, the quarter in which peak sales of Supermix occur. To keep production and sales moving smoothly, the company has the following inventory requirements:

a. The finished goods inventory on hand at the end of each month must be equal to 3,000 units of Supermix plus 20% of the next month's sales. The finished goods inventory on June 30 is budgeted to be 10,000 units.

b. The raw materials inventory on hand at the end of each month must be equal to one-half of the following month's production needs for raw materials. The raw materials inventory on June 30 is budgeted to be 54,000 cc of solvent H300.

c. The company maintains no work in process inventories.
    A sales budget for Supermix for the last six months of the year follows.

	Budgeted Sales in Units
July	35,000
August	40,000
September	50,000
October	30,000
November	20,000
December	10,000

Required:
1. Prepare a production budget for Supermix for the months July, August, September, and October.
2. Examine the production budget that you prepared in (1) above. Why will the company produce more units than it sells in July and August, and fewer units than it sells in September and October?
3. Prepare a direct materials budget showing the quantity of solvent H300 to be purchased for July, August, and September, and for the quarter in total.

EXERCISE 7–11   Cash Budget Analysis [LO7–8]

A cash budget, by quarters, is given below for a retail company (000 omitted). The company requires a minimum cash balance of at least $5,000 to start each quarter.

	Quarter				
	1	2	3	4	Year
Cash balance, beginning	$ 6	$?	$?	$?	$?
Add collections from customers	?	?	96	?	323
Total cash available	71	?	?	?	?
Less disbursements:					
Purchase of inventory	35	45	?	35	?
Selling and administrative expenses	?	30	30	?	113
Equipment purchases	8	8	10	?	36
Dividends	2	2	2	2	?
Total disbursements	?	85	?	?	?
Excess (deficiency) of cash available over disbursements	(2)	?	11	?	?
Financing:					
Borrowings	?	15	—	—	?
Repayments (including interest)*	—	—	(?)	(17)	(?)
Total financing	?	?	?	?	?
Cash balance, ending	$?	$?	$?	$?	$?

*Interest will total $1,000 for the year.

Required:
Fill in the missing amounts in the above table.

Estimated sales for September = $240,000

EXERCISE 7–12   Schedules of Expected Cash Collections and Disbursements; Income Statement; Balance Sheet [LO7–2, LO7–4, LO7–9, LO7–10]

Beech Corporation is a merchandising company that is preparing a master budget for the third quarter of the calendar year. The company's balance sheet as of June 30th is shown below:

Beech Corporation
Balance Sheet
June 30

Assets

Cash	$ 90,000
Accounts receivable	136,000
Inventory	62,000
Plant and equipment, net of depreciation	210,000
Total assets	$498,000

Liabilities and Stockholders' Equity

Accounts payable	$ 71,100
Common stock	327,000
Retained earnings	99,900
Total liabilities and stockholders' equity	$498,000

Beech's managers have made the following additional assumptions and estimates:

1. Estimated sales for July, August, September, and October will be $210,000, $230,000, $220,000, and $240,000, respectively.

2. All sales are on credit and all credit sales are collected. Each month's credit sales are collected 35% in the month of sale and 65% in the month following the sale. All of the accounts receivable at June 30 will be collected in July.

3. Each month's ending inventory must equal 30% of the cost of next month's sales. The cost of goods sold is 60% of sales. The company pays for 40% of its merchandise purchases in the month of the purchase and the remaining 60% in the month following the purchase. All of the accounts payable at June 30 will be paid in July.

4. Monthly selling and administrative expenses are always $60,000. Each month $5,000 of this total amount is depreciation expense and the remaining $55,000 relates to expenses that are paid in the month they are incurred.

5. The company does not plan to borrow money or pay or declare dividends during the quarter ended September 30. The company does not plan to issue any common stock or repurchase its own stock during the quarter ended September 30.

Required:

1. Prepare a schedule of expected cash collections for July, August, and September. Also compute total cash collections for the quarter ended September 30.

2. a. Prepare a merchandise purchases budget for July, August, and September. Also compute total merchandise purchases for the quarter ended September 30.
   b. Prepare a schedule of expected cash disbursements for merchandise purchases for July, August, and September. Also compute total cash disbursements for merchandise purchases for the quarter ended September 30.

3. Prepare an income statement for the quarter ended September 30. Use the absorption format shown in Schedule 9.

4. Prepare a balance sheet as of September 30.

EXERCISE 7–13 Schedules of Expected Cash Collections and Disbursements; Income Statement; Balance Sheet [LO7–2, LO7–4, LO7–9, LO7–10]

Refer to the data for Beech Corporation in Exercise 7–12. The company is considering making the following changes to the assumptions underlying its master budget:

1. Each month's credit sales are collected 45% in the month of sale and 55% in the month following the sale.

2. Each month's ending inventory must equal 20% of the cost of next month's sales.

3. The company pays for 30% of its merchandise purchases in the month of the purchase and the remaining 70% in the month following the purchase.

All other information from Exercise 7–12 that is not mentioned above remains the same.

Required:

Using the new assumptions described above, complete the following requirements:

1. Prepare a schedule of expected cash collections for July, August, and September. Also compute total cash collections for the quarter ended September 30.

2. a. Prepare a merchandise purchases budget for July, August, and September. Also compute total merchandise purchases for the quarter ended September 30.
   b. Prepare a schedule of expected cash disbursements for merchandise purchases for July, August, and September. Also compute total cash disbursements for merchandise purchases for the quarter ended September 30.

3. Prepare an income statement for the quarter ended September 30. Use the absorption format shown in Schedule 9.

4. Prepare a balance sheet as of September 30.

EXERCISE 7–14 Sales and Production Budgets [LO7–2, LO7–3]

The marketing department of Jessi Corporation has submitted the following sales forecast for the upcoming fiscal year (all sales are on account):

TAKE
TWO

	1st Quarter	2nd Quarter	3rd Quarter	4th Quarter
Budgeted unit sales	11,000	12,000	14,000	13,000

Selling price per
unit = $2,500;
Budgeted unit sales in
2nd Quarter = 16,000

The selling price of the company's product is $18.00 per unit. Management expects to collect 65% of sales in the quarter in which the sales are made, 30% in the following quarter, and 5% of sales are expected to be uncollectible. The beginning balance of accounts receivable, all of which is expected to be collected in the first quarter, is $70,200.

The company expects to start the first quarter with 1,650 units in finished goods inventory. Management desires an ending finished goods inventory in each quarter equal to 15% of the next quarter's budgeted sales. The desired ending finished goods inventory for the fourth quarter is 1,850 units.

Required:
1. Prepare the company's sales budget and schedule of expected cash collections.
2. Prepare the company's production budget for the upcoming fiscal year.

EXERCISE 7–15   Direct Labor and Manufacturing Overhead Budgets [LO7–5, LO7–6]
The Production Department of Hruska Corporation has submitted the following forecast of units to be produced by quarter for the upcoming fiscal year:

	1st Quarter	2nd Quarter	3rd Quarter	4th Quarter
Units to be produced	12,000	10,000	13,000	14,000

Each unit requires 0.2 direct labor-hours and direct laborers are paid $12.00 per hour.

In addition, the variable manufacturing overhead rate is $1.75 per direct labor-hour. The fixed manufacturing overhead is $86,000 per quarter. The only noncash element of manufacturing overhead is depreciation, which is $23,000 per quarter.

Required:
1. Prepare the company's direct labor budget for the upcoming fiscal year, assuming that the direct labor workforce is adjusted each quarter to match the number of hours required to produce the forecasted number of units produced.
2. Prepare the company's manufacturing overhead budget.

EXERCISE 7–16   Direct Materials and Direct Labor Budgets [LO7–4, LO7–5]
The production department of Zan Corporation has submitted the following forecast of units to be produced by quarter for the upcoming fiscal year:

Units to be produced in 2nd Quarter = 7,500 units

	1st Quarter	2nd Quarter	3rd Quarter	4th Quarter
Units to be produced	5,000	8,000	7,000	6,000

In addition, the beginning raw materials inventory for the 1st Quarter is budgeted to be 6,000 grams and the beginning accounts payable for the 1st Quarter is budgeted to be $2,880.

Each unit requires 8 grams of raw material that costs $1.20 per gram. Management desires to end each quarter with an inventory of raw materials equal to 25% of the following quarter's production needs. The desired ending inventory for the 4th Quarter is 8,000 grams. Management plans to pay for 60% of raw material purchases in the quarter acquired and 40% in the following quarter. Each unit requires 0.20 direct labor-hours and direct laborers are paid $11.50 per hour.

Required:
1. Prepare the company's direct materials budget and schedule of expected cash disbursements for purchases of materials for the upcoming fiscal year.
2. Prepare the company's direct labor budget for the upcoming fiscal year, assuming that the direct labor workforce is adjusted each quarter to match the number of hours required to produce the forecasted number of units produced.

Alternate problem set is available in the *Connect Library*.       **PROBLEMS**

All applicable problems are available with McGraw-Hill's *Connect Accounting*.

PROBLEM 7–17A   Cash Budget; Income Statement; Balance Sheet [LO7–2, LO7–4, LO7–8, LO7–9, LO7–10]

Minden Company is a wholesale distributor of premium European chocolates. The company's balance sheet as of April 30 is given below:

Minden Company	
Balance Sheet	
April 30	
Assets	
Cash	$ 9,000
Accounts receivable	54,000
Inventory	30,000
Buildings and equipment, net of depreciation	207,000
Total assets	$300,000
Liabilities and Stockholders' Equity	
Accounts payable	$ 63,000
Note payable	14,500
Common stock	180,000
Retained earnings	42,500
Total liabilities and stockholders' equity	$300,000

The company is in the process of preparing a budget for May and has assembled the following data:
a.   Sales are budgeted at $200,000 for May. Of these sales, $60,000 will be for cash; the remainder will be credit sales. One-half of a month's credit sales are collected in the month the sales are made, and the remainder is collected in the following month. All of the April 30 accounts receivable will be collected in May.
b.   Purchases of inventory are expected to total $120,000 during May. These purchases will all be on account. Forty percent of all purchases are paid for in the month of purchase; the remainder are paid in the following month. All of the April 30 accounts payable to suppliers will be paid during May.
c.   The May 31 inventory balance is budgeted at $40,000.
d.   Selling and administrative expenses for May are budgeted at $72,000, exclusive of depreciation. These expenses will be paid in cash. Depreciation is budgeted at $2,000 for the month.
e.   The note payable on the April 30 balance sheet will be paid during May, with $100 in interest. (All of the interest relates to May.)
f.   New refrigerating equipment costing $6,500 will be purchased for cash during May.
g.   During May, the company will borrow $20,000 from its bank by giving a new note payable to the bank for that amount. The new note will be due in one year.

Required:
1.   Prepare a cash budget for May. Support your budget with a schedule of expected cash collections from sales and a schedule of expected cash disbursements for merchandise purchases.
2.   Prepare a budgeted income statement for May. Use the absorption costing income statement format as shown in Schedule 9.
3.   Prepare a budgeted balance sheet as of May 31.

**PROBLEM 7–18A   Cash Budget; Income Statement; Balance Sheet; Changing Assumptions
[LO7–2, LO7–4, LO7–8, LO7–9, LO7–10]**
Refer to the data for Minden Company in Problem 7–17A. The company is considering making the following changes to the assumptions underlying its master budget:
1.   Sales are budgeted for $220,000 for May.
2.   Each month's credit sales are collected 60% in the month of sale and 40% in the month following the sale.
3.   The company pays for 50% of its merchandise purchases in the month of the purchase and the remaining 50% in the month following the purchase.
All other information from Problem 7–17A that is not mentioned above remains the same.

Required:
Using the new assumptions described above, complete the following requirements:
1.   Prepare a cash budget for May. Support your budget with a schedule of expected cash collections from sales and a schedule of expected cash disbursements for merchandise purchases.
2.   Prepare a budgeted income statement for May. Use the absorption costing income statement format as shown in Schedule 9.
4.   Prepare a budgeted balance sheet as of May 31.

PROBLEM 7–19A   Schedules of Expected Cash Collections and Disbursements [LO7–2, LO7–4, LO7–8]
You have been asked to prepare a December cash budget for Ashton Company, a distributor of exercise equipment. The following information is available about the company's operations:

a.   The cash balance on December 1 is $40,000.
b.   Actual sales for October and November and expected sales for December are as follows:

	October	November	December
Cash sales	$65,000	$70,000	$83,000
Sales on account	$400,000	$525,000	$600,000

Sales on account are collected over a three-month period as follows: 20% collected in the month of sale, 60% collected in the month following sale, and 18% collected in the second month following sale. The remaining 2% is uncollectible.
c.   Purchases of inventory will total $280,000 for December. Thirty percent of a month's inventory purchases are paid during the month of purchase. The accounts payable remaining from November's inventory purchases total $161,000, all of which will be paid in December.
d.   Selling and administrative expenses are budgeted at $430,000 for December. Of this amount, $50,000 is for depreciation.
e.   A new web server for the Marketing Department costing $76,000 will be purchased for cash during December, and dividends totaling $9,000 will be paid during the month.
f.   The company maintains a minimum cash balance of $20,000. An open line of credit is available from the company's bank to bolster the cash position as needed.

Required:
1.   Prepare a schedule of expected cash collections for December.
2.   Prepare a schedule of expected cash disbursements for merchandise purchases for December.
3.   Prepare a cash budget for December. Indicate in the financing section any borrowing that will be needed during the month. Assume that any interest will not be paid until the following month.

PROBLEM 7–20A   Evaluating a Company's Budget Procedures [LO7–1]
Springfield Corporation operates on a calendar-year basis. It begins the annual budgeting process in late August, when the president establishes targets for total sales dollars and net operating income before taxes for the next year.
     The sales target is given to the Marketing Department, where the marketing manager formulates a sales budget by product line in both units and dollars. From this budget, sales quotas by product line in units and dollars are established for each of the corporation's sales districts.
     The marketing manager also estimates the cost of the marketing activities required to support the target sales volume and prepares a tentative marketing expense budget.
     The executive vice president uses the sales and profit targets, the sales budget by product line, and the tentative marketing expense budget to determine the dollar amounts that can be devoted to manufacturing

and corporate office expense. The executive vice president prepares the budget for corporate expenses, and then forwards to the Production Department the product-line sales budget in units and the total dollar amount that can be devoted to manufacturing.

The production manager meets with the factory managers to develop a manufacturing plan that will produce the required units when needed within the cost constraints set by the executive vice president. The budgeting process usually comes to a halt at this point because the Production Department does not consider the financial resources allocated to it to be adequate.

When this standstill occurs, the vice president of finance, the executive vice president, the marketing manager, and the production manager meet to determine the final budgets for each of the areas. This normally results in a modest increase in the total amount available for manufacturing costs, while the marketing expense and corporate office expense budgets are cut. The total sales and net operating income figures proposed by the president are seldom changed. Although the participants are seldom pleased with the compromise, these budgets are final. Each executive then develops a new detailed budget for the operations in his or her area.

None of the areas has achieved its budget in recent years. Sales often run below the target. When budgeted sales are not achieved, each area is expected to cut costs so that the president's profit target can still be met. However, the profit target is seldom met because costs are not cut enough. In fact, costs often run above the original budget in all functional areas. The president is disturbed that Springfield has not been able to meet the sales and profit targets. He hired a consultant with considerable relevant industry experience. The consultant reviewed the budgets for the past four years. He concluded that the product-line sales budgets were reasonable and that the cost and expense budgets were adequate for the budgeted sales and production levels.

Required:

1. Discuss how the budgeting process as employed by Springfield Corporation contributes to the failure to achieve the president's sales and profit targets.
2. Suggest how Springfield Corporation's budgeting process could be revised to correct the problem.
3. Should the functional areas be expected to cut their costs when sales volume falls below budget? Explain your answer.

(CMA, adapted)

PROBLEM 7–21A   Schedule of Expected Cash Collections; Cash Budget [LO7–2, LO7–8]

The president of the retailer Prime Products has just approached the company's bank with a request for a $30,000, 90-day loan. The purpose of the loan is to assist the company in acquiring inventories. Because the company has had some difficulty in paying off its loans in the past, the loan officer has asked for a cash budget to help determine whether the loan should be made. The following data are available for the months April through June, during which the loan will be used:

a. On April 1, the start of the loan period, the cash balance will be $24,000. Accounts receivable on April 1 will total $140,000, of which $120,000 will be collected during April and $16,000 will be collected during May. The remainder will be uncollectible.

b. Past experience shows that 30% of a month's sales are collected in the month of sale, 60% in the month following sale, and 8% in the second month following sale. The other 2% represents bad debts that are never collected. Budgeted sales and expenses for the three-month period follow:

	April	May	June
Sales (all on account)	$300,000	$400,000	$250,000
Merchandise purchases	$210,000	$160,000	$130,000
Payroll	$20,000	$20,000	$18,000
Lease payments	$22,000	$22,000	$22,000
Advertising	$60,000	$60,000	$50,000
Equipment purchases	—	—	$65,000
Depreciation	$15,000	$15,000	$15,000

c. Merchandise purchases are paid in full during the month following purchase. Accounts payable for merchandise purchases during March, which will be paid during April, total $140,000.

d. In preparing the cash budget, assume that the $30,000 loan will be made in April and repaid in June. Interest on the loan will total $1,200.

Required:

1. Prepare a schedule of expected cash collections for April, May, and June, and for the three months in total.
2. Prepare a cash budget, by month and in total, for the three-month period.
3. If the company needs a minimum cash balance of $20,000 to start each month, can the loan be repaid as planned? Explain.

PROBLEM 7–22A Cash Budget with Supporting Schedules [LO7–2, LO7–4, LO7–8]

Garden Sales, Inc., sells garden supplies. Management is planning its cash needs for the second quarter. The company usually has to borrow money during this quarter to support peak sales of lawn care equipment, which occur during May. The following information has been assembled to assist in preparing a cash budget for the quarter:

a. Budgeted monthly absorption costing income statements for April–July are

	April	May	June	July
Sales	$600,000	$900,000	$500,000	$400,000
Cost of goods sold	420,000	630,000	350,000	280,000
Gross margin	180,000	270,000	150,000	120,000
Selling and administrative expenses:				
Selling expense	79,000	120,000	62,000	51,000
Administrative expense*	45,000	52,000	41,000	38,000
Total selling and administrative expenses ..	124,000	172,000	103,000	89,000
Net operating income	$ 56,000	$ 98,000	$ 47,000	$ 31,000

*Includes $20,000 of depreciation each month.

b. Sales are 20% for cash and 80% on account.
c. Sales on account are collected over a three-month period with 10% collected in the month of sale; 70% collected in the first month following the month of sale; and the remaining 20% collected in the second month following the month of sale. February's sales totaled $200,000, and March's sales totaled $300,000.
d. Inventory purchases are paid for within 15 days. Therefore, 50% of a month's inventory purchases are paid for in the month of purchase. The remaining 50% is paid in the following month. Accounts payable at March 31 for inventory purchases during March total $126,000.
e. Each month's ending inventory must equal 20% of the cost of the merchandise to be sold in the following month. The merchandise inventory at March 31 is $84,000.
f. Dividends of $49,000 will be declared and paid in April.
g. Land costing $16,000 will be purchased for cash in May.
h. The cash balance at March 31 is $52,000; the company must maintain a cash balance of at least $40,000 at the end of each month.
i. The company has an agreement with a local bank that allows the company to borrow in increments of $1,000 at the beginning of each month, up to a total loan balance of $200,000. The interest rate on these loans is 1% per month and for simplicity we will assume that interest is not compounded. The company would, as far as it is able, repay the loan plus accumulated interest at the end of the quarter.

Required:

1. Prepare a schedule of expected cash collections for April, May, and June, and for the quarter in total.
2. Prepare the following for merchandise inventory:
    a. A merchandise purchases budget for April, May, and June.
    b. A schedule of expected cash disbursements for merchandise purchases for April, May, and June, and for the quarter in total.
3. Prepare a cash budget for April, May, and June as well as in total for the quarter.

PROBLEM 7–23A Cash Budget with Supporting Schedules; Changing Assumptions [LO7–2, LO7–4, LO7–8]

Refer to the data for Garden Sales, Inc., in Problem 7–22A. The company's president is interested in knowing how reducing inventory levels and collecting accounts receivable sooner will impact the cash budget. He revises the cash collection and ending inventory assumptions as follows:

1. Sales continue to be 20% for cash and 80% on credit. However, credit sales from April, May, and June are collected over a three-month period with 25% collected in the month of sale, 65% collected in the

month following sale, and 10% in the second month following sale. Credit sales from February and March are collected during the second quarter using the collection percentages specified in Problem 7–22A.

2. The company maintains its ending inventory levels for April, May, and June at 15% of the cost of merchandise to be sold in the following month. The merchandise inventory at March 31 remains $84,000 and accounts payable for inventory purchases at March 31 remains $126,000.

All other information from Problem 7–22A that is not referred to above remains the same.

Required:

1. Using the president's new assumptions in (1) above, prepare a schedule of expected cash collections for April, May, and June and for the quarter in total.
2. Using the president's new assumptions in (2) above, prepare the following for merchandise inventory:
    a. A merchandise purchases budget for April, May, and June.
    b. A schedule of expected cash disbursements for merchandise purchases for April, May, and June and for the quarter in total.
3. Using the president's new assumptions, prepare a cash budget for April, May, and June, and for the quarter in total.
4. Prepare a brief memorandum for the president explaining how his revised assumptions affect the cash budget.

PROBLEM 7–24A   Behavioral Aspects of Budgeting; Ethics and the Manager [LO7–1]

Norton Company, a manufacturer of infant furniture and carriages, is in the initial stages of preparing the annual budget for next year. Scott Ford has recently joined Norton's accounting staff and is interested to learn as much as possible about the company's budgeting process. During a recent lunch with Marge Atkins, sales manager, and Pete Granger, production manager, Ford initiated the following conversation.

Ford: Since I'm new around here and am going to be involved with the preparation of the annual budget, I'd be interested to learn how the two of you estimate sales and production numbers.

Atkins: We start out very methodically by looking at recent history, discussing what we know about current accounts, potential customers, and the general state of consumer spending. Then, we add that usual dose of intuition to come up with the best forecast we can.

Granger: I usually take the sales projections as the basis for my projections. Of course, we have to make an estimate of what this year's ending inventories will be, which is sometimes difficult.

Ford: Why does that present a problem? There must have been an estimate of ending inventories in the budget for the current year.

Granger: Those numbers aren't always reliable because Marge makes some adjustments to the sales numbers before passing them on to me.

Ford: What kind of adjustments?

Atkins: Well, we don't want to fall short of the sales projections so we generally give ourselves a little breathing room by lowering the initial sales projection anywhere from 5% to 10%.

Granger: So, you can see why this year's budget is not a very reliable starting point. We always have to adjust the projected production rates as the year progresses and, of course, this changes the ending inventory estimates. By the way, we make similar adjustments to expenses by adding at least 10% to the estimates; I think everyone around here does the same thing.

Required:

1. Marge Atkins and Pete Granger have described the use of what is sometimes called *budgetary slack.*
    a. Explain why Atkins and Granger behave in this manner and describe the benefits they expect to realize from the use of budgetary slack.
    b. Explain how the use of budgetary slack can adversely affect Atkins and Granger.
2. As a management accountant, Scott Ford believes that the behavior described by Marge Atkins and Pete Granger may be unethical. By referring to the IMA's Statement of Ethical Professional Practice in the Prologue, explain why the use of budgetary slack may be unethical.

(CMA, adapted)

PROBLEM 7–25A   Schedule of Expected Cash Collections; Cash Budget [LO7–2, LO7–8]

Herbal Care Corp., a distributor of herb-based sunscreens, is ready to begin its third quarter, in which peak sales occur. The company has requested a $40,000, 90-day loan from its bank to help meet cash requirements during the quarter. Since Herbal Care has experienced difficulty in paying off its loans in the past, the loan officer at the bank has asked the company to prepare a cash budget for the quarter. In response to this request, the following data have been assembled:

a.   On July 1, the beginning of the third quarter, the company will have a cash balance of $44,500.

b.   Actual sales for the last two months and budgeted sales for the third quarter follow (all sales are on account):

May (actual)	$250,000
June (actual)	$300,000
July (budgeted)	$400,000
August (budgeted)	$600,000
September (budgeted)	$320,000

Past experience shows that 25% of a month's sales are collected in the month of sale, 70% in the month following sale, and 3% in the second month following sale. The remainder is uncollectible.

c.   Budgeted merchandise purchases and budgeted expenses for the third quarter are given below:

	July	August	September
Merchandise purchases	$240,000	$350,000	$175,000
Salaries and wages	$45,000	$50,000	$40,000
Advertising	$130,000	$145,000	$80,000
Rent payments	$9,000	$9,000	$9,000
Depreciation	$10,000	$10,000	$10,000

Merchandise purchases are paid in full during the month following purchase. Accounts payable for merchandise purchases on June 30, which will be paid during July, total $180,000.

d.   Equipment costing $10,000 will be purchased for cash during July.

e.   In preparing the cash budget, assume that the $40,000 loan will be made in July and repaid in September. Interest on the loan will total $1,200.

Required:

1.   Prepare a schedule of expected cash collections for July, August, and September and for the quarter in total.

2.   Prepare a cash budget, by month and in total, for the third quarter.

3.   If the company needs a minimum cash balance of $20,000 to start each month, can the loan be repaid as planned? Explain.

PROBLEM 7–26A   Cash Budget with Supporting Schedules [LO7–2, LO7–4, LO7–7, LO7–8]
Westex Products is a wholesale distributor of industrial cleaning products. When the treasurer of Westex Products approached the company's bank late in the current year seeking short-term financing, he was told that money was very tight and that any borrowing over the next year would have to be supported by a detailed statement of cash collections and disbursements. The treasurer also was told that it would be very helpful to the bank if borrowers would indicate the quarters in which they would be needing funds, as well as the amounts that would be needed, and the quarters in which repayments could be made.

Because the treasurer is unsure as to the particular quarters in which bank financing will be needed, he has assembled the following information to assist in preparing a detailed cash budget:

a.   Budgeted sales and merchandise purchases for next year, as well as actual sales and purchases for the last quarter of the current year, are

	Sales	Merchandise Purchases
Current Year:		
Fourth quarter actual	$200,000	$126,000
Next Year:		
First quarter estimated	$300,000	$186,000
Second quarter estimated	$400,000	$246,000
Third quarter estimated	$500,000	$305,000
Fourth quarter estimated	$200,000	$126,000

b. All sales are on account. The company normally collects 65% of a quarter's sales before the quarter ends and another 33% in the following quarter. The remainder is uncollectible. This pattern of collections is now being experienced in the current year's fourth-quarter actual data.

c. Eighty percent of a quarter's merchandise purchases are paid for within the quarter. The remainder is paid for in the following quarter.

d. Selling and administrative expenses for next year are budgeted at $50,000 per quarter plus 15% of sales. Of the fixed amount, $20,000 each quarter is depreciation.

e. The company will pay $10,000 in dividends each quarter.

f. Land purchases of $75,000 will be made in the second quarter, and purchases of $48,000 will be made in the third quarter. These purchases will be for cash.

g. The Cash account contained $10,000 at the end of the current year. The treasurer feels that this represents a minimum balance that must be maintained.

h. The company has an agreement with a local bank that allows the company to borrow in increments of $1,000 at the beginning of each quarter, up to a total loan balance of $100,000. The interest rate on these loans is 2.5% per quarter and for simplicity we will assume that interest is not compounded. The company would, as far as it is able, repay the loan plus accumulated interest at the end of the year.

i. At present, the company has no loans outstanding.

Required:

1. Prepare the following by quarter and in total for next year:
    a. A schedule of expected cash collections.
    b. A schedule of expected cash disbursements for merchandise purchases.

2. Compute the expected cash disbursements for selling and administrative expenses, by quarter and in total, for next year.

3. Prepare a cash budget, by quarter and in total, for next year.

PROBLEM 7–27A   Completing a Master Budget [LO7–2, LO7–4, LO7–7, LO7–8, LO7–9, LO7–10]
The following data relate to the operations of Shilow Company, a wholesale distributor of consumer goods:

Current assets as of March 31:	
Cash	$8,000
Accounts receivable	$20,000
Inventory	$36,000
Building and equipment, net	$120,000
Accounts payable	$21,750
Common stock	$150,000
Retained earnings	$12,250

a. The gross margin is 25% of sales.
b. Actual and budgeted sales data:

March (actual)	$50,000
April	$60,000
May	$72,000
June	$90,000
July	$48,000

c. Sales are 60% for cash and 40% on credit. Credit sales are collected in the month following sale. The accounts receivable at March 31 are a result of March credit sales.

d. Each month's ending inventory should equal 80% of the following month's budgeted cost of goods sold.

e. One-half of a month's inventory purchases is paid for in the month of purchase; the other half is paid for in the following month. The accounts payable at March 31 are the result of March purchases of inventory.

f. Monthly expenses are as follows: commissions, 12% of sales; rent, $2,500 per month; other expenses (excluding depreciation), 6% of sales. Assume that these expenses are paid monthly. Depreciation is $900 per month (includes depreciation on new assets).

g. Equipment costing $1,500 will be purchased for cash in April.

h. Management would like to maintain a minimum cash balance of at least $4,000 at the end of each month. The company has an agreement with a local bank that allows the company to borrow in increments of $1,000 at the beginning of each month, up to a total loan balance of $20,000. The interest rate on these loans is 1% per month and for simplicity we will assume that interest is not compounded. The company would, as far as it is able, repay the loan plus accumulated interest at the end of the quarter.

Required:

Using the preceding data:

1.   Complete the following schedule:

Schedule of Expected Cash Collections

	April	May	June	Quarter
Cash sales	$36,000			
Credit sales	20,000	—	—	—
Total collections	$56,000	═	═	═

2.   Complete the following:

Merchandise Purchases Budget

	April	May	June	Quarter
Budgeted cost of goods sold	$45,000*	$54,000		
Add desired ending inventory	43,200†	____	____	____
Total needs	88,200			
Less beginning inventory	36,000	____	____	____
Required purchases	$52,200	═	═	═

*For April sales: $60,000 sales × 75% cost ratio = $45,000.
†$54,000 × 80% = $43,200

Schedule of Expected Cash Disbursements—Merchandise Purchases

	April	May	June	Quarter
March purchases	$21,750			$21,750
April purchases	26,100	$26,100		52,200
May purchases				
June purchases		____	____	____
Total disbursements	$47,850	═	═	═

3.   Complete the following cash budget:

Cash Budget

	April	May	June	Quarter
Beginning cash balance	$ 8,000			
Add cash collections	56,000	____	____	____
Total cash available	64,000	____	____	____
Less cash disbursements:				
For inventory	47,850			
For expenses	13,300			
For equipment	1,500	____	____	____
Total cash disbursements	62,650	____	____	____
Excess (deficiency) of cash	1,350			
Financing:				
Etc.				

4.   Prepare an absorption costing income statement, similar to the one shown in Schedule 9 in the chapter, for the quarter ended June 30.

5.   Prepare a balance sheet as of June 30.

PROBLEM 7–28A   Integration of the Sales, Production, and Direct Materials Budgets [LO7–2, LO7–3, LO7–4]

Milo Company manufactures beach umbrellas. The company is preparing detailed budgets for the third quarter and has assembled the following information to assist in the budget preparation:

a.   The Marketing Department has estimated sales as follows for the remainder of the year (in units):

July	30,000	October	20,000
August	70,000	November	10,000
September	50,000	December	10,000

The selling price of the beach umbrellas is $12 per unit.

b.   All sales are on account. Based on past experience, sales are collected in the following pattern:

> 30% in the month of sale
> 65% in the month following sale
> 5% uncollectible

Sales for June totaled $300,000.

c.   The company maintains finished goods inventories equal to 15% of the following month's sales. This requirement will be met at the end of June.

d.   Each beach umbrella requires 4 feet of Gilden, a material that is sometimes hard to acquire. Therefore, the company requires that the ending inventory of Gilden be equal to 50% of the following month's production needs. The inventory of Gilden on hand at the beginning and end of the quarter will be

June 30	72,000 feet
September 30	? feet

e.   Gilden costs $0.80 per foot. One-half of a month's purchases of Gilden is paid for in the month of purchase; the remainder is paid for in the following month. The accounts payable on July 1 for purchases of Gilden during June will be $76,000.

Required:

1.   Prepare a sales budget, by month and in total, for the third quarter. (Show your budget in both units and dollars.) Also prepare a schedule of expected cash collections, by month and in total, for the third quarter.
2.   Prepare a production budget for each of the months July–October.
3.   Prepare a direct materials budget for Gilden, by month and in total, for the third quarter. Also prepare a schedule of expected cash disbursements for Gilden, by month and in total, for the third quarter.

PROBLEM 7–29A   Completing a Master Budget [LO7–2, LO7–4, LO7–7, LO7–8, LO7–9, LO7–10]

Hillyard Company, an office supplies specialty store, prepares its master budget on a quarterly basis. The following data have been assembled to assist in preparing the master budget for the first quarter:

a.   As of December 31 (the end of the prior quarter), the company's general ledger showed the following account balances:

	Debits	Credits
Cash	$ 48,000	
Accounts receivable	224,000	
Inventory	60,000	
Buildings and equipment (net)	370,000	
Accounts payable		$ 93,000
Common stock		500,000
Retained earnings		109,000
	$702,000	$702,000

b. Actual sales for December and budgeted sales for the next four months are as follows:

December (actual)	$280,000
January	$400,000
February	$600,000
March	$300,000
April	$200,000

c. Sales are 20% for cash and 80% on credit. All payments on credit sales are collected in the month following sale. The accounts receivable at December 31 are a result of December credit sales.
d. The company's gross margin is 40% of sales. (In other words, cost of goods sold is 60% of sales.)
e. Monthly expenses are budgeted as follows: salaries and wages, $27,000 per month: advertising, $70,000 per month; shipping, 5% of sales; other expenses, 3% of sales. Depreciation, including depreciation on new assets acquired during the quarter, will be $42,000 for the quarter.
f. Each month's ending inventory should equal 25% of the following month's cost of goods sold.
g. One-half of a month's inventory purchases is paid for in the month of purchase; the other half is paid in the following month.
h. During February, the company will purchase a new copy machine for $1,700 cash. During March, other equipment will be purchased for cash at a cost of $84,500.
i. During January, the company will declare and pay $45,000 in cash dividends.
j. Management wants to maintain a minimum cash balance of $30,000. The company has an agreement with a local bank that allows the company to borrow in increments of $1,000 at the beginning of each month. The interest rate on these loans is 1% per month and for simplicity we will assume that interest is not compounded. The company would, as far as it is able, repay the loan plus accumulated interest at the end of the quarter.

Required:
Using the data above, complete the following statements and schedules for the first quarter:
1. Schedule of expected cash collections:

	January	February	March	Quarter
Cash sales	$ 80,000			
Credit sales	224,000			
Total cash collections	$304,000			

2. a. Merchandise purchases budget:

	January	February	March	Quarter
Budgeted cost of goods sold	$240,000*	$360,000		
Add desired ending inventory	90,000†			
Total needs	330,000			
Less beginning inventory	60,000			
Required purchases	$270,000			

*$400,000 sales × 60% cost ratio = $240,000.
†$360,000 × 25% = $90,000.

b. Schedule of expected cash disbursements for merchandise purchases:

	January	February	March	Quarter
December purchases	$ 93,000			$ 93,000
January purchases	135,000	135,000		270,000
February purchases		—		
March purchases		—		
Total cash disbursements for purchases	$228,000			

3. Cash budget:

	January	February	March	Quarter
Beginning cash balance	$ 48,000			
Add cash collections	304,000			
Total cash available	352,000			
Less cash disbursements:				
Purchases of inventory	228,000			
Selling and administrative				
expenses	129,000			
Purchases of equipment	—			
Cash dividends	45,000			
Total cash disbursements	402,000			
Excess (deficiency) of cash	(50,000)			
Financing:				
Etc.				

4. Prepare an absorption costing income statement for the quarter ending March 31 as shown in Schedule 9 in the chapter.
5. Prepare a balance sheet as of March 31.

BUILDING YOUR SKILLS

ETHICS CHALLENGE [LO7–1]

Granger Stokes, managing partner of the venture capital firm of Halston and Stokes, was dissatisfied with the top management of PrimeDrive, a manufacturer of computer disk drives. Halston and Stokes had invested $20 million in PrimeDrive, and the return on their investment had been below expectations for several years. In a tense meeting of the board of directors of PrimeDrive, Stokes exercised his firm's rights as the major equity investor in PrimeDrive and fired PrimeDrive's chief executive officer (CEO). He then quickly moved to have the board of directors of PrimeDrive appoint himself as the new CEO.

Stokes prided himself on his hard-driving management style. At the first management meeting, he asked two of the managers to stand and fired them on the spot, just to show everyone who was in control of the company. At the budget review meeting that followed, he ripped up the departmental budgets that had been submitted for his review and yelled at the managers for their "wimpy, do nothing targets." He then ordered everyone to submit new budgets calling for at least a 40% increase in sales volume and announced that he would not accept excuses for results that fell below budget.

Keri Kalani, an accountant working for the production manager at PrimeDrive, discovered toward the end of the year that her boss had not been scrapping defective disk drives that had been returned by customers. Instead, he had been shipping them in new cartons to other customers to avoid booking losses. Quality control had deteriorated during the year as a result of the push for increased volume, and returns of defective disk drives were running as high as 15% of the new drives shipped. When she confronted her boss with her discovery, he told her to mind her own business. And then, to justify his actions, he said, "All of us managers are finding ways to hit Stokes's targets."

Required:
1. Is Granger Stokes using budgets as a planning and control tool?
2. What are the behavioral consequences of the way budgets are being used at PrimeDrive?
3. What, if anything, do you think Keri Kalani should do?

ANALYTICAL THINKING [LO7–1]

Tom Emory and Jim Morris strolled back to their plant from the administrative offices of Ferguson & Son Manufacturing Company. Tom is manager of the machine shop in the company's factory; Jim is manager of the equipment maintenance department.

The men had just attended the monthly performance evaluation meeting for plant department heads. These meetings had been held on the third Tuesday of each month since Robert Ferguson, Jr., the president's son, had become plant manager a year earlier.

As they were walking, Tom Emory spoke: "Boy, I hate those meetings! I never know whether my department's accounting reports will show good or bad performance. I'm beginning to expect the worst. If the accountants say I saved the company a dollar, I'm called 'Sir,' but if I spend even a little too much—boy, do I get in trouble. I don't know if I can hold on until I retire."

Tom had just been given the worst evaluation he had ever received in his long career with Ferguson & Son. He was the most respected of the experienced machinists in the company. He had been with Ferguson & Son for many years and was promoted to supervisor of the machine shop when the company expanded and moved to its present location. The president (Robert Ferguson, Sr.) had often stated that the company's success was due to the high-quality work of machinists like Tom. As supervisor, Tom stressed the importance of craftsmanship and told his workers that he wanted no sloppy work coming from his department.

When Robert Ferguson, Jr., became the plant manager, he directed that monthly performance comparisons be made between actual and budgeted costs for each department. The departmental budgets were intended to encourage the supervisors to reduce inefficiencies and to seek cost reduction opportunities. The company controller was instructed to have his staff "tighten" the budget slightly whenever a department attained its budget in a given month; this was done to reinforce the plant manager's desire to reduce costs. The young plant manager often stressed the importance of continued progress toward attaining the budget; he also made it known that he kept a file of these performance reports for future reference when he succeeded his father.

Tom Emory's conversation with Jim Morris continued as follows:

Emory: I really don't understand. We've worked so hard to meet the budget, and the minute we do so they tighten it on us. We can't work any faster and still maintain quality. I think my men are ready to quit trying. Besides, those reports don't tell the whole story. We always seem to be interrupting the big jobs for all those small rush orders. All that setup and machine adjustment time is killing us. And quite frankly, Jim, you were no help. When our hydraulic press broke down last month, your people were nowhere to be found. We had to take it apart ourselves and got stuck with all that idle time.

Morris: I'm sorry about that, Tom, but you know my department has had trouble making budget, too. We were running well behind at the time of that problem, and if we'd spent a day on that old machine, we would never have made it up. Instead we made the scheduled inspections of the forklift trucks because we knew we could do those in less than the budgeted time.

Emory: Well, Jim, at least you have some options. I'm locked into what the scheduling department assigns to me and you know they're being harassed by sales for those special orders. Incidentally, why didn't your report show all the supplies you guys wasted last month when you were working in Bill's department?

Morris: We're not out of the woods on that deal yet. We charged the maximum we could to other work and haven't even reported some of it yet.

Emory: Well, I'm glad you have a way of getting out of the pressure. The accountants seem to know everything that's happening in my department, sometimes even before I do. I thought all that budget and accounting stuff was supposed to help, but it just gets me into trouble. It's all a big pain. I'm trying to put out quality work; they're trying to save pennies.

Required:
1. Identify the problems that appear to exist in Ferguson & Son Manufacturing Company's budgetary control system and explain how the problems are likely to reduce the effectiveness of the system.
2. Explain how Ferguson & Son Manufacturing Company's budgetary control system could be revised to improve its effectiveness.

(CMA, adapted)

CASE [LO7–2, LO7–4, LO7–8, LO7–9, LO7–10]
You have just been hired as a new management trainee by Earrings Unlimited, a distributor of earrings to various retail outlets located in shopping malls across the country. In the past, the company has done very little in the way of budgeting and at certain times of the year has experienced a shortage of cash.

Since you are well trained in budgeting, you have decided to prepare comprehensive budgets for the upcoming second quarter in order to show management the benefits that can be gained from an integrated budgeting program. To this end, you have worked with accounting and other areas to gather the information assembled below.

The company sells many styles of earrings, but all are sold for the same price—$10 per pair. Actual sales of earrings for the last three months and budgeted sales for the next six months follow (in pairs of earrings):

January (actual)	20,000	June (budget)	50,000
February (actual)	26,000	July (budget)	30,000
March (actual)	40,000	August (budget)	28,000
April (budget)	65,000	September (budget)	25,000
May (budget)	100,000		

The concentration of sales before and during May is due to Mother's Day. Sufficient inventory should be on hand at the end of each month to supply 40% of the earrings sold in the following month.

Suppliers are paid $4 for a pair of earrings. One-half of a month's purchases is paid for in the month of purchase; the other half is paid for in the following month. All sales are on credit, with no discount, and payable within 15 days. The company has found, however, that only 20% of a month's sales are collected in the month of sale. An additional 70% is collected in the following month, and the remaining 10% is collected in the second month following sale. Bad debts have been negligible.

Monthly operating expenses for the company are given below:

Variable:	
Sales commissions	4% of sales
Fixed:	
Advertising	$200,000
Rent	$18,000
Salaries	$106,000
Utilities	$7,000
Insurance	$3,000
Depreciation	$14,000

Insurance is paid on an annual basis, in November of each year.

The company plans to purchase $16,000 in new equipment during May and $40,000 in new equipment during June; both purchases will be for cash. The company declares dividends of $15,000 each quarter, payable in the first month of the following quarter.

A listing of the company's ledger accounts as of March 31 is given below:

Assets	
Cash	$ 74,000
Accounts receivable ($26,000 February sales; $320,000 March sales)	346,000
Inventory	104,000
Prepaid insurance	21,000
Property and equipment (net)	950,000
Total assets	$1,495,000

Liabilities and Stockholders' Equity	
Accounts payable	$ 100,000
Dividends payable	15,000
Common stock	800,000
Retained earnings	580,000
Total liabilities and stockholders' equity	$1,495,000

The company maintains a minimum cash balance of $50,000. All borrowing is done at the beginning of a month; any repayments are made at the end of a month.

The company has an agreement with a bank that allows the company to borrow in increments of $1,000 at the beginning of each month. The interest rate on these loans is 1% per month and for simplicity we will assume that interest is not compounded. At the end of the quarter, the company would pay the bank all of the accumulated interest on the loan and as much of the loan as possible (in increments of $1,000), while still retaining at least $50,000 in cash.

Required:

Prepare a master budget for the three-month period ending June 30. Include the following detailed budgets:

1. a. A sales budget, by month and in total.
   b. A schedule of expected cash collections from sales, by month and in total.
   c. A merchandise purchases budget in units and in dollars. Show the budget by month and in total.
   d. A schedule of expected cash disbursements for merchandise purchases, by month and in total.
2. A cash budget. Show the budget by month and in total. Determine any borrowing that would be needed to maintain the minimum cash balance of $50,000.
3. A budgeted income statement for the three-month period ending June 30. Use the contribution approach.
4. A budgeted balance sheet as of June 30.

COMMUNICATING IN PRACTICE [LO7–1]

In recent years, public universities have experienced major budget cuts due to reduced funding from their state governments. These budget cuts usually occur at the most inopportune time—during the school year when contractual commitments with faculty and staff had been signed, programs had been planned, and students were enrolled and taking classes.

Required:

1. Should the administration be "fair" to all affected and institute across-the-board cuts whenever the state announces a reduction in funding?
2. If not across-the-board cutbacks in programs, then would you recommend more focused reductions, and if so, what priorities would you establish for bringing spending in line with revenues?
3. Since these usually are not one-time-only cutbacks, how would you manage continuous, long-term reductions in budgets extending over a period of years?
4. Should the decision-making process be top-down (centralized with top administrators) or bottom-up (participative)? Why?
5. How should issues such as protect-your-turf mentality, resistance to change, and consensus building be dealt with?

A LOOK BACK

In Chapter 7, we discussed the budgeting process and each of the schedules in the master budget.

A LOOK AT THIS CHAPTER

Chapter 8 begins our discussion of management control and performance measures. We explain how to prepare flexible budgets and how to compare them to actual results for the purposes of computing revenue and spending variances. We also describe how standards are used to isolate the effects of various factors on actual results. In particular, we compute material, labor, and overhead variances.

A LOOK AHEAD

In Chapter 9, we continue the discussion of management control and performance measures by focusing on how decentralized organizations are managed.

8 Flexible Budgets, Standard Costs, and Variance Analysis

LEARNING OBJECTIVES

After studying Chapter 8, you should be able to:

LO8–1 Prepare a flexible budget.

LO8–2 Prepare a report showing revenue and spending variances.

LO8–3 Prepare a flexible budget with more than one cost driver.

LO8–4 Compute the direct materials price and quantity variances and explain their significance.

LO8–5 Compute the direct labor rate and efficiency variances and explain their significance.

LO8–6 Compute the variable manufacturing overhead rate and efficiency variances and explain their significance.

LO8–7 (Appendix 8A) Compute and interpret the fixed overhead budget and volume variances.

LO8–8 (Appendix 8B) Prepare journal entries to record standard costs and variances.

Why Do Companies Need Flexible Budgets?

The difficulty of accurately predicting future financial performance can be readily understood by reading the annual report of any publicly traded company. For example, **Nucor Corporation**, a steel manufacturer headquartered in Charlotte, North Carolina, cites numerous reasons why its actual results may differ from expectations, including the following: (1) changes in the supply and cost of raw materials; (2) changes in the availability and cost of electricity and natural gas; (3) changes in the market demand for steel products; (4) fluctuations in currency conversion rates; (5) significant changes in laws or government regulations; and (6) the cyclical nature of the steel industry.

Source: Nucor Corporation 2011 Annual Report, p. 3.

In the last chapter we explored how budgets are developed before a period begins. In this chapter, we explain how budgets can be adjusted to help guide actual operations and influence the performance evaluation process. For example, an organization's actual expenses will rarely equal its budgeted expenses as estimated at the beginning of the period. The reason is that the actual level of activity (such as unit sales) will rarely be the same as the budgeted activity; therefore, many actual expenses and revenues will naturally differ from what was budgeted. Should a manager be penalized for spending 10% more than budgeted for a variable expense like direct materials if unit sales are 10% higher than budgeted? Of course not. After studying this chapter, you'll know how to adjust a budget to enable meaningful comparisons to actual results.

THE VARIANCE ANALYSIS CYCLE

Companies use the *variance analysis cycle,* as illustrated in Exhibit 8–1, to evaluate and improve performance. The cycle begins with the preparation of performance reports in the accounting department. These reports highlight variances, which are the differences between the actual results and what should have occurred according to the budget. The variances raise questions. Why did this variance occur? Why is this variance larger than it was last period? The significant variances are investigated so that their root causes can be either replicated or eliminated. Then, next period's operations are carried out and the cycle begins again with the preparation of a new performance report for the latest period. The emphasis should be on highlighting superior and unsatisfactory results, finding the root causes of these outcomes, and then replicating the sources of superior achievement and eliminating the sources of unsatisfactory performance. The variance analysis cycle should not be used to assign blame for poor performance.

Managers frequently use the concept of *management by exception* in conjunction with the variance analysis cycle. **Management by exception** is a management system that compares actual results to a budget so that significant deviations can be flagged as exceptions and investigated further. This approach enables managers to focus on the most important variances while bypassing trivial discrepancies between the budget and actual results. For example, a variance of $5 is probably not big enough to warrant attention, whereas a variance of $5,000 might be worth tracking down. Another clue is the size of the variance relative to the amount of spending. A variance that is only 0.1% of spending on an item is probably caused by random factors. On the other hand, a variance of 10% of spending is much more likely to be a signal that something is wrong. In addition to watching for unusually large variances, the pattern of the variances should be monitored. For example, a run of steadily mounting variances should trigger an investigation even though none of the variances is large enough by itself to warrant investigation.

EXHIBIT 8–1
The Variance Analysis Cycle

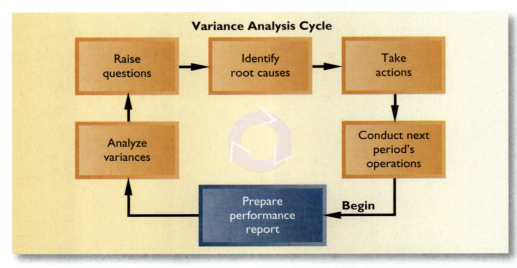

Next, we explain how service organizations use flexible budgets to analyze variances followed by a discussion of how companies can use standard costs for those same purposes.

FLEXIBLE BUDGETS

Characteristics of a Flexible Budget

The budgets that we explored in the last chapter were *planning budgets*. A **planning budget** is prepared before the period begins and is valid for only the planned level of activity. A static planning budget is suitable for planning but is inappropriate for evaluating how well costs are controlled. If the actual level of activity differs from what was planned, it would be misleading to compare actual costs to the static, unchanged planning budget. If activity is higher than expected, variable costs should be higher than expected; and if activity is lower than expected, variable costs should be lower than expected.

Flexible budgets take into account how changes in activity affect costs. A **flexible budget** is an estimate of what revenues and costs should have been, given the actual level of activity for the period. When a flexible budget is used in performance evaluation, actual costs are compared to what the costs *should have been for the actual level of activity during the period* rather than to the static planning budget. This is a very important distinction. If adjustments for the level of activity are not made, it is very difficult to interpret discrepancies between budgeted and actual costs.

LEARNING OBJECTIVE 8–1

Prepare a flexible budget.

---

1. Which of the following statements is true? (You may select more than one answer.)
   a. A planning budget is prepared before the period begins and it is based on the actual level of activity incurred during the period.
   b. A flexible budget is an estimate of what revenues and costs should have been, given the actual level of activity for the period.
   c. The variance analysis cycle includes analyzing differences between actual results and what should have occurred according to the budget.
   d. The management by exception approach enables managers to focus on the most important variances while bypassing trivial discrepancies.

✓ **CONCEPT CHECK**

Winners and Losers from the NBA Lockout

IN BUSINESS

A company's actual net operating income can deviate from the budget for numerous and often uncontrollable reasons. For example, when the **National Basketball Association** (NBA) decided to suspend play because of a dispute between its team owners and players, many small businesses suffered—caterers, sports bars, apparel retailers, and parking lot owners all experienced a drop in revenues. BestSportsApparel.com experienced a substantial drop in NBA apparel sales due to the work stoppage. Rather than hiring 12 extra employees for the NBA season, the company reduced the size of its workforce.

While some companies lost revenues when the NBA shut down, others benefited from the situation. Andrew Zimbalist, professor of economics at Smith College, notes that "local economies are not impacted by sports work stoppages" because people choose to spend their entertainment dollars at other venues such as the theater, the zoo, or the museum.

Source: Emily Maltby and Sarah E. Needleman, "NBA Lockout: Local Firms Lose Big," *The Wall Street Journal*, October 13, 2011, p. B5.

Deficiencies of the Static Planning Budget

To illustrate the difference between a static planning budget and a flexible budget, consider Rick's Hairstyling, an upscale hairstyling salon located in Beverly Hills that is owned and managed by Rick Manzi. Recently Rick has been attempting to get better control of his revenues and costs, and at the urging of his accounting and business adviser, Victoria Kho, he has begun to prepare monthly budgets.

At the end of February, Rick prepared the March budget that appears in Exhibit 8–2. Rick believes that the number of customers served in a month (also known as the number of client-visits) is the best way to measure the overall level of activity in his salon. A customer who comes into the salon and has his or her hair styled is counted as one client-visit.

Note that the term *revenue* is used in the planning budget rather than *sales*. We use the term revenue throughout the chapter because some organizations have sources of revenue other than sales. For example, donations, as well as sales, are counted as revenue in non-profit organizations.

Rick has identified eight major categories of costs—wages and salaries, hairstyling supplies, client gratuities, electricity, rent, liability insurance, employee health insurance, and miscellaneous. Client gratuities consist of flowers, candies, and glasses of champagne that Rick gives to his customers while they are in the salon.

Working with Victoria Kho, Rick estimated a cost formula for each cost. For example, the cost formula for electricity is $1,500 + $0.10q$, where q equals the number of client-visits. In other words, electricity is a mixed cost with a $1,500 fixed element and a $0.10 per client-visit variable element. Once the budgeted level of activity was set at 1,000 client-visits, Rick computed the budgeted amount for each line item in the budget. For example, using the cost formula, he set the budgeted cost for electricity at $1,600 (= $1,500 + $0.10 × 1,000$). To finalize his budget, Rick computed his expected net operating income for March of $16,800.

At the end of March, Rick prepared the income statement in Exhibit 8–3, which shows that 1,100 clients actually visited his salon in March and that his actual net operating income for the month was $21,230. It is important to realize that the actual results are *not* determined by plugging the actual number of client-visits into the revenue and cost formulas. The formulas are simply estimates of what the revenues and costs should be for a given level of activity. What actually happens usually differs from what is supposed to happen.

The first thing Rick noticed when comparing Exhibits 8–2 and 8–3 is that the actual profit of $21,230 (from Exhibit 8-3) was substantially higher than the budgeted profit of $16,800 (from Exhibit 8-2). This was, of course, good news, but Rick wanted to know

EXHIBIT 8–2
Planning Budget

Rick's Hairstyling Planning Budget For the Month Ended March 31	
Budgeted client-visits (q)	1,000
Revenue ($180.00q)	$180,000
Expenses:	
Wages and salaries ($65,000 + $37.00q)	102,000
Hairstyling supplies ($1.50q)	1,500
Client gratuities ($4.10q)	4,100
Electricity ($1,500 + $0.10q)	1,600
Rent ($28,500)	28,500
Liability insurance ($2,800)	2,800
Employee health insurance ($21,300)	21,300
Miscellaneous ($1,200 + $0.20q)	1,400
Total expense	163,200
Net operating income	$ 16,800

EXHIBIT 8–3
Actual Results—Income
Statement

Rick's Hairstyling Income Statement For the Month Ended March 31	
Actual client-visits	1,100
Revenue	$194,200
Expenses:	
Wages and salaries	106,900
Hairstyling supplies	1,620
Client gratuities	6,870
Electricity	1,550
Rent	28,500
Liability insurance	2,800
Employee health insurance	22,600
Miscellaneous	2,130
Total expense	172,970
Net operating income	$ 21,230

more. Business was up by 10%—the salon had 1,100 client-visits instead of the budgeted 1,000 client-visits. Could this alone explain the higher net operating income? The answer is no. An increase in net operating income of 10% would have resulted in net operating income of only $18,480 (= 1.1 × $16,800), not the $21,230 actually earned during the month. What is responsible for this better outcome? Higher prices? Lower costs? Something else? Whatever the cause, Rick would like to know the answer and then hopefully repeat the same performance next month.

In an attempt to analyze what happened in March, Rick prepared the report comparing actual to budgeted costs that appears in Exhibit 8–4. Note that most of the variances in this report are labeled unfavorable (U) rather than favorable (F) even though net

EXHIBIT 8–4
Comparison of Actual Results to
the Static Planning Budget

Rick's Hairstyling Comparison of Actual Results to Planning Budget For the Month Ended March 31	Actual Results	Planning Budget	Variances*
Client-visits	1,100	1,000	
Revenue	$194,200	$180,000	$14,200 F
Expenses:			
Wages and salaries	106,900	102,000	4,900 U
Hairstyling supplies	1,620	1,500	120 U
Client gratuities	6,870	4,100	2,770 U
Electricity	1,550	1,600	50 F
Rent	28,500	28,500	0
Liability insurance	2,800	2,800	0
Employee health insurance	22,600	21,300	1,300 U
Miscellaneous	2,130	1,400	730 U
Total expense	172,970	163,200	9,770 U
Net operating income	$ 21,230	$ 16,800	$ 4,430 F

*The revenue variance is labeled favorable (unfavorable) when the actual revenue is greater than (less than) the planning budget. The expense variances are labeled favorable (unfavorable) when the actual expense is less than (greater than) the planning budget.

operating income was actually higher than expected. For example, wages and salaries show an unfavorable variance of $4,900 because the actual wages and salaries expense was $106,900, whereas the budget called for wages and salaries of $102,000. The problem with the report, as Rick immediately realized, is that it compares revenues and costs at one level of activity (1,000 client-visits) to revenues and costs at a different level of activity (1,100 client-visits). This is like comparing apples to oranges. Because Rick had 100 more client-visits than expected, some of his costs should be higher than budgeted. From Rick's standpoint, the increase in activity was good; however, it appears to be having a negative impact on most of the costs in the report. Rick knew that something would have to be done to make the report more meaningful, but he was unsure of what to do. So he contacted his accountant, Victoria Kho, and asked her to analyze his salon's performance using the data in Exhibits 8–2 and 8–3.

How a Flexible Budget Works

Victoria responded to Rick's request by preparing the flexible budget shown in Exhibit 8–5. Her flexible budget shows what the *revenues and costs should have been given the actual level of activity* in March. She calculated the expenses in her flexible budget by using Rick's cost formulas from Exhibit 8–2 to estimate what each expense should have been for 1,100 client-visits—the actual level of activity. For example, using the cost formula $1,500 + $0.10q, the cost of electricity in March *should have been* $1,610 (= $1,500 + $0.10 × 1,100). Also, notice that the amounts of rent ($28,500), liability insurance ($2,800), and employee health insurance ($21,300) in Victoria's flexible budget equal the corresponding amounts included in Rick's planning budget. This occurs because fixed costs are not affected by the activity level.

We can see from the flexible budget that the net operating income in March *should have been* $30,510, but recall from Exhibit 8–3 that the net operating income was actually only $21,230. The results are not as good as we thought. Why? We will answer that question shortly.

To summarize to this point, Rick had budgeted for a profit of $16,800. The actual profit was quite a bit higher—$21,230. However, Victoria's analysis shows that given the actual number of client-visits in March, the profit should have been even higher—$30,510. What are the causes of these discrepancies? Rick would certainly like to build on the positive factors, while working to reduce the negative factors. But what are they?

EXHIBIT 8–5
Flexible Budget Based on Actual Activity

Rick's Hairstyling
Flexible Budget
For the Month Ended March 31

Actual client-visits (*q*)	1,100
Revenue ($180.00*q*)	$198,000
Expenses:	
Wages and salaries ($65,000 + $37.00*q*)	105,700
Hairstyling supplies ($1.50*q*)	1,650
Client gratuities ($4.10*q*)	4,510
Electricity ($1,500 + $0.10*q*)	1,610
Rent ($28,500)	28,500
Liability insurance ($2,800)	2,800
Employee health insurance ($21,300)	21,300
Miscellaneous ($1,200 + $0.20*q*)	1,420
Total expense	167,490
Net operating income	$ 30,510

FLEXIBLE BUDGET VARIANCES

Recall that the flexible budget based on the actual level of activity in Exhibit 8–5 shows what *should have happened given the actual level of activity.* Therefore, Victoria's next step was to compare actual results to the flexible budget—in essence comparing what actually happened to what should have happened. Her work is shown in Exhibit 8–6.

LEARNING OBJECTIVE 8–2

Prepare a report showing revenue and spending variances

Revenue Variances

Focusing first on revenue, the actual revenue totaled $194,200. However, the flexible budget indicates that, given the actual level of activity, revenue should have been $198,000. Consequently, revenue was $3,800 less than it should have been, given the actual number of client-visits for the month. This discrepancy is labeled as a $3,800 U (unfavorable) variance and is called a *revenue variance.* A **revenue variance** is the difference between the actual total revenue and what the total revenue should have been, given the actual level of activity for the period. If actual revenue exceeds what the revenue should have been, the variance is labeled favorable. If actual revenue is less than what the revenue should have been, the variance is labeled unfavorable. Why would actual revenue be less than or more than it should have been, given the actual level of activity? Basically, the revenue variance is favorable if the average selling price is greater than expected; it is unfavorable if the average selling price is less than expected. This could happen for a variety of reasons including a change in selling price, a different mix of products sold, a change in the amount of discounts given, poor accounting controls, and so on.

EXHIBIT 8–6
Revenue and Spending Variances from Comparing Actual Results to the Flexible Budget

Rick's Hairstyling Revenue and Spending Variances For the Month Ended March 31	Actual Results	Flexible Budget	Revenue and Spending Variances*
Client-visits	1,100	1,100	
Revenue ($180.00q)	$194,200	$198,000	$3,800 U
Expenses:			
Wages and salaries ($65,000 + $37.00q)	106,900	105,700	1,200 U
Hairstyling supplies ($1.50q)	1,620	1,650	30 F
Client gratuities ($4.10q)	6,870	4,510	2,360 U
Electricity ($1,500 + $0.10q)	1,550	1,610	60 F
Rent ($28,500)	28,500	28,500	0
Liability insurance ($2,800)	2,800	2,800	0
Employee health insurance ($21,300)	22,600	21,300	1,300 U
Miscellaneous ($1,200 + $0.20q)	2,130	1,420	710 U
Total expense	172,970	167,490	5,480 U
Net operating income	$ 21,230	$ 30,510	$9,280 U

*The revenue variance is labeled favorable (unfavorable) when the actual revenue is greater than (less than) the flexible budget. The expense variances are labeled favorable (unfavorable) when the actual expense is less than (greater than) the flexible budget.

State of the Union Speech Hurts Corporate Jet Industry

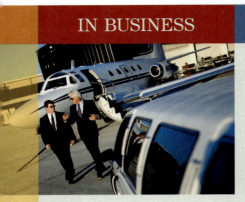

In December 2008, Detroit auto executives flew private corporate jets to Washington D.C. to plead for billions of taxpayer dollars to save their companies. The public outcry was loud and clear: How could companies on the verge of bankruptcy afford to transport their executives in private corporate jets? One month later President Obama's State of the Union speech included criticism of CEOs who "disappear on a private jet."

The impact of these events on the corporate jet manufacturing industry was swift and severe. **Dassault Aviation** had 27 more order cancellations than new orders in the first quarter of 2009. **Cessna Aircraft** had 92 first-quarter order cancellations and laid off 42% of its workforce. Approximately 3,100 jets flooded the resale market compared to 1,800 jets for resale in the first quarter of the prior year. The CEO of Cessna and the president of **Gulfstream Aerospace** went to the White House in May 2009 to seek an end to the rhetoric that was destroying their sales.

These facts illustrate how actual results can be affected by uncontrollable events. The actual first-quarter sales at these companies were substantially lower than their planned sales due to reasons that they could not foresee or control.

Source: Carol Matlack, "Public Flak Grounds Private Jets," *BusinessWeek*, June 8, 2009, p. 13.

Spending Variances

Focusing next on costs, the actual electricity cost was $1,550; however, the flexible budget indicates that electricity costs should have been $1,610 for the 1,100 client-visits in March. Because the cost was $60 less than we would have expected for the actual level of activity during the period, it is labeled as a favorable variance, $60 F. This is an example of a *spending variance*. By definition, a **spending variance** is the difference between the actual amount of the cost and how much a cost should have been, given the actual level of activity. If the actual cost is greater than what the cost should have been, the variance is labeled as unfavorable. If the actual cost is less than what the cost should have been, the variance is labeled as favorable. Why would a cost have a favorable or unfavorable variance? There are many possible explanations including paying a higher price for inputs than should have been paid, using too many inputs for the actual level of activity, a change in technology, and so on. Later in the chapter we will explore these types of explanations in greater detail when we begin discussing standard costs.

Note from Exhibit 8–6 that the overall net operating income variance is $9,280 U (unfavorable). This means that given the actual level of activity for the period, the net operating income was $9,280 lower than it should have been. There are a number of reasons for this. The most prominent is the unfavorable revenue variance of $3,800. Next in line is the $2,360 unfavorable variance for client gratuities. Looking at this in another way, client gratuities were more than 50% larger than they should have been according to the flexible budget. This is a variance that Rick would almost certainly want to investigate further. He may find that this unfavorable variance is not necessarily a bad thing. It is possible, for example, that more lavish use of gratuities led to the 10% increase in client-visits.

Exhibit 8–6 also includes a $1,300 unfavorable variance related to employee health insurance, thereby highlighting how a fixed cost can have a spending variance. While fixed costs do not depend on the level of activity, the actual amount of a fixed cost can differ from the estimated amount included in a flexible budget. For example, perhaps Rick's employee health insurance premiums unexpectedly increased by $1,300 during March.

In conclusion, the revenue and spending variances in Exhibit 8–6 will help Rick better understand why his actual net operating income differs from what should have happened given the actual level of activity.

DECISION POINT

Owner of Micro-Brewery

Hops is an essential ingredient in beer. The brewery's budget for the current month, which was based on the production of 800 barrels of beer, allowed for an expense of $960 for hops. The actual production for the month was 850 barrels of beer and the actual cost of the hops used to produce that beer was $1,020. Hops is a variable cost. Do you think the expense for hops for the month was too high?

FLEXIBLE BUDGETS WITH MULTIPLE COST DRIVERS

At Rick's Hairstyling, we have thus far assumed that there is only one cost driver—the number of client-visits. However, in the activity-based costing chapter, we found that more than one cost driver might be needed to adequately explain all of the costs in an organization. For example, some of the costs at Rick's Hairstyling probably depend more on the number of hours that the salon is open for business than the number of client-visits. Specifically, most of Rick's employees are paid salaries, but some are paid on an hourly basis. None of the employees is paid on the basis of the number of customers actually served. Consequently, the cost formula for wages and salaries would be more accurate if it were stated in terms of the hours of operation rather than the number of client-visits. The cost of electricity is even more complex. Some of the cost is fixed—the heat must be kept at some minimum level even at night when the salon is closed. Some of the cost depends on the number of client-visits—the power consumed by hair dryers depends on the number of customers served. Some of the cost depends on the number of hours the salon is open—the costs of lighting the salon and heating it to a comfortable temperature. Consequently, the cost formula for electricity would be more accurate if it were stated in terms of both the number of client-visits and the hours of operation rather than just in terms of the number of client-visits.

Exhibit 8–7 shows a flexible budget in which these changes have been made. In that flexible budget, two cost drivers are listed—client-visits and hours of operation—where q_1 refers to client-visits and q_2 refers to hours of operation. For example, wages and salaries depend on the hours of operation and its cost formula is $65,000 + $220q_2$. Because the salon actually operated 190 hours, the flexible budget amount for wages and salaries

LEARNING OBJECTIVE 8–3

Prepare a flexible budget with more than one cost driver.

EXHIBIT 8–7
Flexible Budget Based on More than One Cost Driver

Rick's Hairstyling Flexible Budget For the Month Ended March 31	
Actual client-visits (q_1)	1,100
Actual hours of operation (q_2)	190
Revenue (180.00q_1$)	$198,000
Expenses:	
Wages and salaries ($65,000 + $220q_2$)	106,800
Hairstyling supplies (1.50q_1$)	1,650
Client gratuities (4.10q_1$)	4,510
Electricity ($390 + $0.10q_1 + $6.00q_2$)	1,640
Rent ($28,500)	28,500
Liability insurance ($2,800)	2,800
Employee health insurance ($21,300)	21,300
Miscellaneous ($1,200 + $0.20q_1$)	1,420
Total expense	168,620
Net operating income	$ 29,380

is $106,800 (= $65,000 + $220 × 190). The electricity cost depends on both client-visits and the hours of operation and its cost formula is $390 + $0.10q_1 + $6.00q_2$. Because the actual number of client-visits was 1,100 and the salon actually operated for 190 hours, the flexible budget amount for electricity is $1,640 (= $390 + $0.10 × 1,100 + $6.00 × 190). Notice that the net operating income in the flexible budget based on two cost drivers is $29,380, whereas the net operating income in the flexible budget based on one cost driver (see Exhibit 8–5) is $30,510. These two amounts differ because the flexible budget based on two cost drivers is more accurate than the flexible budget based on one driver.

The revised flexible budget based on both client-visits and hours of operation can be used exactly like we used the earlier flexible budget based on just client-visits to compute revenue and spending variances as in Exhibit 8–6. The difference is that because the cost formulas based on more than one cost driver are more accurate than the cost formulas based on just one cost driver, the variances will also be more accurate.

Beyond using more than one cost driver to improve its budgeting and performance analysis process, a company can also decompose its spending variances into two parts—a part that measures how well resources were used and a part that measures how well the acquisition prices of those resources were controlled. For example, at Rick's Hairstyling, an unfavorable spending variance for hairstyling supplies could be due to using too many supplies or paying too much for the supplies, or some combination of the two. *The remainder of the chapter explains how standard cost systems can be used to decompose spending variances into these two parts.* Shortly, we'll transition from our example involving Rick's Hairstyling to an example involving a manufacturing company called The Colonial Pewter Company. Because standard cost systems are frequently used in manufacturing companies, we are shifting our focus accordingly.

CONCEPT CHECK

2. A five-star hotel buys bouquets of flowers to decorate its common areas and guest rooms. Its flexible budget for flowers is $325 per day of operations plus $7.20 per room-day. (A room day is a room rented for one day; a room is decorated with flowers only if it is occupied.) If this month the hotel operated for 30 days and it had 7,680 room-days, what would be the flexible budget amount for flowers for the month?
   a. $55,296
   b. $65,046
   c. $9,750
   d. $332.20
3. Refer to the data in the above question. If the actual spending on flowers for the month was $61,978 and the hotel originally budgeted for 30 operating days and 7,500 room-days, what was the spending variance for the month?
   a. $3,068 Favorable
   b. $3,068 Unfavorable
   c. $1,772 Favorable
   d. $1,772 Unfavorable

STANDARD COSTS—SETTING THE STAGE

A *standard* is a benchmark for measuring performance. Standards are found everywhere. Auto service centers like **Firestone** and **Sears**, for example, often set specific labor time standards for the completion of certain tasks, such as installing a carburetor or doing a valve job, and then measure actual performance against these standards. Fast-food outlets such as **McDonald's** and **Subway** have exacting standards for the quantity of meat going into a sandwich, as well as standards for the cost of the meat. Your doctor evaluates your weight using standards for individuals of your age, height, and gender. The buildings we live in conform to standards set in building codes.

Standards are also widely used in managerial accounting where they relate to the *quantity* and acquisition *price* of inputs used in manufacturing goods or providing services.[1] *Quantity standards* specify how much of an input should be used to make a product or provide a service. *Price standards* specify how much should be paid for each unit of the input. If either the quantity or acquisition price of an input departs significantly from the standard, managers investigate the discrepancy to find the cause of the problem and eliminate it.

Next we'll demonstrate how a company can establish quantity and price standards for direct materials, direct labor, and variable manufacturing overhead and then we'll discuss how those standards can be used to calculate variances and manage operations.

The Colonial Pewter Company makes only one product—an elaborate reproduction of an 18th century pewter statue. The statue is made largely by hand, using traditional metalworking tools. Consequently, the manufacturing process is labor intensive and requires a high level of skill.

Colonial Pewter has recently expanded its workforce to take advantage of unexpected demand for the statue as a gift. The company started with a small cadre of experienced pewter workers but has had to hire less experienced workers as a result of the expansion. The president of the company, J. D. Wriston, has called a meeting to discuss production problems. Attending the meeting are Tom Kuchel, the production manager; Janet Warner, the purchasing manager; and Terry Sherman, the corporate controller.

Colonial Pewter Company

J. D.: I've got a feeling that we aren't getting the production we should out of our new people.

Tom: Give us a chance. Some of the new people have been with the company for less than a month.

Janet: Let me add that production seems to be wasting an awful lot of material—particularly pewter. That stuff is very expensive.

Tom: What about the shipment of defective pewter that you bought—the one with the iron contamination? That caused us major problems.

Janet: How was I to know it was off-grade? Besides, it was a great deal.

J. D.: Calm down everybody. Let's get the facts before we start attacking each other.

Tom: I agree. The more facts the better.

J. D.: Okay, Terry, it's your turn. Facts are the controller's department.

Terry: I'm afraid I can't provide the answers off the top of my head, but if you give me about a week I can set up a system that can routinely answer questions relating to worker productivity, material waste, and input prices.

J. D.: Let's mark it on our calendars.

Setting Direct Materials Standards

Terry Sherman's first task was to prepare quantity and price standards for the company's only significant raw material, pewter ingots. The **standard quantity per unit** defines the amount of direct materials that should be used for each unit of finished product, including an allowance for normal inefficiencies, such as scrap and spoilage.[2] After consulting with the production manager, Tom Kuchel, Terry set the quantity standard for pewter at 3.0 pounds per statue.

---

[1]Throughout the chapter, we assume that "tight but attainable" practical standards are used rather than ideal standards that can only be attained by the most skilled and efficient employees working at peak effort 100% of the time.

[2]Although companies often create "practical" rather than "ideal" materials quantity standards that include allowances for normal inefficiencies such as scrap, spoilage, and rejects, this practice is often criticized because it contradicts the zero defects goal that underlies many process improvement programs. If these types of allowances are built into materials quantity standards, they should be periodically reviewed and reduced over time to reflect improved processes, better training, and better equipment.

The **standard price per unit** defines the price that should be paid for each unit of direct materials and it should reflect the final, delivered cost of those materials. After consulting with purchasing manager Janet Warner, Terry set the standard price of pewter at $4.00 per pound.

Once Terry established the quantity and price standards he computed the standard direct materials cost per statue as follows:

$$3.0 \text{ pounds per statue} \times \$4.00 \text{ per pound} = \$12.00 \text{ per statue}$$

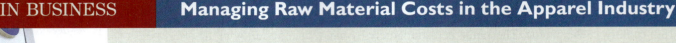

IN BUSINESS Managing Raw Material Costs in the Apparel Industry

A company's raw material costs can rise for numerous and often uncontrollable reasons. For example, severe weather in China, which is the world's largest producer of cotton, can influence the cotton prices paid by **Abercrombie & Fitch**. Rising fuel costs can influence what **Maidenform Brands** pays for its petroleum-based synthetic fabrics. When farmers stop producing cotton in favor of soybeans, it increases the price **Jones Apparel Group** pays for a shrinking supply of cotton.

When faced with rising raw material costs, companies can respond three ways. First, they can maintain existing selling prices and consequently operate with lower margins. Second, they can pass the cost increases along to customers in the form of higher prices. Third, they can try to lower their raw material costs. For example, **Hanesbrands** buys hedging contracts that lock in its cotton prices, thereby insulating the company from future cost increases. **J.C. Penney** is changing the blend of raw materials used in its garments, whereas Maidenform has started buying some of its raw materials from lower-cost producers in Bangladesh.

Source: Elizabeth Holmes and Rachel Dodes, "Cotton Tale: Apparel Prices Set to Rise," *The Wall Street Journal*, May 19, 2010, p. B8.

Setting Direct Labor Standards

Direct labor quantity and price standards are usually expressed in terms of labor-hours or a labor rate. The **standard hours per unit** defines the amount of direct labor-hours that should be used to produce one unit of finished goods. One approach used to determine this standard is for an industrial engineer to do a time and motion study, actually clocking the time required for each task. Throughout the chapter, we'll assume that "tight but attainable" labor standards are used rather than "ideal" standards that can only be attained by the most skilled and efficient employees working at peak effort 100% of the time. Therefore, after consulting with the production manager and considering reasonable allowances for breaks, personal needs of employees, cleanup, and machine downtime, Terry set the standard hours per unit at 0.50 direct labor-hours per statue.[3]

The **standard rate per hour** defines the company's expected direct labor wage rate per hour, including employment taxes and fringe benefits. Using wage records and in consultation with the production manager, Terry Sherman established a standard rate per hour of $22.00. This standard rate reflects the expected "mix" of workers, even though the actual hourly wage rates may vary somewhat from individual to individual due to differing skills or seniority.

Once Terry established the time and rate standards, he computed the standard direct labor cost per statue as follows:

$$0.50 \text{ direct labor-hours per statue} \times \$22.00 \text{ per direct labor-hour} = \$11.00 \text{ per statue}$$

---

[3]Labor quantity standards assume that the production process is labor-paced—if labor works faster, output will go up. However, output in many companies is determined by the processing speed of machines, not by labor efficiency.

EXHIBIT 8–8
Standard Cost Card—Variable
Manufacturing Costs

Inputs	(1) Standard Quantity or Hours	(2) Standard Price or Rate	Standard Cost (1) × (2)
Direct materials.	3.0 pounds	$4.00 per pound	$12.00
Direct labor	0.50 hours	$22.00 per hour	11.00
Variable manufacturing overhead	0.50 hours	$6.00 per hour	3.00
Total standard cost per unit.			$26.00

Setting Variable Manufacturing Overhead Standards

As with direct labor, the quantity and price standards for variable manufacturing overhead are usually expressed in terms of hours and a rate. The *standard hours per unit* for variable overhead measures the amount of the allocation base from a company's predetermined overhead rate that is required to produce one unit of finished goods. In the case of Colonial Pewter, we will assume that the company uses direct labor-hours as the allocation base in its predetermined overhead rate. Therefore, the standard hours per unit for variable overhead is exactly the same as the standard hours per unit for direct labor—0.50 direct labor-hours per statue.

The *standard rate per unit* that a company expects to pay for variable overhead equals *the variable portion of the predetermined overhead rate*. At Colonial Pewter, the variable portion of the predetermined overhead rate is $6.00 per direct labor-hour. Therefore, Terry computed the standard variable manufacturing overhead cost per statue as follows:

0.50 direct labor-hours per statue × $6.00 per direct labor-hour = $3.00 per statue

This $3.00 per unit cost for variable manufacturing overhead appears along with direct materials ($12 per unit) and direct labor ($11 per unit) on the *standard cost card* in Exhibit 8–8. A **standard cost card** shows the standard quantity (or hours) and standard price (or rate) of the inputs required to produce a unit of a specific product. The **standard cost per unit** for all three variable manufacturing costs is computed the same way. The standard quantity (or hours) per unit is multiplied by the standard price (or rate) per unit to obtain the standard cost per unit.

Using Standards in Flexible Budgets

Once Terry Sherman created the standard cost card shown in Exhibit 8–8, he was ready to use this information to calculate direct materials, direct labor, and variable manufacturing overhead variances. Therefore, he gathered the following data for the month of June:

Actual output in June	2,000 statues
Actual direct materials cost in June*	$24,700
Actual direct labor cost in June.	$22,680
Actual variable manufacturing overhead cost in June	$7,140

*There were no beginning or ending inventories of raw materials in June; all materials purchased were used.

Using the above data and the standard cost data from Exhibit 8–8, Terry computed the spending variances shown in Exhibit 8–9. Notice that the actual results and flexible budget columns are each based on the actual output of 2,000 statues. The standard costs of

EXHIBIT 8-9
Spending Variances for
Variable Manufacturing Costs

Colonial Pewter
Spending Variances—Variable Manufacturing Costs Only
For the Month Ended June 30

	Actual Results	Spending Variances	Flexible Budget
Statues produced (q)	2,000		2,000
Direct materials ($12.00q$)	$24,700	$700 U	$24,000
Direct labor ($11.00q$)	$22,680	$680 U	$22,000
Variable manufacturing overhead ($3.00q$)	$7,140	$1,140 U	$6,000

$12.00 per unit for materials, $11.00 per unit for direct labor, and $3.00 per unit for variable manufacturing overhead are each multiplied by the actual output of 2,000 statues to compute the amounts in the flexible budget column. For example, the standard direct labor cost per unit of $11.00 multiplied by 2,000 statues equals the direct labor flexible budget of $22,000.

The spending variances shown in Exhibit 8–9 are computed by taking the amounts in the actual results column and subtracting the amounts in the flexible budget column. For all three variable manufacturing costs, this computation results in a positive number because the actual amount of the cost incurred to produce 2,000 statues exceeds the standard cost allowed for 2,000 statues. Because, in all three instances, the actual cost incurred exceeds the standard cost allowed for the actual level of output, the variance is labeled unfavorable (U). Had any of the actual costs incurred been less than the standard cost allowed for the actual level of output, the corresponding variances would have been labeled favorable (F).

While the information in Exhibit 8–9 is useful, it would be even more useful if the spending variances could be broken down into their price-related and quantity-related components. For example, the direct materials spending variance in the report is $700 unfavorable. This means that, given the actual level of production for the period, direct materials costs were too high by $700—at least according to the standard costs. Was this due to higher than expected prices for materials? Or was it due to too much material being used? The standard cost variances we will be discussing in the rest of the chapter are designed to answer these questions.

A GENERAL MODEL FOR STANDARD COST VARIANCE ANALYSIS

Standard cost variance analysis decomposes spending variances from the flexible budget into two elements—one due to the price paid for the input and the other due to the amount of the input that is used. A **price variance** is the difference between the actual amount paid for an input and the standard amount that should have been paid, multiplied by the actual amount of the input purchased. A **quantity variance** is the difference between how much of an input was actually used and how much should have been used and is stated in dollar terms using the standard price of the input.

Why are standards separated into two categories—price and quantity? Price variances and quantity variances usually have different causes. In addition, different managers are usually responsible for buying and using inputs. For example, in the case of a raw material, the purchasing manager is responsible for its price and the production manager is responsible for the amount of the raw material actually used to make products. Therefore, it is important to clearly distinguish between deviations from price standards (the responsibility of the purchasing manager) and deviations from quantity standards (the responsibility of the production manager).

EXHIBIT 8–10   A General Model for Standard Cost Variance Analysis—Variable Manufacturing Costs

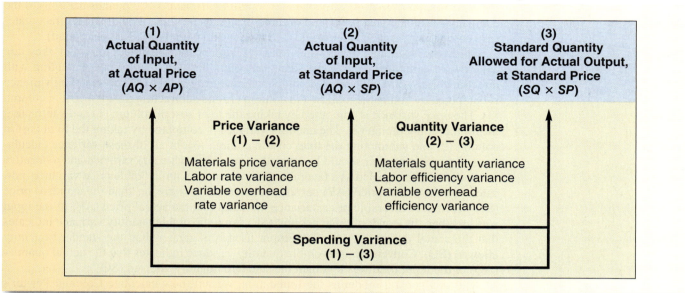

Exhibit 8–10 presents a general model that can be used to decompose the spending variance for a variable cost into a *price variance* and a *quantity variance*.[4] Column (1) in this exhibit corresponds with the Actual Results column in Exhibit 8–9. Column (3) corresponds with the Flexible Budget column in Exhibit 8–9. Column (2) has been inserted into Exhibit 8–10 to enable separating the spending variance into a price variance and a quantity variance.

Three things should be noted from Exhibit 8–10. First, it can be used to compute a price variance and a quantity variance for each of the three variable cost elements—direct materials, direct labor, and variable manufacturing overhead—even though the variances have different names. A price variance is called a *materials price variance* in the case of direct materials, a *labor rate variance* in the case of direct labor, and a *variable overhead rate variance* in the case of variable manufacturing overhead. A quantity variance is called a *materials quantity variance* in the case of direct materials, a *labor efficiency variance* in the case of direct labor, and a *variable overhead efficiency variance* in the case of variable manufacturing overhead.

Second, all three columns in the exhibit are based on the *actual amount of output* produced during the period. Even the flexible budget column depicts the standard cost allowed for the *actual amount of output* produced during the period. The key to understanding the flexible budget column in Exhibit 8–10 is to grasp the meaning of the term *standard quantity allowed (SQ)*. The **standard quantity allowed** (when computing direct materials variances) or **standard hours allowed** (when computing direct labor and variable manufacturing overhead variances) refers to the amount of an input *that should have been used* to manufacture the actual output of finished goods produced during the period. It is computed by multiplying the actual output by the standard quantity (or hours) per unit. The standard quantity (or hours) allowed is then multiplied by the standard price (or rate) per unit of the input to obtain the total cost according to the flexible budget. For example, if a company actually produced 100 units of finished goods during the period and its

---

[4]This general model can always be used to compute direct labor and variable manufacturing overhead variances. However, it can be used to compute direct materials variances only when the actual quantity of materials purchased equals the actual quantity of materials used in production. Later in the chapter, we will explain how to compute direct materials variances when these quantities differ.

standard quantity per unit of finished goods for direct materials is 3 pounds, then its *standard quantity allowed (SQ)* would be 300 pounds (= 100 units × 3 pounds per unit). If the company's standard cost per pound of direct materials is $2.00, then the total direct materials cost in its flexible budget would be $600 (= 300 pounds × $2.00 per pound).

Third, the spending, price, and quantity variances—regardless of what they are called—are computed exactly the same way regardless of whether one is dealing with direct materials, direct labor, or variable manufacturing overhead. The spending variance is computed by taking the total cost in column (1) and subtracting the total cost in column (3). The price variance is computed by taking the total cost in column (1) and subtracting the total cost in column (2). The quantity variance is computed by taking the total cost in column (2) and subtracting the total cost in column (3). In all of these variance calculations, a positive number should be labeled as an unfavorable (U) variance and a negative number should be labeled as a favorable (F) variance. An unfavorable price variance indicates that the actual price (AP) per unit of the input was greater than the standard price (SP) per unit. A favorable price variance indicates that the actual price (AP) of the input was less than the standard price per unit (SP). An unfavorable quantity variance indicates that the actual quantity (AQ) of the input used was greater than the standard quantity allowed (SQ). Conversely, a favorable quantity variance indicates that the actual quantity (AQ) of the input used was less than the standard quantity allowed (SQ).

With this general model as the foundation, we will now calculate Colonial Pewter's price and quantity variances.

USING STANDARD COSTS—DIRECT MATERIALS VARIANCES

LEARNING OBJECTIVE 8–4

Compute the direct materials price and quantity variances and explain their significance.

After determining Colonial Pewter Company's standard costs for direct materials, direct labor, and variable manufacturing overhead, Terry Sherman's next step was to compute the company's variances for June. As discussed in the preceding section, variances are computed by comparing actual costs to standard costs. Terry referred to the standard cost card in Exhibit 8–8 that shows the standard direct materials cost per statue was computed as follows:

$$\text{3.0 pounds per statue} \times \$4.00 \text{ per pound} = \$12.00 \text{ per statue}$$

Colonial Pewter's records for June showed that the actual quantity (AQ) of pewter purchased was 6,500 pounds at an actual price (AP) of $3.80 per pound, for a total cost of $24,700. All of the material purchased was used during June to manufacture 2,000 statues.[5] Using these data and the standard costs from Exhibit 8–8, Terry computed the price and quantity variances shown in Exhibit 8–11.

Notice that the variances in this exhibit are based on three different total costs—$24,700, $26,000, and $24,000. The first, $24,700, is the actual amount paid for the actual amount of pewter purchased. The third total cost figure, $24,000, refers to how much should have been spent on pewter to produce the actual output of 2,000 statues. The standards call for 3 pounds of pewter per statue. Because 2,000 statues were produced, 6,000 pounds of pewter should have been used. This is referred to as the *standard quantity allowed* for the actual output and its computation can be stated in formula form as follows:

> Standard quantity allowed for actual output = Actual output × Standard quantity

If 6,000 pounds of pewter had been purchased at the standard price of $4.00 per pound, the company would have spent $24,000. This is the amount that appears in the company's flexible budget for the month. The difference between the $24,700 actually spent and the $24,000 that should have been spent is the spending variance for the month of $700 U.

---

[5]Throughout this section, we assume zero beginning and ending inventories of materials and that all materials purchased during the period are used during that period. The more general case in which there are beginning and ending inventories of materials and materials are not necessarily used during the period in which they are purchased is considered later in the chapter.

EXHIBIT 8–11 Standard Cost Variance Analysis—Direct Materials
(Note: The quantity of materials purchased equals the quantity used in production.)

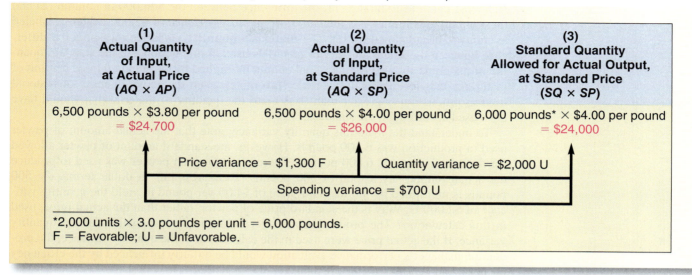

*2,000 units × 3.0 pounds per unit = 6,000 pounds.
F = Favorable; U = Unfavorable.

This variance is unfavorable (denoted by U) because the amount that was actually spent exceeds the amount that should have been spent. Also note that this spending variance agrees with the direct materials spending variance in Exhibit 8–9.

The second total cost figure in Exhibit 8–11, $26,000, is the key that allows us to decompose the spending variance into two distinct elements—one due to price and one due to quantity. It represents how much the company should have spent if it had purchased the actual amount of input, 6,500 pounds, at the standard price of $4.00 a pound rather than the actual price of $3.80 a pound.

The Materials Price Variance

Using the $26,000 total cost figure in column (2) of Exhibit 8–11, we can make two comparisons—one with the total cost of $24,700 in column (1) and one with the total cost of $24,000 in column (3). The difference between the $24,700 in column (1) and the $26,000 in column (2) is the *materials price variance* of $1,300, which is labeled as favorable (denoted by F). A **materials price variance** measures the difference between an input's actual price and its standard price, multiplied by the actual quantity purchased.

To understand the price variance, note that the actual price of $3.80 per pound of pewter is $0.20 less than the standard price of $4.00 per pound. Because 6,500 pounds were purchased, the total amount of the variance is $1,300 (= $0.20 per pound × 6,500 pounds). This variance is labeled favorable (F) because the actual purchase price per pound is less than the standard purchase price per pound. A price variance is labeled unfavorable (U) if the actual purchase price exceeds the standard purchase price.

Generally speaking, the purchasing manager has control over the price paid for goods and is therefore responsible for the materials price variance. Many factors influence the prices paid for goods including how many units are ordered, how the order is delivered, whether the order is a rush order, and the quality of materials purchased. If any of these factors deviates from what was assumed when the standards were set, a price variance can result. For example, purchasing second-grade materials rather than top-grade materials may result in a favorable price variance because the lower-grade materials may be less costly. However, the lower-grade materials may create production problems. It also bears emphasizing that someone other than the purchasing manager could be responsible for a materials price variance. For example, due to production problems beyond the purchasing manager's control, the purchasing manager may have to use express delivery. In these cases, the production manager should be held responsible for the resulting price variances.

The Materials Quantity Variance

Referring again to Exhibit 8–11, the difference between the $26,000 in column (2) and the $24,000 in column (3) is the *materials quantity variance* of $2,000, which is labeled as unfavorable (denoted by U). The **materials quantity variance** measures the difference between the actual quantity of materials used in production and the standard quantity of materials allowed for the actual output, multiplied by the standard price per unit of materials. It is labeled as unfavorable (favorable) when the actual quantity of material used in production is greater than (less than) the quantity of material that should have been used according to the standard.

To understand the materials quantity variance, note that the actual amount of pewter used in production was 6,500 pounds. However, the standard amount of pewter allowed for the actual output is 6,000 pounds. Therefore, too much pewter was used to produce the actual output—by a total of 500 pounds. To express this in dollar terms, the 500 pounds is multiplied by the standard price of $4.00 per pound to yield the quantity variance of $2,000 U. Why is the standard price of pewter, rather than the actual price, used in this calculation? The production manager is ordinarily responsible for the quantity variance. If the actual price were used in the calculation of the quantity variance, the production manager's performance evaluation would be unfairly influenced by the efficiency or inefficiency of the purchasing manager.

Excessive materials usage can result from many factors, including faulty machines, inferior materials quality, untrained workers, and poor supervision. Generally speaking, it is the responsibility of the production manager to see that material usage is kept in line with standards. There may be times, however, when the *purchasing* manager is responsible for an unfavorable materials quantity variance. For example, if the purchasing manager buys inferior materials at a lower price, the materials may be unsuitable for use and may result in excessive waste. Thus, the purchasing manager rather than the production manager would be responsible for the quantity variance.

HELPFUL HINT

The Colonial Pewter Company's materials price and quantity variances can also be computed using the equations shown below where:

AQ = Actual quantity of pounds purchased and used in production
SQ = Standard quantity of pounds allowed for the actual output
AP = Actual price per unit of the input
SP = Standard price per unit of the input

Materials Price Variance:
Materials price variance = $(AQ \times AP) - (AQ \times SP)$
Materials price variance = $AQ(AP - SP)$
Materials price variance = 6,500 pounds ($3.80 per pound − $4.00 per pound)
Materials price variance = $1,300 F

The materials price variance is favorable because the actual price paid per pound was $0.20 less than the standard price per pound.

Materials Quantity Variance:
Materials quantity variance = $(AQ \times SP) - (SQ \times SP)$
Materials quantity variance = $SP(AQ - SQ)$
Materials quantity variance = $4.00 per pound (6,500 pounds − 6,000 pounds)
Materials quantity variance = $2,000 U

The materials quantity variance is unfavorable because the company used 500 more pounds than it should have to make 2,000 statues.

4. Which of the following statements is true? (You may select more than one answer.)
   a. The standard quantity per unit defines the amount of direct materials that should be used for each unit of finished goods.
   b. The "standard quantity allowed for actual output" equals the actual output of finished goods multiplied by the standard quantity per unit.
   c. The materials price variance measures the difference between an input's actual price and its standard price, multiplied by the standard quantity purchased.
   d. The materials quantity variance measures the difference between the actual quantity of materials used in production and the standard quantity of materials allowed for the actual output, multiplied by the standard price per unit of materials.

5. The standard and actual prices per pound of raw material are $4.00 and $4.50, respectively. A total of 10,500 pounds of raw material was purchased and then used to produce 5,000 units. The quantity standard allows two pounds of the raw material per unit produced. What is the materials price variance?
   a. $5,250 favorable
   b. $5,250 unfavorable
   c. $5,000 unfavorable
   d. $5,000 favorable

6. Referring to the facts in question 5 above, what is the material quantity variance?
   a. $5,000 unfavorable
   b. $5,000 favorable
   c. $2,000 favorable
   d. $2,000 unfavorable

CONCEPT CHECK

Customers Speak Loud and Clear

IN BUSINESS

When **ConAgra Foods** raised the price of its Banquet frozen dinners from $1.00 to $1.25, many customers stopped buying the product. The resulting drop in sales contributed to a 40% decline in the company's stock price. It also presented ConAgra with an interesting challenge—lowering its raw material costs so that Banquet frozen dinners could be profitable at the customer-mandated price of $1.00. ConAgra responded by replacing expensive entrees such as barbecued chicken and country-fried pork with less costly choices such as meat patties and rice and beans. It also shrank standard portion sizes and expanded the use of cheaper side items such as mashed potatoes and brownies. However, the company did not sacrifice on variety—it still offers more than 100 Banquet-branded products.

Source: Joseph Weber, "Over a Buck for Dinner? Outrageous," *BusinessWeek*, March 9, 2009, p. 57.

USING STANDARD COSTS—DIRECT LABOR VARIANCES

Terry Sherman's next step in determining Colonial Pewter's variances for June was to compute the direct labor variances for the month. Recall from Exhibit 8–8 that the standard direct labor cost per statue is $11, computed as follows:

LEARNING OBJECTIVE 8–5

Compute the direct labor rate and efficiency variances and explain their significance.

$$0.50 \text{ hours per statue} \times \$22.00 \text{ per hour} = \$11.00 \text{ per statue}$$

In addition, Colonial Pewter's records for June showed that 1,050 direct labor-hours were actually worked. Given that the company paid its direct labor workers a total of $22,680 (including payroll taxes and fringe benefits), the average actual wage rate was $21.60 per hour (= $22,680 ÷ 1,050 hours). Using these data and the standard costs

EXHIBIT 8–12   Standard Cost Variance Analysis—Direct Labor

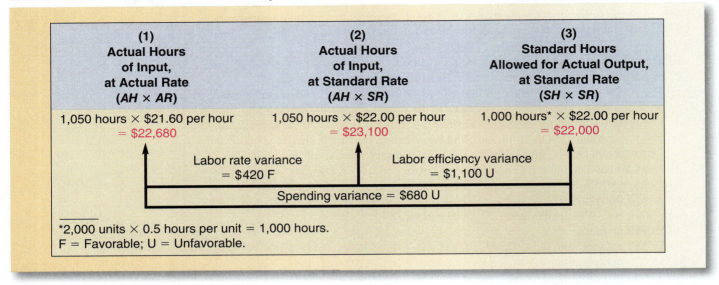

from Exhibit 8–8, Terry computed the direct labor rate and efficiency variances that appear in Exhibit 8–12.

Notice that the column headings in Exhibit 8–12 are the same as those used in Exhibits 8–10 and 8–11, except that in Exhibit 8–12 the terms *rate* and *hours* are used in place of the terms *price* and *quantity*.

The Labor Rate Variance

Using the $23,100 total cost figure in column (2) of Exhibit 8–12, we can make two comparisons—one with the total cost of $22,680 in column (1) and one with the total cost of $22,000 in column (3). The difference between the 22,680 in column (1) and the $23,100 in column (2) is the *labor rate variance* of $420 F. The **labor rate variance** measures the difference between the actual hourly rate and the standard hourly rate, multiplied by the actual number of hours worked during the period.

To understand the labor rate variance, note that the actual hourly rate of $21.60 is $0.40 less than the standard rate of $22.00 per hour. Because 1,050 hours were actually worked, the total amount of the variance is $420 (= $0.40 per hour × 1,050 hours). The variance is labeled favorable (F) because the actual hourly rate is less than the standard hourly rate. If the actual hourly rate had been greater than the standard hourly rate, the variance would have been labeled unfavorable (U).

In most companies, the wage rates paid to workers are quite predictable. Nevertheless, rate variances can arise based on how production supervisors use their direct labor workers. Skilled workers with high hourly rates of pay may be given duties that require little skill and call for lower hourly rates of pay. This will result in an unfavorable labor rate variance because the actual hourly rate of pay will exceed the standard rate specified for the particular task. In contrast, a favorable rate variance would result when workers who are paid at a rate lower than specified in the standard are assigned to the task. However, the lower-paid workers may not be as efficient. Finally, overtime work at premium rates will result in an unfavorable labor rate variance if the overtime premium is charged to the direct labor account.

The Labor Efficiency Variance

Referring back to Exhibit 8–12, the difference between the $23,100 in column (2) and the $22,000 in column (3) is the *labor efficiency variance* of $1,100 unfavorable (U). The **labor efficiency variance** measures the difference between the actual hours used and the standard hours allowed for the actual output, multiplied by the standard hourly rate.

To understand Colonial Pewter's labor efficiency variance, note that the actual amount of hours used in production was 1,050 hours. However, the standard amount of hours allowed for the actual output is 1,000 hours. Therefore, the company used 50 more hours for the actual output than the standards allow. To express this in dollar terms, the 50 hours are multiplied by the standard rate of $22.00 per hour to yield the efficiency variance of $1,100 U.

Cashiers Face the Stopwatch

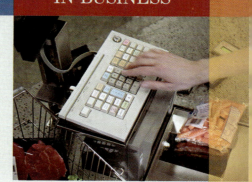

Operations Workforce Optimization (OWO) writes software that uses engineered labor standards to determine how long it should take a cashier to check out a customer. The software measures an employee's productivity by continuously comparing actual customer checkout times to pre-established labor efficiency standards. For example, the cashiers at **Meijer**, a regional retailer located in the Midwest, may be demoted or terminated if they do not meet or exceed labor efficiency standards for at least 95% of customers served. In addition to Meijer, OWO has attracted other clients such as **Gap**, **Limited Brands**, **Office Depot**, **Nike**, and **Toys "R" Us**, based on claims that its software can reduce labor costs by 5–15%. The software has also attracted the attention of the **United Food and Commercial Workers Union**, which represents 27,000 Meijer employees. The union has filed a grievance against Meijer related to its cashier monitoring system.

Source: Vanessa O'Connell, "Stores Count Seconds to Cut Labor Costs," *The Wall Street Journal*, November 17, 2008, pp. A1–A15.

Possible causes of an unfavorable labor efficiency variance include poorly trained or motivated workers; poor-quality materials, requiring more labor time; faulty equipment, causing breakdowns and work interruptions; poor supervision of workers; and inaccurate standards. The managers in charge of production would usually be responsible for control of the labor efficiency variance. However, the purchasing manager could be held responsible if the purchase of poor-quality materials resulted in excessive labor processing time.

Another important cause of an unfavorable labor efficiency variance may be insufficient demand for the company's products. Managers in some companies argue that it is difficult, and perhaps unwise, to constantly adjust the workforce in response to changes in the amount of work that needs to be done. In such companies, the direct labor workforce is essentially fixed in the short run. If demand is insufficient to keep everyone busy, workers are not laid off and an unfavorable labor efficiency variance will often be recorded.

If customer orders are insufficient to keep the workers busy, the work center manager has two options—either accept an unfavorable labor efficiency variance or build inventory. A central lesson of Lean Production is that building inventory with no immediate prospect of sale is a bad idea. Excessive inventory—particularly work in process inventory—leads to high defect rates, obsolete goods, and inefficient operations. As a consequence, when the workforce is basically fixed in the short term, managers must be cautious about how labor efficiency variances are used. Some experts advocate eliminating labor efficiency variances in such situations—at least for the purposes of motivating and controlling workers on the shop floor.

The Colonial Pewter Company's direct labor rate and efficiency variances can also be computed using the equations shown below where:

AH = Actual quantity of hours used in production
SH = Standard quantity of hours allowed for the actual output
AR = Actual rate per direct labor hour
SR = Standard rate per direct labor hour

(continued)

Labor Rate Variance:
Labor rate variance = $(AH \times AR) - (AH \times SR)$
Labor rate variance = $AH(AR - SR)$
Labor rate variance = 1,050 hours ($21.60 per hour − $22.00 per hour)
Labor rate variance = $420 F

The labor rate variance is favorable because the actual hourly rate of $21.60 is $0.40 less than the standard hourly rate of $22.00.

Labor Efficiency Variance:
Labor efficiency variance = $(AH \times SR) - (SH \times SR)$
Labor efficiency variance = $SR(AH - SH)$
Labor efficiency variance = $22.00 per hour (1,050 hours − 1,000 hours)
Labor efficiency variance = $1,100 U

The labor efficiency variance is unfavorable because the company used 50 more hours than it should have to make 2,000 statues.

USING STANDARD COSTS—VARIABLE MANUFACTURING OVERHEAD VARIANCES

LEARNING OBJECTIVE 8–6

Compute the variable manufacturing overhead rate and efficiency variances and explain their significance.

The final step in Terry Sherman's analysis of Colonial Pewter's variances for June was to compute the variable manufacturing overhead variances. The variable portion of manufacturing overhead can be analyzed using the same basic formulas that we used to analyze direct materials and direct labor. Recall from Exhibit 8–8 that the standard variable manufacturing overhead is $3.00 per statue, computed as follows:

$$0.50 \text{ hours per statue} \times \$6.00 \text{ per hour} = \$3.00 \text{ per statue}$$

Also recall that Colonial Pewter's cost records showed that the total actual variable manufacturing overhead cost for June was $7,140 and that 1,050 direct labor-hours were worked in June to produce 2,000 statues. Terry's analysis of this overhead data appears in Exhibit 8–13.

EXHIBIT 8–13 Standard Cost Variance Analysis—Variable Manufacturing Overhead

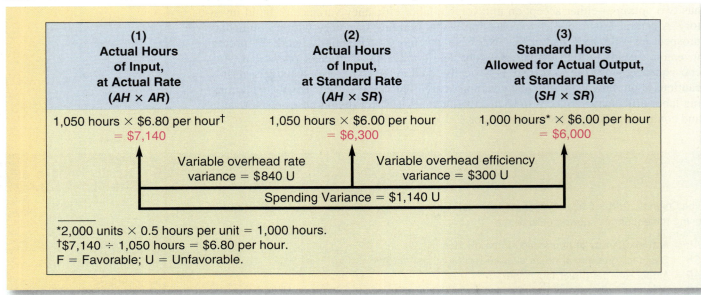

(1) Actual Hours of Input, at Actual Rate (AH × AR)	(2) Actual Hours of Input, at Standard Rate (AH × SR)	(3) Standard Hours Allowed for Actual Output, at Standard Rate (SH × SR)
1,050 hours × $6.80 per hour† = $7,140	1,050 hours × $6.00 per hour = $6,300	1,000 hours* × $6.00 per hour = $6,000

Variable overhead rate variance = $840 U   Variable overhead efficiency variance = $300 U

Spending Variance = $1,140 U

*2,000 units × 0.5 hours per unit = 1,000 hours.
†$7,140 ÷ 1,050 hours = $6.80 per hour.
F = Favorable; U = Unfavorable.

Notice the similarities between Exhibits 8–12 and 8–13. These similarities arise from the fact that direct labor-hours are being used as the base for allocating overhead cost to units of product; thus, the same hourly figures appear in Exhibit 8–13 for variable manufacturing overhead as in Exhibit 8–12 for direct labor. The main difference between the two exhibits is in the standard hourly rate being used, which in this company is much lower for variable manufacturing overhead than for direct labor.

The Variable Manufacturing Overhead Rate and Efficiency Variances

Using the $6,300 total cost figure in column (2) of Exhibit 8–13, we can make two comparisons—one with the total cost of $7,140 in column (1) and one with the total cost of $6,000 in column (3). The difference between the $7,140 in column (1) and the $6,300 in column (2) is the *variable overhead rate variance* of $840 U. The **variable overhead rate variance** measures the difference between the actual variable overhead cost incurred during the period and the standard cost that should have been incurred based on the actual activity of the period. The difference between the $6,300 in column (2) and the $6,000 in column (3) is the *variable overhead efficiency variance* of $300 U. The **variable overhead efficiency variance** measures the difference between the actual level of activity and the standard activity allowed for the actual output, multiplied by the variable part of the predetermined overhead rate.

To understand Colonial Pewter's variable overhead efficiency variance, note that the actual amount of hours used in production was 1,050 hours. However, the standard amount of hours allowed for the actual output is 1,000 hours. Therefore, the company used 50 more hours for the actual output than the standards allow. To express this in dollar terms, the 50 hours are multiplied by the variable part of the predetermined overhead rate of $6.00 per hour to yield the variable overhead efficiency variance of $300 U.

The interpretation of the variable overhead variances is not as clear as the direct materials and direct labor variances. In particular, the variable overhead efficiency variance is exactly the same as the direct labor efficiency variance except for one detail—the rate that is used to translate the variance into dollars. In both cases, the variance is the difference between the actual hours worked and the standard hours allowed for the actual output. In the case of the direct labor efficiency variance, this difference is multiplied by the standard direct labor rate. In the case of the variable overhead efficiency variance, this difference is multiplied by the variable portion of the predetermined overhead rate. So when direct labor is used as the base for overhead, whenever the direct labor efficiency variance is favorable, the variable overhead efficiency variance will also be favorable. And whenever the direct labor efficiency variance is unfavorable, the variable overhead efficiency variance will be unfavorable. Indeed, the variable overhead efficiency variance really doesn't tell us anything about how efficiently overhead resources were used. It depends solely on how efficiently direct labor was used.

HELPFUL HINT

The Colonial Pewter Company's variable overhead rate and efficiency variances can also be computed using the equations shown below where:

AH = Actual quantity of hours used in production
SH = Standard quantity of hours allowed for the actual output
AR = Actual rate per direct labor hour
SR = Standard rate per direct labor hour

(continued)

Variable Overhead Rate Variance:
Variable overhead rate variance = $(AH \times AR) - (AH \times SR)$
Variable overhead rate variance = $AH(AR - SR)$
Variable overhead rate variance = $1,050$ hours ($6.80 - $6.00)
Variable overhead rate variance = 840 U

Variable Overhead Efficiency Variance:
Variable overhead efficiency variance = $(AH \times SR) - (SH \times SR)$
Variable overhead efficiency variance = $SR(AH - SH)$
Variable overhead efficiency variance = $6.00 per hour ($1,050$ hours $- 1,000$ hours)
Variable overhead efficiency variance = 300 U

The variable overhead efficiency variance is unfavorable because the company used 50 more hours than it should have to make 2,000 statues.

MANAGERIAL ACCOUNTING IN ACTION
The Wrap-Up

Colonial Pewter Company

In preparation for the scheduled meeting to discuss his analysis of Colonial Pewter's standard costs and variances, Terry distributed his computations to the management group of Colonial Pewter. This included J. D. Wriston, the president of the company; Tom Kuchel, the production manager; and Janet Warner, the purchasing manager. J. D. Wriston opened the meeting with the following question:

J. D.: Terry, I think I understand what you have done, but just to make sure, would you mind summarizing the highlights of what you found?

Terry: As you can see, the biggest problems are the unfavorable materials quantity variance of $2,000 and the unfavorable labor efficiency variance of $1,100.

J. D.: Tom, you're the production boss. What do you think is causing the unfavorable labor efficiency variance?

Tom: It has to be the new production workers. Our experienced workers shouldn't have much problem meeting the standard of half an hour per unit. We all knew that there would be some inefficiency for a while as we brought new people on board. My plan for overcoming the problem is to pair up each of the new guys with one of our old-timers and have them work together for a while. It would slow down our older guys a bit, but I'll bet the unfavorable variance disappears and our new workers would learn a lot.

J. D.: Sounds good. Now, what about that $2,000 unfavorable materials quantity variance?

Terry: Tom, are the new workers generating a lot of scrap?

Tom: Yeah, I guess so.

J. D.: I think that could be part of the problem. Can you do anything about it?

Tom: I can watch the scrap closely for a few days to see where it's being generated. If it is the new workers, I can have the old-timers work with them on the problem when I team them up.

J. D.: Janet, the favorable materials price variance of $1,300 isn't helping us if it is contributing to the unfavorable materials quantity and labor efficiency variances. Let's make sure that our raw material purchases conform to our quality standards.

Janet: Will do.

J. D.: Good. Let's reconvene in a few weeks to see what has happened. Hopefully, we can get those unfavorable variances under control.

AN IMPORTANT SUBTLETY IN THE MATERIALS VARIANCES

Most companies use the *quantity of materials purchased* to compute the materials price variance and the *quantity of materials used* in production to compute the materials quantity variance. There are two reasons for this practice. First, delaying the computation of the price variance until the materials are used would result in less timely variance reports. Second, computing the price variance when the materials are purchased allows materials to be carried in the inventory accounts at their standard cost. This greatly simplifies bookkeeping. (See Appendix 8B at the end of the chapter for an explanation of how the bookkeeping works in a standard costing system.)[6]

When we computed materials price and quantity variances for Colonial Pewter in Exhibit 8–11, we assumed that 6,500 pounds of materials were purchased and used in production. However, it is very common for a company's quantity of materials purchased to differ from its quantity used in production. When this happens, the materials price variance is computed using the *quantity of materials purchased,* whereas the materials quantity variance is computed using the *quantity of materials used* in production.

To illustrate, assume that during June Colonial Pewter purchased 7,000 pounds of materials at $3.80 per pound instead of 6,500 pounds as assumed earlier in the chapter. Also assume that the company continued to use 6,500 pounds of materials in production and that the standard price remained at $4.00 per pound.

Given these assumptions, Exhibit 8–14 shows how to compute the materials price variance of $1,400 F and the materials quantity variance of $2,000 U. Note that the price variance is based on the amount of the input purchased whereas the quantity variance is based on the quantity of the input used in production. Column (2) of Exhibit 8–14 contains two different total costs for this reason. When the price variance is computed, the total cost used from column (2) is $28,000—which is the cost of the input *purchased,* evaluated at the standard price. When the quantity variance is computed, the total cost used from column (2) is $26,000—which is the cost of the actual input *used,* evaluated at the standard price.

Exhibit 8–14 shows that the price variance is computed on the entire amount of material purchased (7,000 pounds), whereas the quantity variance is computed only on the amount of materials used in production during the month (6,500 pounds). What about the other 500 pounds of material that were purchased during the period, but that have not yet been used? When those materials are used in future periods, a quantity variance will be computed. However, a price variance will not be computed when the materials are finally used because the price variance was computed when the materials were purchased.

Because the price variance is based on the amount purchased and the quantity variance is based on the amount used, the two variances do not generally sum to the spending variance from the flexible budget, which is wholly based on the amount used. We would also like to emphasize that the approach shown in *Exhibit 8–14 can always be used to compute direct materials variances.* However, *Exhibit 8–11 can only be used in the special case when the quantity of materials purchased equals the quantity of materials used.*

---

[6]Standard cost systems are typically used as part of a company's financial reporting system. Therefore, standard cost variance reports are often prepared on a monthly basis as part of the financial closing process. As a consequence, the reports may be produced too infrequently to enable real-time operational improvements. To combat this problem, some companies are now reporting variances and other key operating data daily or even more frequently.

EXHIBIT 8–14   Standard Cost Variance Analysis—Direct Materials
(Note: The quantity of materials purchased does not equal the quantity used in production.)

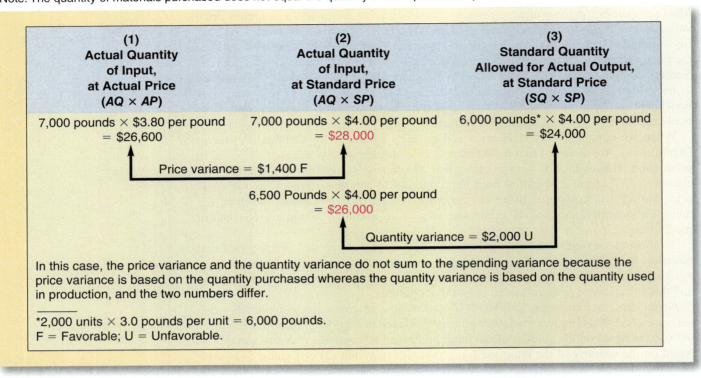

In this case, the price variance and the quantity variance do not sum to the spending variance because the price variance is based on the quantity purchased whereas the quantity variance is based on the quantity used in production, and the two numbers differ.

*2,000 units × 3.0 pounds per unit = 6,000 pounds.
F = Favorable; U = Unfavorable.

HELPFUL HINT

When Colonial Pewter purchases 7,000 pounds of materials and uses 6,500 pounds in production, the materials quantity and price variances can be computed using the equations shown below:

Materials Price Variance:
AQ = Actual quantity of pounds *purchased*
AP = Actual price per unit of the input
SP = Standard price per unit of the input

Materials price variance = (AQ × AP) − (AQ × SP)
Materials price variance = AQ(AP − SP)
Materials price variance = 7,000 pounds ($3.80 per pound − $4.00 per pound)
Materials price variance = $1,400 F

Materials Quantity Variance:
AQ = Actual quantity of pounds *used in production*
SQ = Standard quantity of pounds allowed for the actual output
SP = Standard price per unit of the input

Materials quantity variance = (AQ × SP) − (SQ × SP)
Materials quantity variance = SP(AQ − SQ)
Materials quantity variance = $4.00 per pound (6,500 pounds − 6,000 pounds)
Materials quantity variance = $2,000 U

SUMMARY

LO8–1 Prepare a flexible budget.

A flexible budget is a budget that is adjusted to the actual level of activity. It is the best estimate of what revenues and costs should have been, given the actual level of activity during the period. The flexible budget can be compared to the budget from the beginning of the period or to the actual results.

LO8–2 Prepare a report showing revenue and spending variances.

When actual results are compared to the flexible budget, revenue and spending variances are the result. A favorable revenue variance indicates that revenue was larger than should have been expected, given the actual level of activity. An unfavorable revenue variance indicates that revenue was less than it should have been, given the actual level of activity. A favorable spending variance indicates that the actual cost was less than expected, given the actual level of activity. An unfavorable spending variance indicates that the actual cost was greater than expected, given the actual level of activity.

LO8–3 Prepare a flexible budget with more than one cost driver.

A cost may depend on more than one cost driver. If so, the flexible budget for that cost should be stated in terms of all of the cost drivers.

LO8–4 Compute the direct materials price and quantity variances and explain their significance.

The materials price variance is the difference between the actual price paid for materials and the standard price, multiplied by the quantity purchased. An unfavorable variance occurs whenever the actual price exceeds the standard price. A favorable variance occurs when the actual price is less than the standard price for the input.

The materials quantity variance is the difference between the amount of materials actually used and the amount that should have been used to produce the actual good output of the period, multiplied by the standard price per unit of the input. An unfavorable materials quantity variance occurs when the amount of materials actually used exceeds the amount that should have been used according to the materials quantity standard. A favorable variance occurs when the amount of materials actually used is less than the amount that should have been used according to the standard.

LO8–5 Compute the direct labor rate and efficiency variances and explain their significance.

The direct labor rate variance is the difference between the actual wage rate paid and the standard wage rate, multiplied by the hours worked. An unfavorable variance occurs whenever the actual wage rate exceeds the standard wage rate. A favorable variance occurs when the actual wage rate is less than the standard wage rate.

The labor efficiency variance is the difference between the hours actually worked and the hours that should have been used to produce the actual good output of the period, multiplied by the standard wage rate. An unfavorable labor efficiency variance occurs when the hours actually worked exceed the hours allowed for the actual output. A favorable variance occurs when the hours actually worked are less than hours allowed for the actual output.

LO8–6 Compute the variable manufacturing overhead rate and efficiency variances and explain their significance.

The variable manufacturing overhead rate variance is the difference between the actual variable manufacturing overhead cost incurred and the actual hours worked multiplied by the standard variable manufacturing overhead rate. The variable manufacturing overhead efficiency variance is the difference between the hours actually worked and the hours that should have been used to produce the actual good output of the period, multiplied by the standard variable manufacturing overhead rate.

GUIDANCE ANSWERS TO DECISION POINT

Owner of Micro-Brewery (p. 357)

The cost of hops is a purely variable cost. Since the cost for producing 800 barrels of beer is $960, the cost of hops in one barrel of beer is $1.20 (= $960 ÷ 800 barrels). Therefore, if 850 barrels of beer are produced, the cost of the hops should be $1.20 per barrel times 850 barrels, or $1,020. Since that is how much was actually spent, there is no indication that too much or too little was spent on hops.

GUIDANCE ANSWERS TO CONCEPT CHECKS

1. **Choices b, c, and d.** A planning budget is based on the planned level, not the actual level of activity.
2. **Choice b.** The cost for flowers according to the flexible budget is $65,046 (= $325 per operating day × 30 operating days × $7.20 per room-day × 7,680 room-days).
3. **Choice a.** The spending variance is $3,068 favorable (= $65,046 − $61,978).
4. **Choices a, b, and d.** The materials price variance is based on the actual quantity purchased.
5. **Choice b.** The materials price variance is ($4.50 actual price per pound − $4.00 standard price per pound) × 10,500 pounds purchased = $5,250 unfavorable.
6. **Choice d.** The materials quantity variance is (10,500 pounds used − 10,000 pounds allowed) × $4.00 per pound = $2,000 unfavorable.

REVIEW PROBLEM 1: VARIANCE ANALYSIS USING A FLEXIBLE BUDGET

Harrald's Fish House is a family-owned restaurant that specializes in Scandinavian-style seafood. Data concerning the restaurant's monthly revenues and costs appear below (*q* refers to the number of meals served):

	Formula
Revenue	$16.50*q*
Cost of ingredients	$6.25*q*
Wages and salaries	$10,400
Utilities	$800 + $0.20*q*
Rent	$2,200
Miscellaneous	$600 + $0.80*q*

Required:

1. Prepare the restaurant's planning budget for April assuming that 1,800 meals are served.
2. Assume that 1,700 meals were actually served in April. Prepare a flexible budget for this level of activity.
3. The actual results for April appear below. Compute the revenue and spending variances for the restaurant for April.

Revenue	$27,920
Cost of ingredients	$11,110
Wages and salaries	$10,130
Utilities	$1,080
Rent	$2,200
Miscellaneous	$2,240

Solution to Review Problem

1. The planning budget for April appears below:

Harrald's Fish House
Planning Budget
For the Month Ended April 30

Budgeted meals served (q)	1,800
Revenue ($16.50q)	$29,700
Expenses:	
Cost of ingredients ($6.25q)	11,250
Wages and salaries ($10,400)	10,400
Utilities ($800 + $0.20q)	1,160
Rent ($2,200)	2,200
Miscellaneous ($600 + $0.80q)	2,040
Total expense	27,050
Net operating income	$ 2,650

2. The flexible budget for April appears below:

Harrald's Fish House
Flexible Budget
For the Month Ended April 30

Actual meals served (q)	1,700
Revenue ($16.50q)	$28,050
Expenses:	
Cost of ingredients ($6.25q)	10,625
Wages and salaries ($10,400)	10,400
Utilities ($800 + $0.20q)	1,140
Rent ($2,200)	2,200
Miscellaneous ($600 + $0.80q)	1,960
Total expense	26,325
Net operating income	$ 1,725

3. The revenue and spending variances for April appear below:

Harrald's Fish House
Revenue and Spending Variances
For the Month Ended April 30

	(1) Actual Results	Revenue and Spending Variances (1) − (2)	(2) Flexible Budget
Meals served	1,700		1,700
Revenue ($16.50q)	$27,920	$130 U	$28,050
Expenses:			
Cost of ingredients ($6.25q)	11,110	485 U	10,625
Wages and salaries ($10,400)	10,130	270 F	10,400
Utilities ($800 + $0.20q)	1,080	60 F	1,140
Rent ($2,200)	2,200	0	2,200
Miscellaneous ($600 + $0.80q)	2,240	280 U	1,960
Total expense	26,760	435 U	26,325
Net operating income	$ 1,160	$565 U	$ 1,725

REVIEW PROBLEM 2: STANDARD COSTS

Xavier Company produces a single product. Variable manufacturing overhead is applied to products on the basis of direct labor-hours. The standard costs for one unit of product are as follows:

Direct material: 6 ounces at $0.50 per ounce...................	$ 3.00
Direct labor: 0.6 hours at $30.00 per hour	18.00
Variable manufacturing overhead: 0.6 hours at $10.00 per hour	6.00
Total standard variable cost per unit..........................	$27.00

During June, 2,000 units were produced. The costs associated with June's operations were as follows:

Material purchased: 18,000 ounces at $0.60 per ounce......	$10,800
Material used in production: 14,000 ounces...............	—
Direct labor: 1,100 hours at $30.50 per hour	$33,550
Variable manufacturing overhead costs incurred	$12,980

Required:

Compute the direct materials, direct labor, and variable manufacturing overhead variances.

Solution to Review Problem

Direct Materials Variances

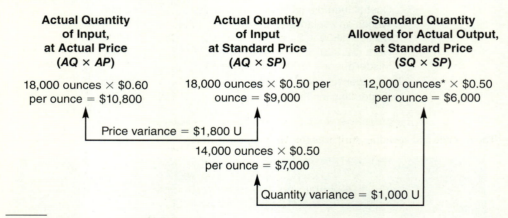

Actual Quantity of Input, at Actual Price (AQ × AP)	Actual Quantity of Input at Standard Price (AQ × SP)	Standard Quantity Allowed for Actual Output, at Standard Price (SQ × SP)
18,000 ounces × $0.60 per ounce = $10,800	18,000 ounces × $0.50 per ounce = $9,000	12,000 ounces* × $0.50 per ounce = $6,000

Price variance = $1,800 U

14,000 ounces × $0.50 per ounce = $7,000

Quantity variance = $1,000 U

_____

*2,000 units × 6 ounces per unit = 12,000 ounces.

Using formulas, the same variances would be computed as follows:

$$\text{Materials price variance} = (\text{AQ} \times \text{AP}) - (\text{AQ} \times \text{SP})$$
$$= \text{AQ}(\text{AP} - \text{SP})$$
$$= 18{,}000 \text{ ounces } (\$0.60 \text{ per ounce} - \$0.50 \text{ per ounce})$$
$$= \$1{,}800 \text{ U}$$

$$\text{Materials quantity variance} = (\text{AQ} \times \text{SP}) - (\text{SQ} \times \text{SP})$$
$$= \text{SP}(\text{AQ} - \text{SQ})$$
$$= \$0.50 \text{ per ounce } (14{,}000 \text{ ounces} - 12{,}000 \text{ ounces})$$
$$= \$1{,}000 \text{ U}$$

Direct Labor Variances

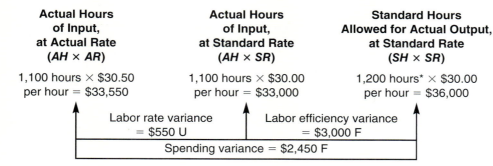

Actual Hours of Input, at Actual Rate ($AH \times AR$)	Actual Hours of Input, at Standard Rate ($AH \times SR$)	Standard Hours Allowed for Actual Output, at Standard Rate ($SH \times SR$)
1,100 hours × $30.50 per hour = $33,550	1,100 hours × $30.00 per hour = $33,000	1,200 hours* × $30.00 per hour = $36,000

Labor rate variance = $550 U   Labor efficiency variance = $3,000 F

Spending variance = $2,450 F

*2,000 units × 0.6 hours per unit =1,200 hours.
F = Favorable; U = Unfavorable.

Using formulas, the same variances can be computed as follows:

$$\text{Labor rate variance} = (AH \times AR) - (AH \times SR)$$
$$= AH(AR - SR)$$
$$= 1,100 \text{ hours } (\$30.50 \text{ per hour} - \$30.00 \text{ per hour})$$
$$= \$550 \text{ U}$$

$$\text{Labor efficiency variance} = (AH \times SR) - (SH \times SR)$$
$$= SR(AH - SH)$$
$$= \$30.00 \text{ per hour } (1,100 \text{ hours} - 1,200 \text{ hours})$$
$$= \$3,000 \text{ F}$$

Variable Manufacturing Overhead Variances

Actual Hours of Input, at Actual Rate ($AH \times AR$)	Actual Hours of Input, at Standard Rate ($AH \times SR$)	Standard Hours Allowed for Actual Output, at Standard Rate ($SH \times SR$)
1,100 hours × $11.80 per hour† = $12,980	1,100 hours × $10.00 per hour = $11,000	1,200 hours* × $10.00 per hour = $12,000

Variable overhead rate variance = $1,980 U   Variable overhead efficiency variance = $1,000 F

Spending variance = $980 U

*2,000 units × 0.6 hours per unit = 1,200 hours.
†$12,980 ÷ 1,100 hours = $11.80 per hour.
F = Favorable; U = Unfavorable.

Using formulas, the same variances can be computed as follows:

$$\text{Variable overhead rate variance} = (AH \times AR) - (AH \times SR)$$
$$= AH(AR - SR)$$
$$= 1,100 \text{ hours } (\$11.80 \text{ per hour} - \$10.00 \text{ per hour})$$
$$= \$1,980 \text{ U}$$

$$\text{Variable overhead efficiency variance} = (AH \times SR) - (SH \times SR)$$
$$= SR(AH - SH)$$
$$= \$10.00 \text{ per hour } (1,100 \text{ hours} - 1,200 \text{ hours})$$
$$= \$1,000 \text{ F}$$

GLOSSARY

Flexible budget   A report showing estimates of what revenues and costs should have been, given the actual level of activity for the period. (p. 351)

Labor efficiency variance   The difference between the actual hours taken to complete a task and the standard hours allowed for the actual output, multiplied by the standard hourly labor rate. (p. 368)

Labor rate variance   The difference between the actual hourly labor rate and the standard rate, multiplied by the number of hours worked during the period. (p. 368)

Management by exception   A management system in which actual results are compared to a budget. Significant deviations from the budget are flagged as exceptions and investigated further. (p. 350)

Materials price variance   The difference between the actual unit price paid for an item and the standard price, multiplied by the quantity purchased. (p. 365)

Materials quantity variance   The difference between the actual quantity of materials used in production and the standard quantity allowed for the actual output, multiplied by the standard price per unit of materials. (p. 366)

Planning budget   A budget created at the beginning of the budgeting period that is valid only for the planned level of activity. (p. 351)

Price variance   A variance that is computed by taking the difference between the actual price and the standard price and multiplying the result by the actual quantity of the input. (p. 362)

Quantity variance   A variance that is computed by taking the difference between the actual quantity of the input used and the amount of the input that should have been used for the actual level of output and multiplying the result by the standard price of the input. (p. 362)

Revenue variance   The difference between how much the revenue should have been, given the actual level of activity, and the actual revenue for the period. A favorable (unfavorable) revenue variance occurs because the revenue is higher (lower) than expected, given the actual level of activity for the period. (p. 355)

Spending variance   The difference between how much a cost should have been, given the actual level of activity, and the actual amount of the cost. A favorable (unfavorable) spending variance occurs because the cost is lower (higher) than expected, given the actual level of activity for the period. (p. 356)

Standard cost card   A detailed listing of the standard amounts of inputs and their costs that are required to produce one unit of a specific product. (p. 361)

Standard cost per unit   The standard quantity allowed of an input per unit of a specific product, multiplied by the standard price of the input. (p. 361)

Standard hours allowed for actual output   The time that should have been taken to complete the period's output. It is computed by multiplying the actual number of units produced by the standard hours per unit. (p. 363)

Standard hours per unit   The amount of direct labor time that should be required to complete a single unit of product, including allowances for breaks, machine downtime, cleanup, rejects, and other normal inefficiencies. (p. 360)

Standard price per unit   The price that should be paid for an input. (p. 360)

Standard quantity allowed for actual output   The amount of an input that should have been used to complete the period's actual output. It is computed by multiplying the actual number of units produced by the standard quantity per unit. (p. 363)

Standard quantity per unit   The amount of an input that should be required to complete a single unit of product, including allowances for normal waste, spoilage, rejects, and other normal inefficiencies. (p. 359)

Standard rate per hour   The labor rate that should be incurred per hour of labor time, including employment taxes and fringe benefits. (p. 360)

Variable overhead efficiency variance   The difference between the actual level of activity (direct labor-hours, machine-hours, or some other base) and the standard activity allowed, multiplied by the variable part of the predetermined overhead rate. (p. 371)

Variable overhead rate variance   The difference between the actual variable overhead cost incurred during a period and the standard cost that should have been incurred based on the actual activity of the period. (p. 371)

QUESTIONS

8–1   What is a static planning budget?

8–2   What is a flexible budget and how does it differ from a static planning budget?

8–3   What are some of the possible reasons that actual results may differ from what had been budgeted at the beginning of a period?

8–4   Why is it difficult to interpret a difference between how much expense was budgeted at the beginning of the period and how much was actually spent?

8–5   What is a revenue variance and what does it mean?

8–6   What is a spending variance and what does it mean?

8–7   What does a flexible budget enable that a simple comparison of the planning budget to actual results does not do?

8–8   How does a flexible budget based on two cost drivers differ from a flexible budget based on a single cost driver?

8–9   What is a quantity standard? What is a price standard?

8–10   Why are separate price and quantity variances computed?

8–11   Who is generally responsible for the materials price variance? The materials quantity variance? The labor efficiency variance?

8–12   The materials price variance can be computed at what two different points in time? Which point is better? Why?

8–13   If the materials price variance is favorable but the materials quantity variance is unfavorable, what might this indicate?

8–14   "Our workers are all under labor contracts; therefore, our labor rate variance is bound to be zero." Discuss.

8–15   What effect, if any, would you expect poor-quality materials to have on direct labor variances?

8–16   If variable manufacturing overhead is applied to production on the basis of direct labor-hours and the direct labor efficiency variance is unfavorable, will the variable overhead efficiency variance be favorable or unfavorable, or could it be either? Explain.

8–17   Why can undue emphasis on labor efficiency variances lead to excess work in process inventories?

Multiple-choice questions are available in the *Connect Library*.

 **APPLYING EXCEL**

Available with McGraw-Hill's *Connect Accounting*.

LO8–4, LO8–5, LO8–6

The Excel worksheet form that appears below is to be used to recreate the main example in the text on pages 361–372. Download the workbook containing this form in the *Connect Library*. On the website you will also receive instructions about how to use this worksheet form.

	A	B	C	D	E	F	G
1	Chapter 8: Applying Excel						
2							
3	Data						
4	*Exhibit 8-8: Standard Cost Card*						
5	Inputs	Standard Quantity		Standard Price			
6	Direct materials	3.0 pounds		$4.00 per pound			
7	Direct labor	0.50 hours		$22.00 per hour			
8	Variable manufacturing overhead	0.50 hours		$6.00 per hour			
9							
10	Actual results:						
11	Actual output	2,000 units					
12	Actual variable manufacturing overhead cost	$7,140					
13		Actual Quantity		Actual price			
14	Actual direct materials cost	6,500 pounds		$3.80 per pound			
15	Actual direct labor cost	1,050 hours		$21.60 per hour			
16							
17	*Enter a formula into each of the cells marked with a ? below*						
18	**Main Example: Chapter 8**						
19							
20	*Exhibit 8-11: Standard Cost Variance Analysis–Direct Materials*						
21	Standard Quantity Allowed for the Actual Output, at Standard Price	? pounds ×		? per pound =		?	
22	Actual Quantity of Input, at Standard Price	? pounds ×		? per pound =		?	
23	Actual Quantity of Input, at Actual Price	? pounds ×		? per pound =		?	
24	Direct materials variances:						
25	Materials quantity variance	?					
26	Materials price variance	?					
27	Materials spending variance	?					
28							
29	*Exhibit 8-12: Standard Cost Variance Analysis–Direct Labor*						
30	Standard Hours Allowed for the Actual Output, at Standard Rate	? hours ×		? per hour =		?	
31	Actual Hours of Input, at Standard Rate	? hours ×		? per hour =		?	
32	Actual Hours of Input, at Actual Rate	? hours ×		? per hour =		?	
33	Direct labor variances:						
34	Labor efficiency variance	?					
35	Labor rate variance	?					
36	Labor spending variance	?					
37							
38	*Exhibit 8-13: Standard Cost Variance Analysis–Variable Manufacturing Overhead*						
39	Standard Hours Allowed for the Actual Output, at Standard Rate	? hours ×		? per hour =		?	
40	Actual Hours of Input, at Standard Rate	? hours ×		? per hour =		?	
41	Actual Hours of Input, at Actual Rate	? hours ×		? per hour =		?	
42	Variable overhead variances:						
43	Variable overhead efficiency variance	?					
44	Variable overhead rate variance	?					
45	Variable overhead spending variance	?					
46							

Chapter 8 Form   Filled in Chapter 8 Form   Chapter 8 Formulas   Chap

You should proceed to the requirements below only after completing your worksheet.

Required:

1. Check your worksheet by changing the direct materials standard quantity in cell B6 to 2.9 pounds, the direct labor quantity standard quantity in cell B7 to 0.6 hours, and the variable manufacturing overhead in cell B8 to 0.6 hours. The materials spending variance should now be $1,500 U, the labor spending variance should now be $3,720 F, and the variable overhead spending variance should now be $60 F. If you do not get these answers, find the errors in your worksheet and correct them.
   a. What is the materials quantity variance? Explain this variance.
   b. What is the labor rate variance? Explain this variance.
2. Revise the data in your worksheet to reflect the results for the subsequent period:

Data Exhibit 8–8: Standard Cost Card		
Inputs	**Standard Quantity**	**Standard Price**
Direct materials..........................	3.0 pounds	$4.00 per pound
Direct labor	0.50 hours	$22.00 per hour
Variable manufacturing overhead.............	0.50 hours	$6.00 per hour
Actual results:		
Actual output..........................	2,100 units	
Actual variable manufacturing overhead cost ..	$5,100	
	Actual Quantity	**Actual Price**
Actual direct materials cost................	6,350 pounds	$4.10 per pound
Actual direct labor cost	1,020 hours	$22.10 per hour

   a. What is the materials quantity variance? What is the materials price variance?
   b. What is the labor efficiency variance? What is the labor rate variance?
   c. What is the variable overhead efficiency variance? What is the variable overhead rate variance?

THE FOUNDATIONAL 15    |ACCOUNTING

Available with McGraw-Hill's *Connect Accounting*.

LO8–1, LO8–2,
LO8–4, LO8–5,
LO8–6

Preble Company manufactures one product. Its variable manufacturing overhead is applied to production based on direct labor-hours and its standard cost card per unit is as follows:

Direct material: 5 pounds at $8.00 per pound...................		$40.00
Direct labor: 2 hours at $14 per hour		28.00
Variable overhead: 2 hours at $5 per hour		10.00
Total standard variable cost per unit.........................		$78.00

The company also established the following cost formulas for its selling expenses:

	Fixed Cost per Month	Variable Cost per Unit Sold
Advertising	$200,000	
Sales salaries and commissions	$100,000	$12.00
Shipping expenses		$3.00

The planning budget for March was based on producing and selling 25,000 units. However, during March the company actually produced and sold 30,000 units and incurred the following costs:

a. Purchased 160,000 pounds of raw materials at a cost of $7.50 per pound. All of this material was used in production.
b. Direct-laborers worked 55,000 hours at a rate of $15.00 per hour.
c. Total variable manufacturing overhead for the month was $280,500.
d. Total advertising, sales salaries and commissions, and shipping expenses were $210,000, $455,000, and $115,000, respectively.

Required:
1. What raw materials cost would be included in the company's flexible budget for March?
2. What is the materials quantity variance for March?
3. What is the materials price variance for March?
4. If Preble had purchased 170,000 pounds of materials at $7.50 per pound and used 160,000 pounds in production, what would be the materials quantity variance for March?
5. If Preble had purchased 170,000 pounds of materials at $7.50 per pound and used 160,000 pounds in production, what would be the materials price variance for March?
6. What direct labor cost would be included in the company's flexible budget for March?
7. What is the direct labor efficiency variance for March?
8. What is the direct labor rate variance for March?
9. What variable manufacturing overhead cost would be included in the company's flexible budget for March?
10. What is the variable overhead efficiency variance for March?
11. What is the variable overhead rate variance for March?
12. What amounts of advertising, sales salaries and commissions, and shipping expenses would be included in the company's flexible budget for March?
13. What is the spending variance related to advertising?
14. What is the spending variance related to sales salaries and commissions?
15. What is the spending variance related to shipping expenses?

EXERCISES

All applicable exercises are available with McGraw-Hill's *Connect Accounting*.

EXERCISE 8–1   Prepare a Flexible Budget [LO8–1]
Puget Sound Divers is a company that provides diving services such as underwater ship repairs to clients in the Puget Sound area. The company's planning budget for May appears below:

Puget Sound Divers Planning Budget For the Month Ended May 31	
Budgeted diving-hours (q)	100
Revenue ($365.00q)	$36,500
Expenses:	
Wages and salaries ($8,000 + $125.00q)	20,500
Supplies ($3.00q)	300
Equipment rental ($1,800 + $32.00q)	5,000
Insurance ($3,400)	3,400
Miscellaneous ($630 + $1.80q)	810
Total expense	30,010
Net operating income	$ 6,490

Actual diving-hours = 110

Required:
During May, the company's activity was actually 105 diving-hours. Prepare a flexible budget for that level of activity.

Actual revenue = $30,000

EXERCISE 8–2   Prepare a Report Showing Revenue and Spending Variances [LO8–2]
Quilcene Oysteria farms and sells oysters in the Pacific Northwest. The company harvested and sold 8,000 pounds of oysters in August. The company's flexible budget for August appears below:

Quilcene Oysteria Flexible Budget For the Month Ended August 31	
Actual pounds (q)	8,000
Revenue ($4.00q).	$32,000
Expenses:	
Packing supplies ($0.50q).	4,000
Oyster bed maintenance ($3,200).	3,200
Wages and salaries ($2,900 + $0.30q) .	5,300
Shipping ($0.80q)	6,400
Utilities ($830).	830
Other ($450 + $0.05q)	850
Total expense	20,580
Net operating income	$ 11,420

The actual results for August appear below:

Quilcene Oysteria Income Statement For the Month Ended August 31	
Actual pounds.	8,000
Revenue	$35,200
Expenses:	
Packing supplies	4,200
Oyster bed maintenance.	3,100
Wages and salaries.	5,640
Shipping	6,950
Utilities	810
Other.	980
Total expense	21,680
Net operating income	$13,520

Required:
Prepare a report showing the company's revenue and spending variances for August.

**Budgeted passengers
= 1,500**

EXERCISE 8–3   Prepare a Flexible Budget with More Than One Cost Driver [LO8–3]
Alyeski Tours operates day tours of coastal glaciers in Alaska on its tour boat the Blue Glacier. Management has identified two cost drivers—the number of cruises and the number of passengers—that it uses in its budgeting and performance reports. The company publishes a schedule of day cruises that it may supplement with special sailings if there is sufficient demand. Up to 80 passengers can be accommodated on the tour boat. Data concerning the company's cost formulas appear below:

	Fixed Cost per Month	Cost per Cruise	Cost per Passenger
Vessel operating costs	$5,200	$480.00	$2.00
Advertising	$1,700		
Administrative costs	$4,300	$24.00	$1.00
Insurance	$2,900		

For example, vessel operating costs should be $5,200 per month plus $480 per cruise plus $2 per passenger. The company's sales should average $25 per passenger. The company's planning budget for July is based on 24 cruises and 1,400 passengers.

Required:
Prepare the company's planning budget for July.

EXERCISE 8–4 Direct Materials Variances [LO8–4]
Bandar Industries Berhad of Malaysia manufactures sporting equipment. One of the company's products, a football helmet for the North American market, requires a special plastic. During the quarter ending June 30, the company manufactured 35,000 helmets, using 22,500 kilograms of plastic. The plastic cost the company $171,000.

According to the standard cost card, each helmet should require 0.6 kilograms of plastic, at a cost of $8 per kilogram.

Standard Kilograms per unit = 0.75

Required:
1. According to the standards, what cost for plastic should have been incurred to make 35,000 helmets? How much greater or less is this than the cost that was incurred?
2. Break down the difference computed in (1) above into a materials price variance and a materials quantity variance.

EXERCISE 8–5 Direct Labor Variances [LO8–5]
SkyChefs, Inc., prepares in-flight meals for a number of major airlines. One of the company's products is grilled salmon in dill sauce with baby new potatoes and spring vegetables. During the most recent week, the company prepared 4,000 of these meals using 960 direct labor-hours. The company paid these direct labor workers a total of $9,600 for this work, or $10.00 per hour.

According to the standard cost card for this meal, it should require 0.25 direct labor-hours at a cost of $9.75 per hour.

Standard direct labor cost per hour = $10.00

Required:
1. According to the standards, what direct labor cost should have been incurred to prepare 4,000 meals? How much does this differ from the actual direct labor cost?
2. Break down the difference computed in (1) above into a labor rate variance and a labor efficiency variance.

EXERCISE 8–6 Variable Overhead Variances [LO8–6]
Logistics Solutions provides order fulfillment services for dot.com merchants. The company maintains warehouses that stock items carried by its dot.com clients. When a client receives an order from a customer, the order is forwarded to Logistics Solutions, which pulls the item from storage, packs it, and ships it to the customer. The company uses a predetermined variable overhead rate based on direct labor-hours.

In the most recent month, 120,000 items were shipped to customers using 2,300 direct labor-hours. The company incurred a total of $7,360 in variable overhead costs.

According to the company's standards, 0.02 direct labor-hours are required to fulfill an order for one item and the variable overhead rate is $3.25 per direct labor-hour.

Required:
1. According to the standards, what variable overhead cost should have been incurred to fill the orders for the 120,000 items? How much does this differ from the actual variable overhead cost?
2. Break down the difference computed in (1) above into a variable overhead rate variance and a variable overhead efficiency variance.

EXERCISE 8–7 Flexible Budget [LO8–1]
Lavage Rapide is a Canadian company that owns and operates a large automatic carwash facility near Montreal. The following table provides data concerning the company's costs:

Planning budget = 8,200 cars washed

	Fixed Cost per Month	Cost per Car Washed
Cleaning supplies		$0.80
Electricity	$1,200	$0.15
Maintenance.		$0.20
Wages and salaries	$5,000	$0.30
Depreciation	$6,000	
Rent	$8,000	
Administrative expenses.	$4,000	$0.10

For example, electricity costs are $1,200 per month plus $0.15 per car washed. The company expects to wash 9,000 cars in August and to collect an average of $4.90 per car washed.

Required:
Prepare the company's planning budget for August.

EXERCISE 8–8　Flexible Budget [LO8–1]
Refer to the data for Lavage Rapide in Exercise 8–7. The company actually washed 8,800 cars in August.

Required:
Prepare the company's flexible budget for August.

EXERCISE 8–9　Prepare a Report Showing Revenue and Spending Variances [LO8–2]
Refer to the data for Lavage Rapide in Exercise 8–7. The actual operating results for August appear below.

Lavage Rapide **Income Statement** **For the Month Ended August 31**	
Actual cars washed.	8,800
Revenue	$43,080
Expenses:	
Cleaning supplies	7,560
Electricity	2,670
Maintenance	2,260
Wages and salaries.	8,500
Depreciation	6,000
Rent	8,000
Administrative expenses	4,950
Total expense	39,940
Net operating income	$ 3,140

Required:
Prepare a report showing the company's revenue and spending variances for August.

EXERCISE 8–10　Direct Labor and Variable Manufacturing Overhead Variances [LO8–5, LO8–6]
Erie Company manufactures a small mp3 player called the Jogging Mate. The company uses standards to control its costs. The labor standards that have been set for one Jogging Mate mp3 player are as follows:

Standard Hours	Standard Rate per Hour	Standard Cost
18 minutes	$12.00	$3.60

During August, 5,750 hours of direct labor time were needed to make 20,000 units of the Jogging Mate. The direct labor cost totaled $73,600 for the month.

Required:
1. According to the standards, what direct labor cost should have been incurred to make 20,000 units of the Jogging Mate? By how much does this differ from the cost that was incurred?
2. Break down the difference in cost from (1) above into a labor rate variance and a labor efficiency variance.
3. The budgeted variable manufacturing overhead rate is $4 per direct labor-hour. During August, the company incurred $21,850 in variable manufacturing overhead cost. Compute the variable overhead rate and efficiency variances for the month.

EXERCISE 8–11 Working Backwards from Labor Variances [LO8–5]

The auto repair shop of Quality Motor Company uses standards to control the labor time and labor cost in the shop. The standard labor cost for a motor tune-up is given below:

Job	Standard Hours	Standard Rate	Standard Cost
Motor tune-up	2.5	$9.00	$22.50

The record showing the time spent in the shop last week on motor tune-ups has been misplaced. However, the shop supervisor recalls that 50 tune-ups were completed during the week, and the controller recalls the following variance data relating to tune-ups:

Labor rate variance.	$87 F
Labor spending variance	$93 U

Required:

1. Determine the number of actual labor-hours spent on tune-ups during the week.
2. Determine the actual hourly rate of pay for tune-ups last week.

(*Hint:* A useful way to proceed would be to work from known to unknown data by using the columnar format shown in Exhibit 8–12.)

EXERCISE 8–12 Working with More Than One Cost Driver [LO8–2, LO8–3]

The Gourmand Cooking School runs short cooking courses at its small campus. Management has identified two cost drivers that it uses in its budgeting and performance reports—the number of courses and the total number of students. For example, the school might run two courses in a month and have a total of 50 students enrolled in those two courses. Data concerning the company's cost formulas appear below:

	Fixed Cost per Month	Cost per Course	Cost per Student
Instructor wages		$3,080	
Classroom supplies			$260
Utilities	$870	$130	
Campus rent	$4,200		
Insurance	$1,890		
Administrative expenses	$3,270	$15	$4

For example, administrative expenses should be $3,270 per month plus $15 per course plus $4 per student. The company's sales should average $800 per student.

The actual operating results for September appear below:

	Actual
Revenue	$32,400
Instructor wages	$9,080
Classroom supplies	$8,540
Utilities	$1,530
Campus rent	$4,200
Insurance	$1,890
Administrative expenses	$3,790

Required:

1. The Gourmand Cooking School expects to run three courses with a total of 45 students in September. Prepare the company's planning budget for this level of activity.
2. The school actually ran three courses with a total of 42 students in September. Prepare the company's flexible budget for this level of activity.
3. Calculate the revenue and spending variances for September.

EXERCISE 8–13   Direct Materials and Direct Labor Variances [LO8–4, LO8–5]

Huron Company produces a commercial cleaning compound known as Zoom. The direct materials and direct labor standards for one unit of Zoom are given below:

	Standard Quantity or Hours	Standard Price or Rate	Standard Cost
Direct materials.	4.6 pounds	$2.50 per pound	$11.50
Direct labor	0.2 hours	$12.00 per hour	$2.40

During the most recent month, the following activity was recorded:
a.   Twenty thousand pounds of material were purchased at a cost of $2.35 per pound.
b.   All of the material purchased was used to produce 4,000 units of Zoom.
c.   750 hours of direct labor time were recorded at a total labor cost of $10,425.

Required:
1.   Compute the materials price and quantity variances for the month.
2.   Compute the labor rate and efficiency variances for the month.

EXERCISE 8–14   Direct Materials Variances [LO8–4]

Refer to the data in Exercise 8–13. Assume that instead of producing 4,000 units during the month, the company produced only 3,000 units, using 14,750 pounds of material. (The rest of the material purchased remained in raw materials inventory.)

Required:
Compute the materials price and quantity variances for the month.

EXERCISE 8–15   Flexible Budgets and Revenue and Spending Variances [LO8–1, LO8–2]

Via Gelato is a popular neighborhood gelato shop. The company has provided the following data concerning its operations:

	Fixed Element per Month	Variable Element per Liter	Actual Total for June
Revenue		$12.00	$71,540
Raw materials.		$4.65	$29,230
Wages	$5,600	$1.40	$13,860
Utilities	$1,630	$0.20	$3,270
Rent	$2,600		$2,600
Insurance	$1,350		$1,350
Miscellaneous.	$650	$0.35	$2,590

While gelato is sold by the cone or cup, the shop measures its activity in terms of the total number of liters of gelato sold. For example, wages should be $5,600 plus $1.40 per liter of gelato sold and the actual wages for June were $13,860. Via Gelato expected to sell 6,000 liters in June, but actually sold 6,200 liters.

Required:
Prepare a report showing Via Gelato revenue and spending variances for June.

EXERCISE 8–16   Flexible Budgets in a Cost Center [LO8–1, LO8–2]

Packaging Solutions Corporation manufactures and sells a wide variety of packaging products. Performance reports are prepared monthly for each department. The planning budget and flexible budget for the Production Department are based on the following formulas, where q is the number of labor-hours worked in a month:

	Cost Formulas
Direct labor	$15.80q
Indirect labor.	$8,200 + $1.60q
Utilities	$6,400 + $0.80q
Supplies	$1,100 + $0.40q
Equipment depreciation	$23,000 + $3.70q
Factory rent.	$8,400
Property taxes.	$2,100
Factory administration	$11,700 + $1.90q

The actual costs incurred in March in the Production Department are listed below:

	Actual Cost Incurred in March
Direct labor.	$134,730
Indirect labor.	$19,860
Utilities	$14,570
Supplies	$4,980
Equipment depreciation	$54,080
Factory rent.	$8,700
Property taxes.	$2,100
Factory administration	$26,470

Required:
1. The company had budgeted for an activity level of 8,000 labor-hours in March. Prepare the Production Department's planning budget for the month.
2. The company actually worked 8,400 labor-hours in March. Prepare the Production Department's flexible budget for the month.
3. Calculate the spending variances for all expense items.

EXERCISE 8–17   Direct Materials and Direct Labor Variances [LO8–4, LO8–5]

Dawson Toys, Ltd., produces a toy called the Maze. The company has recently established a standard cost system to help control costs and has established the following standards for the Maze toy:

> Direct materials: 6 microns per toy at $0.50 per micron
> Direct labor: 1.3 hours per toy at $8.00 per hour

During July, the company produced 3,000 Maze toys. Production data for the month on the toy follow:

Direct materials: 25,000 microns were purchased at a cost of $0.48 per micron. 5,000 of these microns were still in inventory at the end of the month.
Direct labor: 4,000 direct labor-hours were worked at a cost of $36,000.

Required:
1. Compute the following variances for July:
   a. The materials price and quantity variances.
   b. The labor rate and efficiency variances.
2. Prepare a brief explanation of the possible causes of each variance.

Alternate problem set is available in the *Connect Library*.       **PROBLEMS**

All applicable problems are available with McGraw-Hill's *Connect Accounting*.

PROBLEM 8–18A   Comprehensive Variance Analysis [LO8–4, LO8–5, LO8–6]

Miller Toy Company manufactures a plastic swimming pool at its Westwood Plant. The plant has been experiencing problems as shown by its June contribution format income statement below:

	Budgeted	Actual
Sales (15,000 pools).	$450,000	$450,000
Variable expenses:		
Variable cost of goods sold*	180,000	196,290
Variable selling expenses	20,000	20,000
Total variable expenses	200,000	216,290
Contribution margin	250,000	233,710
Fixed expenses:		
Manufacturing overhead	130,000	130,000
Selling and administrative.	84,000	84,000
Total fixed expenses	214,000	214,000
Net operating income	$ 36,000	$ 19,710

*Contains direct materials, direct labor, and variable manufacturing overhead.

Janet Dunn, who has just been appointed general manager of the Westwood Plant, has been given instructions to "get things under control." Upon reviewing the plant's income statement, Ms. Dunn has concluded that the major problem lies in the variable cost of goods sold. She has been provided with the following standard cost per swimming pool:

	Standard Quantity or Hours	Standard Price or Rate	Standard Cost
Direct materials..................	3.0 pounds	$2.00 per pound	$ 6.00
Direct labor......................	0.8 hours	$6.00 per hour	4.80
Variable manufacturing overhead.....	0.4 hours*	$3.00 per hour	1.20
Total standard cost................			$12.00

*Based on machine-hours.

During June the plant produced 15,000 pools and incurred the following costs:

a. Purchased 60,000 pounds of materials at a cost of $1.95 per pound.
b. Used 49,200 pounds of materials in production. (Finished goods and work in process inventories are insignificant and can be ignored.)
c. Worked 11,800 direct labor-hours at a cost of $7.00 per hour.
d. Incurred variable manufacturing overhead cost totaling $18,290 for the month. A total of 5,900 machine-hours was recorded.

It is the company's policy to close all variances to cost of goods sold on a monthly basis.

Required:
1. Compute the following variances for June:
   a. Materials price and quantity variances.
   b. Labor rate and efficiency variances.
   c. Variable overhead rate and efficiency variances.
2. Summarize the variances that you computed in (1) above by showing the net overall favorable or unfavorable variance for the month. What impact did this figure have on the company's income statement? Show computations.
3. Pick out the two most significant variances that you computed in (1) above. Explain to Ms. Dunn possible causes of these variances.

PROBLEM 8–19A More than One Cost Driver [LO8–2, LO8–3]
Milano Pizza is a small neighborhood pizzeria that has a small area for in-store dining as well as offering take-out and free home delivery services. The pizzeria's owner has determined that the shop has two major cost drivers—the number of pizzas sold and the number of deliveries made. Data concerning the pizzeria's costs appear below:

	Fixed Cost per Month	Cost per Pizza	Cost per Delivery
Pizza ingredients		$3.80	
Kitchen staff	$5,220		
Utilities	$630	$0.05	
Delivery person..........			$3.50
Delivery vehicle	$540		$1.50
Equipment depreciation ...	$275		
Rent	$1,830		
Miscellaneous...........	$820	$0.15	

In November, the pizzeria budgeted for 1,200 pizzas at an average selling price of $13.50 per pizza and for 180 deliveries.

Data concerning the pizzeria's operations in November appear below:

	Actual Results
Pizzas.	1,240
Deliveries	174
Revenue	$17,420
Pizza ingredients	$4,985
Kitchen staff	$5,281
Utilities	$984
Delivery person.	$609
Delivery vehicle	$655
Equipment depreciation	$275
Rent	$1,830
Miscellaneous.	$954

Required:
1. Compute the revenue and spending variances for the pizzeria for November.
2. Explain the revenue and spending variances.

PROBLEM 8–20A   Basic Variance Analysis; the Impact of Variances on Unit Costs [LO8–4, LO8–5, LO8–6]

Koontz Company manufactures a number of products. The standards relating to one of these products are shown below, along with actual cost data for May.

	Standard Cost per Unit	Actual Cost per Unit
Direct materials:		
Standard: 1.80 feet at $3.00 per foot.	$5.40	
Actual: 1.80 feet at $3.30 per foot		$5.94
Direct labor:		
Standard: 0.90 hours at $18.00 per hour	16.20	
Actual: 0.92 hours at $17.50 per hour		16.10
Variable overhead:		
Standard: 0.90 hours at $5.00 per hour	4.50	
Actual: 0.92 hours at $4.50 per hour		4.14
Total cost per unit	$26.10	$26.18
Excess of actual cost over standard cost per unit. . .	$0.08	

The production superintendent was pleased when he saw this report and commented: "This $0.08 excess cost is well within the 2 percent limit management has set for acceptable variances. It's obvious that there's not much to worry about with this product."

Actual production for the month was 12,000 units. Variable overhead cost is assigned to products on the basis of direct labor-hours. There were no beginning or ending inventories of materials.

Required:
1. Compute the following variances for May:
   a. Materials price and quantity variances.
   b. Labor rate and efficiency variances.
   c. Variable overhead rate and efficiency variances.
2. How much of the $0.08 excess unit cost is traceable to each of the variances computed in (1) above.
3. How much of the $0.08 excess unit cost is traceable to apparent inefficient use of labor time?
4. Do you agree that the excess unit cost is not of concern?

PROBLEM 8–21A   Multiple Products, Materials, and Processes [LO8–4, LO8–5]

Mickley Corporation produces two products, Alpha6s and Zeta7s, which pass through two operations, Sintering and Finishing. Each of the products uses two raw materials, X442 and Y661. The company uses a standard cost system, with the following standards for each product (on a per unit basis):

	Raw Material		Standard Labor Time	
Product	X442	Y661	Sintering	Finishing
Alpha6	1.8 kilos	2.0 liters	0.20 hours	0.80 hours
Zeta7	3.0 kilos	4.5 liters	0.35 hours	0.90 hours

Information relating to materials purchased and materials used in production during May follows:

Material	Purchases	Purchase Cost	Standard Price	Used in Production
X442.	14,500 kilos	$52,200	$3.50 per kilo	8,500 kilos
Y661.	15,500 liters	$20,925	$1.40 per liter	13,000 liters

The following additional information is available:

a. The company recognizes price variances when materials are purchased.
b. The standard labor rate is $19.80 per hour in Sintering and $19.20 per hour in Finishing.
c. During May, 1,200 direct labor-hours were worked in Sintering at a total labor cost of $27,000, and 2,850 direct labor-hours were worked in Finishing at a total labor cost of $59,850.
d. Production during May was 1,500 Alpha6s and 2,000 Zeta7s.

Required:

1. Prepare a standard cost card for each product, showing the standard cost of direct materials and direct labor.
2. Compute the materials price and quantity variances for each material.
3. Compute the labor rate and efficiency variances for each operation.

PROBLEM 8–22A   Variance Analysis in a Hospital [LO8–4, LO8–5, LO8–6]

John Fleming, chief administrator for Valley View Hospital, is concerned about the costs for tests in the hospital's lab. Charges for lab tests are consistently higher at Valley View than at other hospitals and have resulted in many complaints. Also, because of strict regulations on amounts reimbursed for lab tests, payments received from insurance companies and governmental units have not been high enough to cover lab costs.

Mr. Fleming has asked you to evaluate costs in the hospital's lab for the past month. The following information is available:

a. Two types of tests are performed in the lab—blood tests and smears. During the past month, 1,800 blood tests and 2,400 smears were performed in the lab.
b. Small glass plates are used in both types of tests. During the past month, the hospital purchased 12,000 plates at a cost of $28,200. 1,500 of these plates were unused at the end of the month; no plates were on hand at the beginning of the month.
c. During the past month, 1,150 hours of labor time were recorded in the lab at a cost of $13,800.
d. The lab's variable overhead cost last month totaled $7,820.

Valley View Hospital has never used standard costs. By searching industry literature, however, you have determined the following nationwide averages for hospital labs:

Plates: Two plates are required per lab test. These plates cost $2.50 each and are disposed of after the test is completed.
Labor: Each blood test should require 0.3 hours to complete, and each smear should require 0.15 hours to complete. The average cost of this lab time is $14 per hour.
Overhead: Overhead cost is based on direct labor-hours. The average rate for variable overhead is $6 per hour.

Required:

1. Compute a materials price variance for the plates purchased last month and a materials quantity variance for the plates used last month.
2. For labor cost in the lab:
    a. Compute a labor rate variance and a labor efficiency variance.
    b. In most hospitals, one-half of the workers in the lab are senior technicians and one-half are assistants. In an effort to reduce costs, Valley View Hospital employs only one-fourth senior technicians and three-fourths assistants. Would you recommend that this policy be continued? Explain.
3. Compute the variable overhead rate and efficiency variances. Is there any relation between the variable overhead efficiency variance and the labor efficiency variance? Explain.

PROBLEM 8–23A Flexible Budgets and Spending Variances [LO8–1, LO8–2]

You have just been hired by FAB Corporation, the manufacturer of a revolutionary new garage door opening device. The president has asked that you review the company's costing system and "do what you can to help us get better control of our manufacturing overhead costs." You find that the company has never used a flexible budget, and you suggest that preparing such a budget would be an excellent first step in overhead planning and control.

After much effort and analysis, you determined the following cost formulas and gathered the following actual cost data for March:

	Cost Formula	Actual Cost in March
Utilities	$20,600 plus $0.10 per machine-hour	$24,200
Maintenance.	$40,000 plus $1.60 per machine-hour	$78,100
Supplies	$0.30 per machine-hour	$8,400
Indirect labor.	$130,000 plus $0.70 per machine-hour	$149,600
Depreciation	$70,000	$71,500

During March, the company worked 26,000 machine-hours and produced 15,000 units. The company had originally planned to work 30,000 machine-hours during March.

Required:

1. Prepare a flexible budget for March.
2. Prepare a report showing the spending variances for March. Explain what these variances mean.

PROBLEM 8–24A Comprehensive Variance Analysis [LO8–4, LO8–5, LO8–6]

Marvel Parts, Inc., manufactures auto accessories. One of the company's products is a set of seat covers that can be adjusted to fit nearly any small car. The company has a standard cost system in use for all of its products. According to the standards that have been set for the seat covers, the factory should work 2,850 hours each month to produce 1,900 sets of covers. The standard costs associated with this level of production follow:

	Total	Per Set of Covers
Direct materials.	$42,560	$22.40
Direct labor	$17,100	9.00
Variable manufacturing overhead		
(based on direct labor-hours)	$6,840	3.60
		$35.00

During August, the factory worked only 2,800 direct labor-hours and produced 2,000 sets of covers. The following actual costs were recorded during the month:

	Total	Per Set of Covers
Direct materials (12,000 yards).........	$45,600	$22.80
Direct labor.........................	$18,200	9.10
Variable manufacturing overhead......	$7,000	3.50
		$35.40

At standard, each set of covers should require 5.6 yards of material. All of the materials purchased during the month were used in production.

Required:
Compute the following variances for August:
1. The materials price and quantity variances.
2. The labor rate and efficiency variances.
3. The variable overhead rate and efficiency variances.

PROBLEM 8–25A   Direct Materials and Direct Labor Variances; Computations from Incomplete Data [LO8–4, LO8–5]
Sharp Company manufactures a product for which the following standards have been set:

	Standard Quantity or Hours	Standard Price or Rate	Standard Cost
Direct materials..........	3 feet	$5 per foot	$15
Direct labor.............	? hours	? per hour	?

During March, the company purchased direct materials at a cost of $55,650, all of which were used in the production of 3,200 units of product. In addition, 4,900 hours of direct labor time were worked on the product during the month. The cost of this labor time was $36,750. The following variances have been computed for the month:

Materials quantity variance..............	$4,500 U
Labor spending variance	$1,650 F
Labor efficiency variance	$800 U

Required:
1. For direct materials:
   a. Compute the actual cost per foot for materials for March.
   b. Compute the price variance and the spending variance.
2. For direct labor:
   a. Compute the standard direct labor rate per hour.
   b. Compute the standard hours allowed for the month's production.
   c. Compute the standard hours allowed per unit of product.

(*Hint:* In completing the problem, it may be helpful to move from known to unknown data by using the columnar format shown in Exhibits 8–11 and 8–12.)

BUILDING YOUR SKILLS

ETHICS CHALLENGE [LO8–2]
Tom Kemper is the controller of the Wichita manufacturing facility of Prudhom Enterprises, Inc. The annual cost control report is one of the many reports that must be filed with corporate headquarters and is due at corporate headquarters shortly after the beginning of the New Year. Kemper does not like putting

work off to the last minute, so just before Christmas he prepared a preliminary draft of the cost control report. Some adjustments would later be required for transactions that occur between Christmas and New Year's Day. A copy of the preliminary draft report, which Kemper completed on December 21, follows:

Wichita Manufacturing Facility
Cost Control Report
December 21 Preliminary Draft

	Actual Results	Flexible Budget	Spending Variances
Labor-hours	18,000	18,000	
Direct labor	$ 326,000	$ 324,000	$ 2,000 U
Power	19,750	18,000	1,750 U
Supplies	105,000	99,000	6,000 U
Equipment depreciation	343,000	332,000	11,000 U
Supervisory salaries.........	273,000	275,000	2,000 F
Insurance	37,000	37,000	0
Industrial engineering........	189,000	210,000	21,000 F
Factory building lease........	60,000	60,000	0
Total expense	$1,352,750	$1,355,000	$ 2,250 F

Melissa Ilianovitch, the general manager at the Wichita facility, asked to see a copy of the preliminary draft report. Kemper carried a copy of the report to her office where the following discussion took place:

Ilianovitch: Ouch! Almost all of the variances on the report are unfavorable. The only favorable variances are for supervisory salaries and industrial engineering. How did we have an unfavorable variance for depreciation?

Kemper: Do you remember that milling machine that broke down because the wrong lubricant was used by the machine operator?

Ilianovitch: Yes.

Kemper: We couldn't fix it. We had to scrap the machine and buy a new one.

Ilianovitch: This report doesn't look good. I was raked over the coals last year when we had just a few unfavorable variances.

Kemper: I'm afraid the final report is going to look even worse.

Ilianovitch: Oh?

Kemper: The line item for industrial engineering on the report is for work we hired Ferguson Engineering to do for us. The original contract was for $210,000, but we asked them to do some additional work that was not in the contract. We have to reimburse Ferguson Engineering for the costs of that additional work. The $189,000 in actual costs that appears on the preliminary draft report reflects only their billings up through December 21. The last bill they had sent us was on November 28, and they completed the project just last week. Yesterday I got a call from Laura Sunder over at Ferguson and she said they would be sending us a final bill for the project before the end of the year. The total bill, including the reimbursements for the additional work, is going to be . . .

Ilianovitch: I am not sure I want to hear this.

Kemper: $225,000

Ilianovitch: Wow!

Kemper: The additional work added $15,000 to the cost of the project.

Ilianovitch: I can't turn in a report with an overall unfavorable variance! They'll kill me at corporate headquarters. Call up Laura at Ferguson and ask her not to send the bill until after the first of the year. We have to have that $21,000 favorable variance for industrial engineering on the report.

Required:
What should Tom Kemper do? Explain.

ANALYTICAL THINKING [LO8–4, LO8–5, LO8–6]

Highland Company produces a lightweight backpack that is popular with college students. Standard variable costs relating to a single backpack are given below:

	Standard Quantity or Hours	Standard Price or Rate	Standard Cost
Direct materials.	?	$6 per yard	$?
Direct labor	?	?	?
Variable manufacturing overhead . . .	?	$3 per direct labor-hour	?
Total standard cost			$?

Overhead is applied to production on the basis of direct labor-hours. During March, 1,000 backpacks were manufactured and sold. Selected information relating to the month's production is given below:

	Materials Used	Direct Labor	Variable Manufacturing Overhead
Total standard cost allowed*	$16,800	$10,500	$4,200
Actual costs incurred	$15,000	?	$3,600
Materials price variance	?		
Materials quantity variance	$1,200 U		
Labor rate variance		?	
Labor efficiency variance		?	
Variable overhead rate variance			?
Variable overhead efficiency variance . .			?

*For the month's production.

The following additional information is available for March's production:

Actual direct labor-hours	1,500
Difference between standard and actual cost per backpack produced during March	$0.15 F

Required:

1. What is the standard cost of a single backpack?
2. What was the actual cost per backpack produced during March?
3. How many yards of material are required at standard per backpack?
4. What was the materials price variance for March if there were no beginning or ending inventories of materials?
5. What is the standard direct labor rate per hour?
6. What was the labor rate variance for March? The labor efficiency variance?
7. What was the variable overhead rate variance for March? The variable overhead efficiency variance?
8. Prepare a standard cost card for one backpack.

CASE [LO8–1, LO8–2, LO8–3]

The Little Theatre is a nonprofit organization devoted to staging plays for children. The theater has a very small full-time professional administrative staff. Through a special arrangement with the actors' union, actors and directors rehearse without pay and are paid only for actual performances.

The costs from the current year's planning budget appear on the next page. The Little Theatre had tentatively planned to put on six different productions with a total of 108 performances. For example, one of the productions was *Peter Rabbit,* which had a six-week run with three performances on each weekend.

The Little Theater
Costs from the Planning Budget
For the Year Ended December 31

Budgeted number of productions	6
Budgeted number of performances	108
Actors' and directors' wages	$216,000
Stagehands' wages.	32,400
Ticket booth personnel and ushers' wages. . . .	16,200
Scenery, costumes, and props	108,000
Theater hall rent	54,000
Printed programs	27,000
Publicity	12,000
Administrative expenses.	43,200
Total	$508,800

Some of the costs vary with the number of productions, some with the number of performances, and some are fixed and depend on neither the number of productions nor the number of performances. The costs of scenery, costumes, props, and publicity vary with the number of productions. It doesn't make any difference how many times *Peter Rabbit* is performed, the cost of the scenery is the same. Likewise, the cost of publicizing a play with posters and radio commercials is the same whether there are 10, 20, or 30 performances of the play. On the other hand, the wages of the actors, directors, stagehands, ticket booth personnel, and ushers vary with the number of performances. The greater the number of performances, the higher the wage costs will be. Similarly, the costs of renting the hall and printing the programs will vary with the number of performances. Administrative expenses are more difficult to pin down, but the best estimate is that approximately 75% of the budgeted costs are fixed, 15% depend on the number of productions staged, and the remaining 10% depend on the number of performances.

After the beginning of the year, the board of directors of the theater authorized expanding the theater's program to seven productions and a total of 168 performances. Not surprisingly, actual costs were considerably higher than the costs from the planning budget. (Grants from donors and ticket sales were also correspondingly higher, but are not shown here.) Data concerning the actual costs appear below:

The Little Theater
Actual Costs
For the Year Ended December 31

Actual number of productions.	7
Actual number of performances	168
Actors' and directors' wages	$341,800
Stagehands' wages.	49,700
Ticket booth personnel and ushers' wages. . .	25,900
Scenery, costumes, and props	130,600
Theater hall rent	78,000
Printed programs	38,300
Publicity	15,100
Administrative expenses.	47,500
Total	$726,900

Required:
1. Prepare a flexible budget for The Little Theatre based on the actual activity of the year.
2. Prepare a report for the year that shows the spending variances for all expense items.
3. If you were on the board of directors of the theater, would you be pleased with how well costs were controlled during the year? Why, or why not?
4. The cost formulas provide figures for the average cost per production and average cost per performance. How accurate do you think these figures would be for predicting the cost of a new production or of an additional performance of a particular production?

APPENDIX 8A: PREDETERMINED OVERHEAD RATES AND OVERHEAD ANALYSIS IN A STANDARD COSTING SYSTEM

LEARNING OBJECTIVE 8–7

Compute and interpret the fixed overhead budget and volume variances.

In this appendix, we will investigate how the predetermined overhead rates that we discussed in the job-order costing chapter earlier in the book can be used in a standard costing system. Throughout this appendix, we assume that an absorption costing system is used in which *all* manufacturing costs—both fixed and variable—are included in product costs.

Predetermined Overhead Rates

The data in Exhibit 8A–1 pertain to MicroDrive Corporation, a company that produces miniature electric motors. Note that the company budgeted for 50,000 machine-hours based on production of 25,000 motors. At this level of activity, the budgeted variable manufacturing overhead was $75,000 and the budgeted fixed manufacturing overhead was $300,000.

EXHIBIT 8A–1
MicroDrive Corporation Data

Budgeted production	25,000 motors
Standard machine-hours per motor	2 machine-hours per motor
Budgeted machine-hours (2 machine-hours per motor × 25,000 motors)	50,000 machine-hours
Actual production	20,000 motors
Standard machine-hours allowed for the actual production (2 machine-hours per motor × 20,000 motors)	40,000 machine-hours
Actual machine-hours.	42,000 machine-hours
Budgeted variable manufacturing overhead	$75,000
Budgeted fixed manufacturing overhead	$300,000
Total budgeted manufacturing overhead.	$375,000
Actual variable manufacturing overhead.	$71,400
Actual fixed manufacturing overhead	$308,000
Total actual manufacturing overhead	$379,400

Recall from the job-order costing chapter that the following formula is used to set the predetermined overhead rate at the beginning of the period:

$$\text{Predetermined overhead rate} = \frac{\text{Estimated total manufacturing overhead cost}}{\text{Estimated total amount of the allocation base}}$$

The estimated total amount of the allocation base in the formula for the predetermined overhead rate is called the **denominator activity.**

As discussed in the job-order costing chapter, once the predetermined overhead rate has been determined, it remains unchanged throughout the period, even if the actual level of activity differs from what was estimated. Consequently, the amount of overhead applied to each unit of product is the same regardless of when it is produced during the period.

MicroDrive Corporation uses budgeted machine-hours as its denominator activity in the predetermined overhead rate. Consequently, the company's predetermined overhead rate would be computed as follows:

$$\text{Predetermined overhead rate} = \frac{\$375,000}{50,000 \text{ MHs}} = \$7.50 \text{ per MH}$$

This predetermined overhead rate can be broken down into its variable and fixed components as follows:

$$\text{Variable component of the predetermined overhead rate} = \frac{\$75{,}000}{50{,}000 \text{ MHs}} = \$1.50 \text{ per MH}$$

$$\text{Fixed component of the predetermined overhead rate} = \frac{\$300{,}000}{50{,}000 \text{ MHs}} = \$6.00 \text{ per MH}$$

For every standard machine-hour recorded, work in process is charged with $7.50 of manufacturing overhead, of which $1.50 represents variable manufacturing overhead and $6.00 represents fixed manufacturing overhead. In total, MicroDrive Corporation would apply $300,000 of overhead to work in process as shown below:

$$\text{Overhead applied} = \frac{\text{Predetermined}}{\text{overhead rate}} \times \frac{\text{Standard hours allowed}}{\text{for the actual output}}$$

$$= \$7.50 \text{ per machine-hour} \times 40{,}000 \text{ machine-hours}$$

$$= \$300{,}000$$

Overhead Application in a Standard Cost System

To understand fixed overhead variances, we first have to understand how overhead is applied to work in process in a standard cost system. Recall that in the job-order costing chapter we applied overhead to work in process on the basis of the actual level of activity. This procedure was correct because at the time we were dealing with a normal cost system.[1] However, we are now dealing with a standard cost system. In such a system, overhead is applied to work in process on the basis of the *standard hours allowed for the actual output of the period* rather than on the basis of the actual number of hours worked. Exhibit 8A–2 illustrates this point. In a standard cost system, every unit of a particular product is charged with the same amount of overhead cost, regardless of how much time the unit actually requires for processing.

Budget Variance

Two fixed manufacturing overhead variances are computed in a standard costing system—a *budget variance* and a *volume variance*. These variances are computed in Exhibit 8A–3. The **budget variance** is simply the difference between the actual fixed

Normal Cost System		Standard Cost System	
Manufacturing Overhead		Manufacturing Overhead	
Actual overhead costs incurred.	Applied overhead costs: Actual hours × Predetermined overhead rate.	Actual overhead costs incurred.	Applied overhead costs: Standard hours allowed for actual output × Predetermined overhead rate.
Underapplied or overapplied overhead		Underapplied or overapplied overhead	

EXHIBIT 8A–2
Applied Overhead Costs: Normal Cost System versus Standard Cost System

---

[1]Normal cost systems are discussed on page 74 in the job-order costing chapter.

EXHIBIT 8A–3   Fixed Overhead Variances

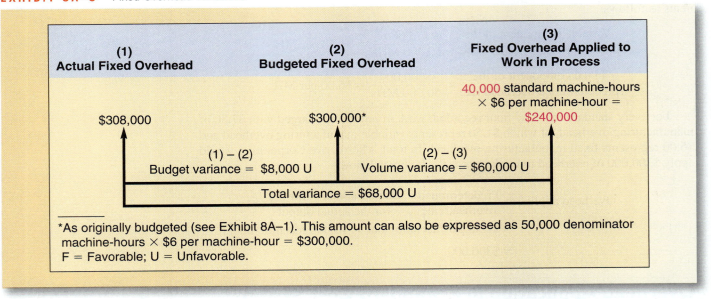

(1) Actual Fixed Overhead	(2) Budgeted Fixed Overhead	(3) Fixed Overhead Applied to Work in Process
		40,000 standard machine-hours × $6 per machine-hour = $240,000
$308,000	$300,000*	

(1) − (2) Budget variance = $8,000 U	(2) − (3) Volume variance = $60,000 U

Total variance = $68,000 U

*As originally budgeted (see Exhibit 8A–1). This amount can also be expressed as 50,000 denominator machine-hours × $6 per machine-hour = $300,000.
F = Favorable; U = Unfavorable.

manufacturing overhead and the budgeted fixed manufacturing overhead for the period. The formula is as follows:

$$\text{Budget variance} = \text{Actual fixed overhead} - \text{Budgeted fixed overhead}$$

If the actual fixed overhead cost exceeds the budgeted fixed overhead cost, the budget variance is labeled unfavorable. If the actual fixed overhead cost is less than the budgeted fixed overhead cost, the budget variance is labeled favorable.

Applying the formula to the MicroDrive Corporation data, the budget variance is computed as follows:

$$\text{Budget variance} = \$308,000 - \$300,000 = \$8,000 \text{ U}$$

According to the budget, the fixed manufacturing overhead should have been $300,000, but it was actually $308,000. Because the actual cost exceeds the budget by $8,000, the variance is labeled as unfavorable; however, this label does not automatically signal ineffective managerial performance. For example, this variance may be the result of waste and inefficiency, or it may be due to an unforeseen yet prudent investment in fixed overhead resources that improves product quality or manufacturing cycle efficiency.

Volume Variance

The **volume variance** is defined by the following formula:

$$\text{Volume variance} = \frac{\text{Budgeted fixed}}{\text{overhead}} - \frac{\text{Fixed overhead applied}}{\text{to work in process}}$$

When the budgeted fixed manufacturing overhead exceeds the fixed manufacturing overhead applied to work in process, the volume variance is labeled as unfavorable. When the budgeted fixed manufacturing overhead is less than the fixed manufacturing overhead applied to work in process, the volume variance is labeled as favorable. As we shall see, caution is advised when interpreting this variance.

To understand the volume variance, we need to understand how fixed manufacturing overhead is applied to work in process in a standard costing system. As discussed earlier, fixed manufacturing overhead is applied to work in process on the basis of the standard hours allowed for the actual output of the period. In the case of MicroDrive Corporation, the company produced 20,000 motors and the standard for each motor is 2 machine-hours. Therefore, the standard hours allowed for the actual output is 40,000 machine-hours (= 20,000 motors × 2 machine-hours). As shown in Exhibit 8A–3, the predetermined fixed manufacturing overhead rate of $6.00 per machine-hour is multiplied by the 40,000 standard machine-hours allowed for the actual output to arrive at $240,000 of fixed manufacturing overhead applied to work in process. Another way to think of this is that the standard for each motor is 2 machine-hours. Because the predetermined fixed manufacturing overhead rate is $6.00 per machine-hour, each motor is assigned $12.00 (= 2 machine-hours × $6.00 per machine-hour) of fixed manufacturing overhead. Consequently, a total of $240,000 of fixed manufacturing overhead is applied to the 20,000 motors that are actually produced. Under either explanation, the volume variance according to the formula is as follows:

$$\text{Volume variance} = \$300,000 - \$240,000 = \$60,000 \text{ U}$$

The key to interpreting the volume variance is to understand that it depends on the difference between the hours used in the denominator to compute the predetermined overhead rate and the standard hours allowed for the actual output of the period. While it is not obvious, the volume variance can also be computed using the following formula:

$$\frac{\text{Volume}}{\text{variance}} = \frac{\text{Fixed component of the}}{\text{predetermined overhead rate}} \times \left(\frac{\text{Denominator}}{\text{hours}} - \frac{\text{Standard hours allowed}}{\text{for the actual output}} \right)$$

In the case of MicroDrive Corporation, the volume variance can be computed using this formula as follows:

$$\text{Volume variance} = \frac{\$6.00 \text{ per}}{\text{machine-hour}} \times \left(\frac{50,000}{\text{machine-hours}} - \frac{40,000}{\text{machine-hours}} \right)$$
$$= \$6.00 \text{ per machine-hour} \times (10,000 \text{ machine-hours})$$
$$= \$60,000 \text{ U}$$

Note that this agrees with the volume variance computed using the earlier formula.

Focusing on this new formula, if the denominator hours exceed the standard hours allowed for the actual output, the volume variance is unfavorable. If the denominator hours are less than the standard hours allowed for the actual output, the volume variance is favorable. Stated differently, the volume variance is unfavorable if the actual level of activity is less than expected. The volume variance is favorable if the actual level of activity is greater than expected. It is important to note that the volume variance does not measure overspending or underspending. A company should incur the same dollar amount of fixed overhead cost regardless of whether the period's activity was above or below the planned (denominator) level.

The volume variance is often viewed as a measure of the utilization of facilities. If the standard hours allowed for the actual output are greater than (less than) the denominator hours, it signals efficient (inefficient) usage of facilities. However, other measures of utilization—such as the percentage of capacity utilized—are easier to compute and understand. Perhaps a better interpretation of the volume variance is that it is the error that occurs when the level of activity is incorrectly estimated and the costing system assumes fixed costs behave as if they are variable. This interpretation may be clearer in the next section that graphically analyzes the fixed manufacturing overhead variances.

Graphic Analysis of Fixed Overhead Variances

Exhibit 8A–4 shows a graphic analysis that offers insights into the fixed overhead budget and volume variances. As shown in the graph, fixed overhead cost is applied to work in process at the predetermined rate of $6.00 for each standard hour of activity. (The applied-cost line is the upward-sloping line on the graph.) Because a denominator level of 50,000 machine-hours was used in computing the $6.00 rate, the applied-cost line crosses the budget-cost line at exactly 50,000 machine-hours. If the denominator hours and the standard hours allowed for the actual output are the same, there is no volume variance. It is only when the standard hours differ from the denominator hours that a volume variance arises.

In MicroDrive's case, the standard hours allowed for the actual output (40,000 hours) are less than the denominator hours (50,000 hours). The result is an unfavorable volume variance because less cost was applied to production than was originally budgeted. If the situation had been reversed and the standard hours allowed for the actual output had exceeded the denominator hours, then the volume variance on the graph would have been favorable.

Cautions in Fixed Overhead Analysis

A volume variance for fixed overhead arises because when applying the costs to work in process, we act *as if* the fixed costs are variable. The graph in Exhibit 8A–4 illustrates this point. Notice from the graph that fixed overhead costs are applied to work in process at a rate of $6 per hour *as if* they are variable. Treating these costs as if they are variable is necessary for product costing purposes, but some real dangers lurk here. Managers can easily be misled into thinking that fixed costs are *in fact* variable.

Keep clearly in mind that fixed overhead costs come in large chunks. Expressing fixed costs on a unit or per hour basis, though necessary for product costing for external reports, is artificial. Increases or decreases in activity in fact have no effect on total fixed costs within the relevant range of activity. Even though fixed costs are expressed on a unit or per

EXHIBIT 8A–4
Graphic Analysis of Fixed Overhead Variances

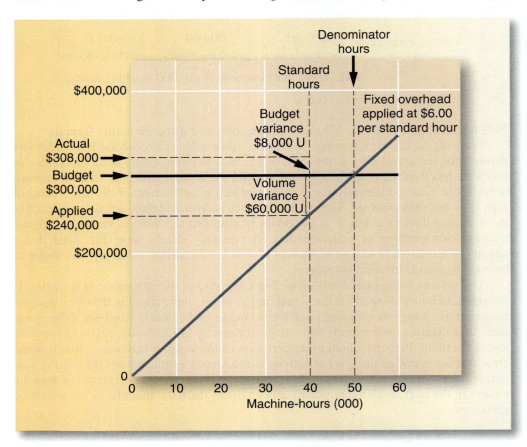

hour basis, they are *not* proportional to activity. In a sense, the volume variance is the error that occurs as a result of treating fixed costs as variable costs in the costing system.

Reconciling Overhead Variances and Underapplied or Overapplied Overhead

In a standard cost system, the underapplied or overapplied overhead for a period equals the sum of the overhead variances. To see this, we will return to the MicroDrive Corporation example.

As discussed earlier, in a standard cost system, overhead is applied to work in process on the basis of the standard hours allowed for the actual output of the period. The following table shows how the underapplied or overapplied overhead for MicroDrive is computed.

Predetermined overhead rate (a)	$7.50 per machine-hour
Standard hours allowed for the actual output [Exhibit 8A–1] (b)	40,000 machine-hours
Manufacturing overhead applied (a) × (b)	$300,000
Total actual manufacturing overhead [Exhibit 8A–1]	$379,400
Manufacturing overhead underapplied or overapplied	$79,400 underapplied

We have already computed the budget variance and the volume variance for this company. We will also need to compute the variable manufacturing overhead variances. The data for these computations are contained in Exhibit 8A–1. Recalling the formulas for the variable manufacturing overhead variances from earlier in this chapter, we can compute the variable overhead rate and efficiency variances as follows:

$$\text{Variable overhead rate variance} = (AH \times AR) - (AH \times SR)$$

$$= AH(AR - SR)$$

$$= \frac{42,000}{\text{machine-hours}} - \left(\frac{\$1.70 \text{ per}}{\text{machine-hour}^2} - \frac{\$1.50 \text{ per}}{\text{machine-hour}} \right)$$

$$= \$8,400 \text{ U}$$

$$\text{Variable overhead efficiency variance} = (AH \times SR) - (SH \times SR)$$

$$= SR(AH - SH)$$

$$= \frac{\$1.50 \text{ per}}{\text{machine-hour}} - \left(\frac{42,000}{\text{machine-hours}} - \frac{40,000 \text{ per}}{\text{machine-hours}} \right)$$

$$= \$3,000 \text{ U}$$

We can now compute the sum of all of the overhead variances as follows:

Variable overhead rate variance	$ 8,400 U
Variable overhead efficiency variance	3,000 U
Fixed overhead budget variance	8,000 U
Fixed overhead volume variance	60,000 U
Total of the overhead variances	$79,400 U

Note that the total of the overhead variances is $79,000, which equals the underapplied overhead of $79,000. In general, if the overhead is underapplied, the total of the standard cost overhead variances is unfavorable. If the overhead is overapplied, the total of the standard cost overhead variances is favorable.

---

[2]AR = $71,400 ÷ 42,000 machine-hours = $1.70 per machine-hour.

GLOSSARY

Budget variance The difference between the actual fixed overhead costs and the budgeted fixed overhead costs for the period. (p. 399)

Denominator activity The level of activity used to compute the predetermined overhead rate. (p. 398)

Volume variance The variance that arises whenever the standard hours allowed for the actual output of a period are different from the denominator activity level that was used to compute the predetermined overhead rate. It is computed by multiplying the fixed component of the predetermined overhead rate by the difference between the denominator hours and the standard hours allowed for the actual output. (p. 400)

APPENDIX 8A EXERCISES AND PROBLEMS  connect
|ACCOUNTING

All applicable exercises and problems are available with McGraw-Hill's *Connect Accounting*.

EXERCISE 8A–1   Fixed Overhead Variances [LO8–7]

Primara Corporation has a standard cost system in which it applies overhead to products based on the standard direct labor-hours allowed for the actual output of the period. Data concerning the most recent year appear below:

Total budgeted fixed overhead cost for the year	$250,000
Actual fixed overhead cost for the year	$254,000
Budgeted standard direct labor-hours (denominator level of activity) . . .	25,000
Actual direct labor-hours	27,000
Standard direct labor-hours allowed for the actual output	26,000

Required:

1. Compute the fixed portion of the predetermined overhead rate for the year.
2. Compute the fixed overhead budget variance and volume variance.

EXERCISE 8A–2   Predetermined Overhead Rate; Overhead Variances [LO8–6, LO8–7]

Norwall Company's variable manufacturing overhead should be $3.00 per standard machine-hour and its fixed manufacturing overhead should be $300,000 per month.

The following information is available for a recent month:

a. The denominator activity of 60,000 machine-hours is used to compute the predetermined overhead rate.
b. At the 60,000 standard machine-hours level of activity, the company should produce 40,000 units of product.
c. The company's actual operating results were

Number of units produced	42,000
Actual machine-hours	64,000
Actual variable manufacturing overhead cost . . .	$185,600
Actual fixed manufacturing overhead cost	$302,400

Required:

1. Compute the predetermined overhead rate and break it down into variable and fixed cost elements.
2. Compute the standard hours allowed for the actual production.
3. Compute the variable overhead rate and efficiency variances and the fixed overhead budget and volume variances.

EXERCISE 8A–3   Applying Overhead in a Standard Costing System [LO8–7]

Privack Corporation has a standard cost system in which it applies overhead to products based on the standard direct labor-hours allowed for the actual output of the period. Data concerning the most recent year appear below:

Variable overhead cost per direct labor-hour	$2.00
Total fixed overhead cost per year	$250,000
Budgeted standard direct labor-hours (denominator level of activity) . . .	40,000
Actual direct labor-hours	39,000
Standard direct labor-hours allowed for the actual output	38,000

Required:
1. Compute the predetermined overhead rate for the year.
2. Determine the amount of overhead that would be applied to the output of the period.

EXERCISE 8A–4   Fixed Overhead Variances [LO8–7]
Selected operating information on three different companies for a recent year is given below:

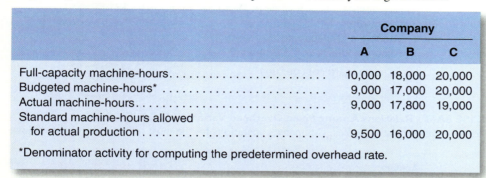

	Company		
	A	B	C
Full-capacity machine-hours....................	10,000	18,000	20,000
Budgeted machine-hours*.......................	9,000	17,000	20,000
Actual machine-hours...........................	9,000	17,800	19,000
Standard machine-hours allowed for actual production...........................	9,500	16,000	20,000

*Denominator activity for computing the predetermined overhead rate.

Required:
For each company, state whether the company would have a favorable or unfavorable volume variance and why.

EXERCISE 8A–5   Using Fixed Overhead Variances [LO8–7]
The standard cost card for the single product manufactured by Cutter, Inc., is given below:

Standard Cost Card—Per Unit	
Direct materials, 3 yards at $6.00 per yard.....................	$ 18
Direct labor, 4 hours at $15.50 per hour.......................	62
Variable overhead, 4 hours at $1.50 per hour	6
Fixed overhead, 4 hours at $5.00 per hour.....................	20
Total standard cost per unit.................................	$106

Manufacturing overhead is applied to production on the basis of standard direct labor-hours. During the year, the company worked 37,000 hours and manufactured 9,500 units of product. Selected data relating to the company's fixed manufacturing overhead cost for the year are shown below:

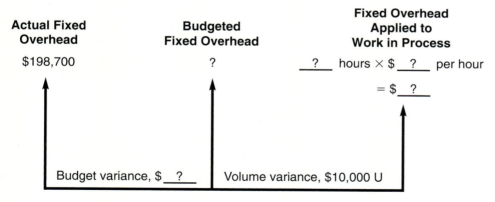

Actual Fixed Overhead	Budgeted Fixed Overhead	Fixed Overhead Applied to Work in Process
$198,700	?	_?_ hours × $_?_ per hour = $ _?_

Budget variance, $ _?_   Volume variance, $10,000 U

Required:
1. What were the standard hours allowed for the year's production?
2. What was the amount of budgeted fixed overhead cost for the year?
3. What was the fixed overhead budget variance for the year?
4. What denominator activity level did the company use in setting the predetermined overhead rate for the year?

EXERCISE 8A–6   Predetermined Overhead Rate [LO8–7]
Operating at a normal level of 30,000 direct labor-hours, Lasser Company produces 10,000 units of product each year. The direct labor wage rate is $12 per hour. Two and one-half yards of direct materials go into each unit of product; the material costs $8.60 per yard. Variable manufacturing overhead should be $1.90 per standard direct labor-hour. Fixed manufacturing overhead should be $168,000 per period.

Required:
1. Using 30,000 direct labor-hours as the denominator activity, compute the predetermined overhead rate and break it down into variable and fixed elements.
2. Complete the standard cost card below for one unit of product:

Direct materials, 2.5 yards at $8.60 per yard	$21.50
Direct labor, ?	?
Variable manufacturing overhead, ?	?
Fixed manufacturing overhead, ?	?
Total standard cost per unit.	$?

EXERCISE 8A–7   Relations Among Fixed Overhead Variances [LO8–7]
Selected information relating to Yost Company's operations for the most recent year is given below:

Activity:	
Denominator activity (machine-hours)	45,000
Standard hours allowed per unit	3
Number of units produced.	14,000
Costs:	
Actual fixed overhead costs incurred.	$267,000
Fixed overhead budget variance	$3,000 F

The company applies overhead cost to products on the basis of standard machine-hours.

Required:
1. What were the standard machine-hours allowed for the actual production?
2. What was the fixed portion of the predetermined overhead rate?
3. What was the volume variance?

PROBLEM 8A–8A   Applying Overhead; Overhead Variances [LO8–6, LO8–7]
Lane Company manufactures a single product that requires a great deal of hand labor. Overhead cost is applied on the basis of standard direct labor-hours. Variable manufacturing overhead should be $2 per standard direct labor-hour and fixed manufacturing overhead should be $480,000 per year.

The company's product requires 3 pounds of material that has a standard cost of $7 per pound and 1.5 hours of direct labor time that has a standard rate of $12 per hour.

The company planned to operate at a denominator activity level of 60,000 direct labor-hours and to produce 40,000 units of product during the most recent year. Actual activity and costs for the year were as follows:

Number of units produced	42,000
Actual direct labor-hours worked.	65,000
Actual variable manufacturing overhead cost incurred	$123,500
Actual fixed manufacturing overhead cost incurred	$483,000

Required:
1. Compute the predetermined overhead rate for the year. Break the rate down into variable and fixed elements.
2. Prepare a standard cost card for the company's product; show the details for all manufacturing costs on your standard cost card.
3. Do the following:
    a. Compute the standard direct labor-hours allowed for the year's production.
    b. Complete the following Manufacturing Overhead T-account for the year:

Manufacturing Overhead

?	?
?	?

4. Determine the reason for any underapplied or overapplied overhead for the year by computing the variable overhead rate and efficiency variances and the fixed overhead budget and volume variances.
5. Suppose the company had chosen 65,000 direct labor-hours as the denominator activity rather than 60,000 hours. State which, if any, of the variances computed in (4) above would have changed, and explain how the variance(s) would have changed. No computations are necessary.

PROBLEM 8A–9A Applying Overhead; Overhead Variances [LO8–6, LO8–7]

Chilczuk, S.A., of Gdansk, Poland, is a major producer of classic Polish sausage. The company uses a standard cost system to help control costs. Manufacturing overhead is applied to production on the basis of standard direct labor-hours. According to the company's flexible budget, the following manufacturing overhead costs should be incurred at an activity level of 35,000 labor-hours (the denominator activity level):

Variable manufacturing overhead cost	$ 87,500
Fixed manufacturing overhead cost	210,000
Total manufacturing overhead cost.	$297,500

During the most recent year, the following operating results were recorded:

Activity:	
Actual labor-hours worked	30,000
Standard labor-hours allowed for output.	32,000
Costs:	
Actual variable manufacturing overhead cost incurred	$78,000
Actual fixed manufacturing overhead cost incurred	$209,400

At the end of the year, the company's Manufacturing Overhead account contained the following data:

Manufacturing Overhead

Actual	287,400	Applied	272,000
	15,400		

Management would like to determine the cause of the $15,400 underapplied overhead.

Required:
1. Compute the predetermined overhead rate. Break the rate down into variable and fixed cost elements.
2. Show how the $272,000 Applied figure in the Manufacturing Overhead account was computed.
3. Analyze the $15,400 underapplied overhead figure in terms of the variable overhead rate and efficiency variances and the fixed overhead budget and volume variances.
4. Explain the meaning of each variance that you computed in (3) above.

PROBLEM 8A–10A Comprehensive Standard Cost Variances [LO8–4, LO8–5, LO8–6, LO8–7]

"Wonderful! Not only did our salespeople do a good job in meeting the sales budget this year, but our production people did a good job in controlling costs as well," said Kim Clark, president of Martell Company. "Our $18,300 overall manufacturing cost variance is only 1.2% of the $1,536,000 standard cost of products made during the year. That's well within the 3% parameter set by management for acceptable variances. It looks like everyone will be in line for a bonus this year."

The company produces and sells a single product. The standard cost card for the product follows:

Standard Cost Card—Per Unit	
Direct materials, 2 feet at $8.45 per foot.	$16.90
Direct labor, 1.4 direct labor-hours at $16 per direct labor-hour	22.40
Variable overhead, 1.4 direct labor-hours at $2.50 per direct labor-hour . . .	3.50
Fixed overhead, 1.4 direct labor-hours at $6 per direct labor-hour	8.40
Standard cost per unit	$51.20

The following additional information is available for the year just completed:

a. The company manufactured 30,000 units of product during the year.

b. A total of 64,000 feet of material was purchased during the year at a cost of $8.55 per foot. All of this material was used to manufacture the 30,000 units. There were no beginning or ending inventories for the year.

c. The company worked 43,500 direct labor-hours during the year at a direct labor cost of $15.80 per hour.

d. Overhead is applied to products on the basis of standard direct labor-hours. Data relating to manufacturing overhead costs follow:

Denominator activity level (direct labor-hours)	35,000
Budgeted fixed overhead costs	$210,000
Actual variable overhead costs incurred.	$108,000
Actual fixed overhead costs incurred	$211,800

Required:

1. Compute the materials price and quantity variances for the year.
2. Compute the labor rate and efficiency variances for the year.
3. For manufacturing overhead compute:
   a. The variable overhead rate and efficiency variances for the year.
   b. The fixed overhead budget and volume variances for the year.
4. Total the variances you have computed, and compare the net amount with the $18,300 mentioned by the president. Do you agree that bonuses should be given to everyone for good cost control during the year? Explain.

PROBLEM 8A–11A Comprehensive Standard Cost Variances [LO8–4, LO8–5, LO8–6, L08–7]

Flandro Company uses a standard cost system and sets predetermined overhead rates on the basis of direct labor-hours. The following data are taken from the company's budget for the current year:

Denominator activity (direct labor-hours)	5,000
Variable manufacturing overhead cost	$25,000
Fixed manufacturing overhead cost	$59,000

The standard cost card for the company's only product is given below:

Direct materials, 3 yards at $4.40 per yard.	$13.20
Direct labor, 1 hour at $12 per hour	12.00
Manufacturing overhead, 140% of direct labor cost	16.80
Standard cost per unit	$42.00

During the year, the company produced 6,000 units of product and incurred the following costs:

Materials purchased, 24,000 yards at $4.80 per yard.	$115,200
Materials used in production (in yards).	18,500
Direct labor cost incurred, 5,800 hours at $13 per hour	$75,400
Variable manufacturing overhead cost incurred	$29,580
Fixed manufacturing overhead cost incurred	$60,400

Required:

1. Redo the standard cost card in a clearer, more usable format by detailing the variable and fixed overhead cost elements.
2. Prepare an analysis of the variances for direct materials and direct labor for the year.
3. Prepare an analysis of the variances for variable and fixed overhead for the year.
4. What effect, if any, does the choice of a denominator activity level have on unit standard costs? Is the volume variance a controllable variance from a spending point of view? Explain.

PROBLEM 8A–12A   Selection of a Denominator; Overhead Analysis; Standard Cost Card [LO8–6, LO8–7]

Morton Company's variable manufacturing overhead should be $4.50 per standard direct labor-hour and fixed manufacturing should be $270,000 per year.

The company manufactures a single product that requires two direct labor-hours to complete. The direct labor wage rate is $15 per hour. Four feet of raw material are required for each unit of product; the standard cost of the material is $8.75 per foot.

Although normal activity is 30,000 direct labor-hours each year, the company expects to operate at a 40,000-hour level of activity this year.

Required:
1. Assume that the company chooses 30,000 direct labor-hours as the denominator level of activity. Compute the predetermined overhead rate, breaking it down into variable and fixed cost elements.
2. Assume that the company chooses 40,000 direct labor-hours as the denominator level of activity. Repeat the computations in (1) above.
3. Complete two standard cost cards as outlined below.

Denominator Activity: 30,000 Direct Labor-Hours

Direct materials, 4 feet at $8.75 per foot. . . .	$35.00
Direct labor, ?	?
Variable manufacturing overhead, ?	?
Fixed manufacturing overhead, ?	?
Standard cost per unit	$?

Denominator Activity: 40,000 Direct Labor-Hours

Direct materials, $4 feet at $8.75 per foot. . .	$35.00
Direct labor, ?	?
Variable manufacturing overhead, ?	?
Fixed manufacturing overhead, ?	?
Standard cost per unit	$?

---

4. Assume that the company actually produces 18,000 units and works 38,000 direct labor-hours during the year. Actual manufacturing overhead costs for the year are

Variable manufacturing overhead cost	$174,800
Fixed manufacturing overhead cost	271,600
Total manufacturing overhead cost.	$446,400

Do the following:
a. Compute the standard direct labor-hours allowed for this year's production.
b. Complete the Manufacturing Overhead account below. Assume that the company uses 30,000 direct labor-hours (normal activity) as the denominator activity figure in computing predetermined overhead rates, as you have done in (1) above.

Manufacturing Overhead

Actual costs	446,400	Applied costs	?
	?		?

c. Determine the cause of the underapplied or overapplied overhead for the year by computing the variable overhead rate and efficiency variances and the fixed overhead budget and volume variances.
5. Looking at the variances you have computed, what appears to be the major disadvantage of using normal activity rather than expected actual activity as a denominator in computing the predetermined overhead rate? What advantages can you see to offset this disadvantage?

APPENDIX 8B: JOURNAL ENTRIES TO RECORD VARIANCES

Although standard costs and variances can be computed and used by management without being formally entered into the accounting records, many organizations prefer to make formal journal entries. Formal entries tend to give variances a greater emphasis than informal, off-the-record computations. This emphasis signals management's desire to keep costs within the limits that have been set. In addition, formal use of standard costs simplifies the bookkeeping process enormously. Inventories and cost of goods sold can be valued at their standard costs—eliminating the need to keep track of the actual cost of each unit.

Direct Materials Variances

To illustrate the journal entries needed to record standard cost variances, we will return to the data contained in Review Problem 2 at the end of the chapter. The entry to record the purchase of direct materials would be as follows:

Raw Materials (18,000 ounces at $0.50 per ounce).	9,000	
Materials Price Variance (18,000 ounces at $0.10 per ounce U)	1,800	
Accounts Payable (18,000 ounces at $0.60 per ounce)		10,800

Notice that the price variance is recognized when purchases are made, rather than when materials are actually used in production and that the materials are carried in the inventory account at standard cost. As direct materials are later drawn from inventory and used in production, the quantity variance is isolated as follows:

Work in Process (12,000 ounces at $0.50 per ounce)	6,000	
Materials Quantity Variance (2,000 ounces U at $0.50 per ounce)	1,000	
Raw Materials (14,000 ounces at $0.50 per ounce)		7,000

Thus, direct materials are added to the Work in Process account at the standard cost of the materials that should have been used to produce the actual output.

Notice that both the price variance and the quantity variance above are unfavorable and are debit entries. If either of these variances had been favorable, it would have appeared as a credit entry.

Direct Labor Variances

Referring again to the cost data in the review problem at the end of the chapter, the journal entry to record the incurrence of direct labor cost would be as follows:

Work in Process (1,200 hours at $30.00 per hour).	36,000	
Labor Rate Variance (1,100 hours at $0.50 U)	550	
Labor Efficiency Variance (100 hours F at $30.00 per hour).		3,000
Wages Payable (1,100 hours at $30.50 per hour).		33,550

Thus, as with direct materials, direct labor costs enter into the Work in Process account at standard, both in terms of the rate and in terms of the hours allowed for the actual production of the period. Note that the unfavorable labor efficiency variance is a debit entry whereas the favorable labor rate variance is a credit entry.

Cost Flows in a Standard Cost System

The flow of costs through the company's accounts are illustrated in Exhibit 8B–1. Note that entries into the various inventory accounts are made at standard cost—not actual cost. The differences between actual and standard costs are entered into special accounts

EXHIBIT 8B–1 Cost Flows in a Standard Cost System

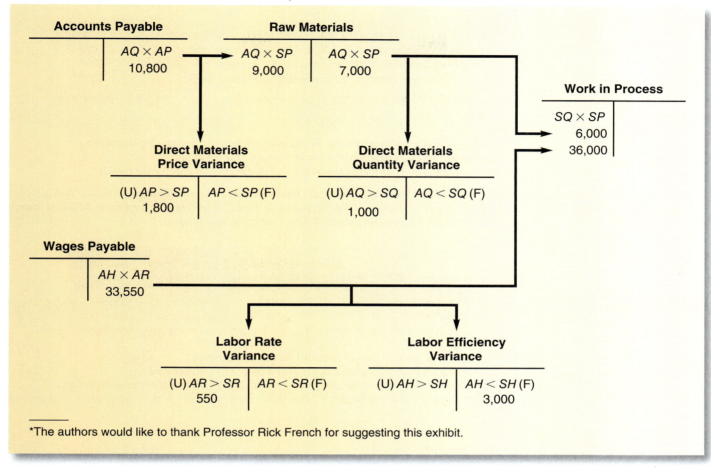

*The authors would like to thank Professor Rick French for suggesting this exhibit.

that accumulate the various standard cost variances. Ordinarily, these standard cost variance accounts are closed out to Cost of Goods Sold at the end of the period. Unfavorable variances increase Cost of Goods Sold, and favorable variances decrease Cost of Goods Sold.

 APPENDIX 8B EXERCISES AND PROBLEMS

All applicable exercises and problems are available with McGraw-Hill's *Connect Accounting*.

EXERCISE 8B–I   Recording Variances in the General Ledger [LO8–8]
Bliny Corporation makes a product with the following standard costs for direct material and direct labor:

Direct material: 2.00 meters at $3.25 per meter	$6.50
Direct labor: 0.40 hours at $12.00 per hour	$4.80

During the most recent month, 5,000 units were produced. The costs associated with the month's production of this product were as follows:

Material purchased: 12,000 meters at $3.15 per meter . .	$37,800
Material used in production: 10,500 meters	—
Direct labor: 1,975 hours at $12.20 per hour	$24,095

The standard cost variances for direct material and direct labor are

Materials price variance: 12,000 meters at $0.10 per meter F	$1,200 F
Materials quantity variance: 500 meters at $3.25 per meter U....	$1,625 U
Labor rate variance: 1,975 hours at $0.20 per hour U	$395 U
Labor efficiency variance: 25 hours at $12.00 per hour F........	$300 F

Required:
1. Prepare the journal entry to record the purchase of materials on account for the month.
2. Prepare the journal entry to record the use of materials for the month.
3. Prepare the journal entry to record the incurrence of direct labor cost for the month.

EXERCISE 8B–2 Direct Materials and Direct Labor Variances; Journal Entries [LO8–4, LO8–5, LO8–8]
Genola Fashions began production of a new product on June 1. The company uses a standard cost system and has established the following standards for one unit of the new product:

	Standard Quantity or Hours	Standard Price or Rate	Standard Cost
Direct materials.....	2.5 yards	$14 per yard	$35.00
Direct labor........	1.6 hours	$8 per hour	$12.80

During June, the following activity was recorded for the new product:
a. Purchasing acquired 10,000 yards of material at a cost of $13.80 per yard.
b. Production used 8,000 yards of the material to manufacture 3,000 units of the new product.
c. Production reported that 5,000 direct labor-hours were worked on the new product at a cost of $43,000.

Required:
1. For direct materials:
   a. Compute the materials price and quantity variances.
   b. Prepare journal entries to record the purchase of materials and the use of materials in production.
2. For direct labor:
   a. Compute the labor rate and efficiency variances.
   b. Prepare a journal entry to record the incurrence of direct labor cost for the month.
3. Post the entries you have prepared to the following T-accounts:

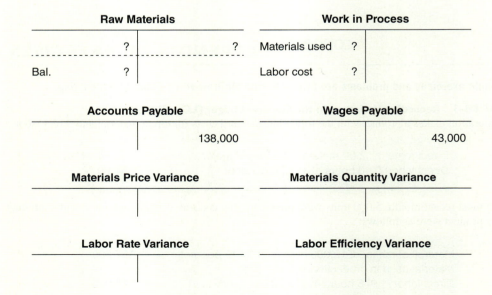

PROBLEM 8B–3A   Comprehensive Variance Analysis; Journal Entries [LO8–4, LO8–5, LO8–6, LO8–8]

Trueform Products, Inc., produces a broad line of sports equipment and uses a standard cost system for control purposes. Last year the company produced 8,000 varsity footballs. The standard costs associated with this football, along with the actual costs incurred last year, are given below (per football):

	Standard Cost	Actual Cost
Direct materials:		
Standard: 3.7 feet at $5.00 per foot.	$18.50	
Actual: 4.0 feet at $4.80 per foot		$19.20
Direct labor:		
Standard: 0.9 hours at $7.50 per hour	6.75	
Actual: 0.8 hours at $8.00 per hour.		6.40
Variable manufacturing overhead:		
Standard: 0.9 hours at $2.50 per hour	2.25	
Actual: 0.8 hours at $2.75 per hour.		2.20
Total cost per football	$27.50	$27.80

The president was elated when he saw that actual costs exceeded standard costs by only $0.30 per football. He stated, "I was afraid that our unit cost might get out of hand when we gave out those raises last year in order to stimulate output. But it's obvious our costs are well under control."

There was no inventory of materials on hand to start the year. During the year, 32,000 feet of materials were purchased and used in production.

Required:
1.   For direct materials:
   a.   Compute the price and quantity variances for the year.
   b.   Prepare journal entries to record all activity relating to direct materials for the year.
2.   For direct labor:
   a.   Compute the rate and efficiency variances.
   b.   Prepare a journal entry to record the incurrence of direct labor cost for the year.
3.   Compute the variable overhead rate and efficiency variances.
4.   Was the president correct in his statement that "our costs are well under control"? Explain.
5.   State possible causes of each variance that you have computed.

PROBLEM 8B–4A   Comprehensive Variance Analysis with Incomplete Data; Journal Entries [LO8–4, LO8–5, LO8–6, LO8–8]

Maple Products, Ltd., manufactures a super-strong hockey stick. The standard cost of one hockey stick is

	Standard Quantity or Hours	Standard Price or Rate	Standard Cost
Direct materials	? feet	$3.00 per foot	$?
Direct labor	2 hours	? per hour	?
Variable manufacturing overhead	? hours	$1.30 per hour	?
Total standard cost			$27.00

Last year, 8,000 hockey sticks were produced and sold. Selected cost data relating to last year's operations follow:

	Dr.	Cr.
Accounts payable—direct materials purchased (60,000 feet).		$174,000
Wages payable (? hours)		$79,200*
Work in process—direct materials	$115.200	
Labor rate variance.		$3,300
Variable overhead efficiency variance	$650	

*Relates to the actual direct labor cost for the year.

The following additional information is available for last year's operations:

a.   No materials were on hand at the start of last year. Some of the materials purchased during the year were still on hand in the warehouse at the end of the year.
b.   The variable manufacturing overhead rate is based on direct labor-hours. Total actual variable manufacturing overhead cost for last year was $19,800.
c.   Actual direct materials usage for last year exceeded the standard by 0.2 feet per stick.

Required:
1.   For direct materials:
     a. Compute the price and quantity variances for last year.
     b. Prepare journal entries to record all activities relating to direct materials for last year.
2.   For direct labor:
     a. Using the rate variance given above, calculate the standard hourly wage rate and compute the efficiency variance for last year.
     b. Prepare a journal entry to record activity relating to direct labor for last year.
3.   Compute the variable overhead rate variance for last year and verify the variable overhead efficiency variance given above.
4.   State possible causes of each variance that you have computed.
5.   Prepare a standard cost card for one hockey stick.

A LOOK BACK

In Chapter 8, we looked at flexible budgets and spending variances. Standards were used to isolate the effects of various factors on actual results. In particular, we computed material, labor, and overhead variances.

A LOOK AT THIS CHAPTER

In Chapter 9, we continue our coverage of performance measurement. Return on investment and residual income measures are used to motivate managers and monitor progress. The balanced scorecard is an integrated set of performance measures that are derived from and support the organization's strategy.

A LOOK AHEAD

In Chapter 10, we concentrate on the identification of differential costs and benefits to aid decision making.

9 Performance Measurement in Decentralized Organizations

CHAPTER OUTLINE

Decentralization in Organizations

- Advantages and Disadvantages of Decentralization

Responsibility Accounting

- Cost, Profit, and Investment Centers

Evaluating Investment Center Performance—Return on Investment

- The Return on Investment (ROI) Formula
- Net Operating Income and Operating Assets Defined
- Understanding ROI
- Criticisms of ROI

Residual Income

- Motivation and Residual Income
- Divisional Comparison and Residual Income

Operating Performance Measures

- Delivery Cycle Time
- Throughput (Manufacturing Cycle) Time
- Manufacturing Cycle Efficiency (MCE)

Balanced Scorecard

- Common Characteristics of Balanced Scorecards
- A Company's Strategy and the Balanced Scorecard
- Tying Compensation to the Balanced Scorecard

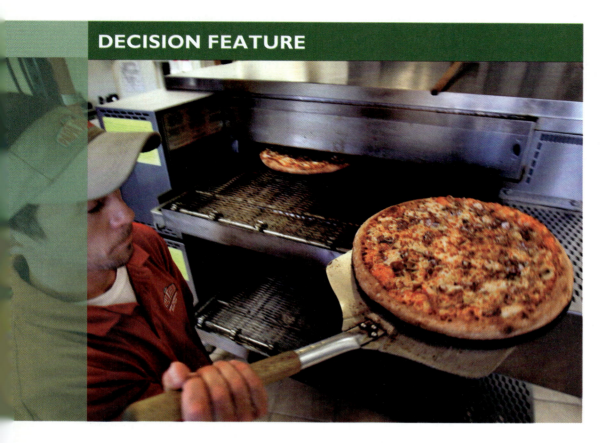

LEARNING OBJECTIVES

After studying Chapter 9, you should be able to:

LO9–1 Compute return on investment (ROI) and show how changes in sales, expenses, and assets affect ROI.

LO9–2 Compute residual income and understand its strengths and weaknesses.

LO9–3 Compute delivery cycle time, throughput time, and manufacturing cycle efficiency (MCE).

LO9–4 Understand how to construct and use a balanced scorecard.

Performance Measures That Drive Financial Results

Companies that wish to achieve strong financial results need to be responsive to employee and customer needs. For example, **Papa John's** uses mystery shoppers and a 10-point scale to measure the quality of 10,000 pizzas per month. The mystery shopper scores, which are tied to executive bonuses, help Papa John's meet the customers' need for high-quality pizza. **American Express** asked its 26,000 call-center employees what they needed to achieve higher job satisfaction—then it responded by delivering flexible schedules, more career development, and higher pay. Collectively, these changes increased the company's service margins by 10%.

This chapter discusses financial measures that companies use to track performance. It also introduces some nonfinancial performance measures, related to customers, employees, and business processes, that companies use to drive financial results.

Sources: Scott Cendrowski, "Papa John's John Schnatter," *Fortune*, September 28, 2009, p. 34; Christopher Tkaczyk, "No. 73: American Express," *Fortune*, August 16, 2010, p. 14.

Except in very small organizations, top managers must delegate some decisions. For example, the CEO of the **Hyatt Hotel** chain cannot be expected to decide whether a particular hotel guest at the Hyatt Hotel on Maui should be allowed to check out later than the normal checkout time. Instead, employees at Maui are authorized to make this decision. As in this example, managers in large organizations have to delegate some decisions to those who are at lower levels in the organization.

DECENTRALIZATION IN ORGANIZATIONS

In a **decentralized organization**, decision-making authority is spread throughout the organization rather than being confined to a few top executives. As noted above, out of necessity all large organizations are decentralized to some extent. Organizations do differ, however, in the extent to which they are decentralized. In strongly centralized organizations, decision-making authority is reluctantly delegated to lower-level managers who have little freedom to make decisions. In strongly decentralized organizations, even the lowest-level managers are empowered to make as many decisions as possible. Most organizations fall somewhere between these two extremes.

Advantages and Disadvantages of Decentralization

The major advantages of decentralization include

1. By delegating day-to-day problem solving to lower-level managers, top management can concentrate on bigger issues, such as overall strategy.
2. Empowering lower-level managers to make decisions puts the decision-making authority in the hands of those who tend to have the most detailed and up-to-date information about day-to-day operations.
3. By eliminating layers of decision making and approvals, organizations can respond more quickly to customers and to changes in the operating environment.
4. Granting decision-making authority helps train lower-level managers for higher-level positions.
5. Empowering lower-level managers to make decisions can increase their motivation and job satisfaction.

The major disadvantages of decentralization include

1. Lower-level managers may make decisions without fully understanding the company's overall strategy.
2. If lower-level managers make their own decisions independently of each other, coordination may be lacking.
3. Lower-level managers may have objectives that clash with the objectives of the entire organization.[1] For example, a manager may be more interested in increasing the size of his or her department, leading to more power and prestige, than in increasing the department's effectiveness.

---

[1]Similar problems exist with top-level managers as well. The shareholders of the company delegate their decision-making authority to the top managers. Unfortunately, top managers may abuse that trust by rewarding themselves and their friends too generously, spending too much company money on palatial offices, and so on. The issue of how to ensure that top managers act in the best interests of the company's owners continues to challenge experts. To a large extent, the owners rely on performance evaluation using return on investment and residual income measures, as discussed later in the chapter, and on bonuses and stock options. The stock market is also an important disciplining mechanism. If top managers squander the company's resources, the price of the company's stock will almost surely fall—possibly resulting in a loss of prestige, bonuses, and a job. And, of course, particularly outrageous self-dealing may land a CEO in court.

4. Spreading innovative ideas may be difficult in a decentralized organization. Someone in one part of the organization may have a terrific idea that would benefit other parts of the organization, but without strong central direction the idea may not be shared with, and adopted by, other parts of the organization.

RESPONSIBILITY ACCOUNTING

Decentralized organizations need *responsibility accounting systems* that link lower-level managers' decision-making authority with accountability for the outcomes of those decisions. The term **responsibility center** is used for any part of an organization whose manager has control over and is accountable for cost, profit, or investments. The three primary types of responsibility centers are *cost centers, profit centers,* and *investment centers.*

Cost, Profit, and Investment Centers

Cost Center   The manager of a **cost center** has control over costs, but not over revenue or the use of investment funds. Service departments such as accounting, finance, general administration, legal, and personnel are usually classified as cost centers. In addition, manufacturing facilities are often considered to be cost centers. The managers of cost centers are expected to minimize costs while providing the level of products and services demanded by other parts of the organization. For example, the manager of a manufacturing facility would be evaluated at least in part by comparing actual costs to how much costs should have been for the actual level of output during the period. Standard cost variances and flexible budget variances, such as those discussed in the previous chapter, are often used to evaluate cost center performance.

Profit Center   The manager of a **profit center** has control over both costs and revenue, but not over the use of investment funds. For example, the manager in charge of a **Six Flags** amusement park would be responsible for both the revenues and costs, and hence the profits, of the amusement park, but may not have control over major investments in the park. Profit center managers are often evaluated by comparing actual profit to targeted or budgeted profit.

Investment Center   The manager of an **investment center** has control over cost, revenue, and investments in operating assets. For example, **General Motors'** vice president of manufacturing in North America would have a great deal of discretion over investments in manufacturing—such as investing in equipment to produce more fuel-efficient engines. Once General Motors' top-level managers and board of directors approve the vice president's investment proposals, he is held responsible for making them pay off. As discussed in the next section, investment center managers are often evaluated using return on investment (ROI) or residual income measures.

1. Managers in which of the following responsibility centers are held responsible for profits? (You may select more than one answer.)
   a. Revenue centers
   b. Cost centers
   c. Profit centers
   d. Investment centers

CONCEPT CHECK

EVALUATING INVESTMENT CENTER PERFORMANCE—RETURN ON INVESTMENT

LEARNING OBJECTIVE 9–1

Compute return on investment (ROI) and show how changes in sales, expenses, and assets affect ROI.

An investment center is responsible for earning an adequate return on investment. The following two sections present two methods for evaluating this aspect of an investment center's performance. The first method, covered in this section, is called *return on investment* (ROI). The second method, covered in the next section, is called *residual income.*

The Return on Investment (ROI) Formula

Return on investment (ROI) is defined as net operating income divided by average operating assets:

$$\text{ROI} = \frac{\text{Net operating income}}{\text{Average operating assets}}$$

The higher a business segment's return on investment (ROI), the greater the profit earned per dollar invested in the segment's operating assets.

Net Operating Income and Operating Assets Defined

Note that *net operating income,* rather than net income, is used in the ROI formula. **Net operating income** is income before interest and taxes and is sometimes referred to as EBIT (earnings before interest and taxes). Net operating income is used in the formula because the base (i.e., denominator) consists of *operating assets.* To be consistent, we use net operating income in the numerator.

    Operating assets include cash, accounts receivable, inventory, plant and equipment, and all other assets held for operating purposes. Examples of assets that are not included in operating assets (i.e., examples of nonoperating assets) include land held for future use, an investment in another company, or a building rented to someone else. These assets are not held for operating purposes and therefore are excluded from operating assets. The operating assets base used in the formula is typically computed as the average of the operating assets between the beginning and the end of the year.

    Most companies use the net book value (i.e., acquisition cost less accumulated depreciation) of depreciable assets to calculate average operating assets. This approach has drawbacks. An asset's net book value decreases over time as the accumulated depreciation increases. This decreases the denominator in the ROI calculation, thus increasing ROI. Consequently, ROI mechanically increases over time. Moreover, replacing old depreciated equipment with new equipment increases the book value of depreciable assets and decreases ROI. Hence, using net book value in the calculation of average operating assets results in a predictable pattern of increasing ROI over time as accumulated depreciation grows and discourages replacing old equipment with new, updated equipment. An alternative to using net book value is the gross cost of the asset, which ignores accumulated depreciation. Gross cost stays constant over time because depreciation is ignored; therefore, ROI does not grow automatically over time, and replacing a fully depreciated asset with a comparably priced new asset will not adversely affect ROI.

    Nevertheless, most companies use the net book value approach to computing average operating assets because it is consistent with their financial reporting practices of recording the net book value of assets on the balance sheet and including depreciation as an operating expense on the income statement. In this text, we will use the net book value approach unless a specific exercise or problem directs otherwise.

Understanding ROI

The equation for ROI, net operating income divided by average operating assets, does not provide much help to managers interested in taking actions to improve their ROI. It only offers two levers for improving performance—net operating income and average operating assets. Fortunately, ROI can also be expressed in terms of **margin** and **turnover** as follows:

$$\text{ROI} = \text{Margin} \times \text{Turnover}$$

where

$$\text{Margin} = \frac{\text{Net operating income}}{\text{Sales}}$$

and

$$\text{Turnover} = \frac{\text{Sales}}{\text{Average operating assets}}$$

Note that the sales terms in the margin and turnover formulas cancel out when they are multiplied together, yielding the original formula for ROI stated in terms of net operating income and average operating assets. So either formula for ROI will give the same answer. However, the margin and turnover formulation provides some additional insights.

Margin and turnover are important concepts in understanding how a manager can affect ROI. All other things the same, margin is ordinarily improved by increasing selling prices, reducing operating expenses, or increasing unit sales. Increasing selling prices and reducing operating expenses both increase net operating income and therefore margin. Increasing unit sales also ordinarily increases the margin because of operating leverage. As discussed in a previous chapter, because of operating leverage, a given percentage increase in unit sales usually leads to an even larger percentage increase in net operating income. Therefore, an increase in unit sales ordinarily has the effect of increasing margin. Some managers tend to focus too much on margin and ignore turnover. However, turnover incorporates a crucial area of a manager's responsibility—the investment in operating assets. Excessive funds tied up in operating assets (e.g., cash, accounts receivable, inventories, plant and equipment, and other assets) depress turnover and lower ROI. In fact, excessive operating assets can be just as much of a drag on ROI as excessive operating expenses, which depress margin.

A Strategy of Scarcity

IN BUSINESS

Old Rip Van Winkle Distillery employs two people, Julian Van Winkle III and his son Preston. Its annual sales of $2 million pale in comparison to larger competitors such as **Makers' Mark** and **Wild Turkey**. Although the company could easily triple its sales volume, it chooses to limit sales to 7,000 cases of bourbon per year. Given that the company's 20-year-old aged whiskey once achieved an unprecedented "99" rating from the **Beverage Tasting Institute of Chicago**, demand for the company's products far exceeds its supply—thereby enabling regular price increases. For example, a fifth of 20-year-old Pappy Van Winkle bourbon sells for $110. In accounting terms, the Old Rip Van Winkle Distillery purposely foregoes turnover in favor of earning large margins on its award-winning products.

Source: Brian Dumaine, "Creating the Ultimate Cult Brand," *Fortune*, February 28, 2011, pp. 21–24.

Many actions involve combinations of changes in sales, expenses, and operating assets. For example, a manager may make an investment in (i.e., increase) operating assets to reduce operating expenses or increase sales. Whether the net effect is favorable or not is judged in terms of its overall impact on ROI.

HELPFUL HINT

To better understand the concepts of margin and turnover, link them to actual companies. For example, the local jewelry store in your hometown relies more on margin than turnover to generate a satisfactory return on investment (ROI). It completes a small number of transactions each day, so to be profitable it needs to earn a high margin per transaction. Conversely, Walmart relies more on turnover than margin to generate its ROI. Walmart completes an enormous number of transactions each day so, even though each transaction earns a very small margin, the company's extraordinary turnover creates a favorable ROI.

For example, suppose that the Montvale Burger Grill expects the following operating results next month:

Sales	$100,000
Operating expenses	$90,000
Net operating income	$10,000
Average operating assets	$50,000

The expected return on investment (ROI) for the month is computed as follows:

$$\text{ROI} = \frac{\text{Net operating income}}{\text{Sales}} \times \frac{\text{Sales}}{\text{Average operating assets}}$$

$$= \frac{\$10,000}{\$100,000} \times \frac{\$100,000}{\$50,000}$$

$$= 10\% \times 2 = 20\%$$

Suppose that the manager of the Montvale Burger Grill is considering investing $2,000 in a state-of-the-art soft-serve ice cream machine that can dispense a number of different flavors. This new machine would boost sales by $4,000, but would require additional operating expenses of $1,000. Thus, net operating income would increase by $3,000, to $13,000. The new ROI would be

$$\text{ROI} = \frac{\text{Net operating income}}{\text{Sales}} \times \frac{\text{Sales}}{\text{Average operating assets}}$$

$$= \frac{\$13,000}{\$104,000} \times \frac{\$104,000}{\$52,000}$$

$$= 12.5\% \times 2 = 25\% \text{ (as compared to 20\% originally)}$$

In this particular example, the investment increases ROI, but that will not always happen. **E.I. du Pont de Nemours and Company** (better known as DuPont) pioneered the use of ROI and recognized the importance of looking at both margin and turnover in assessing a manager's performance. ROI is now widely used as the key measure of investment center performance. ROI reflects in a single figure many aspects of the manager's responsibilities. It can be compared to the returns of other investment centers in the organization, the returns of other companies in the industry, and to the past returns of the investment center itself. DuPont also developed the diagram that appears in Exhibit 9–1. This exhibit helps managers understand how they can improve ROI.

EXHIBIT 9–1   Elements of Return on Investment (ROI)

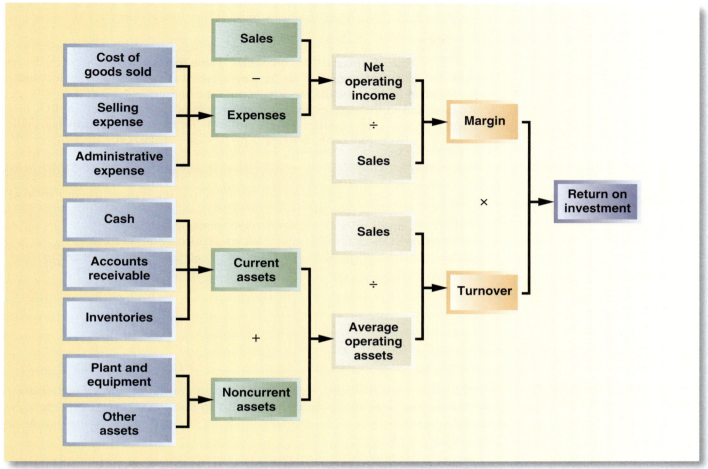

Microsoft Manages in an Economic Downturn

IN BUSINESS

Microsoft responded to tough economic times by lowering its prices, thereby accepting lower margins per unit sold in exchange for higher turnover. For example, Microsoft lowered the price of its Office software from $150 to $100 (after promotional discounts) and realized a 415% increase in unit sales. In China, the company combated huge piracy problems by dropping the price of Office to $29, resulting in an 800% increase in sales. Microsoft established a selling price of $200 for its Windows 7 PC operating system, which was $40 less than the price the company charged for its predecessor Vista PC operating system.

Source: Peter Burrows, "Microsoft's Aggressive New Pricing Strategy," *BusinessWeek*, July 27, 2009, p. 51.

Criticisms of ROI

Although ROI is widely used in evaluating performance, it is subject to the following criticisms:

1. Just telling managers to increase ROI may not be enough. Managers may not know how to increase ROI; they may increase ROI in a way that is inconsistent with the company's strategy; or they may take actions that increase ROI in the short run but harm the company in the long run (such as cutting back on research and development). This is why ROI is best used as part of a balanced scorecard, as discussed later

in this chapter. A balanced scorecard can provide concrete guidance to managers, making it more likely that their actions are consistent with the company's strategy and reducing the likelihood that they will boost short-run performance at the expense of long-term performance.

2. A manager who takes over a business segment typically inherits many committed costs over which the manager has no control. These committed costs may be relevant in assessing the performance of the business segment as an investment but they make it difficult to fairly assess the performance of the manager.

3. As discussed in the next section, a manager who is evaluated based on ROI may reject investment opportunities that are profitable for the whole company but would have a negative impact on the manager's performance evaluation.

CONCEPT CHECK

2. Which of the following statements is false? (You may select more than one answer.)
   a. Margin equals net operating income divided by sales.
   b. Turnover equals sales divided by average operating assets.
   c. Return on investment (ROI) equals margin divided by turnover.
   d. Return on investment (ROI) equals net operating income divided by average operating assets.

RESIDUAL INCOME

LEARNING OBJECTIVE 9–2

Compute residual income and understand its strengths and weaknesses.

Residual income is another approach to measuring an investment center's performance. **Residual income** is the net operating income that an investment center earns above the minimum required return on its operating assets. In equation form, residual income is calculated as follows:

$$\text{Residual income} = \text{Net operating income} - \left(\text{Average operating assets} \times \text{Minimum required rate of return}\right)$$

Economic Value Added (EVA®) is an adaptation of residual income that has been adopted by many companies.[2] Under EVA, companies often modify their accounting principles in various ways. For example, funds used for research and development are often treated as investments rather than as expenses.[3] These complications are best dealt with in a more advanced course; in this text we will not draw any distinction between residual income and EVA.

When residual income or EVA is used to measure performance, the objective is to maximize the total amount of residual income or EVA, not to maximize ROI. This is an important distinction. If the objective were to maximize ROI, then every company should divest all of its products except the single product with the highest ROI.

A wide variety of organizations have embraced some version of residual income or EVA, including **Bausch & Lomb**, **Best Buy**, **Boise Cascade**, **Coca-Cola**, **Dun and Bradstreet**, **Eli Lilly**, **Federal Mogul**, **Georgia-Pacific**, **Hershey Foods**, **Husky**

[2]The basic idea underlying residual income and economic value added has been around for over 100 years. Economic value added has been popularized and trademarked by the consulting firm Stern, Stewart & Co.

[3]Over 100 different adjustments could be made for deferred taxes, LIFO reserves, provisions for future liabilities, mergers and acquisitions, gains or losses due to changes in accounting rules, operating leases, and other accounts, but most companies make only a few. For further details, see John O'Hanlon and Ken Peasnell, "Wall Street's Contribution to Management Accounting: the Stern Stewart EVA® Financial Management System," *Management Accounting Research* 9, 1998, pp. 421–444.

Injection Molding, **J.C. Penney**, **Kansas City Power & Light**, **Olin**, **Quaker Oats**, **Silicon Valley Bank**, **Sprint**, **Toys R Us**, **Tupperware**, and the **United States Postal Service**.

For purposes of illustration, consider the following data for an investment center—the Ketchikan Division of Alaskan Marine Services Corporation.

Alaskan Marine Services Corporation **Ketchikan Division** **Basic Data for Performance Evaluation**	
Average operating assets	$100,000
Net operating income	$20,000
Minimum required rate of return	15%

Alaskan Marine Services Corporation has long had a policy of using ROI to evaluate its investment center managers, but it is considering switching to residual income. The controller of the company, who is in favor of the change to residual income, has provided the following table that shows how the performance of the division would be evaluated under each of the two methods:

Alaskan Marine Services Corporation **Ketchikan Division**		
	Alternative Performance Measures	
	ROI	**Residual Income**
Average operating assets (a)	$100,000	$100,000
Net operating income (b)	$20,000	$20,000
ROI, (b) ÷ (a)	20%	
Minimum required return (15% × $100,000)		15,000
Residual income		$ 5,000

The reasoning underlying the residual income calculation is straightforward. The company is able to earn a rate of return of at least 15% on its investments. Because the company has invested $100,000 in the Ketchikan Division in the form of operating assets, the company should be able to earn at least $15,000 (15% × $100,000) on this investment. Because the Ketchikan Division's net operating income is $20,000, the residual income above and beyond the minimum required return is $5,000. If residual income is adopted as the performance measure to replace ROI, the manager of the Ketchikan Division would be evaluated based on the growth in residual income from year to year.

Motivation and Residual Income

One of the primary reasons why the controller of Alaskan Marine Services Corporation would like to switch from ROI to residual income relates to how managers view new investments under the two performance measurement methods. The residual income approach encourages managers to make investments that are profitable for the entire company but that would be rejected by managers who are evaluated using the ROI formula.

To illustrate this problem with ROI, suppose that the manager of the Ketchikan Division is considering purchasing a computerized diagnostic machine to aid in servicing marine diesel engines. The machine would cost $25,000 and is expected to generate additional operating income of $4,500 a year. From the standpoint of the company, this would be a good investment because it promises a rate of return of 18% ($4,500 ÷ $25,000), which exceeds the company's minimum required rate of return of 15%.

If the manager of the Ketchikan Division is evaluated based on residual income, she would be in favor of the investment in the diagnostic machine as shown below:

Alaskan Marine Services Corporation
Ketchikan Division
Performance Evaluated Using Residual Income

	Present	New Project	Overall
Average operating assets	$100,000	$25,000	$125,000
Net operating income	$20,000	$4,500	$24,500
Minimum required return	15,000	3,750*	18,750
Residual income	$ 5,000	$ 750	$ 5,750

*$25,000 × 15% = $3,750.

Because the project would increase the residual income of the Ketchikan Division by $750, the manager would choose to invest in the new diagnostic machine.

Now suppose that the manager of the Ketchikan Division is evaluated based on ROI. The effect of the diagnostic machine on the division's ROI is computed below:

Alaskan Marine Services Corporation
Ketchikan Division
Performance Evaluated Using ROI

	Present	New Project	Overall
Average operating assets (a)	$100,000	$25,000	$125,000
Net operating income (b)	$20,000	$4,500	$24,500
ROI, (b) ÷ (a)	20%	18%	19.6%

The new project reduces the division's ROI from 20% to 19.6%. This happens because the 18% rate of return on the new diagnostic machine, while above the company's 15% minimum required rate of return, is below the division's current ROI of 20%. Therefore, the new diagnostic machine would decrease the division's ROI even though it would be a good investment from the standpoint of the company as a whole. If the manager of the division is evaluated based on ROI, she will be reluctant to even propose such an investment.

Generally, a manager who is evaluated based on ROI will reject any project whose rate of return is below the division's current ROI even if the rate of return on the project is above the company's minimum required rate of return. In contrast, managers who are evaluated using residual income will pursue any project whose rate of return is above the minimum required rate of return because it will increase their residual income. Because it is in the best interests of the company as a whole to accept any project whose rate of return is above the minimum required rate of return, managers who are evaluated based on residual income will tend to make better decisions concerning investment projects than managers who are evaluated based on ROI.

When managers are evaluated and rewarded based on return on investment (ROI) it can create situations where managers make decisions that are not in the company's best interest. For example, assume that the company establishes a minimum required return of 15%, thereby implying that the company wants its managers to pursue investment opportunities that can earn a return equal to or greater than 15%. However, let's also assume that the manager has historically earned an ROI of 20% and that her bonus is based on her ability to meet or exceed this 20% threshold.

In this situation, the manager and the company will both want to bypass investment opportunities with an ROI less than 15%. They will both want to pursue investment opportunities with an ROI greater than 20%. The problem arises with investment opportunities that earn greater than 15% but less than 20%. The company will want the manager to pursue these opportunities, whereas the manager will want to bypass them because they will reduce her historical ROI and lower her chances of earning a bonus. This problem can be resolved by using residual income to evaluate managerial performance because it would reward the manager for pursuing all investments that exceed the minimum required return of 15%.

Divisional Comparison and Residual Income

The residual income approach has one major disadvantage. It can't be used to compare the performance of divisions of different sizes. Larger divisions often have more residual income than smaller divisions, not necessarily because they are better managed but simply because they are bigger.

As an example, consider the following residual income computations for the Wholesale Division and the Retail Division of Sisal Marketing Corporation:

	Wholesale Division	Retail Division
Average operating assets (a)	$1,000,000	$250,000
Net operating income	$120,000	$40,000
Minimum required return: 10% × (a)	100,000	25,000
Residual income	$ 20,000	$15,000

Observe that the Wholesale Division has slightly more residual income than the Retail Division, but that the Wholesale Division has $1,000,000 in operating assets as compared to only $250,000 in operating assets for the Retail Division. Thus, the Wholesale Division's greater residual income is probably due to its larger size rather than the quality of its management. In fact, it appears that the smaller division may be better managed because it has been able to generate nearly as much residual income with only one-fourth as much in operating assets. When comparing investment centers, it is probably better to focus on the percentage change in residual income from year to year rather than on the absolute amount of the residual income.

CONCEPT CHECK

3. Last year sales were $300,000, net operating income was $75,000, and average operating assets were $500,000. If sales next year remain the same as last year and expenses and average operating assets are reduced by 5%, what will be the return on investment next year?
   a. 12.2%
   b. 18.2%
   c. 0.2%
   d. 25.2%

4. Referring to the facts in question 3 above, if the minimum required rate of return is 12%, what will be the residual income next year?
   a. $26,250
   b. $27,250
   c. $28,250
   d. $29,250

DECISION POINT

Shoe Store Manager

You are the manager of a shoe store in a busy shopping mall. The store is part of a national chain that evaluates its store managers on the basis of return on investment (ROI). As the manager of the store, you have control over costs, pricing, and the inventory you carry. The ROI of your store was 17.21% last year and is projected to be 17.00% this year unless some action is taken. The projected ROI has been computed as follows:

Average operating assets (a)	$2,000,000
Net operating income (b)	$340,000
ROI, (b) ÷ (a)	17.00%

Your bonus this year will depend on improving your ROI performance over last year. The minimum required rate of return on investment for the national chain is 15%.

You are considering two alternatives for improving this year's ROI:

a. Cut inventories (and average operating assets) by $500,000. This will unfortunately result in a reduction in sales, with a negative impact on net operating income of $79,000.

b. Add a new product line that would increase average operating assets by $200,000, but would increase net operating income by $33,000.

Which alternative would result in your earning a bonus for the year? Which alternative is in the best interests of the national chain?

OPERATING PERFORMANCE MEASURES

LEARNING OBJECTIVE 9–3

Compute delivery cycle time, throughput time, and manufacturing cycle efficiency (MCE).

In addition to financial performance measures, organizations use many nonfinancial performance measures. While financial measures pick up the *results* of what people in the organization do, they do not measure what *drives* organizational performance. For example, activity and revenue variances pick up the results of efforts aimed at increasing sales, but they do not measure the actions that actually drive sales such as improving quality, exposing more potential customers to the product, filling customer orders on time, and so on. Consequently, many organizations use a variety of nonfinancial performance measures in addition to financial measures. In this section we will discuss three examples of such measures that are critical to success in many organizations—delivery cycle time, throughput time, and manufacturing cycle efficiency (MCE). Note that while these examples focus on manufacturers, very similar measures can be used by any service organization that experiences a delay between receiving a customer request and responding to that request.

Delivery Cycle Time

The amount of time from when a customer order is received to when the completed order is shipped is called **delivery cycle time**. This time is an important concern to many customers, who would like the delivery cycle time to be as short as possible. Cutting the delivery cycle time may give a company a key competitive advantage—and may be necessary for survival. The formula for computing delivery cycle time is as follows:

$$\text{Delivery cycle time} = \text{Wait time} + \text{Throughput time}$$

Throughput (Manufacturing Cycle) Time

The amount of time required to turn raw materials into completed products is called **throughput time**, or *manufacturing cycle time*. The relation between the delivery cycle time and the throughput (manufacturing cycle) time is illustrated in Exhibit 9–2.

As shown in Exhibit 9–2, the throughput time, or manufacturing cycle time, is made up of process time, inspection time, move time, and queue time. *Process time* is the amount of time work is actually done on the product. *Inspection time* is the amount of time spent ensuring that the product is not defective. *Move time* is the time required to move materials or partially completed products from workstation to workstation. *Queue time* is the amount of time a product spends waiting to be worked on, to be moved, to be inspected, or to be shipped.

As shown at the bottom of Exhibit 9–2, only one of these four activities adds value to the product—process time. The other three activities—inspecting, moving, and queuing—add

EXHIBIT 9–2 Delivery Cycle Time and Throughput (Manufacturing Cycle) Time

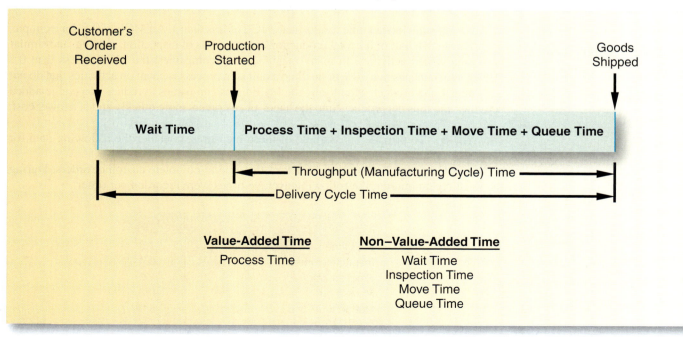

no value and should be eliminated as much as possible. The formula for computing throughput (manufacturing cycle) time is as follows:

$$\text{Throughput (manufacturing cycle) time} =$$
$$\text{Process time} + \text{Inspection time} + \text{Move time} + \text{Queue time}$$

Manufacturing Cycle Efficiency (MCE)

Through concerted efforts to eliminate the *non–value-added* activities of inspecting, moving, and queuing, some companies have reduced their throughput time to only a fraction of previous levels. In turn, this has helped to reduce the delivery cycle time from months to only weeks or hours. Throughput time, which is a key measure in delivery performance, can be put into better perspective by computing the **manufacturing cycle efficiency (MCE)**. The MCE is computed by relating the value-added time to the throughput time. The formula is

$$\text{MCE} = \frac{\text{Value-added time (Process time)}}{\text{Throughput (manufacturing cycle) time}}$$

Any non–value-added time results in an MCE of less than 1. An MCE of 0.5, for example, would mean that half of the total production time consists of inspection, moving, and similar non–value-added activities. In many manufacturing companies, the MCE is less than 0.1 (10%), which means that 90% of the time a unit is in process is spent on activities that do not add value to the product. Monitoring the MCE helps companies to reduce non–value-added activities and thus get products into the hands of customers more quickly and at a lower cost.

Example To provide an example of these measures, consider the following data for Novex Company:

Novex Company keeps careful track of the time to complete customer orders. During the most recent quarter, the following average times were recorded per order:

	Days
Wait time	17.0
Inspection time	0.4
Process time	2.0
Move time	0.6
Queue time	5.0

Goods are shipped as soon as production is completed.

REQUIRED:

1. Compute the throughput time.
2. Compute the manufacturing cycle efficiency (MCE).
3. What percentage of the production time is spent in non–value-added activities?
4. Compute the delivery cycle time.

Solution

1. Throughput time = Process time + Inspection time + Move time + Queue time

$$= 2.0 \text{ days} + 0.4 \text{ days} + 0.6 \text{ days} + 5.0 \text{ days}$$
$$= 8.0 \text{ days}$$

2. Only process time represents value-added time; therefore, MCE would be computed as follows:

$$MCE = \frac{\text{Value-added time}}{\text{Throughput time}} = \frac{2.0 \text{ days}}{8.0 \text{ days}}$$
$$= 0.25$$

   Thus, once put into production, a typical order is actually being worked on only 25% of the time.

3. Because the MCE is 25%, 75% (100% − 25%) of total production time is spent in non–value-added activities.

4. Delivery cycle time = Wait time + Throughput time

$$= 17.0 \text{ days} + 8.0 \text{ days}$$
$$= 25.0 \text{ days}$$

Lean Operating Performance Measures

IN BUSINESS

Watlow Electric Manufacturing Company implemented *lean accounting* to support its lean manufacturing methods. The company stopped providing standard cost variance reports to operating managers because the information was generated too late (at the end of each month) and it could not be understood by frontline employees. Instead, the company began reporting daily and hourly process-oriented measures that helped frontline workers improve performance.

Examples of lean operating performance measures are shown in the table below:

Measure	Description of Measure
On-time delivery percentage	Measures the percentage of orders that customers would define as being delivered on time.
Day-by-the-hour	Measures the quantity of production on an hourly basis to ensure that it is synchronized with customer demand.
First time through percentage	Measures the percentage of completed units that are free of defects.
Number of accidents and injuries	Measures the number of accidents and injuries on the manufacturing floor.
5S audit	Measures the cell workers' ability to keep their work area organized and clean.

Note: 5S stands for Sort, Straighten, Shine, Standardize, and Sustain

Sources: Jan Brosnahan, "Unleash the Power of Lean Accounting," *Journal of Accountancy*, July 2008, pp. 60–66; and Brian Maskell and Frances Kennedy, "Why Do We Need Lean Accounting and How Does It Work?" *Journal of Corporate Accounting and Finance*, March/April 2007, pp. 59–73.

5. Which of the following statements is false? (You may select more than one answer.)
   a. The delivery cycle time will always be equal to or greater than the throughput (manufacturing cycle) time.
   b. A manufacturing cycle efficiency of 1.0 is better than a manufacturing cycle efficiency of 0.1.
   c. The throughput (manufacturing cycle) time increases when the wait time increases.
   d. The delivery cycle time is unaffected by queue time.

BALANCED SCORECARD

LEARNING OBJECTIVE 9–4

Understand how to construct and use a balanced scorecard.

Financial measures, such as ROI and residual income, and operating measures, such as those discussed in the previous section, may be included in a *balanced scorecard*. A **balanced scorecard** consists of an integrated set of performance measures that are derived from and support a company's strategy. A strategy is essentially a theory about how to achieve the organization's goals. For example, Southwest Airlines' strategy is to offer an *operational excellence* customer value proposition that has three key components—low ticket prices, convenience, and reliability. The company operates only one type of aircraft, the Boeing 737, to reduce maintenance and training costs and simplify scheduling. It further reduces costs by not offering meals, seat assignments, or baggage transfers and by booking a large portion of its passenger revenue over the Internet. Southwest also uses point-to-point flights rather than the hub-and-spoke approach of its larger competitors, thereby providing customers convenient, nonstop service to their final destination. Because Southwest serves many less-congested airports such as Chicago Midway, Burbank, Manchester, Oakland, and Providence, it offers quicker passenger check-ins and reliable departures, while maintaining high asset utilization (i.e., the company's average gate turnaround time of 25 minutes enables it to function with fewer planes and gates). Overall, the company's strategy has worked. At a time when Southwest Airlines' larger competitors are struggling, it continues to earn substantial profits.

Under the balanced scorecard approach, top management translates its strategy into performance measures that employees can understand and influence. For example, the amount of time passengers have to wait in line to have their baggage checked might be a performance measure for the supervisor in charge of the Southwest Airlines check-in counter at the Burbank airport. This performance measure is easily understood by the supervisor, and can be improved by the supervisor's actions.

Common Characteristics of Balanced Scorecards

Performance measures used in balanced scorecards tend to fall into the four groups illustrated in Exhibit 9–3: financial, customer, internal business processes, and learning and growth. Internal business processes are what the company does in an attempt to satisfy customers. For example, in a manufacturing company, assembling a product is an internal business process. In an airline, handling baggage is an internal business process. The idea underlying these groupings (as indicated by the vertical arrows in Exhibit 9–3) is that learning is necessary to improve internal business processes; improving business processes is necessary to improve customer satisfaction; and improving customer satisfaction is necessary to improve financial results.

EXHIBIT 9–3   From Strategy to Performance Measures: The Balanced Scorecard

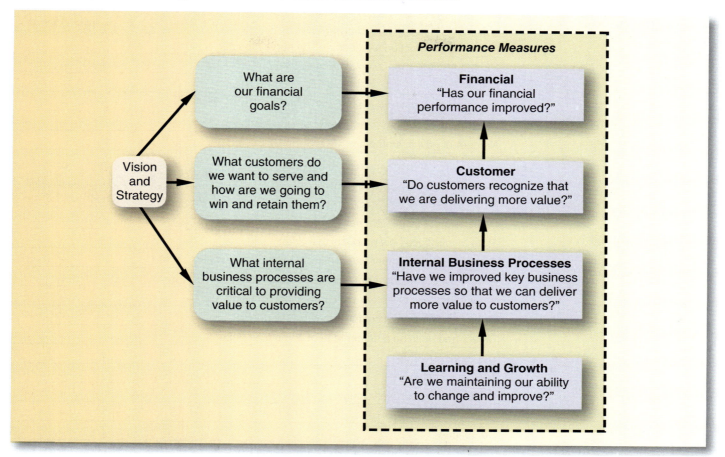

Note that the emphasis in Exhibit 9–3 is on *improvement*—not on just attaining some specific objective such as profits of $10 million. In the balanced scorecard approach, continual improvement is encouraged. If an organization does not continually improve, it will eventually lose out to competitors that do.

Financial performance measures appear at the top of Exhibit 9–3. Ultimately, most companies exist to provide financial rewards to owners. There are exceptions. Some companies—for example, **The Body Shop**—may have loftier goals such as providing environmentally friendly products to consumers. However, even nonprofit organizations must generate enough financial resources to stay in operation.

For several reasons, financial performance measures are not sufficient in themselves—they should be integrated with nonfinancial measures in a well-designed balanced scorecard. First, financial measures are lag indicators that report on the results of past actions. In contrast, nonfinancial measures of key success drivers such as customer satisfaction are leading indicators of future financial performance. Second, top managers are ordinarily responsible for the financial performance measures—not lower-level managers. The supervisor in charge of checking in passengers can be held responsible for how long passengers have to wait in line. However, this supervisor cannot reasonably be held responsible for the entire company's profit. That is the responsibility of the airline's top managers.

Exhibit 9–4 lists some examples of performance measures that can be found on the balanced scorecards of companies. However, few companies, if any, would use all of these performance measures, and almost all companies would add other performance measures. Managers should carefully select performance measures for their own

EXHIBIT 9–4
Examples of Performance
Measures for Balanced
Scorecards

Customer Perspective	
Performance Measure	**Desired Change**
Customer satisfaction as measured by survey results	+
Number of customer complaints	−
Market share	+
Product returns as a percentage of sales	−
Percentage of customers retained from last period	+
Number of new customers	+

Internal Business Processes Perspective	
Performance Measure	**Desired Change**
Percentage of sales from new products	+
Time to introduce new products to market	−
Percentage of customer calls answered within 20 seconds	+
On-time deliveries as a percentage of all deliveries	+
Work in process inventory as a percentage of sales	−
Unfavorable standard cost variances	−
Defect-free units as a percentage of completed units	+
Delivery cycle time	−
Throughput time	−
Manufacturing cycle efficiency	+
Quality costs	−
Setup time	−
Time from call by customer to repair of product	−
Percent of customer complaints settled on first contact	+
Time to settle a customer claim	−

Learning and Growth Perspective	
Performance Measure	**Desired Change**
Suggestions per employee	+
Employee turnover	−
Hours of in-house training per employee	+

company's balanced scorecard, keeping the following points in mind. First and foremost, the performance measures should be consistent with, and follow from, the company's strategy. If the performance measures are not consistent with the company's strategy, people will find themselves working at cross-purposes. Second, the performance measures should be understandable and controllable to a significant extent by those being evaluated. Third, the performance measures should be reported on a frequent and timely basis. For example, data about defects should be reported to the responsible manager at least once a day so that problems can be resolved quickly. Fourth, the scorecard should not have too many performance measures. This can lead to a lack of focus and confusion.

While the entire organization will have an overall balanced scorecard, each responsible individual will have his or her own personal scorecard as well. This scorecard should consist of items the individual can personally influence that relate directly to the performance measures on the overall balanced scorecard. The performance measures on this personal scorecard should not be overly influenced by actions taken by others in the company or by events that are outside of the individual's control. And, focusing on the performance measure should not lead an individual to take actions that are counter to the organization's objectives.

With those broad principles in mind, we will now take a look at how a company's strategy affects its balanced scorecard.

Measuring Customer Loyalty

Bain & Company consultant Fred Reichheld recommends measuring customer loyalty with one question—"On a scale of 0 to 10, how likely is it that you would recommend us to your friends and colleagues?" Customers who choose a score of 9 or 10 are labeled promoters. Those who choose a score of 0 to 6 are categorized as detractors, while those who select 7 or 8 are deemed passively satisfied. The net promoter score measures the difference between the percentages of customers who are promoters and detractors. Reichheld's research suggests that changes in a company's net promoter score correlate with (or move in tandem with) changes in its sales.

General Electric's Healthcare Division used net promoter scores to determine 20% of its managers' bonuses. The metric was eventually rolled out to all General Electric divisions. Other adopters of the net promoter score include **American Express**, consulting firm **BearingPoint**, and software maker **Intuit**.

Source: Jean McGregor, "Would You Recommend Us?" *BusinessWeek,* January 30, 2006, p. 94.

A Company's Strategy and the Balanced Scorecard

Returning to the performance measures in Exhibit 9–3, each company must decide which customers to target and what internal business processes are crucial to attracting and retaining those customers. Different companies, having different strategies, will target different customers with different kinds of products and services. Take the automobile industry as an example. **BMW** stresses engineering and handling; **Volvo**, safety; **Jaguar**, luxury detailing; and **Honda**, reliability. Because of these differences in emphasis, a one-size-fits-all approach to performance measurement won't work even within this one industry. Performance measures must be tailored to the specific strategy of each company.

Suppose, for example, that Jaguar's strategy is to offer distinctive, richly finished luxury automobiles to wealthy individuals who prize handcrafted, individualized products. To deliver this customer intimacy value proposition to its wealthy target customers, Jaguar might create such a large number of options for details, such as leather seats, interior and exterior color combinations, and wooden dashboards, that each car becomes virtually one of a kind. For example, instead of just offering tan or blue leather seats in standard cowhide, the company may offer customers the choice of an almost infinite palette of colors in any of a number of different exotic leathers. For such a system to work effectively, Jaguar would have to be able to deliver a completely customized car within a reasonable amount of time—and without incurring more cost for this customization than the customer is willing to pay. Exhibit 9–5 suggests how Jaguar might reflect this strategy in its balanced scorecard.

If the balanced scorecard is correctly constructed, the performance measures should be linked together on a cause-and-effect basis. Each link can then be read as a hypothesis

EXHIBIT 9–5
A Possible Strategy at Jaguar and
the Balanced Scorecard

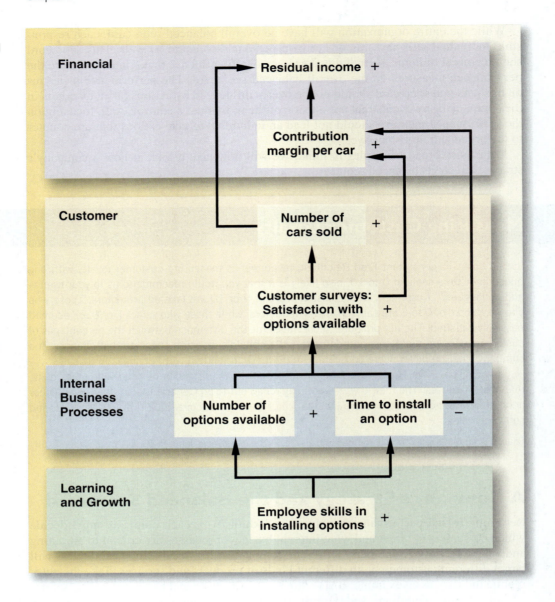

in the form "If we improve this performance measure, then this other performance measure should also improve." Starting from the bottom of Exhibit 9–5, we can read the links between performance measures as follows. If employees acquire the skills to install new options more effectively, then the company can offer more options and the options can be installed in less time. If more options are available and they are installed in less time, then customer surveys should show greater satisfaction with the range of options available. If customer satisfaction improves, then the number of cars sold should increase. In addition, if customer satisfaction improves, the company should be able to maintain or increase its selling prices, and if the time to install options decreases, the costs of installing the options should decrease. Together, this should result in an increase in the contribution margin per car. If the contribution margin per car increases and more cars are sold, the result should be an increase in residual income.

In essence, the balanced scorecard lays out a theory of how the company can take concrete actions to attain its desired outcomes (financial, in this case). The strategy laid out in Exhibit 9–5 seems plausible, but it should be regarded as only a theory. For example, if the company succeeds in increasing the number of options available and in decreasing the time required to install options and yet there is no increase in customer satisfaction, the number of cars sold, the contribution margin per car, or residual income, the strategy would have to be reconsidered. One of the advantages of the balanced scorecard is that it continually tests the theories underlying management's strategy. If a strategy is not working, it should become evident when some of the predicted effects (i.e., more car sales) don't occur. Without this feedback, the organization may drift on indefinitely with an ineffective strategy based on faulty assumptions.

The Wellness Scorecard

IN BUSINESS

Towers Watson estimates that America's average annual health care spending per employee now exceeds $10,000, up from $5,386 in 2002. However, companies that have implemented high-performing corporate wellness programs have annual health care costs that are $1,800 per employee less than other organizations. These high-performing companies create and track wellness performance measures as an important part of managing their programs.

The wellness scorecard is one framework for measuring corporate wellness performance. It has four categories of measures—attitudes, participation, physical results, and financial results—that are connected on a cause-and-effect basis. If employee attitudes toward the company's wellness program improve, then it should increase the rate of employee participation in wellness activities. If employees increase their participation rates, then it should produce physical results, such as lower obesity rates, lower incidents of diabetes, and increased smoking cessation rates. These physical improvements should produce positive financial results for the company, such as lower medical, pharmaceutical, and disability disbursements.

Sources: Towers Perrin, "2010 Health Care Cost Survey," www.towerswatson.com; and Peter C. Brewer, Angela Gallo, and Melanie R. Smith, "Getting Fit with Corporate Wellness Programs," *Strategic Finance*, May 2010, pp. 27–33.

Tying Compensation to the Balanced Scorecard

Incentive compensation for employees, such as bonuses, can, and probably should, be tied to balanced scorecard performance measures. However, this should be done only after the organization has been successfully managed with the scorecard for some time—perhaps a year or more. Managers must be confident that the performance measures are reliable, sensible, understood by those who are being evaluated, and not easily manipulated. As Robert Kaplan and David Norton, the originators of the balanced scorecard concept point out, "compensation is such a powerful lever that you have to be pretty confident that you have the right measures and have good data for the measures before making the link."[4]

6. Which of the following statements is true? (You may select more than one answer.)
   a. The balanced scorecard contains four categories of performance measures.
   b. The balanced scorecard focuses on nonfinancial performance measures and excludes financial performance measures.
   c. The performance measures in a balanced scorecard should be linked together on a cause-and-effect basis.
   d. The balanced scorecard is derived from and supports a company's strategy.

CONCEPT CHECK

[4]Lori Calabro, "On Balance: A CFO Interview," *CFO*, February 2001, pp. 73–78.

SUMMARY

LO9–1 Compute return on investment (ROI) and show how changes in sales, expenses, and assets affect ROI.

Return on investment (ROI) is defined as net operating income divided by average operating assets. Alternatively, it can be defined as the product of margin and turnover, where margin is net operating income divided by sales and turnover is sales divided by average operating assets.

The relations among sales, expenses, assets, and ROI are complex. The effect of a change in any one variable on the others will depend on the specific circumstances. Nevertheless, an increase in sales often leads to an increase in ROI via the effect of sales on net operating income. If the organization has significant fixed costs, then a given percentage increase in sales is likely to have an even larger percentage effect on net operating income.

LO9–2 Compute residual income and understand its strengths and weaknesses.

Residual income is the difference between net operating income and the minimum required return on average operating assets. The minimum required return on average operating assets is computed by applying the minimum rate of return to the average operating assets.

A major advantage of residual income over ROI is that it encourages investment in projects whose rates of return are above the minimum required rate of return for the entire organization, but below the segment's current ROI.

LO9–3 Compute delivery cycle time, throughput time, and manufacturing cycle efficiency (MCE).

In addition to financial measures, companies use operating performance measures to assess their performance. The delivery cycle time is the amount of time from when a customer order is received to when the completed order is shipped. The amount of time required to turn raw materials into completed products is called throughput time. The manufacturing cycle efficiency (MCE) measures the value-added time divided by the throughput time. Any non–value-added time results in an MCE of less than 1.

LO9–4 Understand how to construct and use a balanced scorecard.

A balanced scorecard is an integrated system of performance measures designed to support an organization's strategy. The various measures in a balanced scorecard should be linked on a plausible cause-and-effect basis from the very lowest level up through the organization's ultimate objectives. The balanced scorecard is essentially a theory about how specific actions taken by various people in the organization will further the organization's objectives. The theory should be viewed as tentative and subject to change if the actions do not in fact result in improvements in the organization's financial and other goals. If the theory changes, then the performance measures on the balanced scorecard should also change. The balanced scorecard is a dynamic measurement system that evolves as an organization learns more about what works and what doesn't work and refines its strategy accordingly.

GUIDANCE ANSWERS TO DECISION POINT

Shoe Store Manager (p. 428)

The effects of the two alternatives on your store's ROI for the year can be computed as follows:

	Present	Alternative (a)	Overall
Average operating assets (a)	$2,000,000	$(500,000)	$1,500,000
Net operating income (b)	$340,000	$(79,000)	$261,000
ROI, (b) ÷ (a)	17.00%	15.80%	17.40%

	Present	Alternative (b)	Overall
Average operating assets (a)	$2,000,000	$200,000	$2,200,000
Net operating income (b)	$340,000	$33,000	$373,000
ROI, (b) ÷ (a)	17.00%	16.50%	16.95%

Alternative (a) would increase your store's ROI to 17.40%—beating last year's ROI and hence earning you a bonus. Alternative (b) would actually decrease your store's ROI and would result in no bonus for the year. So to earn the bonus, you would select Alternative (a). However, this alternative is not in the best interests of the national chain since the ROI of the lost sales is 15.8%, which exceeds the national chain's minimum required rate of return of 15%. Rather, it would be in the national chain's interests to adopt Alternative (b)—the addition of a new product line. The ROI on these sales would be 16.5%, which exceeds the minimum required rate of return of 15%.

GUIDANCE ANSWERS TO CONCEPT CHECKS

1. **Choices c and d.** Both profit and investment center managers are held responsible for profits. In addition, an investment center manager is held responsible for earning an adequate return on investment or residual income.
2. **Choice c.** Return on investment equals margin times turnover.
3. **Choice b.** The net operating income would be $300,000 − ($225,000 × 95%) = $86,250. The return on investment would be ($86,250 ÷ ($500,000 × 95%) = 18.2%.
4. **Choice d.** The residual income would be $86,250 − ($475,000 × 12%) = $29,250.
5. **Choices c and d.** The throughput (manufacturing cycle) time is unaffected by the wait time. The delivery cycle time is influenced by the queue time.
6. **Choices a, c, and d.** The balanced scorecard includes financial measures.

REVIEW PROBLEM: RETURN ON INVESTMENT (ROI) AND RESIDUAL INCOME

The Magnetic Imaging Division of Medical Diagnostics, Inc., has reported the following results for last year's operations:

Sales	$25 million
Net operating income	$3 million
Average operating assets	$10 million

Required:
1. Compute the Magnetic Imaging Division's margin, turnover, and ROI.
2. Top management of Medical Diagnostics, Inc., has set a minimum required rate of return on average operating assets of 25%. What is the Magnetic Imaging Division's residual income for the year?

Solution to Review Problem
1. The required calculations follow:

$$\text{Margin} = \frac{\text{Net operating income}}{\text{Sales}}$$

$$= \frac{\$3,000,000}{\$25,000,000}$$

$$= 12\%$$

$$\text{Turnover} = \frac{\text{Sales}}{\text{Average operating assets}}$$

$$= \frac{\$25,000,000}{\$10,000,000}$$

$$= 2.5$$

$$\text{ROI} = \text{Margin} \times \text{Turnover}$$

$$= 12\% \times 2.5$$

$$= 30\%$$

2. The Magnetic Imaging Division's residual income is computed as follows:

Average operating assets	$10,000,000
Net operating income	$3,000,000
Minimum required return (25% × $10,000,000)	2,500,000
Residual income	$ 500,000

GLOSSARY

Balanced scorecard An integrated set of performance measures that are derived from and support the organization's strategy. (p. 432)

Cost center A business segment whose manager has control over cost but has no control over revenue or investments in operating assets. (p. 419)

Decentralized organization An organization in which decision-making authority is not confined to a few top executives but rather is spread throughout the organization. (p. 418)

Delivery cycle time The elapsed time from receipt of a customer order to when the completed goods are shipped to the customer. (p. 429)

Economic Value Added (EVA) A concept similar to residual income in which a variety of adjustments may be made to GAAP financial statements for performance evaluation purposes. (p. 424)

Investment center A business segment whose manager has control over cost, revenue, and investments in operating assets. (p. 419)

Manufacturing cycle efficiency (MCE) Process (value-added) time as a percentage of throughput time. (p. 430)

Margin Net operating income divided by sales. (p. 421)

Net operating income Income before interest and income taxes have been deducted. (p. 420)

Operating assets Cash, accounts receivable, inventory, plant and equipment, and all other assets held for operating purposes. (p. 420)

Profit center A business segment whose manager has control over cost and revenue but has no control over investments in operating assets. (p. 419)

Residual income The net operating income that an investment center earns above the minimum required return on its operating assets. (p. 424)

Responsibility center Any business segment whose manager has control over costs, revenues, or investments in operating assets. (p. 419)

Return on investment (ROI) Net operating income divided by average operating assets. It also equals margin multiplied by turnover. (p. 420)

Throughput time The amount of time required to turn raw materials into completed products. (p. 429)

Turnover Sales divided by average operating assets. (p. 421)

QUESTIONS

9–1 What is meant by the term *decentralization?*

9–2 What benefits result from decentralization?

9–3 Distinguish between a cost center, a profit center, and an investment center.

9–4 What is meant by the terms *margin* and *turnover* in ROI calculations?

9–5 What is meant by residual income?

9–6 In what way can the use of ROI as a performance measure for investment centers lead to bad decisions? How does the residual income approach overcome this problem?

9–7 What is the difference between delivery cycle time and throughput time? What four elements make up throughput time? What elements of throughput time are value-added and what elements are non–value-added?

9–8 What does a manufacturing cycle efficiency (MCE) of less than 1 mean? How would you interpret an MCE of 0.40?

9–9 Why do the measures used in a balanced scorecard differ from company to company?

9–10 Why does the balanced scorecard include financial performance measures as well as measures of how well internal business processes are doing?

Multiple-choice questions are available in the *Connect Library.*

Available with McGraw-Hill's *Connect Accounting*.

The Excel worksheet form that appears below is to be used to recreate the Review Problem in the text on pages 439–440. Download the workbook containing this form in the *Connect Library*. *On the website you will also receive instructions about how to use this worksheet form.*

LO9–1, LO9–2

	A	B	C	D
1	Chapter 9: Applying Excel			
2				
3	Data			
4	Sales	$25,000,000		
5	Net operating income	$3,000,000		
6	Average operating assets	$10,000,000		
7	Minimum required rate of return	25%		
8				
9	*Enter a formula into each of the cells marked with a ? below*			
10	**Review Problem: Return on Investment (ROI) and Residual Income**			
11				
12	*Compute the ROI*			
13	Margin	?		
14	Turnover	?		
15	ROI	?		
16				
17	*Compute the residual income*			
18	Average operating assets	?		
19	Net operating income	?		
20	Minimum required return	?		
21	Residual income	?		
22				

Chapter 9 Form   Filled in Chapter 9 Form

You should proceed to the requirements below only after completing your worksheet.

Required:
1. Check your worksheet by changing the average operating assets in cell B6 to $8,000,000. The ROI should now be 38% and the residual income should now be $1,000,000. If you do not get these answers, find the errors in your worksheet and correct them.

    Explain why the ROI and the residual income both increase when the average operating assets decrease.
2. Revise the data in your worksheet as follows:

Data	
Sales	$1,200
Net operating income	$72
Average operating assets	$500
Minimum required rate of return	15%

a. What is the ROI?
b. What is the residual income?
c. Explain the relationship between the ROI and the residual income?

THE FOUNDATIONAL 15 ![connect ACCOUNTING]

Available with McGraw-Hill's *Connect Accounting.*

Westerville Company reported the following results from last year's operations:

Sales	$1,000,000
Variable expenses	300,000
Contribution margin	700,000
Fixed expenses	500,000
Net operating income	$ 200,000
Average operating assets	$625,000

This year, the company has a $120,000 investment opportunity with the following cost and revenue characteristics:

Sales	$200,000
Contribution margin ratio	60% of sales
Fixed expenses	$90,000

The company's minimum required rate of return is 15%.

Required:

1. What is last year's margin?
2. What is last year's turnover?
3. What is last year's return on investment (ROI)?
4. What is the margin related to this year's investment opportunity?
5. What is the turnover related to this year's investment opportunity?
6. What is the ROI related to this year's investment opportunity?
7. If the company pursues the investment opportunity and otherwise performs the same as last year, what margin will it earn this year?
8. If the company pursues the investment opportunity and otherwise performs the same as last year, what turnover will it earn this year?
9. If the company pursues the investment opportunity and otherwise performs the same as last year, what ROI will it earn this year?
10. If Westerville's chief executive officer will earn a bonus only if her ROI from this year exceeds her ROI from last year, would she pursue the investment opportunity? Would the owners of the company want her to pursue the investment opportunity?
11. What is last year's residual income?
12. What is the residual income of this year's investment opportunity?
13. If the company pursues the investment opportunity and otherwise performs the same as last year, what residual income will it earn this year?
14. If Westerville's chief executive officer will earn a bonus only if her residual income from this year exceeds her residual income from last year, would she pursue the investment opportunity?
15. Assume that the contribution margin ratio of the investment opportunity was 50% instead of 60%. If Westerville's chief executive officer will earn a bonus only if her residual income from this year exceeds her residual income from last year, would she pursue the investment opportunity? Would the owners of the company want her to pursue the investment opportunity?

EXERCISES ![connect ACCOUNTING]

TAKE TWO

Sales = $8,000,000

All applicable exercises are available with McGraw-Hill's *Connect Accounting.*

EXERCISE 9–1 Compute the Return on Investment (ROI) [LO9–1]

Alyeska Services Company, a division of a major oil company, provides various services to the operators of the North Slope oil field in Alaska. Data concerning the most recent year appear below:

Sales	$7,500,000
Net operating income	$600,000
Average operating assets	$5,000,000

Required:
1. Compute the margin for Alyeska Services Company.
2. Compute the turnover for Alyeska Services Company.
3. Compute the return on investment (ROI) for Alyeska Services Company.

EXERCISE 9–2   Residual Income [LO9–2]

Juniper Design Ltd. of Manchester, England, is a company specializing in providing design services to residential developers. Last year the company had net operating income of $600,000 on sales of $3,000,000. The company's average operating assets for the year were $2,800,000 and its minimum required rate of return was 18%.

Minimum required rate of return = 15%

Required:
Compute the company's residual income for the year.

EXERCISE 9–3   Measures of Internal Business Process Performance [LO9–3]

Management of Mittel Rhein AG of Köln, Germany, would like to reduce the amount of time between when a customer places an order and when the order is shipped. For the first quarter of operations during the current year the following data were reported:

Process time = 4.8 days

Inspection time	0.3 days
Wait time (from order to start of production)	14.0 days
Process time	2.7 days
Move time	1.0 days
Queue time	5.0 days

Required:
1. Compute the throughput time.
2. Compute the manufacturing cycle efficiency (MCE) for the quarter.
3. What percentage of the throughput time was spent in non–value-added activities?
4. Compute the delivery cycle time.
5. If by using Lean Production all queue time during production is eliminated, what will be the new MCE?

EXERCISE 9–4   Building a Balanced Scorecard [LO9–4]

Lost Peak ski resort was for many years a small, family-owned resort serving day skiers from nearby towns. Lost Peak was recently acquired by Western Resorts, a major ski resort operator. The new owners have plans to upgrade the resort into a destination resort for vacationers. As part of this plan, the new owners would like to make major improvements in the Powder 8 Lodge, the resort's on-the-hill cafeteria. The menu at the lodge is very limited—hamburgers, hot dogs, chili, tuna fish sandwiches, pizzas, french fries, and packaged snacks. With little competition, the previous owners of the resort had felt no urgency to upgrade the food service at the lodge. If skiers want lunch on the mountain, the only alternatives are the Powder 8 Lodge or a brown bag lunch brought from home.

As part of the deal when acquiring Lost Peak, Western Resorts agreed to retain all of the current employees of the resort. The manager of the lodge, while hardworking and enthusiastic, has very little experience in the restaurant business. The manager is responsible for selecting the menu, finding and training employees, and overseeing daily operations. The kitchen staff prepare food and wash dishes. The dining room staff take orders, serve as cashiers, and clean the dining room area.

Shortly after taking over Lost Peak, management of Western Resorts held a day-long meeting with all of the employees of the Powder 8 Lodge to discuss the future of the ski resort and the new management's plans for the lodge. At the end of this meeting, management and lodge employees created a balanced scorecard for the lodge that would help guide operations for the coming ski season. Almost everyone who participated in the meeting seemed to be enthusiastic about the scorecard and management's plans for the lodge.

The following performance measures were included on the balanced scorecard for the Powder 8 Lodge:

a. Weekly Powder 8 Lodge sales.
b. Weekly Powder 8 Lodge profit.
c. Number of menu items.
d. Dining area cleanliness as rated by a representative from Western Resorts management.

e. Customer satisfaction with menu choices as measured by customer surveys
f. Customer satisfaction with service as measured by customer surveys
g. Average time to take an order
h. Average time to prepare an order
i. Percentage of kitchen staff completing a basic cooking course at the local community college
j. Percentage of dining room staff completing a basic hospitality course at the local community college

Western Resorts will pay for the costs of staff attending courses at the local community college.

Required:
1. Using the above performance measures, construct a balanced scorecard for the Powder 8 Lodge. Use Exhibit 9–5 as a guide. Use arrows to show causal links and indicate with a + or − whether the performance measure should increase or decrease.
2. What hypotheses are built into the balanced scorecard for the Powder 8 Lodge? Which of these hypotheses do you believe are most questionable? Why?
3. How will management know if one of the hypotheses underlying the balanced scorecard is false?

EXERCISE 9–5 Return on Investment (ROI) [LO9–1]
Provide the missing data in the following table for a distributor of martial arts products:

	Division		
	Alpha	Bravo	Charlie
Sales	$?	$11,500,000	$?
Net operating income	$?	$ 920,000	$210,000
Average operating assets	$800,000	$?	$?
Margin	4%	?	7%
Turnover	5	?	?
Return on investment (ROI)	?	20%	14%

Osaka net operating income = $200,000

EXERCISE 9–6 Contrasting Return on Investment (ROI) and Residual Income [LO9–1, LO9–2]
Meiji Isetan Corp. of Japan has two regional divisions with headquarters in Osaka and Yokohama. Selected data on the two divisions follow:

	Division	
	Osaka	Yokohama
Sales	$3,000,000	$9,000,000
Net operating income	$210,000	$720,000
Average operating assets	$1,000,000	$4,000,000

Required:
1. For each division, compute the return on investment (ROI) in terms of margin and turnover. Where necessary, carry computations to two decimal places.
2. Assume that the company evaluates performance using residual income and that the minimum required rate of return for any division is 15%. Compute the residual income for each division.
3. Is Yokohama's greater amount of residual income an indication that it is better managed? Explain.

EXERCISE 9–7 Creating a Balanced Scorecard [LO9–4]
Ariel Tax Services prepares tax returns for individual and corporate clients. As the company has gradually expanded to 10 offices, the founder Max Jacobs has begun to feel as though he is losing control of

operations. In response to this concern, he has decided to implement a performance measurement system that will help control current operations and facilitate his plans of expanding to 20 offices.

Jacobs describes the keys to the success of his business as follows:

"Our only real asset is our people. We must keep our employees highly motivated and we must hire the 'cream of the crop.' Interestingly, employee morale and recruiting success are both driven by the same two factors—compensation and career advancement. In other words, providing superior compensation relative to the industry average coupled with fast-track career advancement opportunities keeps morale high and makes us a very attractive place to work. It drives a high rate of job offer acceptances relative to job offers tendered."

"Hiring highly qualified people and keeping them energized ensures operational success, which in our business is a function of productivity, efficiency, and effectiveness. Productivity boils down to employees being billable rather than idle. Efficiency relates to the time required to complete a tax return. Finally, effectiveness is critical to our business in the sense that we cannot tolerate errors. Completing a tax return quickly is meaningless if the return contains errors."

"Our growth depends on acquiring new customers through word-of-mouth from satisfied repeat customers. We believe that our customers come back year after year because they value error-free, timely, and courteous tax return preparation. Common courtesy is an important aspect of our business! We call it service quality, and it all ties back to employee morale in the sense that happy employees treat their clients with care and concern."

"While sales growth is obviously important to our future plans, growth without a corresponding increase in profitability is useless. Therefore, we understand that increasing our profit margin is a function of cost-efficiency as well as sales growth. Given that payroll is our biggest expense, we must maintain an optimal balance between staffing levels and the revenue being generated. As I alluded to earlier, the key to maintaining this balance is employee productivity. If we can achieve cost-efficient sales growth, we should eventually have 20 profitable offices!"

Required:

1. Create a balanced scorecard for Ariel Tax Services. Link your scorecard measures using the framework from Exhibit 9–5. Indicate whether each measure is expected to increase or decrease. Feel free to create measures that may not be specifically mentioned in the chapter, but make sense given the strategic goals of the company.

2. What hypotheses are built into the balanced scorecard for Ariel Tax Services? Which of these hypotheses do you believe are most questionable and why?

3. Discuss the potential advantages and disadvantages of implementing an internal business process measure called *total dollar amount of tax refunds generated*. Would you recommend using this measure in Ariel's balanced scorecard?

4. Would it be beneficial to attempt to measure each office's individual performance with respect to the scorecard measures that you created? Why or why not?

EXERCISE 9–8   Computing and Interpreting Return on Investment (ROI) [LO9–1]

Selected operating data for two divisions of Outback Brewing, Ltd., of Australia are given below:

	Division	
	Queensland	New South Wales
Sales	$4,000,000	$7,000,000
Average operating assets	$2,000,000	$2,000,000
Net operating income	$360,000	$420,000
Property, plant, and equipment (net)	$950,000	$800,000

Required:

1. Compute the rate of return for each division using the return on investment (ROI) formula stated in terms of margin and turnover.

2. Which divisional manager seems to be doing the better job? Why?

EXERCISE 9–9 Return on Investment (ROI) and Residual Income Relations [LO9–1, LO9–2]

A family friend has asked your help in analyzing the operations of three anonymous companies operating in the same service sector industry. Supply the missing data in the table below:

	Company		
	A	**B**	**C**
Sales	$9,000,000	$7,000,000	$4,500,000
Net operating income	$?	$ 280,000	$?
Average operating assets	$3,000,000	$?	$1,800,000
Return on investment (ROI)	18%	14%	?
Minimum required rate of return:			
Percentage	16%	?	15%
Dollar amount	$?	$ 320,000	$?
Residual income	$?	$?	$ 90,000

EXERCISE 9–10 Cost-Volume-Profit Analysis and Return on Investment (ROI) [LO9–1]

Posters.com is a small Internet retailer of high-quality posters. The company has $1,000,000 in operating assets and fixed expenses of $150,000 per year. With this level of operating assets and fixed expenses, the company can support sales of up to $3,000,000 per year. The company's contribution margin ratio is 25%, which means that an additional dollar of sales results in additional contribution margin, and net operating income, of 25 cents.

Required:

1. Complete the following table showing the relation between sales and return on investment (ROI).

Sales	Net Operating Income	Average Operating Assets	ROI
$2,500,000	$475,000	$1,000,000	?
$2,600,000	$?	$1,000,000	?
$2,700,000	$?	$1,000,000	?
$2,800,000	$?	$1,000,000	?
$2,900,000	$?	$1,000,000	?
$3,000,000	$?	$1,000,000	?

2. What happens to the company's return on investment (ROI) as sales increase? Explain.

EXERCISE 9–11 Effects of Changes in Profits and Assets on Return on Investment (ROI) [LO9–1]

Fitness Fanatics is a regional chain of health clubs. The managers of the clubs, who have authority to make investments as needed, are evaluated based largely on return on investment (ROI). The company's Springfield Club reported the following results for the past year:

Sales	$1,400,000
Net operating income	$70,000
Average operating assets	$350,000

Average operating assets = $200,000

Required:

The following questions are to be considered independently. Carry out all computations to two decimal places.

1. Compute the Springfield club's return on investment (ROI).
2. Assume that the manager of the club is able to increase sales by $70,000 and that, as a result, net operating income increases by $18,200. Further assume that this is possible without any increase in operating assets. What would be the club's return on investment (ROI)?
3. Assume that the manager of the club is able to reduce expenses by $14,000 without any change in sales or operating assets. What would be the club's return on investment (ROI)?
4. Assume that the manager of the club is able to reduce operating assets by $70,000 without any change in sales or net operating income. What would be the club's return on investment (ROI)?

EXERCISE 9–12 Evaluating New Investments Using Return on Investment (ROI) and Residual Income [LO9–1, LO9–2]

Selected sales and operating data for three divisions of different structural engineering firms are given as follows:

	Division A	Division B	Division C
Sales	$12,000,000	$14,000,000	$25,000,000
Average operating assets	$3,000,000	$7,000,000	$5,000,000
Net operating income	$600,000	$560,000	$800,000
Minimum required rate of return	14%	10%	16%

TAKE TWO

Minimum required rate of return for all divisions = 17%

Required:
1. Compute the return on investment (ROI) for each division using the formula stated in terms of margin and turnover.
2. Compute the residual income for each division.
3. Assume that each division is presented with an investment opportunity that would yield a 15% rate of return.
   a. If performance is being measured by ROI, which division or divisions will probably accept the opportunity? Reject? Why?
   b. If performance is being measured by residual income, which division or divisions will probably accept the opportunity? Reject? Why?

EXERCISE 9–13 Effects of Changes in Sales, Expenses, and Assets on ROI [LO9–1]

CommercialServices.com Corporation provides business-to-business services on the Internet. Data concerning the most recent year appear below:

Sales	$3,000,000
Net operating income	$150,000
Average operating assets	$750,000

TAKE TWO

Net operating income = $300,000

Required:
Consider each question below independently. Carry out all computations to two decimal places.
1. Compute the company's return on investment (ROI).
2. The entrepreneur who founded the company is convinced that sales will increase next year by 50% and that net operating income will increase by 200%, with no increase in average operating assets. What would be the company's ROI?
3. The chief financial officer of the company believes a more realistic scenario would be a $1,000,000 increase in sales, requiring a $250,000 increase in average operating assets, with a resulting $200,000 increase in net operating income. What would be the company's ROI in this scenario?

Alternate problem set is available in the Connect Library.

PROBLEMS

All applicable problems are available with McGraw-Hill's *Connect Accounting*.

PROBLEM 9–14A Measures of Internal Business Process Performance [LO9–3]

DataSpan, Inc., automated its plant at the start of the current year and installed a flexible manufacturing system. The company is also evaluating its suppliers and moving toward Lean Production. Many adjustment problems have been encountered, including problems relating to performance measurement. After much study, the company has decided to use the performance measures below, and it has gathered data relating to these measures for the first four months of operations.

	Month			
	1	**2**	**3**	**4**
Throughput time (days)	?	?	?	?
Delivery cycle time (days)	?	?	?	?
Manufacturing cycle efficiency (MCE) ..	?	?	?	?
Percentage of on-time deliveries	91%	86%	83%	79%
Total sales (units)	3,210	3,072	2,915	2,806

Management has asked for your help in computing throughput time, delivery cycle time, and MCE. The following average times have been logged over the last four months:

	Average per Month (in days)			
	1	2	3	4
Move time per unit	0.4	0.3	0.4	0.4
Process time per unit	2.1	2.0	1.9	1.8
Wait time per order before start				
of production	16.0	17.5	19.0	20.5
Queue time per unit	4.3	5.0	5.8	6.7
Inspection time per unit	0.6	0.7	0.7	0.6

Required:
1. For each month, compute the following:
   a. The throughput time.
   b. The MCE.
   c. The delivery cycle time.
2. Evaluate the company's performance over the last four months.
3. Refer to the move time, process time, and so forth, given above for month 4.
   a. Assume that in month 5 the move time, process time, and so forth, are the same as in month 4, except that through the use of Lean Production the company is able to completely eliminate the queue time during production. Compute the new throughput time and MCE.
   b. Assume in month 6 that the move time, process time, and so forth, are again the same as in month 4, except that the company is able to completely eliminate both the queue time during production and the inspection time. Compute the new throughput time and MCE.

PROBLEM 9–15A Return on Investment (ROI) and Residual Income [LO9–1, LO9–2]
Financial data for Joel de Paris, Inc., for last year follow:

Joel de Paris, Inc.
Balance Sheet

	Beginning Balance	Ending Balance
Assets		
Cash	$ 140,000	$ 120,000
Accounts receivable	450,000	530,000
Inventory	320,000	380,000
Plant and equipment, net	680,000	620,000
Investment in Buisson, S.A.	250,000	280,000
Land (undeveloped)	180,000	170,000
Total assets	$2,020,000	$2,100,000
Liabilities and Stockholders' Equity		
Accounts payable	$ 360,000	$ 310,000
Long-term debt	1,500,000	1,500,000
Stockholders' equity	160,000	290,000
Total liabilities and stockholders' equity	$2,020,000	$2,100,000

Joel de Paris, Inc.
Income Statement

Sales		$4,050,000
Operating expenses		3,645,000
Net operating income		405,000
Interest and taxes:		
Interest expense	$150,000	
Tax expense	110,000	260,000
Net income		$ 145,000

The company paid dividends of $15,000 last year. The "Investment in Buisson, S.A.," on the balance sheet represents an investment in the stock of another company.

Required:
1. Compute the company's margin, turnover, and return on investment (ROI) for last year.
2. The board of directors of Joel de Paris, Inc., has set a minimum required rate of return of 15%. What was the company's residual income last year?

PROBLEM 9–16A   Creating a Balanced Scorecard [LO9–4]

Mason Paper Company (MPC) manufactures commodity grade papers for use in computer printers and photocopiers. MPC has reported net operating losses for the last two years due to intense price pressure from much larger competitors. The MPC management team—including Kristen Townsend (CEO), Mike Martinez (vice president of Manufacturing), Tom Andrews (vice president of Marketing), and Wendy Chen (CFO)—is contemplating a change in strategy to save the company from impending bankruptcy. Excerpts from a recent management team meeting are shown below:

Townsend: As we all know, the commodity paper manufacturing business is all about economies of scale. The largest competitors with the lowest cost per unit win. The limited capacity of our older machines prohibits us from competing in the high-volume commodity paper grades. Furthermore, expanding our capacity by acquiring a new paper-making machine is out of the question given the extraordinarily high price tag. Therefore, I propose that we abandon cost reduction as a strategic goal and instead pursue manufacturing flexibility as the key to our future success.

Chen: Manufacturing flexibility? What does that mean?

Martinez: It means we have to abandon our "crank out as many tons of paper as possible" mentality. Instead, we need to pursue the low-volume business opportunities that exist in the nonstandard, specialized paper grades. To succeed in this regard, we'll need to improve our flexibility in three ways. First, we must improve our ability to switch between paper grades. Right now, we require an average of four hours to change over to another paper grade. Timely customer deliveries are a function of changeover performance. Second, we need to expand the range of paper grades that we can manufacture. Currently, we can only manufacture three paper grades. Our customers must perceive that we are a "one-stop shop" that can meet all of their paper grade needs. Third, we will need to improve our yields (e.g., tons of acceptable output relative to total tons processed) in the nonstandard paper grades. Our percentage of waste within these grades will be unacceptably high unless we do something to improve our processes. Our variable costs will go through the roof if we cannot increase our yields!

Chen: Wait just a minute! These changes are going to destroy our equipment utilization numbers!

Andrews: You're right Wendy; however, equipment utilization is not the name of the game when it comes to competing in terms of flexibility. Our customers don't care about our equipment utilization. Instead, as Mike just alluded to, they want just-in-time delivery of smaller quantities of a full range of paper grades. If we can shrink the elapsed time from order placement to order delivery and expand our product offerings, it will increase sales from current customers and bring in new customers. Furthermore, we will be able to charge a premium price because of the limited competition within this niche from our cost-focused larger competitors. Our contribution margin per ton should drastically improve!

Martinez: Of course, executing the change in strategy will not be easy. We'll need to make a substantial investment in training because ultimately it is our people who create our flexible manufacturing capabilities.

Chen: If we adopt this new strategy, it is definitely going to impact how we measure performance. We'll need to create measures that motivate our employees to make decisions that support our flexibility goals.

Townsend: Wendy, you hit the nail right on the head. For our next meeting, could you pull together some potential measures that support our new strategy?

Required:
1. Contrast MPC's previous manufacturing strategy with its new manufacturing strategy.
2. Generally speaking, why would a company that changes its strategic goals need to change its performance measurement system as well? What are some examples of measures that would have been appropriate for MPC prior to its change in strategy? Why would those measures fail to support MPC's new strategy?
3. Construct a balanced scorecard that would support MPC's new manufacturing strategy. Use arrows to show the causal links between the performance measures and show whether the

performance measure should increase or decrease over time. Feel free to create measures that may not be specifically mentioned in the chapter, but nonetheless make sense given the strategic goals of the company.

4. What hypotheses are built into MPC's balanced scorecard? Which of these hypotheses do you believe are most questionable and why?

PROBLEM 9–17A   Comparison of Performance Using Return on Investment (ROI) [LO9–1]

Comparative data on three companies in the same service industry are given below:

	Company		
	A	**B**	**C**
Sales	$600,000	$500,000	$?
Net operating income	$ 84,000	$ 70,000	$?
Average operating assets	$300,000	$?	$1,000,000
Margin	?	?	3.5%
Turnover	?	?	2
ROI	?	7%	?

Required:

1. What advantages are there to breaking down the ROI computation into two separate elements, margin and turnover?

2. Fill in the missing information above, and comment on the relative performance of the three companies in as much detail as the data permit. Make *specific recommendations* about how to improve the ROI.

(Adapted from National Association of Accountants, *Research Report No. 35,* p. 34)

PROBLEM 9–18A   Return on Investment (ROI) and Residual Income [LO9–1, LO9–2]

"I know headquarters wants us to add that new product line," said Dell Havasi, manager of Billings Company's Office Products Division. "But I want to see the numbers before I make any move. Our division's return on investment (ROI) has led the company for three years, and I don't want any letdown."

Billings Company is a decentralized wholesaler with five autonomous divisions. The divisions are evaluated on the basis of ROI, with year-end bonuses given to the divisional managers who have the highest ROIs. Operating results for the company's Office Products Division for the most recent year are given below:

Sales	$10,000,000
Variable expenses	6,000,000
Contribution margin	4,000,000
Fixed expenses	3,200,000
Net operating income	$ 800,000
Divisional operating assets	$ 4,000,000

The company had an overall return on investment (ROI) of 15% last year (considering all divisions). The Office Products Division has an opportunity to add a new product line that would require an additional investment in operating assets of $1,000,000. The cost and revenue characteristics of the new product line per year would be

Sales	$2,000,000
Variable expenses	60% of sales
Fixed expenses	$640,000

Required:
1. Compute the Office Products Division's ROI for the most recent year; also compute the ROI as it would appear if the new product line is added.
2. If you were in Dell Havasi's position, would you accept or reject the new product line? Explain.
3. Why do you suppose headquarters is anxious for the Office Products Division to add the new product line?
4. Suppose that the company's minimum required rate of return on operating assets is 12% and that performance is evaluated using residual income.
   a. Compute the Office Products Division's residual income for the most recent year; also compute the residual income as it would appear if the new product line is added.
   b. Under these circumstances, if you were in Dell Havasi's position, would you accept or reject the new product line? Explain.

PROBLEM 9–19A Internal Business Process Performance Measures [LO9–3]

Tombro Industries is in the process of automating one of its plants and developing a flexible manufacturing system. The company is finding it necessary to make many changes in operating procedures. Progress has been slow, particularly in trying to develop new performance measures for the factory.

In an effort to evaluate performance and determine where improvements can be made, management has gathered the following data relating to activities over the last four months:

	Month			
	1	2	3	4
Quality control measures:				
Number of defects	185	163	124	91
Number of warranty claims	46	39	30	27
Number of customer complaints	102	96	79	58
Material control measures:				
Purchase order lead time	8 days	7 days	5 days	4 days
Scrap as a percent of total cost	1%	1%	2%	3%
Machine performance measures:				
Machine downtime as a percentage of availability	3%	4%	4%	6%
Use as a percentage of availability	95%	92%	89%	85%
Setup time (hours)	8	10	11	12
Delivery performance measures:				
Throughput time	?	?	?	?
Manufacturing cycle efficiency (MCE)	?	?	?	?
Delivery cycle time	?	?	?	?
Percentage of on-time deliveries	96%	95%	92%	89%

The president has read in industry journals that throughput time, MCE, and delivery cycle time are important measures of performance, but no one is sure how they are computed. You have been asked to assist the company, and you have gathered the following data relating to these measures:

	Average per Month (in days)			
	1	2	3	4
Wait time per order before start of production	9.0	11.5	12.0	14.0
Inspection time per unit	0.8	0.7	0.7	0.7
Process time per unit	2.1	2.0	1.9	1.8
Queue time per unit	2.8	4.4	6.0	7.0
Move time per unit	0.3	0.4	0.4	0.5

Required:
1. For each month, compute the following performance measures:
   a. Throughput time.
   b. MCE.
   c. Delivery cycle time.

2. Using the performance measures given in the main body of the problem and the performance measures computed in (1) above, do the following:
    a. Identify areas where the company seems to be improving.
    b. Identify areas where the company seems to be deteriorating.
3. Refer to the inspection time, process time, and so forth, given for month 4.
    a. Assume that in month 5 the inspection time, process time, and so forth, are the same as for month 4, except that the company is able to completely eliminate the queue time during production using Lean Production. Compute the new throughput time and MCE.
    b. Assume that in month 6 the inspection time, process time, and so forth, are the same as in month 4, except that the company is able to eliminate both the queue time during production and the inspection time using Lean Production. Compute the new throughput time and MCE.

PROBLEM 9–20A   Return on Investment (ROI) Analysis [LO9–1]

The contribution format income statement for Huerra Company for last year is given below:

	Total	Unit
Sales	$4,000,000	$80.00
Variable expenses	2,800,000	56.00
Contribution margin	1,200,000	24.00
Fixed expenses	840,000	16.80
Net operating income	360,000	7.20
Income taxes @ 30%	108,000	2.16
Net income	$ 252,000	$ 5.04

The company had average operating assets of $2,000,000 during the year.

Required:

1. Compute the company's return on investment (ROI) for the period using the ROI formula stated in terms of margin and turnover.
    For each of the following questions, indicate whether the margin and turnover will increase, decrease, or remain unchanged as a result of the events described, and then compute the new ROI figure. Consider each question separately, starting in each case from the data used to compute the original ROI in (1) above.
2. Using Lean Production, the company is able to reduce the average level of inventory by $400,000. (The released funds are used to pay off short-term creditors.)
3. The company achieves a cost savings of $32,000 per year by using less costly materials.
4. The company issues bonds and uses the proceeds to purchase $500,000 in machinery and equipment at the beginning of the period. Interest on the bonds is $60,000 per year. Sales remain unchanged. The new, more efficient equipment reduces production costs by $20,000 per year.
5. As a result of a more intense effort by salespeople, sales are increased by 20%; operating assets remain unchanged.
6. Obsolete inventory carried on the books at a cost of $40,000 is scrapped and written off as a loss.
7. The company uses $200,000 of cash (received on accounts receivable) to repurchase and retire some of its common stock.

PROBLEM 9–21A   Creating Balanced Scorecards that Support Different Strategies [LO9–4]

The Midwest Consulting Group (MCG) helps companies build balanced scorecards. As part of its marketing efforts, MCG conducts an annual balanced scorecard workshop for prospective clients. As MCG's newest employee, your boss has asked you to participate in this year's workshop by explaining to attendees how a company's strategy determines the measures that are appropriate for its balanced scorecard. Your boss has provided you with the excerpts below from the annual reports of two current MCG clients. She has asked you to use these excerpts in your portion of the workshop.

Excerpt from Applied Pharmaceuticals' annual report:

The keys to our business are consistent and timely new product introductions and manufacturing process integrity. The new product introduction side of the equation is a function of research and development (R&D) yield (e.g., the number of marketable drug compounds created relative to the total number of potential compounds pursued). We seek to optimize our R&D yield and first-to-market capability by investing in state-of-the-art technology, hiring the highest possible percentage of the "best and the brightest" engineers that we pursue, and providing world-class training to those engineers. Manufacturing process integrity is all about establishing world-class quality specifications and then relentlessly engaging in prevention and appraisal activities to minimize defect rates. Our customers must have an awareness of and respect for our brand image of being "first to market and first in quality." If we deliver on this pledge to our customers, then our financial goal of increasing our return on stockholders' equity should take care of itself.

Excerpt from Destination Resorts International's annual report:

Our business succeeds or fails based on the quality of the service that our front-line employees provide to customers. Therefore, it is imperative that we strive to maintain high employee morale and minimize employee turnover. In addition, it is critical that we train our employees to use technology to create one seamless worldwide experience for our repeat customers. Once an employee enters a customer preference (e.g., provide two extra pillows in the room, deliver fresh brewed coffee to the room at 8:00 A.M., etc.) into our database, our worldwide workforce strives to ensure that a customer will never need to repeat it at any of our destination resorts. If we properly train and retain a motivated workforce, we should see continuous improvement in our percentage of error-free repeat customer check-ins, the time taken to resolve customer complaints, and our independently assessed room cleanliness. This in turn should drive improvement in our customer retention, which is the key to meeting our revenue growth goals.

Required:

1. Based on the excerpts above, compare and contrast the strategies of Applied Pharmaceuticals and Destination Resorts International.
2. Select balanced scorecard measures for each company and link the scorecard measures using the framework from Exhibit 9–5. Use arrows to show the causal links between the performance measures and show whether the performance measure should increase or decrease over time. Feel free to create measures that may not be specifically mentioned in the chapter, but nonetheless make sense given the strategic goals of each company.
3. What hypotheses are built into each balanced scorecard? Why do the hypotheses differ between the two companies?

PROBLEM 9–22A   Perverse Effects of Some Performance Measures [LO9–4]

There is often more than one way to improve a performance measure. Unfortunately, some of the actions taken by managers to make their performance look better may actually harm the organization. For example, suppose the marketing department is held responsible only for increasing the performance measure "total revenues." Increases in total revenues may be achieved by working harder and smarter, but they can also usually be achieved by simply cutting prices. The increase in volume from cutting prices almost always results in greater total revenues; however, it does not always lead to greater total profits. Those who design performance measurement systems need to keep in mind that managers who are under pressure to perform may take actions to improve performance measures that have negative consequences elsewhere.

Required:

For each of the following situations, describe actions that managers might take to show improvement in the performance measure but which do not actually lead to improvement in the organization's overall performance.

1. Concerned with the slow rate at which new products are brought to market, top management of a consumer electronics company introduces a new performance measure—speed-to-market. The research and development department is given responsibility for this performance measure, which measures the average amount of time a product is in development before it is released to the market for sale.
2. The CEO of an airline company is dissatisfied with the amount of time that her ground crews are taking to unload luggage from airplanes. To solve the problem, she decides to measure the average elapsed time from when an airplane parks at the gate to when all pieces of luggage are unloaded from the airplane. For each month that an airport's ground crew can lower its "average elapsed time" relative to the prior month, the CEO pays a lump-sum bonus to be split equally among members of the crew.

3. A manufacturing company has been plagued by the chronic failure to ship orders to customers by the promised date. To solve this problem, the production manager has been given the responsibility of increasing the percentage of orders shipped on time. When a customer calls in an order, the production manager and the customer agree to a delivery date. If the order is not completed by that date, it is counted as a late shipment.

4. Concerned with the productivity of employees, the board of directors of a large multinational corporation has dictated that the manager of each subsidiary will be held responsible for increasing the revenue per employee of his or her subsidiary.

BUILDING YOUR SKILLS

CASE [LO9–4]

Haglund Department Store is located in the downtown area of a small city. While the store had been profitable for many years, it is facing increasing competition from large national chains that have set up stores on the outskirts of the city. Recently the downtown area has been undergoing revitalization, and the owners of Haglund Department Store are somewhat optimistic that profitability can be restored.

In an attempt to accelerate the return to profitability, management of Haglund Department Store is in the process of designing a balanced scorecard for the company. Management believes the company should focus on two key problems. First, customers are taking longer and longer to pay the bills they incur using the department store's charge card, and the company has far more bad debts than are normal for the industry. If this problem were solved, the company would have more cash to make much needed renovations. Investigation has revealed that much of the problem with late payments and unpaid bills results from customers disputing incorrect charges on their bills. These incorrect charges usually occur because salesclerks incorrectly enter data on the charge account slip. Second, the company has been incurring large losses on unsold seasonal apparel. Such items are ordinarily resold at a loss to discount stores that specialize in such distress items.

The meeting in which the balanced scorecard approach was discussed was disorganized and ineffectively led—possibly because no one other than one of the vice presidents had read anything about how to build a balanced scorecard. Nevertheless, a number of potential performance measures were suggested by various managers. These potential performance measures are

a. Percentage of charge account bills containing errors.
b. Percentage of salesclerks trained to correctly enter data on charge account slips.
c. Average age of accounts receivables.
d. Profit per employee.
e. Customer satisfaction with accuracy of charge account bills from monthly customer survey.
f. Total sales revenue.
g. Sales per employee.
h. Travel expenses for buyers for trips to fashion shows.
i. Unsold inventory at the end of the season as a percentage of total cost of sales.
j. Courtesy shown by junior staff members to senior staff members based on surveys of senior staff.
k. Percentage of suppliers making just-in-time deliveries.
l. Sales per square foot of floor space.
m. Written-off accounts receivable (bad debts) as a percentage of sales.
n. Quality of food in the staff cafeteria based on staff surveys.
o. Percentage of employees who have attended the city's cultural diversity workshop.
p. Total profit.

Required:

1. As someone with more knowledge of the balanced scorecard than almost anyone else in the company, you have been asked to build an integrated balanced scorecard. In your scorecard, use only performance measures listed previously. You do not have to use all of the performance measures suggested by the managers, but you should build a balanced scorecard that reveals a strategy for dealing with the problems with accounts receivable and with unsold merchandise. Construct the balanced scorecard following the format used in Exhibit 9–5. Do not be concerned with whether a specific performance measure falls within the learning and growth, internal business process, customer, or financial perspective. However, use arrows to show the causal links between performance measures within your

balanced scorecard and explain whether the performance measures should show increases or decreases.

2. Assume that the company adopts your balanced scorecard. After operating for a year, some performance measures show improvements, but not others. What should management do next?

3. a. Suppose that customers express greater satisfaction with the accuracy of their charge account bills but the performance measures for the average age of accounts receivable and for bad debts do not improve. Explain why this might happen.

   b. Suppose that the performance measures for the average age of accounts receivable, bad debts, and unsold inventory improve, but total profits do not. Explain why this might happen. Assume in your answer that the explanation lies within the company.

COMMUNICATING IN PRACTICE [LO9–1, LO9–2, LO9–3]

How do the performance measurement and compensation systems of service companies compare with those of manufacturers? Ask the manager of your local McDonald's, Wendy's, Burger King, or other fast-food chain if he or she could spend some time discussing the performance measures that the company uses to evaluate store managers and how the performance measures tie in with their compensation.

Required:

After asking the following questions, write a brief memorandum to your instructor that summarizes what you discovered during your interview with the manager of the franchise.

1. What are the national chain's goals, that is, the broad, long-range plans of the company (e.g., to increase market share)?

2. What performance measures are used to help motivate the store managers and monitor progress toward achieving the corporation's goals?

3. Are the performance measures consistent with the store manager's compensation plan?

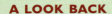

A LOOK BACK

We concluded our coverage of performance measures in Chapter 9 by focusing on decentralized organizations. Return on investment (ROI) and residual income are used to motivate the managers of investment centers and to monitor the performance of these centers.

A LOOK AT THIS CHAPTER

We continue our coverage of decision making in Chapter 10 by focusing on the use of differential analysis when analyzing alternatives. In general, only those costs and benefits that differ between alternatives are relevant in a decision. This basic idea is applied in a wide variety of situations in this chapter.

A LOOK AHEAD

Common approaches to making major investment decisions, which can have significant long-term implications for any organization, are discussed in Chapter 11.

10 Differential Analysis: The Key to Decision Making

CHAPTER OUTLINE

DECISION FEATURE

Moving Manufacturing Operations Overseas

A survey from **Ventoro Institute LLC** found that many companies expect to realize an 80% cost savings when moving manufacturing operations overseas. However, in this same survey, companies reported an average actual cost savings of less than 10%. Some of the problems encountered by these companies included miscommunications with offshore manufacturers, shipping delays, intellectual property infringement, and substandard product quality. William Botts, vice chairman of **Vegas Valley Angels** (an angel-investing group), suggests that companies with labor-intensive manufacturing processes are most likely to benefit from sending manufacturing operations overseas because the bulk of potential cost savings relate to labor costs.

Source: Small Talk, "Kelly Spors Answers Questions on Protecting Ideas, Cutting Off Junk Mail, and Overseas Manufacturing," *The Wall Street Journal*, March 17, 2008, p. R2.

Managers must decide what products to sell, whether to make or buy component parts, what prices to charge, what channels of distribution to use, whether to accept special orders at special prices, and so forth. Making such decisions is often a difficult task that is complicated by numerous alternatives and massive amounts of data, only some of which may be relevant.

Every decision involves choosing from among at least two alternatives. In making a decision, the costs and benefits of one alternative must be compared to the costs and benefits of other alternatives. The key to making such comparisons is *differential analysis*—focusing on the costs and benefits that *differ* between the alternatives. A difference in cost between any two alternatives is known as a **differential cost**. A difference in revenue between any two alternatives is known as **differential revenue**. Differential costs and revenues are relevant to decision making, whereas costs and revenues that do not differ between alternatives are irrelevant to decision making. Because differential costs and differential revenues are the only inputs that are relevant to decision making, they are also often referred to as **relevant costs** and **relevant benefits**.

Distinguishing between relevant and irrelevant costs and benefits is critical for two reasons. First, irrelevant data can be ignored—saving decision makers tremendous amounts of time and effort. Second, bad decisions can easily result from erroneously including irrelevant costs and benefits when analyzing alternatives. To be successful in decision making, managers must be able to tell the difference between relevant and irrelevant data and must be able to correctly use the relevant data in analyzing alternatives. The purpose of this chapter is to develop these skills by illustrating their use in a wide range of decision-making situations. These decision-making skills are as important in your personal life as they are to managers. After completing your study of this chapter, you should be able to think more clearly about decisions in many facets of your life.

COST CONCEPTS FOR DECISION MAKING

Identifying Relevant Costs and Benefits

LEARNING OBJECTIVE 10–1

Identify relevant and irrelevant costs and benefits in a decision.

Only those costs and benefits that differ in total between alternatives are relevant in a decision. If the total amount of a cost will be the same regardless of the alternative selected, then the decision has no effect on the cost, so the cost can be ignored. To elaborate on this point, we'd like to define the terms *avoidable cost, sunk cost,* and *opportunity cost,* and illustrate the concept of *future costs that do not differ between alternatives.*

Assume you are trying to decide whether to go to a movie or rent a DVD for the evening. The rent on your apartment is irrelevant. Whether you go to a movie or rent a DVD, the rent on your apartment will be exactly the same and is therefore irrelevant to the decision. On the other hand, the cost of the movie ticket and the cost of renting the DVD would be relevant in the decision because they are *avoidable costs.*

An **avoidable cost** is a cost that can be eliminated by choosing one alternative over another. By choosing the alternative of going to the movie, the cost of renting the DVD can be avoided. By choosing the alternative of renting the DVD, the cost of the movie ticket can be avoided. Therefore, the cost of the movie ticket and the cost of renting the DVD are both avoidable costs. On the other hand, the rent on your apartment is not an avoidable cost of either alternative. You would continue to rent your apartment under either alternative. Avoidable costs are relevant costs. Unavoidable costs are irrelevant costs.

To refine the notion of relevant costs a little further, two broad categories of costs are never relevant in decisions—sunk costs and future costs that do not differ between the alternatives. As we learned in Chapter 1, a **sunk cost** is a cost that has already been incurred and cannot be avoided regardless of what a manager decides to do. For example, suppose a company purchased a five-year-old truck for $12,000. The amount paid for the truck is a sunk cost because it has already been incurred and the transaction cannot be undone. Even though it is perhaps counterintuitive, the amount the company paid for the truck is irrelevant in making decisions such as whether to keep, sell, or replace the truck. Furthermore, any depreciation expense related to the truck is *irrelevant in making decisions*. This is true because depreciation is a noncash expense that simply spreads the cost of the truck over its useful life. Sunk costs are always the same no matter what alternatives are being considered; therefore, they are irrelevant and should be ignored when making decisions.

Future costs that do not differ between alternatives should also be ignored. Continuing with the example discussed earlier, suppose you plan to order a pizza after you go to the movie theater or you rent a DVD. If you are going to buy the same pizza regardless of your choice of entertainment, the cost of the pizza is irrelevant to the choice of whether you go to the movie theater or rent a DVD. Notice, the cost of the pizza is not a sunk cost because it has not yet been incurred. Nonetheless, the cost of the pizza is irrelevant to the entertainment decision because it is a future cost that does not differ between the alternatives.

Opportunity costs also need to be considered when making decisions. An **opportunity cost** is the potential benefit that is given up when one alternative is selected over another. For example, if you were considering giving up a high-paying summer job to travel overseas, the forgone wages would be an opportunity cost of traveling abroad. Opportunity costs are not usually found in accounting records, but they are costs that must be explicitly considered in every decision a manager makes.

To summarize, only those costs and benefits that differ between alternatives are relevant in a decision. Differential costs are also referred to as relevant costs or avoidable costs. The key to successful decision making is to focus on relevant costs and benefits as well as opportunity costs while ignoring everything else—including sunk costs and future costs and benefits that do not differ between the alternatives.

Industrial Motion Heads East

IN BUSINESS

Eric Kozlowski and Brian Pfeifer founded **Industrial Motion Inc.** in Rancho Santa Margarita, California; however, after 10 years in California, they decided to cut costs by relocating the company to Mooresville, North Carolina. In Mooresville, the company's 42 employees are paid salaries of $35,000–$45,000 instead of the $60,000 paid to employees in California; furthermore, worker's compensation insurance is one-tenth of the amount paid in California. Property taxes and the cost of real estate are 50% less in Mooresville compared to Rancho Santa Margarita. Even the company's security system in Mooresville costs only $25 per month instead of $280 per month in California.

Source: Simona Covel, "Moving Across the Country to Cut Costs," *The Wall Street Journal*, January 10, 2008, p. B4.

Different Costs for Different Purposes

We need to recognize a fundamental concept from the outset of our discussion—costs that are relevant in one decision situation are not necessarily relevant in another. This means that *managers need different costs for different purposes*. For one purpose, a particular group of costs may be relevant; for another purpose, an entirely different group of costs may be relevant. Thus, *each* decision situation must be carefully analyzed to isolate the relevant costs. Otherwise, irrelevant data may cloud the situation and lead to a bad decision.

The concept of "different costs for different purposes" is basic to managerial accounting; we shall frequently see its application in the pages that follow.

An Example of Identifying Relevant Costs and Benefits

Cynthia is currently a student in an MBA program in Boston and would like to visit a friend in New York City over the weekend. She is trying to decide whether to drive or take the train. Because she is on a tight budget, she wants to carefully consider the costs of the two alternatives. If one alternative is far less expensive than the other, that may be decisive in her choice. By car, the distance between her apartment in Boston and her friend's apartment in New York City is 230 miles. Cynthia has compiled the following list of items to consider:

Automobile Costs		
Item	Annual Cost of Fixed Items	Cost per Mile (based on 10,000 miles per year)
(a) Annual straight-line depreciation on car [($24,000 original cost − $10,000 estimated resale value in 5 years)/5 years]	$2,800	$0.280
(b) Cost of gasoline ($3.30 per gallon ÷ 33 miles per gallon)		0.100
(c) Annual cost of auto insurance and license	$1,380	0.138
(d) Maintenance and repairs		0.065
(e) Parking fees at school ($45 per month × 8 months)	$360	0.036
(f) Total average cost per mile		$0.619

Additional Data	
Item	
(g) Reduction in the resale value of car due solely to wear and tear	$0.026 per mile
(h) Cost of round-trip train ticket from Boston to New York City	$104
(i) Benefit of relaxing and being able to study during the train ride rather than having to drive	?
(j) Cost of putting the dog in a kennel while gone	$40
(k) Benefit of having a car available in New York City	?
(l) Hassle of parking the car in New York City	?
(m) Cost of parking the car in New York City	$25 per day

Which costs and benefits are relevant in this decision? Remember, only those costs and benefits that differ between alternatives are relevant. Everything else is irrelevant and can be ignored.

Start at the top of the list with item (a): the original cost of the car is a sunk cost. This cost has already been incurred and therefore can never differ between alternatives. Consequently, it is irrelevant and should be ignored. The same is true of the accounting depreciation of $2,800 per year, which simply spreads the sunk cost across five years.

Item (b), the cost of gasoline consumed by driving to New York City, is a relevant cost. If Cynthia takes the train, this cost would not be incurred. Hence, the cost differs between alternatives and is therefore relevant.

Item (c), the annual cost of auto insurance and license, is not relevant. Whether Cynthia takes the train or drives on this particular trip, her annual auto insurance premium and her auto license fee will remain the same.[1]

---

[1]If Cynthia has an accident while driving to New York City or back, this might affect her insurance premium when the policy is renewed. The increase in the insurance premium would be a relevant cost of this particular trip, but the normal amount of the insurance premium is not relevant in any case.

Item (d), the cost of maintenance and repairs, is relevant. While maintenance and repair costs have a large random component, over the long run they should be more or less proportional to the number of miles the car is driven. Thus, the average cost of $0.065 per mile is a reasonable estimate to use.

Item (e), the monthly fee that Cynthia pays to park at her school during the academic year is not relevant. Regardless of which alternative she selects—driving or taking the train—she will still need to pay for parking at school.

Item (f) is the total average cost of $0.619 per mile. As discussed above, some elements of this total are relevant, but some are not relevant. Because it contains some irrelevant costs, it would be incorrect to estimate the cost of driving to New York City and back by simply multiplying the $0.619 by 460 miles (230 miles each way × 2). This erroneous approach would yield a cost of driving of $284.74. Unfortunately, such mistakes are often made in both personal life and in business. Because the total cost is stated on a per-mile basis, people are easily misled. Often people think that if the cost is stated as $0.619 per mile, the cost of driving 100 miles is $61.90. But it is not. Many of the costs included in the $0.619 cost per mile are sunk and/or fixed and will not increase if the car is driven another 100 miles. The $0.619 is an average cost, not an incremental cost. Beware of such unitized costs (i.e., costs stated in terms of a dollar amount per unit, per mile, per direct labor-hour, per machine-hour, and so on)—they are often misleading.

Item (g), the decline in the resale value of the car that occurs as a consequence of driving more miles, is relevant in the decision. Because she uses the car, its resale value declines, which is a real cost of using the car that should be taken into account. Cynthia estimated this cost by accessing the *Kelly Blue Book* website at www.kbb.com. The reduction in resale value of an asset through use or over time is often called *real or economic depreciation*. This is different from accounting depreciation, which attempts to match the sunk cost of an asset with the periods that benefit from that cost.

Item (h), the $104 cost of a round-trip ticket on the train, is relevant in this decision. If she drives, she would not have to buy the ticket.

Item (i) is relevant to the decision, even if it is difficult to put a dollar value on relaxing and being able to study while on the train. It is relevant because it is a benefit that is available under one alternative but not under the other.

Item (j), the cost of putting Cynthia's dog in the kennel while she is gone, is irrelevant in this decision. Whether she takes the train or drives to New York City, she will still need to put her dog in a kennel.

Like item (i), items (k) and (l) are relevant to the decision even if it is difficult to measure their dollar impacts.

Item (m), the cost of parking in New York City, is relevant to the decision.

Bringing together all of the relevant data, Cynthia would estimate the relevant costs of driving and taking the train as follows:

Relevant financial cost of driving to New York City:	
Gasoline (460 miles × $0.100 per mile)	$ 46.00
Maintenance and repairs (460 miles × $0.065 per mile)	29.90
Reduction in the resale value of car due solely to wear and tear (460 miles × $0.026 per mile)	11.96
Cost of parking the car in New York City (2 days × $25 per day)	50.00
Total	$137.86
Relevant financial cost of taking the train to New York City:	
Cost of round-trip train ticket from Boston to New York City	$104.00

What should Cynthia do? From a purely financial standpoint, it would be cheaper by $33.86 ($137.86 − $104.00) to take the train than to drive. Cynthia has to decide if the convenience of having a car in New York City outweighs the additional cost and the disadvantages of being unable to relax and study on the train and the hassle of finding parking in the city.

In this example, we focused on identifying the relevant costs and benefits—everything else was ignored. In the next example, we include all of the costs and benefits—relevant or not. Nonetheless, we'll still get the correct answer because the irrelevant costs and benefits will cancel out when we compare the alternatives.

IN BUSINESS

Understanding the Importance of Qualitative Factors

SAS is a privately held $2.26 billion company located on a 200-acre campus in Cary, North Carolina. The company has an on-site medical facility (including a lab for blood tests) that is staffed by doctors, nurse practitioners, physical therapists, and a nutritionist. The company also has an infant day care, a Montessori school, a hair salon, a dry cleaning shop, a fitness center, and jogging and biking trails on campus. Employees that use the day care pay $360 per month per child for the service and SAS covers the remaining $720 per month per child that it costs to retain 120 teachers and staffers.

Although it may be difficult to quantify the benefits of these investments, SAS firmly believes that retaining happy and healthy employees is instrumental to its success. Mary Simmons, a SAS software developer says, "At lunch I will go out and bike 20 miles. Then I'll get back and all of a sudden a thought comes to my brain, and I solve something I was struggling with."

Source: Christopher Tkaczyk, "Offer Affordable (Awesome) Day Care," *Fortune,* August 17, 2009, p. 26.

Reconciling the Total and Differential Approaches

Oak Harbor Woodworks is considering a new labor-saving machine that rents for $3,000 per year. The machine will be used on the company's butcher block production line. Data concerning the company's annual sales and costs of butcher blocks with and without the new machine are shown below:

	Current Situation	Situation with the New Machine
Units produced and sold..........................	5,000	5,000
Selling price per unit...............................	$40	$40
Direct materials cost per unit	$14	$14
Direct labor cost per unit..........................	$8	$5
Variable overhead cost per unit	$2	$2
Fixed expenses, other..............................	$62,000	$62,000
Fixed expenses, rental of new machine	—	$3,000

Given the data above, the net operating income for the product under the two alternatives can be computed as shown in Exhibit 10–1.

Note that the net operating income is $12,000 higher with the new machine, so that is the better alternative. Note also that the $12,000 advantage for the new machine can be obtained in two different ways. It is the difference between the $30,000 net operating income with the new machine and the $18,000 net operating income for the current situation. It is also the sum of the differential costs and benefits as shown in the last column of Exhibit 10–1 ($15,000 + $(3,000) = $12,000). A positive number in the Differential Costs and Benefits column indicates that the difference between the alternatives favors the new machine; a negative number indicates that the difference favors the current

EXHIBIT 10–1
Total and Differential Costs

	Current Situation	Situation with New Machine	Differential Costs and Benefits
Sales (5,000 units × $40 per unit)	$200,000	$200,000	$ 0
Variable expenses:			
Direct materials (5,000 units × $14 per unit) . . .	70,000	70,000	0
Direct labor (5,000 units × $8 per unit;			
5,000 units × $5 per unit)	40,000	25,000	15,000
Variable overhead (5,000 units × $2 per unit) . . .	10,000	10,000	0
Total variable expenses	120,000	105,000	
Contribution margin	80,000	95,000	
Fixed expenses:			
Other.	62,000	62,000	0
Rental of new machine	0	3,000	(3,000)
Total fixed expenses.	62,000	65,000	
Net operating income	$ 18,000	$ 30,000	$12,000

situation. A zero in that column simply means that the total amount for the item is exactly the same for both alternatives. Thus, because the difference in the net operating incomes equals the sum of the differences for the individual items, any cost or benefit that is the same for both alternatives will have no impact on which alternative is preferred. This is the reason that costs and benefits that do not differ between alternatives are irrelevant and can be ignored. If we properly account for them, they will cancel out when we compare the alternatives.

We could have arrived at the same solution much more quickly by completely ignoring the irrelevant costs and benefits.

- The selling price per unit and the number of units sold do not differ between the alternatives. Therefore, the total sales revenues are exactly the same for the two alternatives as shown in Exhibit 10–1. Because the sales revenues are exactly the same, they have no effect on the difference in net operating income between the two alternatives. That is shown in the last column in Exhibit 10–1, which shows a $0 differential benefit.

- The direct materials cost per unit, the variable overhead cost per unit, and the number of units produced and sold do not differ between the alternatives. Consequently, the total direct materials cost and the total variable overhead cost are the same for the two alternatives and can be ignored.

- The "other" fixed expenses do not differ between the alternatives, so they can be ignored as well.

Indeed, the only costs that do differ between the alternatives are direct labor costs and the fixed rental cost of the new machine. Hence, the two alternatives can be compared based only on these relevant costs:

Net Advantage of Renting the New Machine	
Decrease in direct labor costs (5,000 units at a cost savings of $3 per unit) . . .	$15,000
Increase in fixed expenses.	(3,000)
Net annual cost savings from renting the new machine	$12,000

If we focus on just the relevant costs and benefits, we get exactly the same answer as when we listed all of the costs and benefits—including those that do not differ between the alternatives and, hence, are irrelevant. We get the same answer because the only costs

464 Chapter 10

and benefits that matter in the final comparison of the net operating incomes are those that differ between the two alternatives and, hence, are not zero in the last column of Exhibit 10–1. Those two relevant costs are both included in the above analysis that quantifies the net advantage of renting the new machine.

Why Isolate Relevant Costs?

In the preceding example, we used two different approaches to analyze the alternatives. First, we considered all costs, both those that were relevant and those that were not; and second, we considered only the relevant costs. We obtained the same answer under both approaches. It would be natural to ask, "Why bother to isolate relevant costs when total costs will do the job just as well?" Isolating relevant costs is desirable for at least two reasons.

First, only rarely will enough information be available to prepare a detailed income statement for both alternatives. Assume, for example, that you are called on to make a decision relating to a portion of a single business process in a multidepartmental, multi-product company. Under these circumstances, it would be virtually impossible to prepare an income statement of any type. You would have to rely on your ability to recognize which costs are relevant and which are not in order to assemble the data necessary to make a decision.

Second, mingling irrelevant costs with relevant costs may cause confusion and distract attention from the information that is really critical. Furthermore, the danger always exists that an irrelevant piece of data may be used improperly, resulting in an incorrect decision. The best approach is to ignore irrelevant data and base the decision entirely on relevant data.

Relevant cost analysis, combined with the contribution approach to the income statement, provides a powerful tool for making decisions. We will investigate various uses of this tool in the remaining sections of this chapter.

CONCEPT CHECK

1. Which of the following statements is false? (You may select more than one answer.)
   a. Under some circumstances, a sunk cost may be a relevant cost.
   b. Future costs that do not differ between alternatives are irrelevant.
   c. The same cost may be relevant or irrelevant depending on the decision context.
   d. Only variable costs are relevant costs. Fixed costs cannot be relevant costs.
2. Assume that in October you bought a $450 nonrefundable airline ticket to Telluride, Colorado, for a 5-day/4-night winter ski vacation. You now have an opportunity to buy an airline ticket for a 5-day/4-night winter ski vacation in Stowe, Vermont, for $400 that includes a free ski lift ticket. The price of your lift ticket for the Telluride vacation would be $300. The price of a hotel room in Telluride is $180 per night. The price of a hotel room in Stowe is $150 per night. Which of the following costs is not relevant in a decision of whether to proceed with the planned trip to Telluride or to change to a trip to Stowe?
   a. The $450 airline ticket to Telluride.
   b. The $400 airline ticket to Stowe.
   c. The $300 lift ticket for the Telluride vacation.
   d. The $180 per night hotel room in Telluride.
3. Based on the facts in question 2 above, does a differential cost analysis favor Telluride or Stowe, and by how much?
   a. Stowe by $470.
   b. Stowe by $20.
   c. Telluride by $70.
   d. Telluride by $20.

ADDING AND DROPPING PRODUCT LINES AND OTHER SEGMENTS

Decisions relating to whether product lines or other segments of a company should be dropped and new ones added are among the most difficult that a manager has to make. In such decisions, many qualitative and quantitative factors must be considered. Ultimately, however, any final decision to drop a business segment or to add a new one hinges primarily on the impact the decision will have on net operating income. To assess this impact, costs must be carefully analyzed.

LEARNING OBJECTIVE 10–2

Prepare an analysis showing whether a product line or other business segment should be added or dropped.

An Illustration of Cost Analysis

Exhibit 10–2 provides sales and cost information for the preceding month for the Discount Drug Company and its three major product lines—drugs, cosmetics, and housewares. A quick review of this exhibit suggests that dropping the housewares segment would increase the company's overall net operating income by $8,000. However, this would be a flawed conclusion because the data in Exhibit 10–2 do not distinguish between fixed expenses that can be avoided if a product line is dropped and common fixed expenses that cannot be avoided by dropping any particular product line.

In this scenario, the two alternatives under consideration are keeping the housewares product line and dropping the housewares product line. Therefore, only those costs that differ between these two alternatives (i.e., that can be avoided by dropping the housewares product line) are relevant. In deciding whether to drop housewares, it is crucial to identify which costs can be avoided, and hence are relevant to the decision, and which costs cannot be avoided, and hence are irrelevant. The decision should be analyzed as follows.

If the housewares line is dropped, then the company will lose $20,000 per month in contribution margin, but by dropping the line it may be possible to avoid some fixed costs such as salaries or advertising costs. If dropping the housewares line enables the company to avoid more in fixed costs than it loses in contribution margin, then its overall net operating income will improve by eliminating the product line. On the other hand, if the company is not able to avoid as much in fixed costs as it loses in contribution margin, then the housewares line should be kept. In short, the manager should ask, "What costs can I avoid if I drop this product line?"

As we have seen from our earlier discussion, not all costs are avoidable. For example, some of the costs associated with a product line may be sunk costs. Other costs may be allocated fixed costs that will not differ in total regardless of whether the product line is dropped or retained.

	Total	**Product Line** Drugs	Cosmetics	Housewares
Sales.....................	$250,000	$125,000	$75,000	$50,000
Variable expenses	105,000	50,000	25,000	30,000
Contribution margin	145,000	75,000	50,000	20,000
Fixed expenses:				
Salaries..................	50,000	29,500	12,500	8,000
Advertising	15,000	1,000	7,500	6,500
Utilities	2,000	500	500	1,000
Depreciation—fixtures.......	5,000	1,000	2,000	2,000
Rent	20,000	10,000	6,000	4,000
Insurance	3,000	2,000	500	500
General administrative	30,000	15,000	9,000	6,000
Total fixed expenses..........	125,000	59,000	38,000	28,000
Net operating income (loss)	$ 20,000	$ 16,000	$12,000	$(8,000)

EXHIBIT 10–2
Discount Drug Company Product Lines

To show how to proceed in a product-line analysis, suppose that Discount Drug Company has analyzed the fixed costs being charged to the three product lines and determined the following:

1. The salaries expense represents salaries paid to employees working directly on the product. All of the employees working in housewares would be discharged if the product line is dropped.
2. The advertising expense represents advertisements that are specific to each product line and are avoidable if the line is dropped.
3. The utilities expense represents utilities costs for the entire company. The amount charged to each product line is an allocation based on space occupied and is not avoidable if the product line is dropped.
4. The depreciation expense represents depreciation on fixtures used to display the various product lines. Although the fixtures are nearly new, they are custom-built and will have no resale value if the housewares line is dropped.
5. The rent expense represents rent on the entire building housing the company; it is allocated to the product lines on the basis of sales dollars. The monthly rent of $20,000 is fixed under a long-term lease agreement.
6. The insurance expense is for insurance carried on inventories within each of the three product lines. If housewares is dropped, the related inventories will be liquidated and the insurance premiums will decrease proportionately.
7. The general administrative expense represents the costs of accounting, purchasing, and general management, which are allocated to the product lines on the basis of sales dollars. These costs will not change if the housewares line is dropped.

With this information, management can determine that $15,000 of the fixed expenses associated with the housewares product line are avoidable and $13,000 are not:

Fixed Expenses	Total Cost Assigned to Housewares	Not Avoidable*	Avoidable
Salaries	$ 8,000		$ 8,000
Advertising	6,500		6,500
Utilities	1,000	$ 1,000	
Depreciation—fixtures	2,000	2,000	
Rent	4,000	4,000	
Insurance	500		500
General administrative	6,000	6,000	
Total	$28,000	$13,000	$15,000

*These fixed costs represent either sunk costs or future costs that will not change whether the housewares line is retained or discontinued.

As stated earlier, if the housewares product line were dropped, the company would lose the product's contribution margin of $20,000, but would save its associated avoidable fixed expenses. We now know that those avoidable fixed expenses total $15,000. Therefore, dropping the housewares product line would result in a $5,000 *reduction* in net operating income as shown below:

Contribution margin lost if the housewares line is discontinued (see Exhibit 10–2)..	$(20,000)
Fixed expenses that can be avoided if the housewares line is discontinued (see above)...	15,000
Decrease in overall company net operating income.....................	$ (5,000)

In this case, the fixed costs that can be avoided by dropping the housewares product line ($15,000) are less than the contribution margin that will be lost ($20,000). Therefore, based on the data given, the housewares line should not be discontinued unless a more profitable use can be found for the floor and counter space that it is occupying.

A Comparative Format

This decision can also be approached by preparing comparative income statements showing the effects of either keeping or dropping the product line. Exhibit 10–3 contains such an analysis for the Discount Drug Company. As shown in the last column of the exhibit, if the housewares line is dropped, then overall company net operating income will decrease by $5,000 each period. This is the same answer, of course, as we obtained when we focused just on the lost contribution margin and avoidable fixed costs.

Beware of Allocated Fixed Costs

Go back to Exhibit 10–2. Does this exhibit suggest that the housewares product line should be kept—as we have just concluded? No, it does not. Exhibit 10–2 suggests that the housewares product line is losing money. Why keep a product line that is showing a loss? The explanation for this apparent inconsistency lies in part with the common fixed costs that are being allocated to the product lines. One of the great dangers in allocating common fixed costs is that such allocations can make a product line (or other business segment) look less profitable than it really is. In this instance, allocating the common fixed costs among all product lines makes the housewares product line appear to be unprofitable. However, as we have just shown, dropping the product line would result in a decrease in the company's overall net operating income. This point can be seen clearly if we redo

	Keep Housewares	Drop Housewares	Difference: Net Operating Income Increase (or Decrease)
Sales.	$50,000	$ 0	$(50,000)
Variable expenses	30,000	0	30,000
Contribution margin	20,000	0	(20,000)
Fixed expenses:			
Salaries.	8,000	0	8,000
Advertising	6,500	0	6,500
Utilities	1,000	1,000	0
Depreciation—fixtures.	2,000	2,000	0
Rent	4,000	4,000	0
Insurance	500	0	500
General administrative	6,000	6,000	0
Total fixed expenses.	28,000	13,000	15,000
Net operating loss.	$ (8,000)	$(13,000)	$ (5,000)

EXHIBIT 10–3
A Comparative Format for Product-Line Analysis

EXHIBIT 10–4
Discount Drug Company Product
Lines—Recast in Contribution
Format (from Exhibit 10–2)

		Product Line		
	Total	**Drugs**	**Cosmetics**	**Housewares**
Sales....................	$250,000	$125,000	$75,000	$50,000
Variable expenses	105,000	50,000	25,000	30,000
Contribution margin	145,000	75,000	50,000	20,000
Traceable fixed expenses:				
Salaries.................	50,000	29,500	12,500	8,000
Advertising	15,000	1,000	7,500	6,500
Depreciation—fixtures.......	5,000	1,000	2,000	2,000
Insurance	3,000	2,000	500	500
Total traceable fixed expenses ..	73,000	33,500	22,500	17,000
Product-line segment margin ...	72,000	$ 41,500	$27,500	$ 3,000*
Common fixed expenses:				
Utilities	2,000			
Rent	20,000			
General administrative	30,000			
Total common fixed expenses ..	52,000			
Net operating income	$ 20,000			

*If the housewares line is dropped, the company will lose the $3,000 segment margin
generated by this product line. In addition, we have seen that the $2,000 depreciation on
the fixtures is a sunk cost that cannot be avoided. The sum of these two figures
($3,000 + $2,000 = $5,000) would be the decrease in the company's overall profits if the
housewares line were discontinued. Of course, the company may later choose to drop the
product if circumstances change—such as a pending decision to replace the fixtures.

Exhibit 10–2 by eliminating the allocation of the common fixed costs. Exhibit 10–4 uses
the segmented approach from Chapter 6 to estimate the profitability of the product lines.

Exhibit 10–4 gives us a much different perspective of the housewares line than does
Exhibit 10–2. As shown in Exhibit 10–4, the housewares line is covering all of its own
traceable fixed costs and generating a $3,000 segment margin toward covering the com-
mon fixed costs of the company. Unless another product line can be found that will generate a segment margin greater than $3,000, the company would be better off keeping the
housewares line. By keeping the product line, the company's overall net operating income
will be higher than if the product line were dropped.

Additionally, managers may choose to retain an unprofitable product line if the line
helps sell other products, or if it serves as a "magnet" to attract customers. Bread, for
example, may not be an especially profitable line in some food stores, but customers
expect it to be available, and many of them would undoubtedly shift their buying elsewhere if a particular store decided to stop carrying it.

CONCEPT CHECK

4. Which of the following statements is true? (You may select more than one answer.)
   a. Common fixed costs should be allocated to business segments when making deci-
      sions because all of a company's costs need to be covered to be profitable.
   b. When making decisions, common fixed costs should be allocated to business seg-
      ments based on each segment's sales revenue because this reflects each segment's
      "ability to bear" additional costs.
   c. Common fixed costs should not be allocated to business segments for decision-
      making purposes.
   d. When making decisions, allocating common fixed costs to segments may under-
      state the true profitability of those segments.

THE MAKE OR BUY DECISION

LEARNING OBJECTIVE 10–3

Prepare a make or buy analysis.

Providing a product or service to a customer involves many steps. For example, consider all of the steps that are necessary to develop and sell a product such as tax preparation software in retail stores. First the software must be developed, which involves highly skilled software engineers and a great deal of project management effort. Then the product must be put into a form that can be delivered to customers. This involves burning the application onto a blank CD or DVD, applying a label, and packaging the result in an attractive box. Then the product must be distributed to retail stores. Then the product must be sold. And finally, help lines and other forms of after-sale service may have to be provided. And we should not forget that the blank CD or DVD, the label, and the box must of course be made by someone before any of this can happen. All of these activities, from development, to production, to after-sales service are called a *value chain.*

Separate companies may carry out each of the activities in the value chain or a single company may carry out several. When a company is involved in more than one activity in the entire value chain, it is **vertically integrated**. Some companies control all of the activities in the value chain from producing basic raw materials right up to the final distribution of finished goods and provision of after-sales service. Other companies are content to integrate on a smaller scale by purchasing many of the parts and materials that go into their finished products. A decision to carry out one of the activities in the value chain internally, rather than to buy externally from a supplier, is called a **make or buy decision**. Quite often these decisions involve whether to buy a particular part or to make it internally. Make or buy decisions also involve decisions concerning whether to outsource development tasks, after-sales service, or other activities.

An Example of Make or Buy

To provide an illustration of a make or buy decision, consider Mountain Goat Cycles. The company is now producing the heavy-duty gear shifters used in its most popular line of mountain bikes. The company's Accounting Department reports the following costs of producing 8,000 units of the shifter internally each year:

	Per Unit	8,000 Units
Direct materials.	$ 6	$ 48,000
Direct labor	4	32,000
Variable overhead.	1	8,000
Supervisor's salary	3	24,000
Depreciation of special equipment	2	16,000
Allocated general overhead	5	40,000
Total cost	$21	$168,000

An outside supplier has offered to sell 8,000 shifters a year to Mountain Goat Cycles for a price of only $19 each, or a total of $152,000 (= 8,000 shifters × $19 each). Should the company stop producing the shifters internally and buy them from the outside supplier? As always, the focus should be on the relevant costs—those that differ between the alternatives. And the costs that differ between the alternatives consist of the costs that could be avoided by purchasing the shifters from the outside supplier. If the costs that can be avoided by purchasing the shifters from the outside supplier total less than $152,000, then the company should continue to manufacture its own shifters and reject the outside supplier's offer. On the other hand, if the costs that can be avoided by purchasing the shifters from the outside supplier total more than $152,000 the outside supplier's offer should be accepted.

Note that depreciation of special equipment is listed as one of the costs of producing the shifters internally. Because the equipment has already been purchased, this depreciation is a sunk cost and is therefore irrelevant. If the equipment could be sold, its salvage value would be relevant. Or if the machine could be used to make other products, this could be relevant as well. However, we will assume that the equipment has no salvage value and that it has no other use except making the heavy-duty gear shifters.

Also note that the company is allocating a portion of its general overhead costs to the shifters. Any portion of this general overhead cost that would actually be eliminated if the gear shifters were purchased rather than made would be relevant in the analysis. However, it is likely that the general overhead costs allocated to the gear shifters are in fact common to all items produced in the factory and would continue unchanged even if the shifters were purchased from the outside. Such allocated common costs are not relevant costs (because they do not differ between the make or buy alternatives) and should be eliminated from the analysis along with the sunk costs.

The variable costs of producing the shifters can be avoided by buying the shifters from the outside supplier so they are relevant costs. We will assume in this case that the variable costs include direct materials, direct labor, and variable overhead. The supervisor's salary is also relevant if it could be avoided by buying the shifters. Exhibit 10–5 contains the relevant cost analysis of the make or buy decision assuming that the supervisor's salary can indeed be avoided.

Because the avoidable costs related to making the shifters is $40,000 less than the total amount that would be paid to buy them from the outside supplier, Mountain Goat Cycles should reject the outside supplier's offer. However, the company may wish to consider one additional factor before coming to a final decision—the opportunity cost of the space now being used to produce the shifters.

EXHIBIT 10–5
Mountain Goat Cycles Make or Buy Analysis

	Total Relevant Costs—8,000 units	
	Make	**Buy**
Direct materials (8,000 units × $6 per unit)	$ 48,000	
Direct labor (8,000 units × $4 per unit)	32,000	
Variable overhead (8,000 units × $1 per unit)	8,000	
Supervisor's salary	24,000	
Depreciation of special equipment (not relevant)		
Allocated general overhead (not relevant)		
Outside purchase price		$152,000
Total cost	$112,000	$152,000
Difference in favor of continuing to make	$40,000	

Use the following three steps to quantify the financial impact of make or buy decisions:

Step 1: Calculate the total amount that would be paid to the supplier if the buy option is chosen.

Step 2: Calculate the total differential manufacturing costs. These are the variable manufacturing costs and traceable fixed manufacturing costs that will be incurred if the company chooses to make, but avoided if the company chooses to buy.

Step 3: Calculate the difference between the amounts from steps 1 and 2. If the amount from step 1 exceeds the amount from step 2, then choose the make option. If the amount from step 1 is less than the amount from step 2, then choose the buy option.

While you may need to add additional steps when solving complex problems, these three steps will help organize your analysis.

OPPORTUNITY COST

If the space now being used to produce the shifters *would otherwise be idle,* then Mountain Goat Cycles should continue to produce its own shifters and the supplier's offer should be rejected, as stated above. Idle space that has no alternative use has an opportunity cost of zero.

But what if the space now being used to produce shifters could be used for some other purpose? In that case, the space would have an opportunity cost equal to the segment margin that could be derived from the best alternative use of the space.

To illustrate, assume that the space now being used to produce shifters could be used to produce a new cross-country bike that would generate a segment margin of $60,000 per year. Under these conditions, Mountain Goat Cycles should accept the supplier's offer and use the available space to produce the new product line:

	Make	Buy
Total annual cost (see Exhibit 10–5)	$112,000	$152,000
Opportunity cost—segment margin forgone on a potential new product line	60,000	
Total cost	$172,000	$152,000
Difference in favor of purchasing from the outside supplier		$20,000

Opportunity costs are not recorded in the organization's general ledger because they do not represent actual dollar outlays. Rather, they represent economic benefits that are *forgone* as a result of pursuing some course of action. The opportunity cost for Mountain Goat Cycles is sufficiently large in this case to change the decision.

Vice President of Production

You are faced with a make or buy decision. The company currently makes a component for one of its products but is considering whether it should instead purchase the component. If the offer from an outside supplier were accepted, the company would no longer need to rent the machinery currently being used to manufacture the component. You realize that the annual rental cost is a fixed cost, but recall some sort of warning about fixed costs. Is the annual rental cost relevant to this make or buy decision?

Is There Such a Thing as a $1 Bus Ticket?

When **Megabus** and **Greyhound's Bolt Bus** sell tickets for $1 it begs the question—how can that be profitable? The answer lies in understanding the concept of opportunity costs. The bus companies use computer algorithms to determine how many empty seats ordinarily exist on a given bus route. Since the incremental cost of allowing a customer to occupy a seat that would otherwise be empty is zero, the $1 price provides bus companies with additional contribution margin. Of course, only a few $1 tickets are available for each trip on a given bus route. Furthermore, these deeply discounted tickets must be purchased well in advance of the travel date. All other customers pay a higher fare that enables the bus company to earn a profit on its routes.

Source: Anne VanderMey, "What's Up With $1 Bus Tickets?" *Fortune*, November 7, 2011, p. 27.

SPECIAL ORDERS

Managers must often evaluate whether a *special order* should be accepted, and if the order is accepted, the price that should be charged. A **special order** is a one-time order that is not considered part of the company's normal ongoing business. To illustrate, Mountain Goat Cycles has just received a request from the Seattle Police Department to produce 100 specially modified mountain bikes at a price of $558 each. The bikes would be used to patrol some of the more densely populated residential sections of the city. Mountain Goat Cycles can easily modify its City Cruiser model to fit the specifications of the Seattle Police. The normal selling price of the City Cruiser bike is $698, and its unit product cost is $564 as shown below:

Direct materials.	$372
Direct labor	90
Manufacturing overhead	102
Unit product cost.	$564

The variable portion of the above manufacturing overhead is $12 per unit. The order would have no effect on the company's total fixed manufacturing overhead costs.

The modifications requested by the Seattle Police Department consist of welded brackets to hold radios, nightsticks, and other gear. These modifications would require $34 in incremental variable costs. In addition, the company would have to pay a graphics design studio $2,400 to design and cut stencils that would be used for spray painting the Seattle Police Department's logo and other identifying marks on the bikes.

This order should have no effect on the company's other sales. The production manager says that she can handle the special order without disrupting any of the company's regular scheduled production.

What effect would accepting this order have on the company's net operating income?

Only the incremental costs and benefits are relevant. Because the existing fixed manufacturing overhead costs would not be affected by the order, they are not relevant. The incremental net operating income can be computed as follows:

	Per Unit	Total 100 Bikes
Incremental revenue	$558	$55,800
Less incremental costs:		
Variable costs:		
Direct materials	372	37,200
Direct labor	90	9,000
Variable manufacturing overhead	12	1,200
Special modifications.	34	3,400
Total variable cost	$508	50,800
Fixed cost:		
Purchase of stencils		2,400
Total incremental cost.		53,200
Incremental net operating income		$ 2,600

Therefore, even though the $558 price on the special order is below the normal $564 unit product cost and the order would require additional costs, the order would increase net operating income. In general, a special order is profitable if the incremental revenue from the special order exceeds the incremental costs of the order. However, it is important to make sure that there is indeed idle capacity and that the special order does not cut into normal unit sales or undercut prices on normal sales. For example, if the company was operating at capacity, opportunity costs would have to be taken into account, as well as the incremental costs that have already been detailed above.

HELPFUL HINT

Use the following three steps to quantify the financial impact of accepting a special order:
Step 1: Calculate the total revenue generated by the special order.
Step 2: Calculate the total incremental costs that will be incurred to produce the special order.
Step 3: Take the amount in step 1 and subtract from it the amount in step 2. If the result is a positive number, then accept the special order. If it is a negative number, then reject the special order.
While you may need to add additional steps when solving complex problems, these three steps will help organize your analysis.

CONCEPT CHECK

5. A company has received a special order from a customer to make 5,000 units of a customized product. The direct materials cost per unit of the customized product is $15, the direct labor cost per unit is $5, and the manufacturing overhead per unit is $18, including $6 of variable manufacturing overhead. If the company has sufficient available manufacturing capacity, what is the minimum price that can be accepted for the special order?

   a. $24   b. $26   c. $32   d. $38

6. Refer to the facts from question 5; however, in answering this question assume that the company is operating at 100% of its capacity without the special order. If the company normally manufactures only one product that has a contribution margin of $20 per unit and that consumes 2 minutes of the constrained resource per unit, what is the opportunity cost (stated in terms of forgone contribution margin) of accepting the special order? Assume the special order would require 1.5 minutes of the constrained resource per unit.

   a. $25,000   b. $50,000   c. $75,000   d. $100,000

UTILIZATION OF A CONSTRAINED RESOURCE

What Is a Constraint?

A **constraint** is anything that prevents you from getting more of what you want. Every individual and every organization faces at least one constraint, so it is not difficult to find examples of constraints. You may not have enough time to study thoroughly for every subject *and* to go out with your friends on the weekend, so time is your constraint. **United Airlines** has only a limited number of loading gates available at its busy Chicago O'Hare hub, so its constraint is loading gates. **Vail Resorts** has only a limited amount of land to develop as homesites and commercial lots at its ski areas, so its constraint is land.

As an example, long waiting periods for surgery are a chronic problem in the **National Health Service (NHS)**, the government-funded provider of health care in the United Kingdom. The diagram in Exhibit 10–6 illustrates a simplified version of the steps followed by a surgery patient. The number of patients who can be processed through each step in a day is indicated in the exhibit. For example, appointments for outpatient visits can be made for as many as 100 referrals from general practitioners in a day.

The constraint, or **bottleneck**, in the system is determined by the step that limits total output because it has the smallest capacity—in this case surgery. The total number of patients processed through the entire system cannot exceed 15 per day—the maximum number of patients who can be treated in surgery. No matter how hard managers, doctors, and nurses try to improve the processing rate elsewhere in the system, they will never succeed in driving down wait lists until the capacity of surgery is increased. In fact, improvements elsewhere in the system—particularly before the constraint—are likely to result in even longer waiting times and more frustrated patients and health care providers. Thus, to be effective, improvement efforts must be focused on the constraint. A business process, such as the process for serving surgery patients, is like a chain. If you want to increase the strength of a chain, what is the most effective way to do this? Should you concentrate your efforts on strengthening the strongest link, all the links, or the weakest link? Clearly, focusing your effort on the weakest link will bring the biggest benefit.

The procedure to follow to strengthen the chain is clear. First, identify the weakest link, which is the constraint. In the case of the NHS, the constraint is surgery. Second, do not place a greater strain on the system than the weakest link can handle—if you do, the chain will break. In the case of the NHS, more referrals than surgery can accommodate lead to unacceptably long waiting lists. Third, concentrate improvement efforts on strengthening the weakest link. In the case of the NHS, this means finding ways to increase the number of surgeries that can be performed in a day. Fourth, if the improvement efforts are successful, eventually the weakest link will improve to the point where it is no longer the weakest link. At that point, the new weakest link (i.e., the new constraint) must be identified, and improvement efforts must be shifted over to that link. This simple sequential process provides a powerful strategy for optimizing business processes.

EXHIBIT 10–6   Processing Surgery Patients at an NHS Facility (simplified)*

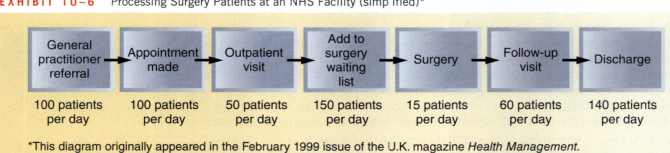

*This diagram originally appeared in the February 1999 issue of the U.K. magazine *Health Management*.

Contribution Margin per Unit of the Constrained Resource

LEARNING OBJECTIVE 10–5

Determine the most profitable use of a constrained resource.

Managers routinely face the problem of deciding how constrained resources are going to be used. A department store, for example, has a limited amount of floor space and therefore cannot stock every product that may be available. A manufacturer has a limited number of machine-hours and a limited number of direct labor-hours at its disposal. Because the company cannot fully satisfy demand, managers must decide which products or services should be cut back. In other words, managers must decide which products or services make the best use of the constrained resource. Fixed costs are usually unaffected by such choices, so the course of action that will maximize the company's total contribution margin should ordinarily be selected.

If some products must be cut back because of a constraint, the key to maximizing the total contribution margin may seem obvious—favor the products with the highest unit contribution margins. Unfortunately, that is not quite correct. Rather, the correct solution is to favor the products that provide the highest *contribution margin per unit of the constrained resource*. To illustrate, in addition to its other products, Mountain Goat Cycles makes saddlebags for bicycles called *panniers*. These panniers come in two models—a touring model and a mountain model. Cost and revenue data for the two models of panniers follow:

	Mountain Pannier	Touring Pannier
Selling price per unit.	$25	$30
Variable cost per unit	10	18
Contribution margin per unit	$15	$12
Contribution margin (CM) ratio	60%	40%

The mountain pannier appears to be much more profitable than the touring pannier. It has a $15 per unit contribution margin as compared to only $12 per unit for the touring model, and it has a 60% CM ratio as compared to only 40% for the touring model.

But now let us add one more piece of information—the plant that makes the panniers is operating at capacity. This does not mean that every machine and every person in the plant is working at the maximum possible rate. Because machines have different capacities, some machines will be operating at less than 100% of capacity. However, if the plant as a whole cannot produce any more units, some machine or process must be operating at capacity. The machine or process that is limiting overall output is called the bottleneck—it is the constraint.

At Mountain Goat Cycles, the bottleneck (i.e., constraint) is a stitching machine. The mountain pannier requires two minutes of stitching time per unit, and the touring pannier requires one minute of stitching time per unit. The stitching machine is available for 12,000 minutes per month, and the company can sell up to 4,000 mountain panniers and 7,000 touring panniers per month. Producing up to this demand for both products would require 15,000 minutes, as shown below:

	Mountain Pannier	Touring Pannier	Total
Monthly demand (a)	4,000 units	7,000 units	
Stitching machine time required to produce one unit (b)	2 minutes	1 minute	
Total stitching time required (a) × (b)	8,000 minutes	7,000 minutes	15,000 minutes

Producing up to demand would require 15,000 minutes, but only 12,000 minutes are available. This simply confirms that the stitching machine is the bottleneck. By definition, because the stitching machine is a bottleneck, the stitching machine does not have enough capacity to satisfy the existing demand for mountain panniers and touring panniers Therefore, some orders for the products will have to be turned down. Naturally, managers will want to know which product is less profitable. To answer this question, they should focus on the contribution margin per unit of the constrained resource. This figure is computed by dividing a product's contribution margin per unit by the amount of the constrained resource required to make a unit of that product. These calculations are carried out below for the mountain and touring panniers:

	Mountain Pannier	Touring Pannier
Contribution margin per unit (a)	$15.00	$12.00
Stitching machine time required to produce one unit (b)	2 minutes	1 minute
Contribution margin per unit of the constrained resource, (a) ÷ (b)	$7.50 per minute	$12.00 per minute

It is now easy to decide which product is less profitable and should be deemphasized. Each minute on the stitching machine that is devoted to the touring pannier results in an increase of $12.00 in contribution margin and profits. The comparable figure for the mountain pannier is only $7.50 per minute. Therefore, the touring model should be emphasized. Even though the mountain model has the larger contribution margin per unit and the larger CM ratio, the touring model provides the larger contribution margin in relation to the constrained resource.

To verify that the touring model is indeed the more profitable product, suppose an hour of additional stitching time is available and that unfilled orders exist for both products. The additional hour on the stitching machine could be used to make either 30 mountain panniers (60 minutes ÷ 2 minutes per mountain pannier) or 60 touring panniers (60 minutes ÷ 1 minute per touring pannier), with the following profit implications:

	Mountain Pannier	Touring Pannier
Contribution margin per unit	$ 15	$ 12
Additional units that can be processed in one hour	× 30	× 60
Additional contribution margin	$450	$720

Because the additional contribution margin would be $720 for the touring panniers and only $450 for the mountain panniers, the touring panniers make the most profitable use of the company's constrained resource—the stitching machine.

The stitching machine is available for 12,000 minutes per month, and producing the touring panniers is the most profitable use of the stitching machine. Therefore, to maximize profits, the company should produce all of the touring panniers the market will demand (7,000 units) and use any remaining capacity to produce mountain panniers. The computations to determine how many mountain panniers can be produced are as follows:

Monthly demand for touring panniers (a)	7,000 units
Stitching machine time required to produce one touring pannier (b)	1 minute
Total stitching time required to produce touring panniers (a) × (b).	7,000 minutes
Remaining stitching time available (12,000 minutes − 7,000 minutes) (c).	5,000 minutes
Stitching machine time required to produce one mountain pannier (d) . . .	2 minutes
Production of mountain panniers (c) ÷ (d)	2,500 units

Therefore, profit would be maximized by producing 7,000 touring panniers and then using the remaining capacity to produce 2,500 mountain panniers.

This example clearly shows that looking at each product's unit contribution margin alone is not enough; the contribution margin must be viewed in relation to the amount of the constrained resource each product requires.

HELPFUL HINT

Use the following four steps to help determine the most profitable use of a constrained resource:
Step 1: Calculate each product's contribution margin per unit.
Step 2: Identify the constraining resource and the quantity of that resource that is consumed to make one unit of each product.
Step 3: Calculate each product's contribution margin per unit of the constraining resource.
Step 4: Rank the products from the highest contribution margin per unit of the constraining resource to the lowest.
If you start by completing these four steps, it will help you compute the most profitable use of a constrained resource.

Managing Constraints

Effectively managing an organization's constraints is a key to increased profits. As discussed above, when a constraint exists in the production process, managers can increase profits by producing the products with the highest contribution margin per unit of the constrained resource. However, they can also increase profits by increasing the capacity of the bottleneck operation.

LEARNING OBJECTIVE 10–6

Determine the value of obtaining more of the constrained resource.

When a manager increases the capacity of the bottleneck, it is called **relaxing (or elevating) the constraint**. In the case of Mountain Goat Cycles, the company is currently working one eight-hour shift. To relax the constraint, the stitching machine operator could be asked to work overtime. No one else would have to work overtime. Because all of the other operations involved in producing panniers have excess capacity, up to a point, the additional panniers processed through the stitching machine during overtime could be finished during normal working hours in the other operations.

The benefits from relaxing the constraint are often enormous and can be easily quantified—the key is the contribution margin per unit of the constrained resource that we have already computed. This number, which was originally stated in terms of minutes in the Mountain Goat Cycles example, is restated below in terms of hours for easier interpretation:

	Mountain Pannier	Touring Pannier
Contribution margin per unit of the constrained resource (in minutes). . .	$7.50 per minute × 60 minutes per hour	$12.00 per minute × 60 minutes per hour
Contribution margin per unit of the constrained resource (in hours) . . .	= $450 per hour	= $720 per hour

So what is the value of relaxing the constraint—the time on the stitching machine? The manager should first ask, "What would I do with additional capacity at the bottleneck if it were available?" If the time were to be used to make additional mountain panniers, it would be worth $450 per hour. If the time were to be used to make additional touring panniers, it would be worth $720 per hour. In this latter case, the company should be willing to pay an overtime *premium* to the stitching machine operator of up to $720 per hour! Suppose, for example, that the stitching machine operator is paid $20 per hour during normal working hours and time-and-a-half, or $30 per hour, for overtime. In this case, the premium for overtime is only $10 per hour, whereas in principle, the company should be willing to pay a premium of up to $720 per hour. The difference between what the company should be willing to pay as a premium, $720 per hour, and what it would actually have to pay, $10 per hour, is pure profit of $710 per hour.

To reinforce this concept, suppose that there are only unfilled orders for the mountain pannier. How much would it be worth to the company to run the stitching machine overtime in this situation? Because the additional capacity would be used to make the mountain pannier, the value of that additional capacity would drop to $7.50 per minute or $450 per hour. Nevertheless, the value of relaxing the constraint would still be quite high and the company should be willing to pay an overtime premium of up to $450 per hour.

These calculations indicate that managers should pay great attention to the bottleneck operation. If a bottleneck machine breaks down or is ineffectively utilized, the losses to the company can be quite large. In our example, for every minute the stitching machine is down due to breakdowns or setups, the company loses between $7.50 and $12.00.[2] The losses on an hourly basis are between $450 and $720! In contrast, there is no such loss of contribution margin if time is lost on a machine that is not a bottleneck—such machines have excess capacity anyway.

The implications are clear. Managers should focus much of their attention on managing the bottleneck. As we have discussed, managers should emphasize products that most profitably utilize the constrained resource. They should also make sure that products are processed smoothly through the bottleneck, with minimal lost time due to breakdowns and setups. And they should try to find ways to increase the capacity at the bottleneck.

The capacity of a bottleneck can be effectively increased in a number of ways, including:

- Working overtime on the bottleneck.
- Subcontracting some of the processing that would be done at the bottleneck.
- Investing in additional machines at the bottleneck.
- Shifting workers from processes that are not bottlenecks to the process that is the bottleneck.
- Focusing business process improvement efforts on the bottleneck.
- Reducing defective units. Each defective unit that is processed through the bottleneck and subsequently scrapped takes the place of a good unit that could have been sold.

The last three methods of increasing the capacity of the bottleneck are particularly attractive because they are essentially free and may even yield additional cost savings.

CONCEPT CHECK

7.   When a company has a constraint and wishes to maximize profits, it should favor the products that have the highest
     a. Gross margin per unit.
     b. Gross margin per unit of the constraining resource.
     c. Contribution margin per unit.
     d. Contribution margin per unit of the constraining resource.

---

[2]Setups are required when production switches from one product to another. For example, consider a company that makes automobile side panels. The panels are painted before shipping them to an automobile manufacturer for final assembly. The customer might require 100 blue panels, 50 black panels, and 20 yellow panels. Each time the color is changed, the painting equipment must be purged of the old paint color, cleaned with solvents, and refilled with the new paint color. This takes time. In fact, some equipment may require such lengthy and frequent setups that it is unavailable for actual production more often than not.

Boeing Is Constrained by a Supplier

Boeing Co. had to delay delivery of its model 777 airplanes to **Emirates** airline because the German supplier **Sell GmbH** could not provide the equipment for cooking galleys to Boeing on time. The production bottleneck forced Emirates to repeatedly postpone its planned expansion into the U.S. west coast. It also forced Boeing to accept payment delays for airplanes that sell for more than $200 million apiece. In response, Sell GmbH hired 250 more employees and invested millions of euros in new machine tools and factory space to expand its production capacity.

Source: Daniel Michaels and J. Lynn Lunsford, "Lack of Seats, Galleys Stalls Boeing, Airbus," *The Wall Street Journal,* August 8, 2008, pp. B1 and B4.

JOINT PRODUCT COSTS AND THE CONTRIBUTION APPROACH

In some industries, a number of end products are produced from a single raw material input. For example, in the petroleum refining industry a large number of products are extracted from crude oil, including gasoline, jet fuel, home heating oil, lubricants, asphalt, and various organic chemicals. Another example is provided by the Santa Maria Wool Cooperative of New Mexico. The company buys raw wool from local sheepherders, separates the wool into three grades—coarse, fine, and superfine—and then dyes the wool using traditional methods that rely on pigments from local materials. Exhibit 10–7 contains a diagram of the production process.

At Santa Maria Wool Cooperative, coarse wool, fine wool, and superfine wool are produced from one input—raw wool. Two or more products that are produced from a common input are known as **joint products**. The **split-off point** is the point in the manufacturing process at which the joint products can be recognized as separate products. This does not occur at Santa Maria Wool Cooperative until the raw wool has gone through the separating process. The term **joint cost** is used to describe the costs incurred up to the split-off point. At Santa Maria Wool Cooperative, the joint costs are the $200,000 cost of the raw wool and the $40,000 cost of separating the wool. The undyed wool is called an *intermediate product* because it is not finished at this point. Nevertheless, a market does exist for undyed wool—although at a significantly lower price than finished, dyed wool.

> **LEARNING OBJECTIVE 10–7**
>
> Prepare an analysis showing whether joint products should be sold at the split-off point or processed further.

The Pitfalls of Allocation

Joint costs are common costs that are incurred to simultaneously produce a variety of end products. These joint costs are often allocated among the different products at the split-off point. A typical approach is to allocate the joint costs according to the relative sales value of the end products.

EXHIBIT 10–7 Santa Maria Wool Cooperative

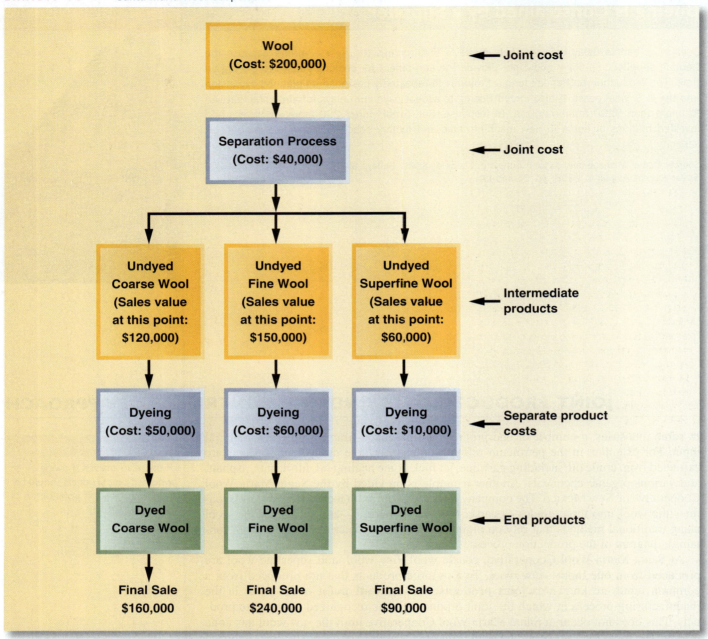

Although allocation of joint product costs is needed for some purposes, such as balance sheet inventory valuation, allocations of this kind are extremely misleading for decision making. The In Business box "Getting It All Wrong" (see page 481) illustrates an incorrect decision that resulted from using such an allocated joint cost. You should stop now and read that box before proceeding further.

Sell or Process Further Decisions

Joint costs are irrelevant in decisions regarding what to do with a product from the split-off point forward. Once the split-off point is reached, the joint costs have already been incurred

Getting It All Wrong

IN BUSINESS

A company located on the Gulf of Mexico produces soap products. Its six main soap product lines are produced from common inputs. Joint product costs up to the split-off point constitute the bulk of the production costs for all six product lines. These joint product costs are allocated to the six product lines on the basis of the relative sales value of each line at the split-off point.

A waste product results from the production of the six main product lines. The company loaded the waste onto barges and dumped it into the Gulf of Mexico because the waste was thought to have no commercial value. The dumping was stopped, however, when the company's research division discovered that with some further processing the waste could be sold as a fertilizer ingredient. The further processing costs $175,000 per year. The waste was then sold to fertilizer manufacturers for $300,000.

The accountants responsible for allocating manufacturing costs included the sales value of the waste product along with the sales value of the six main product lines in their allocation of the joint product costs at the split-off point. This allocation resulted in the waste product being allocated $150,000 in joint product cost. This $150,000 allocation, when added to the further processing costs of $175,000 for the waste, made it appear that the waste product was unprofitable—as shown in the table below. When presented with this analysis, the company's management decided that further processing of the waste should be stopped. The company went back to dumping the waste in the Gulf.

Sales value of the waste product after further processing	$300,000
Less costs assigned to the waste product	325,000
Net loss.	$ (25,000)

and nothing can be done to avoid them. Furthermore, even if the product were disposed of in a landfill without any further processing, all of the joint costs must be incurred to obtain the other products that come out of the joint process. None of the joint costs are avoidable by disposing of any one of the products that emerge from the split-off point. Therefore, none of the joint costs are economically attributable to any one of the intermediate or end products. The joint costs are a common cost of all of the intermediate and end products and should not be allocated to them for purposes of making decisions about the individual products. In the case of the soap company in the accompanying In Business box "Getting It All Wrong," the $150,000 in allocated joint costs should not have influenced what was done with the waste product from the split-off point forward. Even ignoring the negative environmental impact of dumping the waste in the Gulf of Mexico, a correct analysis would have shown that the company was making money by further processing the waste into a fertilizer ingredient. The analysis should have been done as follows:

	Dump in Gulf	Process Further
Sales value of fertilizer ingredient.	0	$300,000
Additional processing costs	0	175,000
Contribution margin	0	$125,000
Advantage of processing further.		$125,000

Decisions of this type are known as **sell or process further decisions**. It is profitable to continue processing a joint product after the split-off point *so long as the incremental revenue from such processing exceeds the incremental processing cost incurred after the split-off point.* Joint costs that have already been incurred up to the split-off point are always irrelevant in decisions concerning what to do from the split-off point forward.

To provide a detailed example of the sell or process further decision, return to the data for Santa Maria Wool Cooperative in Exhibit 10–7. We can answer several important questions using this data. First, is the company making money if it runs the entire process from beginning to end? Assuming there are no costs other than those displayed in Exhibit 10–7, the company is indeed making money as follows:

Analysis of the profitability of the overall operation:		
Combined final sales value ($160,000 + $240,000 + $90,000) . . .		$490,000
Less costs of producing the end products:		
Cost of wool	$200,000	
Cost of separating wool	40,000	
Combined costs of dyeing ($50,000 + $60,000 + $10,000) . . .	120,000	360,000
Profit		$130,000

Note that the joint costs of buying the wool and separating the wool *are* relevant when considering the profitability of the entire operation. This is because these joint costs *could* be avoided if the entire operation were shut down. However, these joint costs are *not* relevant when considering the profitability of any one product. As long as the process is being run to make the other products, no additional joint costs are incurred to make the specific product in question.

Even though the company is making money overall, it may be losing money on one or more of the products. If the company buys wool and runs the separation process, it will get all three intermediate products. Nothing can be done about that. However, each of these products can be sold *as is* without further processing. It may be that the company would be better off selling one or more of the products prior to dyeing to avoid the dyeing costs. The appropriate way to make this choice is to compare the incremental revenues to the incremental costs from further processing as follows:

Analysis of sell or process further:	**Coarse Wool**	**Fine Wool**	**Superfine Wool**
Final sales value after further processing	$160,000	$240,000	$90,000
Less sales value at the split-off point	120,000	150,000	60,000
Incremental revenue from further processing	40,000	90,000	30,000
Less cost of further processing (dyeing)	50,000	60,000	10,000
Profit (loss) from further processing	$ (10,000)	$ 30,000	$20,000

As this analysis shows, the company would be better off selling the undyed coarse wool as is rather than processing it further. The other two products should be processed further and dyed before selling them.

Note that the joint costs of the wool ($200,000) and of the wool separation process ($40,000) play no role in the decision to sell or further process the intermediate products. These joint costs are relevant in a decision of whether to buy wool and to run the wool separation process, but they are not relevant in decisions about what to do with the intermediate products once they have been separated.

For each end product, use the following three steps to make sell or process further decisions:

Step 1: Calculate the sales value if processed further minus the sales value at the split-off point.

Step 2: Determine the cost of further processing beyond the split-off point.

Step 3: Take the amount in step 1 and subtract from it the amount in step 2. If the result is a positive number, then choose to process further. If it is a negative number, then choose to sell at the split-off point.

While you may need to add additional steps when solving complex problems, these three steps will help organize your analysis.

CONCEPT CHECK

8. It is profitable to continue processing a joint product after the split-off point so long as
   a. The incremental revenue from such processing exceeds the incremental processing costs incurred after the split-off point.
   b. The incremental revenue from such processing exceeds the incremental processing costs incurred before the split-off point.
   c. The incremental revenue from such processing exceeds the allocated joint costs attributable to the product.
   d. The incremental revenue from such processing exceeds the sum of the allocated joint costs attributable to the product and the incremental processing costs incurred after the split-off point.

SUMMARY

LO10–1 Identify relevant and irrelevant costs and benefits in a decision.

Every decision involves a choice from among at least two alternatives. Only those costs and benefits that differ in total between the alternatives are relevant; costs and benefits that are the same for all alternatives are not affected by the decision and can be ignored. Only future costs that differ between alternatives are relevant. Sunk costs are always irrelevant.

LO10–2 Prepare an analysis showing whether a product line or other business segment should be added or dropped.

A decision of whether a product line or other segment should be dropped should focus on the differences in the costs and benefits between dropping or retaining the product line or segment. Caution should be exercised when using reports in which common fixed costs have been allocated among segments. If these common fixed costs are unaffected by the decision of whether to add or drop the segment, they are irrelevant and should be removed before determining the real profitability of a segment.

LO10–3 Prepare a make or buy analysis.

When deciding whether to make or buy a component, focus on the costs and benefits that differ between those two alternatives. As in other decisions, sunk costs—such as the depreciation on old equipment—should be ignored. Future costs that do not differ between alternatives—such as allocations of common fixed costs like general overhead—should be ignored.

LO10–4 Prepare an analysis showing whether a special order should be accepted.

When deciding whether to accept or reject a special order, focus on the benefits and costs that differ between those two alternatives. Specifically, a special order should be accepted when the incremental revenue from the sale exceeds the incremental cost. As always, sunk costs and future costs that do not differ between the alternatives are irrelevant.

LO10–5 Determine the most profitable use of a constrained resource.

When demand for a company's products and services exceeds its ability to supply them, the company has a bottleneck. The bottleneck, whether it is a particular material, skilled labor, or a specific machine, is a constrained resource. Since the company is unable to make everything it could sell, managers must decide what the company will make and what the company will not make. In this situation, the profitability of a product is best measured by its contribution margin per unit of the constrained resource. The products with the highest contribution margin per unit of the constrained resource should be favored.

LO10–6 Determine the value of obtaining more of the constrained resource.

Managers should focus their attention on effectively managing the constraint. This involves making the most profitable use of the constrained resource and increasing the amount of the constrained resource that is available. The value of relaxing the constraint is determined by the contribution margin per unit of the constrained resource for the work that would be done if more of the resource were available.

LO10–7 Prepare an analysis showing whether joint products should be sold at the split-off point or processed further.

Managers should recommend further processing of an intermediate product so long as the incremental revenue from such processing exceeds the incremental processing cost incurred after the split-off point. Joint costs are irrelevant in decisions regarding what to do with a product from the split-off point forward. Once the split-off point is reached, the joint costs have already been incurred and nothing can be done to avoid them.

GUIDANCE ANSWER TO DECISION POINT

Vice President of Production (p. 471)

The annual rental cost for the machinery is an *avoidable* fixed cost. An avoidable fixed cost is a cost that can be eliminated in whole or in part by choosing one alternative over another. Because the annual rental cost of the machinery can be avoided if the company purchases the components from an outside supplier, it is relevant to this decision.

GUIDANCE ANSWERS TO CONCEPT CHECKS

1. **Choices a and d.** Sunk costs are always irrelevant. Fixed costs can be relevant costs.
2. **Choice a.** The cost of the airline ticket to Telluride is a sunk cost; it has already been incurred and the ticket is nonrefundable.
3. **Choice b.** The cost of going to Stowe would be $1,000 [$400 + ($150 per night × 4 nights)] whereas the incremental cost of going to Telluride would be $1,020 [$300 + ($180 per night × 4 nights)]. Note that the $450 cost of flying to Telluride is irrelevant at this point because it is a sunk cost. The analysis favors Stowe by $20.
4. **Choices c and d.** Common fixed costs should not be allocated to segments when making decisions. Doing so will understate the true profitability of each segment.
5. **Choice b.** The minimum price would be $15 direct materials + $5 direct labor + $6 variable manufacturing overhead = $26.
6. **Choice c.** The special order requires 7,500 minutes (5,000 units × 1.5 minutes per unit). Accepting the special order would require sacrificing 3,750 units (7,500 minutes ÷ 2 minutes per unit) of the regular product. The forgone contribution margin would be 3,750 units × $20 per unit = $75,000.
7. **Choice d.** Gross margin includes fixed costs that are not relevant to this situation. The contribution margin per unit overlooks the constraining resource.
8. **Choice a.** Any costs incurred before the split-off point are not relevant to sell or process further decisions.

REVIEW PROBLEM: RELEVANT COSTS

Charter Sports Equipment manufactures round, rectangular, and octagonal trampolines. Sales and expense data for the past month follow:

| | Total | Trampoline | | |
		Round	Rectangular	Octagonal
Sales........................	$1,000,000	$140,000	$500,000	$360,000
Variable expenses	410,000	60,000	200,000	150,000
Contribution margin	590,000	80,000	300,000	210,000
Fixed expenses:				
Advertising—traceable	216,000	41,000	110,000	65,000
Depreciation of special equipment ..	95,000	20,000	40,000	35,000
Line supervisors' salaries	19,000	6,000	7,000	6,000
General factory overhead*	200,000	28,000	100,000	72,000
Total fixed expenses..............	530,000	95,000	257,000	178,000
Net operating income (loss)	$ 60,000	$ (15,000)	$ 43,000	$ 32,000

*A common fixed cost that is allocated on the basis of sales dollars.

Management is concerned about the continued losses shown by the round trampolines and wants a recommendation as to whether or not the line should be discontinued. The special equipment used to produce the trampolines has no resale value. If the round trampoline model is dropped, the two line supervisors assigned to the model would be discharged.

Required:

1. Should production and sale of the round trampolines be discontinued? The company has no other use for the capacity now being used to produce the round trampolines. Show computations to support your answer.

2. Recast the above data in a format that would be more useful to management in assessing the profitability of the various product lines.

Solution to Review Problem

1. No, production and sale of the round trampolines should not be discontinued. Computations to support this answer follow:

Contribution margin lost if the round trampolines are discontinued		$(80,000)
Less fixed expenses that can be avoided:		
Advertising—traceable	$41,000	
Line supervisors' salaries	6,000	47,000
Decrease in net operating income for the company as a whole....		$(33,000)

The depreciation of the special equipment is a sunk cost, and therefore, it is not relevant to the decision. The general factory overhead is allocated and will presumably continue regardless of whether or not the round trampolines are discontinued; thus, it is not relevant.

2. If management wants a clearer picture of the profitability of the segments, the general factory overhead should not be allocated. It is a common cost and, therefore, should be deducted from the total product-line segment margin. A more useful income statement format would be as follows:

			Trampoline	
	Total	Round	Rectangular	Octagonal
Sales.	$1,000,000	$140,000	$500,000	$360,000
Variable expenses	410,000	60,000	200,000	150,000
Contribution margin	590,000	80,000	300,000	210,000
Traceable fixed expenses:				
Advertising—traceable	216,000	41,000	110,000	65,000
Depreciation of special equipment . . .	95,000	20,000	40,000	35,000
Line supervisors' salaries	19,000	6,000	7,000	6,000
Total traceable fixed expenses	330,000	67,000	157,000	106,000
Product-line segment margin	260,000	$ 13,000	$143,000	$104,000
Common fixed expenses	200,000			
Net operating income	$ 60,000			

GLOSSARY

Avoidable cost A cost that can be eliminated by choosing one alternative over another in a decision. This term is synonymous with *differential cost* and *relevant cost*. (p. 458)

Bottleneck A machine or some other part of a process that limits the total output of the entire system. (p. 474)

Constraint A limitation under which a company must operate, such as limited available machine time or raw materials, that restricts the company's ability to satisfy demand. (p. 474)

Differential cost A difference in cost between any two alternatives. (p. 458)

Differential revenue A difference in revenue between any two alternatives. (p. 458)

Joint costs Costs that are incurred up to the split-off point in a process that produces joint products. (p. 479)

Joint products Two or more products that are produced from a common input. (p. 479)

Make or buy decision A decision concerning whether an item should be produced internally or purchased from an outside supplier. (p. 469)

Opportunity cost The potential benefit that is given up when one alternative is selected over another. (p. 459)

Relaxing (or elevating) the constraint An action that increases the amount of a constrained resource. Equivalently, an action that increases the capacity of the bottleneck. (p. 477)

Relevant benefit A benefit that differs between alternatives in a decision. *Differential revenue* is a *relevant benefit*. (p. 458)

Relevant cost A difference in cost between any two alternatives. Synonyms are *avoidable cost, differential cost,* and *incremental cost.* (p. 458)

Sell or process further decision A decision as to whether a joint product should be sold at the split-off point or sold after further processing. (p. 482)

Special order A one-time order that is not considered part of the company's normal ongoing business. (p. 472)

Split-off point That point in the manufacturing process where some or all of the joint products can be recognized as individual products. (p. 479)

Sunk cost Any cost that has already been incurred and that cannot be changed by any decision made now or in the future. (p. 458)

Vertical integration The involvement by a company in more than one of the activities in the entire value chain from development through production, distribution, sales, and after-sales service. (p. 469)

QUESTIONS

10–1 What is a *relevant cost?*

10–2 Define the following terms: *incremental cost, opportunity cost,* and *sunk cost.*

10–3 Are variable costs always relevant costs? Explain.

10–4 "Sunk costs are easy to spot—they're the fixed costs associated with a decision." Do you agree? Explain.

10–5 "Variable costs and differential costs mean the same thing." Do you agree? Explain.

10–6 "All future costs are relevant in decision making." Do you agree? Why?

10–7 Prentice Company is considering dropping one of its product lines. What costs of the product line would be relevant to this decision? What costs would be irrelevant?

10–8 "If a product is generating a loss, then it should be discontinued." Do you agree? Explain.

10–9   What is the danger in allocating common fixed costs among products or other segments of an organization?

10–10 How does opportunity cost enter into a make or buy decision?

10–11 Give at least four examples of possible constraints.

10–12 How will relating product contribution margins to the amount of the constrained resource they consume help a company maximize its profits?

10–13 Define the following terms: *joint products, joint costs,* and *split-off point.*

10–14 From a decision-making point of view, should joint costs be allocated among joint products?

10–15 What guideline should be used in determining whether a joint product should be sold at the split-off point or processed further?

10–16 Airlines sometimes offer reduced rates during certain times of the week to members of a businessperson's family if they accompany him or her on trips. How does the concept of relevant costs enter into the decision by the airline to offer reduced rates of this type?

Multiple-choice questions are available in the *Connect Library*.

APPLYING EXCEL

LO10–7

Available with McGraw-Hill's *Connect Accounting*.

The Excel worksheet form that appears below is to be used to recreate the example in the text on pages 479–482. Download the workbook containing this form in the *Connect Library*. On the website you will also receive instructions about how to use this worksheet form.

	A	B	C	D	E
1	Chapter 10: Applying Excel				
2					
3	Data				
4	Exhibit 10-7 Santa Maria Wool Cooperative				
5	Cost of wool	$200,000			
6	Cost of separation process	$40,000			
7	Sales value of intermediate products at split-off point:				
8	Undyed coarse wool	$120,000			
9	Undyed fine wool	$150,000			
10	Undyed superfine wool	$60,000			
11	Costs of further processing (dyeing) intermediate products:				
12	Undyed coarse wool	$50,000			
13	Undyed fine wool	$60,000			
14	Undyed superfine wool	$10,000			
15	Sales value of end products:				
16	Dyed coarse wool	$160,000			
17	Dyed fine wool	$240,000			
18	Dyed superfine wool	$90,000			
19					
20	*Enter a formula into each of the cells marked with a ? below*				
21	**Example: Joint Product Costs and the Contribution Approach**				
22					
23	*Analysis of the profitability of the overall operation:*				
24	Combined final sales value		?		
25	Less costs of producing the end products:				
26	Cost of wool	?			
27	Cost of separation process	?			
28	Combined costs of dyeing	?	?		
29	Profit		?		
30					
31	*Analysis of sell or process further:*				
32		Coarse	Fine	Superfine	
33		Wool	Wool	Wool	
34	Final sales value after further processing	?	?	?	
35	Less sales value at the split-off point	?	?	?	
36	Incremental revenue from further processing	?	?	?	
37	Less cost of further processing (dyeing)	?	?	?	
38	Profit (loss) from further processing	?	?	?	
39					

⏮ ◀ ▶ ⏭   Chapter 10 Form / Filled in Chapter 10 Form / Chapter

You should proceed to the requirements on the next page only after completing your worksheet.

Required:

1. Check your worksheet by changing the cost of further processing undyed coarse wool in cell B12 to $30,000. The overall profit from processing all intermediate products into final products should now be $150,000 and the profit from further processing coarse wool should now be $10,000. If you do not get these answers, find the errors in your worksheet and correct them.

    How should operations change in response to this change in cost?

2. In industries that process joint products, the costs of the raw materials inputs and the sales values of intermediate and final products are often volatile. Change the data area of your worksheet to match the following:

Data	
Exhibit 10–7 Santa Maria Wool Cooperative	
Cost of wool	$290,000
Cost of separation process.	$40,000
Sales value of intermediate products at split-off point:	
Undyed coarse wool	$100,000
Undyed fine wool	$110,000
Undyed superfine wool	$90,000
Costs of further processing (dyeing) intermediate products:	
Undyed coarse wool	$50,000
Undyed fine wool	$60,000
Undyed superfine wool	$10,000
Sales value of end products:	
Dyed coarse wool	$180,000
Dyed fine wool.	$210,000
Dyed superfine wool	$90,000

a. What is the overall profit if all intermediate products are processed into final products?
b. What is the profit from further processing each of the intermediate products?
c. With these new costs and selling prices, what recommendations would you make concerning the company's operations? If your recommendation is followed, what should be the overall profit of the company?

THE FOUNDATIONAL 15

Available with McGraw-Hill's *Connect Accounting*.

LO10–2, LO10–3, LO10–4, LO10–5, LO10–6

Cane Company manufactures two products called Alpha and Beta that sell for $120 and $80, respectively. Each product uses only one type of raw material that costs $6 per pound. The company has the capacity to annually produce 100,000 units of each product. Its unit costs for each product at this level of activity are given below:

	Alpha	Beta
Direct materials.	$ 30	$12
Direct labor	20	15
Variable manufacturing overhead	7	5
Traceable fixed manufacturing overhead	16	18
Variable selling expenses	12	8
Common fixed expenses	15	10
Total cost per unit	$100	$68

The company considers its traceable fixed manufacturing overhead to be avoidable, whereas its common fixed expenses are deemed unavoidable and have been allocated to products based on sales dollars.

Required:

(Answer each question independently unless instructed otherwise.)

1. What is the total amount of traceable fixed manufacturing overhead for the Alpha product line and for the Beta product line?

2. What is the company's total amount of common fixed expenses?

3. Assume that Cane expects to produce and sell 80,000 Alphas during the current year. One of Cane's sales representatives has found a new customer that is willing to buy 10,000 additional Alphas for a price of $80 per unit. If Cane accepts the customer's offer, how much will its profits increase or decrease?

4. Assume that Cane expects to produce and sell 90,000 Betas during the current year. One of Cane's sales representatives has found a new customer that is willing to buy 5,000 additional Betas for a price of $39 per unit. If Cane accepts the customer's offer, how much will its profits increase or decrease?

5. Assume that Cane expects to produce and sell 95,000 Alphas during the current year. One of Cane's sales representatives has found a new customer that is willing to buy 10,000 additional Alphas for a price of $80 per unit. If Cane accepts the customer's offer, it will decrease Alpha sales to regular customers by 5,000 units. Should Cane accept this special order?

6. Assume that Cane normally produces and sells 90,000 Betas per year. If Cane discontinues the Beta product line, how much will profits increase or decrease?

7. Assume that Cane normally produces and sells 40,000 Betas per year. If Cane discontinues the Beta product line, how much will profits increase or decrease?

8. Assume that Cane normally produces and sells 60,000 Betas and 80,000 Alphas per year. If Cane discontinues the Beta product line, its sales representatives could increase sales of Alpha by 15,000 units. If Cane discontinues the Beta product line, how much would profits increase or decrease?

9. Assume that Cane expects to produce and sell 80,000 Alphas during the current year. A supplier has offered to manufacture and deliver 80,000 Alphas to Cane for a price of $80 per unit. If Cane buys 80,000 units from the supplier instead of making those units, how much will profits increase or decrease?

10. Assume that Cane expects to produce and sell 50,000 Alphas during the current year. A supplier has offered to manufacture and deliver 50,000 Alphas to Cane for a price of $80 per unit. If Cane buys 50,000 units from the supplier instead of making those units, how much will profits increase or decrease?

11. How many pounds of raw material are needed to make one unit of Alpha and one unit of Beta?

12. What contribution margin per pound of raw material is earned by Alpha and Beta?

13. Assume that Cane's customers would buy a maximum of 80,000 units of Alpha and 60,000 units of Beta. Also assume that the company's raw material available for production is limited to 160,000 pounds. How many units of each product should Cane produce to maximize its profits?

14. If Cane follows your recommendation in requirement 13, what total contribution margin will it earn?

15. If Cane uses its 160,000 pounds of raw materials as you recommended in requirement 13, up to how much should it be willing to pay per pound for additional raw materials?

EXERCISES

All applicable exercises are available with McGraw-Hill's _Connect Accounting_.

EXERCISE 10–1   Identifying Relevant Costs [LO10–1]
A number of costs are listed below that may be relevant in decisions faced by the management of Svahn, AB, a Swedish manufacturer of sailing yachts:

Item	Case 1 Relevant	Case 1 Not Relevant	Case 2 Relevant	Case 2 Not Relevant
a. Sales revenue.				
b. Direct materials.				
c. Direct labor				
d. Variable manufacturing overhead				
e. Depreciation—Model B100 machine				
f. Book value—Model B100 machine				
g. Disposal value—Model B100 machine				
h. Market value—Model B300 machine (cost) . . .				
i. Fixed manufacturing overhead (general)				
j. Variable selling expense				
k. Fixed selling expense				
l. General administrative overhead				

Required:

Copy the information above onto your answer sheet and place an X in the appropriate column to indicate whether each item is relevant or not relevant in the following situations. Requirement 1 relates to Case 1 above, and requirement 2 relates to Case 2.

1. The company chronically has no idle capacity and the old Model B100 machine is the company's constraint. Management is considering purchasing a Model B300 machine to use in addition to the company's present Model B100 machine. The old Model B100 machine will continue to be used to capacity as before, with the new Model B300 machine being used to expand production. This will increase the company's production and sales. The increase in volume will be large enough to require increases in fixed selling expenses and in general administrative overhead, but not in the fixed manufacturing overhead.

2. The old Model B100 machine is not the company's constraint, but management is considering replacing it with a new Model B300 machine because of the potential savings in direct materials with the new machine. The Model B100 machine would be sold. This change will have no effect on production or sales, other than some savings in direct materials costs due to less waste.

EXERCISE 10–2 Dropping or Retaining a Segment [LO10–2]

The Regal Cycle Company manufactures three types of bicycles—a dirt bike, a mountain bike, and a racing bike. Data on sales and expenses for the past quarter follow:

	Total	Dirt Bikes	Mountain Bikes	Racing Bikes
Sales.	$300,000	$90,000	$150,000	$60,000
Variable manufacturing and selling expenses . .	120,000	27,000	60,000	33,000
Contribution margin	180,000	63,000	90,000	27,000
Fixed expenses:				
Advertising, traceable	30,000	10,000	14,000	6,000
Depreciation of special equipment	23,000	6,000	9,000	8,000
Salaries of product-line managers	35,000	12,000	13,000	10,000
Allocated common fixed expenses*	60,000	18,000	30,000	12,000
Total fixed expenses	148,000	46,000	66,000	36,000
Net operating income (loss)	$ 32,000	$17,000	$ 24,000	$ (9,000)

*Allocated on the basis of sales dollars.

Management is concerned about the continued losses shown by the racing bikes and wants a recommendation as to whether or not the line should be discontinued. The special equipment used to produce racing bikes has no resale value and does not wear out.

Required:

1. Should production and sale of the racing bikes be discontinued? Explain. Show computations to support your answer.
2. Recast the above data in a format that would be more usable to management in assessing the long-run profitability of the various product lines.

EXERCISE 10–3 Make or Buy a Component [LO10–3]

Troy Engines, Ltd., manufactures a variety of engines for use in heavy equipment. The company has always produced all of the necessary parts for its engines, including all of the carburetors. An outside supplier has offered to sell one type of carburetor to Troy Engines, Ltd., for a cost of $35 per unit. To evaluate this offer, Troy Engines, Ltd., has gathered the following information relating to its own cost of producing the carburetor internally:

	Per Unit	15,000 Units per Year
Direct materials.	$14	$210,000
Direct labor	10	150,000
Variable manufacturing overhead	3	45,000
Fixed manufacturing overhead, traceable	6*	90,000
Fixed manufacturing overhead, allocated	9	135,000
Total cost	$42	$630,000

*One-third supervisory salaries; two-thirds depreciation of special equipment (no resale value).

Required:
1.   Assuming that the company has no alternative use for the facilities that are now being used to produce the carburetors, should the outside supplier's offer be accepted? Show all computations.
2.   Suppose that if the carburetors were purchased, Troy Engines, Ltd., could use the freed capacity to launch a new product. The segment margin of the new product would be $150,000 per year. Should Troy Engines, Ltd., accept the offer to buy the carburetors for $35 per unit? Show all computations.

EXERCISE 10–4   Evaluating a Special Order [LO10–4]

Imperial Jewelers is considering a special order for 20 handcrafted gold bracelets to be given as gifts to members of a wedding party. The normal selling price of a gold bracelet is $189.95 and its unit product cost is $149.00 as shown below:

Special price = $139.95

Direct materials.	$ 84.00
Direct labor	45.00
Manufacturing overhead.	20.00
Unit product cost.	$149.00

Most of the manufacturing overhead is fixed and unaffected by variations in how much jewelry is produced in any given period. However, $4.00 of the overhead is variable with respect to the number of bracelets produced. The customer who is interested in the special bracelet order would like special filigree applied to the bracelets. This filigree would require additional materials costing $2.00 per bracelet and would also require acquisition of a special tool costing $250 that would have no other use once the special order is completed. This order would have no effect on the company's regular sales and the order could be fulfilled using the company's existing capacity without affecting any other order.

Required:
What effect would accepting this order have on the company's net operating income if a special price of $169.95 per bracelet is offered for this order? Should the special order be accepted at this price?

EXERCISE 10–5   Utilizing a Constrained Resource [LO10–5]

Outdoor Luggage Inc. makes high-end hard-sided luggage for sports equipment. Data concerning three of the company's most popular models appear below.

	Ski Guard	Golf Guard	Fishing Guard
Selling price per unit.	$200	$300	$255
Variable cost per unit	$60	$140	$55
Plastic injection molding machine processing			
time required to produce one unit	2 minutes	5 minutes	4 minutes
Pounds of plastic pellets per unit	7 pounds	4 pounds	8 pounds

Required:
1.   The total time available on the plastic injection molding machine is the constraint in the production process. Which product would be the most profitable use of this constraint? Which product would be the least profitable use of this constraint?
2.   A severe shortage of plastic pellets has required the company to cut back its production so much that the plastic injection molding machine is no longer the bottleneck. Instead, the constraint is the total available pounds of plastic pellets. Which product would be the most profitable use of this constraint? Which product would be the least profitable use of this constraint?
3.   Which product has the largest contribution margin per unit? Why wouldn't this product be the most profitable use of the constrained resource in either case?

EXERCISE 10–6   Managing a Constrained Resource [LO10–6]

Portsmouth Company makes fine colonial reproduction furniture. Upholstered furniture is one of its major product lines and the bottleneck on this production line is time in the upholstery shop. Upholstering is a craft that takes years of experience to master and the demand for upholstered furniture far exceeds the company's capacity in the upholstering shop. Information concerning three of the company's upholstered chairs appears below:

	Recliner	Sofa	Love Seat
Selling price per unit.	$1,400	$1,800	$1,500
Variable cost per unit	$800	$1,200	$1,000
Upholstery shop time required to produce one unit	8 hours	10 hours	5 hours

Required:

1. More time could be made available in the upholstery shop by asking the employees who work in this shop to work overtime. Assuming that this extra time would be used to produce sofas, up to how much should the company be willing to pay per hour to keep the upholstery shop open after normal working hours?

2. A small nearby upholstering company has offered to upholster furniture for Portsmouth at a fixed charge of $45 per hour. The management of Portsmouth is confident that this upholstering company's work is high quality and their craftsmen should be able to work about as quickly as Portsmouth's own craftsmen on the simpler upholstering jobs such as the love seat. Should management accept this offer? Explain.

EXERCISE 10–7   Sell or Process Further [LO10–7]

Additional processing costs for A = $57,000 and B = $102,000

Dorsey Company manufactures three products from a common input in a joint processing operation. Joint processing costs up to the split-off point total $350,000 per quarter. The company allocates these costs to the joint products on the basis of their relative sales value at the split-off point. Unit selling prices and total output at the split-off point are as follows:

Product	Selling Price	Quarterly Output
A.............	$16 per pound	15,000 pounds
B.............	$8 per pound	20,000 pounds
C.............	$25 per gallon	4,000 gallons

Each product can be processed further after the split-off point. Additional processing requires no special facilities. The additional processing costs (per quarter) and unit selling prices after further processing are given below:

Product	Additional Processing Costs	Selling Price
A............	$63,000	$20 per pound
B............	$80,000	$13 per pound
C............	$36,000	$32 per gallon

Required:

Which product or products should be sold at the split-off point and which product or products should be processed further? Show computations.

EXERCISE 10–8   Utilization of a Constrained Resource [LO10–5, LO10–6]

Barlow Company manufactures three products: A, B, and C. The selling price, variable costs, and contribution margin for one unit of each product follow:

Product C direct material cost per unit = $16

	Product		
	A	B	C
Selling price	$180	$270	$240
Variable expenses:			
Direct materials.........................	24	72	32
Other variable expenses.................	102	90	148
Total variable expenses	126	162	180
Contribution margin	$ 54	$108	$ 60
Contribution margin ratio	30%	40%	25%

The same raw material is used in all three products. Barlow Company has only 5,000 pounds of raw material on hand and will not be able to obtain any more of it for several weeks due to a strike in its supplier's plant. Management is trying to decide which product(s) to concentrate on next week in filling its backlog of orders. The material costs $8 per pound.

Required:

1. Compute the amount of contribution margin that will be obtained per pound of material used in each product.
2. Which orders would you recommend that the company work on next week—the orders for product A, product B, or product C? Show computations.
3. A foreign supplier could furnish Barlow with additional stocks of the raw material at a substantial premium over the usual price. If there is unfilled demand for all three products, what is the highest price that Barlow Company should be willing to pay for an additional pound of materials? Explain.

EXERCISE 10–9   Special Order [LO10–4]

Delta Company produces a single product. The cost of producing and selling a single unit of this product at the company's normal activity level of 60,000 units per year is as follows:

Direct materials.	$5.10
Direct labor	$3.80
Variable manufacturing overhead	$1.00
Fixed manufacturing overhead	$4.20
Variable selling and administrative expense.	$1.50
Fixed selling and administrative expense	$2.40

The normal selling price is $21 per unit. The company's capacity is 75,000 units per year. An order has been received from a mail-order house for 15,000 units at a special price of $14.00 per unit. This order would not affect regular sales.

Required:

1. If the order is accepted, by how much will annual profits be increased or decreased? (The order will not change the company's total fixed costs.)
2. Assume the company has 1,000 units of this product left over from last year that are inferior to the current model. The units must be sold through regular channels at reduced prices. What unit cost is relevant for establishing a minimum selling price for these units? Explain.

EXERCISE 10–10   Make or Buy a Component [LO10–3]

For many years Futura Company has purchased the starters that it installs in its standard line of farm tractors. Due to a reduction in output, the company has idle capacity that could be used to produce the starters. The chief engineer has recommended against this move, however, pointing out that the cost to produce the starters would be greater than the current $8.40 per unit purchase price:

	Per Unit	Total
Direct materials.	$3.10	
Direct labor	2.70	
Supervision.	1.50	$60,000
Depreciation	1.00	$40,000
Variable manufacturing overhead	0.60	
Rent	0.30	$12,000
Total production cost.	$9.20	

A supervisor would have to be hired to oversee production of the starters. However, the company has sufficient idle tools and machinery that no new equipment would have to be purchased. The rent charge above is based on space utilized in the plant. The total rent on the plant is $80,000 per period. Depreciation is due to obsolescence rather than wear and tear.

Required:

Prepare computations showing how much profits will increase or decrease as a result of making the starters.

EXERCISE 10–11   Make or Buy a Component [LO10–3]

Han Products manufactures 30,000 units of part S-6 each year for use on its production line. At this level of activity, the cost per unit for part S-6 is as follows:

Annual rental = $50,000

Direct materials.	$ 3.60
Direct labor	10.00
Variable manufacturing overhead	2.40
Fixed manufacturing overhead	9.00
Total cost per part.	$25.00

An outside supplier has offered to sell 30,000 units of part S-6 each year to Han Products for $21 per part. If Han Products accepts this offer, the facilities now being used to manufacture part S-6 could be rented to another company at an annual rental of $80,000. However, Han Products has determined that two-thirds of the fixed manufacturing overhead being applied to part S-6 would continue even if part S-6 were purchased from the outside supplier.

Required:

Prepare computations showing how much profits will increase or decrease if the outside supplier's offer is accepted.

EXERCISE 10–12   Utilization of a Constrained Resource [LO10–5]

Benoit Company produces three products, A, B, and C. Data concerning the three products follow (per unit):

Direct material cost per unit for product C = $18

	Product		
	A	B	C
Selling price	$80	$56	$70
Variable expenses:			
Direct materials.	24	15	9
Other variable expenses	24	27	40
Total variable expenses	48	42	49
Contribution margin	$32	$14	$21
Contribution margin ratio	40%	25%	30%

Demand for the company's products is very strong, with far more orders each month than the company can produce with the available raw materials. The same material is used in each product. The material costs $3 per pound with a maximum of 5,000 pounds available each month.

Required:

Which orders would you advise the company to accept first, those for A, for B, or for C? Which orders second? Third?

EXERCISE 10–13   Sell or Process Further [LO10–7]

Wexpro, Inc., produces several products from processing 1 ton of clypton, a rare mineral. Material and processing costs total $60,000 per ton, one-fourth of which is allocated to product X15. Seven thousand units of product X15 are produced from each ton of clypton. The units can either be sold at the split-off point for $9 each, or processed further at a total cost of $9,500 and then sold for $12 each.

Cost of further processing = $22,000

Required:

Should product X15 be processed further or sold at the split-off point?

EXERCISE 10–14   Identification of Relevant Costs [LO10–1]

Kristen Lu purchased a used automobile for $8,000 at the beginning of last year and incurred the following operating costs:

Depreciation ($8,000 ÷ 5 years)	$1,600
Insurance	$1,200
Garage rent	$360
Automobile tax and license	$40
Variable operating cost	$0.14 per mile

The variable operating cost consists of gasoline, oil, tires, maintenance, and repairs. Kristen estimates that, at her current rate of usage, the car will have zero resale value in five years, so the annual straight-line depreciation is $1,600. The car is kept in a garage for a monthly fee.

Required:
1. Kristen drove the car 10,000 miles last year. Compute the average cost per mile of owning and operating the car.
2. Kristen is unsure about whether she should use her own car or rent a car to go on an extended cross-country trip for two weeks during spring break. What costs above are relevant in this decision? Explain.
3. Kristen is thinking about buying an expensive sports car to replace the car she bought last year. She would drive the same number of miles regardless of which car she owns and would rent the same parking space. The sports car's variable operating costs would be roughly the same as the variable operating costs of her old car. However, her insurance and automobile tax and license costs would go up. What costs are relevant in estimating the incremental cost of owning the more expensive car? Explain.

EXERCISE 10–15 Dropping or Retaining a Segment [LO10–2]
Thalassines Kataskeves, S.A., of Greece makes marine equipment. The company has been experiencing losses on its bilge pump product line for several years. The most recent quarterly contribution format income statement for the bilge pump product line follows:

TAKE
TWO

Sales = $690,000, Variable expenses are unchanged

Thalassines Kataskeves, S.A. **Income Statement—Bilge Pump** **For the Quarter Ended March 31**		
Sales		$850,000
Variable expenses:		
Variable manufacturing expenses	$330,000	
Sales commissions	42,000	
Shipping	18,000	
Total variable expenses		390,000
Contribution margin		460,000
Fixed expenses:		
Advertising	270,000	
Depreciation of equipment (no resale value)	80,000	
General factory overhead	105,000*	
Salary of product-line manager	32,000	
Insurance on inventories	8,000	
Purchasing department	45,000[†]	
Total fixed expenses		540,000
Net operating loss		$ (80,000)

*Common costs allocated on the basis of machine-hours.
[†]Common costs allocated on the basis of sales dollars.

Discontinuing the bilge pump product line would not affect sales of other product lines and would have no effect on the company's total general factory overhead or total Purchasing Department expenses.

Required:
Would you recommend that the bilge pump product line be discontinued? Support your answer with appropriate computations.

EXERCISE 10–16   Identification of Relevant Costs [LO10–1]

Bill has just returned from a duck hunting trip. He has brought home eight ducks. Bill's friend, John, disapproves of duck hunting, and to discourage Bill from further hunting, John has presented him with the following cost estimate per duck:

Camper and equipment:	
Cost, $12,000; usable for eight seasons; 10 hunting trips per season	$150
Travel expense (pickup truck):	
100 miles at $0.31 per mile (gas, oil, and tires—$0.21 per mile; depreciation and insurance—$0.10 per mile)	31
Shotgun shells (two boxes)	20
Boat:	
Cost, $2,320, usable for eight seasons; 10 hunting trips per season	29
Hunting license:	
Cost, $30 for the season; 10 hunting trips per season	3
Money lost playing poker:	
Loss, $24 (Bill plays poker every weekend)	24
Bottle of whiskey:	
Cost, $15 (used to ward off the cold)	15
Total cost	$272
Cost per duck ($272 ÷ 8 ducks)	$ 34

Required:

1. Assuming that the duck hunting trip Bill has just completed is typical, what costs are relevant to a decision as to whether Bill should go duck hunting again this season?
2. Suppose that Bill gets lucky on his next hunting trip and shoots 10 ducks in the amount of time it took him to shoot 8 ducks on his last trip. How much would it have cost him to shoot the last two ducks? Explain.
3. Which costs are relevant in a decision of whether Bill should give up hunting? Explain.

EXERCISE 10–17   Dropping or Retaining a Segment [LO10–2]

Bed & Bath, a retailing company, has two departments, Hardware and Linens. The company's most recent monthly contribution format income statement follows:

		Department	
	Total	**Hardware**	**Linens**
Sales.	$4,000,000	$3,000,000	$1,000,000
Variable expenses	1,300,000	900,000	400,000
Contribution margin	2,700,000	2,100,000	600,000
Fixed expenses.	2,200,000	1,400,000	800,000
Net operating income (loss)	$ 500,000	$ 700,000	$ (200,000)

A study indicates that $340,000 of the fixed expenses being charged to Linens are sunk costs or allocated costs that will continue even if the Linens Department is dropped. In addition, the elimination of the Linens Department will result in a 10% decrease in the sales of the Hardware Department.

Required:

If the Linens Department is dropped, what will be the effect on the net operating income of the company as a whole?

Alternate problem set is available in the *Connect Library*.

PROBLEMS

All applicable problems are available with McGraw-Hill's *Connect Accounting*.

PROBLEM 10–18A   Relevant Cost Analysis in a Variety of Situations [LO10–2, LO10–3, LO10–4]

Andretti Company has a single product called a Dak. The company normally produces and sells 60,000 Daks each year at a selling price of $32 per unit. The company's unit costs at this level of activity are given below:

Direct materials.	$10.00	
Direct labor	4.50	
Variable manufacturing overhead	2.30	
Fixed manufacturing overhead	5.00	($300,000 total)
Variable selling expenses	1.20	
Fixed selling expenses	3.50	($210,000 total)
Total cost per unit	$26.50	

A number of questions relating to the production and sale of Daks follow. Each question is independent.

Required:

1. Assume that Andretti Company has sufficient capacity to produce 90,000 Daks each year without any increase in fixed manufacturing overhead costs. The company could increase its sales by 25% above the present 60,000 units each year if it were willing to increase the fixed selling expenses by $80,000. Would the increased fixed selling expenses be justified?

2. Assume again that Andretti Company has sufficient capacity to produce 90,000 Daks each year. A customer in a foreign market wants to purchase 20,000 Daks. Import duties on the Daks would be $1.70 per unit, and costs for permits and licenses would be $9,000. The only selling costs that would be associated with the order would be $3.20 per unit shipping cost. Compute the per unit break-even price on this order.

3. The company has 1,000 Daks on hand that have some irregularities and are therefore considered to be "seconds." Due to the irregularities, it will be impossible to sell these units at the normal price through regular distribution channels. What unit cost figure is relevant for setting a minimum selling price? Explain.

4. Due to a strike in its supplier's plant, Andretti Company is unable to purchase more material for the production of Daks. The strike is expected to last for two months. Andretti Company has enough material on hand to operate at 30% of normal levels for the two-month period. As an alternative, Andretti could close its plant down entirely for the two months. If the plant were closed, fixed manufacturing overhead costs would continue at 60% of their normal level during the two-month period and the fixed selling expenses would be reduced by 20%. What would be the impact on profits of closing the plant for the two-month period?

5. An outside manufacturer has offered to produce Daks and ship them directly to Andretti's customers. If Andretti Company accepts this offer, the facilities that it uses to produce Daks would be idle; however, fixed manufacturing overhead costs would be reduced by 75%. Because the outside manufacturer would pay for all shipping costs, the variable selling expenses would be only two-thirds of their present amount. Compute the unit cost that is relevant for comparison to the price quoted by the outside manufacturer.

PROBLEM 10–19A   Dropping or Retaining a Segment [LO10–2]

Jackson County Senior Services is a nonprofit organization devoted to providing essential services to seniors who live in their own homes within the Jackson County area. Three services are provided for seniors—home nursing, Meals On Wheels, and housekeeping. Data on revenue and expenses for the past year follow:

	Total	Home Nursing	Meals On Wheels	House-keeping
Revenues	$900,000	$260,000	$400,000	$240,000
Variable expenses	490,000	120,000	210,000	160,000
Contribution margin	410,000	140,000	190,000	80,000
Fixed expenses:				
Depreciation	68,000	8,000	40,000	20,000
Liability insurance	42,000	20,000	7,000	15,000
Program administrators' salaries	115,000	40,000	38,000	37,000
General administrative overhead* . . .	180,000	52,000	80,000	48,000
Total fixed expenses	405,000	120,000	165,000	120,000
Net operating income (loss)	$ 5,000	$ 20,000	$ 25,000	$(40,000)

*Allocated on the basis of program revenues.

The head administrator of Jackson County Senior Services, Judith Miyama, is concerned about the organization's finances and considers the net operating income of $5,000 last year to be razor-thin. (Last year's results were very similar to the results for previous years and are representative of what would be expected in the future.) She feels that the organization should be building its financial reserves at a more rapid rate in order to prepare for the next inevitable recession. After seeing the above report, Ms. Miyama asked for more information about the financial advisability of perhaps discontinuing the housekeeping program.

The depreciation in housekeeping is for a small van that is used to carry the housekeepers and their equipment from job to job. If the program were discontinued, the van would be donated to a charitable organization. None of the general administrative overhead would be avoided if the housekeeping program were dropped, but the liability insurance and the salary of the program administrator would be avoided.

Required:
1. Should the Housekeeping program be discontinued? Explain. Show computations to support your answer.
2. Recast the above data in a format that would be more useful to management in assessing the long-run financial viability of the various services.

PROBLEM 10–20A　Sell or Process Further [LO10–7]
(Prepared from a situation suggested by Professor John W. Hardy.) Lone Star Meat Packers is a major processor of beef and other meat products. The company has a large amount of T-bone steak on hand, and it is trying to decide whether to sell the T-bone steaks as they are initially cut or to process them further into filet mignon and the New York cut.

If the T-bone steaks are sold as initially cut, the company figures that a 1-pound T-bone steak would yield the following profit:

Selling price ($2.25 per pound)	$2.25
Less joint costs incurred up to the split-off point where T-bone steak can be identified as a separate product	1.80
Profit per pound	$0.45

As mentioned above, instead of being sold as initially cut, the T-bone steaks could be further processed into filet mignon and New York cut steaks. Cutting one side of a T-bone steak provides the filet mignon, and cutting the other side provides the New York cut. One 16-ounce T-bone steak cut in this way will yield one 6-ounce filet mignon and one 8-ounce New York cut; the remaining ounces are waste. The cost of processing the T-bone steaks into these cuts is $0.25 per pound. The filet mignon can be sold for $4.00 per pound, and the New York cut can be sold for $2.80 per pound.

Required:
1. Determine the profit per pound from processing the T-bone steaks into filet mignon and New York cut steaks.
2. Would you recommend that the T-bone steaks be sold as initially cut or processed further? Why?

PROBLEM 10–21A Dropping or Retaining a Flight [LO10–2]

Profits have been decreasing for several years at Pegasus Airlines. In an effort to improve the company's performance, consideration is being given to dropping several flights that appear to be unprofitable.

A typical income statement for one round-trip of one such flight (flight 482) is as follows:

Ticket revenue (175 seats × 40% occupancy × $200 ticket price).....................	$14,000	100.0%
Variable expenses ($15 per person)...................	1,050	7.5
Contribution margin	12,950	92.5%
Flight expenses:		
Salaries, flight crew.............................	1,800	
Flight promotion	750	
Depreciation of aircraft	1,550	
Fuel for aircraft	5,800	
Liability insurance	4,200	
Salaries, flight assistants.......................	1,500	
Baggage loading and flight preparation	1,700	
Overnight costs for flight crew and assistants at destination.....................	300	
Total flight expenses............................	17,600	
Net operating loss...............................	$ (4,650)	

The following additional information is available about flight 482:

a. Members of the flight crew are paid fixed annual salaries, whereas the flight assistants are paid based on the number of round trips they complete.

b. One-third of the liability insurance is a special charge assessed against flight 482 because in the opinion of the insurance company, the destination of the flight is in a "high-risk" area. The remaining two-thirds would be unaffected by a decision to drop flight 482.

c. The baggage loading and flight preparation expense is an allocation of ground crews' salaries and depreciation of ground equipment. Dropping flight 482 would have no effect on the company's total baggage loading and flight preparation expenses.

d. If flight 482 is dropped, Pegasus Airlines has no authorization at present to replace it with another flight.

e. Aircraft depreciation is due entirely to obsolescence. Depreciation due to wear and tear is negligible.

f. Dropping flight 482 would not allow Pegasus Airlines to reduce the number of aircraft in its fleet or the number of flight crew on its payroll.

Required:

1. Prepare an analysis showing what impact dropping flight 482 would have on the airline's profits.
2. The airline's scheduling officer has been criticized because only about 50% of the seats on Pegasus' flights are being filled compared to an industry average of 60%. The scheduling officer has explained that Pegasus' average seat occupancy could be improved considerably by eliminating about 10% of its flights, but that doing so would reduce profits. Explain how this could happen.

PROBLEM 10–22A Accept or Reject a Special Order [LO10–4]

Polaski Company manufactures and sells a single product called a Ret. Operating at capacity, the company can produce and sell 30,000 Rets per year. Costs associated with this level of production and sales are given below:

	Unit	Total
Direct materials.................	$15	$ 450,000
Direct labor.....................	8	240,000
Variable manufacturing overhead..	3	90,000
Fixed manufacturing overhead....	9	270,000
Variable selling expense.........	4	120,000
Fixed selling expense...........	6	180,000
Total cost	$45	$1,350,000

The Rets normally sell for $50 each. Fixed manufacturing overhead is constant at $270,000 per year within the range of 25,000 through 30,000 Rets per year.

Required:
1. Assume that due to a recession, Polaski Company expects to sell only 25,000 Rets through regular channels next year. A large retail chain has offered to purchase 5,000 Rets if Polaski is willing to accept a 16% discount off the regular price. There would be no sales commissions on this order; thus, variable selling expenses would be slashed by 75%. However, Polaski Company would have to purchase a special machine to engrave the retail chain's name on the 5,000 units. This machine would cost $10,000. Polaski Company has no assurance that the retail chain will purchase additional units in the future. Determine the impact on profits next year if this special order is accepted.
2. Refer to the original data. Assume again that Polaski Company expects to sell only 25,000 Rets through regular channels next year. The U.S. Army would like to make a one-time-only purchase of 5,000 Rets. The Army would pay a fixed fee of $1.80 per Ret, and it would reimburse Polaski Company for all costs of production (variable and fixed) associated with the units. Because the army would pick up the Rets with its own trucks, there would be no variable selling expenses associated with this order. If Polaski Company accepts the order, by how much will profits increase or decrease for the year?
3. Assume the same situation as that described in (2) above, except that the company expects to sell 30,000 Rets through regular channels next year. Thus, accepting the U.S. Army's order would require giving up regular sales of 5,000 Rets. If the Army's order is accepted, by how much will profits increase or decrease from what they would be if the 5,000 Rets were sold through regular channels?

PROBLEM 10–23A   Make or Buy Decision [LO10–3]
Silven Industries, which manufactures and sells a highly successful line of summer lotions and insect repellents, has decided to diversify in order to stabilize sales throughout the year. A natural area for the company to consider is the production of winter lotions and creams to prevent dry and chapped skin.

After considerable research, a winter products line has been developed. However, Silven's president has decided to introduce only one of the new products for this coming winter. If the product is a success, further expansion in future years will be initiated.

The product selected (called Chap-Off) is a lip balm that will be sold in a lipstick-type tube. The product will be sold to wholesalers in boxes of 24 tubes for $8 per box. Because of excess capacity, no additional fixed manufacturing overhead costs will be incurred to produce the product. However, a $90,000 charge for fixed manufacturing overhead will be absorbed by the product under the company's absorption costing system.

Using the estimated sales and production of 100,000 boxes of Chap-Off, the Accounting Department has developed the following cost per box:

Direct material	$3.60
Direct labor	2.00
Manufacturing overhead	1.40
Total cost	$7.00

The costs above include costs for producing both the lip balm and the tube that contains it. As an alternative to making the tubes, Silven has approached a supplier to discuss the possibility of purchasing the tubes for Chap-Off. The purchase price of the empty tubes from the supplier would be $1.35 per box of 24 tubes. If Silven Industries accepts the purchase proposal, direct labor and variable manufacturing overhead costs per box of Chap-Off would be reduced by 10% and direct materials costs would be reduced by 25%.

Required:
1. Should Silven Industries make or buy the tubes? Show calculations to support your answer.
2. What would be the maximum purchase price acceptable to Silven Industries? Explain.
3. Instead of sales of 100,000 boxes, revised estimates show a sales volume of 120,000 boxes. At this new volume, additional equipment must be acquired to manufacture the tubes at an annual rental of $40,000. Assuming that the outside supplier will not accept an order for less than 120,000 boxes, should Silven Industries make or buy the tubes? Show computations to support your answer.
4. Refer to the data in (3) above. Assume that the outside supplier will accept an order of any size for the tubes at $1.35 per box. How, if at all, would this change your answer? Show computations.
5. What qualitative factors should Silven Industries consider in determining whether they should make or buy the tubes?

(CMA, adapted)

PROBLEM 10–24A   Shutting Down or Continuing to Operate a Plant [LO10–2]

(Note: This type of decision is similar to keeping or dropping a product line.)

Birch Company normally produces and sells 30,000 units of RG-6 each month. RG-6 is a small electrical relay used as a component part in the automotive industry. The selling price is $22 per unit, variable costs are $14 per unit, fixed manufacturing overhead costs total $150,000 per month, and fixed selling costs total $30,000 per month.

Employment-contract strikes in the companies that purchase the bulk of the RG-6 units have caused Birch Company's sales to temporarily drop to only 8,000 units per month. Birch Company estimates that the strikes will last for two months, after which time sales of RG-6 should return to normal. Due to the current low level of sales, Birch Company is thinking about closing down its own plant during the strike, which would reduce its fixed manufacturing overhead costs by $45,000 per month and its fixed selling costs by 10%. Start-up costs at the end of the shutdown period would total $8,000. Because Birch Company uses Lean Production methods, no inventories are on hand.

Required:

1. Assuming that the strikes continue for two months, would you recommend that Birch Company close its own plant? Explain. Show computations.
2. At what level of sales (in units) for the two-month period should Birch Company be indifferent between closing the plant or keeping it open? Show computations. (Hint: This is a type of break-even analysis, except that the fixed cost portion of your break-even computation should include only those fixed costs that are relevant [i.e., avoidable] over the two-month period.)

PROBLEM 10–25A   Utilization of a Constrained Resource [LO10–5, LO10–6]

The Walton Toy Company manufactures a line of dolls and a doll dress sewing kit. Demand for the dolls is increasing, and management requests assistance from you in determining an economical sales and production mix for the coming year. The company has provided the following data:

Product	Demand Next Year (units)	Selling Price per Unit	Direct Materials	Direct Labor
Debbie	50,000	$13.50	$4.30	$3.20
Trish	42,000	$5.50	$1.10	$2.00
Sarah	35,000	$21.00	$6.44	$5.60
Mike	40,000	$10.00	$2.00	$4.00
Sewing kit.	325,000	$8.00	$3.20	$1.60

The following additional information is available:

a. The company's plant has a capacity of 130,000 direct labor-hours per year on a single-shift basis. The company's present employees and equipment can produce all five products.
b. The direct labor rate of $8 per hour is expected to remain unchanged during the coming year.
c. Fixed costs total $520,000 per year. Variable overhead costs are $2 per direct labor-hour.
d. All of the company's nonmanufacturing costs are fixed.
e. The company's finished goods inventory is negligible and can be ignored.

Required:

1. Determine the contribution margin per direct labor-hour expended on each product.
2. Prepare a schedule showing the total direct labor-hours that will be required to produce the units estimated to be sold during the coming year.
3. Examine the data you have computed in (1) and (2) above. How would you allocate the 130,000 direct labor-hours of capacity to Walton Toy Company's various products?
4. What is the highest total contribution margin that the company can earn if it makes optimal use of its constrained resource?
5. What is the highest price, in terms of a rate per hour, that Walton Toy Company would be willing to pay for additional capacity (that is, for added direct labor time)?
6. Assume again that the company does not want to reduce sales of any product. Identify ways in which the company could obtain the additional output.

(CMA, adapted)

PROBLEM 10–26A   Close or Retain a Store [LO10–2]
Superior Markets, Inc., operates three stores in a large metropolitan area. A segmented absorption costing income statement for the company for the last quarter is given below:

Superior Markets, Inc.
Income Statement
For the Quarter Ended September 30

	Total	North Store	South Store	East Store
Sales	$3,000,000	$720,000	$1,200,000	$1,080,000
Cost of goods sold	1,657,200	403,200	660,000	594,000
Gross margin	1,342,800	316,800	540,000	486,000
Selling and administrative expenses:				
Selling expenses	817,000	231,400	315,000	270,600
Administrative expenses	383,000	106,000	150,900	126,100
Total expenses	1,200,000	337,400	465,900	396,700
Net operating income (loss)	$ 142,800	$(20,600)	$ 74,100	$ 89,300

The North Store has consistently shown losses over the past two years. For this reason, management is giving consideration to closing the store. The company has asked you to make a recommendation as to whether the store should be closed or kept open. The following additional information is available for your use:

a.   The breakdown of the selling and administrative expenses is as follows:

	Total	North Store	South Store	East Store
Selling expenses:				
Sales salaries	$239,000	$ 70,000	$ 89,000	$ 80,000
Direct advertising	187,000	51,000	72,000	64,000
General advertising*	45,000	10,800	18,000	16,200
Store rent	300,000	85,000	120,000	95,000
Depreciation of store fixtures	16,000	4,600	6,000	5,400
Delivery salaries	21,000	7,000	7,000	7,000
Depreciation of delivery equipment	9,000	3,000	3,000	3,000
Total selling expenses	$817,000	$231,400	$315,000	$270,600

*Allocated on the basis of sales dollars.

	Total	North Store	South Store	East Store
Administrative expenses:				
Store management salaries	$ 70,000	$ 21,000	$ 30,000	$ 19,000
General office salaries*	50,000	12,000	20,000	18,000
Insurance on fixtures and inventory	25,000	7,500	9,000	8,500
Utilities	106,000	31,000	40,000	35,000
Employment taxes	57,000	16,500	21,900	18,600
General office—other*	75,000	18,000	30,000	27,000
Total administrative expenses	$383,000	$106,000	$150,900	$126,100

*Allocated on the basis of sales dollars.

b. The lease on the building housing the North Store can be broken with no penalty.
c. The fixtures being used in the North Store would be transferred to the other two stores if the North Store were closed.
d. The general manager of the North Store would be retained and transferred to another position in the company if the North Store were closed. She would be filling a position that would otherwise be filled by hiring a new employee at a salary of $11,000 per quarter. The general manager of the North Store would be retained at her normal salary of $12,000 per quarter. All other employees in the store would be discharged.
e. The company has one delivery crew that serves all three stores. One delivery person could be discharged if the North Store were closed. This person's salary is $4,000 per quarter. The delivery equipment would be distributed to the other stores. The equipment does not wear out through use, but does eventually become obsolete.
f. The company's employment taxes are 15% of salaries.
g. One-third of the insurance in the North Store is on the store's fixtures.
h. The "General office salaries" and "General office—other" relate to the overall management of Superior Markets, Inc. If the North Store were closed, one person in the general office could be discharged because of the decrease in overall workload. This person's compensation is $6,000 per quarter.

Required:

1. Prepare a schedule showing the change in revenues and expenses and the impact on the company's overall net operating income that would result if the North Store were closed.
2. Assuming that the store space can't be subleased, what recommendation would you make to the management of Superior Markets, Inc.?
3. Disregard requirement 2. Assume that if the North Store were closed, at least one-fourth of its sales would transfer to the East Store, due to strong customer loyalty to Superior Markets. The East Store has enough capacity to handle the increased sales. You may assume that the increased sales in the East Store would yield the same gross margin as a percentage of sales as present sales in that store. What effect would these factors have on your recommendation concerning the North Store? Show all computations to support your answer.

PROBLEM 10–27A   Sell or Process Further [LO10–7]

Come-Clean Corporation produces a variety of cleaning compounds and solutions for both industrial and household use. While most of its products are processed independently, a few are related, such as the company's Grit 337 and its Sparkle silver polish.

Grit 337 is a coarse cleaning powder with many industrial uses. It costs $1.60 a pound to make, and it has a selling price of $2.00 a pound. A small portion of the annual production of Grit 337 is retained in the factory for further processing. It is combined with several other ingredients to form a paste that is marketed as Sparkle silver polish. The silver polish sells for $4.00 per jar.

This further processing requires one-fourth pound of Grit 337 per jar of silver polish. The additional direct costs involved in the processing of a jar of silver polish are

Other ingredients	$0.65
Direct labor	1.48
Total direct cost	$2.13

Overhead costs associated with processing the silver polish are

Variable manufacturing overhead cost	25% of direct labor cost
Fixed manufacturing overhead cost (per month):	
Production supervisor	$3,000
Depreciation of mixing equipment	$1,400

The production supervisor has no duties other than to oversee production of the silver polish. The mixing equipment is special-purpose equipment acquired specifically to produce the silver polish. Its resale value is negligible and it does not wear out through use.

Direct labor is a variable cost at Come-Clean Corporation.

Advertising costs for the silver polish total $4,000 per month. Variable selling costs associated with the silver polish are 7.5% of sales.

Due to a recent decline in the demand for silver polish, the company is wondering whether its continued production is advisable. The sales manager feels that it would be more profitable to sell all of the Grit 337 as a cleaning powder.

Required:

1. What is the incremental contribution margin per jar from further processing of Grit 337 into silver polish?
2. What is the minimum number of jars of silver polish that must be sold each month to justify the continued processing of Grit 337 into silver polish? Explain. Show all computations.

(CMA, adapted)

PROBLEM 10–28A   Make or Buy Analysis [LO10–3]

"In my opinion, we ought to stop making our own drums and accept that outside supplier's offer," said Wim Niewindt, managing director of Antilles Refining, N.V., of Aruba. "At a price of $18 per drum, we would be paying $5 less than it costs us to manufacture the drums in our own plant. Since we use 60,000 drums a year, that would be an annual cost savings of $300,000." Antilles Refining's current cost to manufacture one drum is given below (based on 60,000 drums per year):

Direct materials.	$10.35
Direct labor	6.00
Variable overhead.	1.50
Fixed overhead ($2.80 general company overhead, $1.60 depreciation and, $0.75 supervision)	5.15
Total cost per drum.	$23.00

A decision about whether to make or buy the drums is especially important at this time because the equipment being used to make the drums is completely worn out and must be replaced. The choices facing the company are

Alternative 1: Rent new equipment and continue to make the drums. The equipment would be rented for $135,000 per year.

Alternative 2: Purchase the drums from an outside supplier at $18 per drum.

The new equipment would be more efficient than the equipment that Antilles Refining has been using and, according to the manufacturer, would reduce direct labor and variable overhead costs by 30%. The old equipment has no resale value. Supervision cost ($45,000 per year) and direct materials cost per drum would not be affected by the new equipment. The new equipment's capacity would be 90,000 drums per year.

The company's total general company overhead would be unaffected by this decision.

Required:

1. To assist the managing director in making a decision, prepare an analysis showing the total cost and the cost per drum for each of the two alternatives given above. Assume that 60,000 drums are needed each year. Which course of action would you recommend to the managing director?
2. Would your recommendation in (1) above be the same if the company's needs were (a) 75,000 drums per year or (b) 90,000 drums per year? Show computations to support your answer, with costs presented on both a total and a per unit basis.
3. What other factors would you recommend that the company consider before making a decision?

CASE [LO10–7]

The Scottie Sweater Company produces sweaters under the "Scottie" label. The company buys raw wool and processes it into wool yarn from which the sweaters are woven. One spindle of wool yarn is required to produce one sweater. The costs and revenues associated with the sweaters are given below:

		Per Sweater
Selling price		$30.00
Cost to manufacture:		
Raw materials:		
Buttons, thread, lining	$ 2.00	
Wool yarn	16.00	
Total raw materials	18.00	
Direct labor	5.80	
Manufacturing overhead	8.70	32.50
Manufacturing profit (loss)		$ (2.50)

Originally, all of the wool yarn was used to produce sweaters, but in recent years a market has developed for the wool yarn itself. The yarn is purchased by other companies for use in production of wool blankets and other wool products. Since the development of the market for the wool yarn, a continuing dispute has existed in the Scottie Sweater Company as to whether the yarn should be sold simply as yarn or processed into sweaters. Current cost and revenue data on the yarn are given below:

		Per Spindle of Yarn
Selling price		$20.00
Cost to manufacture:		
Raw materials (raw wool)	$7.00	
Direct labor	3.60	
Manufacturing overhead	5.40	16.00
Manufacturing profit		$ 4.00

The market for sweaters is temporarily depressed, due to unusually warm weather in the western states where the sweaters are sold. This has made it necessary for the company to discount the selling price of the sweaters to $30 from the normal $40 price. Since the market for wool yarn has remained strong, the dispute has again surfaced over whether the yarn should be sold outright rather than processed into sweaters. The sales manager thinks that the production of sweaters should be discontinued; she is upset about having to sell sweaters at a $2.50 loss when the yarn could be sold for a $4.00 profit. However, the production superintendent does not want to close down a large portion of the factory. He argues that the company is in the sweater business, not the yarn business, and that the company should focus on its core strength.

All of the manufacturing overhead costs are fixed and would not be affected even if sweaters were discontinued. Manufacturing overhead is assigned to products on the basis of 150% of direct labor cost. Materials and direct labor costs are variable.

Required:
1. Would you recommend that the wool yarn be sold outright or processed into sweaters? Support your answer with appropriate computations and explain your reasoning.
2. What is the lowest price that the company should accept for a sweater? Support your answer with appropriate computations and explain your reasoning.

ETHICS CHALLENGE [LO10–2]

Haley Romeros had just been appointed vice president of the Rocky Mountain Region of the Bank Services Corporation (BSC). The company provides check processing services for small banks. The banks send checks presented for deposit or payment to BSC, which records the data on each check in a computerized database. BSC then sends the data electronically to the nearest Federal Reserve Bank check-clearing center where the appropriate transfers of funds are made between banks. The Rocky Mountain Region has three check processing centers, which are located in Billings, Montana; Great Falls, Montana; and Clayton, Idaho. Prior to her promotion to vice president, Ms. Romeros had been the manager of a check processing center in New Jersey.

Immediately after assuming her new position, Ms. Romeros requested a complete financial report for the just-ended fiscal year from the region's controller, John Littlebear. Ms. Romeros specified that the financial report should follow the standardized format required by corporate headquarters for all regional performance reports. That report follows:

Bank Services Corporation (BSC)
Rocky Mountain Region
Financial Performance

| | Total | Check Processing Centers | | |
		Billings	Great Falls	Clayton
Sales.	$50,000,000	$20,000,000	$18,000,000	$12,000,000
Operating expenses:				
Direct labor	32,000,000	12,500,000	11,000,000	8,500,000
Variable overhead	850,000	350,000	310,000	190,000
Equipment depreciation	3,900,000	1,300,000	1,400,000	1,200,000
Facility expense	2,800,000	900,000	800,000	1,100,000
Local administrative expense*	450,000	140,000	160,000	150,000
Regional administrative expense†	1,500,000	600,000	540,000	360,000
Corporate administrative expense‡ . . .	4,750,000	1,900,000	1,710,000	1,140,000
Total operating expense	46,250,000	17,690,000	15,920,000	12,640,000
Net operating income (loss)	$ 3,750,000	$ 2,310,000	$ 2,080,000	$ (640,000)

*Local administrative expenses are the administrative expenses incurred at the check processing centers.
†Regional administrative expenses are allocated to the check processing centers based on sales.
‡Corporate administrative expenses are charged to segments of the company such as the Rocky Mountain Region and the check processing centers at the rate of 9.5% of their sales.

Upon seeing this report, Ms. Romeros summoned John Littlebear for an explanation.

Romeros: What's the story on Clayton? It didn't have a loss the previous year did it?

Littlebear: No, the Clayton facility has had a nice profit every year since it was opened six years ago, but Clayton lost a big contract this year.

Romeros: Why?

Littlebear: One of our national competitors entered the local market and bid very aggressively on the contract. We couldn't afford to meet the bid. Clayton's costs—particularly their facility expenses— are just too high. When Clayton lost the contract, we had to lay off a lot of employees, but we could not reduce the fixed costs of the Clayton facility.

Romeros: Why is Clayton's facility expense so high? It's a smaller facility than either Billings or Great Falls and yet its facility expense is higher.

Littlebear: The problem is that we are able to rent suitable facilities very cheaply at Billings and Great Falls. No such facilities were available at Clayton; we had them built. Unfortunately, there were big cost overruns. The contractor we hired was inexperienced at this kind of work and in fact went bankrupt before the project was completed. After hiring another contractor to finish the work, we were way over budget. The large depreciation charges on the facility didn't matter at first because we didn't have much competition at the time and could charge premium prices.

Romeros: Well we can't do that anymore. The Clayton facility will obviously have to be shut down. Its business can be shifted to the other two check processing centers in the region.

Littlebear: I would advise against that. The $1,200,000 in depreciation at the Clayton facility is misleading. That facility should last indefinitely with proper maintenance. And it has no resale value; there is no other commercial activity around Clayton.

Romeros: What about the other costs at Clayton?

Littlebear: If we shifted Clayton's business over to the other two processing centers in the region, we wouldn't save anything on direct labor or variable overhead costs. We might save $90,000 or so in local administrative expense, but we would not save any regional administrative expense and corporate headquarters would still charge us 9.5% of our sales as corporate administrative expense.

In addition, we would have to rent more space in Billings and Great Falls in order to handle the work transferred from Clayton; that would probably cost us at least $600,000 a year. And don't forget that it will cost us something to move the equipment from Clayton to Billings and Great Falls. And the move will disrupt service to customers.

Romeros: I understand all of that, but a money-losing processing center on my performance report is completely unacceptable.

Littlebear: And if you shut down Clayton, you are going to throw some loyal employees out of work.

Romeros: That's unfortunate, but we have to face hard business realities.

Littlebear: And you would have to write off the investment in the facilities at Clayton.

Romeros: I can explain a write-off to corporate headquarters; hiring an inexperienced contractor to build the Clayton facility was my predecessor's mistake. But they'll have my head at headquarters if I show operating losses every year at one of my processing centers. Clayton has to go. At the next corporate board meeting, I am going to recommend that the Clayton facility be closed.

Required:

1. From the standpoint of the company as a whole, should the Clayton processing center be shut down and its work redistributed to other processing centers in the region? Explain.
2. Do you think Haley Romeros's decision to shut down the Clayton facility is ethical? Explain.
3. What influence should the depreciation on the facilities at Clayton have on prices charged by Clayton for its services?

ANALYTICAL THINKING [LO10–1, LO10–3, LO10–5]

TufStuff, Inc., sells a wide range of drums, bins, boxes, and other containers that are used in the chemical industry. One of the company's products is a heavy-duty corrosion-resistant metal drum, called the WVD drum, used to store toxic wastes. Production is constrained by the capacity of an automated welding machine that is used to make precision welds. A total of 2,000 hours of welding time is available annually on the machine. Because each drum requires 0.4 hours of welding machine time, annual production is limited to 5,000 drums. At present, the welding machine is used exclusively to make the WVD drums. The accounting department has provided the following financial data concerning the WVD drums:

WVD Drums		
Selling price per drum		$149.00
Cost per drum:		
Direct materials..............................	$52.10	
Direct labor ($18 per hour)	3.60	
Manufacturing overhead	4.50	
Selling and administrative expense.............	29.80	90.00
Margin per drum..............................		$ 59.00

Management believes 6,000 WVD drums could be sold each year if the company had sufficient manufacturing capacity. As an alternative to adding another welding machine, management has considered buying additional drums from an outside supplier. Harcor Industries, Inc., a supplier of quality products, would be able to provide up to 4,000 WVD-type drums per year at a price of $138 per drum, which TufStuff would resell to its customers at its normal selling price after appropriate relabeling.

Megan Flores, TufStuff's production manager, has suggested that the company could make better use of the welding machine by manufacturing bike frames, which would require only 0.5 hours of welding machine time per frame and yet sell for far more than the drums. Megan believes that TufStuff could sell up to 1,600 bike frames per year to bike manufacturers at a price of $239 each. The accounting department has provided the following data concerning the proposed new product:

Bike Frames		
Selling price per frame		$239.00
Cost per frame:		
Direct materials	$99.40	
Direct labor ($18 per hour)	28.80	
Manufacturing overhead	36.00	
Selling and administrative expense	47.80	212.00
Margin per frame		$ 27.00

The bike frames could be produced with existing equipment and personnel. Manufacturing overhead is allocated to products on the basis of direct labor-hours. Most of the manufacturing overhead consists of fixed common costs such as rent on the factory building, but some of it is variable. The variable manufacturing overhead has been estimated at $1.35 per WVD drum and $1.90 per bike frame. The variable manufacturing overhead cost would not be incurred on drums acquired from the outside supplier.

Selling and administrative expenses are allocated to products on the basis of revenues. Almost all of the selling and administrative expenses are fixed common costs, but it has been estimated that variable selling and administrative expenses amount to $0.75 per WVD drum whether made or purchased and would be $1.30 per bike frame.

All of the company's employees—direct and indirect—are paid for full 40-hour workweeks and the company has a policy of laying off workers only in major recessions.

Required:
1. Would you be comfortable relying on the financial data provided by the accounting department for making decisions related to the WVD drums and bike frames? Why?
2. Compute the contribution margin per unit for:
   a. Purchased WVD drums.
   b. Manufactured WVD drums.
   c. Manufactured bike frames.
3. Determine the number of WVD drums (if any) that should be purchased and the number of WVD drums and/or bike frames (if any) that should be manufactured. What is the increase in net operating income that would result from this plan over current operations?

   As soon as your analysis was shown to the top management team at TufStuff, several managers got into an argument concerning how direct labor costs should be treated when making this decision. One manager argued that direct labor is always treated as a variable cost in textbooks and in practice and has always been considered a variable cost at TufStuff. After all, "direct" means you can directly trace the cost to products. "If direct labor is not a variable cost, what is?" Another manager argued just as strenuously that direct labor should be considered a fixed cost at TufStuff. No one had been laid off in over a decade, and for all practical purposes, everyone at the plant is on a monthly salary. Everyone classified as direct labor works a regular 40-hour workweek and overtime has not been necessary since the company adopted Lean Production techniques. Whether the welding machine is used to make drums or frames, the total payroll would be exactly the same. There is enough slack, in the form of idle time, to accommodate any increase in total direct labor time that the bike frames would require.
4. Redo requirements (2) and (3) making the opposite assumption about direct labor from the one you originally made. In other words, if you treated direct labor as a variable cost, redo the analysis treating it as a fixed cost. If you treated direct labor as a fixed cost, redo the analysis treating it as a variable cost.
5. What do you think is the correct way to treat direct labor cost in this situation—as variable or as fixed? Explain.

A LOOK BACK

Chapter 10 used the basic decision-making framework, which focuses on differential costs and benefits, to analyze a wide variety of situations.

A LOOK AT THIS CHAPTER

Chapter 11 expands coverage of decision making by focusing on decisions about investments in long-term projects. It illustrates a variety of techniques used by managers faced with these decisions.

A LOOK AHEAD

Chapter 12 covers the statement of cash flows. It addresses how to classify various types of cash inflows and outflows along with the interpretation of information reported on that financial statement.

11

Capital Budgeting Decisions

CHAPTER OUTLINE

Commercial Delivery Fleets Adopt Electric Trucks

Staples, **Frito-Lay**, and **AT&T** have begun purchasing electric delivery trucks even though they cost $30,000 more than diesel delivery trucks. Staples is willing to make the more expensive up-front investment because it expects each electric truck to incur lower operating costs. For example, it estimates that electric trucks will save $2,450 per year in maintenance costs and $6,500 per year in fuel costs. It also expects to replace each electric truck's brakes every four or five years instead of every one or two years with diesel trucks. In total, Staples expects each electric delivery truck to save $60,000 over its 10-year useful life.

Source: Mike Ramsey, "As Electric Vehicles Arrive, Firms See Payback in Trucks," *The Wall Street Journal,* December 8, 2010, pp. B1–B2.

Managers often consider decisions that involve an investment today in the hope of realizing future profits. For example, **Yum! Brands, Inc.**, makes an investment when it opens a new Pizza Hut restaurant. **L. L. Bean** makes an investment when it installs a new computer to handle customer billing. **Ford** makes an investment when it redesigns a vehicle such as the F-150 pickup truck. **Merck & Co.** invests in medical research. **Amazon.com** makes an investment when it redesigns its website. All of these investments require spending now with the expectation of additional future net cash inflows.

The term **capital budgeting** is used to describe how managers plan significant investments in projects that have long-term implications such as the purchase of new equipment or the introduction of new products. Most companies have many more potential projects than can actually be funded. Hence, managers must carefully select those projects that promise the greatest future return. How well managers make these capital budgeting decisions is a critical factor in the long-run financial health of the organization. This chapter provides in-depth discussion of three methods for making capital budgeting decisions—the *payback method,* the *net present value method,* and the *simple rate of return method.*

CAPITAL BUDGETING—AN OVERVIEW

Typical Capital Budgeting Decisions

Any decision that involves a cash outlay now in order to obtain a future return is a capital budgeting decision. Typical capital budgeting decisions include:

1. Cost reduction decisions. Should new equipment be purchased to reduce costs?
2. Expansion decisions. Should a new plant, warehouse, or other facility be acquired to increase capacity and sales?
3. Equipment selection decisions. Which of several available machines should be purchased?
4. Lease or buy decisions. Should new equipment be leased or purchased?
5. Equipment replacement decisions. Should old equipment be replaced now or later?

Capital budgeting decisions fall into two broad categories—*screening decisions* and *preference decisions.* **Screening decisions** relate to whether a proposed project is acceptable—whether it passes a preset hurdle. For example, a company may have a policy of accepting projects only if they provide a return of at least 20% on the investment. The required rate of return is the minimum rate of return a project must yield to be acceptable. **Preference decisions**, by contrast, relate to selecting from among several acceptable alternatives. To illustrate, a company may be considering several different machines to replace an existing machine on the assembly line. The choice of which machine to purchase is a preference decision.

Cash Flows versus Net Operating Income

The first two capital budgeting methods discussed in the chapter—the payback method, and the net present value method—both focus on analyzing the *cash flows* associated with capital investment projects, whereas the simple rate of return method focuses on *incremental net operating income.* To better prepare you to apply the payback and net present value methods, we'd like to define the most common types of cash outflows and cash inflows that accompany capital investment projects.

Typical Cash Outflows   Most projects have at least three types of cash outflows. First, they often require an immediate cash outflow in the form of an initial investment in equipment, other assets, and installation costs. Any salvage value realized from the sale of old equipment can be recognized as a reduction in the initial investment or as a cash inflow. Second, some projects require a company to expand its working capital. **Working capital** is current assets (e.g., cash, accounts receivable, and inventory) less current liabilities. When a company takes on a new project, the balances in the current asset accounts often increase. For example, opening a new Nordstrom's department store requires additional cash in sales registers and more inventory. These additional working capital needs are treated as part of the initial investment in a project. Third, many projects require periodic outlays for repairs and maintenance and additional operating costs.

Typical Cash Inflows   Most projects also have at least three types of cash inflows. First, a project will normally increase revenues or reduce costs. Either way, the amount involved should be treated as a cash inflow for capital budgeting purposes. Notice that from a cash flow standpoint, a reduction in costs is equivalent to an increase in revenues. Second, cash inflows are also frequently realized from selling equipment for its salvage value when a project ends, although the company may actually have to pay to dispose of some low-value or hazardous items. Third, any working capital that was tied up in the project can be released for use elsewhere at the end of the project and should be treated as a cash inflow at that time. Working capital is released, for example, when a company sells off its inventory or collects its accounts receivable.

The Time Value of Money

Beyond defining a capital project's cash outflows and inflows, it is also important to consider when those cash flows occur. For example, if someone offered to give you $1,000 dollars today that you could save toward your eventual retirement or $1,000 dollars a year from now that you could save toward your future retirement, which alternative would you choose? In all likelihood, you would choose to receive $1,000 today because you could invest it and have more than $1,000 dollars a year from now. This simple example illustrates an important capital budgeting concept known as *the time value of money*. The **time value of money** recognizes that a dollar today is worth more than a dollar a year from now if for no other reason than you could put the dollar in a bank today and have more than a dollar a year from now. Because of the time value of money, capital investments that promise earlier cash flows are preferable to those that promise later cash flows.

Although the payback method focuses on cash flows, it does not recognize the time value of money. In other words, it treats a dollar received today as being of equal value to a dollar received at any point in the future. Conversely, the net present value method not only focuses on cash flows, but it also recognizes the time value of those cash flows. It uses a technique called *discounting cash flows* to translate the value of future cash flows to their lesser present value. If you are not familiar with the concept of discounting cash flows and the use of present value tables, you should read Appendix 11A: The Concept of Present Value, at the end of the chapter, before studying the net present value method.

HELPFUL HINT

The simple rate of return method uses net operating income to evaluate capital budgeting proposals, whereas the payback and net present value methods are cash flow-based modes of analysis. The payback method ignores the time value of money. Conversely, the net present value method acknowledges the time value of money by discounting cash flows to their present value.

Investing in a Vineyard: A Cash Flows Perspective

When Michael Evans was contemplating moving to Buenos Aires, Argentina, to start a company called the **Vines of Mendoza**, he had to estimate the project's initial cash outlays and compare them to its future net cash inflows. The initial cash outlays included $2.9 million to buy 1,046 acres of land and to construct a tasting room, $300,000 for a well and irrigation system, $30,000 for underground power lines, and $285,000 for 250,000 grape plants. The annual operating costs included $1,500 per acre for pruning, mowing, and irrigation and $114 per acre for harvesting.

In terms of future cash inflows, Evans hopes to sell his acreage to buyers who want to grow their own grapes and make their own wine while avoiding the work involved with doing so. He intends to charge buyers a one-time fee of $55,000 per planted acre. The buyers would also reimburse Evans for his annual operating costs per acre plus a 25% markup. In a good year, buyers should be able to get 250 cases of wine from their acre of grapevines.

Source: Helen Coster, "Planting Roots," *Forbes*, March 1, 2010, pp. 42–44.

THE PAYBACK METHOD

The payback method of evaluating capital budgeting projects focuses on the *payback period*. The **payback period** is the length of time that it takes for a project to recover its initial cost from the net cash inflows that it generates. This period is sometimes referred to as "the time that it takes for an investment to pay for itself." The basic premise of the payback method is that the more quickly the cost of an investment can be recovered, the more desirable is the investment.

The payback period is expressed in years. *When the annual net cash inflow is the same every year,* the following formula can be used to compute the payback period:

$$\text{Payback period} = \frac{\text{Investment required}}{\text{Annual net cash inflow}} \tag{1}$$

To illustrate the payback method, consider the following data:

Example A: York Company needs a new milling machine. The company is considering two machines: machine A and machine B. Machine A costs $15,000, has a useful life of ten years, and will reduce operating costs by $5,000 per year. Machine B costs only $12,000, will also reduce operating costs by $5,000 per year, but has a useful life of only five years.

Required:
Which machine should be purchased according to the payback method?

$$\text{Machine A payback period} = \frac{\$15,000}{\$5,000} = 3.0 \text{ years}$$

$$\text{Machine B payback period} = \frac{\$12,000}{\$5,000} = 2.4 \text{ years}$$

According to the payback calculations, York Company should purchase machine B because it has a shorter payback period than machine A.

Evaluation of the Payback Method

The payback method is not a true measure of the profitability of an investment. Rather, it simply tells a manager how many years are required to recover the original investment. Unfortunately, a shorter payback period does not always mean that one investment is more desirable than another.

To illustrate, refer back to Example A on the previous page. Machine B has a shorter payback period than machine A, but it has a useful life of only 5 years rather than 10 years for machine A. Machine B would have to be purchased twice—once immediately and then again after the fifth year—to provide the same service as just one machine A. Under these circumstances, machine A would probably be a better investment than machine B, even though machine B has a shorter payback period. Unfortunately, the payback method ignores all cash flows that occur after the payback period.

A further criticism of the payback method is that it does not consider the time value of money. A cash inflow to be received several years in the future is weighed the same as a cash inflow received right now. To illustrate, assume that for an investment of $8,000 you can purchase either of the two following streams of cash inflows:

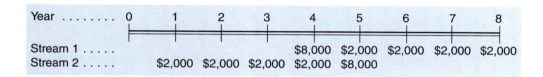

Year	0	1	2	3	4	5	6	7	8
Stream 1					$8,000	$2,000	$2,000	$2,000	$2,000
Stream 2		$2,000	$2,000	$2,000	$2,000	$8,000			

Which stream of cash inflows would you prefer to receive in return for your $8,000 investment? Each stream has a payback period of 4.0 years. Therefore, if payback alone is used to make the decision, the streams would be considered equally desirable. However, from a time value of money perspective, stream 2 is much more desirable than stream 1.

On the other hand, under certain conditions the payback method can be very useful. For one thing, it can help identify which investment proposals are in the "ballpark." That is, it can be used as a screening tool to help answer the question, "Should I consider this proposal further?" If a proposal doesn't provide a payback within some specified period, then there may be no need to consider it further. In addition, the payback period is often important to new companies that are "cash poor." When a company is cash poor, a project with a short payback period but a low rate of return might be preferred over another project with a high rate of return but a long payback period. The reason is that the company may simply need a faster return of its cash investment. And finally, the payback method is sometimes used in industries where products become obsolete very rapidly—such as consumer electronics. Because products may last only a year or two, the payback period on investments must be very short.

An Extended Example of Payback

As shown by formula (1) on page 514, the payback period is computed by dividing the investment in a project by the project's annual net cash inflows. If new equipment is replacing old equipment, then any salvage value to be received when disposing of the old equipment should be deducted from the cost of the new equipment, and only the *incremental* investment should be used in the payback computation. In addition, any depreciation deducted in arriving at the project's net operating income must be added back to obtain the project's expected annual net cash inflow. To illustrate, consider the following data:

Example B: Goodtime Fun Centers, Inc., operates amusement parks. Some of the vending machines in one of its parks provide very little revenue, so the company is considering removing the machines and installing equipment to dispense soft ice cream. The equipment would cost $80,000 and have an eight-year useful life with no salvage value. Incremental annual revenues and costs associated with the sale of ice cream would be as follows:

Sales	$150,000
Variable expenses	90,000
Contribution margin	60,000
Fixed expenses:	
Salaries	27,000
Maintenance	3,000
Depreciation	10,000
Total fixed expenses	40,000
Net operating income	$ 20,000

The vending machines can be sold for a $5,000 scrap value. The company will not purchase equipment unless it has a payback period of three years or less. Does the ice cream dispenser pass this hurdle?

Exhibit 11–1 computes the payback period for the ice cream dispenser. Several things should be noted. First, depreciation is added back to net operating income to obtain the annual net cash inflow from the new equipment. Depreciation is not a cash outlay; thus, it must be added back to adjust net operating income to a cash basis. Second, the payback computation deducts the salvage value of the old machines from the cost of the new equipment so that only the incremental investment is used in computing the payback period.

Because the proposed equipment has a payback period of less than three years, the company's payback requirement has been met.

EXHIBIT 11–1
Computation of the Payback Period

Step 1: *Compute the annual net cash inflow.* Because the annual net cash inflow is not given, it must be computed before the payback period can be determined:

Net operating income	$20,000
Add: Noncash deduction for depreciation	10,000
Annual net cash inflow	$30,000

Step 2: *Compute the payback period.* Using the annual net cash inflow from above, the payback period can be determined as follows:

Cost of the new equipment	$80,000
Less salvage value of old equipment	5,000
Investment required	$75,000

$$\text{Payback period} = \frac{\text{Investment required}}{\text{Annual net cash inflow}}$$

$$= \frac{\$75,000}{\$30,000} = 2.5 \text{ years}$$

Payback and Uneven Cash Flows

When the cash flows associated with an investment project change from year to year, the simple payback formula that we outlined earlier cannot be used. Instead, the payoff period can be computed as follows (assuming that cash inflows occur evenly throughout the year): Payback period = Number of years up to the year in which the investment is paid off + (Unrecovered investment at the beginning of the year in which the investment is paid off ÷ Cash inflow in the period in which the investment is paid off). To illustrate how to apply this formula, consider the following data:

Year	Investment	Cash Inflow
1	$4,000	$1,000
2		$0
3		$2,000
4	$2,000	$1,000
5		$500
6		$3,000
7		$2,000

What is the payback period on this investment? The answer is 5.5 years, computed as follows: 5 + ($1,500 ÷ $3,000) = 5.5 years. In essence, we are tracking the unrecovered investment year by year as shown in Exhibit 11–2. By the middle of the sixth year, sufficient cash inflows will have been realized to recover the entire investment of $6,000 ($4,000 + $2,000).

Year	Investment	Cash Inflow	Unrecovered Investment*
1	$4,000	$1,000	$3,000
2		$0	$3,000
3		$2,000	$1,000
4	$2,000	$1,000	$2,000
5		$500	$1,500
6		$3,000	$0
7		$2,000	$0

*Year X unrecovered investment = Year X−1 unrecovered investment + Year X investment − Year X cash inflow

EXHIBIT 11–2
Payback and Uneven Cash Flows

CONCEPT CHECK

1. Which of the following statements is true? (You may select more than one answer.)
   a. The time value of money recognizes that a dollar received today is worth more than a dollar received a year from now.
   b. Working capital is noncurrent assets minus current assets.
   c. The simple rate of return method focuses on incremental net operating income.
   d. The cost of capital is the average rate of return the company must pay to its long-term creditors and its shareholders for the use of their funds.
2. Which of the following statements is true? (You may select more than one answer.)
   a. The payback period increases as the cost of capital increases.
   b. The payback period is the length of time that it takes for a project to recover its initial cost from the net cash inflows that it generates.
   c. The equation for computing the payback period includes a company's net operating income.
   d. The payback method relies on discounted cash flows.

THE NET PRESENT VALUE METHOD

LEARNING OBJECTIVE 11–2

Evaluate the acceptability of an investment project using the net present value method.

As previously mentioned, the *net present value method* uses discounted cash flows to analyze capital budgeting decisions. It compares the present value of a project's cash inflows to the present value of its cash outflows. The difference between the present value of these cash flows, called the **net present value**, determines whether or not a project is an acceptable investment.

When performing net present value analysis, managers usually make two important assumptions. First, they assume that all cash flows other than the initial investment occur at the end of periods. This assumption is somewhat unrealistic because cash flows typically occur *throughout* a period rather than just at its end; however, it simplifies the computations considerably. Second, managers assume that all cash flows generated by an investment project are immediately reinvested at a rate of return equal to the rate used to discount the future cash flows, also known as the *discount rate*. If this condition is not met, the net present value computations will not be accurate.

To illustrate net present analysis, consider the following data:

> **Example C:** Harper Company is contemplating the purchase of a machine capable of performing some operations that are now performed manually. The machine will cost $50,000, and it will last for five years. At the end of the five-year period, the machine will be sold for its salvage value of $5,000. Use of the machine will reduce labor costs by $18,000 per year. Harper Company requires a minimum pretax return of 18% on all investment projects.[1]

Should the machine be purchased? Harper Company must determine whether a cash investment now of $50,000 can be justified if it will result in an $18,000 reduction in cost in each of the next five years. It may appear that the answer is obvious because the total cost savings is $90,000 ($18,000 per year × 5 years). However, the company can earn an 18% return by investing its money elsewhere. It is not enough that the cost reductions cover just the original cost of the machine; they must also yield a return of at least 18% or the company would be better off investing the money elsewhere.

To determine whether the investment is desirable, the stream of annual $18,000 cost savings and the machine's salvage value of $5,000 should be discounted to their present values and then compared to the cost of the new machine. Exhibit 11–3 demonstrates a four-step approach for performing these computations. First, it calculates the present

EXHIBIT 11–3
Net Present Value Analysis Using Discount Factors from Exhibit 11B-1 and 11B-2 in Appendix 11B

	A	B	C	D
1				Year(s)	
2		Now	1-5	5
3	Initial investment	$ (50,000)		
4	Annual cost savings		$ 18,000	
5	Salvage value of the new machine			$ 5,000
6	Total cash flows (a)	$ (50,000)	$ 18,000	$ 5,000
7	Discount factor (18%) (b)	1.000	3.127	0.437
8	Present value of the cash flows (a) × (b)	$ (50,000)	$ 56,286	$ 2,185
9	Net present value (SUM B8:D8)	$ 8,471		
10				
11	Note: The discount factor come from Exhibits 11B-1 and 11B-2 in Appendix 11B.			
12				

K ◀ ▶ ▶I Exhibit 11-3 / Exhibit 11-4 / Exhibit 11-

---

[1] For simplicity, we ignore inflation and taxes. The impact of income taxes on capital budgeting decisions is discussed in more advanced texts.

value of the initial investment by multiplying $50,000 by 1.000, the present value factor for any cash flow that occurs immediately. Second, it calculates the present value of the annual cost savings by multiplying $18,000 by 3.127, the present value factor of a five-year annuity at the discount rate of 18%, to obtain $56,286. Third, it calculates the present value of the machine's salvage value by multiplying $5,000 by 0.437, the present value factor of a single sum to be received in five years at the discount rate of 18%, to obtain $2,185. Finally, cells B8 through D8 are added together to derive the net present value of $8,471.[2]

Exhibit 11–4 demonstrates an alternative approach for performing these same calculations. This alternative approach also begins by calculating the present value of the initial investment by multiplying $50,000 by 1.000, the present value factor for any cash flow that occurs immediately. However, rather than calculating the present value of the annual cost savings using a discount factor of 3.127 from Exhibit 11B–2, it discounts the annual cost savings in Years 1–5 and the machine's salvage value in Year 5 to their present values using the discount factors from Exhibit 11B–1. For example, the $18,000 cost savings in Year 3 is multiplied by the discount factor of 0.609 to derive this future cash flow's present value of $10,962. As another example, the $23,000 of total cash flows in Year 5 is multiplied by the discount factor of 0.437 to determine these future cash flows' present value of $10,051. The present values in cells B8 through G8 are then added together to compute the project's net present value of $8,471.

The methods described in Exhibits 11–3 and 11–4 are mathematically equivalent—they both produced a net present value of $8,471. The only difference between these two exhibits relates to the discounting of the annual labor cost savings. In Exhibit 11–3, the labor cost savings are discounted to their present value using the annuity factor of 3.127, whereas in Exhibit 11–4, these cost savings are discounted using five separate factors that sum to 3.127 (0.847 + 0.718 + 0.609 + 0.516 + 0.437 = 3.127). In other words, the calculations are equivalent.

While you should feel free to use either of these methods when performing net present value calculations, from this point forward we'll be emphasizing the approach used in Exhibit 11–4 for two reasons. First, most managers use an approach similar to Exhibit 11–4 when performing net present value calculations. They use Microsoft Excel to summarize each year's cash flows in a separate column and then they discount each year's cash flows to their present values using the factors shown in Exhibit 11B–1. Second, many students believe that the approach shown in Exhibit 11–4 is easier to understand than competing methods when the net present value computations become increasingly complex.

---

[2]In this chapter, we use the discount factors from Appendix 11B, which have been rounded to three decimal places, for all present value calculations. However, Microsoft Excel can also be used to calculate discount factors that are not rounded to three decimal places. These unrounded discount factors provide solutions that slightly differ from those derived using the tables in Appendix 11B.

EXHIBIT 11–4
Net Present Value Analysis Using Discount Factors from Exhibit 11B-1 in Appendix 11B

	A	B	C	D	E	F	G
1						Year	
2		Now	1	2	3	4	5
3	Initial investment	$(50,000)					
4	Annual labor cost savings		$18,000	$18,000	$18,000	$18,000	$ 18,000
5	Salvage value of new machine						$ 5,000
6	Total cash flows (a)	$(50,000)	$18,000	$18,000	$18,000	$18,000	$ 23,000
7	Discount factor (18%) (b)	1.000	0.847	0.718	0.609	0.516	0.437
8	Present value of cash flows (a) × (b)	$(50,000)	$15,246	$12,924	$10,962	$ 9,288	$ 10,051
9	Net present value (SUM B8:G8)	$ 8,471					
10							
11	Note: The discount factors come from Exhibit 11B-1 in Appendix 11B.						
12							

Exhibit 11-3 Exhibit 11-4 Exhibit 11-5 Exhibit 11-6 Exhibit 11-7 Exhibit 11-8 Exhibit 11-9

Once you have computed a net present value using either of the approaches that we just demonstrated, you'll need to interpret your findings. For example, because Harper Company's proposed project has a positive net present value of $8,471, it implies that the company should purchase the new machine. A positive net present value indicates that the project's return exceeds the discount rate. A negative net present value indicates that the project's return is less than the discount rate. Therefore, if the company's minimum required rate of return is used as the discount rate, a project with a positive net present value has a return that exceeds the minimum required rate of return and is acceptable. Conversely, a project with a negative net present value has a return that is less than the minimum required rate of return and is unacceptable. In sum:

If the Net Present Value Is	Then the Project Is . . .
Positive	Acceptable because its return is greater than the required rate of return.
Zero	Acceptable because its return is equal to the required rate of return.
Negative	Not acceptable because its return is less than the required rate of return.

To improve your understanding of the minimum required rate of return, it bears emphasizing that a company's *cost of capital* is usually regarded as its minimum required rate of return. The **cost of capital** is the average rate of return that the company must pay to its long-term creditors and its shareholders for the use of their funds. If a project's rate of return is less than the cost of capital, the company does not earn enough to compensate its creditors and shareholders. Therefore, any project with a rate of return less than the cost of capital should be rejected.

The cost of capital serves as a *screening device.* When the cost of capital is used as the discount rate in net present value analysis, any project with a negative net present value does not cover the company's cost of capital and should be discarded as unacceptable.

Recovery of the Original Investment

The net present value method automatically provides for return of the original investment. Whenever the net present value of a project is positive, the project will recover the original cost of the investment plus sufficient excess cash inflows to compensate the organization for tying up funds in the project. To demonstrate this point, consider the following situation:

Example D: Carver Hospital is considering the purchase of an attachment for its X-ray machine that will cost $3,169. The attachment will be usable for four years, after which time it will have no salvage value. It will increase net cash inflows by $1,000 per year in the X-ray department. The hospital's board of directors requires a rate of return of at least 10% on such investments.

A net present value analysis of the desirability of purchasing the X-ray attachment is presented in Exhibit 11–5. Notice that the attachment has exactly a 10% return on the original investment because the net present value is zero at a 10% discount rate.

Each annual $1,000 cash inflow arising from use of the attachment is made up of two parts. One part represents a recovery of a portion *of* the original $3,169 paid for the attachment, and the other part represents a return *on* this investment. The breakdown of each year's $1,000 cash inflow between recovery *of* investment and return *on* investment is shown in Exhibit 11–6.

The first year's $1,000 cash inflow consists of a return *on* investment of $317 (a 10% return *on* the $3,169 original investment), plus a $683 return *of* that investment. Because the amount of the unrecovered investment decreases each year, the dollar amount of the return on investment also decreases each year. By the end of the fourth year, all $3,169 of the original investment has been recovered.

EXHIBIT 11–5 Carver Hospital—Net Present Value Analysis of X-Ray Attachment

	A	B	C	D	E	F
1				Year		
2		Now	1	2	3	4
3	Initial investment	$ (3,169)				
4	Annual net cash inflow	_____	$1,000	$1,000	$1,000	$1,000
5	Total cash flows (a)	$ (3,169)	$1,000	$1,000	$1,000	$1,000
6	Discount factor (10%) (b)	1.000	0.909	0.826	0.751	0.683
7	Present value of cash flows (a) × (b)	$ (3,169)	$ 909	$ 826	$ 751	$ 683
8	Net present value (SUM B7:F7)	$ 0				
9						
10	Note: The discount factors come from Exhibit 11B-1 in Appendix 11B.					
11						

Exhibit 11-3 / Exhibit 11-4 / **Exhibit 11-5** / Exhibit 11-6 / Exhibit 11-7 / Exhibit 11-8 / Exhibit 11-

EXHIBIT 11–6 Carver Hospital—Breakdown of Annual Cash Inflows

	A	B	C	D	E	F	G
1		(1)	(2)	(3)	(4)	(5)	
2	Year	Investment Outstanding during the Year	Cash Inflow	Return on Investment (1) × 10%	Recovery of Investment during the Year (2) – (3)	Unrecovered Investment at the End of the Year (1) – (4)	
3	1	$3,169	$1,000	$317	$683	$2,486	
4	2	$2,486	$1,000	$249	$751	$1,735	
5	3	$1,735	$1,000	$174	$826	$909	
6	4	$909	$1,000	$91	$909	$0	
7	Total investment recovered				$3,169		
8							

Exhibit 11-3 / Exhibit 11-4 / Exhibit 11-5 / **Exhibit 11-6** / Exhibit 11-7 / Exhibit 11-8 / Exhibit 11-9

Cooling Servers Naturally

IN BUSINESS

Google consumes more than 2 terawatt hours of electricity per year, which is greater than the annual electricity consumption of 200,000 American homes. A large part of Google's electricity consumption relates to running and cooling its huge number of servers. In an effort to lower its electricity bill, Google invested €200 million to build a server storage facility in the Baltic Sea coastal community of Hamina, Finland. Hamina's low electricity rates coupled with its persistently low ambient air temperatures will lower Google's annual electricity bills considerably. Shortly after Google's facility opened in Hamina, **Facebook** opened a five-acre data center in Luleá. Sweden, where the average temperature is 35 degrees Fahrenheit.

Source: Sven Grunberg and Niclas Rolander, "For Data Center, Google Goes for the Cold," The *Wall Street Journal,* September 12, 2011, p. B10.

An Extended Example of the Net Present Value Method

Example E provides an extended example of how the net present value method is used to analyze a proposed project. This example helps tie together and reinforce many of the ideas discussed thus far.

Example E: Under a special licensing arrangement, Swinyard Corporation has an opportunity to market a new product for a five-year period. The product would be purchased from the manufacturer, with Swinyard responsible for promotion and distribution costs. The licensing arrangement could be renewed at the end of the five-year period. After careful study, Swinyard estimated the following costs and revenues for the new product:

Cost of equipment needed	$60,000
Working capital needed	$100,000
Overhaul of the equipment in four years	$5,000
Salvage value of the equipment in five years	$10,000
Annual revenues and costs:	
Sales revenues	$200,000
Cost of goods sold	$125,000
Out-of-pocket operating costs (for salaries,	
advertising, and other direct costs)	$35,000

At the end of the five-year period, if Swinyard decides not to renew the licensing arrangement the working capital would be released for investment elsewhere. Swinyard uses a 14% discount rate. Would you recommend that the new product be introduced?

This example involves a variety of cash inflows and cash outflows. The solution is given in Exhibit 11–7.

Notice how the working capital is handled in this exhibit. It is counted as a cash outflow at the beginning of the project and as a cash inflow when it is released at the end of

EXHIBIT 11–7   The Net Present Value Method—An Extended Example

	A	B	C	D	E	F	G
1					Year		
2		Now	1	2	3	4	5
3	Purchase of equipment	$ (60,000)					
4	Investment in working capital	$ (100,000)					
5	Sales		$ 200,000	$ 200,000	$ 200,000	$ 200,000	$ 200,000
6	Cost of goods sold		$(125,000)	$(125,000)	$(125,000)	$(125,000)	$(125,000)
7	Out-of-pocket costs for salaries, advertising, etc.		$ (35,000)	$ (35,000)	$ (35,000)	$ (35,000)	$ (35,000)
8	Overhaul of equipment					$ (5,000)	
9	Salvage value of the equipment						$ 10,000
10	Working capital released						$ 100,000
11	Total cash flows (a)	$ (160,000)	$ 40,000	$ 40,000	$ 40,000	$ 35,000	$ 150,000
12	Discount factor (14%) (b)	1.000	0.877	0.769	0.675	0.592	$ 0.519
13	Present value of cash flows (a) × (b)	$ (160,000)	$ 35,080	$ 30,760	$ 27,000	$ 20,720	$ 77,850
14	Net present value (SUM B13:G13)	$ 31,410					
15							
16	Note: The discount factors come from Exhibit 11B-1 in Appendix 11B.						
17							

Exhibit 11-3   Exhibit 11-4   Exhibit 11-5   Exhibit 11-6   Exhibit 11-7   Exhibit 11-8   Exhibit 11-9

the project. Also notice how the sales revenues, cost of goods sold, and out-of-pocket costs are handled. **Out-of-pocket costs** are actual cash outlays for salaries, advertising, and other operating expenses.

Because the net present value of the proposal is positive, the new product is acceptable.

EXPANDING THE NET PRESENT VALUE METHOD

So far, all of our examples have involved an evaluation of a single investment project. In the following section we use the *total-cost approach* to explain how the net present value method can be used to evaluate two alternative projects.

The total-cost approach is the most flexible method for comparing competing projects. To illustrate the mechanics of the approach, consider the following data:

Example F: Harper Ferry Company operates a high-speed passenger ferry service across the Mississippi River. One of its ferryboats is in poor condition. This ferry can be renovated at an immediate cost of $200,000. Further repairs and an overhaul of the motor will be needed three years from now at a cost of $80,000. In all, the ferry will be usable for 5 years if this work is done. At the end of 5 years, the ferry will have to be scrapped at a salvage value of $60,000. The scrap value of the ferry right now is $70,000. It will cost $300,000 each year to operate the ferry, and revenues will total $400,000 annually.

As an alternative, Harper Ferry Company can purchase a new ferryboat at a cost of $360,000. The new ferry will have a life of 5 years, but it will require some repairs costing $30,000 at the end of 3 years. At the end of 5 years, the ferry will have a scrap value of $60,000. It will cost $210,000 each year to operate the ferry, and revenues will total $400,000 annually.

Harper Ferry Company requires a return of at least 14% on all investment projects.

Should the company purchase the new ferry or renovate the old ferry? Exhibit 11–8 shows the solution using the total-cost approach.

Two points should be noted from the exhibit. First, *all* cash inflows and *all* cash outflows are included in the solution under each alternative. No effort has been made to isolate those cash flows that are relevant to the decision and those that are not relevant. The inclusion of all cash flows associated with each alternative gives the approach its name—the *total-cost* approach.

Second, notice that a net present value is computed for each alternative. This is a strength of the total-cost approach because an unlimited number of alternatives can be compared side by side to determine the best option. For example, another alternative for Harper Ferry Company would be to get out of the ferry business entirely. If management desired, the net present value of this alternative could be computed to compare with the alternatives shown in Exhibit 11–8. Still other alternatives might be available to the

EXHIBIT 11–8 The Total-Cost Approach to Project Selection

	A	B	C	D	E	F	G	H
					Year			
1	Keep the old ferry:							
2		Now	1	2	3	4	5	
3	Renovation	$ (200,000)						
4	Annual revenues		$ 400,000	$ 400,000	$ 400,000	$ 400,000	$ 400,000	
5	Annual cash operating costs		$ (300,000)	$ (300,000)	$ (300,000)	$ (300,000)	$ (300,000)	
6	Repairs in three years				$ (80,000)			
7	Salvage value of old ferry						$ 60,000	
8	Total cash flows (a)	$ (200,000)	$ 100,000	$ 100,000	$ 20,000	$ 100,000	$ 160,000	
9	Discount factor (14%) (b)	1.000	0.877	0.769	0.675	0.592	0.519	
10	Present value of cash flows (a) × (b)	$ (200,000)	$ 87,700	$ 76,900	$ 13,500	$ 59,200	$ 83,040	
11	Net present value (SUM B10:G10)	$ 120,340						
12								
13	Buy the new ferry:				Year			
14		Now	1	2	3	4	5	
15	Initial investment	$ (360,000)						
16	Salvage value of the old ferry	$ 70,000						
17	Annual revenues		$ 400,000	$ 400,000	$ 400,000	$ 400,000	$ 400,000	
18	Annual cash operating costs		$ (210,000)	$ (210,000)	$ (210,000)	$ (210,000)	$ (210,000)	
19	Repairs in three years				$ (30,000)			
20	Salvage value of new ferry						$ 60,000	
21	Total cash flows (a)	$ (290,000)	$ 190,000	$ 190,000	$ 160,000	$ 190,000	$ 250,000	
22	Discount factor (14%) (b)	1.000	0.877	0.769	0.675	0.592	0.519	
23	Present value of cash flows (a) × (b)	$ (290,000)	$ 166,630	$ 146,110	$ 108,000	$ 112,480	$ 129,750	
24	Net present value (SUM B23:G23)	$ 372,970						
25								
26	Net present value in favor of buying the new ferry (B24–B11)	$ 252,630						
27								
28	Note: The discount factors come from Exhibit 11B-1 in Appendix 11B.							
29								

Exhibit 11-3 | Exhibit 11-4 | Exhibit 11-5 | Exhibit 11-6 | Exhibit 11-7 | **Exhibit 11-8** | Exhibit 11-9

company. In the case at hand, given only two alternatives, the data indicate that the net present value in favor of buying the new ferry is $252,630.[3]

Least-Cost Decisions

Some decisions do not involve any revenues. For example, a company may be trying to decide whether to buy or lease an executive jet. The choice would be made on the basis of which alternative—buying or leasing—would be least costly. In situations such as these, where no revenues are involved, the most desirable alternative is the one with the *least total cost* from a present value perspective. Hence, these are known as least-cost decisions. To illustrate a least-cost decision, consider the following data:

Example G: Val-Tek Company is considering replacing an old threading machine with a new threading machine that would substantially reduce annual operating costs. Selected data relating to the old and new machines are presented below:

	Old Machine	New Machine
Purchase cost when new	$200,000	$250,000
Salvage value now	$30,000	—
Annual cash operating costs	$150,000	$90,000
Overhaul needed immediately	$40,000	—
Salvage value in six years	$0	$50,000
Remaining life	6 years	6 years

Val-Tek Company uses a 10% discount rate.

---

[3]The alternative with the highest net present value is not always the best choice, although it is the best choice in this case. For further discussion, see the section Preference Decisions—The Ranking of Investment Projects.

EXHIBIT 11–9   Least-Cost Decision: A Net Present Value Analysis

	A	B	C	D	E	F	G	H
1	Keep the old machine:					Year		
2		Now	1	2	3	4	5	6
3	Overhaul needed now	$ (40,000)						
4	Annual cash operating costs		$ (150,000)	$ (150,000)	$ (150,000)	$(150,000)	$(150,000)	$(150,000)
5	Total cash flows (a)	$ (40,000)	$ (150,000)	$ (150,000)	$ (150,000)	$(150,000)	$(150,000)	$(150,000)
6	Discount factor (10%) (b)	1.000	0.909	0.826	0.751	0.683	0.621	0.564
7	Present value of cash flows (a) × (b)	$ (40,000)	$ (136,350)	$ (123,900)	$ (112,650)	$(102,450)	$ (93,150)	$ (84,600)
8	Net present value (SUM B7:H7)	$ (693,100)						
9								
10	Buy the new machine:					Year		
11		Now	1	2	3	4	5	6
12	Initial investment	$ (250,000)						
13	Salvage value of the old machine	$ 30,000						
14	Annual cash operating costs		$ (90,000)	$ (90,000)	$ (90,000)	$ (90,000)	$ (90,000)	$ (90,000)
15	Salvage value of new machine							$ 50,000
16	Total cash flows (a)	$ (220,000)	$ (90,000)	$ (90,000)	$ (90,000)	$ (90,000)	$ (90,000)	$ (40,000)
17	Discount factor (10%) (b)	1.000	0.909	0.826	0.751	0.683	0.621	0.564
18	Present value of cash flows (a) × (b)	$ (220,000)	$ (81,810)	$ (74,340)	$ (67,590)	$ (61,470)	$ (55,890)	$ (22,560)
19	Net present value (SUM B18:H18)	$ (583,660)						
20								
21	Net present value in favor of buying the new machine	$ 109,440						
22								
23	Note: The discount factors come from Exhibit 11B-1 in Appendix 11B.							
24								

Exhibit 11–4 Exhibit 11–5 Exhibit 11–6 Exhibit 11–7 Exhibit 11–8 Exhibit 11–9

Exhibit 11–9 analyzes the alternatives using the total-cost approach. Because this is a least-cost decision, the present values are negative for both alternatives. However, the present value of the alternative of buying the new machine is $109,440 higher than the other alternative. Therefore, buying the new machine is the less costly alternative.

3. Which of the following statements is false? (You may select more than one answer.)
   a. The total-cost and incremental-cost approaches to net present value analysis can occasionally lead to conflicting results.
   b. Least-cost decisions do not involve any revenues.
   c. The present value of a dollar increases as the time of receipt extends further into the future.
   d. The higher the discount rate, the lower the present value of a dollar received in the future.

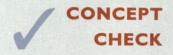

CONCEPT CHECK

Home Construction Goes Green—Or Does It?

IN BUSINESS

Many homebuyers like the idea of building environmentally friendly homes until they get the bill. Specpan, an Indianapolis research firm, estimates a "green" home costs 10%–19% more than a comparable conventional home. For example, installing solar-electric glass-faced tiles on a roof costs $15,000 per 100 square feet compared to $1,200 per 100 square feet for standard fiber-cement tiles. Environmentally friendly interior paint costs $35–$42 per gallon compared to $20–$32 per gallon for standard latex paint. To further complicate this least-cost decision, the average homeowner lives in a house only seven years before moving. Within this time frame, many green investments appear to be financially unattractive. Nonetheless, the American Institute of Architects reports that 63% of their clients expressed an interest in renewable flooring materials such as cork and bamboo, up from 53% a year earlier.

Source: June Fletcher, "The Price of Going Green," *The Wall Street Journal*, February 29, 2008, p. W8.

DECISION POINT

Financing the Sports Car

Assume you would like to buy a new sports car that can be purchased for $21,495 in cash or acquired from the dealer via a leasing arrangement. Under the terms of the lease, you would have to make a payment of $2,078 when the lease is signed and then monthly payments of $300 for 24 months. At the end of the 24-month lease, you can choose to buy the car you have leased for an additional payment of $13,776. If you do not make that final payment, the car reverts to the dealer.

You have enough cash to make the initial payment on the lease, but not enough to buy the car for cash. However, you could borrow the additional cash from a credit union for 1% per month. Do you think you should borrow money from a credit union to purchase the car or should you sign a lease with the dealer?

Hints: The net present value of the cash purchase option, including any payments to the credit union, is $21,495 using 1% per month as the discount rate. (Accept this statement as true; don't try to do the computations to verify it.) Determine the net present value of the lease, using 1% per month as the discount rate. The present value of an annuity of $1 for 24 periods at 1% per period is 21.243 and the present value of a single payment of $1 at the end of 24 periods at 1% per period is 0.788.

PREFERENCE DECISIONS—THE RANKING OF INVESTMENT PROJECTS

LEARNING OBJECTIVE 11–3

Rank investment projects in order of preference.

Recall that when considering investment opportunities, managers must make two types of decisions—screening decisions and preference decisions. Screening decisions, which come first, pertain to whether or not a proposed investment is acceptable. Preference decisions come *after* screening decisions and attempt to answer the following question: "How do the remaining investment proposals, all of which have been screened and provide an acceptable rate of return, rank in terms of preference? That is, which one(s) would be *best* for the company to accept?"

Sometimes preference decisions are called rationing decisions, or ranking decisions. Limited investment funds must be rationed among many competing alternatives. Hence, the alternatives must be ranked.

The net present value of one project cannot be directly compared to the net present value of another project unless the initial investments are equal. For example, assume that a company is considering two competing investments, as shown below:

	Investment	
	A	**B**
Investment required	$(10,000)	$(5,000)
Present value of cash inflows	11,000	6,000
Net present value	$ 1,000	$ 1,000

Although each project has a net present value of $1,000, the projects are not equally desirable if the funds available for investment are limited. The project requiring an investment of only $5,000 is much more desirable than the project requiring an investment of $10,000. This fact can be highlighted by dividing the net present value of the project by the investment required. The result, shown below in equation form, is called the **project profitability index**.

$$\text{Project profitability index} = \frac{\text{Net present value of the project}}{\text{Investment required}} \qquad (2)$$

The project profitability indexes for the two investments on the previous page would be computed as follows:

	Investment	
	A	B
Net present value (a)	$1,000	$1,000
Investment required (b)	$10,000	$5,000
Project profitability index, (a) ÷ (b)	0.10	0.20

When using the project profitability index to rank competing investments projects, the preference rule is: *The higher the project profitability index, the more desirable the project.*[4] Applying this rule to the two investments above, investment B should be chosen over investment A.

The project profitability index is an application of the techniques for utilizing constrained resources discussed in an earlier chapter. In this case, the constrained resource is the limited funds available for investment, and the project profitability index is similar to the contribution margin per unit of the constrained resource.

A few details should be clarified with respect to the computation of the project profitability index. The "Investment required" refers to any cash outflows that occur at the beginning of the project, reduced by any salvage value recovered from the sale of old equipment. The "Investment required" also includes any investment in working capital that the project may need.

THE INTERNAL RATE OF RETURN METHOD

The *internal rate of return* method is a popular alternative to the net present value method. The **internal rate of return** is the rate of return promised by an investment over its useful life. It is computed by finding the discount rate at which the net present value of the investment is zero. The internal rate of return can be used either to screen projects or to rank them. Any project whose internal rate of return is less than the cost of capital is rejected and, in general, the higher a project's rate of return, the more desirable it is.

For technical reasons that are discussed in more advanced texts, the net present value method is generally considered to be more reliable than the internal rate of return method for both screening and ranking projects.

THE NET PRESENT VALUE METHOD AND INCOME TAXES

Our discussion of the net present value method has assumed that there are no income taxes. In most countries—including the United States—income taxes, both on individual income and on business income, are a fact of life.

---

[4]Because of the "lumpiness" of projects, the project profitability index ranking may not be perfect. Nevertheless, it is a good starting point. Furthermore, these complexities are beyond the scope of this book.

Income taxes affect net present value analysis in two ways. First, income taxes affect the cost of capital in that the cost of capital should reflect the *after-tax* cost of long-term debt and of equity. Second, net present value analysis should focus on *after-tax cash flows*. The effects of income taxes on both revenues and expenses should be fully reflected in the analysis. This includes taking into account the tax deductibility of depreciation. Whereas depreciation is not itself a cash flow, it reduces taxable income and therefore income taxes, which *are* a cash flow. The techniques for adjusting the cost of capital and cash flows for income taxes are beyond the scope of this book and are covered in more advanced texts.

THE SIMPLE RATE OF RETURN METHOD

LEARNING OBJECTIVE 11–4

Compute the simple rate of return for an investment.

The **simple rate of return** method is the final capital budgeting technique discussed in the chapter. This method is also often referred to as the accounting rate of return or the unadjusted rate of return. We will begin by explaining how to compute the simple rate of return followed by a discussion of this method's limitations and its impact on the behavior of investment center managers.

To obtain the simple rate of return, the annual incremental net operating income generated by a project is divided by the initial investment in the project, as shown below.

$$\text{Simple rate of return} = \frac{\text{Annual incremental net operating income}}{\text{Initial investment}} \qquad (3)$$

The annual incremental net operating income included in the numerator should be reduced by the depreciation charges that result from making the investment. Furthermore, the initial investment shown in the denominator should be reduced by any salvage value realized from the sale of old equipment.

> **Example H:** Brigham Tea, Inc., is a processor of low-acid tea. The company is contemplating purchasing equipment for an additional processing line that would increase revenues by $90,000 per year. Incremental cash operating expenses would be $40,000 per year. The equipment would cost $180,000 and have a nine-year life with no salvage value.

To apply the formula for the simple rate of return, we must first determine the annual incremental net operating income from the project:

Annual incremental revenues		$90,000
Annual incremental cash operating expenses	$40,000	
Annual depreciation ($180,000 − $0)/9	20,000	
Annual incremental expenses		60,000
Annual incremental net operating income		$30,000

Given that the annual incremental net operating income from the project is $30,000 and the initial investment is $180,000, the simple rate of return is 16.7% as shown below:

$$\text{Simple rate of return} = \frac{\text{Annual incremental net operating income}}{\text{Initial investment}}$$
$$= \frac{\$30,000}{\$180,000}$$
$$= 16.7\%$$

> **Example I:** Midwest Farms, Inc., hires people on a part-time basis to sort eggs. The cost of hand sorting is $30,000 per year. The company is investigating an egg-sorting machine that would cost $90,000 and have a 15-year useful life. The machine would

have negligible salvage value, and it would cost $10,000 per year to operate and maintain. The egg-sorting equipment currently being used could be sold now for a scrap value of $2,500.

This project is slightly different from the preceding project because it involves cost reductions with no additional revenues. Nevertheless, the annual incremental net operating income can be computed by treating the annual cost savings as if it were incremental revenues as follows:

Annual incremental cost savings		$30,000
Annual incremental cash operating expenses	$10,000	
Annual depreciation ($90,000 − $0)/15	6,000	
Annual incremental expenses		16,000
Annual incremental net operating income		$14,000

Thus, even though the new equipment would not generate any additional revenues, it would reduce costs by $14,000 a year. This would have the effect of increasing net operating income by $14,000 a year.

Finally, the salvage value of the old equipment offsets the initial cost of the new equipment as follows:

Cost of the new equipment	$90,000
Less salvage value of the old equipment	2,500
Initial investment	$87,500

Given the annual incremental net operating income of $14,000 and the initial investment of $87,500, the simple rate of return is 16.0% computed as follows:

$$\text{Simple rate of return} = \frac{\text{Annual incremental net operating income}}{\text{Initial investment}}$$

$$= \frac{\$14,000}{\$87,500}$$

$$= 16.0\%$$

The simple rate of return suffers from two important limitations. First, it focuses on accounting net operating income rather than cash flows. Thus, if a project does not have constant incremental revenues and expenses over its useful life, the simple rate of return will fluctuate from year to year, thereby possibly causing the same project to appear desirable in some years and undesirable in others. Second, the simple rate of return method does not involve discounting cash flows. It considers a dollar received 10 years from now to be as valuable as a dollar received today.

Given these limitations, it is reasonable to wonder why we bothered discussing this method. First of all, in spite of its limitations, some companies use the simple rate of return to evaluate capital investment proposals. Therefore, you should be familiar with this approach so that you can properly critique it in the event that you encounter it in practice. More importantly, you need to understand how the simple rate of return method influences the behavior of investment center managers who are evaluated and rewarded based on their return on investment (ROI).

For example, assume the following three facts. First, assume that you are an investment center manager whose pay raises are based solely on ROI. Second, assume that last year your division had an ROI of 20%. Third, assume that your division has the chance to pursue a capital budgeting project that will have a positive net present value and a simple rate of return of 17%. Given these three assumptions, would you choose to accept this project or reject it? Although the company would want you to accept it because of its positive net present value, you would probably choose to reject it because the simple rate of return of 17% is less than your prior year's ROI of 20%. This basic example illustrates how a project's simple rate of return can influence the decisions made by investment center managers. It also highlights an important challenge faced by organizations, namely designing performance measurement systems that align employee actions with organizational goals.

CONCEPT CHECK

4. If a $300,000 investment has a project profitability index of 0.25, what is the net present value of the project?
   a. $75,000
   b. $225,000
   c. $25,000
   d. $275,000
5. Which of the following statements is true? (You may select more than one answer.)
   a. The project profitability index is used to make screening decisions.
   b. The internal rate of return is the rate of return promised by an investment over its useful life.
   c. A project's simple rate of return can fluctuate from year to year.
   d. The simple rate of return typically equals a company's cost of capital.

POSTAUDIT OF INVESTMENT PROJECTS

After an investment project has been approved and implemented, a *postaudit* should be conducted. A **postaudit** involves checking whether or not expected results are actually realized. This is a key part of the capital budgeting process because it helps keep managers honest in their investment proposals. Any tendency to inflate the benefits or downplay the costs in a proposal should become evident after a few postaudits have been conducted. The postaudit also provides an opportunity to reinforce and possibly expand successful projects and to cut losses on floundering projects.

The same capital budgeting method should be used in the postaudit as was used in the original approval process. That is, if a project was approved on the basis of a net present value analysis, then the same procedure should be used in performing the postaudit. However, the data used in the postaudit analysis should be *actual observed data* rather than estimated data. This gives management an opportunity to make a side-by-side comparison to see how well the project has succeeded. It also helps assure that estimated data received on future proposals will be carefully prepared because the persons submitting the data knows that their estimates will be compared to actual results in the postaudit process. Actual results that are far out of line with original estimates should be carefully reviewed.

Royal Caribbean Cruises Launches *Oasis of the Seas*

Royal Caribbean Cruises invested $1.4 billion to build the *Oasis of the Seas,* a cruise ship that carries 5,400 passengers and stands 20 stories above the sea. The vessel is a third larger than any other cruise ship and contains 21 pools, 24 restaurants, 13 retail shops, and 300-foot water slides. The company hopes the ship's extraordinary amenities will attract large numbers of customers willing to pay premium prices. However, the economic downturn has caused many customers to refrain from spending on lavish vacations.

Source: Mike Esterl, "Huge Cruise Ships Prepare for Launch but Face Uncertain Waters," *The Wall Street Journal,* December 4, 2009, pp. B1–B2.

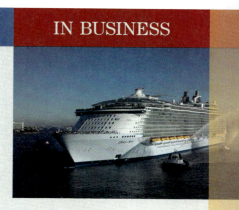

SUMMARY

LO11–1 Determine the payback period for an investment.

The payback period is the number of periods that are required to recover the investment in a project from the project's net cash inflows. The payback period is most useful for projects whose useful lives are short and uncertain. Generally speaking it is not a reliable method for evaluating investment opportunities because it ignores the time value of money and all cash flows that occur after the investment has been recovered.

LO11–2 Evaluate the acceptability of an investment project using the net present value method.

Investment decisions should take into account the time value of money because a dollar today is more valuable than a dollar received in the future. In the net present value method, future cash flows are discounted to their present value so that they can be compared with current cash outlays. The difference between the present value of the cash inflows and the present value of the cash outflows is called the project's net present value. If the net present value of the project is negative, the project is rejected. The company's cost of capital is often used as the discount rate in the net present value method.

LO11–3 Rank investment projects in order of preference.

After screening out projects whose net present values are negative, the company may still have more projects than can be supported with available funds. The remaining projects can be ranked using the project profitability index, which is computed by dividing the net present value of the project by the required initial investment.

LO11–4 Compute the simple rate of return for an investment.

The simple rate of return is determined by dividing a project's accounting net operating income by the initial investment in the project. The simple rate of return is not a reliable guide for evaluating potential projects because it ignores the time value of money. While this method has important limitations, it can influence the decision-making process of investment center managers who are evaluated and rewarded based on their return on investment (ROI).

GUIDANCE ANSWER TO DECISION POINT

Financing the Sports Car (p. 526)

The formal analysis, using the least-cost approach, appears below:

Item	Month(s)	Amount of Cash Flows	1% Factor	Present Value of Cash Flows
Pay cash for the car:				
Cash payment	Now	$(21,495)	1.000	$(21,495)
Net present value				$(21,495)
Lease the car:				
Cash payment on lease signing	Now	$(2,078)	1.000	$ (2,078)
Monthly lease payment	1–24	$(300)	21.243	(6,373)
Final payment	24	$(13,776)	0.788	(10,855)
Net present value				$(19,306)
Net present value in favor of leasing				$ 2,189

The leasing alternative is $2,189 less costly, in terms of net present value, than the cash purchase alternative. In addition, the leasing alternative has the advantage that you can choose to not make the final payment of $13,776 at the end of 24 months if for some reason you decide you do not want to keep the car. For example, if the resale value of the car at that point is far less than $13,776, you may choose to return the car to the dealer and save the $13,776. If, however, you had purchased the car outright, you would not have this option—you could only realize the resale value. Because of this "real option," the leasing alternative is even more valuable than the net present value calculations indicate. Therefore, you should lease the car rather than pay cash (and borrow from the credit union).

GUIDANCE ANSWERS TO CONCEPT CHECKS

1. **Choices a, c, and d.** Working capital is current assets minus current liabilities.
2. **Choice b.** The payback method focuses on cash flows rather than net operating income and it does not discount those cash flows; therefore, it is not affected by the cost of capital.
3. **Choices a and c.** The total-cost and incremental-cost approaches to net present value analysis produce the same results. The present value of a dollar decreases as the time of receipt extends farther into the future.
4. **Choice a.** The net present value of the project is $300,000 × 0.25 = $75,000.
5. **Choices b and c.** The project profitability index is used to make preference decisions. The simple rate of return is unrelated to a company's cost of capital.

REVIEW PROBLEM: COMPARISON OF CAPITAL BUDGETING METHODS

Lamar Company is considering a project that would have a five-year life and require a $2,400,000 investment in equipment. At the end of five years, the project would terminate and the equipment would have no salvage value. The project would provide net operating income each year as follows:

Sales	$3,200,000
Variable expenses	1,800,000
Contribution margin	1,400,000
Fixed expenses:	
Advertising, salaries, and other	
fixed out-of-pocket costs $700,000	
Depreciation 300,000	
Total fixed expenses	1,000,000
Net operating income	$ 400,000

The company's discount rate is 12%.

Required:
1. Compute the annual net cash inflow from the project.
2. Compute the project's net present value. Is the project acceptable?
3. Compute the project's payback period.
4. Compute the project's simple rate of return.

Solution to Review Problem
1. The annual net cash inflow can be computed by deducting the cash expenses from sales:

Sales	$3,200,000
Variable expenses	1,800,000
Contribution margin	1,400,000
Advertising, salaries, and other fixed	
out-of-pocket costs	700,000
Annual net cash inflow	$ 700,000

Or the annual net cash inflow can be computed by adding depreciation back to net operating income:

Net operating income	$400,000
Add: Noncash deduction for depreciation	300,000
Annual net cash inflow	$700,000

2. The net present value is computed as follows:

	A	B	C	D	E	F	G
1						Year	
2		Now	1	2	3	4	5
3	Initial investment	$ (2,400,000)					
4	Sales		$ 3,200,000	$ 3,200,000	$ 3,200,000	$ 3,200,000	$ 3,200,000
5	Variable expenses		$(1,800,000)	$(1,800,000)	$(1,800,000)	$(1,800,000)	$(1,800,000)
6	Fixed out-of-pocket costs		$ (700,000)	$ (700,000)	$ (700,000)	$ (700,000)	$ (700,000)
7	Total cash flows (a)	$ (2,400,000)	$ 700,000	$ 700,000	$ 700,000	$ 700,000	$ 700,000
8	Discount factor (12%) (b)	1.000	0.893	0.797	0.712	0.636	0.567
9	Present value of cash flows (a) × (b)	$ (2,400,000)	$ 625,100	$ 557,900	$ 498,400	$ 445,200	$ 396,900
10	Net present value (SUM B9:G9)	$ 123,500					
11							
12	Note: The discount factors come from Exhibit 11B-1 in Appendix 11B.						
13							

Sheet1 Sheet2 Sheet3

Or, it can also be computed as follows:

	A	B	C
1			Years
2		Now	1-5
3	Initial investment	$ (2,400,000)	
4	Sales		$ 3,200,000
5	Variable expenses		$ (1,800,000)
6	Fixed out-of-pocket costs		$ (700,000)
7	Total cash flows (a)	$ (2,400,000)	$ 700,000
8	Discount factor (12%) (b)	1.000	3.605
9	Present value of the cash flows (a) × (b)	$ (2,400,000)	$2,523,500
10	Net present value (SUM B9:C9)	$123,500	
11			
12	Note: The discount factor comes from Exhibit 11B-2 in Appendix 11B.		
13			

Yes, the project is acceptable because it has a positive net present value.

3. The formula for the payback period is as follows:

$$\text{Payback period} = \frac{\text{Investment required}}{\text{Annual net cash flow}}$$
$$= \frac{\$2,400,000}{\$700,000}$$
$$= 3.4 \text{ years}$$

4. The formula for the simple rate of return is as follows:

$$\text{Simple rate of return} = \frac{\text{Annual incremental net operating income}}{\text{Initial investment}}$$
$$= \frac{\$400,000}{\$2,400,000}$$
$$= 16.7\%$$

GLOSSARY

Capital budgeting The process of planning significant investments in projects that have long-term implications such as the purchase of new equipment or the introduction of a new product. (p. 512)

Cost of capital The average rate of return a company must pay to its long-term creditors and shareholders for the use of their funds. (p. 520)

Internal rate of return The discount rate at which the net present value of an investment project is zero; the rate of return of a project over its useful life. (p. 527)

Net present value The difference between the present value of an investment project's cash inflows and the present value of its cash outflows. (p. 518)

Out-of-pocket costs Actual cash outlays for salaries, advertising, repairs, and similar costs. (p. 523)

Payback period The length of time that it takes for a project to fully recover its initial cost out of the net cash inflows that it generates. (p. 514)

Postaudit The follow-up after a project has been approved and implemented to determine whether expected results were actually realized. (p. 530)

Preference decision A decision in which the alternatives must be ranked. (p. 512)

Project profitability index The ratio of the net present value of a project's cash flows to the investment required. (p. 527)

Screening decision A decision as to whether a proposed investment project is acceptable. (p. 512)

Simple rate of return The rate of return computed by dividing a project's annual incremental net operating income by the initial investment required. (p. 528)

Time value of money The concept that a dollar today is worth more than a dollar a year from now. (p. 513)

Working capital Current assets less current liabilities. (p. 513)

11–1 What is the difference between capital budgeting screening decisions and capital budgeting preference decisions?

11–2 What is meant by the term *time value of money?*

11–3 What is meant by the term *discounting?*

11–4 Why isn't accounting net income used in the net present value and internal rate of return methods of making capital budgeting decisions?

11–5 Why are discounted cash flow methods of making capital budgeting decisions superior to other methods?

11–6 What is net present value? Can it ever be negative? Explain.

11–7 Identify two simplifying assumptions associated with discounted cash flow methods of making capital budgeting decisions.

11–8 If a company has to pay interest of 14% on long-term debt, then its cost of capital is 14%. Do you agree? Explain.

11–9 Explain how the cost of capital serves as a screening tool when using (*a*) the net present value method and (*b*) the internal rate of return method.

11–10 As the discount rate increases, the present value of a given future cash flow also increases. Do you agree? Explain.

11–11 Refer to Exhibit 11–7. Is the return on this investment proposal exactly 14%, more than 14%, or less than 14%? Explain.

11–12 How is the project profitability index computed, and what does it measure?

11–13 What is meant by the term *payback period?* How is the payback period determined? How can the payback method be useful?

11–14 What is the major criticism of the payback and simple rate of return methods of making capital budgeting decisions?

Multiple-choice questions are available in the *Connect Library*.

APPLYING EXCEL

Available with McGraw-Hill's *Connect Accounting*.

LO11–2

The Excel worksheet form that appears below is to be used to recreate Example E and Exhibit 11–7 on pages 522–523. Download the workbook containing this form in the *Connect Library*. On the website you will also receive instructions about how to use this worksheet form.

	A	B	C	D	E	F	G
1	Chapter 11: Applying Excel						
2							
3	**Data**						
4	**Example E**						
5	Cost of equipment needed	$60,000					
6	Working capital needed	$100,000					
7	Overhaul of equipment in four years	$5,000					
8	Salvage value of the equipment in five years	$10,000					
9	Annual revenues and costs:						
10	Sales revenues	$200,000					
11	Cost of goods sold	$125,000					
12	Out-of-pocket operating costs	$35,000					
13	Discount rate	14%					
14							
15	*Enter a formula into each of the cells marked with a ? below*						
16	**Exhibit 11-7**						
17					Years		
18		Now	1	2	3	4	5
19	Purchase of equipment	?					
20	Investment in working capital	?					
21	Sales		?	?	?	?	?
22	Cost of goods sold		?	?	?	?	?
23	Out-of-pocket operating costs		?	?	?	?	?
24	Overhaul of equipment					?	
25	Salvage value of the equipment						?
26	Working capital released						?
27	Total cash flows (a)	?	?	?	?	?	?
28	Discount factor (14%) (b)	?	?	?	?	?	?
29	Present value of cash flows (a) x (b)	?	?	?	?	?	?
30	Net present value	?					
31							
32	*Use the formulas from Appendix 11B:*						
33	Present value of $1 = 1/(1+r)^n						
34	Present value of an annuity of $1 = (1/r)*(1-(1/(1+r)^n))						
35	where n is the number of years and r is the discount rate						
36							

⏮ ◀ ▶ ▶⏭ Chapter 11 Form ╱ Filled in Chapter 11 Form ╱ Chapter 11 Formulas ╱ Chap ◀

You should proceed to the requirements below only after completing your worksheet. Note that you may get a slightly different net present value from that shown in the text due to the precision of the calculations.

Required:

1. Check your worksheet by changing the discount rate to 10%. The net present value should now be between $56,495 and $56,518—depending on the precision of the calculations. If you do not get an answer in this range, find the errors in your worksheet and correct them.

    Explain why the net present value has fallen as a result of reducing the discount rate from 14% to 10%.

2. The company is considering another project involving the purchase of new equipment. Change the data area of your worksheet to match the following:

Data	
Example E	
Cost of equipment needed	$120,000
Working capital needed	$80,000
Overhaul of equipment in four years	$40,000
Salvage value of the equipment in five years ..	$20,000
Annual revenues and costs:	
Sales revenues	$255,000
Cost of goods sold	$160,000
Out-of-pocket operating costs	$50,000
Discount rate	14%

a. What is the net present value of the project?
b. Experiment with changing the discount rate in one percent increments (e.g., 13%, 12%, 15%, etc.). At what interest rate does the net present value turn from negative to positive?

THE FOUNDATIONAL 15

Available with McGraw-Hill's *Connect Accounting*.

Cardinal Company is considering a project that would require a $2,975,000 investment in equipment with a useful life of five years. At the end of five years, the project would terminate and the equipment would be sold for its salvage value of $300,000. The company's discount rate is 14%. The project would provide net operating income each year as follows:

Sales	$2,735,000
Variable expenses	1,000,000
Contribution margin	1,735,000
Fixed expenses:	
Advertising, salaries, and other fixed	
out-of-pocket costs $735,000	
Depreciation 535,000	
Total fixed expenses	1,270,000
Net operating income	$ 465,000

Required:

1. Which item(s) in the income statement shown above will not affect cash flows?
2. What are the project's annual net cash inflows?
3. What is the present value of the project's annual net cash inflows?
4. What is the present value of the equipment's salvage value at the end of five years?
5. What is the project's net present value?

6. What is the project profitability index for this project? (Round your answer to the nearest whole percent.)
7. What is the project's payback period?
8. What is the project's simple rate of return for each of the five years?
9. If the company's discount rate was 16% instead of 14%, would you expect the project's net present value to be higher than, lower than, or the same as your answer to question 4? No computations are necessary
10. If the equipment's salvage value was $500,000 instead of $300,000, would you expect the project's payback period to be higher than, lower than, or the same as your answer to question 7? No computations are necessary.
11. If the equipment's salvage value was $500,000 instead of $300,000, would you expect the project's net present value to be higher than, lower than, or the same as your answer to question 4? No computations are necessary.
12. If the equipment's salvage value was $500,000 instead of $300,000, what would be the project's simple rate of return?
13. Assume a postaudit showed that all estimates (including total sales) were exactly correct except for the variable expense ratio, which actually turned out to be 45%. What was the project's actual net present value?
14. Assume a postaudit showed that all estimates (including total sales) were exactly correct except for the variable expense ratio, which actually turned out to be 45%. What was the project's actual payback period?
15. Assume a postaudit showed that all estimates (including total sales) were exactly correct except for the variable expense ratio, which actually turned out to be 45%. What was the project's actual simple rate of return?

EXERCISES

All applicable exercises are available with McGraw-Hill's *Connect Accounting*.

EXERCISE 11–1 Payback Method [LO11–1]

The management of Unter Corporation, an architectural design firm, is considering an investment with the following cash flows:

Year	Investment	Cash Inflow
1	$15,000	$1,000
2	$8,000	$2,000
3		$2,500
4		$4,000
5		$5,000
6		$6,000
7		$5,000
8		$4,000
9		$3,000
10		$2,000

Investment in year
1 = $17.500

Required:
1. Determine the payback period of the investment.
2. Would the payback period be affected if the cash inflow in the last year were several times as large?

EXERCISE 11–2 Net Present Value Method [LO11–2]

The management of Kunkel Company is considering the purchase of a $27,000 machine that would reduce operating costs by $7,000 per year. At the end of the machine's five-year useful life, it will have zero scrap value. The company's required rate of return is 12%.

Required rate of
return = 10%

Required:
1. Determine the net present value of the investment in the machine.
2. What is the difference between the total, undiscounted cash inflows and cash outflows over the entire life of the machine?

EXERCISE 11–3 Preference Ranking [LO11–3]
Information on four investment proposals is given below:

	Investment Proposal			
	A	**B**	**C**	**D**
Investment required	$(90,000)	$(100,000)	$(70,000)	$(120,000)
Present value of cash inflows	126,000	138,000	105,000	160,000
Net present value	$ 36,000	$ 38,000	$ 35,000	$ 40,000
Life of the project	5 years	7 years	6 years	6 years

Required:
1. Compute the project profitability index for each investment proposal.
2. Rank the proposals in terms of preference.

EXERCISE 11–4 Simple Rate of Return Method [LO11–4]
The management of Ballard MicroBrew is considering the purchase of an automated bottling machine for $120,000. The machine would replace an old piece of equipment that costs $30,000 per year to operate. The new machine would cost $12,000 per year to operate. The old machine currently in use could be sold now for a scrap value of $40,000. The new machine would have a useful life of 10 years with no salvage value.

Useful life of new
machine = 8 years

Required:
Compute the simple rate of return on the new automated bottling machine.

EXERCISE 11–5 Net Present Value Analysis of Two Alternatives [LO11–2]
Perit Industries has $100,000 to invest. The company is trying to decide between two alternative uses of the funds. The alternatives are

	Project A	Project B
Cost of equipment required	$100,000	$0
Working capital investment required	$0	$100,000
Annual cash inflows	$21,000	$16,000
Salvage value of equipment in six years	$8,000	$0
Life of the project	6 years	6 years

The working capital needed for project B will be released at the end of six years for investment elsewhere. Perit Industries' discount rate is 14%.

Required:
Which investment alternative (if either) would you recommend that the company accept? Show all computations using the net present value method. Prepare separate computations for each project.

EXERCISE 11–6 Payback Period and Simple Rate of Return [LO11–1, LO11-4]
Nick's Novelties, Inc., is considering the purchase of new electronic games to place in its amusement houses. The games would cost a total of $300,000, have an eight-year useful life, and have a total salvage value of $20,000. The company estimates that annual revenues and expenses associated with the games would be as follows:

Revenues = $210,000

Revenues		$200,000
Less operating expenses:		
Commissions to amusement houses	$100,000	
Insurance	7,000	
Depreciation	35,000	
Maintenance	18,000	160,000
Net operating income		$ 40,000

Required:
1. Assume that Nick's Novelties, Inc., will not purchase new games unless they provide a payback period of five years or less. Would the company purchase the new games?
2. Compute the simple rate of return promised by the games. If the company requires a simple rate of return of at least 12%, will the games be purchased?

EXERCISE 11–7   Net Present Value Analysis and Simple Rate of Return [LO11–2, LO11–4]

Derrick Iverson is a divisional manager for Holston Company. His annual pay raises are largely determined by his division's return on investment (ROI), which has been above 20% each of the last three years. Derrick is considering a capital budgeting project that would require a $3,000,000 investment in equipment with a useful life of five years and no salvage value. Holston Company's discount rate is 15%. The project would provide net operating income each year for five years as follows:

Sales		$2,500,000
Variable expenses		1,000,000
Contribution margin		1,500,000
Fixed expenses:		
Advertising, salaries, and other fixed out-of-pocket costs	$600,000	
Depreciation	600,000	
Total fixed expenses		1,200,000
Net operating income		$ 300,000

Required:
1. Compute the project's net present value.
2. Compute the project's simple rate of return.
3. Would the company want Derrick to pursue this investment opportunity? Would Derrick be inclined to pursue this investment opportunity? Explain.

EXERCISE 11–8   Basic Net Present Value Analysis [LO11–2]

Kathy Myers frequently purchases stocks and bonds, but she is uncertain how to determine the rate of return that she is earning. For example, three years ago she paid $13,000 for 200 shares of Malti Company's common stock. She received a $420 cash dividend on the stock at the end of each year for three years. At the end of three years, she sold the stock for $16,000. Kathy would like to earn a return of at least 14% on all of her investments. She is not sure whether the Malti Company stock provided a 14% return and would like some help with the necessary computations.

TAKE
TWO

Required:
Using the net present value method, determine whether or not the Malti Company stock provided a 14% return. Round all computations to the nearest whole dollar.

Dividend = $500 per year

EXERCISE 11–9   Preference Ranking of Investment Projects [LO11–3]

Oxford Company has limited funds available for investment and must ration the funds among four competing projects. Selected information on the four projects follows:

Project	Investment Required	Net Present Value	Life of the Project (years)	Internal Rate of Return (percent)
A	$160,000	$44,323	7	18%
B	$135,000	$42,000	12	16%
C	$100,000	$35,035	7	20%
D	$175,000	$38,136	3	22%

The net present values above have been computed using a 10% discount rate. The company wants your assistance in determining which project to accept first, second, and so forth.

Required:

1. Compute the project profitability index for each project.
2. In order of preference, rank the four projects in terms of:
   a. Net present value.
   b. Project profitability index.
   c. Internal rate of return.
3. Which ranking do you prefer? Why?

EXERCISE 11–10   Basic Payback Period and Simple Rate of Return Computations [LO11–1, LO11–4]

A piece of laborsaving equipment has just come onto the market that Mitsui Electronics, Ltd., could use to reduce costs in one of its plants in Japan. Relevant data relating to the equipment follow:

Purchase cost of the equipment	$432,000
Annual cost savings that will be provided by the equipment	$90,000
Life of the equipment	12 years

Required:

1. Compute the payback period for the equipment. If the company requires a payback period of four years or less, would the equipment be purchased?
2. Compute the simple rate of return on the equipment. Use straight-line depreciation based on the equipment's useful life. Would the equipment be purchased if the company's required rate of return is 14%?

EXERCISE 11–11   Comparison of Projects Using Net Present Value [LO11–2]

Labeau Products, Ltd., of Perth, Australia, has $35,000 to invest. The company is trying to decide between two alternative uses for the funds as follows:

	Invest in Project X	Invest in Project Y
Investment required	$35,000	$35,000
Annual cash inflows	$12,000	
Single cash inflow at the end of 6 years		$90,000
Life of the project	6 years	6 years

Discount rate = 15%

The company's discount rate is 18%.

Required:

Which alternative would you recommend that the company accept? Show all computations using the net present value approach. Prepare separate computations for each project.

PROBLEMS

connect
|ACCOUNTING

All applicable problems are available with McGraw-Hill's *Connect Accounting*.

PROBLEM 11–12A   Basic Net Present Value Analysis [LO11–2]

Windhoek Mines, Ltd., of Namibia, is contemplating the purchase of equipment to exploit a mineral deposit on land to which the company has mineral rights. An engineering and cost analysis has been made, and it is expected that the following cash flows would be associated with opening and operating a mine in the area:

Cost of new equipment and timbers	$275,000
Working capital required	$100,000
Annual net cash receipts	$120,000*
Cost to construct new roads in three years	$40,000
Salvage value of equipment in four years	$65,000

*Receipts from sales of ore, less out-of-pocket costs for salaries, utilities, insurance, and so forth.

The mineral deposit would be exhausted after four years of mining. At that point, the working capital would be released for reinvestment elsewhere. The company's required rate of return is 20%.

Required:
Determine the net present value of the proposed mining project. Should the project be accepted? Explain.

PROBLEM 11–13A Net Present Value Analysis; Simple Rate of Return [LO11–2, LO11–4]
Casey Nelson is a divisional manager for Pigeon Company. His annual pay raises are largely determined by his division's return on investment (ROI), which has been above 20% each of the last three years. Casey is considering a capital budgeting project that would require a $3,500,000 investment in equipment with a useful life of five years and no salvage value. Pigeon Company's discount rate is 16%. The project would provide net operating income each year for five years as follows:

Sales		$3,400,000
Variable expenses		1,600,000
Contribution margin		1,800,000
Fixed expenses:		
Advertising, salaries, and other fixed out-of-pocket costs	$700,000	
Depreciation	700,000	
Total fixed expenses		1,400,000
Net operating income		$ 400,000

Required:
1. What is the project's net present value?
2. What is the project's simple rate of return?
3. Would the company want Casey to pursue this investment opportunity? Would Casey be inclined to pursue this investment opportunity? Explain.

PROBLEM 11–14A Net Present Value Analysis [LO11–2]
Oakmont Company has an opportunity to manufacture and sell a new product for a four-year period. The company's discount rate is 15%. After careful study, Oakmont estimated the following costs and revenues for the new product:

Cost of equipment needed	$130,000
Working capital needed	$60,000
Overhaul of the equipment in two years	$8,000
Salvage value of the equipment in four years	$12,000
Annual revenues and costs:	
Sales revenues	$250,000
Variable expenses	$120,000
Fixed out-of-pocket operating costs	$70,000

When the project concludes in four years the working capital will be released for investment elsewhere within the company.

Required:
Calculate the net present value of this investment opportunity.

PROBLEM 11–15A Simple Rate of Return; Payback [LO11–1, LO11–4]
Paul Swanson has an opportunity to acquire a franchise from The Yogurt Place, Inc., to dispense frozen yogurt products under The Yogurt Place name. Mr. Swanson has assembled the following information relating to the franchise:

a. A suitable location in a large shopping mall can be rented for $3,500 per month.
b. Remodeling and necessary equipment would cost $270,000. The equipment would have a 15-year life and an $18,000 salvage value. Straight-line depreciation would be used, and the salvage value would be considered in computing depreciation.

c. Based on similar outlets elsewhere, Mr. Swanson estimates that sales would total $300,000 per year. Ingredients would cost 20% of sales.

d. Operating costs would include $70,000 per year for salaries, $3,500 per year for insurance, and $27,000 per year for utilities. In addition, Mr. Swanson would have to pay a commission to The Yogurt Place, Inc., of 12.5% of sales.

Required:

1. Prepare a contribution format income statement that shows the expected net operating income each year from the franchise outlet.

2. Compute the simple rate of return promised by the outlet. If Mr. Swanson requires a simple rate of return of at least 12%, should he acquire the franchise?

3. Compute the payback period on the outlet. If Mr. Swanson wants a payback of four years or less, will he acquire the franchise?

PROBLEM 11–16A   Net Present Value Analysis [LO11–2]

"I'm not sure we should lay out $250,000 for that automated welding machine," said Jim Alder, president of the Superior Equipment Company. "That's a lot of money, and it would cost us $80,000 for software and installation, and another $3,000 every month just to maintain the thing. In addition, the manufacturer admits that it would cost $45,000 more at the end of three years to replace worn-out parts."

"I admit it's a lot of money," said Franci Rogers, the controller. "But you know the turnover problem we've had with the welding crew. This machine would replace six welders at a cost savings of $108,000 per year. And we would save another $6,500 per year in reduced material waste. When you figure that the automated welder would last for six years, I'm sure the return would be greater than our 16% required rate of return."

"I'm still not convinced," countered Mr. Alder. "We can only get $12,000 scrap value out of our old welding equipment if we sell it now, and in six years the new machine will only be worth $20,000 for parts. But have your people work up the figures and we'll talk about them at the executive committee meeting tomorrow."

Required:

1. Compute the annual net cost savings promised by the automated welding machine.

2. Using the data from (1) above and other data from the problem, compute the automated welding machine's net present value. Would you recommend purchasing the automated welding machine? Explain.

PROBLEM 11–17A   Preference Ranking of Investment Projects [LO11–3]

The management of Revco Products is exploring four different investment opportunities. Information on the four projects under study follows:

	Project Number			
	1	**2**	**3**	**4**
Investment required	$(270,000)	$(450,000)	$(360,000)	$(480,000)
Present value of cash inflows at a 10% discount rate	336,140	522,970	433,400	567,270
Net present value	$ 66,140	$ 72,970	$ 73,400	$ 87,270
Life of the project	6 years	3 years	12 years	6 years
Internal rate of return	18%	19%	14%	16%

Because the company's required rate of return is 10%, a 10% discount rate has been used in the present value computations above. Limited funds are available for investment, so the company can't accept all of the available projects.

Required:

1. Compute the project profitability index for each investment project.

2. Rank the four projects according to preference, in terms of:
    a. Net present value
    b. Project profitability index
    c. Internal rate of return

3. Which ranking do you prefer? Why?

PROBLEM 11–18A Basic Net Present Value Analysis [LO11–2]

The Sweetwater Candy Company would like to buy a new machine that would automatically "dip" chocolates. The dipping operation is currently done largely by hand. The machine the company is considering costs $120,000. The manufacturer estimates that the machine would be usable for five years but would require the replacement of several key parts at the end of the third year. These parts would cost $9,000, including installation. After five years, the machine could be sold for $7,500.

The company estimates that the cost to operate the machine will be $7,000 per year. The present method of dipping chocolates costs $30,000 per year. In addition to reducing costs, the new machine will increase production by 6,000 boxes of chocolates per year. The company realizes a contribution margin of $1.50 per box. A 20% rate of return is required on all investments.

Required:
1. What are the annual net cash inflows that will be provided by the new dipping machine?
2. Compute the new machine's net present value. Round all dollar amounts to the nearest whole dollar.

PROBLEM 11–19A Comprehensive Problem [LO11–1, LO11–2, LO11–3, LO11–4]

Lou Barlow, a divisional manager for Sage Company, has an opportunity to manufacture and sell one of two new products for a five-year period. His annual pay raises are determined by his division's return on investment (ROI), which has exceeded 18% each of the last three years. He has computed the cost and revenue estimates for each product as follows:

	Product A	Product B
Initial investment:		
Cost of equipment (zero salvage value)	$170,000	$380,000
Annual revenues and costs:		
Sales revenues	$250,000	$350,000
Variable expenses	$120,000	$170,000
Depreciation expense	$34,000	$76,000
Fixed out-of-pocket operating costs	$70,000	$50,000

The company's discount rate is 16%.

Required:
1. Calculate the payback period for each product.
2. Calculate the net present value for each product.
3. Calculate the project profitability index for each product.
4. Calculate the simple rate of return for each product.
5. Which of the two products should Lou's division pursue? Why?

PROBLEM 11–20A Simple Rate of Return; Payback [LO11–1, LO11–4]

The Elberta Fruit Farm of Ontario has always hired transient workers to pick its annual cherry crop. Francie Wright, the farm manager, has just received information on a cherry picking machine that is being purchased by many fruit farms. The machine is a motorized device that shakes the cherry tree, causing the cherries to fall onto plastic tarps that funnel the cherries into bins. Ms. Wright has gathered the following information to decide whether a cherry picker would be a profitable investment for the Elberta Fruit Farm:
a. Currently, the farm is paying an average of $40,000 per year to transient workers to pick the cherries.
b. The cherry picker would cost $94,500, and it would have an estimated 12-year useful life. The farm uses straight-line depreciation on all assets and considers salvage value in computing depreciation deductions. The estimated salvage value of the cherry picker is $4,500.
c. Annual out-of-pocket costs associated with the cherry picker would be cost of an operator and an assistant, $14,000; insurance, $200; fuel, $1,800; and a maintenance contract, $3,000.

Required:
1. Determine the annual savings in cash operating costs that would be realized if the cherry picker were purchased.
2. Compute the simple rate of return expected from the cherry picker. Would the cherry picker be purchased if Elberta Fruit Farm's required rate of return is 16%?
3. Compute the payback period on the cherry picker. The Elberta Fruit Farm will not purchase equipment unless it has a payback period of five years or less. Would the cherry picker be purchased?

PROBLEM 11–21A   Net Present Value Analysis of a Lease or Buy Decision [LO11–2]

The Riteway Ad Agency provides cars for its sales staff. In the past, the company has always purchased its cars from a dealer and then sold the cars after three years of use. The company's present fleet of cars is three years old and will be sold very shortly. To provide a replacement fleet, the company is considering two alternatives:

Purchase alternative: The company can purchase the cars, as in the past, and sell the cars after three years of use. Ten cars will be needed, which can be purchased at a discounted price of $17,000 each. If this alternative is accepted, the following costs will be incurred on the fleet as a whole:

Annual cost of servicing, taxes, and licensing . . .	$3,000
Repairs, first year	$1,500
Repairs, second year	$4,000
Repairs, third year	$6,000

At the end of three years, the fleet could be sold for one-half of the original purchase price.

Lease alternative: The company can lease the cars under a three-year lease contract. The lease cost would be $55,000 per year (the first payment due at the end of Year 1). As part of this lease cost, the owner would provide all servicing and repairs, license the cars, and pay all the taxes. Riteway would be required to make a $10,000 security deposit at the beginning of the lease period, which would be refunded when the cars were returned to the owner at the end of the lease contract.

Riteway Ad Agency's required rate of return is 18%.

Required:

1.   Use the total-cost approach to determine the present value of the cash flows associated with each alternative. Round all dollar amounts to the nearest whole dollar.
2.   Which alternative should the company accept?

PROBLEM 11–22A   Simple Rate of Return; Payback [LO11–1, LO11–4]

Sharkey's Fun Center contains a number of electronic games as well as a miniature golf course and various rides located outside the building. Paul Sharkey, the owner, would like to construct a water slide on one portion of his property. Mr. Sharkey has gathered the following information about the slide:

a.   Water slide equipment could be purchased and installed at a cost of $330,000. According to the manufacturer, the slide would be usable for 12 years after which it would have no salvage value.
b.   Mr. Sharkey would use straight-line depreciation on the slide equipment.
c.   To make room for the water slide, several rides would be dismantled and sold. These rides are fully depreciated, but they could be sold for $60,000 to an amusement park in a nearby city.
d.   Mr. Sharkey has concluded that about 50,000 more people would use the water slide each year than have been using the rides. The admission price would be $3.60 per person (the same price that the Fun Center has been charging for the old rides).
e.   Based on experience at other water slides, Mr. Sharkey estimates that annual incremental operating expenses for the slide would be salaries, $85,000; insurance, $4,200; utilities, $13,000; and maintenance, $9,800.

Required:

1.   Prepare an income statement showing the expected net operating income each year from the water slide.
2.   Compute the simple rate of return expected from the water slide. Based on this computation, would the water slide be constructed if Mr. Sharkey requires a simple rate of return of at least 14% on all investments?
3.   Compute the payback period for the water slide. If Mr. Sharkey accepts any project with a payback period of five years or less, would the water slide be constructed?

PROBLEM 11–23A   Net Present Value Analysis [LO11–2]

In five years, Kent Duncan will retire. He is exploring the possibility of opening a self-service car wash. The car wash could be managed in the free time he has available from his regular occupation, and it could be closed easily when he retires. After careful study, Mr. Duncan has determined the following:

a.   A building in which a car wash could be installed is available under a five-year lease at a cost of $1,700 per month.
b.   Purchase and installation costs of equipment would total $200,000. In five years the equipment could be sold for about 10% of its original cost.

c. An investment of an additional $2,000 would be required to cover working capital needs for cleaning supplies, change funds, and so forth. After five years, this working capital would be released for investment elsewhere.

d. Both a wash and a vacuum service would be offered with a wash costing $2.00 and the vacuum costing $1.00 per use.

e. The only variable costs associated with the operation would be 20 cents per wash for water and 10 cents per use of the vacuum for electricity.

f. In addition to rent, monthly costs of operation would be cleaning, $450; insurance, $75; and maintenance, $500.

g. Gross receipts from the wash would be about $1,350 per week. According to the experience of other car washes, 60% of the customers using the wash would also use the vacuum.

Mr. Duncan will not open the car wash unless it provides at least a 10% return.

Required:

1. Assuming that the car wash will be open 52 weeks a year, compute the expected annual net cash receipts (gross cash receipts less cash disbursements) from its operation. (Do not include the cost of the equipment, the working capital, or the salvage value in these computations.)

2. Would you advise Mr. Duncan to open the car wash? Show computations using the net present value method of investment analysis. Round all dollar figures to the nearest whole dollar.

PROBLEM 11–24A Net Present Value [LO11–2]

Bilboa Freightlines, S.A., of Panama, has a small truck that it uses for intracity deliveries. The truck is worn out and must be either overhauled or replaced with a new truck. The company has assembled the following information:

	Present Truck	New Truck
Purchase cost new	$21,000	$30,000
Remaining book value	$11,500	
Overhaul needed now	$7,000	
Annual cash operating costs	$10,000	$6,500
Salvage value-now	$9,000	
Salvage value-five years from now ...	$1,000	$4,000

If the company keeps and overhauls its present delivery truck, then the truck will be usable for five more years. If a new truck is purchased, it will be used for five years, after which it will be traded in on another truck. The new truck would be diesel-operated, resulting in a substantial reduction in annual operating costs, as shown above.

The company computes depreciation on a straight-line basis. All investment projects are evaluated using a 16% discount rate.

Required:

Should Bilboa Freightlines keep the old truck or purchase the new one? Use the total-cost approach to net present value in making your decision. Round to the nearest whole dollar.

PROBLEM 11–25A Net Present Value Analysis of Securities [LO11–2]

Linda Clark received $175,000 from her mother's estate. She placed the funds into the hands of a broker, who purchased the following securities on Linda's behalf:

a. Common stock was purchased at a cost of $95,000. The stock paid no dividends, but it was sold for $160,000 at the end of three years.

b. Preferred stock was purchased at its par value of $30,000. The stock paid a 6% dividend (based on par value) each year for three years. At the end of three years, the stock was sold for $27,000.

c. Bonds were purchased at a cost of $50,000. The bonds paid annual interest of $6,000. After three years, the bonds were sold for $52,700.

The securities were all sold at the end of three years so that Linda would have funds available to open a new business venture. The broker stated that the investments had earned more than a 16% return, and he gave Linda the following computations to support his statement:

Common stock:	
Gain on sale ($160,000 − $95,000)	$65,000
Preferred stock:	
Dividends paid (6% × $30,000 × 3 years) . .	5,400
Loss on sale ($27,000 − $30,000)	(3,000)
Bonds:	
Interest paid ($6,000 × 3 years)	18,000
Gain on sale ($52,700 − $50,000)	2,700
Net gain on all investments	$88,100

$$\frac{\$88,100 \div 3 \text{ years}}{\$175,000} = 16.8\%$$

Required:
1. Using a 16% discount rate, compute the net present value of each of the three investments. On which investment(s) did Linda earn a 16% rate of return? (Round computations to the nearest whole dollar.)
2. Considering all three investments together, did Linda earn a 16% rate of return? Explain.
3. Linda wants to use the $239,700 proceeds ($160,000 + $27,000 + $52,700 = $239,700) from sale of the securities to open a retail store under a 12-year franchise contract. What annual net cash inflow must the store generate for Linda to earn a 14% return over the 12-year period? Round computations to the nearest whole dollar.

BUILDING YOUR SKILLS

ETHICS CHALLENGE

The Fore Corporation is an integrated food processing company that has operations in over two dozen countries. Fore's corporate headquarters is in Chicago, and the company's executives frequently travel to visit Fore's foreign and domestic facilities.

Fore has a fleet of aircraft that consists of two business jets with international range and six smaller turboprop aircraft that are used on shorter flights. Company policy is to assign aircraft to trips on the basis of minimizing cost, but the practice is to assign the aircraft based on the organizational rank of the traveler. Fore offers its aircraft for short-term lease or for charter by other organizations whenever Fore itself does not plan to use the aircraft. Fore surveys the market often in order to keep its lease and charter rates competitive.

William Earle, Fore's vice president of finance, has claimed that a third business jet can be justified financially. However, some people in the controller's office have surmised that the real reason for a third business jet was to upgrade the aircraft used by Earle. Presently, the people outranking Earle keep the two business jets busy with the result that Earle usually flies in smaller turboprop aircraft.

The third business jet would cost $11 million. A capital expenditure of this magnitude requires a formal proposal with projected cash flows and net present value computations using Fore's minimum required rate of return. If Fore's president and the finance committee of the board of directors approve the proposal, it will be submitted to the full board of directors. The board has final approval on capital expenditures exceeding $5 million and has established a firm policy of rejecting any discretionary proposal that has a negative net present value.

Earle asked Rachel Arnett, assistant corporate controller, to prepare a proposal on a third business jet. Arnett gathered the following data:

- Acquisition cost of the aircraft, including instrumentation and interior furnishing.
- Operating cost of the aircraft for company use.
- Projected avoidable commercial airfare and other avoidable costs from company use of the plane.
- Projected value of executive time saved by using the third business jet.
- Projected contribution margin from incremental lease and charter activity.
- Estimated resale value of the aircraft.

When Earle reviewed Arnett's completed proposal and saw the large negative net present value figure, he returned the proposal to Arnett. With a glare, Earle commented, "You must have made an error. The proposal should look better than that."

Feeling some pressure, Arnett went back and checked her computations; she found no errors. However, Earle's message was clear. Arnett discarded her projections that she believed were reasonable and replaced them with figures that had a remote chance of actually occurring but were more favorable to the proposal. For example, she used first-class airfares to refigure the avoidable commercial airfare costs, even though company policy was to fly coach. She found revising the proposal to be distressing.

The revised proposal still had a negative net present value. Earle's anger was evident as he told Arnett to revise the proposal again, and to start with a $100,000 positive net present value and work backwards to compute supporting projections.

Required:
1. Explain whether Rachel Arnett's revision of the proposal was in violation of the IMA's Statement of Ethical Professional Practice.
2. Was William Earle in violation of the IMA's Statement of Ethical Professional Practice by telling Arnett specifically how to revise the proposal? Explain your answer.
3. Identify specific internal controls that Fore Corporation could implement to prevent unethical behavior on the part of the vice president of finance.

(CMA, adapted)

CASE [LO11–2]

Matheson Electronics has just developed a new electronic device that it believes will have broad market appeal. The company has performed marketing and cost studies that revealed the following information:
a. New equipment would have to be acquired to produce the device. The equipment would cost $315,000 and have a six-year useful life. After six years, it would have a salvage value of about $15,000.
b. Sales in units over the next six years are projected to be as follows:

Year	Sales in Units
1	9,000
2	15,000
3	18,000
4–6	22,000

c. Production and sales of the device would require working capital of $60,000 to finance accounts receivable, inventories, and day-to-day cash needs. This working capital would be released at the end of the project's life.
d. The devices would sell for $35 each; variable costs for production, administration, and sales would be $15 per unit.
e. Fixed costs for salaries, maintenance, property taxes, insurance, and straight-line depreciation on the equipment would total $135,000 per year. (Depreciation is based on cost less salvage value.)
f. To gain rapid entry into the market, the company would have to advertise heavily. The advertising program would be

Year	Amount of Yearly Advertising
1–2	$180,000
3	$150,000
4–6	$120,000

g. The company's required rate of return is 14%.

Required:
1. Compute the net cash inflow (cash receipts less yearly cash operating expenses) anticipated from sale of the device for each year over the next six years.
2. Using the data computed in (1) above and other data provided in the problem, determine the net present value of the proposed investment. Would you recommend that Matheson accept the device as a new product?

APPENDIX 11A: THE CONCEPT OF PRESENT VALUE

A dollar received today is more valuable than a dollar received a year from now for the simple reason that if you have a dollar today, you can put it in the bank and have more than a dollar a year from now. Because dollars today are worth more than dollars in the future, cash flows that are received at different times must be valued differently.

The Mathematics of Interest

If a bank pays 5% interest, then a deposit of $100 today will be worth $105 one year from now. This can be expressed as follows:

$$F_1 = P(1 + r) \tag{1}$$

where F_1 = the balance at the end of one period, P = the amount invested now, and r = the rate of interest per period.

In the case where $100 is deposited in a savings account that earns 5% interest, $P = \$100$ and $r = 0.05$. Under these conditions, $F_1 = \$105$.

The $100 present outlay is called the **present value** of the $105 amount to be received in one year. It is also known as the *discounted value* of the future $105 receipt. The $100 represents the value in present terms of $105 to be received a year from now when the interest rate is 5%.

Compound Interest   What if the $105 is left in the bank for a second year? In that case, by the end of the second year the original $100 deposit will have grown to $110.25.

Original deposit	$100.00
Interest for the first year:	
$100 × 0.05	5.00
Balance at the end of the first year	105.00
Interest for the second year:	
$105 × 0.05	5.25
Balance at the end of the second year	$110.25

Notice that the interest for the second year is $5.25, as compared to only $5.00 for the first year. This difference arises because interest is being paid on interest during the second year. That is, the $5.00 interest earned during the first year has been left in the account and has been added to the original $100 deposit when computing interest for the second year. This is known as **compound interest**. In this case, the compounding is annual. Interest can be compounded on a semiannual, quarterly, monthly, or even more frequent basis. The more frequently compounding is done, the more rapidly the balance will grow.

We can determine the balance in an account after n periods of compounding using the following equation:

$$F_n = P(1 + r)^n \tag{2}$$

where n = the number of periods of compounding.

If $n = 2$ years and the interest rate is 5% per year, then the balance in two years will be computed as follows:

$$F_2 = \$100(1 + 0.05)^2$$

$$F_2 = \$110.25$$

EXHIBIT 11A–1
The Relationship between
Present Value and Future Value

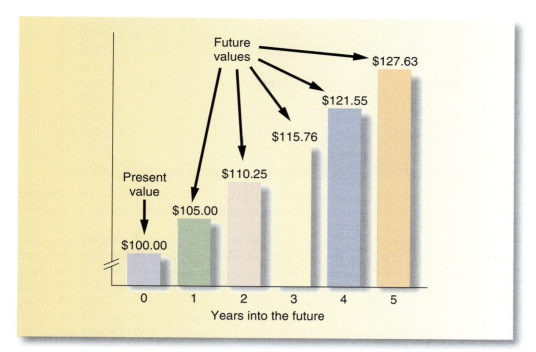

Present Value and Future Value

Present Value and Future Value   Exhibit 11A–1 shows the relationship between present value and future value. As shown in the exhibit, if $100 is deposited in a bank at 5% interest compounded annually, it will grow to $127.63 by the end of five years.

Computation of Present Value

An investment can be viewed in two ways—either in terms of its future value or in terms of its present value. We have seen from our computations above that if we know the present value of a sum (such as our $100 deposit), the future value in n years can be computed by using equation (2). But what if the situation is reversed and we know the *future* value of some amount but we do not know its present value?

For example, assume that you are to receive $200 two years from now. You know that the future value of this sum is $200 because this is the amount that you will be receiving in two years. But what is the sum's present value—what is it worth *right now?* The present value of any sum to be received in the future can be computed by turning equation (2) around and solving for P:

$$P = \frac{F_n}{(1 + r)^n} \qquad (3)$$

In our example, $F_n = 200 (the amount to be received in the future), $r = 0.05$ (the annual rate of interest), and $n = 2$ (the number of years in the future that the amount will be received).

$$P = \frac{$200}{(1 + 0.05)^2}$$

$$P = \frac{$200}{1.1025}$$

$$P = $181.40$$

As shown by the computation above, the present value of a $200 amount to be received two years from now is $181.40 if the interest rate is 5%. In effect, $181.40 received *right now* is equivalent to $200 received two years from now.

The process of finding the present value of a future cash flow, which we have just completed, is called **discounting**. We have *discounted* the $200 to its present value of

Present Value of a Series of Cash Receipts

Year	Factor at 12% (Exhibit 11B–1)	Interest Received	Present Value
1	0.893	$15,000	$13,395
2	0.797	$15,000	11,955
3	0.712	$15,000	10,680
4	0.636	$15,000	9,540
5	0.567	$15,000	8,505
			$54,075

$181.40. The 5% interest that we have used to find this present value is called the **discount rate**. Discounting future sums to their present value is a common practice in business, particularly in capital budgeting decisions.

If you have a power key (y^x) on your calculator, the above calculations are fairly easy. However, some of the present value formulas we will be using are more complex. Fortunately, tables are available in which many of the calculations have already been done. For example, Exhibit 11B–1 in Appendix 11B shows the discounted present value of $1 to be received at various periods in the future at various interest rates. The table indicates that the present value of $1 to be received two periods from now at 5% is 0.907. Because in our example we want to know the present value of $200 rather than just $1, we need to multiply the factor in the table by $200:

$$\$200 \times 0.907 = \$181.40$$

This answer is the same as we obtained earlier using the formula in equation (3).

Present Value of a Series of Cash Flows

Although some investments involve a single sum to be received (or paid) at a single point in the future, other investments involve a *series* of cash flows. A series of identical cash flows is known as an **annuity**. To provide an example, assume that a company has just purchased some government bonds. The bonds will yield interest of $15,000 each year and will be held for five years. What is the present value of the stream of interest receipts from the bonds? As shown in Exhibit 11A–2, if the discount rate is 12%, the present value of this stream is $54,075. The discount factors used in this exhibit were taken from Exhibit 11B–1 in Appendix 11B.

Exhibit 11A–2 illustrates two important points. First, the present value of the $15,000 interest declines the further it is into the future. The present value of $15,000 received a year from now is $13,395, as compared to only $8,505 if received five years from now. This point underscores the time value of money.

The second point is that the computations used in Exhibit 11A–2 involved unnecessary work. The same present value of $54,075 could have been obtained more easily by referring to Exhibit 11B–2 in Appendix 11B. Exhibit 11B–2 contains the present value of $1 to be received each year over a *series* of years at various interest rates. Exhibit 11B–2 has been derived by simply adding together the factors from Exhibit 11B–1, as follows:

Year	Factors at 12% (from Exhibit 11B–1)
1	0.893
2	0.797
3	0.712
4	0.636
5	0.567
	3.605

The sum of these five factors is 3.605. Notice from Exhibit 11B–2 that the factor for $1 to be received each year for five years at 12% is also 3.605. If we use this factor and multiply it by the $15,000 annual cash inflow, then we get the same $54,075 present value that we obtained earlier in Exhibit 11A–2.

$$\$15,000 \times 3.605 = \$54,075$$

Therefore, when computing the present value of a series of equal cash flows that begins at the end of period 1, Exhibit 11B–2 should be used.

To summarize, the present value tables in Appendix 11B should be used as follows:

Exhibit 11B–1: This table should be used to find the present value of a single cash flow (such as a single payment or receipt) occurring in the future.

Exhibit 11B–2: This table should be used to find the present value of a series of identical cash flows beginning at the end of the current period and continuing into the future.

The use of both of these tables is illustrated in various exhibits in the main body of the chapter. *When a present value factor appears in an exhibit, you should take the time to trace it back into either Exhibit 11B–1 or Exhibit 11B–2 to get acquainted with the tables and how they work.*

REVIEW PROBLEM: BASIC PRESENT VALUE COMPUTATIONS

Each of the following situations is independent. Work out your own solution to each situation, and then check it against the solution provided.

1. John plans to retire in 12 years. Upon retiring, he would like to take an extended vacation, which he expects will cost at least $40,000. What lump-sum amount must he invest now to have $40,000 at the end of 12 years if the rate of return is as follows:
    a. Eight percent?
    b. Twelve percent?
2. The Morgans would like to send their daughter to a music camp at the end of each of the next five years. The camp costs $1,000 a year. What lump-sum amount would have to be invested now to have $1,000 at the end of each year if the rate of return is as follows:
    a. Eight percent?
    b. Twelve percent?
3. You have just received an inheritance from a relative. You can either receive a $200,000 lump-sum amount at the end of 10 years or receive $14,000 at the end of each year for the next 10 years. If your discount rate is 12%, which alternative would you prefer?

Solution to Review Problem

1. a. The amount that must be invested now would be the present value of the $40,000, using a discount rate of 8%. From Exhibit 11B–1 in Appendix 11B, the factor for a discount rate of 8% for 12 periods is 0.397. Multiplying this discount factor by the $40,000 needed in 12 years will give the amount of the present investment required: $40,000 × 0.397 = $15,880.
    b. We will proceed as we did in (*a*) above, but this time we will use a discount rate of 12%. From Exhibit 11B–1 in Appendix 11B, the factor for a discount rate of 12% for 12 periods is 0.257. Multiplying this discount factor by the $40,000 needed in 12 years will give the amount of the present investment required: $40,000 × 0.257 = $10,280.
        Notice that as the discount rate (desired rate of return) increases, the present value decreases.
2. This part differs from (1) above in that we are now dealing with an annuity rather than with a single future sum. The amount that must be invested now is the present value of the $1,000 needed at the end of each year for five years. Because we are dealing with an annuity, or a series of annual cash flows, we must refer to Exhibit 11B–2 in Appendix 11B for the appropriate discount factor.

a. From Exhibit 11B–2 in Appendix 11B, the discount factor for 8% for five periods is 3.993. Therefore, the amount that must be invested now to have $1,000 available at the end of each year for five years is $1,000 × 3.993 = $3,993.

b. From Exhibit 11B–2 in Appendix 11B, the discount factor for 12% for five periods is 3.605. Therefore, the amount that must be invested now to have $1,000 available at the end of each year for five years is $1,000 × 3.605 = $3,605.

Again, notice that as the discount rate increases, the present value decreases. When the rate of return increases, less must be invested today to yield a given amount in the future.

3. For this part we will need to refer to both Exhibits 11B–1 and 11B–2 in Appendix 11B. From Exhibit 11B–1, we will need to find the discount factor for 12% for 10 periods, then apply it to the $200,000 lump sum to be received in 10 years. From Exhibit 11B–2, we will need to find the discount factor for 12% for 10 periods, then apply it to the series of $14,000 payments to be received over the 10-year period. Whichever alternative has the higher present value is the one that should be selected.

$$\$200,000 \times 0.322 = \$64,400$$

$$\$14,000 \times 5.650 = \$79,100$$

Thus, you should prefer to receive the $14,000 per year for 10 years rather than the $200,000 lump sum. This means that you could invest the $14,000 received at the end of each year at 12% and have *more* than $200,000 at the end of 10 years.

GLOSSARY (APPENDIX 11A)

Annuity   A series of identical cash flows. (p. 550)
Compound interest   The process of paying interest on interest in an investment. (p. 548)
Discount rate   The rate of return that is used to find the present value of a future cash flow. (p. 550)
Discounting   The process of finding the present value of a future cash flow. (p. 549)
Present value   The value now of an amount that will be received in some future period. (p. 548)

APPENDIX 11A EXERCISES

All applicable exercises are available with McGraw-Hill's *Connect Accounting*.

EXERCISE 11A–1   Basic Present Value Concepts [LO11–5]
Annual cash inflows that will arise from two competing investment projects are given below:

Year	Investment A	Investment B
1	$ 3,000	$12,000
2	6,000	9,000
3	9,000	6,000
4	12,000	3,000
	$30,000	$30,000

The discount rate is 18%.

Required:
Compute the present value of the cash inflows for each investment.

EXERCISE 11A–2   Basic Present Value Concepts [LO11–5]
Julie has just retired. Her company's retirement program has two options as to how retirement benefits can be received. Under the first option, Julie would receive a lump sum of $150,000 immediately as her full retirement benefit. Under the second option, she would receive $14,000 each year for 20 years plus a lump-sum payment of $60,000 at the end of the 20-year period.

Required:

If she can invest money at 12%, which option would you recommend that she accept? Use present value analysis.

EXERCISE 11A–3   Basic Present Value Concepts [LO11–5]

In three years, when he is discharged from the Air Force, Steve wants to buy an $8,000 power boat.

Required:

What lump-sum amount must Steve invest now to have the $8,000 at the end of three years if he can invest money at:
1.   Ten percent?
2.   Fourteen percent?

EXERCISE 11A–4   Basic Present Value Concepts [LO11–5]

Fraser Company will need a new warehouse in five years. The warehouse will cost $500,000 to build.

Required:

What lump-sum amount should the company invest now to have the $500,000 available at the end of the five-year period? Assume that the company can invest money at:
1.   Ten percent.
2.   Fourteen percent.

EXERCISE 11A–5   Basic Present Value Concepts [LO11–5]

The Atlantic Medical Clinic can purchase a new computer system that will save $7,000 annually in billing costs. The computer system will last for eight years and have no salvage value.

Required:

Up to how much should the Atlantic Medical Clinic be willing to pay for the new computer system if the clinic's required rate of return is as follows:
1.   Sixteen percent?
2.   Twenty percent?

EXERCISE 11A–6   Basic Present Value Concepts [LO11–5]

The Caldwell Herald newspaper reported the following story: Frank Ormsby of Caldwell is the state's newest millionaire. By choosing the six winning numbers on last week's state lottery, Mr. Ormsby has won the week's grand prize totaling $1.6 million. The State Lottery Commission has indicated that Mr. Ormsby will receive his prize in 20 annual installments of $80,000 each.

Required:

1.   If Mr. Ormsby can invest money at a 12% rate of return, what is the present value of his winnings?
2.   Is it correct to say that Mr. Ormsby is the "state's newest millionaire"? Explain your answer.

APPENDIX 11B: PRESENT VALUE TABLES

EXHIBIT 11B–1 Present Value of \$1; $\dfrac{1}{(1+r)^n}$

Periods	4%	5%	6%	7%	8%	9%	10%	11%	12%	13%	14%	15%	16%	17%	18%	19%	20%	21%	22%	23%	24%	25%
1	0.962	0.952	0.943	0.935	0.926	0.917	0.909	0.901	0.893	0.885	0.877	0.870	0.862	0.855	0.847	0.840	0.833	0.826	0.820	0.813	0.806	0.800
2	0.925	0.907	0.890	0.873	0.857	0.842	0.826	0.812	0.797	0.783	0.769	0.756	0.743	0.731	0.718	0.706	0.694	0.683	0.672	0.661	0.650	0.640
3	0.889	0.864	0.840	0.816	0.794	0.772	0.751	0.731	0.712	0.693	0.675	0.658	0.641	0.624	0.609	0.593	0.579	0.564	0.551	0.537	0.524	0.512
4	0.855	0.823	0.792	0.763	0.735	0.708	0.683	0.659	0.636	0.613	0.592	0.572	0.552	0.534	0.516	0.499	0.482	0.467	0.451	0.437	0.423	0.410
5	0.822	0.784	0.747	0.713	0.681	0.650	0.621	0.593	0.567	0.543	0.519	0.497	0.476	0.456	0.437	0.419	0.402	0.386	0.370	0.355	0.341	0.328
6	0.790	0.746	0.705	0.666	0.630	0.596	0.564	0.535	0.507	0.480	0.456	0.432	0.410	0.390	0.370	0.352	0.335	0.319	0.303	0.289	0.275	0.262
7	0.760	0.711	0.665	0.623	0.583	0.547	0.513	0.482	0.452	0.425	0.400	0.376	0.354	0.333	0.314	0.296	0.279	0.263	0.249	0.235	0.222	0.210
8	0.731	0.677	0.627	0.582	0.540	0.502	0.467	0.434	0.404	0.376	0.351	0.327	0.305	0.285	0.266	0.249	0.233	0.218	0.204	0.191	0.179	0.168
9	0.703	0.645	0.592	0.544	0.500	0.460	0.424	0.391	0.361	0.333	0.308	0.284	0.263	0.243	0.225	0.209	0.194	0.180	0.167	0.155	0.144	0.134
10	0.676	0.614	0.558	0.508	0.463	0.422	0.386	0.352	0.322	0.295	0.270	0.247	0.227	0.208	0.191	0.176	0.162	0.149	0.137	0.126	0.116	0.107
11	0.650	0.585	0.527	0.475	0.429	0.388	0.350	0.317	0.287	0.261	0.237	0.215	0.195	0.178	0.162	0.148	0.135	0.123	0.112	0.103	0.094	0.086
12	0.625	0.557	0.497	0.444	0.397	0.356	0.319	0.286	0.257	0.231	0.208	0.187	0.168	0.152	0.137	0.124	0.112	0.102	0.092	0.083	0.076	0.069
13	0.601	0.530	0.469	0.415	0.368	0.326	0.290	0.258	0.229	0.204	0.182	0.163	0.145	0.130	0.116	0.104	0.093	0.084	0.075	0.068	0.061	0.055
14	0.577	0.505	0.442	0.388	0.340	0.299	0.263	0.232	0.205	0.181	0.160	0.141	0.125	0.111	0.099	0.088	0.078	0.069	0.062	0.055	0.049	0.044
15	0.555	0.481	0.417	0.362	0.315	0.275	0.239	0.209	0.183	0.160	0.140	0.123	0.108	0.095	0.084	0.074	0.065	0.057	0.051	0.045	0.040	0.035
16	0.534	0.458	0.394	0.339	0.292	0.252	0.218	0.188	0.163	0.141	0.123	0.107	0.093	0.081	0.071	0.062	0.054	0.047	0.042	0.036	0.032	0.028
17	0.513	0.436	0.371	0.317	0.270	0.231	0.198	0.170	0.146	0.125	0.108	0.093	0.080	0.069	0.060	0.052	0.045	0.039	0.034	0.030	0.026	0.023
18	0.494	0.416	0.350	0.296	0.250	0.212	0.180	0.153	0.130	0.111	0.095	0.081	0.069	0.059	0.051	0.044	0.038	0.032	0.028	0.024	0.021	0.018
19	0.475	0.396	0.331	0.277	0.232	0.194	0.164	0.138	0.116	0.098	0.083	0.070	0.060	0.051	0.043	0.037	0.031	0.027	0.023	0.020	0.017	0.014
20	0.456	0.377	0.312	0.258	0.215	0.178	0.149	0.124	0.104	0.087	0.073	0.061	0.051	0.043	0.037	0.031	0.026	0.022	0.019	0.016	0.014	0.012
21	0.439	0.359	0.294	0.242	0.199	0.164	0.135	0.112	0.093	0.077	0.064	0.053	0.044	0.037	0.031	0.026	0.022	0.018	0.015	0.013	0.011	0.009
22	0.422	0.342	0.278	0.226	0.184	0.150	0.123	0.101	0.083	0.068	0.056	0.046	0.038	0.032	0.026	0.022	0.018	0.015	0.013	0.011	0.009	0.007
23	0.406	0.326	0.262	0.211	0.170	0.138	0.112	0.091	0.074	0.060	0.049	0.040	0.033	0.027	0.022	0.018	0.015	0.012	0.010	0.009	0.007	0.006
24	0.390	0.310	0.247	0.197	0.158	0.126	0.102	0.082	0.066	0.053	0.043	0.035	0.028	0.023	0.019	0.015	0.013	0.010	0.008	0.007	0.006	0.005
25	0.375	0.295	0.233	0.184	0.146	0.116	0.092	0.074	0.059	0.047	0.038	0.030	0.024	0.020	0.016	0.013	0.010	0.009	0.007	0.006	0.005	0.004
26	0.361	0.281	0.220	0.172	0.135	0.106	0.084	0.066	0.053	0.042	0.033	0.026	0.021	0.017	0.014	0.011	0.009	0.007	0.006	0.005	0.004	0.003
27	0.347	0.268	0.207	0.161	0.125	0.098	0.076	0.060	0.047	0.037	0.029	0.023	0.018	0.014	0.011	0.009	0.007	0.006	0.005	0.004	0.003	0.002
28	0.333	0.255	0.196	0.150	0.116	0.090	0.069	0.054	0.042	0.033	0.026	0.020	0.016	0.012	0.010	0.008	0.006	0.005	0.004	0.003	0.002	0.002
29	0.321	0.243	0.185	0.141	0.107	0.082	0.063	0.048	0.037	0.029	0.022	0.017	0.014	0.011	0.008	0.006	0.005	0.004	0.003	0.002	0.002	0.002
30	0.308	0.231	0.174	0.131	0.099	0.075	0.057	0.044	0.033	0.026	0.020	0.015	0.012	0.009	0.007	0.005	0.004	0.003	0.003	0.002	0.002	0.001
40	0.208	0.142	0.097	0.067	0.046	0.032	0.022	0.015	0.011	0.008	0.005	0.004	0.003	0.002	0.001	0.001	0.001	0.000	0.000	0.000	0.000	0.000

Periods	4%	5%	6%	7%	8%	9%	10%	11%	12%	13%	14%	15%	16%	17%	18%	19%	20%	21%	22%	23%	24%	25%
1	0.962	0.952	0.943	0.935	0.926	0.917	0.909	0.901	0.893	0.885	0.877	0.870	0.862	0.855	0.847	0.840	0.833	0.826	0.820	0.813	0.806	0.800
2	1.886	1.859	1.833	1.808	1.783	1.759	1.736	1.713	1.690	1.668	1.647	1.626	1.605	1.585	1.566	1.547	1.528	1.509	1.492	1.474	1.457	1.440
3	2.775	2.723	2.673	2.624	2.577	2.531	2.487	2.444	2.402	2.361	2.322	2.283	2.246	2.210	2.174	2.140	2.106	2.074	2.042	2.011	1.981	1.952
4	3.630	3.546	3.465	3.387	3.312	3.240	3.170	3.102	3.037	2.974	2.914	2.855	2.798	2.743	2.690	2.639	2.589	2.540	2.494	2.448	2.404	2.362
5	4.452	4.329	4.212	4.100	3.993	3.890	3.791	3.696	3.605	3.517	3.433	3.352	3.274	3.199	3.127	3.058	2.991	2.926	2.864	2.803	2.745	2.689
6	5.242	5.076	4.917	4.767	4.623	4.486	4.355	4.231	4.111	3.998	3.889	3.784	3.685	3.589	3.498	3.410	3.326	3.245	3.167	3.092	3.020	2.951
7	6.002	5.786	5.582	5.389	5.206	5.033	4.868	4.712	4.564	4.423	4.288	4.160	4.039	3.922	3.812	3.706	3.605	3.508	3.416	3.327	3.242	3.161
8	6.733	6.463	6.210	5.971	5.747	5.535	5.335	5.146	4.968	4.799	4.639	4.487	4.344	4.207	4.078	3.954	3.837	3.726	3.619	3.518	3.421	3.329
9	7.435	7.108	6.802	6.515	6.247	5.995	5.759	5.537	5.328	5.132	4.946	4.772	4.607	4.451	4.303	4.163	4.031	3.905	3.786	3.673	3.566	3.463
10	8.111	7.722	7.360	7.024	6.710	6.418	6.145	5.889	5.650	5.426	5.216	5.019	4.833	4.659	4.494	4.339	4.192	4.054	3.923	3.799	3.682	3.571
11	8.760	8.306	7.887	7.499	7.139	6.805	6.495	6.207	5.938	5.687	5.453	5.234	5.029	4.836	4.656	4.486	4.327	4.177	4.035	3.902	3.776	3.656
12	9.385	8.863	8.384	7.943	7.536	7.161	6.814	6.492	6.194	5.918	5.660	5.421	5.197	4.988	4.793	4.611	4.439	4.278	4.127	3.985	3.851	3.725
13	9.986	9.394	8.853	8.358	7.904	7.487	7.103	6.750	6.424	6.122	5.842	5.583	5.342	5.118	4.910	4.715	4.533	4.362	4.203	4.053	3.912	3.780
14	10.563	9.899	9.295	8.745	8.244	7.786	7.367	6.982	6.628	6.302	6.002	5.724	5.468	5.229	5.008	4.802	4.611	4.432	4.265	4.108	3.962	3.824
15	11.118	10.380	9.712	9.108	8.559	8.061	7.606	7.191	6.811	6.462	6.142	5.847	5.575	5.324	5.092	4.876	4.675	4.489	4.315	4.153	4.001	3.859
16	11.652	10.838	10.106	9.447	8.851	8.313	7.824	7.379	6.974	6.604	6.265	5.954	5.668	5.405	5.162	4.938	4.730	4.536	4.357	4.189	4.033	3.887
17	12.166	11.274	10.477	9.763	9.122	8.544	8.022	7.549	7.120	6.729	6.373	6.047	5.749	5.475	5.222	4.990	4.775	4.576	4.391	4.219	4.059	3.910
18	12.659	11.690	10.828	10.059	9.372	8.756	8.201	7.702	7.250	6.840	6.467	6.128	5.818	5.534	5.273	5.033	4.812	4.608	4.419	4.243	4.080	3.928
19	13.134	12.085	11.158	10.336	9.604	8.950	8.365	7.839	7.366	6.938	6.550	6.198	5.877	5.584	5.316	5.070	4.843	4.635	4.442	4.263	4.097	3.942
20	13.590	12.462	11.470	10.594	9.818	9.129	8.514	7.963	7.469	7.025	6.623	6.259	5.929	5.628	5.353	5.101	4.870	4.657	4.460	4.279	4.110	3.954
21	14.029	12.821	11.764	10.836	10.017	9.292	8.649	8.075	7.562	7.102	6.687	6.312	5.973	5.665	5.384	5.127	4.891	4.675	4.476	4.292	4.121	3.963
22	14.451	13.163	12.042	11.061	10.201	9.442	8.772	8.176	7.645	7.170	6.743	6.359	6.011	5.696	5.410	5.149	4.909	4.690	4.488	4.302	4.130	3.970
23	14.857	13.489	12.303	11.272	10.371	9.580	8.883	8.266	7.718	7.230	6.792	6.399	6.044	5.723	5.432	5.167	4.925	4.703	4.499	4.311	4.137	3.976
24	15.247	13.799	12.550	11.469	10.529	9.707	8.985	8.348	7.784	7.283	6.835	6.434	6.073	5.746	5.451	5.182	4.937	4.713	4.507	4.318	4.143	3.981
25	15.622	14.094	12.783	11.654	10.675	9.823	9.077	8.422	7.843	7.330	6.873	6.464	6.097	5.766	5.467	5.195	4.948	4.721	4.514	4.323	4.147	3.985
26	15.983	14.375	13.003	11.826	10.810	9.929	9.161	8.488	7.896	7.372	6.906	6.491	6.118	5.783	5.480	5.206	4.956	4.728	4.520	4.328	4.151	3.988
27	16.330	14.643	13.211	11.987	10.935	10.027	9.237	8.548	7.943	7.409	6.935	6.514	6.136	5.798	5.492	5.215	4.964	4.734	4.524	4.332	4.154	3.990
28	16.663	14.898	13.406	12.137	11.051	10.116	9.307	8.602	7.984	7.441	6.961	6.534	6.152	5.810	5.502	5.223	4.970	4.739	4.528	4.335	4.157	3.992
29	16.984	15.141	13.591	12.278	11.158	10.198	9.370	8.650	8.022	7.470	6.983	6.551	6.166	5.820	5.510	5.229	4.975	4.743	4.531	4.337	4.159	3.994
30	17.292	15.372	13.765	12.409	11.258	10.274	9.427	8.694	8.055	7.496	7.003	6.566	6.177	5.829	5.517	5.235	4.979	4.746	4.534	4.339	4.160	3.995
40	19.793	17.159	15.046	13.332	11.925	10.757	9.779	8.951	8.244	7.634	7.105	6.642	6.233	5.871	5.548	5.258	4.997	4.760	4.544	4.347	4.166	3.999

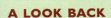

A LOOK BACK

Capital budgeting decisions involve significant investments in long-term projects. Chapter 11 covered various techniques used for capital budgeting decisions.

A LOOK AT THIS CHAPTER

The statement of cash flows provides invaluable information. After addressing the classification of various types of cash inflows and outflows, we discuss how to prepare the statement of cash flows and how to interpret it.

A LOOK AHEAD

Chapter 13 explains how managers use financial statements to assess the financial health of their companies. It describes how to prepare comparative and common-size form financial statements and how to compute and interpret financial ratios.

12

Statement of Cash Flows

CHAPTER OUTLINE

LEARNING OBJECTIVES

After studying Chapter 12, you should be able to:

LO12–1 Classify cash inflows and outflows as relating to operating, investing, or financing activities.

LO12–2 Prepare a statement of cash flows using the indirect method to determine the net cash provided by operating activities.

LO12–3 Compute free cash flow.

LO12–4 (Appendix 12A) Use the direct method to determine the net cash provided by operating activities.

Understanding Cash Flows

In 2011, The Kroger Company, the largest food and drug retailer in the United States, reported net income of $596 million. During the same year the company spent $1.9 billion for plant and equipment, paid dividends totaling $257 million, paid off $547 million of long-term debt, and spent $1.5 billion to purchase shares of its own common stock. At first glance, these figures may seem confusing because Kroger is spending amounts of money that far exceed its net income. In this chapter you'll learn about the statement of cash flows that explains the relationship between a company's net income and its cash inflows and outflows.

Source: The Kroger Company, 2011 Form 10-K Annual Report, www.sec.gov/edgar/searchedgar/companysearch.html.

Three major financial statements are required for external reports—an income statement, a balance sheet, and a statement of cash flows. The **statement of cash flows** highlights the major activities that impact cash flows and, hence, affect the overall cash balance. Managers focus on cash for a very good reason—without sufficient cash at the right times, a company may miss golden investment opportunities or may even go bankrupt.

The statement of cash flows answers questions that cannot be easily answered by looking at the income statement and balance sheet. For example, where did **Delta Airlines** get the cash to pay a dividend of nearly $140 million in a year in which, according to its income statement, it lost more than $1 billion? How was **The Walt Disney Company** able to invest nearly $800 million to expand and renovate its theme parks despite a loss of more than $500 million on its investment in EuroDisney? Where did **The Kroger Company** get $1.9 billion to invest in plant and equipment in a year when its net income was only $596 million? The answers to such questions can be found on the statement of cash flows.

The statement of cash flows is a valuable analytical tool for managers as well as for investors and creditors, although managers tend to be more concerned with forecasted statements of cash flows that are prepared as part of the budgeting process. The statement of cash flows can be used to answer crucial questions such as the following:

1. Is the company generating sufficient positive cash flows from its ongoing operations to remain viable?
2. Will the company be able to repay its debts?
3. Will the company be able to pay its usual dividend?
4. Why do net income and net cash flow differ?
5. To what extent will the company have to borrow money in order to make needed investments?

Managers prepare the statement of cash flows by applying a fundamental principle of double-entry bookkeeping—the change in the cash balance must equal the changes in all other balance sheet accounts besides cash.[1] This principle ensures that properly analyzing the changes in all noncash balance sheet accounts always quantifies the cash inflows and outflows that explain the change in the cash balance. Our goal in this chapter is to translate this fairly complex principle into a small number of concepts and steps that simplify the process of preparing and interpreting a statement of cash flows.

Before delving into the specifics of how to prepare the statement of cash flows, we need to review two basic equations that apply to all asset, contra asset, liability, and stockholders' equity accounts:

> *Basic Equation for Asset Accounts*
> Beginning balance + Debits − Credits = Ending balance
>
> *Basic Equation for Contra Asset, Liability, and Stockholders' Equity Accounts*
> Beginning balance − Debits + Credits = Ending balance

These equations will help you compute various cash inflows and outflows that are reported in the statement of cash flows and they'll be referred to throughout the chapter.

---

[1]The statement of cash flows is based on the following fundamental balance sheet and income statement equations:
(1) Change in cash + Changes in noncash assets = Changes in liabilities + Changes in stockholders' equity
(2) Net cash flow = Change in cash
(3) Changes in stockholders' equity = Net income − Dividends + Changes in capital stock
These three equations can be used to derive the following equation:
(4) Net cash flow = Net income − Changes in noncash assets + Changes in liabilities − Dividends + Changes in capital stock.
Essentially, the statement of cash flows, which explains net cash flow, is constructed by starting with net income and then adjusting it for changes in noncash balance sheet accounts.

THE STATEMENT OF CASH FLOWS: KEY CONCEPTS

The statement of cash flows summarizes all of a company's cash inflows and outflows during a period, thereby explaining the change in its cash balance. In a statement of cash flows, cash is broadly defined to include both cash and cash equivalents. **Cash equivalents** consist of short-term, highly liquid investments such as Treasury bills, commercial paper, and money market funds that are made solely for the purpose of generating a return on temporarily idle funds. Most companies invest their excess cash reserves in these types of interest-bearing assets that can be easily converted into cash. Because such assets are equivalent to cash, they are included with cash in a statement of cash flows.

The remainder of this section discusses four key concepts that you'll need to understand to prepare a statement of cash flows. These four concepts include organizing the statement of cash flows, distinguishing between the direct and indirect methods of preparing a portion of the statement of cash flows, completing the three-step process underlying the indirect method, and recording gross cash flows where appropriate within a statement of cash flows.[2]

Apple's Cash Stash

IN BUSINESS

Apple Inc. accumulated $76.2 billion in cash and short-term investments. Its investors had a variety of opinions about how the company should use this money. Some investors wanted Apple to explore acquisition targets in the music industry. Others believed Apple should invest in start-up companies that are developing emerging technologies, such as improved batteries for the iPhone. Still others felt the company should use some of its cash for dividend payouts or stock repurchases.

This example illustrates the never-ending cycle of managing a business. Once a company succeeds in generating positive cash flows, it immediately raises another question in the minds of investors—what are you planning to do for me now?

Sources: Peter Burrows, "Apple's Cash Conundrum," *BusinessWeek*, August 11, 2008, p. 32; and Yukari Iwatani Kane, "For Apple, a $76 Billion Dilemma," *The Wall Street Journal*, July 21, 2011, p. B9.

Organizing the Statement of Cash Flows

To make it easier to compare data from different companies, U.S. generally accepted accounting principles (GAAP) and International Financial Reporting Standards (IFRS) require companies to follow prescribed rules when preparing the statement of cash flows. One of these rules requires organizing the statement into three sections that report cash

LEARNING OBJECTIVE 12–1

Classify cash inflows and outflows as relating to operating, investing, or financing activities.

---

[2]Another concept that relates to the statement of cash flows is direct exchange transactions, which refer to transactions where noncurrent balance sheet items are swapped. For example, a company might issue common stock in a direct exchange for property. Direct exchange transactions are not reported on the statement of cash flows; however, they are disclosed in a separate schedule that accompanies the statement. More advanced accounting courses cover this topic in greater detail. We will not include direct exchange transactions in this chapter.

EXHIBIT 12–1
Cash Inflows and Outflows
Resulting from Operating,
Investing, and Financing
Activities

	Cash Inflow	Cash Outflow
Operating activities		
Collecting cash from customers	√	
Paying suppliers for inventory purchases		√
Paying bills to insurers, utility providers, etc		√
Paying wages and salaries to employees.		√
Paying taxes to governmental bodies		√
Paying interest to lenders		√
Investing activities		
Buying property, plant, and equipment.		√
Selling property, plant, and equipment	√	
Buying stocks and bonds as a long-term investment		√
Selling stocks and bonds held for long-term investment . . .	√	
Lending money to another entity		√
Collecting the principal on a loan to another entity.	√	
Financing activities		
Borrowing money from a creditor	√	
Repaying the principal amount of a debt		√
Collecting cash from the sale of common stock	√	
Paying cash to repurchase your own common stock		√
Paying a dividend to stockholders		√

flows resulting from *operating activities, investing activities,* and *financing activities.* **Operating activities** generate cash inflows and outflows related to revenue and expense transactions that affect net income. **Investing activities** generate cash inflows and outflows related to acquiring or disposing of noncurrent assets such as property, plant, and equipment, long-term investments, and loans to another entity. **Financing activities** generate cash inflows and outflows related to borrowing from and repaying principal to creditors and completing transactions with the company's owners, such as selling or repurchasing shares of common stock and paying dividends. The most common types of cash inflows and outflows resulting from these three activities are summarized in Exhibit 12–1.[3]

Operating Activities: Direct or Indirect Method?

U.S. GAAP and IFRS allow companies to compute the net amount of cash inflows and outflows resulting from operating activities, which is known formally as the **net cash provided by operating activities,** using either the *direct* or *indirect* method. Both of these methods have the same purpose, which is to translate accrual-based net income to a cash basis. However, they approach this task in two different ways.

Under the **direct method,** the income statement is reconstructed on a cash basis from top to bottom. For example, cash collected from customers is listed instead of revenue, and payments to suppliers is listed instead of cost of goods sold. In essence, cash receipts are counted as revenues and cash disbursements pertaining to operating activities are counted as expenses. The difference between the cash receipts and cash disbursements is the net cash provided by operating activities.

Under the **indirect method,** net income is adjusted to a cash basis. That is, rather than directly computing cash sales, cash expenses, and so forth, these amounts are derived *indirectly* by removing from net income any items that do not affect cash flows. The

---

[3]Operating cash inflows can also include interest income and dividend income; however, in this chapter we will limit our scope to cash receipts from sales to customers.

indirect method has an advantage over the direct method because it shows the reasons for any differences between net income and net cash provided by operating activities.

Although both methods result in the same amount of net cash provided by operating activities, only about 1% of companies use the direct method and the remaining 99% use the indirect method.[4] If a company uses the direct method to prepare its statement of cash flows, then it must also provide a supplementary report that uses the indirect method. However, if a company chooses to use the indirect method, there is no requirement that it also report results using the direct method. Because the direct method requires more work, very few companies choose this approach. Therefore, we will explain the direct method in Appendix 12A, and we will cover the indirect method in the main body of the chapter.

CONCEPT CHECK

1. Which of the following statements is true about the basic equation for asset accounts? (You may select more than one answer.)
   a. Debits are added to the beginning balance.
   b. Debits are subtracted from the beginning balance.
   c. Credits are added to the beginning balance.
   d. Credits are subtracted from the beginning balance.
2. Which of the following is not a cash equivalent? (You may select more than one answer.)
   a. Accounts receivable
   b. Treasury bills
   c. Commercial paper
   d. Money market funds
3. Which of the following statements is true? (You may select more than one answer.)
   a. The direct method of preparing the operating activities section of the statement of cash flows starts with net income and adjusts it to a cash basis.
   b. The basic equations for contra assets and liabilities are the same.
   c. Investing activities generate cash inflows and outflows related to acquiring or disposing of noncurrent assets.
   d. Financing activities include paying dividends.

The Indirect Method: A Three-Step Process

The indirect method adjusts net income to net cash provided by operating activities using a three-step process.

Step 1   The first step is to *add depreciation charges* to net income. Depreciation charges are the credits to the Accumulated Depreciation account during the period—the sum total of the entries that have increased Accumulated Depreciation. Why do we do this? Because Accumulated Depreciation is a noncash balance sheet account and we must adjust net income for all of the changes in the noncash balance sheet accounts that have occurred during the period.

To compute the credits to the Accumulated Depreciation account we use the equation for contra assets that was mentioned earlier:

Basic Equation for Contra Asset Accounts
Beginning balance − Debits + Credits = Ending balance

For example, assume the Accumulated Depreciation account had beginning and ending balances of $300 and $500, respectively. Also, assume that the company sold equipment with accumulated depreciation of $70 during the period. Given that we use debits to the

[4]American Institute of Certified Public Accountants, *Accounting Trends and Techniques: 2007* (Jersey City, NJ, 2007), p. 503.

Accumulated Depreciation account to record accumulated depreciation on assets that have been sold or retired, the depreciation that needs to be added to net income is computed as follows:

$$\text{Beginning balance} - \text{Debits} + \text{Credits} = \text{Ending balance}$$

$$\$300 - \$70 + \text{Credits} = \$500$$

$$\text{Credits} = \$500 - \$300 + \$70$$

$$\text{Credits} = \$270$$

The same logic can be depicted using an Accumulated Depreciation T-account. Given that we know the account's beginning and ending balances and the amount of the debit that would have been recorded for the sale of equipment, the credit side of the T-account must equal $270.

Accumulated Depreciation

		Beg. Bal.	$300
Sale of equipment	70		270
		End. Bal.	$500

For service and merchandising companies, the credits to the Accumulated Depreciation T-account equal the debits to the Depreciation Expense account. For these companies, the adjustment in step one consists of adding depreciation expense to net income. However, for manufacturing companies, some of the credits to the Accumulated Depreciation T-account relate to depreciation on production assets that are debited to work in process inventories rather than depreciation expense. For these companies, the depreciation charges do not simply equal depreciation expense.

Because depreciation is added back to net income on the statement of cash flows, some people erroneously conclude that a company can increase its cash flow by simply increasing its depreciation expense. This is false; a company cannot increase its net cash provided by operating activities by increasing its depreciation expense. If it increases its depreciation expense by X dollars, then net income will decline by X dollars and the amount of the adjustment in step one of this process will increase by X dollars. The decline in net income and the increase in the amount of the adjustment in step one exactly offset each other, resulting in zero impact on the net cash provided by operating activities.

HELPFUL HINT

When completing step one in the indirect method, do not assume that the change in the balance of the Accumulated Depreciation account equals the amount of the required adjustment. Instead, you must check to see if any depreciable assets were sold during the period. If so, the amount of accumulated depreciation on the asset that was sold needs to be included in the basic equation for contra asset accounts or included on the debit side of the Accumulated Depreciation T-account when determining the amount of the adjustment.

Step 2   The second step is to *analyze net changes in noncash balance sheet accounts that impact net income.* Exhibit 12–2 provides general guidelines for how to analyze current asset and current liability accounts.[5] For each account shown in the exhibit, you'll begin by referring to the balance sheet to compute the change in the account balance from the beginning to the end of the period. Then, you will either add each of these amounts to

---

[5]Other accounts such as Interest Payable can impact these computations. However, for simplicity, in this chapter we will focus on the accounts shown in Exhibit 12–2.

	Increase in Account Balance	Decrease in Account Balance
Current Assets		
Accounts receivable	Subtract	Add
Inventory	Subtract	Add
Prepaid expenses	Subtract	Add
Current Liabilities		
Accounts payable	Add	Subtract
Accrued liabilities	Add	Subtract
Income taxes payable	Add	Subtract

EXHIBIT 12–2
General Guidelines for Analyzing How Changes in Noncash Balance Sheet Accounts Affect Net Income on the Statement of Cash Flows

net income or subtract them from net income as shown in Exhibit 12–2. Notice that changes in all current asset accounts (Accounts Receivable, Inventory, and Prepaid Expenses) result in the same type of adjustment to net income. If an asset account balance increases during the period, then the amount of the increase is subtracted from net income. If an asset account balance decreases during the period, then the amount of the decrease is added to net income. The current liability accounts (Accounts Payable, Accrued Liabilities, and Income Taxes Payable) are handled in the opposite fashion. If a liability account balance increases, then the amount of the increase is added to net income. If a liability account balance decreases, then the amount of the decrease is subtracted from net income.

Keep in mind that the purpose of these adjustments is to translate net income to a cash basis. For example, the change in the accounts receivable balance measures the difference between credit sales and cash collections from customers who purchased on account. When the accounts receivable balance increases it means that the amount of credit sales exceeds the amount of cash collected from customers. In this case, the change in the accounts receivable balance is subtracted from net income because it reflects the amount by which credit sales exceeds cash collections from customers. When the accounts receivable balance decreases it means that cash collected from customers exceeds credit sales. In this case, the change in the accounts receivable balance is added to net income because it reflects the amount by which cash collections from customers exceeds credit sales.

The other accounts shown in Exhibit 12–2 have a similar underlying logic. The inventory and accounts payable adjustments translate cost of goods sold to cash paid for inventory purchases. The prepaid expenses and accrued liabilities adjustments translate selling and administrative expenses to a cash basis. The income taxes payable adjustment translates income tax expense to a cash basis.

HELPFUL HINT

Beyond memorizing the adjustments shown in Exhibit 12–2, you should understand the reasons for them. The adjustment pertaining to accounts receivable quantifies the difference between sales, as reported on the income statement, and cash collections from customers. The adjustments related to inventory and accounts payable quantify the difference between cost of goods sold and cash paid to suppliers. The adjustments related to prepaid expenses and accrued liabilities help quantify the difference between selling and administrative expenses and cash paid for those expenses. Finally, the adjustment pertaining to income taxes payable quantifies the difference between income tax expense and income tax payments.

Step 3   The third step in computing the net cash provided by operating activities is to *adjust for gains/losses* included in the income statement. Under U.S. GAAP and IFRS rules, the cash proceeds from the sale of noncurrent assets must be included in the investing activities section of the statement of cash flows. To comply with these rules, the gains and losses pertaining to the sale of noncurrent assets must be removed from net income as reported in the operating activities section of the statement of cash flows. To make this adjustment, subtract gains from net income and add losses to net income in the operating activities section.

4. Which of the following statements is false? (You may select more than one answer.)
   a. Depreciation charges are subtracted from net income.
   b. An increase in inventory is subtracted from net income.
   c. A loss on the sale of an asset is subtracted from net income.
   d. A decrease in accrued liabilities is subtracted from net income.
5. Assume that a company's beginning and ending balances in its Accumulated Depreciation account are $2,000 and $2,900, respectively. Also assume that the company sold a piece of equipment that had an original cost of $400 and accumulated depreciation of $350 for cash proceeds of $75. How much depreciation would the company add to net income in the operating activities section of its statement of cash flows?
   a. $550
   b. $500
   c. $1,300
   d. $1,250
6. Refer to the data in question 5 above. Which of the following choices is true?
   a. The company should subtract a gain of $25 from net income.
   b. The company should add a gain of $25 to net income.
   c. The company should subtract a loss of $25 from net income.
   d. The company should add a loss of $25 to net income.

Investing and Financing Activities: Gross Cash Flows

U.S. GAAP and IFRS require that the investing and financing sections of the statement of cash flows disclose gross cash flows. To illustrate, suppose **Macy's Department Stores** purchases $50 million in property during the year and sells other property for $30 million. Instead of showing the net change of $20 million, the company must show the gross amounts of both the purchases and sales. The $50 million purchase would be disclosed as a cash outflow and the $30 million sale would be reported as a cash inflow in the investing section of the statement of cash flows. Similarly, if **Alcoa** receives $80 million from selling long-term bonds and then pays out $30 million to retire other bonds, the two transactions must be reported separately in the financing section of the statement of cash flows rather than being netted against each other.

The gross method of reporting cash flows is not used in the operating activities section of the statement of cash flows, where debits and credits are netted against each other. For example, if **Sears** adds $600 million to its accounts receivable as a result of sales during the year and $520 million of accounts receivable are collected, only the net increase of $80 million is reported on the statement of cash flows.

To compute gross cash flows for the investing and financing activities sections of the statement of cash flows, you'll begin by calculating the changes in the balance of each applicable balance sheet account. As with the current assets, when a noncurrent asset account balance (including Property, Plant, and Equipment; Long-Term Investments; and Loans to Other Entities) increases, it signals the need to subtract cash outflows in the investing activities section of the statement of cash flows. If the balance in a noncurrent asset account decreases during the period, then it signals the need to add cash inflows. The liability and equity accounts (Bonds Payable and Common Stock) are handled in the opposite fashion. If a liability or equity account balance increases, then it signals a need to add cash inflows to the financing activities section of the statement of cash flows. If a liability or equity account balance decreases, then it signals a need to subtract cash outflows. Exhibit 12–3 summarizes these general guidelines.

	Increase in Account Balance	Decrease in Account Balance
Noncurrent Assets (Investing activities)		
Property, plant, and equipment	Subtract	Add
Long-term investments	Subtract	Add
Loans to other entities	Subtract	Add
Liabilities and Stockholders' Equity (Financing activities)		
Bonds payable	Add	Subtract
Common stock	Add	Subtract
Retained earnings	*	*
*Requires further analysis to quantify cash dividends paid.		

EXHIBIT 12–3
General Guidelines for Analyzing How Changes in Noncash Balance Sheet Accounts Affect the Investing and Financing Sections of the Statement of Cash Flows

While these guidelines provide a helpful starting point, to properly calculate each account's *gross* cash inflows and outflows you'll need to analyze the transactions that occurred within that account during the period. We will illustrate how to do this using Property, Plant, and Equipment and Retained Earnings.

Property, Plant, and Equipment

When a company purchases property, plant, or equipment it debits the Property, Plant, and Equipment account for the amount of the purchase. When it sells or disposes of these kinds of assets, it credits the Property, Plant, and Equipment account for the original cost of the asset. To compute the cash outflows related to Property, Plant, and Equipment we use the basic equation for assets mentioned earlier:

Basic Equation for Asset Accounts
Beginning balance + Debits − Credits = Ending balance

For example, assume that a company's beginning and ending balances in its Property, Plant, and Equipment account are $1,000 and $1,800, respectively. In addition, during the period the company sold a piece of equipment for $40 cash that originally cost $100 and had accumulated depreciation of $70. The company recorded a gain on the sale of $10, which had been included in net income.

We start by calculating the $800 increase in the Property, Plant, and Equipment account. This increase signals the need to subtract cash outflows in the investing activities section of the statement of cash flows. In fact, it may be tempting to conclude that the proper way to analyze Property, Plant, and Equipment in this instance is to record an $800 cash outflow corresponding with the $800 increase in the account balance. However, that would only be correct if the company did not sell any property, plant, and equipment during the year. Because the company did sell equipment, we must use the basic equation for asset accounts to compute the cash outflows as follows:

Beginning balance + Debits − Credits = Ending balance

$1,000 + Debits − $100 = $1,800

Debits = $1,800 − $1,000 + $100

Debits = $900

The same logic can be depicted using a Property, Plant, and Equipment T-account. Given that we know the account's beginning and ending balances and the amount of the credit that would have been recorded to write off the *original cost* of the equipment that was sold, the additions to the account, as summarized on the debit side of the T-account, must equal $900.

Property, Plant, and Equipment

Beg. Bal.	$1,000		
Additions	900	Sale of equipment	100
End. Bal.	$1,800		

So, instead of reporting an $800 cash outflow pertaining to Property, Plant, and Equipment in the investing activities section of the statement of cash flows, the proper accounting requires subtracting the $10 gain on the sale of equipment from net income in the operating activities section of the statement. It also requires disclosing a $40 cash inflow from the sale of equipment and a $900 cash outflow for additions to Property, Plant and Equipment in the investing activities section of the statement.

CONCEPT CHECK

7. Assume that a company's beginning and ending balances in its Property, Plant, and Equipment account are $5,000 and $6,000, respectively. Also assume that the company sold a piece of equipment that originally cost $700 and had accumulated depreciation of $450 for cash proceeds of $500. Based solely on the available information, what is the company's net cash provided by (used in) investing activities?
    a. $1,200
    b. $1,500
    c. $(1,200)
    d. $(1,500)

Retained Earnings   When a company earns net income it credits the Retained Earnings account and when it pays a dividend it debits the Retained Earnings account. To compute the amount of a cash dividend payment we use the basic equation for stockholders' equity accounts mentioned earlier:

Basic Equation for Stockholders' Equity Accounts
Beginning balance − Debits + Credits = Ending balance

For example, assume that a company's beginning and ending balances in its Retained Earnings account are $2,000 and 3,000, respectively. In addition, the company reported net income of $1,200 and paid a cash dividend, but we don't know how much. We start by calculating the $1,000 increase in the Retained Earnings account. However, this amount reflects the net income earned during the period as well as the amount of the dividend payment. Therefore, we must use the equation above to calculate the amount of the dividend payment as follows:

Beginning balance − Debits + Credits = Ending balance

$2,000 − Debits + $1,200 = $3,000

$3,200 = $3,000 + Debits

Debits = $200

The same logic can be depicted using a Retained Earnings T-account. Given that we know the account's beginning and ending balances and the net income that would have been recorded on the credit side of the T-account, the dividend, as reported on the debit side of the T-account, must equal $200.

Retained Earnings

		Beg. Bal.	$2,000
Dividend	200	Net income	1,200
		End. Bal.	$3,000

So, instead of erroneously reporting a $1,000 cash flow pertaining to the overall change in Retained Earnings, the proper accounting requires disclosing net income of $1,200 within the operating activities section of the statement of cash flows and a $200 cash dividend in the financing activities section of the statement.

HELPFUL HINT

Net income is the first number recorded on a statement of cash flows prepared using the indirect method. However, how would you determine net income if it was not explicitly disclosed within an exercise or problem? The secret is to use the basic equation for stockholders' equity accounts to determine the credit to the Retained Earnings account. Input into this equation the beginning and ending balances in Retained Earnings as well as the debit pertaining to cash dividends and then solve for the credit to the account—which corresponds to net income.

Lowe's Takes Steps to Satisfy Investors

IN BUSINESS

Lowe's told investors that it will buy back $18 billion of its own stock over five years, thereby lowering the company's total shares outstanding by about a third. Lowe's also informed investors that it plans to payout 35% of its earnings in dividends over the next five years. Previously, the company was returning 31% of its profits to shareholders in the form of dividends. Lowe's made these decisions with respect to its financing activities to "keep investors interested in its shares as it prepares for an extended period of slowing new-store growth."

Source: Maxwell Murphy, "Lowe's Puts Emphasis on Buybacks, Payout" *The Wall Street Journal,* December 8, 2010, p. B6A.

Summary of Key Concepts

Exhibit 12–4 summarizes the four key concepts just discussed. The first key concept is that the statement of cash flows is divided into three sections: operating activities, investing activities, and financing activities. The net cash used or provided by these three types of activities is combined to derive the net increase/decrease in cash and cash equivalents, which explains the change in the cash balance. The second key concept is that the operating activities section of the statement of cash flows can be prepared using the direct or indirect method. The direct method translates sales, cost of goods sold, selling and administrative expenses, and income tax expense to a cash basis. The indirect method begins with accrual-based net income and adjusts it to a cash basis. The third key concept is that the indirect method requires three steps to compute net cash provided by operating activities. The first step is to add back depreciation to net income. The second step is to analyze net changes in noncash balance sheet accounts that impact net income. The third step is to adjust for gains or losses included in the income statement. The fourth key concept is to record gross cash inflows and outflows in the investing and financing activities sections of the statement of cash flows.[6]

---

[6]This chapter adopts two simplifications related to common stock transactions. First, it always assumes that companies issue no-par value common stock, thus the chapter excludes Additional Paid-In Capital. Second, the chapter assumes that stock repurchases are recorded with a debit to the Common Stock account rather than a debit to the contra equity account called Treasury Stock.

EXHIBIT 12–4   Summary of Key Concepts Needed to Prepare a Statement of Cash Flows

Key Concept #1		Key Concept #2	
The statement of cash flows is divided into three sections:		U.S. GAAP and IFRS allow two methods for preparing the operating activities section of the statement of cash flows:	
Operating activities		**Direct Method (Appendix 12A)**	
Net cash provided by (used in) operating activities	$xx	Cash receipts from customers	$ xx
Investing activities		Cash paid for inventory purchases	(xx)
Net cash provided by (used in) investing activities	xx	Cash paid for selling and administrative expenses	(xx)
		Cash paid for income taxes	(xx)
Financing activities			
Net cash provided by (used in) financing activities	xx	Net cash provided by (used in) operating activities	$ xx
		Indirect Method	
Net increase/decrease in cash and cash equivalents	xx	Net income	$ xx
Beginning cash and cash equivalents	xx	Various adjustments (+/−)	xx
Ending cash and cash equivalents	$xx	Net cash provided by (used in) operating activities	$ xx

Key Concept #3		Key Concept #4	
Computing the net cash provided by operating activities using the indirect method is a three step process:		The investing and financing sections of the statement of cash flows must report gross cash flows:	
Operating activities		Net cash provided by (used in) operating activities	$xx
Net income	$xx	**Investing activities**	
Adjustments to convert net income to a cash basis:		Purchase of property, plant, and equipment	(xx)
		Sale of property, plant, and equipment	xx
Step 1 — Add: Depreciation	xx	Purchase of long-term investments	(xx)
		Sale of long-term investments	xx
		Net cash provided by (used in) investing activities	(xx)
Step 2 — Analyze net changes in noncash balance sheet accounts:			
Increase in current asset accounts	(xx)	**Financing activities**	
Decrease in current asset accounts	xx	Issuance of bonds payable	xx
Increase in current liability accounts	xx	Repaying principal on bonds payable	(xx)
Decrease in current liability accounts	(xx)	Issuance of common stock	xx
		Purchase own shares of common stock	(xx)
Step 3 — Adjust for gains/losses:		Paying a dividend	(xx)
Gain on sale	(xx)	Net cash provided by (used in) financing activities	xx
Loss on sale	xx	Net increase/decrease in cash and cash equivalents	xx
Net cash provided by (used in) operating activities	$xx	Beginning cash and cash equivalents	xx
		Ending cash and cash equivalents	$xx

AN EXAMPLE OF A STATEMENT OF CASH FLOWS

To illustrate the ideas introduced in the preceding section, we will now construct a statement of cash flows for a merchandising company called Apparel, Inc. The company's income statement and balance sheet are shown in Exhibits 12–5 and 12–6, respectively.

Let's also assume the following facts with respect to Apparel, Inc.:

1. The company sold a store that had an original cost of $15 million and accumulated depreciation of $10 million. The cash proceeds from the sale were $8 million. The gain on the sale was $3 million.
2. The company did not issue any new bonds during the year.
3. The company did not repurchase any of its own common stock during the year.
4. The company paid a cash dividend during the year.

EXHIBIT 12–5
Apparel, Inc., Income Statement

Apparel, Inc.
Income Statement
(dollars in millions)

Sales	$3,638
Cost of goods sold	2,469
Gross margin	1,169
Selling and administrative expenses	941
Net operating income	228
Nonoperating items: Gain on sale of store	3
Income before taxes	231
Income taxes	91
Net income	$ 140

EXHIBIT 12–6
Apparel, Inc., Balance Sheet

Apparel, Inc.
Comparative Balance Sheet
(dollars in millions)

	Ending Balance	Beginning Balance	Change
Assets			
Current assets:			
Cash and cash equivalents	$ 91	$ 29	+62
Accounts receivable	637	654	−17
Inventory	586	537	+49
Total current assets	1,314	1,220	
Property, plant, and equipment	1,517	1,394	+123
Less accumulated depreciation	654	561	+93
Net property, plant, and equipment	863	833	
Total assets	$ 2,177	$2,053	
Liabilities and Stockholders' Equity			
Current liabilities:			
Accounts payable	$ 264	$ 220	+44
Accrued liabilities	193	190	+3
Income taxes payable	75	71	+4
Total current liabilities	532	481	
Bonds payable	479	520	−41
Total liabilities	1,011	1,001	
Stockholders' equity:			
Common stock	157	155	+2
Retained earnings	1,009	897	+112
Total stockholders' equity	1,166	1,052	
Total liabilities and stockholders' equity	$2,177	$2,053	

Notice that the balance sheet in Exhibit 12–6 includes the amount of the change in each balance sheet account. For example, the beginning and ending balances in Cash and Cash Equivalents are $29 million and $91 million, respectively. This is a $62 million increase in the account balance. A similar computation is performed for all other balance sheet accounts. Study the changes in these account balances because we will be referring to them in the forthcoming pages. For example, keep in mind that the purpose of Apparel's statement of cash flows is to disclose the operating, investing, and financing cash flows underlying the $62 million increase in Cash and Cash Equivalents shown in Exhibit 12–6. *Also, please be advised that although the changes in account balances are computed for you in Exhibit 12–6, you'll ordinarily need to compute these amounts yourself before attempting to construct the statement of cash flows.*

Operating Activities

This section uses the three-step process explained earlier to construct Apparel's operating activities section of the statement of cash flows.

Step 1   The first step in computing Apparel's net cash provided by operating activities is to *add depreciation* to net income. The balance sheet in Exhibit 12–6 shows Apparel's Accumulated Depreciation account had beginning and ending balances of $561 million and $654 million, respectively. We also know from the assumptions listed on page 568 that Apparel sold a store during the year that had $10 million of accumulated depreciation. Given these facts, we can use the basic equation for contra assets (introduced on page 558) to determine that Apparel needs to add $103 million of depreciation to its net income:

$$\text{Beginning balance} - \text{Debits} + \text{Credits} = \text{Ending balance}$$

$$\$561 \text{ million} - \$10 \text{ million} + \text{Credits} = \$654 \text{ million}$$

$$\text{Credits} = \$654 \text{ million} - \$561 \text{ million} + \$10 \text{ million}$$

$$\text{Credits} = \$103 \text{ million}$$

Step 2   The second step in computing net cash provided by operating activities is to *analyze net changes in noncash balance sheet accounts* that impact net income. Exhibit 12–7 explains the five adjustments Apparel needs to make to complete this step. For your ease of reference, the top half of Exhibit 12–7 reproduces an excerpt of the general guidelines for completing this step that were previously summarized in Exhibit 12–2. The bottom half of Exhibit 12–7 applies the general guidelines from the top half of the exhibit to Apparel's balance sheet. For example, Exhibit 12–6 shows that Apparel's Accounts Receivable balance decreased by $17 million. The top half of Exhibit 12–7 says that decreases in accounts receivable are added to net income. This explains why the bottom half of Exhibit 12–7 includes a plus sign in front of Apparel's $17 million decrease in Accounts Receivable. Similarly, Exhibit 12–6 shows that Apparel's Inventory balance increased by $49 million. When inventory increases, the amount of the increase is subtracted from net income. This explains why the bottom half of Exhibit 12–7 includes a minus sign in front of Apparel's $49 million increase in Inventory. Similar logic can be used to explain why the increases from Exhibit 12–6 in Accounts Payable (+44), Accrued Liabilities (+3), and Income Taxes Payable (+4) all result in the additions to Apparel's net income that are shown in the bottom half of Exhibit 12–7.

EXHIBIT 12–7
Apparel, Inc.: Analyzing How Net Changes in Noncash Balance Sheet Accounts Affect Net Income on the Statement of Cash Flows

	Increase in Account Balance	Decrease in Account Balance
General Guidelines from Exhibit 12–2		
Current Assets		
Accounts receivable	Subtract	Add
Inventory	Subtract	Add
Current Liabilities		
Accounts payable	Add	Subtract
Accrued liabilities	Add	Subtract
Income taxes payable	Add	Subtract
	Increase in Account Balance	**Decrease in Account Balance**
Apparel's Account Analysis		
Current Assets		
Accounts receivable		+17
Inventory	−49	
Current Liabilities		
Accounts payable	+44	
Accrued liabilities	+3	
Income taxes payable	+4	

Apparel, Inc.
(dollars in millions)

Operating Activities

Net income		$140
Adjustments to convert net income to a cash basis:		
Step 1 → Depreciation	103	
Decrease in accounts receivable	17	
Increase in inventory	(49)	
Step 2 → Increase in accounts payable	44	
Increase in accrued liabilities	3	
Increase in income taxes payable	4	
Step 3 → Gain on sale of store	(3)	119
Net cash provided by operating activities		$259

Step 3   The third step in computing the net cash provided by operating activities is to *adjust for gains/losses* included in the income statement. Apparel reported a $3 million gain on its income statement in Exhibit 12–5; therefore, this amount needs to be subtracted from net income. Subtracting the gain on sale removes the gain from the operating activities section of the statement of cash flows. The entire amount of the cash proceeds related to this sale will be recorded in the investing activities section of the statement.

Exhibit 12–8 shows the operating activities section of Apparel's statement of cash flows. Take a moment to trace each of the numbers that we just computed to this exhibit. The total amount of the adjustments to net income is $119 million, which results in net cash provided by operating activities of $259 million.

Investing Activities

Apparel's investing cash flows pertain to its Property, Plant, and Equipment account, which according to Exhibit 12–6 had beginning and ending balances of $1,394 million and $1,517 million, respectively, for an increase of $123 million. This increase suggests that Apparel purchased equipment; however, it does not capture the gross cash flows that need to be reported in the statement of cash flows.

The assumptions on page 568 says that Apparel sold a store that had an original cost of $15 million for $8 million in cash. The cash inflow from this sale needs to be recorded in the investing activities section of the statement of cash flows. To compute the cash outflows related to purchases of property, plant, and equipment we use the basic equation for assets that was mentioned in the beginning of the chapter:

$$\text{Beginning balance} + \text{Debits} - \text{Credits} = \text{Ending balance}$$

$$\$1{,}394 \text{ million} + \text{Debits} - \$15 \text{ million} = \$1{,}517 \text{ million}$$

$$\text{Debits} = \$1{,}517 \text{ million} - \$1{,}394 \text{ million} + \$15 \text{ million}$$

$$\text{Debits} = \$138 \text{ million}$$

Notice the credits in the equation above include the original cost of the store that was sold. When the cash outflows of $138 million are combined with the $8 million of cash proceeds from the sale of the store, Apparel's net cash used in investing activities is $130 million.

Financing Activities

Exhibit 12–9 explains how to compute Apparel's financing cash flows related to its Bonds Payable and Common Stock balance sheet accounts. The top half of the exhibit reproduces an excerpt of the general guidelines for analyzing financing cash flows that was previously summarized in Exhibit 12–3. The bottom half of Exhibit 12–9 applies the general guidelines from the top half of the exhibit to these two accounts from Apparel's balance sheet. We will analyze each account in turn.

EXHIBIT 12–9
Apparel, Inc.: Analyzing How
Changes in Noncash Balance
Sheet Accounts Affect Financing
Cash Flows on the Statement of
Cash Flows

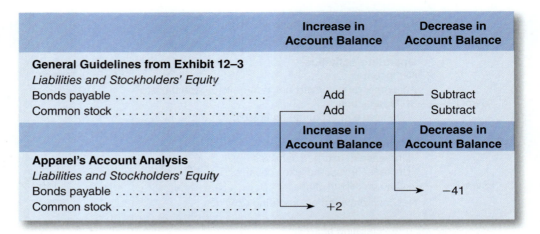

Exhibit 12–6 shows that Apparel's Bonds Payable balance decreased by $41 million. Because, as stated on page 568, Apparel did not issue any bonds during the year, we can conclude that the $41 million decrease in the account is due solely to retiring bonds payable. The top half of Exhibit 12–9 says that a decrease in Bonds Payable signals the need to subtract cash outflows in the investing activities section of the statement of cash flows. This explains why the bottom half of the exhibit includes a minus sign in front of Apparel's $41 million decrease in Bonds Payable. Similarly, Exhibit 12–6 shows that Apparel's Common Stock balance increased by $2 million. Because, as stated on page 568, Apparel did not repurchase any of its own stock during the year, we can conclude that the $2 million increase in the account is due solely to issuing common stock. The top half of Exhibit 12–9 says that increases in common stock signal the need to add cash inflows in the investing activities section of the statement of cash flows. This explains why the bottom half of the exhibit includes a plus sign in front of Apparel's $2 million increase in Common Stock.

The final financing cash outflow for Apparel is its dividend payment to common stockholders. The dividend payment can be computed using the basic equation for stockholders' equity accounts mentioned at the beginning of the chapter:

$$\text{Beginning balance} - \text{Debits} + \text{Credits} = \text{Ending balance}$$

$$\$897 \text{ million} - \text{Debits} + \$140 \text{ million} = \$1{,}009 \text{ million}$$

$$\$1{,}037 \text{ million} = \$1{,}009 \text{ million} + \text{Debits}$$

$$\text{Debits} = \$28 \text{ million}$$

When the cash outflows of $69 million (= $41 million + $28 million) are combined with the cash inflows of $2 million, Apparel's net cash used in financing activities is $67 million.

Exhibit 12–10 shows Apparel's statement of cash flows. The operating activities section of this statement is carried over from Exhibit 12–8. Take a moment to trace the investing and financing cash flows just discussed to Exhibit 12–10. Notice that the net change in cash and cash equivalents ($62 million) is calculated using the following equation:

Net change in cash and cash equivalents	=	Net cash provided by (used in) operating activities	+	Net cash provided by (used in) investing activities	+	Net cash provided by (used in) financing activities

$$\text{Net change in cash and cash equivalents} = \$259 \text{ million} + \$(130 \text{ million}) + \$(67 \text{ million})$$

$$\text{Net change in cash and cash equivalents} = \$62 \text{ million}$$

This amount agrees with the $62 million change in the Cash and Cash Equivalents account shown on the balance sheet in Exhibit 12–6.

Apparel, Inc. Statement of Cash Flows—Indirect Method (dollars in millions)		
Operating Activities		
Net income		$140
Adjustments to convert net income to a cash basis:		
Depreciation	103	
Decrease in accounts receivable	17	
Increase in inventory	(49)	
Increase in accounts payable	44	
Increase in accrued liabilities	3	
Increase in income taxes payable	4	
Gain on sale of store	(3)	119
Net cash provided by operating activities		259
Investing Activities		
Additions to property, plant, and equipment	(138)	
Proceeds from sale of store	8	
Net cash used in investing activities.		(130)
Financing Activities		
Retirement of bonds payable	(41)	
Issuance of common stock	2	
Cash dividends paid	(28)	
Net cash used in financing activities		(67)
Net increase in cash and cash equivalents		62
Beginning cash and cash equivalents		29
Ending cash and cash equivalents		$ 91

EXHIBIT 12–10
Apparel, Inc. Statement of Cash Flows

Seeing the Big Picture

In the beginning of the chapter, we mentioned that a statement of cash flows is prepared by analyzing the changes in noncash balance sheet accounts. We then presented a method of preparing a statement of cash flows. This method simplified the process of creating the statement of cash flows, and now we will show that it is equivalent to analyzing the changes in noncash balance sheet accounts.

Exhibit 12–11 uses T-accounts to summarize how the changes in Apparel, Inc.'s non-cash balance sheet accounts quantify the cash inflows and outflows that explain the change in its cash balance. The top portion of the exhibit is Apparel's Cash T-account and the bottom portion provides T-accounts for the company's remaining balance sheet accounts. Notice that the net cash provided by operating activities ($259 million) and the net increase in cash and cash equivalents ($62 million) shown in the Cash T-account agree with the corresponding figures in the statement of cash flows shown in Exhibit 12–10.

We will explain Exhibit 12–11 in five steps. Entry (1) records Apparel's net income ($140 million) in the credit side of the Retained Earnings account and the debit side of the Cash account. The net income of $140 million shown in the Cash T-account will be adjusted until it reflects the $62 million net increase in cash and cash equivalents. Entry (2) adds the depreciation of $103 million to net income. Entries (3) through (7) adjust net income for the changes in the current asset and current liability accounts. Entries (8) through (11) summarize the cash outflows and inflows related to the additions to property, plant, and equipment, the retirement of bonds payable, the payment of the cash dividend, and the issuance of common stock. Entry (12) records the sale of the store. Notice that the gain on the sale ($3 million) is recorded in the credit side of the Cash T-account. This is equivalent to subtracting the gain from net income so that the entire amount of the cash proceeds from the sale ($8 million) can be recorded in the investing activities section of the statement of cash flows.

EXHIBIT 12–11   T-Accounts after Posting of Account Changes—Apparel, Inc. (in millions)

Cash

Net income	(1)	140	49	(4)	Increase in inventory
Depreciation	(2)	103	3	(12)	Gain on sale of store
Decrease in accounts receivable	(3)	17			
Increase in accounts payable	(5)	44			
Increase in accrued liabilities	(6)	3			
Increase in income taxes payable	(7)	4			
Net cash provided by operating activities		259			
Proceeds from sale of store	(12)	8	138	(8)	Additions to property, plant, and equipment
Increase in common stock	(11)	2	41	(9)	Decrease in bonds payable
			28	(10)	Cash dividends paid
Net increase in cash and cash equivalents		62			

Accounts Receivable					Inventory					Property, Plant, and Equipment					Accumulated Depreciation		
Bal.	654				Bal.	537				Bal.	1,394					561	Bal.
		17	(3)		(4)	49				(8)	138	15	(12)	(12)	10	103	(2)
Bal.	637				Bal.	586				Bal.	1,517					654	Bal.

Accounts Payable				Accrued Liabilities				Income Taxes Payable		
	220	Bal.			190	Bal.			71	Bal.
	44	(5)			3	(6)			4	(7)
	264	Bal.			193	Bal.			75	Bal.

Bonds Payable				Common Stock				Retained Earnings		
	520	Bal.			155	Bal.			897	Bal.
(9)	41				2	(11)	(10)	28	140	(1)
	479	Bal.			157	Bal.			1,009	Bal.

IN BUSINESS   **Four Seasons Hotels Struggle to Manage Their Debt**

When the **Four Seasons Maui**'s occupancy rate fell from 79% to 60%, its net cash flow plummeted to $10.9 million in the first three quarters of the year. The hotel's owner was unable to make its annual debt payment of $23.6 million, so it worked with lenders to restructure the terms of their loan agreement. Other Four Seasons hotels faced similar problems. For example, the **Four Seasons San Francisco** teetered on the brink of foreclosure until its owner brought in a new co-owner called **Westbrook Partners LLC** to pay $35 million of its $90 million mortgage. Similarly, the owner of the **Four Seasons Dallas** faced a cash shortage that forced it to restructure the terms of its $183 million mortgage.

Source: Kris Hudson, "Four Seasons Maui on Ropes," *The Wall Street Journal,* March 22, 2010, p. B2.

INTERPRETING THE STATEMENT OF CASH FLOWS

Managers can derive many useful insights by studying the statement of cash flows. In this section, we will discuss two guidelines managers should use when interpreting the statement of cash flows.

Consider a Company's Specific Circumstances

A statement of cash flows should be evaluated in the context of a company's specific circumstances. To illustrate this point, let's consider two examples related to start-up companies and companies with growing versus declining sales. Start-up companies are usually unable to generate positive cash flows from operations; therefore, they rely on issuing stock and taking out loans to fund investing activities. This means that start-up companies often have negative net cash provided by operating activities and large spikes in net cash used for investing activities and net cash provided by financing activities. However, as a start-up company matures, it should begin generating enough cash to sustain day-to-day operations and maintain its plant and equipment without issuing additional stock or borrowing money. This means the net cash provided by operating activities should swing from a negative to a positive number. The net cash used for investing activities should decline somewhat and stabilize and the net cash provided by financing activities should decrease.

A company with growing sales would understandably have an increase in its accounts receivable, inventory, and accounts payable balances. On the other hand, if a company with declining sales has increases in these account balances, it could signal trouble. Perhaps accounts receivable is increasing because the company is attempting to boost sales by selling to customers who can't pay their bills. Perhaps the increase in inventory suggests the company is stuck with large amounts of obsolete inventory. Accounts payable may be increasing because the company is deferring payments to suppliers in an effort to inflate its net cash provided by operating activities. Notice that the plausible interpretations of these changes in account balances depend on the company's circumstances.

Owner

DECISION POINT

You are the owner of a small manufacturing company. The company started selling its products internationally this year, which has resulted in a very significant increase in sales revenue and net income during the last two months of the year. The operating activities section of the company's statement of cash flows shows a negative number (that is, cash was *used* rather than *provided* by operations). Would you be concerned?

Consider the Relationships among Numbers

While each number in a statement of cash flows provides useful information, managers derive the most meaningful insights by examining the relationships among numbers.

For example, some managers study their company's trends in cash flow margins by comparing the net cash provided by operating activities to sales. The goal is to continuously increase the operating cash flows earned per sales dollar. If we refer back to Apparel's income statement in Exhibit 12–5 and its statement of cash flows in Exhibit 12–10, we can determine that its cash flow margin is about $0.07 per dollar of sales (= $259 ÷ $3,638). Managers also compare the net cash provided by operating activities to the ending balance of current liabilities. If the net cash provided by operating activities is greater than (less than) the current liabilities, it indicates the company did (did not) generate enough operating cash flow to pay its bills at the end of the period. Apparel's net cash provided by operating activities of $259 million (see Exhibit 12–10) was not enough to pay its year-end current liabilities of $481 million (see Exhibit 12–6).

As a third example, managers compare the additions to property, plant, and equipment in the investing activities section of the statement of cash flows to the depreciation included in the operating activities section of the statement. If the additions to property, plant, and equipment are consistently less than depreciation, it suggests the company is not investing enough money to maintain its noncurrent assets. If we refer back to Apparel's statement of cash flows in Exhibit 12–10, its additions to property, plant, and equipment ($138 million) are greater than its depreciation ($103 million). This suggests that Apparel is investing more than enough money to maintain its noncurrent assets.

LEARNING OBJECTIVE 12–3

Compute free cash flow.

Free Cash Flow   *Free cash flow* is a measure used by managers to look at the relationship among three numbers from the statement of cash flows—net cash provided by operating activities, additions to property, plant, and equipment (also called capital expenditures), and dividends. **Free cash flow** measures a company's ability to fund its capital expenditures for property, plant, and equipment and its dividends from its net cash provided by operating activities.[7] The equation for computing free cash flow is as follows:

$$\text{Free cash flow} = \text{Net cash provided by operating activities} - \text{Capital expenditures} - \text{Dividends}$$

Using this equation and the statement of cash flows shown in Exhibit 12–10, we can compute Apparel's free cash flow (in millions) as follows:

$$\text{Free cash flow} = \$259 - \$138 - \$28$$

$$\text{Free cash flow} = \$93$$

The interpretation of free cash flow is straightforward. A positive number indicates that the company generated enough cash flow from its operating activities to fund its capital expenditures and dividend payments. A negative number suggests that the company needed to obtain cash from other sources, such as borrowing money from lenders or issuing shares of common stock, to fund its investments in property, plant, and equipment and its dividend payments. Negative free cash flow does not automatically signal poor performance. As previously discussed, a new company with enormous growth prospects would be expected to have negative free cash flow during its start-up phase. However, even new companies will eventually need to generate positive free cash flow to survive.

Earnings Quality   Managers and investors often look at the relationship between net income and net cash provided by operating activities to help assess the extent to which a company's earnings truly reflects operational performance. Managers generally perceive that earnings are of higher quality, or more indicative of operational performance, when the earnings (1) are not unduly influenced by inflation, (2) are computed using conservative accounting principles and estimates, and (3) are correlated with net cash provided by operating activities. When a company's net income and net cash provided by operating activities move in tandem with one another (in other words, are correlated with one another), it suggests that earnings result from changes in sales and operating expenses. Conversely, if a company's net income is steadily increasing and its net cash provided by operating activities is declining, it suggests that net income is being influenced by factors unrelated to operational performance, such as nonrecurring transactions or aggressive accounting principles and estimates.

[7]For a summary of alternative definitions of free cash flow, see John Mills, Lynn Bible, and Richard Mason, "Defining Free Cash Flow," *CPA Journal,* January 2002, pp. 36–42.

8. Which of the following statements is true with respect to earnings quality? (You may select more than one answer.)

    a. Managers generally perceive that earnings are of higher quality when earnings are not unduly influenced by inflation.

    b. Managers generally perceive that earnings are of higher quality when earnings are computed using aggressive estimates.

    c. Managers generally perceive that earnings are of higher quality when earnings move in the opposite direction to net cash provided by operating activities.

    d. Managers generally perceive that earnings are of higher quality when earnings are computed using conservative accounting principles.

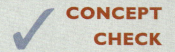

CONCEPT CHECK

Amazon.com Boosts Cash Flows

IN BUSINESS

Amazon.com immediately receives cash from its customers when sales occur on its website. When the company stretched the number of days taken to pay its suppliers from 63 to 72 days, this created a huge jump in the company's accounts payable balance, which helped increase free cash flow from $346 million to $1.36 billion. In one quarter, Amazon.com's sales increased 28%, but its accounts payable nearly doubled, causing a 116% increase in free cash flow. Do you think managers should increase cash flows by delaying payments to suppliers? Would it promote a cooperative relationship with suppliers?

Source: Martin Peers, "Amazon's Astute Timing," *The Wall Street Journal*, October 30, 2009, p. C10.

SUMMARY

LO12–1 Classify cash inflows and outflows as relating to operating, investing, or financing activities.

The statement of cash flows is organized into three sections: operating activities, investing activities, and financing activities. Operating activities generate cash inflows and outflows related to revenue and expense transactions that affect net income. Investing activities generate cash inflows and outflows related to acquiring or disposing of noncurrent assets. Financing activities generate cash inflows and outflows related to borrowing from and repaying principal to creditors and completing transactions with the company's owners.

LO12–2 Prepare a statement of cash flows using the indirect method to determine the net cash provided by operating activities.

The net cash provided by operating activities can be depicted using either the direct or indirect method. Under the direct method, the income statement is reconstructed on a cash basis from top to bottom. For example, cash collected from customers is listed instead of revenue, and payments to suppliers is listed instead of cost of goods sold. Under the indirect method, net income is adjusted to a cash basis. That is, rather than directly computing cash sales, cash expenses, and so forth, these amounts are derived indirectly by removing from net income any items that do not affect cash flows.

The indirect method adjusts net income to net cash provided by operating activities using a three-step process. The first step is to add depreciation charges to net income. The second step is to analyze net changes in noncash balance sheet accounts that impact net income. The third step is to adjust for gains/losses included in the income statement.

The investing and financing sections of the statement of cash flows record gross cash flows rather than net cash flows. The net increase in cash and cash equivalents shown on the statement of cash flows agrees with the change in the Cash account shown on the balance sheet.

LO12–3 Compute free cash flow.

Free cash flow is the net cash provided by operating activities less capital expenditures and dividends.

GUIDANCE ANSWER TO DECISION POINT

Owner (p. 575)

Even though the company reported net income, the net effect of the company's operations was to *consume* rather than *generate* cash during the year. Cash disbursements relating to the company's operations exceeded the amount of cash receipts from operations. If the company generated a significant amount of sales just before the end of the year, it is quite possible that cash has not yet been received from the customers. In fact, given that the additional sales were international, a longer collection period would be expected. Nevertheless, as owner, you probably would want to ensure that the company's credit-granting policies and procedures were adhered to when these sales were made, and you should also monitor the length of time it takes to collect accounts receivable.

GUIDANCE ANSWERS TO CONCEPT CHECKS

1. **Choices a and d.** Debits are added to the beginning balance and credits are subtracted.
2. **Choice a.** Accounts receivable is a current asset, but it is not a cash equivalent.
3. **Choices b, c, and d.** The indirect method starts with net income and adjusts it to a cash basis.
4. **Choices a and c.** Depreciation charges are added to net income. A loss on the sale of an asset should be added to net income.
5. **Choice d.** Using the basic equation for contra assets, $2,000 − $350 + Credits = $2,900. The credits = $1,250.
6. **Choice a.** The cash proceeds from the sale of the asset were $75 and the book value of the asset that was sold is $50 (= $400 − $350). The $25 difference between these two amounts is the gain on the sale of the asset and it should be subtracted from net income in the operating activities section of the statement of cash flows.
7. **Choice c.** Using the basic equation for assets, $5,000 + Debits − $700 = $6,000. The debits equal $1,700 and this amount relates to purchases of noncurrent assets. Since the company sold an asset for $500 and it purchased noncurrent assets for $1,700, its net cash provided by (used in) investing activities is $(1,200).
8. **Choices a and d.** Earnings quality is higher when managers use conservative estimates. It is also higher when earnings move in the same direction as net cash provided by operating activities.

REVIEW PROBLEM

Rockford Company's comparative balance sheet for 2015 and the company's income statement for the year follow:

Rockford Company
Comparative Balance Sheet
(dollars in millions)

	2015	2014
Assets		
Current assets:		
Cash and cash equivalents	$ 26	$ 10
Accounts receivable	180	270
Inventory	205	160
Prepaid expenses	17	20
Total current assets	428	460
Property, plant, and equipment	430	309
Less accumulated depreciation	218	194
Net property, plant, and equipment	212	115
Long-term investments	60	75
Total assets	$700	$650
Liabilities and Stockholders' Equity		
Current liabilities:		
Accounts payable	$230	$310
Accrued liabilities	70	60
Income taxes payable	15	8
Total current liabilities	315	378
Bonds payable	135	40
Total liabilities	450	418
Stockholders' equity:		
Common stock	140	140
Retained earnings	110	92
Total stockholders' equity	250	232
Total liabilities and stockholders' equity ...	$700	$650

Rockford Company
Income Statement
For the Year Ended December 31, 2015
(dollars in millions)

Sales	$1,000
Cost of goods sold	530
Gross margin	470
Selling and administrative expenses	352
Net operating income	118
Nonoperating items:	
Loss on sale of equipment	4
Income before taxes	114
Income taxes	48
Net income	$ 66

Additional data:
1. Rockford paid a cash dividend in 2015.
2. The $4 million loss on sale of equipment reflects a transaction in which equipment with an original cost of $12 million and accumulated depreciation of $5 million was sold for $3 million in cash.
3. Rockford did not purchase any long-term investments during the year. There was no gain or loss on the sale of long-term investments.
4. Rockford did not retire any bonds payable during 2015, or issue or repurchase any common stock.

Required:
1. Using the indirect method, determine the net cash provided by operating activities for 2015.
2. Construct a statement of cash flows for 2015.

Solution to Review Problem
The first task you should complete before turning your attention to the problem's specific requirements is to compute the changes in each balance sheet account as shown below (all amounts are in millions):

Rockford Company Comparative Balance Sheet (dollars in millions)			
	2015	**2014**	**Change**
Assets			
Current assets:			
Cash and cash equivalents	$ 26	$ 10	−16
Accounts receivable	180	270	−90
Inventory	205	160	+45
Prepaid expenses	17	20	−3
Total current assets	428	460	
Property, plant, and equipment	430	309	+121
Less accumulated depreciation	218	194	+24
Net property, plant, and equipment	212	115	
Long-term investments	60	75	−15
Total assets	$700	$650	
Liabilities and Stockholders' Equity			
Current liabilities:			
Accounts payable	$230	$310	−80
Accrued liabilities	70	60	+10
Income taxes payable	15	8	−7
Total current liabilities	315	378	
Bonds payable	135	40	+95
Total liabilities	450	418	
Stockholders' equity:			
Common stock	140	140	+0
Retained earnings	110	92	+18
Total stockholders' equity	250	232	
Total liabilities and stockholders' equity	$700	$650	

Requirement 1:
You should perform three steps to compute the net cash provided by operating activities.

Step 1: Add depreciation to net income.
　　　To complete this step, apply the following equation:

$$\text{Beginning balance} - \text{Debits} + \text{Credits} = \text{Ending balance}$$

$$\$194 \text{ million} - \$5 \text{ million} + \text{Credits} = \$218 \text{ million}$$

$$\text{Credits} = \$218 \text{ million} - \$194 \text{ million} + \$5 \text{ million}$$

$$\text{Credits} = \$29 \text{ million}$$

Step 2: Analyze net changes in noncash balance sheet accounts that affect net income.
To complete this step, apply the logic from Exhibit 12–2 as follows:

	Increase in Account Balance	Decrease in Account Balance
Current Assets		
Accounts receivable		+90
Inventory	−45	
Prepaid expenses		+3
Current Liabilities		
Accounts payable		−80
Accrued liabilities	+10	
Income taxes payable	+7	

Step 3: Adjust for gains/losses included in the income statement.
Rockford's $4 million loss on the sale of equipment must be added to net income.

Having completed these three steps, the operating activities section of the statement of cash flows would appear as follows:

Rockford Company		
Statement of Cash Flows—Indirect Method		
For the Year Ended December 31, 2015		
(dollars in millions)		
Operating Activities:		
Net income		$66
Adjustments to convert net income to a cash basis:		
Depreciation	$29	
Decrease in accounts receivable	90	
Increase in inventory	(45)	
Decrease in prepaid expenses	3	
Decrease in accounts payable	(80)	
Increase in accrued liabilities	10	
Increase in income taxes payable	7	
Loss on sale of equipment	4	18
Net cash provided by operating activities		$84

Requirement 2:

To finalize the statement of cash flows, we must complete the investing and financing sections of the statement. This requires analyzing the Property, Plant, and Equipment, Long-Term Investments, Bonds Payable, Common Stock and Retained Earnings accounts. The table below is based on Exhibit 12–3 and it captures the changes in four account balances for Rockford.

	Increase in Account Balance	Decrease in Account Balance
Noncurrent Assets (Investing activities)		
Property, plant, and equipment	−121	
Long-term investments		+15
Liabilities and Stockholders' Equity		
(Financing activities)		
Bonds payable	+95	
Common stock	No change	No change
Retained earnings	*	*
*Requires further analysis to quantify cash dividends paid.		

The data at the beginning of the problem state that Rockford did not purchase any long-term investments during the year and that there was no gain or loss on the sale of long-term investments. This means that the $15 million decrease in Long-Term Investments corresponds with a $15 million cash inflow from the sale of long-term investments that is recorded in the investing section of the statement of cash flows. The data also state that Rockford did not retire any bonds payable during the year; therefore, the $95 million increase in Bonds Payable must be due to issuing bonds payable. This cash inflow is recorded in the financing section of the statement of cash flows.

The Common Stock account had no activity during the period, so it does not impact the statement of cash flows. This leaves two accounts that require further analysis—Property, Plant, and Equipment and Retained Earnings.

The company sold equipment that had an original cost of $12 million for $3 million in cash. The cash proceeds from the sale need to be recorded in the investing activities section of the statement of cash flows. The cash outflows related to Rockford's investing activities can be computed using the following equation:

$$\text{Beginning balance} + \text{Debits} - \text{Credits} = \text{Ending balance}$$

$$\$309 \text{ million} + \text{Debits} - \$12 \text{ million} = \$430 \text{ million}$$

$$\text{Debits} = \$430 \text{ million} - \$309 \text{ million} + \$12 \text{ million}$$

$$\text{Debits} = \$133 \text{ million}$$

Rockford's Retained Earnings account and the basic equation for stockholders' equity can be used to compute the company's dividend payment as follows:

$$\text{Beginning balance} - \text{Debits} + \text{Credits} = \text{Ending balance}$$

$$\$92 \text{ million} - \text{Debits} + \$66 \text{ million} = \$110 \text{ million}$$

$$\$158 \text{ million} = \$110 \text{ million} + \text{Debits}$$

$$\text{Debits} = \$48 \text{ million}$$

The company's complete statement of cash flows is shown below. Notice that the net increase in cash and cash equivalents ($16 million) equals the change in the Cash and Cash Equivalents account balance.

Rockford Company
Statement of Cash Flows—Indirect Method
For the Year Ended December 31, 2015
(dollars in millions)

Operating Activities:		
Net income		$ 66
Adjustments to convert net income to a cash basis:		
Depreciation	$ 29	
Decrease in accounts receivable	90	
Increase in inventory	(45)	
Decrease in prepaid expenses	3	
Decrease in accounts payable	(80)	
Increase in accrued liabilities	10	
Increase in income taxes payable	7	
Loss on sale of equipment	4	18
Net cash provided by operating activities		84
Investing Activities:		
Additions to property, plant, and equipment	(133)	
Decrease in long-term investments	15	
Proceeds from sale of equipment	3	
Net cash used in investing activities		(115)
Financing Activities:		
Increase in bonds payable	95	
Cash dividends paid	(48)	
Net cash provided by financing activities		47
Net increase in cash and cash equivalents		16
Beginning cash and cash equivalents		10
Ending cash and cash equivalents		$ 26

GLOSSARY

Cash equivalents Short-term, highly liquid investments such as Treasury bills, commercial paper, and money market funds, that are made solely for the purpose of generating a return on temporarily idle funds. (p. 559)

Direct method A method of computing the net cash provided by operating activities in which the income statement is reconstructed on a cash basis from top to bottom. (p. 560)

Financing activities These activities generate cash inflows and outflows related to borrowing from and repaying principal to creditors and completing transactions with the company's owners, such as selling or repurchasing shares of common stock and paying dividends. (p. 560)

Free cash flow A measure that assesses a company's ability to fund its capital expenditures and dividends from its net cash provided by operating activities. (p. 576)

Indirect method A method of computing the net cash provided by operating activities that starts with net income and adjusts it to a cash basis. (p. 560)

Investing activities These activities generate cash inflows and outflows related to acquiring or disposing of noncurrent assets such as property, plant, and equipment, long-term investments, and loans to another entity. (p. 560)

Net cash provided by operating activities The net result of the cash inflows and outflows arising from day-to-day operations. (p. 560)

Operating activities These activities generate cash inflows and outflows related to revenue and expense transactions that affect net income. (p. 560)

Statement of cash flows A financial statement that highlights the major activities that impact cash flows and, hence, affect the overall cash balance. (p. 558)

QUESTIONS

12–1 What is the purpose of a statement of cash flows?

12–2 What are *cash equivalents,* and why are they included with cash on a statement of cash flows?

12–3 What are the three major sections on a statement of cash flows, and what type of cash inflows and outflows should be included in each section?

12–4 What general guidelines can you provide for interpreting the statement of cash flows?

12–5 If an asset is sold at a gain, why is the gain subtracted from net income when computing the net cash provided by operating activities under the indirect method?

12–6 Why aren't transactions involving accounts payable considered to be financing activities?

12–7 Assume that a company repays a $300,000 loan from its bank and then later in the same year borrows $500,000. What amount(s) would appear on the statement of cash flows?

12–8 How do the direct and the indirect methods differ in their approach to computing the net cash provided by operating activities?

12–9 A business executive once stated, "Depreciation is one of our biggest operating cash inflows." Do you agree? Explain.

12–10 If the Accounts Receivable balance increases during a period, how will this increase be recognized using the indirect method of computing the net cash provided by operating activities?

12–11 Would a sale of equipment for cash be considered a financing activity or an investing activity? Why?

12–12 What is the difference between net cash provided by operating activities and free cash flow?

Multiple-choice questions are available in the *Connect Library.*

 |ACCOUNTING **THE FOUNDATIONAL 15**

Available with McGraw-Hill's *Connect Accounting.*

LO12–1, LO12–2

Ravenna Company is a merchandiser that uses the indirect method to prepare the operating activities section of its statement of cash flows. Its balance sheet for this year is as follows:

	Ending Balance	Beginning Balance
Cash	$ 48,000	$ 57,000
Accounts receivable	41,000	44,000
Inventory	55,000	50,000
Total current assets	144,000	151,000
Property, plant, and equipment	150,000	140,000
Less accumulated depreciation	50,000	35,000
Net property, plant, and equipment	100,000	105,000
Total assets	$244,000	$256,000
Accounts payable	$ 32,000	$ 57,000
Income taxes payable	25,000	28,000
Bonds payable	60,000	50,000
Common stock	70,000	60,000
Retained earnings	57,000	61,000
Total liabilities and stockholders' equity	$244,000	$256,000

During the year, Ravenna paid a $6,000 cash dividend and it sold a piece of equipment for $3,000 that had originally cost $6,000 and had accumulated depreciation of $4,000. The company did not retire any bonds or repurchase any of its own common stock during the year.

Required:

1. What is the amount of the net increase or decrease in cash and cash equivalents that would be shown on the company's statement of cash flows?
2. What net income would the company include on its statement of cash flows?
3. How much depreciation would the company add to net income on its statement of cash flows?
4. (To help answer this question, create an Accounts Receivable T-account and insert the beginning and ending balances.) If the company debited Accounts Receivable and credited Sales for $600,000 during the year, what is the total amount of credits recorded in Accounts Receivable during the year? What does the amount of these credits represent?
5. What is the amount and direction (+ or −) of the accounts receivable adjustment to net income in the operating activities section of the statement of cash flows? What does this adjustment represent?
6. (To help answer this question, create T-accounts for Inventory and Accounts Payable and insert their beginning and ending balances.) If the company debited Cost of Goods Sold and credited Inventory for $400,000 during the year, what is the total amount of inventory purchases recorded on the debit side of the Inventory T-account and the credit side of the Accounts Payable T-account? What is the total amount of the debits recorded in the Accounts Payable T-account during the year? What does the amount of these debits represent?
7. What is the combined amount and direction (+ or −) of the inventory and accounts payable adjustments to net income in the operating activities section of the statement of cash flows? What does this amount represent?
8. (To help answer this question, create an Income Taxes Payable T-account and insert the beginning and ending balances.) If the company debited Income Tax Expense and credited Income Taxes Payable $700 during the year, what is the total amount of the debits recorded in the Income Taxes Payable account? What does the amount of these debits represent?
9. What is the amount and direction (+ or −) of the income taxes payable adjustment to net income in the operating activities section of the statement of cash flows? What does this adjustment represent?
10. Would the operating activities section of the company's statement of cash flows contain an adjustment for a gain or a loss? What would be the amount and direction (+ or −) of the adjustment?
11. What is the amount of net cash provided by operating activities in the company's statement of cash flows?
12. What is the amount of gross cash outflows reported in the investing section of the company's statement of cash flows?
13. What is the company's net cash provided by (used in) investing activities?
14. What is the amount of gross cash inflows reported in the financing section of the company's statement of cash flows?
15. What is the company's net cash provided by (used in) financing activities?

EXERCISES

All applicable exercises are available with McGraw-Hill's *Connect Accounting.*

EXERCISE 12–1 Classifying Transactions [LO12–1]
Below are certain events that took place at Hazzard, Inc., last year:

a. Collected cash from customers.
b. Paid cash to repurchase its own stock.
c. Borrowed money from a creditor.
d. Paid suppliers for inventory purchases.
e. Repaid the principal amount of a debt.
f. Paid interest to lenders.
g. Paid a cash dividend to stockholders.
h. Sold common stock.
i. Loaned money to another entity.
j. Paid taxes to the government.
k. Paid wages and salaries to employees.
l. Purchased equipment with cash.
m. Paid bills to insurers and utility providers.

Required:
Prepare an answer sheet with the following headings:

Transaction	Activity		
	Operating	Investing	Financing
a.			
b.			
Etc.			

Enter the cash inflows and outflows above on your answer sheet and indicate how each of them would be classified on a statement of cash flows. Place an X in the Operating, Investing, or Financing column as appropriate.

EXERCISE 12–2 Net Cash Provided by Operating Activities [LO12–2]
For the just completed year, Hanna Company had net income of $35,000. Balances in the company's current asset and current liability accounts at the beginning and end of the year were as follows:

	December 31	
	End of Year	Beginning of Year
Current assets:		
Cash	$30,000	$40,000
Accounts receivable	$125,000	$106,000
Inventory	$213,000	$180,000
Prepaid expenses	$6,000	$7,000
Current liabilities:		
Accounts payable	$210,000	$195,000
Accrued liabilities	$4,000	$6,000
Income taxes payable	$34,000	$30,000

The Accumulated Depreciation account had total credits of $20,000 during the year. Hanna Company did not record any gains or losses during the year.

Required:
Using the indirect method, determine the net cash provided by operating activities for the year.

EXERCISE 12–3 Calculating Free Cash Flow [LO12–3]

Apex Company prepared the statement of cash flows for the current year that is shown below:

Apex Company		
Statement of Cash Flows—Indirect Method		
Operating activities:		
Net income		$ 40,000
Adjustments to convert net income to cash basis:		
Depreciation	$ 22,000	
Increase in accounts receivable	(60,000)	
Increase in inventory	(25,000)	
Decrease in prepaid expenses	9,000	
Increase in accounts payable	55,000	
Decrease in accrued liabilities	(12,000)	
Increase in income taxes payable	5,000	(6,000)
Net cash provided by operating activities		34,000
Investing activities:		
Proceeds from the sale of equipment	14,000	
Loan to Thomas Company	(40,000)	
Additions to plant and equipment	(110,000)	
Net cash used for investing activities		(136,000)
Financing activities:		
Increase in bonds payable	90,000	
Increase in common stock	40,000	
Cash dividends	(30,000)	
Net cash provided by financing activities		100,000
Net decrease in cash		(2,000)
Beginning cash balance		27,000
Ending cash balance		$ 25,000

Required:

Compute Apex Company's free cash flow for the current year.

EXERCISE 12–4 Prepare a Statement of Cash Flows [LO12–1, LO12–2]

The following changes took place last year in Pavolik Company's balance sheet accounts:

Asset and Contra Asset Accounts			**Liabilities and Equity Accounts**		
Cash	$5	D	Accounts payable	$35	I
Accounts receivable	$110	I	Accrued liabilities	$4	D
Inventory	$70	D	Income taxes payable	$8	I
Prepaid expenses	$9	I	Bonds payable	$150	I
Long-term investments	$6	D	Common stock	$80	D
Property, plant, and equipment	$185	I	Retained earnings	$54	I
Accumulated depreciation	$60	I			
D = Decrease; I = Increase					

   Long-term investments that had cost the company $6 were sold during the year for $16 and land that had cost $15 was sold for $9. In addition, the company declared and paid $30 in cash dividends during the year. Besides the sale of land, no other sales or retirements of plant and equipment took place during the year. Pavolik did not retire any bonds during the year or issue any new common stock.

The company's income statement for the year follows:

Sales	$700
Cost of goods sold	400
Gross margin	300
Selling and administrative expenses	184
Net operating income	116
Nonoperating items:	
Loss on sale of land ... $(6)	
Gain on sale of investments ... 10	4
Income before taxes	120
Income taxes	36
Net income	$ 84

The company's beginning cash balance was $90 and its ending balance was $85.

Required:
1. Use the indirect method to determine the net cash provided by operating activities for the year.
2. Prepare a statement of cash flows for the year.

EXERCISE 12–5 Net Cash Provided by Operating Activities [LO12–2]
Changes in various accounts and gains and losses on the sale of assets during the year for Argon Company are given below:

Item	Amount
Accounts receivable	$90,000 decrease
Inventory	$120,000 increase
Prepaid expenses	$3,000 decrease
Accounts payable	$65,000 decrease
Accrued liabilities	$8,000 increase
Income taxes payable	$12,000 increase
Sale of equipment	$7,000 gain
Sale of long-term investments	$10,000 loss

Required:
Prepare an answer sheet using the following column headings:

Item	Amount	Add	Subtract

For each item, place an X in the Add or Subtract column to indicate whether the dollar amount should be added to or subtracted from net income under the indirect method when computing the net cash provided by operating activities for the year.

EXERCISE 12–6 Prepare a Statement of Cash Flows; Free Cash Flow [LO12–1, LO12–2, LO12–3]
Comparative financial statement data for Carmono Company follow:

	This Year	Last Year
Assets		
Cash	$ 3	$ 6
Accounts receivable	22	24
Inventory	50	40
Total current assets	75	70
Property, plant, and equipment	240	200
Less accumulated depreciation	65	50
Net property, plant, and equipment	175	150
Total assets	$250	$220
Liabilities and Stockholders' Equity		
Accounts payable	$ 40	$ 36
Common stock	150	145
Retained earnings	60	39
Total liabilities and stockholders' equity	$250	$220

For this year, the company reported net income as follows:

Sales	$275
Cost of goods sold	150
Gross margin	125
Selling and administrative expenses	90
Net income	$ 35

This year Carmono declared and paid a cash dividend. There were no sales of property, plant, and equipment during this year. The company did not repurchase any of its own stock this year.

Required:
1. Using the indirect method, prepare a statement of cash flows for this year.
2. Compute Carmono's free cash flow for this year.

PROBLEMS

All applicable problems are available with McGraw-Hill's *Connect Accounting.*

PROBLEM 12–7A   **Prepare a Statement of Cash Flows [LO12–1, LO12–2]**
Comparative financial statements for Weaver Company follow:

Weaver Company Comparative Balance Sheet December 31, 2015 and 2014		
	2015	**2014**
Assets		
Cash	$ 9	$ 15
Accounts receivable	340	240
Inventory	125	175
Prepaid expenses	10	6
Total current assets	484	436
Property, plant, and equipment	610	470
Less accumulated depreciation	93	85
Net property, plant, and equipment	517	385
Long-term investments	16	19
Total assets	$1,017	$840
Liabilities and Stockholders' Equity		
Accounts payable	$ 310	$230
Accrued liabilities	60	72
Income taxes payable	40	34
Total current liabilities	410	336
Bonds payable	290	180
Total liabilities	700	516
Common stock	210	250
Retained earnings	107	74
Total stockholders' equity	317	324
Total liabilities and stockholders' equity	$1,017	$840

Weaver Company
Income Statement
For the Year Ended December 31, 2015

Sales		$800
Cost of goods sold		500
Gross margin		300
Selling and administrative expenses . . .		213
Net operating income		87
Nonoperating items:		
Gain on sale of investments	$7	
Loss on sale of equipment	(4)	3
Income before taxes		90
Income taxes		27
Net income		$ 63

During 2015, Weaver sold some equipment for $20 that had cost $40 and on which there was accumulated depreciation of $16. In addition, the company sold long-term investments for $10 that had cost $3 when purchased several years ago. A cash dividend was paid during 2015 and the company repurchased $40 of its own stock. Weaver did not retire any bonds during 2015.

Required:
1. Using the indirect method, determine the net cash provided by operating activities for 2015.
2. Using the information in (1) above, along with an analysis of the remaining balance sheet accounts, prepare a statement of cash flows for 2015.

PROBLEM 12–8A **Classification of Transactions [LO12–1]**
Below are several transactions that took place in Seneca Company last year:
a. Paid suppliers for inventory purchases.
b. Bought equipment for cash.
c. Paid cash to repurchase its own stock.
d. Collected cash from customers.
e. Paid wages to employees.
f. Equipment was sold for cash.
g. Common stock was sold for cash to investors.
h. Cash dividends were declared and paid.
i. A long-term loan was made to a supplier.
j. Income taxes were paid to the government.
k. Interest was paid to a lender.
l. Bonds were retired by paying the principal amount due.

Required:
Prepare an answer sheet with the following headings:

	Activity			Cash	Cash
Transaction	Operating	Investing	Financing	Inflow	Outflow
a.					
b.					
Etc.					

Enter the transactions from the previous page on your answer sheet and indicate how each of them would be classified on a statement of cash flows. As appropriate, place an X in the Operating, Investing, or Financing column. Also, place on X in the Cash Inflow or Cash Outflow column.

PROBLEM 12–9A   Understanding a Statement of Cash Flows [LO12–1, LO12–2]
Brock Company is a merchandiser that prepared the statement of cash flows and income statement provided below:

Brock Company		
Statement of Cash Flows—Indirect Method		
Operating Activities		
Net income		$ 275
Adjustments to convert net income to a cash basis:		
Depreciation	140	
Increase in accounts receivable	(24)	
Decrease in inventory	39	
Decrease in accounts payable	(45)	
Decrease in accrued liabilities	(5)	
Increase in income taxes payable	6	
Gain on sale of equipment	(4)	107
Net cash provided by operating activities		382
Investing Activities		
Additions to property, plant, and equipment	(150)	
Proceeds from sale of equipment	19	
Net cash used in investing activities		(131)
Financing Activities		
Issuance of bonds payable	40	
Issuance of common stock	4	
Cash dividends paid	(35)	
Net cash provided by financing activities		9
Net increase in cash and cash equivalents		260
Beginning cash and cash equivalents		170
Ending cash and cash equivalents		$ 430

Brock Company	
Income Statement	
Net sales	$5,200
Cost of goods sold	2,980
Gross margin	2,220
Selling and administrative expenses	1,801
Net operating income	419
Nonoperating items: Gain on sale of equipment	4
Income before taxes	423
Income taxes	148
Net income	$ 275

Required:

Assume that you have been asked to teach a workshop to the employees within Brock Company's Marketing Department. The purpose of your workshop is to explain how the statement of cash flows differs from the income statement. Your audience is expecting you to explain the logic underlying each number included in the statement of cash flows. Prepare a memo that explains the format of the statement of cash flows and the rationale for each number included in Brock's statement of cash flows.

PROBLEM 12–10A **Prepare a Statement of Cash Flows; Free Cash Flow [LO12–1, LO12–2, LO12–3]**

Joyner Company's income statement for Year 2 follows:

Sales	$900,000
Cost of goods sold	500,000
Gross margin	400,000
Selling and administrative expenses	328,000
Net operating income	72,000
Gain on sale of equipment	8,000
Income before taxes	80,000
Income taxes	24,000
Net income	$ 56,000

Its balance sheet amounts at the end of Years 1 and 2 are as follows:

	Year 2	Year 1
Assets		
Cash	$ 4,000	$ 21,000
Accounts receivable	250,000	170,000
Inventory	310,000	260,000
Prepaid expenses	7,000	14,000
Total current assets	571,000	465,000
Property, plant, and equipment	510,000	400,000
Less accumulated depreciation	132,000	120,000
Net property, plant, and equipment	378,000	280,000
Loan to Hymans Company	40,000	0
Total assets	$989,000	$745,000
Liabilities and Stockholders' Equity		
Accounts payable	$310,000	$250,000
Accrued liabilities	20,000	30,000
Income taxes payable	45,000	42,000
Total current liabilities	375,000	322,000
Bonds payable	190,000	70,000
Total liabilities	565,000	392,000
Common stock	300,000	270,000
Retained earnings	124,000	83,000
Total stockholders' equity	424,000	353,000
Total liabilities and stockholders' equity	$989,000	$745,000

Equipment that had cost $40,000 and on which there was accumulated depreciation of $30,000 was sold during Year 2 for $18,000. The company declared and paid a cash dividend during Year 2. It did not retire any bonds or repurchase any of its own stock.

Required:
1.   Using the indirect method, compute the net cash provided by operating activities for Year 2.
2.   Prepare a statement of cash flows for Year 2.
3.   Compute the free cash flow for Year 2.
4.   Briefly explain why cash declined so sharply during the year.

PROBLEM 12–11A   Missing Data; Statement of Cash Flows [LO12–1, LO12–2]
Yoric Company listed the net changes in its balance sheet accounts for the past year as follows:

	Debits > Credits by:	Credits > Debits by:
Cash	$ 17,000	
Accounts receivable	110,000	
Inventory		$ 65,000
Prepaid expenses		8,000
Long-term loans to subsidiaries		30,000
Long-term investments..................	80,000	
Plant and equipment....................	220,000	
Accumulated depreciation		5,000
Accounts payable		32,000
Accrued liabilities	9,000	
Income taxes payable		16,000
Bonds payable		400,000
Common stock	170,000	
Retained earnings		50,000
	$606,000	$606,000

The following additional information is available about last year's activities:
a.   Net income for the year was $ _____?_____.
b.   The company sold equipment during the year for $15,000. The equipment originally cost $50,000 and it had $37,000 in accumulated depreciation at the time of sale.
c.   Cash dividends of $20,000 were declared and paid during the year.
d.   The beginning and ending balances in the Plant and Equipment and Accumulated Depreciation accounts are given below:

	Beginning	Ending
Plant and equipment	$1,580,000	$1,800,000
Accumulated depreciation	$675,000	$680,000

e.   The balance in the Cash account at the beginning of the year was $23,000; the balance at the end of the year was $ _____?_____.
f.   If data are not given explaining the change in an account, make the most reasonable assumption as to the cause of the change.

Required:
Using the indirect method, prepare a statement of cash flows for the year.

PROBLEM 12–12A Prepare a Statement of Cash Flows [LO12–1, LO12–2]

A comparative balance sheet and an income statement for Burgess Company are given below:

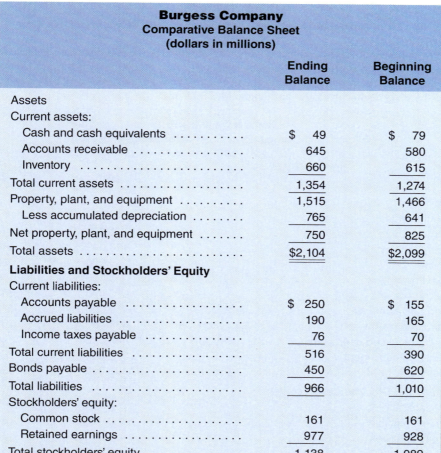

Burgess Company
Comparative Balance Sheet
(dollars in millions)

	Ending Balance	Beginning Balance
Assets		
Current assets:		
Cash and cash equivalents	$ 49	$ 79
Accounts receivable	645	580
Inventory	660	615
Total current assets	1,354	1,274
Property, plant, and equipment	1,515	1,466
Less accumulated depreciation	765	641
Net property, plant, and equipment	750	825
Total assets	$2,104	$2,099
Liabilities and Stockholders' Equity		
Current liabilities:		
Accounts payable	$ 250	$ 155
Accrued liabilities	190	165
Income taxes payable	76	70
Total current liabilities	516	390
Bonds payable	450	620
Total liabilities	966	1,010
Stockholders' equity:		
Common stock	161	161
Retained earnings	977	928
Total stockholders' equity	1,138	1,089
Total liabilities and stockholders' equity	$2,104	$2,099

Burgess Company
Income Statement
(dollars in millions)

Net sales	$3,600
Cost of goods sold	2,550
Gross margin	1,050
Selling and administrative expenses	875
Net operating income	175
Nonoperating items: Gain on sale of equipment...	3
Income before taxes	178
Income taxes	63
Net income	$ 115

Burgess also provided the following information:
1. The company sold equipment that had an original cost of $13 million and accumulated depreciation of $8 million. The cash proceeds from the sale were $8 million. The gain on the sale was $3 million.
2. The company did not issue any new bonds during the year.
3. The company paid a cash dividend during the year.
4. The company did not complete any common stock transactions during the year.

Required:
1. Using the indirect method, prepare a statement of cash flows for the year.

2. Assume that Burgess had sales of $3,800, net income of $135, and net cash provided by operating activities of $150 in the prior year (all numbers are stated in millions). Prepare a memo that summarizes your interpretations of Burgess's financial performance.

PROBLEM 12–13A   Prepare and Interpret a Statement of Cash Flows; Free Cash Flow [LO12–1, LO12–2, LO12–3]

Mary Walker, president of Rusco Company, considers $14,000 to be the minimum cash balance for operating purposes. As can be seen from the following statements, only $8,000 in cash was available at the end of 2015. Since the company reported a large net income for the year, and also issued both bonds and common stock, the sharp decline in cash is puzzling to Ms. Walker.

Rusco Company
Comparative Balance Sheet
July 31, 2015 and 2014

	2015	2014
Assets		
Current assets:		
Cash	$ 8,000	$ 21,000
Accounts receivable	120,000	80,000
Inventory	140,000	90,000
Prepaid expenses	5,000	9,000
Total current assets	273,000	200,000
Long-term investments	50,000	70,000
Plant and equipment	430,000	300,000
Less accumulated depreciation	60,000	50,000
Net plant and equipment	370,000	250,000
Total assets	$693,000	$520,000
Liabilities and Stockholders' Equity		
Current liabilities:		
Accounts payable	$123,000	$ 60,000
Accrued liabilities	8,000	17,000
Income taxes payable	20,000	12,000
Total current liabilities	151,000	89,000
Bonds payable	70,000	0
Total liabilities	221,000	89,000
Stockholders' equity:		
Common stock	366,000	346,000
Retained earnings	106,000	85,000
Total stockholders' equity	472,000	431,000
Total liabilities and stockholders' equity	$693,000	$520,000

Rusco Company
Income Statement
For the Year Ended July 31, 2015

Sales		$500,000
Cost of goods sold		300,000
Gross margin		200,000
Selling and administrative expenses		158,000
Net operating income		42,000
Nonoperating items:		
Gain on sale of investments	$10,000	
Loss on sale of equipment	(2,000)	8,000
Income before taxes		50,000
Income taxes		20,000
Net income		$ 30,000

The following additional information is available for the year 2015.
a. The company declared and paid a cash dividend.
b. Equipment was sold during the year for $8,000. The equipment had originally cost $20,000 and had accumulated depreciation of $10,000.
c. Long-term investments that had cost $20,000 were sold during the year for $30,000.
d. The company did not retire any bonds payable or repurchase any of its common stock.

Required:
1. Using the indirect method, compute the net cash provided by operating activities for 2015.
2. Using the data from (1) above, and other data from the problem as needed, prepare a statement of cash flows for 2015.
3. Compute free cash flow for 2015.
4. Explain the major reasons for the decline in the company's cash balance.

PROBLEM 12–14A   Prepare and Interpret a Statement of Cash Flows [LO12–1, LO12–2]
A comparative balance sheet for Lomax Company containing data for the last two years is as follows:

Lomax Company Comparative Balance Sheet		
	This Year	**Last Year**
Assets		
Current assets:		
Cash and cash equivalents	$ 61,000	$ 40,000
Accounts receivable	710,000	530,000
Inventory	848,000	860,000
Prepaid expenses	10,000	5,000
Total current assets	1,629,000	1,435,000
Property, plant, and equipment	3,170,000	2,600,000
Less accumulated depreciation	810,000	755,000
Net property, plant, and equipment	2,360,000	1,845,000
Long-term investments	60,000	110,000
Loans to subsidiaries	214,000	170,000
Total assets	$4,263,000	$3,560,000
Liabilities and Stockholders' Equity		
Current liabilities:		
Accounts payable	$ 970,000	$ 670,000
Accrued liabilities	65,000	82,000
Income taxes payable	95,000	80,000
Total current liabilities	1,130,000	832,000
Bonds payable	820,000	600,000
Total liabilities	1,950,000	1,432,000
Stockholders' equity:		
Common stock	1,740,000	1,650,000
Retained earnings	573,000	478,000
Total stockholders' equity	2,313,000	2,128,000
Total liabilities and stockholders' equity	$4,263,000	$3,560,000

The following additional information is available about the company's activities during this year:
a. The company declared and paid a cash dividend this year.
b. Bonds with a principal balance of $350,000 were repaid during this year.
c. Equipment was sold during this year for $70,000. The equipment had cost $130,000 and had $40,000 in accumulated depreciation on the date of sale.

d.   Long-term investments were sold during the year for $110,000. These investments had cost $50,000 when purchased several years ago.
e.   The subsidiaries did not repay any outstanding loans during the year.
f.   Lomax did not repurchase any of its own stock during the year.

The company reported net income this year as follows:

Sales		$2,000,000
Cost of goods sold		1,300,000
Gross margin		700,000
Selling and administrative expenses		490,000
Net operating income		210,000
Nonoperating items:		
Gain on sale of investments	$60,000	
Loss on sale of equipment	(20,000)	40,000
Income before taxes		250,000
Income taxes		80,000
Net income		$ 170,000

Required:
1.   Using the indirect method, prepare a statement of cash flows for this year.
2.   What problems relating to the company's activities are revealed by the statement of cash flows that you have prepared?

BUILDING YOUR SKILLS

COMMUNICATING IN PRACTICE [LO12–2, LO12–3,]
Use an online yellow pages directory to find a company in your area that has a website on which it has an annual report, including a statement of cash flows. Make an appointment with the controller or chief financial officer of the company. Before your meeting, find out as much as you can about the organization's operations from its website.

Required
After asking the following questions, write a brief memorandum to your instructor that summarizes the information obtained from the company's website and addresses what you found out during your interview.
1.   Does the company use the direct method or the indirect method to determine the net cash provided by operating activities when preparing its statement of cash flows? Why?
2.   How is the information reported on the statement of cash flows used for decision-making purposes?

APPENDIX 12A: THE DIRECT METHOD OF DETERMINING THE NET CASH PROVIDED BY OPERATING ACTIVITIES

LEARNING OBJECTIVE 12–4

Use the direct method to determine the net cash provided by operating activities.

To compute the net cash provided by operating activities under the direct method, we must reconstruct the income statement on a cash basis from top to bottom. Exhibit 12A–1 shows the adjustments that must be made to adjust sales, expenses, and so forth, to a cash basis. To illustrate, we have included in the exhibit the Apparel, Inc., data from the chapter.

Note that the net cash provided by operating activities of $259 million agrees with the amount computed in the chapter by the indirect method. The two amounts agree because the direct and indirect methods are just different roads to the same destination. The investing and financing activities sections of the statement will be exactly the same as shown for the indirect method in Exhibit 12–10. The only difference between the indirect and direct methods is in the operating activities section.

Similarities and Differences in the Handling of Data

Although we arrive at the same destination under either the direct or indirect method, not all data are handled the same way in the two adjustment processes. Stop for a moment, flip back to the bottom half of Exhibit 12–7 on page 570 and compare the adjustments described in that exhibit to the adjustments made for the direct method in Exhibit 12A–1. The adjustments for accounts that affect revenue (which includes only accounts receivable in our example) are handled the same way in the two methods. In either case, increases in the accounts are subtracted and decreases are added. However, the adjustments for accounts that affect expenses (which include all remaining accounts in Exhibit 12–7) are handled in opposite ways in the indirect and direct methods. This is because under the indirect method the adjustments are made to *net income,* whereas under the direct method the adjustments are made to the *expense accounts* themselves.

To illustrate this difference, note the handling of inventory and depreciation in the indirect and direct methods. Under the indirect method (Exhibit 12–7 on page 570), an increase in the Inventory account ($49) is *subtracted* from net income in computing the amount of net cash provided by operating activities. Under the direct method (Exhibit 12A–1), an increase in inventory is *added* to cost of goods sold. The reason for the difference can be explained as follows: An increase in inventory means that the period's inventory purchases exceeded the cost of goods sold included in the income statement. Therefore, to adjust net income to a cash basis, we must either subtract this increase from net income (indirect method) or we must add this increase to cost of goods sold (direct method). Either way, we will end up with the same figure for net cash provided by operating activities. Similarly,

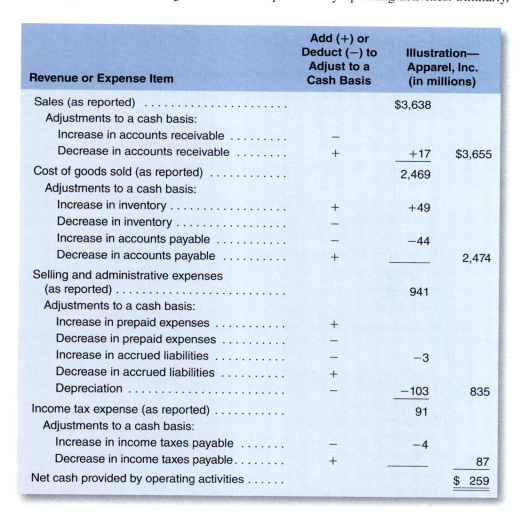

Revenue or Expense Item	Add (+) or Deduct (−) to Adjust to a Cash Basis	Illustration— Apparel, Inc. (in millions)	
Sales (as reported)		$3,638	
Adjustments to a cash basis:			
Increase in accounts receivable	−		
Decrease in accounts receivable	+	+17	$3,655
Cost of goods sold (as reported)		2,469	
Adjustments to a cash basis:			
Increase in inventory	+	+49	
Decrease in inventory	−		
Increase in accounts payable	−	−44	
Decrease in accounts payable	+		2,474
Selling and administrative expenses (as reported)		941	
Adjustments to a cash basis:			
Increase in prepaid expenses	+		
Decrease in prepaid expenses	−		
Increase in accrued liabilities	−	−3	
Decrease in accrued liabilities	+		
Depreciation	−	−103	835
Income tax expense (as reported)		91	
Adjustments to a cash basis:			
Increase in income taxes payable	−	−4	
Decrease in income taxes payable	+		87
Net cash provided by operating activities		$ 259	

EXHIBIT 12A–1
General Model: Direct Method of Determining the Net Cash Provided by Operating Activities

depreciation is added to net income under the indirect method to cancel out its effect (Exhibit 12–8), whereas it is subtracted from selling and administrative expenses under the direct method to cancel out its effect (Exhibit 12A–1). These differences in the handling of data are true for all other expense items in the two methods.

In the matter of gains and losses on sale of assets, no adjustments are needed under the direct method. These gains and losses are simply ignored because they are not part of sales, cost of goods sold, selling and administrative expenses, or income taxes. Observe that in Exhibit 12A–1, Apparel's $3 million gain on the sale of the store is not listed as an adjustment in the operating activities section.

Special Rules—Direct and Indirect Methods

As stated earlier, when the direct method is used, U.S. GAAP and IFRS require a reconciliation between net income and the net cash provided by operating activities, as determined by the indirect method. Thus, *when a company elects to use the direct method, it must also present the indirect method* in a separate schedule accompanying the statement of cash flows.

On the other hand, if a company elects to use the indirect method to compute the net cash provided by operating activities, then it must also provide a special breakdown of data. The company must provide a separate disclosure of the amount of interest and the amount of income taxes paid during the year. This separate disclosure is required so that users can take the data provided by the indirect method and make estimates of what the amounts for sales, income taxes, and so forth, would have been if the direct method had been used instead.

APPENDIX 12A: EXERCISES AND PROBLEMS

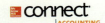

All applicable exercises and problems are available with McGraw-Hill's *Connect Accounting.*

EXERCISE 12A–1   Adjust Net Income to a Cash Basis [LO12–4]
Refer to the data for Pavolik Company in Exercise 12–4.

Required:
Use the direct method to convert the company's income statement to a cash basis.

EXERCISE 12A–2   Net Cash Provided by Operating Activities [LO12–4]
Wiley Company's income statement for Year 2 follows:

Sales	$150,000
Cost of goods sold	90,000
Gross margin	60,000
Selling and administrative expenses	40,000
Income before taxes	20,000
Income taxes	8,000
Net income	$ 12,000

The company's selling and administrative expense for Year 2 includes $7,500 of depreciation expense. Selected balance sheet accounts for Wiley at the end of Years 1 and 2 are as follows:

	Year 2	Year 1
Current Assets		
Accounts receivable	$40,000	$30,000
Inventory	$54,000	$45,000
Prepaid expenses	$8,000	$6,000
Current Liabilities		
Accounts payable	$35,000	$28,000
Accrued liabilities	$5,000	$8,000
Income taxes payable	$2,000	$2,500

Required:
1. Using the direct method, convert the company's income statement to a cash basis.
2. Assume that during Year 2 Wiley had a $9,000 gain on sale of investments and a $3,000 loss on the sale of equipment. Explain how these two transactions would affect your computations in (1) above.

EXERCISE 12A–3 Net Cash Provided by Operating Activities [LO12–4]
Refer to the data for Carmono Company in Exercise 12–6.

Required:
Using the direct method, convert the company's income statement to a cash basis.

EXERCISE 12A–4 Net Cash Provided by Operating Activities [LO12–4]
Refer to the data for Hanna Company in Exercise 12–2. The company's income statement for the year appears below:

Sales	$350,000
Cost of goods sold	140,000
Gross margin	210,000
Selling and administrative expenses	160,000
Income before taxes	50,000
Income taxes	15,000
Net income	$ 35,000

Required:
Using the direct method (and the data from Exercise 12–2), convert the company's income statement to a cash basis.

PROBLEM 12A–5A Prepare and Interpret a Statement of Cash Flows [LO12–1, LO12–4]
Refer to the financial statements for Rusco Company in Problem 12–13. Because the Cash account decreased so dramatically during 2015, the company's executive committee is anxious to see how the income statement would appear on a cash basis.

Required:
1. Using the direct method, adjust the company's income statement for 2015 to a cash basis.
2. Using the data from (1) above, and other data from the problem as needed, prepare a statement of cash flows for 2015.
3. Briefly explain the major reasons for the sharp decline in cash during the year.

PROBLEM 12A–6A Prepare a Statement of Cash Flows [LO12–1, LO12–4]
Refer to the financial statement data for Weaver Company in Problem 12–7.

Required:
1. Using the direct method, adjust the company's income statement for 2015 to a cash basis.
2. Using the information obtained in (1) above, along with an analysis of the remaining balance sheet accounts, prepare a statement of cash flows for 2015.

PROBLEM 12A–7A Prepare and Interpret a Statement of Cash Flows [LO12–1, LO12–4]
Refer to the financial statement data for Joyner Company in Problem 12–10. Sam Conway, president of the company, considers $15,000 to be the minimum cash balance for operating purposes. As can be seen from the balance sheet data, only $4,000 in cash was available at the end of the current year. The sharp decline is puzzling to Mr. Conway, particularly because sales and profits are at a record high.

Required:
1. Using the direct method, adjust the company's income statement to a cash basis for Year 2.
2. Using the data from (1) above and other data from the problem as needed, prepare a statement of cash flows for Year 2.
3. Explain why cash declined so sharply during the year.

A LOOK BACK

In Chapter 12 we showed how to construct the statement of cash flows and discussed how to interpret it.

A LOOK AT THIS CHAPTER

In Chapter 13 we focus on how managers analyze financial statements to better understand the financial health of their companies. We discuss the use of trend data, comparisons with other organizations, and financial ratios.

13 Financial Statement Analysis

CHAPTER OUTLINE

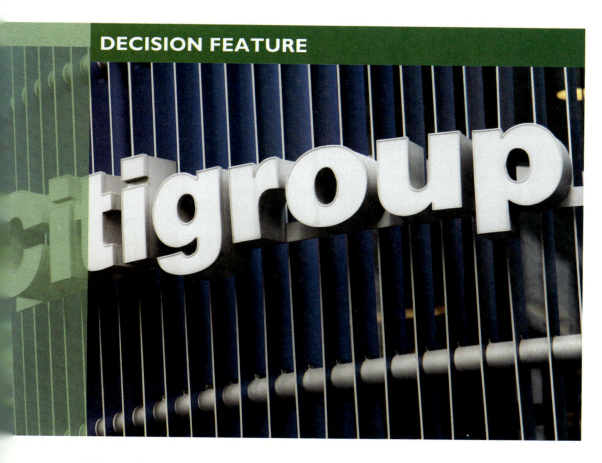

LEARNING OBJECTIVES

After studying Chapter 13, you should be able to:

LO13–1 Prepare and interpret financial statements in comparative and common-size form.

LO13–2 Compute and interpret financial ratios that managers use to assess liquidity.

LO13–3 Compute and interpret financial ratios that managers use for asset management purposes.

LO13–4 Compute and interpret financial ratios that managers use for debt management purposes.

LO13–5 Compute and interpret financial ratios that managers use to assess profitability.

LO13–6 Compute and interpret financial ratios that managers use to assess market performance.

Keeping an Eye on Dividends

When the economy sours, investors look closely at a company's ability to pay dividends. In 2008, 36 of the Standard & Poor's 500 companies suspended $33.3 billion of dividend payments. Citigroup sliced its dividend 41%, Washington Mutual (now part of **JPMorgan Chase**) reduced its quarterly dividend per share from 15 cents to a penny, and **CIT Group** slashed its dividend by 60%. Some companies increase their market appeal during difficult economic times by remaining committed to generous dividend payments. For example, in 2008 Adrian Darley, of **Ignis Asset Management**, recommended investing in **Vivendi, France Telecom**, and **Deutsche Telekom** because these companies committed to making scheduled dividend payments that ranged from 4.9% to 7.2% of their respective stock prices.

Sources: Andrea Tryphonides, "Dividends Replace P/Es as Stock Guides," *The Wall Street Journal*, November 24, 2008, p. C2; Tom Lauricella, "Keeping the Cash: Slowdown Triggers Stingy Dividends," *The Wall Street Journal*, April 21, 2008, p. C1; and Annelena Lobb, "Investors Lick Wounds from Dividend Cuts," *The Wall Street Journal*, November 7, 2008, p. C1.

Stockholders, creditors, and managers are examples of stakeholders that use *financial statement analysis* to evaluate a company's financial health and future prospects. Stockholders and creditors analyze a company's financial statements to estimate its potential for earnings growth, stock price appreciation, making dividend payments, and paying principal and interest on loans. Managers use financial statement analysis for two reasons. First, it enables them to better understand how their company's financial results will be interpreted by stockholders and creditors for the purposes of making investing and lending decisions. Second, financial statement analysis provides managers with valuable feedback regarding their company's performance. For example, managers may study trends in their company's financial statements to assess whether performance has been improving or declining. Or, they may use financial statement analysis to benchmark their company's performance against world-class competitors.

In this chapter, we'll explain how managers prepare financial statements in comparative and common-size form and how they use financial ratios to assess their company's liquidity, asset management, debt management, profitability, and market performance.

LIMITATIONS OF FINANCIAL STATEMENT ANALYSIS

This section discusses two limitations of financial statement analysis that managers should always keep in mind—comparing financial data across companies and looking beyond ratios when formulating conclusions.

Comparing Financial Data across Companies

Comparisons of one company with another can provide valuable clues about the financial health of an organization. Unfortunately, differences in accounting methods between companies sometimes make it difficult to compare their financial data. For example, if one company values its inventories by the LIFO method and another company by the average cost method, then direct comparisons of their financial data such as inventory valuations and cost of goods sold may be misleading. Sometimes enough data are presented in footnotes to the financial statements to restate data to a comparable basis. Otherwise, managers should keep in mind any lack of comparability. Even with this limitation in mind, comparing key ratios with other companies and with industry averages often helps managers identify opportunities for improvement.

Looking beyond Ratios

Ratios should not be viewed as an end, but rather as a *starting point*. They raise many questions and point to opportunities for further analysis, but they rarely answer any questions by themselves. In addition to financial ratios, managers should consider various internal factors, such as employee learning and growth, business process performance, and customer satisfaction as well as external factors like industry trends, technological changes, changes in consumer tastes, and changes in broad economic indicators.

STATEMENTS IN COMPARATIVE AND COMMON-SIZE FORM

LEARNING OBJECTIVE 13–1

Prepare and interpret financial statements in comparative and common-size form.

An item on a balance sheet or income statement has little meaning by itself. Suppose a company's sales for a year were $250 million. In isolation, that is not particularly useful information. How does that stack up against last year's sales? How do the sales relate to the cost of goods sold? In making these kinds of comparisons, three analytical techniques are widely used:

1. Dollar and percentage changes on statements (*horizontal analysis*).
2. Common-size statements (*vertical analysis*).
3. Ratios.

The first and second techniques are discussed in this section; the third technique is discussed in the remainder of the chapter. Throughout the chapter, we will illustrate these analytical techniques using the financial statements of Brickey Electronics, a producer of specialized electronic components.

Dollar and Percentage Changes on Statements

Horizontal analysis (also known as **trend analysis**) involves analyzing financial data over time, such as computing year-to-year dollar and percentage changes within a set of financial statements. Exhibits 13–1 and 13–2 show Brickey Electronics' financial

EXHIBIT 13–1

Brickey Electronics Comparative Balance Sheet (dollars in thousands)	This Year	Last Year	Increase (Decrease)	
			Amount	Percent
Assets				
Current assets:				
Cash..........................	$ 1,200	$ 2,350	$(1,150)	(48.9)%*
Accounts receivable, net	6,000	4,000	2,000	50.0%
Inventory......................	8,000	10,000	(2,000)	(20.0)%
Prepaid expenses................	300	120	180	150.0%
Total current assets	15,500	16,470	(970)	(5.9)%
Property and equipment:				
Land..........................	4,000	4,000	0	0.0%
Buildings and equipment, net	12,000	8,500	3,500	41.2%
Total property and equipment	16,000	12,500	3,500	28.0%
Total assets	$31,500	$28,970	$ 2,530	8.7%
Liabilities and Stockholders' Equity				
Current liabilities:				
Accounts payable	$ 5,800	$ 4,000	$ 1,800	45.0%
Accrued payables	900	400	500	125.0%
Notes payable, short term	300	600	(300)	(50.0)%
Total current liabilities	7,000	5,000	2,000	40.0%
Long-term liabilities:				
Bonds payable, 8%..............	7,500	8,000	(500)	(6.3)%
Total liabilities...................	14,500	13,000	1,500	11.5%
Stockholders' equity:				
Common stock, $12 par..........	6,000	6,000	0	0.0%
Additional paid-in capital	3,000	3,000	0	0.0%
Total paid-in capital	9,000	9,000	0	0.0%
Retained earnings	8,000	6,970	1,030	14.8%
Total stockholders' equity	17,000	15,970	1,030	6.4%
Total liabilities and stockholders' equity..............	$31,500	$28,970	$ 2,530	8.7%

*The changes between this year and last year are expressed as a percentage of the dollar amount for last year. For example, Cash decreased by $1,150 between this year and last year. This decrease expressed in percentage form is computed as follows: $1,150 ÷ $2,350 = 48.9%. Other percentage figures in this exhibit and Exhibit 13–2 are computed in the same way.

EXHIBIT 13–2

					Increase (Decrease)	
Brickey Electronics **Comparative Income Statement and Reconciliation of Retained Earnings** **(dollars in thousands)**						
			This Year	**Last Year**	**Amount**	**Percent**
Sales			$52,000	$48,000	$4,000	8.3%
Cost of goods sold			36,000	31,500	4,500	14.3%
Gross margin			16,000	16,500	(500)	(3.0)%
Selling and administrative expenses:						
Selling expenses			7,000	6,500	500	7.7%
Administrative expenses			5,860	6,100	(240)	(3.9)%
Total selling and administrative expenses			12,860	12,600	260	2.1%
Net operating income			3,140	3,900	(760)	(19.5)%
Interest expense			640	700	(60)	(8.6)%
Net income before taxes			2,500	3,200	(700)	(21.9)%
Income taxes (30%)			750	960	(210)	(21.9)%
Net income			1,750	2,240	$ (490)	(21.9)%
Dividends to common stockholders, $1.44 per share			720	720		
Net income added to retained earnings			1,030	1,520		
Beginning retained earnings			6,970	5,450		
Ending retained earnings			$ 8,000	$ 6,970		

statements in this *comparative form*. The dollar changes highlight the changes that are the most important economically; the percentage changes highlight the changes that are the most unusual.

Horizontal analysis can be even more useful when data from a number of years are used to compute *trend percentages*. To compute **trend percentages,** a base year is selected and the data for all years are stated as a percentage of that base year. To illustrate, consider the sales and net income of **McDonald's Corporation**, the world's largest food service retailer, with more than 31,000 restaurants worldwide:

	2002	2003	2004	2005	2006	2007	2008	2009	2010	2011
Sales (millions)	$14,527	$16,154	$17,889	$19,117	$20,895	$22,787	$23,522	$22,745	$24,075	$27,006
Net income (millions)	$893	$1,471	$2,279	$2,602	$3,544	$2,395	$4,313	$4,551	$4,946	$5,503

By simply looking at these data, you can see that sales increased every year except 2009 and net income increased every year except 2007. However, recasting these data into trend percentages aids interpretation:

	2002	2003	2004	2005	2006	2007	2008	2009	2010	2011
Sales.	100%	111%	123%	132%	144%	157%	162%	157%	166%	186%
Net income	100%	165%	255%	291%	397%	268%	483%	510%	554%	616%

In the above table, both sales and net income have been restated as a percentage of the 2002 sales and net income. For example, the 2008 sales of $23,522 are 162% of the 2002 sales of $14,527. This trend analysis is particularly striking when the data are plotted as in Exhibit 13–3. McDonald's sales growth was impressive throughout the 10-year period, but net income was far more erratic. Notice that net income plummeted in 2007 and then fully recovered by 2008. In 2011, McDonald's earned record sales and profits.

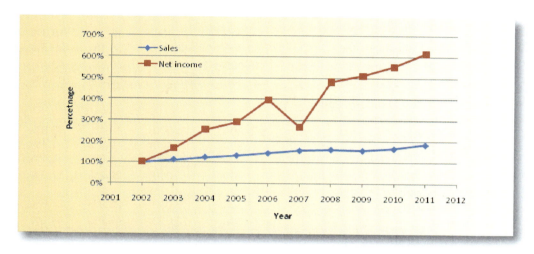

EXHIBIT 13–3
McDonald's Corporation: Trend Analysis of Sales and Net Income

Common-Size Statements

Horizontal analysis, which was discussed in the previous section, examines changes in financial statement accounts over time. **Vertical analysis** focuses on the relations among financial statement accounts at a given point in time. A **common-size financial statement** is a vertical analysis in which each financial statement account is expressed as a percentage. In income statements, all items are usually expressed as a percentage of sales. In balance sheets, all items are usually expressed as a percentage of total assets. Exhibit 13–4 contains Brickey Electronics' common-size balance sheet and Exhibit 13–5 contains its common-size income statement.

Notice from Exhibit 13–4 that placing all assets in common-size form clearly shows the relative importance of the current assets as compared to the noncurrent assets. It also shows that significant changes have taken place in the composition of the current assets over the last year. For example, accounts receivable have increased in relative importance and both cash and inventory have declined in relative importance. Judging from the sharp increase in accounts receivable, the deterioration in the cash balance may be a result of an inability to collect from customers.

The common-size income statement in Exhibit 13–5 states each line item as a percentage of sales. For example, the administrative expenses were 12.7% of sales last year and 11.3% of sales this year. If the quality and efficiency of Brickey's administrative services is holding constant or improving over time, then these two percentages suggest that this year Brickey managed its administrative resources more cost-effectively than last year. Beyond

EXHIBIT 13–4

Brickey Electronics
Common-Size Comparative Balance Sheet
(dollars in thousands)

	This Year	Last Year	Common-Size Percentages This Year	Common-Size Percentages Last Year
Assets				
Current assets:				
Cash.	$ 1,200	$ 2,350	3.8%*	8.1%
Accounts receivable, net.	6,000	4,000	19.0%	13.8%
Inventory.	8,000	10,000	25.4%	34.5%
Prepaid expenses.	300	120	1.0%	0.4%
Total current assets	15,500	16,470	49.2%	56.9%
Property and equipment:				
Land	4,000	4,000	12.7%	13.8%
Buildings and equipment, net	12,000	8,500	38.1%	29.3%
Total property and equipment	16,000	12,500	50.8%	43.1%
Total assets	$31,500	$28,970	100.0%	100.0%
Liabilities and Stockholders' Equity				
Current liabilities:				
Accounts payable	$ 5,800	$ 4,000	18.4%	13.8%
Accrued payables	900	400	2.9%	1.4%
Notes payable, short term	300	600	1.0%	2.1%
Total current liabilities	7,000	5,000	22.2%	17.3%
Long-term liabilities:				
Bonds payable, 8%	7,500	8,000	23.8%	27.6%
Total liabilities	14,500	13,000	46.0%	44.9%
Stockholders' equity:				
Common stock, $12 par	6,000	6,000	19.0%	20.7%
Additional paid-in capital	3,000	3,000	9.5%	10.4%
Total paid-in capital.	9,000	9,000	28.6%	31.1%
Retained earnings.	8,000	6,970	25.4%	24.0%
Total stockholders' equity	17,000	15,970	54.0%	55.1%
Total liabilities and stockholders' equity	$31,500	$28,970	100.0%	100.0%

*Each asset account on a common-size statement is expressed as a percentage of total assets, and each liability and equity account is expressed as a percentage of total liabilities and stockholders' equity. For example, the percentage figure above for this year's Cash balance is computed as follows: $1,200 ÷ $31,500 = 3.8%. All common-size percentages have been rounded to one decimal place.

administrative expenses, managers also have a keen interest in other percentages disclosed in a common-size income statement and those will be discussed in a later section related to profitability ratios.

HELPFUL HINT

Common-size balance sheets express each balance sheet account as a percentage of total assets. Common-size income statements express each income statement account as a percentage of sales.

EXHIBIT 13–5

Brickey Electronics
Common-Size Comparative Income Statement
(dollars in thousands)

	This Year	Last Year	Common-Size Percentages* This Year	Common-Size Percentages* Last Year
Sales	$52,000	$48,000	100.0%	100.0%
Cost of goods sold	36,000	31,500	69.2%	65.6%
Gross margin	16,000	16,500	30.8%	34.4%
Selling and administrative expenses:				
Selling expenses	7,000	6,500	13.5%	13.5%
Administrative expenses	5,860	6,100	11.3%	12.7%
Total selling and administrative expenses	12,860	12,600	24.7%	26.3%
Net operating income	3,140	3,900	6.0%	8.1%
Interest expense	640	700	1.2%	1.5%
Net income before taxes	2,500	3,200	4.8%	6.7%
Income taxes (30%)	750	960	1.4%	2.0%
Net income	$ 1,750	$ 2,240	3.4%	4.7%

*Note that the percentage figures for each year are expressed as a percentage of total sales for the year. For example, the percentage figure for this year's cost of goods sold is computed as follows: $36,000 ÷ $52,000 = 69.2%. All common-size percentages have been rounded to one decimal place.

RATIO ANALYSIS—LIQUIDITY

Liquidity refers to how quickly an asset can be converted to cash. Liquid assets can be converted to cash quickly, whereas ill-liquid assets cannot. Companies need to continuously monitor the amount of their liquid assets relative to the amount that they owe short-term creditors, such as suppliers. If a company's liquid assets are not enough to support timely payments to short-term creditors, this presents an important management problem that, if not remedied, can lead to bankruptcy.

    This section uses Brickey Electronics' financial statements to explain one measure and two ratios that managers use to analyze their company's liquidity and its ability to pay short-term creditors. *As you proceed through this section, keep in mind that all calculations are performed for this year rather than last year.*

Working Capital

The excess of current assets over current liabilities is known as **working capital.**

Working capital = Current assets − Current liabilities

The working capital for Brickey Electronics is computed as follows:

Working capital = $15,500,000 − $7,000,000 = $8,500,000

    Managers need to interpret working capital from two perspectives. On one hand, if a company has ample working capital, it provides some assurance that the company can pay its creditors in full and on time. On the other hand, maintaining large amounts of working capital isn't free. Working capital must be financed with long-term debt and equity—both of which are expensive. Furthermore, a large and growing working capital balance may indicate troubles, such as excessive growth in inventories. Therefore, managers often want to minimize working capital while retaining the ability to pay short-term creditors.

Current Ratio

A company's working capital is frequently expressed in ratio form. A company's current assets divided by its current liabilities is known as the **current ratio:**

$$\text{Current ratio} = \frac{\text{Current assets}}{\text{Current liabilities}}$$

For Brickey Electronics, the current ratio is computed as follows:

$$\text{Current ratio} = \frac{\$15{,}500{,}000}{\$7{,}000{,}000} = 2.21$$

Although widely regarded as a measure of short-term debt-paying ability, the current ratio must be interpreted with great care. A *declining* ratio might be a sign of a deteriorating financial condition, or it might be the result of eliminating obsolete inventories or other stagnant current assets. An *improving* ratio might be the result of stockpiling inventory, or it might indicate an improving financial situation. In short, the current ratio is useful, but tricky to interpret.

The general rule of thumb calls for a current ratio of at least 2. However, many companies successfully operate with a current ratio below 2. The adequacy of a current ratio depends heavily on the *composition* of the assets. For example, as we see in the table below, both Worthington Corporation and Greystone, Inc., have current ratios of 2. However, they are not in comparable financial condition. Greystone is more likely to have difficulty meeting its current financial obligations because almost all of its current assets consist of inventory rather than more liquid assets such as cash and accounts receivable.

	Worthington Corporation	Greystone, Inc.
Current assets:		
Cash	$ 25,000	$ 2,000
Accounts receivable, net	60,000	8,000
Inventory	85,000	160,000
Prepaid expenses	5,000	5,000
Total current assets (a)	$175,000	$175,000
Current liabilities (b)	$ 87,500	$ 87,500
Current ratio, (a) ÷ (b)	2	2

Acid-Test (Quick) Ratio

The **acid-test (quick) ratio** is a more rigorous test of a company's ability to meet its short-term debts than the current ratio. Inventories and prepaid expenses are excluded from total current assets, leaving only the more liquid (or "quick") assets to be divided by current liabilities.

$$\text{Acid-test ratio} = \frac{\text{Cash} + \text{Marketable securities} + \text{Accounts receivable} + \text{Short-term notes receivable}}{\text{Current liabilities}}$$

The acid-test ratio measures how well a company can meet its obligations without having to liquidate or depend too heavily on its inventory. Ideally, each dollar of liabilities should be backed by at least $1 of quick assets. However, acid-test ratios as low as 0.3 are common.

The acid-test ratio for Brickey Electronics is computed below:

$$\text{Acid-test ratio} = \frac{\$1,200,000 + \$0 + \$6,000,000 + \$0}{\$7,000,000} = 1.03$$

Although Brickey Electronics' acid-test ratio is within the acceptable range, a manager might be concerned about several trends revealed in the company's balance sheet. Notice in Exhibit 13–1 that short-term debts are rising, while the cash balance is declining. Perhaps the lower cash balance is a result of the substantial increase in accounts receivable. In short, as with the current ratio, the acid-test ratio should be interpreted with one eye on its basic components.

RATIO ANALYSIS—ASSET MANAGEMENT

A company's assets are funded by lenders and stockholders, both of whom expect those assets to be deployed efficiently and effectively. In this section, we'll describe various measures and ratios that managers use to assess their company's asset management performance. *All forthcoming calculations will be performed for this year.*

> **LEARNING OBJECTIVE 13–3**
>
> Compute and interpret financial ratios that managers use for asset management purposes.

Accounts Receivable Turnover

The *accounts receivable turnover* and *average collection period* ratios measure how quickly credit sales are converted into cash. The **accounts receivable turnover** is computed by dividing sales on account (i.e., credit sales) by the average accounts receivable balance for the year:

$$\text{Accounts receivable turnover} = \frac{\text{Sales on account}}{\text{Average accounts receivable balance}}$$

Assuming that all of Brickey Electronics' sales were on account, its accounts receivable turnover is computed as follows:

$$\text{Accounts receivable turnover} = \frac{\$52,000,000}{(\$6,000,000 + \$4,000,000)/2} = 10.4$$

The accounts receivable turnover can then be divided into 365 days to determine the average number of days required to collect an account (known as the **average collection period**).

$$\text{Average collection period} = \frac{365 \text{ days}}{\text{Accounts receivable turnover}}$$

The average collection period for Brickey Electronics is computed as follows:

$$\text{Average collection period} = \frac{365 \text{ days}}{10.4} = 35 \text{ days}$$

This means that on average it takes 35 days to collect a credit sale. Whether this is good or bad depends on the credit terms Brickey Electronics is offering its customers. Many customers will tend to withhold payment for as long as the credit terms allow. If the credit terms are 30 days, then a 35-day average collection period would usually be viewed as very good. On the other hand, if the company's credit terms are 10 days, then a 35-day average collection period is worrisome. A long collection period may result from having too many old uncollectible accounts, failing to bill promptly or follow up on late accounts, lax credit checks, and so on. In practice, average collection periods ranging all the way from 10 days to 180 days are common, depending on the industry.

IN BUSINESS

The Challenge of Collecting Cash from Customers

When the economy soured **Caroline's Desserts** saw the percentage of its customers who make late payments jump from 2% to 18%. These late payments decreased the company's accounts receivable turnover, which in turn forced the company's owner to delay hiring more employees, to delay new equipment purchases, and to pay bills using personal funds. Similarly, the weak economy caused a large portion of **Quality Service Associates Inc.**'s customers to begin paying for their purchases in 45–60 days instead of the normal 30–45 days. The company's president said the "extra 15 to 20 days that people are not paying has had a pretty significant impact on my ability to keep up with my vendors."

Source: Simona Covel and Kelly K. Spors, "To Help Collect the Bills , Firms Try the Soft Touch," *The Wall Street Journal,* January 22, 2009, pp. B1 and B6.

Inventory Turnover

The **inventory turnover ratio** measures how many times a company's inventory has been sold and replaced during the year. It is computed by dividing the cost of goods sold by the average level of inventory [(Beginning inventory balance + Ending inventory balance) ÷ 2]:

$$\text{Inventory turnover} = \frac{\text{Cost of goods sold}}{\text{Average inventory balance}}$$

Brickey's inventory turnover is computed as follows:

$$\text{Inventory turnover} = \frac{\$36,000,000}{(\$8,000,000 + \$10,000,000)/2} = 4.0$$

The number of days needed on average to sell the entire inventory (called the **average sale period**) can be computed by dividing 365 by the inventory turnover:

$$\text{Average sale period} = \frac{365 \text{ days}}{\text{Inventory turnover}}$$

$$= \frac{365 \text{ days}}{4 \text{ times}} = 91\tfrac{1}{4} \text{ days}$$

The average sale period varies from industry to industry. Grocery stores, with significant perishable stocks, tend to turn over their inventory quickly. On the other hand, jewelry stores tend to turn over their inventory slowly. In practice, average sale periods of 10 days to 90 days are common, depending on the industry.

A company whose inventory turnover ratio is much slower than the average for its industry may have too much inventory or the wrong sorts of inventory. Some managers argue that they must buy in large quantities to take advantage of quantity discounts. But these discounts must be compared to the added costs of insurance, taxes, financing, and risks of obsolescence and deterioration that result from carrying added inventories.

Operating Cycle

The **operating cycle** measures the elapsed time from when inventory is received from suppliers to when cash is received from customers. It is computed as follows:

$$\text{Operating cycle} = \text{Average sale period} + \text{Average collection period}$$

Brickey Electronics' operating cycle is computed as follows:

$$\text{Operating cycle} = 91\tfrac{1}{4} \text{ days} + 35 \text{ days} = 126\tfrac{1}{4} \text{ days}$$

A manager's goal is to reduce the operating cycle because it puts cash receipts in the company's possession sooner. In fact, if a company can shrink its operating cycle to fewer days than its average payment period for suppliers, it means the company is receiving cash from customers before it has to pay suppliers for inventory purchases. For example, if a company's operating cycle is 10 days and its average payment period to suppliers is 30 days, the company is receiving cash from customers 20 days before it pays its suppliers. In this example, the company could earn interest income on cash collections for 20 days before paying a portion of those receipts to suppliers. Conversely, if a company's operating cycle is much longer than its average payment period for suppliers, it creates the need to borrow money to fund its inventories and accounts receivable. In the case of Brickey Electronics, its operating cycle is very high, thereby suggesting that it needs to borrow money to fund its working capital.

Inventory Management in the Apparel Industry

IN BUSINESS

Many apparel retailers such as **Aéropostale** are practicing a three-step inventory management tactic known as chasing. First, the retailer orders very small quantities of its new clothing styles from its suppliers. Second, the retailer determines which of its new clothing styles are popular with customers. Third, the retailer chases consumer demand by asking suppliers to very quickly ramp-up production of its most popular clothing styles. This tactic, if properly executed, enables retailers to not only reduce their average sale period and operating cycle, but it also helps them minimize price markdowns related to excess inventories and forgone sales related to out-of-stock items. Of course, tension inevitably arises with suppliers who greatly prefer large order quantities and 6–9 month lead times.

Source: Elizabeth Holmes, "Tug-of-War in Apparel World," *The Wall Street Journal*, July 16, 2010, pp. B1–B2.

1. Jones Company's sales are $1,000,000 and 80% of those sales are on credit. The beginning and ending accounts receivable balances are $100,000 and $140,000, respectively. What is the company's accounts receivable turnover?
    a. 3.33
    b. 6.67
    c. 8.33
    d. 10.67

2. Jones Company's sales are $1,000,000 and the gross margin percentage is 60%. The beginning and ending inventory balances are $240,000 and $260,000, respectively. What is the inventory turnover?
    a. 1.60
    b. 2.40
    c. 3.40
    d. 3.60

3. Based on the information in question 2, what is Jones Company's average sale period?
    a. 152 days
    b. 140 days
    c. 228 days
    d. 175 days

4. Based on the information in questions 1–3, what is Jones Company's operating cycle?
    a. 295 days
    b. 283 days
    c. 243 days
    d. 307 days

Total Asset Turnover

The **total asset turnover** is a ratio that compares total sales to average total assets. It measures how efficiently a company's assets are being used to generate sales. This ratio expands beyond current assets to include noncurrent assets, such as property, plant, and equipment. It is computed as follows:

$$\text{Total asset turnover} = \frac{\text{Sales}}{\text{Average total assets}}$$

Brickey Electronics' total asset turnover is computed as follows:

$$\text{Total asset turnover} = \frac{\$52,000,000}{(\$31,500,000 + \$28,970,000)/2} = 1.72$$

A company's goal is to increase its total asset turnover. To do so, it must either increase sales or reduce its investment in assets. If a company's accounts receivable turnover and inventory turnover are increasing, but its total asset turnover is decreasing, it suggests the problem may relate to noncurrent asset utilization and efficiency. It also bears emphasizing that if all else holds constant, a company's total asset turnover will increase over time simply because the accumulated depreciation on plant and equipment grows over time.

RATIO ANALYSIS—DEBT MANAGEMENT

Managers need to evaluate their company's debt management choices from the vantage point of two stakeholders—long-term creditors and common stockholders. Long-term creditors are concerned with a company's ability to repay its loans over the long-run. For example, if a company paid out all of its available cash in the form of dividends, then nothing would be left to pay back creditors. Consequently, creditors often seek protection by requiring that borrowers agree to various restrictive covenants, or rules. These restrictive covenants typically include restrictions on dividend payments as well as rules stating that the company must maintain certain financial ratios at specified levels. Although restrictive covenants are widely used, they do not ensure that creditors will be paid when loans come due. The company still must generate sufficient earnings to cover payments.

> **LEARNING OBJECTIVE 13–4**
>
> Compute and interpret financial ratios that managers use for debt management purposes.

Stockholders look at debt from a *financial leverage* perspective. **Financial leverage** refers to borrowing money to acquire assets in an effort to increase sales and profits. A company can have either positive or negative financial leverage depending on the difference between its rate of return on total assets and the rate of return that it must pay its creditors. If the company's rate of return on total assets exceeds the rate of return the company pays its creditors, *financial leverage is positive*. If the rate of return on total assets is less than the rate of return the company pays its creditors, *financial leverage is negative*. We will explore whether Brickey Electronics has positive or negative financial leverage later in the chapter. For now, you need to understand that if a company has positive financial leverage, having debt can substantially benefit common stockholders. Conversely, if a company has negative financial leverage, common stockholders suffer. Given the potential benefits of maintaining positive financial leverage, managers do not try to avoid debt, rather they often seek to maintain a level of debt that is considered to be normal within their industry.

In this section, we explain three ratios that managers use for debt management purposes, times interest earned ratio, debt-to-equity ratio, and the equity multiplier. *All calculations are performed for this year.*

Times Interest Earned Ratio

The most common measure of a company's ability to provide protection to its long-term creditors is the **times interest earned ratio.** It is computed by dividing earnings before interest expense and income taxes (i.e., net operating income) by interest expense:

$$\text{Times interest earned} = \frac{\text{Earnings before interest expense and income taxes}}{\text{Interest expense}}$$

For Brickey Electronics, the times interest earned ratio for this year is computed as follows:

$$\text{Times interest earned} = \frac{\$3,140,000}{\$640,000} = 4.9$$

The times interest earned ratio is based on earnings before interest expense and income taxes because that is the amount of earnings that is available for making interest payments. Interest expenses are deducted *before* income taxes are determined; creditors have first claim on the earnings before taxes are paid.

A times interest earned ratio of less than 1 is inadequate because interest expense exceeds the earnings that are available for paying that interest. In contrast, a times interest earned ratio of 2 or more may be considered sufficient to protect long-term creditors.

Debt-to-Equity Ratio

The **debt-to-equity ratio** is one type of leverage ratio that indicates the relative proportions of debt and equity at one point in time on a company's balance sheet. As the debt-to-equity ratio increases, it indicates that a company is increasing its financial leverage. In other words, it is relying on a greater proportion of debt rather than equity to fund its assets. The debt-to-equity ratio is measured as follows:

$$\text{Debt-to-equity ratio} = \frac{\text{Total liabilities}}{\text{Stockholders' equity}}$$

Brickey's debt-to-equity ratio for this year is computed as follows:

$$\text{Debt-to-equity ratio} = \frac{\$14,500,000}{\$17,000,000} = 0.85$$

At the end of this year, Brickey Electronics' creditors were providing 85 cents for each $1 being provided by stockholders.

Creditors and stockholders have different views about the optimal debt-to-equity ratio. Ordinarily, stockholders would like a lot of debt to take advantage of positive financial leverage. On the other hand, because equity represents the excess of total assets over total liabilities, and hence a buffer of protection for creditors, creditors would like to see less debt and more equity. In practice, debt-to-equity ratios from 0.0 (no debt) to 3.0 are common. Generally speaking, in industries with little financial risk, managers maintain high debt-to-equity ratios. In industries with more financial risk, managers maintain lower debt-to-equity ratios.

Equity Multiplier

The **equity multiplier** is another type of leverage ratio that indicates the portion of a company's assets funded by equity. Similar to the debt-to-equity ratio, as the equity multiplier increases, it indicates that a company is increasing its financial leverage. In other words, it is relying on a greater proportion of debt rather than equity to fund its assets. Instead of measuring amounts in the numerator and denominator at one point in time (as is done with the debt-to-equity ratio), the equity multiplier focuses on average amounts maintained throughout the year and it is measured as follows:

$$\text{Equity multiplier} = \frac{\text{Average total assets}}{\text{Average stockholders' equity}}$$

Brickey's equity multiplier for this year is computed as follows:

$$\text{Equity multiplier} = \frac{(\$31,500,000 + \$28,970,000)/2}{(\$17,000,000 + \$15,970,000)/2} = 1.83$$

The debt-to-equity ratio and the equity multiplier provide signals about how a company is managing its mix of debt and equity. We have introduced the equity multiplier because it will be used in the next section of the chapter to provide further insight into how companies measure and interpret what will be defined as return on equity (ROE).

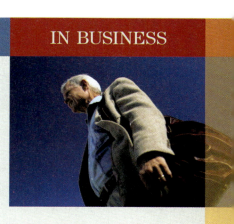

Chuck Bidwell and Jennifer Guarino bought **J.W. Hulme Company** to expand the business into luxury briefcases, backpacks, and handbags. The co-owners planned to grow the company's catalog mailing list tenfold to 10,000 households while doubling its product assortment to 250 items. To finance this growth strategy, the company borrowed more than $2 million, causing its debt-to-equity ratio to jump from 2.94 to 5.53. When the company subsequently sought $250,000 in additional loans to finance its next round of catalogs, lenders were apprehensive. The company's most recent annual sales of $1.5 million fell $500,000 short of the owners' projections. Furthermore, inventory levels had ballooned to $1 million signaling declining demand for the company's products.

Source: Julie Jargon, "On Front Lines of Debt Crisis, Luggage Maker Fights for Life," *The Wall Street Journal,* January 9, 2009, pp. A1 and A8.

5. Total assets are $1,500,000 and stockholders' equity is $900,000. What is the debt-to-equity ratio?
   a. 0.33
   b. 0.50
   c. 0.60
   d. 0.67

CONCEPT CHECK

RATIO ANALYSIS—PROFITABILITY

Managers pay close attention to the amount of profits that their companies earn. However, when analyzing ratios, they tend to focus on the amount of profit earned relative to some other amount such as sales, total assets, or total stockholder's equity. When profits are stated as a percentage of another number, such as sales, it helps managers draw informed conclusions about how the organization is performing over time. For example, if a company had profits in Years 1 and 2 of $10 and $20, respectively, it would be naïve to immediately assume that the company's performance has improved. In other words, if we further assume that sales in Year 1 are $100 and sales in Year 2 are $1,000, it would be troubling to see that the company converted $900 of additional sales into only $10 dollars of additional profit. In this section, we develop this idea further by discussing four profitability ratios commonly used by managers—gross margin percentage, net profit margin percentage, return on total assets, and return on equity. *All forthcoming calculations are performed for this year.*

> **LEARNING OBJECTIVE 13–5**
>
> Compute and interpret financial ratios that managers use to assess profitability.

Gross Margin Percentage

Exhibit 13–5 shows that Brickey's cost of goods sold as a percentage of sales increased from 65.6% last year to 69.2% this year. Or looking at this from a different viewpoint, the *gross margin percentage* declined from 34.4% last year to 30.8% this year. Managers and investors pay close attention to this measure of profitability. The **gross margin percentage** is computed as follows:

$$\text{Gross margin percentage} = \frac{\text{Gross margin}}{\text{Sales}}$$

The gross margin percentage should be more stable for retailing companies than for other companies because the cost of goods sold in retailing excludes fixed costs. When fixed costs are included in the cost of goods sold, the gross margin percentage should increase and decrease with sales volume. With increases in sales volume, fixed costs are spread across more units and the gross margin percentage should improve.

Net Profit Margin Percentage

Exhibit 13–5 shows that Brickey's *net profit margin percentage* decreased from 4.7% last year to 3.4% this year. The **net profit margin percentage** is widely used by managers and it is computed as follows:

$$\text{Net profit margin percentage} = \frac{\text{Net income}}{\text{Sales}}$$

The gross profit margin percentage and the net profit margin percentage state the gross margin and net income as a percentage of sales. The gross margin percentage focuses on only one type of expense (cost of goods sold) and its impact on performance, whereas the net profit margin percentage also looks at how selling and administrative expenses, interest expense, and income tax expense have influenced performance. The remaining ratios in this section look at profitability relative to amounts reported on the balance sheet rather than sales.

Return on Total Assets

The **return on total assets** is a measure of operating performance that is defined as follows:

$$\text{Return on total assets} = \frac{\text{Net income} + [\text{Interest expense} \times (1 - \text{Tax rate})]}{\text{Average total assets}}$$

Interest expense is added back to net income to show what earnings would have been if the company had no debt. With this adjustment, a manager can evaluate his company's return on assets over time without the analysis being influenced by changes in the company's mix of debt and equity over time. Furthermore, this adjustment enables managers to draw more meaningful comparisons with other companies that have differing amounts of debt. Notice that the interest expense is placed on an after-tax basis by multiplying it by the factor (1 − Tax rate).

The return on total assets for Brickey Electronics is computed as follows (from Exhibits 13–1 and 13–2):

$$\text{Return on total assets} = \frac{\$1,750,000 + [\$640,000 \times (1 - 0.30)]}{(\$31,500,000 + \$28,970,000)/2} = 7.3\%$$

Brickey Electronics has earned a return of 7.3% on average total assets employed during this year.

Return on Equity

The return on total assets looks at profits relative to total assets, whereas the *return on equity* looks at profits relative to the book value of stockholders' equity. The **return on equity** is computed as follows:

$$\text{Return on equity} = \frac{\text{Net income}}{\text{Average stockholders' equity}}$$

Brickey Electronics' return on equity for this year would be computed as follows:

$$\text{Return on equity} = \frac{\$1,750,000}{(\$17,000,000 + \$15,970,000)/2} = 10.6\%$$

Now that we have computed return on total assets and return on equity, we can take a moment to see financial leverage in operation for Brickey Electronics. Notice from Exhibit 13–1 that the company pays 8% interest on its bonds payable. The after-tax interest cost of these bonds is only 5.6% [8% interest rate × (1 − 0.30) = 5.6%]. As shown earlier, the company's after-tax return on total assets is 7.3%. Because the return on total assets of 7.3% is greater than the 5.6% after-tax interest cost of the bonds, leverage is positive and the difference goes to the stockholders. This explains in part why the return on equity of 10.6% is greater than the return on total assets of 7.3%.

It also bears emphasizing that many managers and investors take a more in-depth look at return on equity using principles pioneered by **E.I. du Pont de Nemours and Company** (better known as DuPont). This approach recognizes that return on equity is influenced by three elements—operating efficiency (as measured by net profit margin percentage), asset usage efficiency (as measured by total asset turnover), and financial leverage (as measured by the equity multiplier). The following equation computes Brickey Electronics' return on equity using these three elements:

$$\text{Return on equity} = \frac{\text{Net profit margin}}{\text{percentage}} \times \frac{\text{Total asset}}{\text{turnover}} \times \frac{\text{Equity}}{\text{multiplier}}$$

$$\text{Return on equity} = \frac{\text{Net income}}{\text{Sales}} \times \frac{\text{Sales}}{\text{Average total assets}} \times \frac{\text{Average total assets}}{\text{Average stockholders' equity}}$$

$$\text{Return on equity} = 3.37\% \times 1.72 \times 1.83 = 10.6\%$$

Notice that the sales and average total asset figures cancel, so we are left with net income divided by average stockholders' equity. While this equation is a little bit more complex, its return on equity of 10.6% agrees with the initial return on equity computation performed earlier. Also notice that this equation uses a net profit margin percentage of 3.37% rather than the rounded net profit margin percentage of 3.4% shown in Exhibit 13–5. The total asset turnover of 1.72 was previously computed on page 612 and the equity multiplier of 1.83 was previously computed on page 614.

6. Orvil Company's net profit margin percentage is 4.5%, its total asset turnover is 2.4, and its equity multiplier is 1.5. What is the company's return on equity?
   a. 2.8%
   b. 7.2%
   c. 16.2%
   d. 10.7%

CONCEPT CHECK

RATIO ANALYSIS—MARKET PERFORMANCE

This section summarizes five ratios that common stockholders use to assess a company's performance. Given that common stockholders are the ones who own the company, it logically follows that managers should have a thorough understanding of the measures that their owners will use to judge their performance. *All calculations are performed for this year.*

Earnings per Share

An investor buys a stock in the hope of realizing a return in the form of either dividends or future increases in the value of the stock. Because earnings form the basis for dividend payments and future increases in the value of shares, investors are interested in a company's *earnings per share.*

Earnings per share is computed by dividing net income by the average number of common shares outstanding during the year.

$$\text{Earnings per share} = \frac{\text{Net income}}{\text{Average number of common shares outstanding}}$$

Using the data in Exhibits 13–1 and 13–2, Brickey Electronics' earnings per share would be computed as follows:

$$\text{Earnings per share} = \frac{\$1,750,000}{(500,000 \text{ shares*} + 500,000 \text{ shares})/2} = \$3.50 \text{ per share}$$

*$6,000,000 total par value ÷ $12 par value per share = 500,000 shares.

HELPFUL HINT

The number of common shares outstanding is calculated by taking the dollar amount of common stock shown in the balance sheet and dividing it by the common stock's par value per share.

Price-Earnings Ratio

The **price-earnings ratio** expresses the relationship between a stock's market price per share and its earnings per share. If we assume that Brickey Electronics' stock has a market price of $40 per share at the end of this year, then its price-earnings ratio would be computed as follows:

$$\text{Price-earnings ratio} = \frac{\text{Market price per share}}{\text{Earnings per share}}$$

$$= \frac{\$40 \text{ per share}}{\$3.50 \text{ per share}} = 11.43$$

The price-earnings ratio is 11.43; that is, the stock is selling for about 11.43 times its current earnings per share.

A high price-earnings ratio means that investors are willing to pay a premium for the company's stock—presumably because the company is expected to have higher than average future earnings growth. Conversely, if investors believe a company's future earnings growth prospects are limited, the company's price-earnings ratio would be relatively low. In the late 1990s, the stock prices of some dot.com companies—particularly those with little or no earnings—were selling at levels that resulted in huge and nearly unprecedented price-earnings ratios. Many commentators cautioned that these price-earnings ratios were unsustainable in the long run—and they were right. The stock prices of almost all dot.com companies subsequently crashed.

Dividend Payout and Yield Ratios

Investors in a company's stock make money in two ways—increases in the market value of the stock and dividends. In general, earnings should be retained in a company and not paid out in dividends as long as the rate of return on funds invested inside the company exceeds the rate of return that stockholders could earn on alternative investments outside the company. Therefore, companies with excellent prospects of profitable growth often pay little or no dividend. Companies with little opportunity for profitable growth, but with steady, dependable earnings, tend to pay out a higher percentage of their cash flow from operations as dividends.

The Dividend Payout Ratio   The **dividend payout ratio** quantifies the percentage of current earnings being paid out in dividends. This ratio is computed by dividing the dividends per share by the earnings per share for common stock:

$$\text{Dividend payout ratio} = \frac{\text{Dividends per share}}{\text{Earnings per share}}$$

For Brickey Electronics, the dividend payout ratio is computed as follows:

$$\text{Dividend payout ratio} = \frac{\$1.44 \text{ per share (see Exhibit 13–2)}}{\$3.50 \text{ per share}} = 41.1\%$$

There is no such thing as a "right" dividend payout ratio, although the ratio tends to be similar for companies within the same industry. As noted above, companies with ample growth opportunities at high rates of return tend to have low payout ratios, whereas companies with limited reinvestment opportunities tend to have higher payout ratios.

The Dividend Yield Ratio   The **dividend yield ratio** is computed by dividing the current dividends per share by the current market price per share:

$$\text{Dividend yield ratio} = \frac{\text{Dividends per share}}{\text{Market price per share}}$$

Because the market price for Brickey Electronics' stock is $40 per share, the dividend yield is computed as follows:

$$\text{Dividend yield ratio} = \frac{\$1.44 \text{ per share}}{\$40 \text{ per share}} = 3.6\%$$

The dividend yield ratio measures the rate of return (in the form of cash dividends only) that would be earned by an investor who buys common stock at the current market price. A low dividend yield ratio is neither bad nor good by itself.

Book Value per Share

Book value per share measures the amount that would be distributed to holders of each share of common stock if all assets were sold at their balance sheet carrying amounts (i.e., book values) and if all creditors were paid off. Book value per share is based entirely on historical costs. The formula for computing it is

$$\text{Book value per share} = \frac{\text{Total stockholders' equity}}{\text{Number of common shares outstanding}}$$

The book value per share of Brickey Electronics' common stock is computed as follows:

$$\text{Book value per share} = \frac{\$17,000,000}{500,000 \text{ shares}} = \$34 \text{ per share}$$

If this book value is compared with the $40 market value of Brickey Electronics' stock, then the stock may appear to be overpriced. However, as we discussed earlier, market prices reflect expectations about future earnings and dividends, whereas book value largely reflects the results of events that have occurred in the past. Ordinarily, the market value of a stock exceeds its book value. For example, in one year, **Microsoft**'s common stock often traded at over 4 times its book value, and **Coca-Cola**'s market value was over 17 times its book value.

DECISION POINT   Portfolio Manager

Assume that you work for a mutual fund and have the responsibility of selecting stocks to include in its investment portfolio. You have been analyzing the financial statements of a chain of retail clothing stores and noticed that the company's current ratio has increased, but its acid-test (quick) ratio has decreased. In addition, the company's accounts receivable turnover has decreased and its inventory turnover ratio has decreased. Finally, the company's price-earnings ratio is at an all-time high. Would you recommend buying stock in this company?

SUMMARY OF RATIOS AND SOURCES OF COMPARATIVE RATIO DATA

Exhibit 13–6 contains a summary of the ratios discussed in this chapter. The formula for each ratio and a summary comment on each ratio's significance are included in the exhibit.

Exhibit 13–7 (page 622) contains a listing of public sources that provide comparative ratio data organized by industry. These sources are used extensively by managers, investors, and analysts. The **EDGAR** database listed in Exhibit 13–7 is a particularly rich source of data. It contains copies of all reports filed by companies with the SEC since about 1995—including annual reports filed as Form 10-K.

EXHIBIT 13-6   Summary of Ratios

Ratio	Formula	Significance
Working capital	Current assets − Current liabilities	Measures the company's ability to repay current liabilities using only current assets
Current ratio	Current assets ÷ Current liabilities	Test of short-term debt-paying ability
Acid-test ratio	(Cash + Marketable securities + Accounts receivable + Short-term notes receivable) ÷ Current liabilities	Test of short-term debt-paying ability without having to rely on inventory
Accounts receivable turnover	Sales on account ÷ Average accounts receivable balance	Measures how many times a company's accounts receivable have been turned into cash during the year
Average collection period	365 days ÷ Accounts receivable turnover	Measures the average number of days taken to collect an account receivable
Inventory turnover	Cost of goods sold ÷ Average inventory balance	Measures how many times a company's inventory has been sold during the year
Average sale period	365 days ÷ Inventory turnover	Measures the average number of days taken to sell the inventory one time
Operating cycle	Average sale period + Average collection period	Measures the elapsed time from when inventory is received from suppliers to when cash is received from customers
Total asset turnover	Sales ÷ Average total assets	Measures how efficiently assets are being used to generate sales
Times interest earned	Earnings before interest expense and income taxes ÷ Interest expense	Measures the company's ability to make interest payments
Debt-to-equity ratio	Total liabilities ÷ Stockholders' equity	Measures the amount of assets being provided by creditors for each dollar of assets being provided by the stockholders
Equity multiplier	Average total assets ÷ Average stockholders' equity	Measures the portion of a company's assets funded by equity
Gross margin percentage	Gross margin ÷ Sales	Measures profitability before selling and administrative expenses
Net profit margin percentage	Net income ÷ Sales	A broad measure of profitability
Return on total assets	{Net income + [Interest expense × (1 − Tax rate)]} ÷ Average total assets	Measures how well assets have been employed by management
Return on equity	Net income ÷ Average stockholders' equity	When compared to the return on total assets, measures the extent to which financial leverage is working for or against common stockholders
Earnings per share	Net income ÷ Average number of common shares outstanding	Affects the market price per share, as reflected in the price-earnings ratio
Price-earnings ratio	Market price per share ÷ Earnings per share	An index of whether a stock is relatively cheap or relatively expensive in relation to current earnings
Dividend payout ratio	Dividends per share ÷ Earnings per share	An index showing whether a company pays out most of its earnings in dividends or reinvests the earnings internally
Dividend yield ratio	Dividends per share ÷ Market price per share	Shows the return in terms of cash dividends being provided by a stock
Book value per share	Total stockholders' equity ÷ Number of common shares outstanding	Measures the amount that would be distributed to common stockholders if all assets were sold at their balance sheet carrying amounts and if all creditors were paid off

EXHIBIT 13–7   Sources of Financial Ratios

Source	Content
Almanac of Business and Industrial Financial Ratios, Aspen Publishers; published annually	An exhaustive source that contains common-size income statements and financial ratios by industry and by the size of companies within each industry.
AMA Annual Statement Studies, Risk Management Association; published annually.	A widely used publication that contains common-size statements and financial ratios on individual companies; the companies are arranged by industry.
EDGAR, Securities and Exchange Commission; website that is continually updated; www.sec.gov	An exhaustive Internet database that contains reports filed by companies with the SEC; these reports can be downloaded.
FreeEdgar, EDGAR Online, Inc.; website that is continually updated; www.freeedgar.com	A site that allows you to search SEC filings; financial information can be downloaded directly into Excel worksheets.
Hoover's Online, Hoovers, Inc.; website that is continually updated; www.hoovers.com	A site that provides capsule profiles for 10,000 U.S. companies with links to company websites, annual reports, stock charts, news articles, and industry information.
Industry Norms & Key Business Ratios, Dun & Bradstreet; published annually	Fourteen commonly used financial ratios are computed for over 800 major industry groupings.
Mergent Industrial Manual and Mergent Bank and Finance Manual; published annually	An exhaustive source that contains financial ratios on all companies listed on the New York Stock Exchange, the American Stock Exchange, and regional American exchanges.
Standard & Poor's Industry Survey, Standard & Poor's; published annually	Various statistics, including some financial ratios, are given by industry and for leading companies within each industry grouping.

SUMMARY

LO13–1 Prepare and interpret financial statements in comparative and common-size form.

Raw data from financial statements should be standardized so that the data can be compared over time and across companies. For example, all of the financial data for a company can be expressed as a percentage of the data in some base year. This makes it easier to spot trends over time. To make it easier to compare companies, common-size financial statements are often used in which income statement data are expressed as a percentage of sales and balance sheet data are expressed as a percentage of total assets.

LO 13–2 Compute and interpret financial ratios that managers use to assess liquidity.

Managers need to be concerned with their company's ability to repay its debts in the near future. Consequently, they focus on the relation between current assets and current liabilities using measures such as working capital, the current ratio, and the acid-test (quick) ratio.

LO13–3 Compute and interpret financial ratios that managers use for asset management purposes.

Managers need to ensure that their companies use current and noncurrent assets efficiently. The accounts receivable turnover, inventory turnover, and operating cycle help managers assess how quickly their companies are able to translate inventories and credit sales into cash. The total asset turnover is another measure of efficiency that compares sales to the average total assets used to generate those sales.

LO13–4 Compute and interpret financial ratios that managers use for debt management purposes.

Managers need to ensure that their companies can repay long-term creditors. They often track the times interest earned ratio to assess the company's ability to use current operations to make interest payments to those lenders. They also measure the debt-to-equity ratio and the equity multiplier to better understand their company's use of financial leverage.

LO13–5 Compute and interpret financial ratios that managers use to assess profitability.

Profitability is a fundamental measure of organizational performance. The gross margin percentage states the gross margin as a percentage of sales. Similarly, the net profit margin percentage states the net income as a percentage of sales. The return on total assets and return on equity look at net income relative to information contained on the balance sheet—either average total assets or average total stockholders' equity. Generally speaking, companies seek to continually increase all of these measures.

LO13–6 Compute and interpret financial ratios that managers use to assess market performance.

Managers need to understand their company's performance through the eyes of common stockholders. They assess stock market performance using measures such as earnings per share, price-earnings ratio, dividend payout and dividend yield ratios, and book value per share. Generally speaking, the higher these ratios, the better it is for the company and its common stockholders.

GUIDANCE ANSWER TO DECISION POINT

Portfolio Manager (p. 620)

All of the ratios—current ratio, acid-test (quick) ratio, accounts receivable turnover, and inventory turnover ratio—indicate deteriorating operations. And yet the company's price-earnings ratio is at an all-time high, suggesting that the stock market is optimistic about the company's future and its stock price. It would be risky to invest in this company without digging deeper and finding out what has caused the deteriorating operating ratios.

GUIDANCE ANSWERS TO CONCEPT CHECKS

1. **Choice b.** The accounts receivable turnover is $800,000 of credit sales ÷ $120,000 average accounts receivable balance = 6.67.
2. **Choice a.** First, calculate the cost of goods sold as follows: $1,000,000 × (1 − 0.60) = $400,000. Next, the inventory turnover is calculated as follows: $400,000 of cost of goods sold ÷ $250,000 average inventory = 1.60.
3. **Choice c.** The inventory turnover is 1.60. So, 365 days divided by 1.60 = 228 days (rounded).
4. **Choice b.** The accounts receivable turnover is 6.67. So, the average collection period is 365 days divided by 6.67, or approximately 55 days. The average sale period of 228 days plus the average collection period of 55 days equal the operating cycle of 283 days.
5. **Choice d.** Total assets of $1,500,000 − $900,000 of stockholders' equity = $600,000 of total liabilities. The debt-to-equity ratio is $600,000 ÷ $900,000 = 0.67.
6. **Choice c.** The net profit margin percentage of 4.5% times the total asset turnover of 2.4 times the equity multiplier of 1.5 equals the return on equity of 16.2%.

REVIEW PROBLEM: SELECTED RATIOS AND FINANCIAL LEVERAGE

Mulligan Corporation's financial statements are as follows:

Mulligan Corporation
Comparative Balance Sheet
(dollars in millions)

	This Year	Last Year
Assets		
Current assets:		
Cash	$ 281	$ 313
Marketable securities	157	141
Accounts receivable	288	224
Inventories	692	636
Other current assets	278	216
Total current assets	1,696	1,530
Property and equipment, net	2,890	2,288
Other assets	758	611
Total assets	$5,344	$4,429
Liabilities and Stockholders' Equity		
Current liabilities:		
Accounts payable	$ 391	$ 341
Short-term bank loans	710	700
Accrued payables	757	662
Other current liabilities	298	233
Total current liabilities	2,156	1,936
Long-term liabilities	904	265
Total liabilities	3,060	2,201
Stockholders' equity:		
Common stock and additional paid-in capital	40	40
Retained earnings	2,244	2,188
Total stockholders' equity	2,284	2,228
Total liabilities and stockholders' equity	$5,344	$4,429

Mulligan Corporation
Income Statement
(dollars in millions)

	This Year
Sales	$9,411
Cost of goods sold	3,999
Gross margin	5,412
Selling and administrative expenses:	
Store operating expenses	3,216
Other operating expenses	294
Depreciation and amortization	467
General and administrative expenses	489
Total selling and administrative expenses	4,466
Net operating income	946
Plus interest and other income	110
Interest expense	0
Net income before taxes	1,056
Income taxes (about 36%)	384
Net income	$ 672

Required:
1. Compute the return on total assets.
2. Compute the return on equity.
3. Is Mulligan's financial leverage positive or negative? Explain.
4. Compute the current ratio.
5. Compute the acid-test ratio.
6. Compute the inventory turnover.
7. Compute the average sale period.
8. Compute the debt-to-equity ratio.
9. Compute the total asset turnover.
10. Compute the net profit margin percentage.

Solution to Review Problem

1. Return on total assets:

$$\text{Return on total assets} = \frac{\text{Net income} + [\text{Interest expense} \times (1 - \text{Tax rate})]}{\text{Average total assets}}$$

$$= \frac{\$672 + [\$0 \times (1 - 0.36)]}{(\$5,344 + \$4,429)/2} = 13.8\% \text{ (rounded)}$$

2. Return on equity:

$$\text{Return on equity} = \frac{\text{Net income}}{\text{Average stockholders' equity}}$$

$$= \frac{\$672}{(\$2,284 + \$2,228)/2} = 29.8\% \text{ (rounded)}$$

3. The company has positive financial leverage because the return on equity of 29.8% is greater than the return on total assets of 13.8%. The positive financial leverage was obtained from current and long-term liabilities.

4. Current ratio:

$$\text{Current ratio} = \frac{\text{Current assets}}{\text{Current liabilities}}$$

$$= \frac{\$1,696}{\$2,156} = 0.79 \text{ (rounded)}$$

5. Acid-test ratio:

$$\text{Acid-test ratio} = \frac{\text{Cash} + \text{Marketable securities} + \text{Accounts receivable} + \text{Short-term notes receivable}}{\text{Current liabilities}}$$

$$= \frac{\$281 + \$157 + \$288 + \$0}{\$2,156} = 0.34 \text{ (rounded)}$$

6. Inventory turnover:

$$\text{Inventory turnover} = \frac{\text{Cost of goods sold}}{\text{Average inventory balance}}$$

$$= \frac{\$3,999}{(\$692 + \$636)/2} = 6.02 \text{ (rounded)}$$

7. Average sale period:

$$\text{Average sale period} = \frac{365 \text{ days}}{\text{Inventory turnover}}$$

$$= \frac{365 \text{ days}}{6.02} = 61 \text{ days (rounded)}$$

8. Debt-to-equity ratio:

$$\text{Debt-to-equity ratio} = \frac{\text{Total liabilities}}{\text{Stockholders' equity}}$$

$$= \frac{\$2,156 + \$904}{\$2,284} = 1.34 \text{ (rounded)}$$

9. Total asset turnover:

$$\text{Total asset turnover} = \frac{\text{Sales}}{\text{Average total assets}}$$

$$\text{Total asset turnover} = \frac{\$9,411}{(\$5,344 + \$4,429)/2} = 1.93 \text{ (rounded)}$$

10. Net profit margin percentage:

$$\text{Net profit margin percentage} = \frac{\text{Net income}}{\text{Sales}}$$

$$\text{Net profit margin percentage} = \frac{\$672}{\$9,411} = 7.1\% \text{ (rounded)}$$

GLOSSARY

(Note: Definitions and formulas for all financial ratios are shown in Exhibit 13–6. These definitions and formulas are not repeated here.)

Common-size financial statements   A statement that shows the items appearing on it in percentage form as well as in dollar form. On the income statement, the percentages are based on total sales; on the balance sheet, the percentages are based on total assets. (p. 605)

Financial leverage   A difference between the rate of return on assets and the rate paid to creditors. (p. 613)

Horizontal analysis   A side-by-side comparison of two or more years' financial statements. (p. 603)

Trend analysis   See *Horizontal analysis*. (p. 603)

Trend percentages   Several years of financial data expressed as a percentage of performance in a base year. (p. 604)

Vertical analysis   The presentation of a company's financial statements in common-size form. (p. 605)

QUESTIONS

13–1   Distinguish between horizontal and vertical analysis of financial statement data.

13–2   What is the basic purpose for examining trends in a company's financial ratios and other data? What other kinds of comparisons might an analyst make?

13–3   Assume that two companies in the same industry have equal earnings. Why might these companies have different price-earnings ratios? If a company has a price-earnings ratio of 20 and reports earnings per share for the current year of $4, at what price would you expect to find the stock selling on the market?

13–4   Would you expect a company in a rapidly growing technological industry to have a high or low dividend payout ratio?

13–5   What is meant by the dividend yield on a common stock investment?

13–6   What is meant by the term financial leverage?

13–7   The president of a plastics company was quoted in a business journal as stating, "We haven't had a dollar of interest-paying debt in over 10 years. Not many companies can say that." As a stockholder in this company, how would you feel about its policy of not taking on debt?

13–8   If a stock's market value exceeds its book value, then the stock is overpriced. Do you agree? Explain.

13–9   A company seeking a line of credit at a bank was turned down. Among other things, the bank stated that the company's 2 to 1 current ratio was not adequate. Give reasons why a 2 to 1 current ratio might not be adequate.

Multiple-choice questions are available in the *Connect Library.*

THE FOUNDATIONAL 15    connect
|ACCOUNTING

LO13–2, LO13–3, LO13–4, LO13–5, LO13–6

Available with McGraw-Hill's *Connect Accounting.*

Markus Company's common stock sold for $2.75 per share at the end of this year. The company paid a common stock dividend of $0.55 per share this year. It also provided the following *data excerpts* from this year's financial statements:

	Ending Balance	Beginning Balance
Cash	$35,000	$30,000
Accounts receivable	$60,000	$50,000
Inventory.	$55,000	$60,000
Current assets	$150,000	$140,000
Total assets.	$450,000	$460,000
Current liabilities.	$60,000	$40,000
Total liabilities	$130,000	$120,000
Common stock, $1 par value	$120,000	$120,000
Total stockholders' equity	$320,000	$340,000
Total liabilities and stockholders' equity	$450,000	$460,000

	This Year
Sales (all on account).	$700,000
Cost of goods sold	$400,000
Gross margin	$300,000
Net operating income	$140,000
Interest expense.	$8,000
Net income	$92,400

Required:
1. What is the earnings per share?
2. What is the price-earnings ratio?
3. What is the dividend payout ratio and the dividend yield ratio?
4. What is the return on total assets (assuming a 30% tax rate)?
5. What is the return on equity?
6. What is the book value per share at the end of this year?
7. What is the amount of working capital and the current ratio at the end of this year?
8. What is the acid-test ratio at the end of this year?
9. What is the accounts receivable turnover and the average collection period?
10. What is the inventory turnover and the average sale period?
11. What is the company's operating cycle?
12. What is the total asset turnover?
13. What is the times interest earned ratio?
14. What is the debt-to-equity ratio at the end of this year?
15. What is the equity multiplier?

 **EXERCISES**

All applicable exercises are available with McGraw-Hill's *Connect Accounting*.

EXERCISE 13–1   Common-Size Income Statement [LO13–1]
A comparative income statement is given below for McKenzie Sales, Ltd., of Toronto:

McKenzie Sales, Ltd. Comparative Income Statement		
	This Year	Last Year
Sales	$8,000,000	$6,000,000
Cost of goods sold	4,984,000	3,516,000
Gross margin	3,016,000	2,484,000
Selling and administrative expenses:		
Selling expenses	1,480,000	1,092,000
Administrative expenses	712,000	618,000
Total expenses	2,192,000	1,710,000
Net operating income	824,000	774,000
Interest expense	96,000	84,000
Net income before taxes	$ 728,000	$ 690,000

Members of the company's board of directors are surprised to see that net income increased by only $38,000 when sales increased by two million dollars.

Required:
1. Express each year's income statement in common-size percentages. Carry computations to one decimal place.
2. Comment briefly on the changes between the two years.

EXERCISE 13–2   Financial Ratios for Assessing Liquidity [LO13–2]
Comparative financial statements for Weller Corporation, a merchandising company, for the fiscal year ending December 31 appear below. The company did not issue any new common stock during the year. A total of 800,000 shares of common stock were outstanding. The interest rate on the bond payable was 12%, the income tax rate was 40%, and the dividend per share of common stock was $0.75 last year and $0.40 this year. The market value of the company's common stock at the end of the year was $18. All of the company's sales are on account.

Weller Corporation Comparative Balance Sheet (dollars in thousands)	This Year	Last Year
Assets		
Current assets:		
Cash	$ 1,280	$ 1,560
Accounts receivable, net	12,300	9,100
Inventory	9,700	8,200
Prepaid expenses	1,800	2,100
Total current assets	25,080	20,960
Property and equipment:		
Land	6,000	6,000
Buildings and equipment, net	19,200	19,000
Total property and equipment	25,200	25,000
Total assets	$50,280	$45,960
Liabilities and Stockholders' Equity		
Current liabilities:		
Accounts payable	$ 9,500	$ 8,300
Accrued liabilities	600	700
Notes payable, short term	300	300
Total current liabilities	10,400	9,300
Long-term liabilities:		
Bonds payable	5,000	5,000
Total liabilities	15,400	14,300
Stockholders' equity:		
Common stock	800	800
Additional paid-in capital	4,200	4,200
Total paid-in capital	5,000	5,000
Retained earnings	29,880	26,660
Total stockholders' equity	34,880	31,660
Total liabilities and stockholders' equity	$50,280	$45,960

Weller Corporation
Comparative Income Statement and Reconciliation
(dollars in thousands)

	This Year	Last Year
Sales	$79,000	$74,000
Cost of goods sold	52,000	48,000
Gross margin	27,000	26,000
Selling and administrative expenses:		
Selling expenses	8,500	8,000
Administrative expenses	12,000	11,000
Total selling and administrative expenses	20,500	19,000
Net operating income	6,500	7,000
Interest expense	600	600
Net income before taxes	5,900	6,400
Income taxes	2,360	2,560
Net income	3,540	3,840
Dividends to common stockholders	320	600
Net income added to retained earnings	3,220	3,240
Beginning retained earnings	26,660	23,420
Ending retained earnings	$29,880	$26,660

Required:
Compute the following financial data and ratios for this year:
1. Working capital.
2. Current ratio.
3. Acid-test ratio.

EXERCISE 13–3 Financial Ratios for Asset Management [LO13–3]
Refer to the data in Exercise 13–2 for Weller Corporation.

Required:
Compute the following financial data for this year:
1. Accounts receivable turnover. (Assume that all sales are on account.)
2. Average collection period.
3. Inventory turnover.
4. Average sale period.
5. Operating cycle.
6. Total asset turnover.

EXERCISE 13–4 Financial Ratios for Debt Management [LO13–4]
Refer to the data in Exercise 13–2 for Weller Corporation.

Required:
Compute the following financial ratios for this year:
1. Times interest earned ratio.
2. Debt-to-equity ratio.
3. Equity multiplier.

EXERCISE 13–5 Financial Ratios for Assessing Profitability [LO13–5]
Refer to the data in Exercise 13–2 for Weller Corporation.

Required:
Compute the following financial data for this year:
1. Gross margin percentage.
2. Net profit margin percentage.
3. Return on total assets.
4. Return on equity.

EXERCISE 13–6   Financial Ratios for Assessing Market Performance [LO13–6]
Refer to the data in Exercise 13–2 for Weller Corporation.

Required:
Compute the following financial data for this year:
1.   Earnings per share.
2.   Price-earnings ratio.
3.   Dividend payout ratio.
4.   Dividend yield ratio.
5.   Book value per share.

EXERCISE 13–7   Trend Percentages [LO13–1]
Rotorua Products, Ltd., of New Zealand markets agricultural products for the burgeoning Asian consumer market. The company's current assets, current liabilities, and sales have been reported as follows over the last five years (Year 5 is the most recent year):

	Year 1	Year 2	Year 3	Year 4	Year 5
Sales	$1,800,000	$1,980,000	$2,070,000	$2,160,000	$2,250,000
Cash	$ 50,000	$ 65,000	$ 48,000	$ 40,000	$ 30,000
Accounts receivable, net	300,000	345,000	405,000	510,000	570,000
Inventory	600,000	660,000	690,000	720,000	750,000
Total current assets	$ 950,000	$1,070,000	$1,143,000	$1,270,000	$1,350,000
Current liabilities	$ 400,000	$ 440,000	$ 520,000	$ 580,000	$ 640,000

Required:
1.   Express all of the asset, liability, and sales data in trend percentages. (Show percentages for each item.) Use Year 1 as the base year and carry computations to one decimal place.
2.   Comment on the results of your analysis.

EXERCISE 13–8   Selected Financial Ratios [LO13–2, LO13–3, LO13–4]
The financial statements for Castile Products, Inc., are given below:

Castile Products, Inc.
Balance Sheet
December 31

Assets
Current assets:	
Cash	$ 6,500
Accounts receivable, net	35,000
Merchandise inventory	70,000
Prepaid expenses	3,500
Total current assets	115,000
Property and equipment, net	185,000
Total assets	$300,000

Liabilities and Stockholders' Equity
Liabilities:	
Current liabilities	$ 50,000
Bonds payable, 10%	80,000
Total liabilities	130,000
Stockholders' equity:	
Common stock, $5 per value	30,000
Retained earnings	140,000
Total stockholders' equity	170,000
Total liabilities and equity	$300,000

Castile Products, Inc.	
Income Statement	
For the Year Ended December 31	
Sales	$420,000
Cost of goods sold	292,500
Gross margin	127,500
Selling and administrative expenses	89,500
Net operating income	38,000
Interest expense	8,000
Net income before taxes	30,000
Income taxes (30%)	9,000
Net income	$ 21,000

Account balances at the beginning of the year were accounts receivable, $25,000; and inventory, $60,000. All sales were on account.

Required:
Compute the following financial data and ratios:
1. Working capital.
2. Current ratio.
3. Acid-test ratio.
4. Debt-to-equity ratio.
5. Times interest earned ratio.
6. Average collection period.
7. Average sale period.
8. Operating cycle.

EXERCISE 13–9   Financial Ratios for Assessing Profitability and Managing Debt [LO13–4, LO13–5]

Refer to the financial statements for Castile Products, Inc., in Exercise 13–8. Assets at the beginning of the year totaled $280,000, and the stockholders' equity totaled $161,600.

Required:
Compute the following:
1. Gross margin percentage.
2. Net profit margin percentage.
3. Return on total assets.
4. Return on equity.
5. Was financial leverage positive or negative for the year? Explain.

EXERCISE 13–10   Financial Ratios for Assessing Market Performance [LO13–6]

Refer to the financial statements for Castile Products, Inc., in Exercise 13–8. In addition to the data in these statements, assume that Castile Products, Inc., paid dividends of $2.10 per share during the year. Also assume that the company's common stock had a market price of $42 at the end of the year and there was no change in the number of outstanding shares of common stock during the year.

Required:
Compute financial ratios as follows:
1. Earnings per share.
2. Dividend payout ratio.
3. Dividend yield ratio.
4. Price-earnings ratio.
5. Book value per share.

EXERCISE 13–11   Financial Ratios for Assessing Profitability and Managing Debt [LO13–4, LO13–5]

Selected financial data from the June 30 year-end statements of Safford Company are given below:

Total assets	$3,600,000
Long-term debt (12% interest rate)	$500,000
Total stockholders' equity	$2,400,000
Interest paid on long-term debt	$60,000
Net income	$280,000

Total assets at the beginning of the year were $3,000,000; total stockholders' equity was $2,200,000. The company's tax rate is 30%.

Required:
1. Compute the return on total assets.
2. Compute the return on equity.
3. Is financial leverage positive or negative? Explain.

EXERCISE 13–12 Selected Financial Measures for Assessing Liquidity [LO13–2]
Norsk Optronics, ALS, of Bergen, Norway, had a current ratio of 2.5 on June 30 of the current year. On that date, the company's assets were

Cash	$ 90,000
Accounts receivable, net	260,000
Inventory	490,000
Prepaid expenses	10,000
Plant and equipment, net	800,000
Total assets	$1,650,000

Required:
1. What was the company's working capital on June 30?
2. What was the company's acid-test ratio on June 30?
3. The company paid an account payable of $40,000 immediately after June 30.
   a. What effect did this transaction have on working capital? Show computations.
   b. What effect did this transaction have on the current ratio? Show computations.

PROBLEMS

  Alternate problem set is available in the *Connect Library.*

All applicable problems are available with McGraw-Hill's *Connect Accounting.*

PROBLEM 13–13A Effects of Transactions on Various Financial Ratios [LO13–2, LO13–3, LO13–4, LO13–5, LO13–6]
In the right-hand column below, certain financial ratios are listed. To the left of each ratio is a business transaction or event relating to the operating activities of Delta Company (each transaction should be considered independently).

Business Transaction or Event	Ratio
1. Declared a cash dividend.	Current ratio
2. Sold inventory on account at cost.	Acid-test ratio
3. Issued bonds with an interest rate of 8%. The company's return on assets is 10%.	Return on equity
4. Net income decreased by 10% between last year and this year. Long-term debt remained unchanged.	Times interest earned
5. Paid a previously declared cash dividend.	Current ratio
6. The market price of the company's common stock dropped from $24.50 to $20.00. The dividend paid per share remained unchanged.	Dividend payout ratio
7. Obsolete inventory totaling $100,000 was written off as a loss.	Inventory turnover ratio
8. Sold inventory for cash at a profit.	Debt-to-equity ratio
9. Changed customer credit terms from 2/10, n/30 to 2/15, n/30 to comply with a change in industry practice.	Accounts receivable turnover ratio
10. Issued a stock dividend to common stockholders.	Book value per share
11. The market price of the company's common stock increased from $24.50 to $30.00.	Book value per share
12. Paid $40,000 on accounts payable.	Working capital
13. Issued a stock dividend to common stockholders.	Earnings per share
14. Paid accounts payable.	Debt-to-equity ratio
15. Purchased inventory on account.	Acid-test ratio
16. Wrote off an uncollectible account against the Allowance for Bad Debts.	Current ratio
17. The market price of the company's common stock increased from $24.50 to $30.00. Earnings per share remained unchanged.	Price-earnings ratio
18. The market price of the company's common stock increased from $24.50 to $30.00. The dividend paid per share remained unchanged.	Dividend yield ratio

Required:

Indicate the effect that each business transaction or event would have on the ratio listed opposite to it. State the effect in terms of increase, decrease, or no effect on the ratio involved, and give the reason for your answer. In all cases, assume that the current assets exceed the current liabilities both before and after the event or transaction. Use the following format for your answers:

Effect on Ratio	Reason for Increase, Decrease, or No Effect
1.	
Etc.	

PROBLEM 13–14A   Effects of Transactions on Various Ratios [LO13–2]

Denna Company's working capital accounts at the beginning of the year follow:

Cash	$50,000
Marketable securities	$30,000
Accounts receivable, net	$200,000
Inventory	$210,000
Prepaid expenses	$10,000
Accounts payable	$150,000
Notes due within one year	$30,000
Accrued liabilities	$20,000

During the year, Denna Company completed the following transactions:

x.   Paid a cash dividend previously declared, $12,000.
a.   Issued additional shares of common stock for cash, $100,000.
b.   Sold inventory costing $50,000 for $80,000, on account.
c.   Wrote off uncollectible accounts in the amount of $10,000, reducing the accounts receivable balance accordingly.
d.   Declared a cash dividend, $15,000.
e.   Paid accounts payable, $50,000.
f.   Borrowed cash on a short-term note with the bank, $35,000.
g.   Sold inventory costing $15,000 for $10,000 cash.
h.   Purchased inventory on account, $60,000.
i.   Paid off all short-term notes due, $30,000.
j.   Purchased equipment for cash, $15,000.
k.   Sold marketable securities costing $18,000 for cash, $15,000.
l.   Collected cash on accounts receivable, $80,000.

Required:

1.   Compute the following amounts and ratios as of the beginning of the year:
   a. Working capital.
   b. Current ratio.
   c. Acid-test ratio.
2.   Indicate the effect of each of the transactions given above on working capital, the current ratio, and the acid-test ratio. Give the effect in terms of increase, decrease, or none. Item (x) is given below as an example of the format to use:

	The Effect on		
Transaction	Working Capital	Current Ratio	Acid-Test Ratio
(x) Paid a cash dividend previously declared	None	Increase	Increase

PROBLEM 13–15A   Comprehensive Ratio Analysis [LO13–2, LO13–3, LO13–4, LO13–5, LO13–6]

You have just been hired as a financial analyst for Lydex Company, a manufacturer of safety helmets. Your boss has asked you to perform a comprehensive analysis of the company's financial statements, including comparing Lydex's performance to its major competitors. The company's financial statements for the last two years are as follows:

Lydex Company Comparative Balance Sheet	This Year	Last Year
Assets		
Current assets:		
Cash	$ 960,000	$ 1,260,000
Marketable securities	0	300,000
Accounts receivable, net	2,700,000	1,800,000
Inventory	3,900,000	2,400,000
Prepaid expenses	240,000	180,000
Total current assets	7,800,000	5,940,000
Plant and equipment, net	9,300,000	8,940,000
Total assets	$17,100,000	$14,880,000
Liabilities and Stockholders' Equity		
Liabilities:		
Current liabilities	$ 3,900,000	$ 2,760,000
Note payable, 10%	3,600,000	3,000,000
Total liabilities	7,500,000	5,760,000
Stockholders' equity:		
Common stock, $78 par value	7,800,000	7,800,000
Retained earnings	1,800,000	1,320,000
Total stockholders' equity	9,600,000	9,120,000
Total liabilities and stockholders' equity . . .	$17,100,000	$14,880,000

Lydex Company Comparative Income Statement and Reconciliation	This Year	Last Year
Sales (all on account)	$15,750,000	$12,480,000
Cost of goods sold	12,600,000	9,900,000
Gross margin	3,150,000	2,580,000
Selling and administrative expenses	1,590,000	1,560,000
Net operating income	1,560,000	1,020,000
Interest expense	360,000	300,000
Net income before taxes	1,200,000	720,000
Income taxes (30%)	360,000	216,000
Net income	840,000	504,000
Common dividends	360,000	252,000
Net income retained	480,000	252,000
Beginning retained earnings	1,320,000	1,068,000
Ending retained earnings	$ 1,800,000	$ 1,320,000

To begin your assigment you gather the following financial data and ratios that are typical of companies in Lydex Company's industry:

Current ratio	2.3
Acid-test ratio	1.2
Average collection period	30 days
Average sale period	60 days
Return on assets	9.5%
Debt-to-equity ratio	0.65
Times interest earned ratio	5.7
Price-earnings ratio	10

Required:
1. You decide first to assess the company's performance in terms of debt management and profitability. Compute the following for both this year and last year:
    a. The times interest earned ratio.
    b. The debt-to-equity ratio.
    c. The gross margin percentage.
    d. The return on total assets. (Total assets at the beginning of last year were $12,960,000.)
    e. The return on equity. (Stockholders' equity at the beginning of last year totaled $9,048,000. There has been no change in common stock over the last two years.)
    f. Is the company's financial leverage positive or negative? Explain.
2. You decide next to assess the company's stock market performance. Assume that Lydex's stock price at the end of this year is $72 per share and that at the end of last year it was $40. For both this year and last year, compute:
    a. The earnings per share.
    b. The dividend yield ratio.
    c. The dividend payout ratio.
    d. The price-earnings ratio. How do investors regard Lydex Company as compared to other companies in the industry? Explain.
    e. The book value per share of common stock. Does the difference between market value per share and book value per share suggest that the stock at its current price is a bargain? Explain.
3. You decide, finally, to assess the company's liquidity and asset management. For both this year and last year, compute:
    a. Working capital.
    b. The current ratio.
    c. The acid-test ratio.
    d. The average collection period. (The accounts receivable at the beginning of last year totaled $1,560,000.)
    e. The average sale period. (The inventory at the beginning of last year totaled $1,920,000.)
    f. The operating cycle.
    g. The total asset turnover. (The total assets at the beginning of last year totaled $14,500,000.)
4. Prepare a brief memo that summarizes how Lydex is performing relative to its competitors.

PROBLEM 13–16A Common-Size Financial Statements [LO13–1]
Refer to the financial statement data for Lydex Company given in Problem 13–15.

Required:
For both this year and last year:
1. Present the balance sheet in common-size format.
2. Present the income statement in common-size format down through net income.
3. Comment on the results of your analysis.

PROBLEM 13–17A Interpretation of Financial Ratios [LO13–2, LO13–3, LO13–5, LO13–6]
Pecunious Products, Inc.'s financial results for the past three years are summarized below:

	Year 3	Year 2	Year 1
Sales trend	128.0	115.0	100.0
Current ratio	2.5	2.3	2.2
Acid-test ratio	0.8	0.9	1.1
Accounts receivable turnover	9.4	10.6	12.5
Inventory turnover	6.5	7.2	8.0
Dividend yield	7.1%	6.5%	5.8%
Dividend payout ratio	40%	50%	60%
Return on total assets	12.5%	11.0%	9.5%
Return on equity	14.0%	10.0%	7.8%
Dividends paid per share*	$1.50	$1.50	$1.50

*There have been no changes in common stock outstanding over the three-year period.

Your boss has asked you to review these results and then answer the following questions:
a. Is it becoming easier for the company to pay its bills as they come due?
b. Are customers paying their accounts at least as fast now as they were in Year 1?
c. Is the total of the accounts receivable increasing, decreasing, or remaining constant?
d. Is the level of inventory increasing, decreasing, or remaining constant?

e. Is the market price of the company's stock going up or down?
f. Is the earnings per share increasing or decreasing?
g. Is the price-earning ratio going up or down?
h. Is the company employing financial leverage to the advantage of the common stockholders?

Required:
Provide answers to each of the questions raised by your boss.

PROBLEM 13–18A Common-Size Statements and Financial Ratios for a Loan Application [LO13–1, LO13–2, LO13–3, LO13–4]

Paul Sabin organized Sabin Electronics 10 years ago to produce and sell several electronic devices on which he had secured patents. Although the company has been fairly profitable, it is now experiencing a severe cash shortage. For this reason, it is requesting a $500,000 long-term loan from Gulfport State Bank, $100,000 of which will be used to bolster the Cash account and $400,000 of which will be used to modernize equipment. The company's financial statements for the two most recent years follow:

Sabin Electronics Comparative Balance Sheet	This Year	Last Year
Assets		
Current assets:		
Cash	$ 70,000	$ 150,000
Marketable securities	0	18,000
Accounts receivable, net	480,000	300,000
Inventory	950,000	600,000
Prepaid expenses	20,000	22,000
Total current assets	1,520,000	1,090,000
Plant and equipment, net	1,480,000	1,370,000
Total assets	$3,000,000	$2,460,000
Liabilities and Stockholders' Equity		
Liabilities:		
Current liabilities	$ 800,000	$ 430,000
Bonds payable, 12%	600,000	600,000
Total liabilities	1,400,000	1,030,000
Stockholders' equity:		
Common stock, $15 par	750,000	750,000
Retained earnings	850,000	680,000
Total stockholders' equity	1,600,000	1,430,000
Total liabilities and equity	$3,000,000	$2,460,000

Sabin Electronics Comparative Income Statement and Reconciliation	This Year	Last Year
Sales	$5,000,000	$4,350,000
Cost of goods sold	3,875,000	3,450,000
Gross margin	1,125,000	900,000
Selling and administrative expenses	653,000	548,000
Net operating income	472,000	352,000
Interest expense	72,000	72,000
Net income before taxes	400,000	280,000
Income taxes (30%)	120,000	84,000
Net income	280,000	196,000
Common dividends	110,000	95,000
Net income retained	170,000	101,000
Beginning retained earnings	680,000	579,000
Ending retained earnings	$ 850,000	$ 680,000

During the past year, the company introduced several new product lines and raised the selling prices on a number of old product lines in order to improve its profit margin. The company also hired a new sales manager, who has expanded sales into several new territories. Sales terms are 2/10, n/30. All sales are on account.

Required:
1. To assist in approaching the bank about the loan, Paul has asked you to compute the following ratios for both this year and last year:
   a. The amount of working capital.
   b. The current ratio.
   c. The acid-test ratio.
   d. The average collection period. (The accounts receivable at the beginning of last year totaled $250,000.)
   e. The average sale period. (The inventory at the beginning of last year totaled $500,000.)
   f. The operating cycle.
   g. The total asset turnover. (The total assets at the beginning of last year were $2,420,000.)
   h. The debt-to-equity ratio.
   i. The times interest earned ratio.
   j. The equity multiplier. (The total stockholders' equity at the beginning of last year totaled $1,420,000.)
2. For both this year and last year:
   a. Present the balance sheet in common-size format.
   b. Present the income statement in common-size format down through net income.
3. Paul Sabin has also gathered the following financial data and ratios that are typical of companies in the electronics industry:

Current ratio	2.5
Acid-test ratio	1.3
Average collection period	18 days
Average sale period	60 days
Debt-to-equity ratio	0.90
Times interest earned ratio	6.0

Comment on the results of your analysis in (1) and (2) above and compare Sabin Electronics' performance to the benchmarks from the electronics industry. Do you think that the company is likely to get its loan application approved?

PROBLEM 13–19A Financial Ratios for Assessing Profitability and Market Performance [LO13–2]
Refer to the financial statements and other data in Problem 13–18. Assume that Paul Sabin has asked you to assess his company's profitability and stock market performance.

Required:
1. You decide first to assess the company's stock market performance. For both this year and last year, compute:
   a. The earnings per share. There has been no change in common stock over the last two years.
   b. The dividend yield ratio. The company's stock is currently selling for $40 per share; last year it sold for $36 per share.
   c. The dividend payout ratio.
   d. The price-earnings ratio. How do investors regard Sabin Electronics as compared to other companies in the industry if the industry norm for the price-earnings ratio is 12? Explain.
   e. The book value per share of common stock. Does the difference between market value and book value suggest that the stock is overpriced? Explain.
2. You decide next to assess the company's profitability. Compute the following for both this year and last year:
   a. The gross margin percentage.
   b. The net profit margin percentage.
   c. The return on total assets. (Total assets at the beginning of last year were $2,300,000.)

   d. The return on equity. (Stockholders' equity at the beginning of last year was $1,329,000.)

   e. Is the company's financial leverage positive or negative? Explain.

3. Comment on the company's profit performance and stock market performance over the two-year period.

BUILDING YOUR SKILLS

ETHICS CHALLENGE [LO13–2, LO13–4]

Venice InLine, Inc., was founded by Russ Perez to produce a specialized in-line skate he had designed for doing aerial tricks. Up to this point, Russ has financed the company with his own savings and with cash generated by his business. However, Russ now faces a cash crisis. In the year just ended, an acute shortage of high-impact roller bearings developed just as the company was beginning production for the Christmas season. Russ had been assured by his suppliers that the roller bearings would be delivered in time to make Christmas shipments, but the suppliers were unable to fully deliver on this promise. As a consequence, Venice InLine had large stocks of unfinished skates at the end of the year and was unable to fill all of the orders that had come in from retailers for the Christmas season. Consequently, sales were below expectations for the year, and Russ does not have enough cash to pay his creditors.

Well before the accounts payable were due, Russ visited a local bank and inquired about obtaining a loan. The loan officer at the bank assured Russ that there should not be any problem getting a loan to pay off his accounts payable—providing that on his most recent financial statements the current ratio was above 2.0, the acid-test ratio was above 1.0, and net operating income was at least four times the interest on the proposed loan. Russ promised to return later with a copy of his financial statements.

Russ would like to apply for a $80,000 six-month loan bearing an interest rate of 10% per year. The unaudited financial reports of the company appear below:

Venice InLine, Inc. Comparative Balance Sheet As of December 31 (dollars in thousands)	This Year	Last Year
Assets		
Current assets:		
Cash	$ 70	$150
Accounts receivable, net	50	40
Inventory	160	100
Prepaid expenses	10	12
Total current assets	290	302
Property and equipment	270	180
Total assets	$560	$482
Liabilities and Stockholders' Equity		
Current liabilities:		
Accounts payable	$154	$ 90
Accrued liabilities	10	10
Total current liabilities	164	100
Long-term liabilities	—	—
Total liabilities	164	100
Stockholders' equity:		
Common stock and additional paid-in		
capital	100	100
Retained earnings	296	282
Total stockholders' equity	396	382
Total liabilities and stockholders' equity	$560	$482

Venice InLine, Inc.
Income Statement
For the Year Ended December 31
(dollars in thousands)

	This Year
Sales (all on account)	$420
Cost of goods sold	290
Gross margin	130
Selling and administrative expenses:	
Selling expenses	42
Administrative expenses	68
Total selling and administrative expenses . .	110
Net operating income	20
Interest expense	—
Net income before taxes	20
Income taxes (30%)	6
Net income	$ 14

Required:

1. Based on the unaudited financial statements and the statement made by the loan officer, would the company qualify for the loan?
2. Last year Russ purchased and installed new, more efficient equipment to replace an older plastic injection molding machine. Russ had originally planned to sell the old machine but found that it is still needed whenever the plastic injection molding process is a bottleneck. When Russ discussed his cash flow problems with his brother-in-law, he suggested to Russ that the old machine be sold or at least reclassified as inventory on the balance sheet because it could be readily sold. At present, the machine is carried in the Property and Equipment account and could be sold for its net book value of $45,000. The bank does not require audited financial statements. What advice would you give to Russ concerning the machine?

ANALYTICAL THINKING [LO13–2, LO13–3, LO13–4, LO13–5, LO13–6]

Incomplete financial statements for Pepper Industries follow:

Pepper Industries
Balance Sheet
March 31

Current assets:	
Cash	$?
Accounts receivable, net	?
Inventory	?
Total current assets	?
Plant and equipment, net	?
Total assets	$?
Liabilities:	
Current liabilities	$ 320,000
Bonds payable, 10%	?
Total liabilities	?
Stockholders' equity:	
Common stock, $5 par value	?
Retained earnings	?
Total stockholders' equity	?
Total liabilities and stockholders equity	$?

Pepper Industries
Income Statement
For the Year Ended March 31

Sales	$4,200,000
Cost of goods sold	?
Gross margin	?
Selling and administrative expenses	?
Net operating income	?
Interest expense	80,000
Net income before taxes	?
Income taxes (30%)	?
Net income	$?

The following additional information is available about the company:

a. All sales during the year were on account.
b. There was no change in the number of shares of common stock outstanding during the year.
c. The interest expense on the income statement relates to the bonds payable; the amount of bonds outstanding did not change during the year.
d. Selected balances at the *beginning* of the current year were

Accounts receivable	$270,000
Inventory	$360,000
Total assets	$1,800,000

e. Selected financial ratios computed from the statements above for the current year are

Earnings per share	$2.30
Debt-to-equity ratio	0.875
Accounts receivable turnover ..	14.0
Current ratio	2.75
Return on total assets	18.0%
Times interest earned ratio	6.75
Acid-test ratio	1.25
Inventory turnover	6.5

Required:
Compute the missing amounts on the company's financial statements. (*Hint:* What's the difference between the acid-test ratio and the current ratio?)

TEAMWORK IN ACTION [LO13–1, LO13–2, LO13–3, LO13–4, LO13–5, LO13–6]
Obtain the most recent annual report or SEC filing 10-K of a publicly traded company that interests you. It may be a local company or it may be a company in an industry that you would like to know more about. Using the annual report, compute as many of the financial ratios covered in this chapter as you can for at least the past two years. This may pose some difficulties—particularly because companies often use different terms for many income statement and balance sheet items than were shown in the chapter. Nevertheless, do the best that you can. After you have computed the financial ratios, summarize the company's performance for the current year. Has it improved, gotten worse, or remained about the same? Do the ratios indicate any potential problems or any areas that have shown significant improvement? What recommendations, if any, would you make to a bank about extending short-term credit to this company? What recommendations, if any, would you make to an insurance company about extending long-term credit to this company? What recommendations, if any, would you make to an investor about buying or selling this company's stock?

PHOTO CREDITS

Design Element: © McGraw-Hill Education.

Chapter Opener Image: © PixelEmbargo/Getty Images.

Frontmatter

Page iv: © Peter C. Brewer; p. v(top): © Ray H. Garrison, (bottom): © Eric W. Noreen; p. x: © Courtesy of University Tees, Inc.; p. xi: © Rob Melnychuk/Getty Images.

Prologue

Page 11: © Irene Alastruey/Author's Image/Punchstock; p. 12: © Imagestate Media (John Foxx)/Imagestate; p. 16: © MIGUEL MEDINA/Getty Images.

Chapter 1

Page 23: © Purestock/SuperStock; p. 26: © Digital Vision/PunchStock; p. 27: © Patrick Kane/AP Images; p. 30: © Sandee Noreen; p. 40: © flickr RF/Getty Images.

Chapter 2

Page 67: © Courtesy of University Tees, Inc.; p. 69: © Sandee Noreen; p. 94: © Copyright 2013 - FastWrap USA - All Rights Reserved.

Chapter 3

Page 121: © Jeff Greenberg/Alamy; p. 127: © Sandee Noreen; p. 132: © Stock Connection Blue/Alamy.

Chapter 4

Page 161: © Dejan Krsmanovic/Alamy; p. 164: © Yves Logghe/AP Images.

Chapter 5

Page 191: © Comstock Images; p. 206: © Yellow Dog Productions/Getty Images; p. 210: © LM Otero/AP Images; p. 215: © Digital Stock/Corbis.

Chapter 6

Page 243: Bloomberg/Getty Images; p. 253: © Photodisc/Getty Images; p. 257: © TRBfoto/Getty Images; p. 266: © Duncan Smith/Getty Images.

Chapter 7

Page 293: © Sandee Noreen; p. 309: © Photodisc/Getty Images; p. 313: © Eric Noreen.

Chapter 8

Page 349: © Michael Sears/MCT/Newscom; p. 356: © Francisco Cruz/Purestock/Superstock; p. 360: © Woods Wheatcroft/Getty Images; p. 369: © Rob Melnychuk/Getty Images.

Chapter 9

Page 417: © ZUMA Press, Inc/Alamy; p. 421: © John Burke/Getty Images; p. 435: © TongRo Images/Alamy; p. 437: © JGI/Tom Grill/Blend Images/Getty Images.

Chapter 10

Page 457: © jhphoto/AP Images; p. 470: © Asia Images Group/PictureIndia/Getty Images; p. 479: © McGraw-Hill Education. Andrew Resek, photographer.

Chapter 11

Page 511: © David Goldman/AP Images; p. 514: © Royalty-Free/Corbis; p. 525: © Ingram Publishing/SuperStock; p. 531: © Anonymous/AP Images.

Chapter 12

Page 557: © Bloomberg/Getty Images; p. 559: © McGraw-Hill Education. Jill Braaten, photographer; p. 577: © Photodisc/Getty Images.

Chapter 13

Page 601: © Mary Altaffer/AP Images; p. 615: © Photodisc/Getty Images.

INDEX